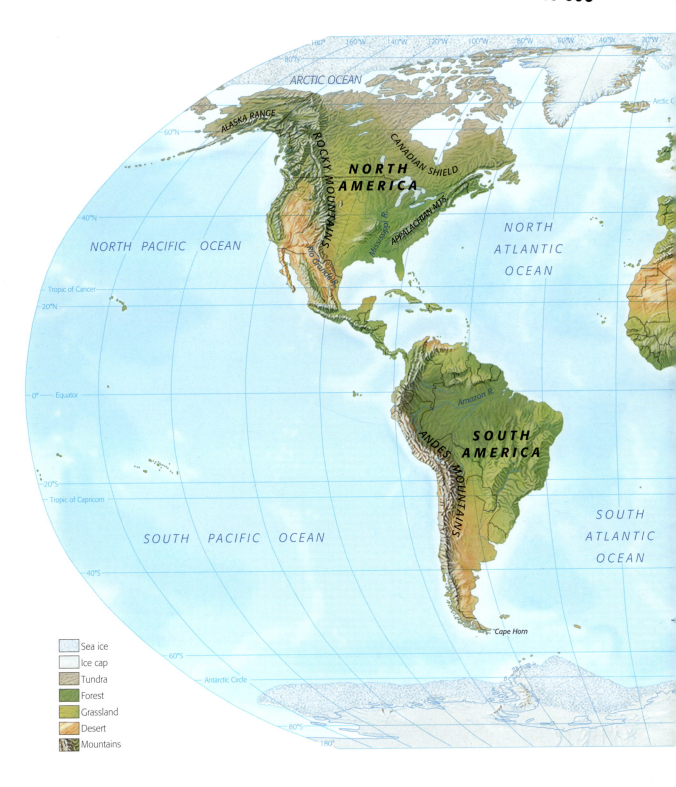

W9-AYW-093

ARCTIC OCEAN

ALASKA RANGE

ROCKY MOUNTAINS

CANADIAN SHIELD

NORTH AMERICA

APPALACHIAN MTS.

Mississippi R.

Rio Grande R.

NORTH PACIFIC OCEAN

NORTH ATLANTIC OCEAN

Tropic of Cancer

Arctic

Equator

Amazon R.

SOUTH AMERICA

ANDES MOUNTAINS

Tropic of Capricorn

SOUTH PACIFIC OCEAN

SOUTH ATLANTIC OCEAN

Cape Horn

Antarctic Circle

Sea ice
Ice cap
Tundra
Forest
Grassland
Desert
Mountains

ABBREVIATIONS

AUS.	AUSTRIA
BEL.	BELGIUM
B. H.	BOSNIA AND HERZEGOVINA
CR.	CROATIA
CZ.	CZECH REPUBLIC
DEN.	DENMARK
HUNG.	HUNGARY
K.	KOSOVO
LUX.	LUXEMBOURG
MAC.	MACEDONIA
MO.	MONTENEGRO
NETH.	NETHERLANDS
SE.	SERBIA
SLK.	SLOVAKIA
SLN.	SLOVENIA
SWITZ.	SWITZERLAND

Voyages in World History

BRIEF EDITION

WADSWORTH
CENGAGE Learning

Voyages in World History Brief Edition, Volume 2: Since 1500
Hansen/Curtis

Senior Publisher: Suzanne Jeans

Acquiring Sponsoring Editor: Brooke Barbier

Associate Editor: Adrienne Zicht

Assistant Editor: Lauren Floyd

Editorial Assistant: Katie Coaster

Senior Media Editor: Lisa M. Ciccolo

Marketing Coordinator: Lorreen R. Towle

Marketing Communications Manager:
Glenn McGibbon

Senior Content Project Manager:
Carol Newman

Senior Art Director: Cate Barr

Senior Manufacturing Planner:
Sandee Milewski

Senior Rights Acquisition Specialist:
Jennifer Meyer Dare

Production Service/Compositor:
Integra Software Services

Text Designer: Cia Boynton/Boynton Hue
Studio

Cover Designer: Cabbage Design

Cover Image: *New Delhi Railway Station, 1995*
(w/c on paper) by Olivia Fraser/ Private
Collection/ The Bridgeman Art Library

For product information and technology assistance, contact us at
Cengage Learning Customer & Sales Support, 1-800-354-9706

For permission to use material from this text or product, submit all requests online at **www.cengage.com/permissions.**
Further permissions questions can be e-mailed to
permissionrequest@cengage.com.

Library of Congress Control Number: 2011924526

ISBN-13: 978-1-111-35235-6

ISBN-10: 1-111-35235-6

Wadsworth
20 Channel Center Street
Boston, MA 02210
USA

Cengage Learning is a leading provider of customized learning solutions with office locations around the globe, including Singapore, the United Kingdom, Australia, Mexico, Brazil and Japan. Locate your local office at **international.cengage.com/region**

Cengage Learning products are represented in Canada by Nelson Education, Ltd.

For your course and learning solutions, visit **www.cengage.com.**

Purchase any of our products at your local college store or at our preferred online store **www.cengagebrain.com.**
Instructors: Please visit **login.cengage.com** and log in to access instructor-specific resources.

Printed in Canada
1 2 3 4 5 6 7 15 14 13 12 11

Voyages in World History

BRIEF EDITION

Volume 2: Since 1500

Valerie Hansen

Yale University

Kenneth R. Curtis

California State University Long Beach

WADSWORTH
CENGAGE Learning™

Australia • Brazil • Japan • Korea • Mexico • Singapore • Spain • United Kingdom • United States

Brief Contents

Contents

CHAPTER *23*

The Industrial Revolution and European Politics, 1780-1880

502

TRAVELER: Alexander Herzen 502

CHAPTER *24*

China, Japan, and India Confront the Modern World, 1800-1910

526

TRAVELER: Fukuzawa Yûkichi 526

CHAPTER *25*

State Building and Social Change in the Americas, 1830-1895   *550*

CHAPTER *26*

The New Imperialism in Africa and Southeast Asia, 1830-1914   *576*

CHAPTER *27*

War, Revolution, and Global Uncertainty, 1905-1928   *600*

CHAPTER *28* ## Responses to Global Crisis, 1920-1939 *624*

TRAVELER: Halide Edib **624**

CHAPTER *29* ## The Second World War and the Origins of the Cold War, 1939-1949 *648*

TRAVELER: Nancy Wake **648**

CHAPTER *30* ## The Cold War and Decolonization, 1949-1975 *670*

TRAVELER: Ernesto Guevara, 1951 **670**

CHAPTER 31   # Toward a New World Order, 1975–2000   696

TRAVELER: Nelson Mandela **696**

CHAPTER 32   # Voyage into the Twenty-First Century   722

TRAVELER: Mira Nair **722**

Maps

Movement of Ideas

Preface

What makes this book different from other world history textbooks?

- Each chapter opens with a narrative about a traveler, and their story is woven throughout to bring the traveler to life for the student as they follow the figure on his or her journey. The *Voyages Map App, Aplia*™ then continues the journey online by using Google Earth™ to transport students to historic sites and locations visited by the travelers, allowing students to explore the past and make connections to the world today.
- The book's theme of movement highlights cultural contact and is reinforced in both the *Voyages Map App, Aplia*™ and in the primary source feature, Movement of Ideas, which introduces students to textual sources by contrasting two different explanations of the same idea, which teaches analytical skills.
- The print text fully integrates with an online experience, including the *Voyages Map App, Aplia*™ (an interactive learning solution that provides assignable, gradable primary source activities; writing and map tutorials; and customized, chapter-based questions), and *CourseMate* (featuring interactive learning, study, and exam prep tools, plus Engagement Tracker and an interactive eBook). Each digital learning solution was created as an extension of the book and fully complements each chapter.
- *CourseReader: World History* is available with the text, and allows you to build your own customized online reader from thousands of primary and secondary sources, readings, and audio and video clips from multiple disciplines. *Hansen's Editor's Choice CourseReader* is also available and offers a select group of primary sources that have been hand-picked by the *Voyages* editors to be the perfect complement to the Hansen book and course.
- Innovative maps in the text show the travelers' routes while inviting students to think analytically about geography and its role in world history, and the *Voyages Map App* brings the maps to life online, following the routes and providing a Journey Quiz to help students evaluate their understanding of the locations and events.
- A beautiful, engaging design features an on-page glossary, a pronunciation guide, and chapter-opening focus questions and chapter summaries (which can be downloaded as MP3 files). These tools help students grasp and retain the main ideas of the chapters as well as learn on-the-go.

This world history textbook will, we hope, be enjoyable for students to read and for instructors to teach. We have focused on thirty-two different people and the journeys they took, starting ten thousand years ago with Kennewick Man (Chapter 1) and concluding in the twenty-first century with the film director Mira Nair. Each of the thirty-two chapters (one for each week of the school year) introduces multiple themes. First, the travelers' narratives introduce the home society and the new civilizations they visited. Our major theme is the movement of people, ideas, trade goods, and artistic motifs and the results of these contacts. We introduce other evidence, often drawn from primary sources, to help students reason like historians.

This brief edition of *Voyages* retains the features that make this textbook unique (like the all-important primary source feature, Movement of Ideas), but we have moved two features, Visual Evidence and World History in Today's World (described below), to the book's website, where they serve to integrate the book with the students' online journey, and enhance the overall learning experience by teaching students to analyze historical evidence and relate historical developments to current issues.

The chapter-opening narratives enhance the scope and depth of the topics covered. The travelers take us to Mesopotamia with Gilgamesh, to Africa with the hajj pilgrim Ibn Battuta, to Peru with the cross-dressing soldier and adventurer Catalina de Erauso, to the Americas with the African Olaudah Equiano, and to Britain during the Industrial Revolution with the Russian socialist Alexander Herzen. They wrote vivid accounts, often important primary sources about these long ago events that shaped our world.

Chapter 12, for example, tells the story of the Chinese poet Li Qingzhao. She lived during the Song dynasty (960–1275) and experienced firsthand China's commercial revolution and calamitous warfare. Her eyewitness account of her husband's death brings this pivotal period in Chinese history to life. Students also learn about the contacts between China and Japan, Korea, and Vietnam during this time of economic growth. In Chapter 24, the focus is on the great Japanese reformer Fukuzawa Yûkichi, an influential participant in the revolutionary changes that accompanied his country's Meiji Restoration (1868).

Students new to world history, or to history in general, will find it easier, we hope, to focus on the experience of thirty-two individuals before focusing on the broader themes of a new society each week. The interactive *Voyages Map App* further engages the new student by guiding them in an online journey through historic sites, bringing the travelers' explorations to life and reinforcing the themes of the book.

Instead of a canned list of dates, each chapter covers the important topics at a sensible and careful pace, without compromising coverage or historical rigor. Students compare the traveler's perceptions with alternative sources, and so awaken their interest in the larger developments. Our goal was to select the most compelling topics and engaging illustrations from the entire record of human civilization, presented in a clear spatial and temporal framework, to counter the view of history as an interminable compendium of geographical place names and facts.

We have chosen a range of travelers, both male and female, from all over the world. Many travelers were well-born and well-educated, and many were not. The Scandinavian explorers Thorfinn and Gudrid Karlsefni (Chapter 10) and the blind Chinese sailor Xie Qinggao (Chapter 20) were born into ordinary families. These individuals help cast our world history in a truly global format, avoiding the Eurocentrism that prompted the introduction of world history courses in the first place.

Our goal in writing *Voyages in World History* was to focus on the experience of individual travelers, and hopefully make students enthusiastic about world history, while achieving the right balance between the traveler's experience and the course material. After circulating draft chapters to over 120 instructors of the course, we found that most agreed on the basic topics to be covered. The long process of revision resulted in our giving less space to the traveler and more to the basic theme and topical coverage of the book. We realized that we had achieved the right balance when the reviewers asked for more information about the travelers.

Our book is self-contained but open-ended, should instructors or their students wish to do more reading. Some instructors may decide to devote some time in their lectures to the travelers, who are indeed fascinating; students, we hope, will naturally be inclined to write term papers about them, and to further explore the travelers' journeys online with the *Voyages Map App*. Almost all of these travel accounts are available in English translation, listed in the suggested readings at the end of each chapter. If instructors assign readings in addition to the textbook, they can assign those travel accounts from the world area with which they are most familiar. Where an Europeanist might assign additional readings from Herodotus, for example, an Asianist might prefer to assign the narratives of the Buddhist pilgrim Xuanzang.

We aspire to answer many of the unmet needs of professors and students in world history. Because our book is not encyclopedic, and because each chapter begins with a narrative of a trip, our book is more readable than its competitors, which strain for all-inclusive coverage. They pack so many names and facts into their text that they leave little time to introduce beginning students to historical method. Because our book gives students a chance to read primary sources in depth, particularly in the Movement of Ideas feature (described below), instructors can spend class time teaching students how to reason historically—not just imparting the details of a given national history. Each chapter includes discussion questions that make it easier for instructors new to world history to facilitate interactive learning. Each chapter closes with answers to those questions: a feature in response to student views as expressed in focus groups.

Our approach particularly suits the needs of young professors who have been trained in only one geographic area of history. Our book does not presuppose that instructors already have broad familiarity with the history of each important world civilization.

Volume 1, which covers material from the first hominids to 1500, introduces students to the important regions and societies of the world: ancient Africa and the Americas (Chapter 1), Mesopotamia and Egypt (Chapter 2), India (Chapter 3), China (Chapter 4), and the Americas again, as well as the islands of the Pacific (Chapter 5). The next section of the book emphasizes the rise of world religions: Zoroastrianism in the Persian Empire (Chapter 6); Rome's adoption of Christianity (Chapter 7); the spread of Buddhism and Hinduism in East, South, and Southeast Asia (Chapter 8); and the rise of Islam (Chapter 9). The final third of Volume 1 focuses on the parallel commercial revolutions in Europe and China (Chapters 12 and 13) and the gradual increase in knowledge about other societies resulting from the Vikings' voyages to Iceland, Greenland, and Newfoundland (Chapter 10); Ibn Battuta's trips in North, Central, and East Africa (Chapter 11); the Mongol conquest (Chapter 14); and the Spanish and Portuguese voyages to the Americas (Chapter 15). Because many of the people who traveled long distances in the premodern world did so for religious reasons, several of the travelers in Volume 1 are pilgrims. Their experiences help to reinforce student's understanding of the traditions of different world religions.

Volume 2 explores the development of the increasingly interconnected modern world, with the rise and fall of empires a persistent theme. We explore the new maritime trade routes that connected Europe to Asia (Chapter 16) and the relationship between religion and politics in both the Christian and Muslim empires of western Eurasia (Chapter 17). The analysis of the colonial Americas (Chapter 18) is expanded by Chapter 19's discussion of Africa and the Atlantic slave trade. The expansion of Asian empires (Chapter 20) is complemented by an analysis of the relationship between science and empire in the Pacific Ocean and around the world (Chapter 21). The role of revolutions in modern history is addressed in Chapters 22 and 23. Chapters 24 through 26 address the global impact of the Industrial Revolution in Asia, the Americas,

Africa, and Southeast Asia. The twentieth century is explored (Chapters 27–31) with an emphasis on the common experiences of globalized humanity through world wars, economic upheavals, and the bitter divisions of the Cold War. Though we cannot properly assess twenty-first century conditions using the historian's tools, Chapter 32 attempts to lay out some of the main challenges and opportunities we face today.

Theme and Approach

Our theme of movement and contact is key to world history because world historians focus on connections among the different societies of the past. The movement of people, whether in voluntary migrations or forced slavery, has been one of the most fruitful topics for world historians, as are the experiences of individual travelers like Ibn Battuta or Simón Bolívar. Their reactions to the people they met on their long journeys reveal much about their home societies as well as about the societies they visited.

Our focus on individual travelers illustrates the increasing ease of contact among different civilizations with the passage of time. This theme highlights the developments that resulted from improved communications, travel among different places, the movement of trade goods, and the mixing of peoples: the movement of world religions, mass migrations, and the spread of diseases like the plague. The book shows how travel has changed over time—how the distance covered by travelers has increased at the same time that the duration of trips has decreased. As a result, more and more people have been able to go to societies distant from their own.

The book and its integrated online components examine the different reasons for travel over the centuries. While some people were captured in battle and forced to go to new places, others visited different societies to teach or to learn the beliefs of a new religion like Buddhism, Christianity, or Islam. This theme, of necessity, treats questions about the environment: how far and over what terrain did early man travel? How did sailors learn to use monsoon winds to their advantage? What were the effects of technological breakthroughs like steamships, trains, and airplanes— and the use of fossil fuels to power them? Because students can link the experience of individual travelers to this theme, movement provides the memorable organizing principle for the book, a principle that is reinforced in the interactive online journeys offered by the *Voyages Map App.*

Having a single theme allows us to provide broad coverage of the most important topics in world history. Students who use this book will learn which empires and nations were most important. We offer comparisons of the different empires under consideration so that students will understand that empires became increasingly complex over time, especially as central governments took advantage of new technologies to register and to control their subjects. Students need not commit long lists of rulers' names to memory: instead they focus on those leaders who created innovative political structures. After an opening chapter on the peopling of the world, the book begins with the very ancient empires (like Mesopotamia and Egypt) that did not control large swathes of territory and progress to those that did—like Qin dynasty China, Achaemenid Persia, and ancient Rome. It examines the political structures of empire: What was the relationship of the central government to the provinces? How were taxes collected and spent? How were officials recruited? Such questions remained remarkably persistent into the modern period, when societies around the world had to contend with rising Western empires.

The focus on the structure of empire helps students to remember the different civilizations they have studied, to explore the borrowing that occurred among various empires, and to understand how the empires were structured differently. This focus fits well with travel because the different travelers were able to make certain journeys because of the political situation at the time. For example, William of Rubruck was able to travel across all of Eurasia because of the unification brought by the Mongol empire, while Jean de Chardin's tavels from France to Iran were facilitated by the size and strength of the Ottoman Empire.

Many rulers patronized religions to increase their control over the people they ruled, allowing us to introduce the teachings of the major world religions. Students will learn how originally regional or national religions moved across political borders to become world religions. Volume 1 introduces the religions of Judaism (Chapter 2), Buddhism (Chapters 3 and 9), Confucianism (Chapter 4), Christianity (Chapters 6 and 10), Hinduism (Chapter 8), and Islam (Chapter 9). Volume 2 provides context for today's complex interplay of religion and politics (Chapter 17) and the complex cultural outcomes that occurred when such religions expanded into new world regions (Chapters 16 and 18). The renewed contemporary focus on religion, as seen in the rise of fundamentalist movements in various parts of the world, is analyzed in the two final chapters.

Our focus on travelers offers an opportunity to explore their involvement with religion. Some chapters examine the experience of religious travelers—such as the Chinese monk Xuanzang who journeyed to India and Matteo Ricci who hoped to convert the Chinese emperor to Christianity. Other travelers did not travel for religious reasons, but they had their own religious beliefs, encountered the religious traditions of the peoples they conquered, and sparked religious exchanges. Because the different chapters of the book pay close attention to the religious traditions of diverse societies, students gain a familiarity with the primary religious traditions of the world.

Students of world history need to understand how societies have been structured and how these ways of organizing society have changed over the past five thousand years. Abandoning the egalitarian structures of the distant past, Sumerian and Egyptian civilizations and their successors developed more hierarchical societies. Between 500 and 1500 both Europe and China moved from land-based aristocracies toward bureaucracy, but European and Chinese governments conceived of bureaucracy very differently. Some societies had extensive slavery; others did not.

Because the travelers were acutely aware of the differences between their own societies and those they visited, they provide crucial comparisons, although their observations were not always correct. For example, in the early seventh century the Chinese pilgrim Xuanzang described the Indian caste system as though it were rigidly structured, but he was not aware of groups who had changed the status of their caste.

Each chapter devotes extensive space to the experience of women. Because in many societies literacy among women was severely limited, especially in the premodern era, we have included as many women travelers as possible: the slave girl and eventual wife of the caliph, Khaizuran (Chapter 9), Leif Eriksson's sister-in-law Gudrid (Chapter 10), the Chinese poet Li Qingzhao (Chapter 12), Heloise (Chapter 13), Catalina de Erauso (Chapter 18), Pauline Johnson-Tekahionwake (Chapter 25), Louise Bryant (Chapter 27), Halide Edib (Chapter 28), Nancy Wake (Chapter 29), and Mira Nair (Chapter 32). In addition, each chapter provides extensive coverage of gender so that students can grasp the experience of ordinary women.

Features

We see the features of this book as an opportunity to help students better understand the main text, and to expand that understanding as they explore the integrated online features. Each chapter opens with a map feature about the route of the chapter's traveler and, within the chapter, presents Movement of Ideas. Both World History in Today's World and Visual Evidence are available on the web.

Chapter Opening Map

At the beginning of each chapter is a map illustrating the route of the traveler. With their imaginative graphics, these chapter-opening maps look more like the maps in a travel book than the usual textbook maps, and they come to life even further online with the *Voyages Map App,* which guides the students as they retrace and explore the travelers' routes. This opening section of each chapter also provides a biographical sketch for each traveler, a portrait, and an extended passage from his or her writings (or, if not available, an extended passage about the individual). This feature aims to capture the student's attention at the outset of each chapter.

Movement of Ideas

This primary source feature offers an introduction, an extensive excerpt from one or more primary sources, and discussion questions. The chosen passages emphasize the movement of ideas, usually by contrasting two different explanations of the same idea. This feature aims to develop the core historical skill of analyzing original sources. Topics include "Doing What Is Right in *The Avesta* and the Bible" and "Fascism and Youth."

World History in Today's World

Available for each chapter on the book's website, this brief feature picks one element of modern life that originated in the period under study. Each subject is especially relatable to students ("The World's First Beer," "Japanese Baseball," and "The Coffeehouse in World History") and highlights their relationship to the past. This feature should provide material to trigger discussion and help instructors explain why world history matters and how relevant it is to students' lives today.

Visual Evidence

This feature, also found for each chapter on the web, guides students as they continue their historical journey online and learn to examine either an artifact, a work of art, or a photograph and to glean historical information from them. These features are illustrated with pictures or photographs and help students understand the importance of the find or the artwork. A close-up photograph of the Chinese terracotta warriors, for example, shows students how the figurines were mass-produced yet have individual features. Portraits of George Washington and Napoleon Bonaparte lead students to analyze the symbolism they contain to view the portraits as *representations* of political power. Discussion questions help students analyze the information presented.

Ancillaries

A wide array of supplements accompanies this text to help students better master the material and to help instructors teach from the book:

Instructor's Resources

PowerLecture DVD with ExamView® and JoinIn® This dual platform, all-in-one multimedia resource includes the Instructor's Resource Manual; Test Bank (prepared by Candace Gregory-Abbott of California State University-Sacramento; includes key term identification, multiple-choice, and essay questions); Microsoft® PowerPoint® slides of both lecture outlines and images and maps from the text that can be used as offered, or customized by importing personal lecture slides or other material; and *JoinIn®* PowerPoint® slides with clicker content. Also included is ExamView, an easy-to-use assessment and tutorial system that allows instructors to create, deliver, and customize tests in minutes. Instructors can build tests with as many as 250 questions using up to 12 question types, and using ExamView's complete word-processing capabilities, they can enter an unlimited number of new questions or edit existing ones.

eInstructor's Resource Manual Prepared by Salvador Diaz of Santa Rosa Junior College, this manual has many features including instructional objectives, chapter outlines, lecture topics and suggestions for discussion, classroom activities and writing assignments, analyzing primary sources, activities for the traveler, audiovisual bibliographies, suggested readings, and Internet resources. Available on the instructor's companion website.

WebTutor™ on Blackboard® or WebCT® With WebTutor's text-specific, pre-formatted content and total flexibility, instructors can easily create and manage their own custom course website. WebTutor's course management tool gives instructors the ability to provide virtual office hours, post syllabi, set up threaded discussions, track student progress with the quizzing material, and much more. For students, WebTutor offers real-time access to a full array of study tools, including animations and videos that bring the book's topics to life, plus chapter outlines, summaries, learning objectives, glossary flashcards (with audio), practice quizzes, and web links.

CourseMate Cengage Learning's History CourseMate brings course concepts to life with interactive learning, study tools, and exam preparation tools (including MP3 downloads and a pronunciation guide) that support the printed textbook. Use Engagement Tracker to monitor student engagement in the course and watch student comprehension soar as your class works with the printed textbook and the textbook-specific website. An interactive eBook allows students to take notes, highlight, search, and interact with embedded media (such as quizzes, flashcards, and videos). Access to the History Resource Center, a "virtual reader," provides students with hundreds of primary sources. Learn more at www.cengage.com/coursemate.

Aplia™ is an online interactive learning solution that improves comprehension and outcomes by increasing student effort and engagement. Founded by a professor to enhance his own courses, Aplia provides assignable, gradable primary source activities and writing and map tutorials in addition to customized, chapter-based questions. Detailed, immediate explanations accompany every question, and innovative teaching materials make it easy to engage students and track their progress. Our easy to use system has been used by more than 1,000,000 students at over 1800 institutions. Additional features include "flipbook" navigation that allows students to easily scan the contents; a course management system that allows you to post announcements, upload course materials, host student discussions, e-mail students, and manage your gradebook; and personalized support from a knowledgeable, and friendly team. The Aplia support team also offers assistance in customizing our assignments to your course schedule. To learn more, visit www.aplia.com.

Wadsworth World History Resource Center Wadsworth's World History Resource Center gives your students access to a "virtual reader" with hundreds of primary sources including speeches, letters, legal documents and transcripts, poems, maps, simulations, timelines, and additional images that bring history to life, along with interactive assignable exercises. A map feature including Google Earth™ coordinates and exercises will aid in student comprehension of geography and use of maps. Students can compare the traditional textbook map with an aerial view of the location today. It's an ideal resource for study, review, and research. In addition to this map feature, the resource center also provides blank maps for student review and testing.

CourseReader: World History is Cengage Learning's easy, affordable way to build your own online customizable reader. Through a partnership with Gale, *CourseReader: World History* searches thousands of primary and secondary sources, readings, and audio and video clips from multiple disciplines. Select exactly and only the material you want your students to work with. Each selection can be listened to (using the "Listen" button), to accommodate varied learning styles. Additionally, an instructor can choose to add her own notes to readings, to direct students' attention or ask them questions about a particular passage. Each primary source is accompanied by an introduction and questions to help students understand the reading. *Hansen's Editor's Choice CourseReader* is also available and offers a select group of primary sources that have been hand-picked by the *Voyages* editors to be the perfect complement to the Hansen book and course.

Student Resources

Voyages Map App Created by Dr. Nishikant Sonwalkar of Synaptic Global Learning, this interactive app guides you through the voyages taken by historical travelers, allowing you to explore and examine the past. Using Google Earth™, you will be transported to historic sites and locations visited by the travelers and learn about each location's monuments, architecture, and historic significance. The app includes review questions, flash cards, and timelines to help you further understand the travelers and their importance. After visiting the historic sites and analyzing the map from each chapter, a Journey Quiz will help you evaluate your own understanding of the location and events. The *Voyages App* is available with CourseMate and for purchase at the iTunes store.

Companion Website Prepared by Elizabeth Propes, of Tennessee Tech University, this website provides a variety of resources to help you review for class. These study tools include glossary, crossword puzzles, short quizzes, essay questions, critical thinking questions, primary sources links, and weblinks.

WebTutor™ on Blackboard® or WebCT® WebTutor™ offers real-time access to an interactive eBook and a full array of study tools, including animations and videos that bring the book's topics to life, plus chapter outlines, summaries, learning objectives, glossary flashcards (with audio), practice quizzes, and web links.

CourseMate The more you study, the better the results. Make the most of your study time by accessing everything you need to succeed in one place. Read your textbook, take notes, review flashcards, watch videos, download MP3s, review a pronunciation guide, and take practice quizzes—online with CourseMate. In addition you can access the History Resource Center, a "virtual reader" that provides you with hundreds of primary sources.

Aplia™ is an online interactive learning solution that helps you improve comprehension—and your grade—by integrating a variety of mediums and tools such as video, tutorials, practice tests and interactive eBook. Founded by a professor to enhance his own courses, Aplia provides automatically graded assignments with detailed, immediate explanations on every question, and innovative teaching materials. More than 1,000,000 students like you have used Aplia at over 1,800 institutions. Aplia™ should be purchased only when assigned by your instructor as part of your course.

CourseReader: World History allows your instructor to build an affordable, online customizable reader for your course by searching thousands of primary and secondary sources, readings, and audio and video clips from multiple disciplines. Each selection can be listened to (using the "Listen" button), to accommodate varied learning styles, and each primary source is accompanied by an introduction and questions to help you understand the reading. *Hansen's Editor's Choice CourseReader* is also available and offers a select group of primary sources that have been hand-picked by the *Voyages* editors to be the perfect complement to the Hansen book and course.

Wadsworth World History Resource Center Wadsworth's World History Resource Center gives you access to a "virtual reader" with hundreds of primary sources including speeches, letters, legal documents and transcripts, poems, maps, simulations, timelines, and additional images that bring history to life, along with interactive assignable exercises. A map feature including Google Earth™ coordinates and exercises will aid in your comprehension of geography and use of maps. You can compare the traditional textbook map with an aerial view of the location today. It's an ideal resource for study, review, and research. In addition to this map feature, the resource center also provides blank maps for student review and testing.

Rand McNally Historical Atlas of the World This valuable resource features over 70 maps that portray the rich panoply of the world's history from preliterate times to the present. They show how cultures and civilization were linked and how they interacted. The maps make it clear that history is not static. Rather, it is about change and movement across time. The maps show change by presenting the dynamics of expansion, cooperation, and conflict. This atlas includes maps that display the world from the beginning of civilization; the political development of all major areas of the world; expanded coverage of Africa, Latin America, and the Middle East; the current Islamic World; and the world population change in 1900 and 2000.

Writing for College History Prepared by Robert M. Frakes, Clarion University. This brief handbook for survey courses in American history, Western Civilization/European history, and world civilization guides students through the various types of writing assignments they encounter in a history class. Providing examples of student writing and candid assessments of student work, this text focuses on the rules and conventions of writing for the college history course.

The History Handbook Prepared by Carol Berkin of Baruch College, City University of New York and Betty Anderson of Boston University. This book teaches students both basic and history-specific study skills such as how to read primary sources, research historical topics, and correctly cite sources. Substantially less expensive than comparable skill-building texts, *The History Handbook* also offers tips for Internet research and evaluating online sources.

Doing History: Research and Writing in the Digital Age Prepared by Michael J. Galgano, J. Chris Arndt, and Raymond M. Hyser of James Madison University. Whether you're starting down the path as a history major, or simply looking for a straightforward and systematic guide to writing a successful paper, you'll find this text to be an indispensible handbook to historical research. This text's "soup to nuts" approach to researching and writing about history addresses every step of the process, from locating your sources and gathering information, to writing clearly and making proper use of various citation styles to avoid plagiarism. You'll also learn how to make the most of every tool available to you—especially the technology that helps you conduct the process efficiently and effectively.

The Modern Researcher Prepared by Jacques Barzun and Henry F. Graff of Columbia University. This classic introduction to the techniques of research and the art of expression is used widely in history courses, but is also appropriate for writing and research methods courses in other departments. Barzun and Graff thoroughly cover every aspect of research, from the selection of a topic through the gathering, analysis, writing, revision, and publication of findings presenting the process not as a set of rules but through actual cases that put the subtleties of research in a useful context. Part One covers the principles and methods of research; Part Two covers writing, speaking, and getting one's work published.

Acknowledgments

It is a pleasure to thank the many instructors who read and critiqued the manuscript through its development:

Tamer Balci, University of Texas–Pan American; Christopher Bellitto, Kean University; Robert Bond, Cuyumaca College; Marjan Boogert, Manchester College; Gail Bossenga, College of William and Mary; James Brodman, University of Central Arkansas; Robert Brown, Tunxis Community College; Daniel Bubb, Gonzaga University; Paul Buckingham, Morrisville State College; William Burns, George Washington University; Annette Chamberlin, Virginia Western Community College; Patricia Colman, Moorpark College; Sara Combs, Virginia Highlands Community College; Marcie Cowley, Grand Valley State University–Allendale; Matthew Crawford, Kent State University; Salvador Diaz, Santa Rosa Junior College; Jeffrey Dym, California State University–Sacramento; Christine Firpo, California Polytechnic State University–San Luis Obispo; Nancy Fitch, California State University–Fullerton; Kenneth Hall, Ball State University; Jack Hayes, Norwich University; Cecily Heisser, University of San Diego; Gustavo Jimenez, Los Angeles Mission College; Luke Kelly, University of Utah; Seth Kendall, Georgia Gwinnett College; Jeffrey Kinkley, Saint John's University; Michael Kinney, Calhoun Community College; Claudia Liebeskind, Florida State University; John Lyons, Joliet Junior College; Mary Lyons-Barrett, University of Nebraska–Omaha and Metropolitan Community College; Anupama

Mande ,Fullerton College; Adrian Mandzy, Morehead State University; Susan Maneck, Jackson State University; Kate Martin, Cape Cod Community College; Susan Maurer, Nassau Community College; Robert McMichael, Wayland Baptist University; David Meier, Dickinson State University; Robert Montgomery, Baldwin Wallace College; William Palmer, Marshall University; Vera Parham, University of Hawaii; Sean Perrone, Saint Anselm College; Elizabeth Propes, Tennessee Tech University; Robert Przygrodzki, Saint Xavier University; Anne Christina Rose, Grand Valley State University–Allendale; John Ryder, Radford University; Jeffrey Smith, Lindenwood University; Anthony Steinhoff, University of Tennessee–Chattanooga; Frans Van Liere, Calvin College; Peter Von Sivers, University of Utah; Joshua Weiner, American River College; Timothy Wesley, Pennsylvania State University; Robert Wilcox, Northern Kentucky University; Deborah Wilson, University of Southern Indiana, Kenneth Wong, Quinsigamond Community College; Stella Xu, Roanoke College

Valerie Hansen would also like to thank the following for their guidance on specific chapters: Benjamin Foster, Yale University; Karen Foster, Yale University; Stephen Colvin, London University; Phyllis Granoff, Yale University; Stanley Insler, Yale University; Mridu Rai, Yale University; Thomas R. H. Havens, Northeastern University; Charles Wheeler, University of California, Irvine; Haydon Cherry, Yale University; Marcello A. Canuto, Yale University; William Fash, Harvard University; Stephen Houston, Brown University; Mary Miller, Yale University; Stephen Colvin, University of London; Frank Turner, Yale University; Kevin van Bladel, University of Southern California; Anders Winroth, Yale University; Paul Freedman, Yale University; Frederick S. Paxton, Connecticut College; Francesca Trivellato, Yale University; Stuart Schwartz, Yale University; and Koichi Shinohara, Yale University.

The study of world history is indeed a voyage, and Kenneth Curtis would like to thank the following for helping identify guideposts along the way. First, thanks to colleagues in the World History Association and the Advanced Placement World History program, especially Ross Dunn, San Diego State University; Patrick Manning, University of Pittsburgh; Peter Stearns, George Mason University; Jerry Bentley, University of Hawai'i; Merry Wiesner-Hanks, University of Wisconsin–Milwaukee; Alan Karras, University of California, Berkeley; Omar Ali, Vanderbilt University; Heather Streets, Washington State University; Laura Mitchell, University of California, Irvine; Anand Yang, University of Washington; Heidi Roupp, Ane Lintvedt, Sharon Cohen, Jay Harmon, Anton Striegl, Michelle Foreman, Chris Wolf, Saroja Ringo, Esther Adams, Linda Black, and Bill Ziegler. He would also like to acknowledge the support of his colleagues in the history department at California State University Long Beach, especially those who aided with sources, translations, or interpretive guidance: Houri Berberian, Timothy Keirn, Craig Hendricks, Margaret Kuo, Andrew Jenks, Ali Igmen, Sharlene Sayegh, and Donald Schwartz. He also benefited from the feedback of the students who read early drafts of the modern history chapters and gave valuable feedback, with a special nod to those graduate students—Charlie Dodson, Patrick Giloogly, Daniel Lynch—who brought their passion for world history teaching in the public schools to the seminar table, and to Colin Rutherford for his help with the pedagogy.

The authors would like to thank the many publishing professionals at Cengage Learning who facilitated the publication of this book, in particular: Nancy Blaine who took us from proposal to finished textbook and who came up with the idea of a brief edition; Jean Woy, for her acute historical judgment; Jennifer Sutherland for her work on the Comprehensive Edition; Jan Fitter, for skillfully and elegantly abridging Chapters 1-16 for the brief edition; Margaret Manos, for equally skillfully and elegantly abridging Chapters 17-32; Adrienne Zicht, for preparing the chapters for publication and working with production and permissions to develop the brief edition; Linda Sykes, for her extraordinary photo research that makes this such a beautiful book; and Carol Newman and Heather Johnson, for shepherding the book through the final pre-publication process.

In closing, Valerie would like to thank Brian Vivier for doing so much work on Volume 1; the title of "research assistant" does not convey even a fraction of what he did, always punctually and cheerfully. She dedicates this book to her children, Lydia, Claire, and Bret Hansen Stepanek, and their future educations.

Kenneth Curtis would like to thank Francine Curtis for her frontline editing skills and belief in the project, and his mother Elizabeth J. Curtis and siblings Jane, Sara, Margaret, Jim, Steve, and Ron for their love and support. In recognition of his father's precious gift of curiosity, Ken dedicates this book to the memory of James Gavin Curtis.

About the Authors

Valerie Hansen

Since her graduate work in premodern Chinese history at the University of Pennsylvania, Valerie Hansen has used nontraditional sources to capture the experience of ordinary people. Professor of History at Yale, she teaches the history of premodern China, the Silk Road, and the world. *Changing Gods in Medieval China* drew on temple inscriptions and ghost stories to shed light on popular religious practice in the Song dynasty (1127–1276), while *Negotiating Daily Life in Traditional China* used contracts to probe Chinese understandings of the law both in this world and the next. Her textbook *The Open Empire: China to 1600* draws on archaeological finds, literature, and art to explore Chinese interactions with the outside world. With grants from the National Endowment for the Humanities and the Fulbright Association, she has traveled to China to collect materials for her current research project: a new history of the Silk Road.

Kenneth R. Curtis

Kenneth R. Curtis received his Ph.D. from the University of Wisconsin–Madison in African and Comparative World History. His research focuses on colonial to post-colonial transitions in East Africa, with a particular focus on the coffee economy of Tanzania. He is Professor of History and Liberal Studies at California State University Long Beach, where he has taught world history at the introductory level, in special courses designed for future middle and high school teachers, and in graduate seminars. He has worked to advance the teaching of world history at the collegiate and secondary levels in collaboration with the World History Association, the California History/Social Science Project, and the College Board's Advanced Placement World History course.

Note on Spelling

Students taking world history will encounter many new names of people, terms, and places. We have retained only the most important of these. The most difficult, of course, are those from languages that use either different alphabets or no alphabet at all (like Chinese) and that have multiple variant spellings in English. As a rule, we have opted to give names in the native language of whom we are writing, not in other languages. In addition, we have kept accents and diacritic marks to a minimum, using them only when absolutely necessary. For example, we give the name of the world's first city (in Turkey) as Catalhoyuk, not Çatalhüyük.

In sum, our goal has been to avoid confusing the reader, even if specific decisions may not make sense to expert readers. To help readers, we provide a pronunciation guide on the first appearance of any term or name whose pronunciation is not obvious from the spelling. There is also an audio pronunciation guide on the text's accompanying website. A few explanations for specific regions follow.

The Americas

The peoples living in the Americas before 1492 had no common language and no shared identity. Only after 1492 with the arrival of Columbus and his men did outsiders label the original residents of the Americas as a single group. For this reason, any word for the inhabitants of North and South America is inaccurate. We try to refer to individual peoples whenever possible. When speaking in general terms, we use the word "Amerindian" because it has no pejorative overtones and is not confusing.

Many place names in Spanish-speaking regions have a form in both Spanish and in the language of the indigenous peoples; whenever possible we have opted for the indigenous word. For example, we write about the Tiwanaku culture in the Andes, not Tiahuanaco. In some cases, we choose the more familiar term, such as Inca and Cuzco, rather than the less-familiar spellings Inka and Cusco. We retain the accents for modern place names.

East Asia

For Chinese, we have used the pinyin system of Romanization, not the older Wade-Giles version. Students and instructors may wish to consult an online pinyin/Wade-Giles conversion program if they want to check a spelling. We use the pinyin throughout but, on the first appearance of a name, alert readers to nonstandard spellings, such as Chiang Kai-shek and Sun Yat-sen, that have already entered English.

For other Asian languages, we have used the most common romanization systems (McCune-Reischauer for Korean, Hepburn for Japanese) and have dropped diacritical marks. Because we prefer to use the names that people called themselves, we use Chinggis Khan, for the ruler of the Mongols (not Genghis Khan, which is Persian) and the Turkish Timur the Lame (rather than Tamerlane, his English name).

West Asia and North Africa

Many romanization systems for Arabic and related languages like Ottoman Turkish or Persian use an apostrophe to indicate specific consonants (*ain* and *hamza*). Because it is difficult for a native speaker of English to hear these differences, we have omitted these apostrophes. For this reason, we use Quran (not Qur'an).

15 Maritime Expansion in the Atlantic World, 1400–1600

...istopher Columbus
...etropolitan Museum of Art / Art
...ce, NY)

With two of his ships separated from the third in a storm and uncertain that he would make it back to Spain, **Christopher Columbus** (1451–1506) summarized his journey and then wrapped the parchment document in cloth, sealed it with wax, and dropped it overboard in a wine casket. He survived the storm and returned to Spain, where he presented a long letter describing his first voyage to his backers Queen Isabella (1451–1504) and King Ferdinand (1452–1516) of Spain. Columbus's voyage connected Europe with the Americas in a way that no previous contact had; the resulting exchange of plants, animals, people, and disease shaped the modern world. In his letter describing the people he encountered in the Caribbean, he voices the twin motivations of the Spanish and the Portuguese in search of gold, they also hoped to convert the indigenous peoples to Christianity.

Hispaniola is a wonder. The mountains and hills, the plains and the meadow lands are both fertile and beautiful. They are most suitable for planting crops and for raising cattle of all kinds, and there are good sites for building towns and villages. The harbors are incredibly fine and there are many great rivers with broad channels and the majority contain gold....

The inhabitants of this island, and all the rest that I discovered or heard of, go naked, as their mothers bore them, men and women alike. A few of the women, however, cover a single place with a leaf of a

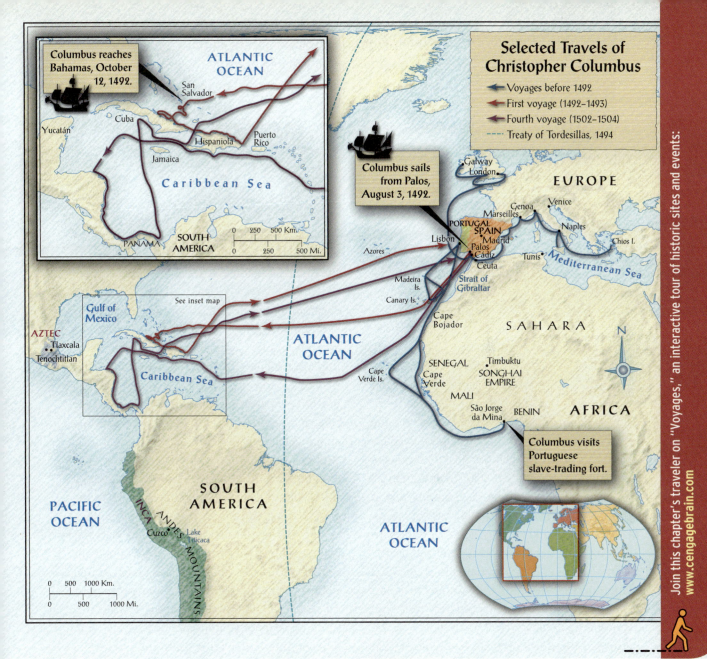

Selected Travels of Christopher Columbus

→ Voyages before 1492
→ First voyage (1492–1493)
→ Fourth voyage (1502–1504)
--- Treaty of Tordesillas, 1494

Columbus reaches Bahamas, October 12, 1492.

Columbus sails from Palos, August 3, 1492.

Columbus visits Portuguese slave-trading fort.

ATLANTIC OCEAN

San Salvador

Cuba

Yucatán

Hispaniola

Puerto Rico

Jamaica

Caribbean Sea

PANAMA

SOUTH AMERICA

0   250   500 Km.
0   250   500 Mi.

EUROPE

Galway
London

Genoa   Venice

Marseilles   Naples

PORTUGAL   SPAIN   Chios I.

Lisbon   Madrid   Tunis   Mediterranean Sea

Palos   Cádiz
Ceuta

Azores   Strait of Gibraltar

Madeira Is.

Canary Is.

Cape Bojador

SAHARA

SENEGAL   Timbuktu
Cape   SONGHAI
Verde   EMPIRE

MALI   AFRICA

Cape Verde Is.   São Jorge da Mina   BENIN

See inset map

Gulf of Mexico

AZTEC
Tlaxcala
Tenochtitlan

Caribbean Sea

ATLANTIC OCEAN

ATLANTIC OCEAN

SOUTH AMERICA

PACIFIC OCEAN

INCA   ANDES MOUNTAINS
Cuzco   Lake Titicaca

0   500   1000 Km.
0   500   1000 Mi.

N

Join this chapter's traveler on "Voyages," an interactive tour of historic sites and events:
www.cengagebrain.com

	1300	1350	1400	1450	1500	1550	1600

Lifetime of Christopher Columbus
1451   1506

MEXICO AND CARIBBEAN
Aztec settle Tenochtitlan 1325
Triple Alliance — Aztec Empire 1428
Viceroyalty of New Spain
1521

SOUTH AMERICA
Inca settle Cuzco 1400
Inca Empire 1438
1532
Viceroyalty of Peru 1543

Cabral reaches Brazil 1500
Portuguese organize settlement of Brazil 1533

CONQUEST AND EXCHANGE
Portugal settles Azores 1350
Portugal begins Atlantic slave trade 1444
Columbus reaches Hispaniola 1492
Conquest of Aztec 1519–1521
Conquest of Inca 1532   1550

Gutenberg Bible printed 1454
Columbus brings European plants and animals to America 1493
First smallpox in America 1518

plant or piece of cotton which they weave for the purpose. They have no iron or steel or arms and are not capable of using them, not because they are not strong and well built but because they are amazingly timid....

I gave them a thousand pretty things that I had brought, in order to gain their love and incline them to become Christians.[1]

Christopher Columbus
(1451–1506) Spanish navigator who visited European colonies in the Mediterranean, the Atlantic Ocean, and the west coast of Africa before voyaging to the island of Hispaniola in 1492. Made three subsequent voyages before being removed as viceroy in 1499.

In search of gold, they also hoped to convert the indigenous peoples to Christianity.

At the time of his first voyage to the Americas, Columbus was in his early forties. Born in Genoa, Italy, as a teenager he had sailed on wooden boats to the different settlements of Genoese and Venetian merchants in the Mediterranean. Later, in his thirties, he lived for three years in the Madeira Islands, a Portuguese possession off the African coast in the Atlantic, and visited the Portuguese slave-trading fort at Sao Jorge da Mina on the west coast of Africa. Madeira, the world's largest sugar producer in 1492, used indigenous peoples from the nearby Canary Islands and African slaves to work on its plantations. While in the Canary Islands, Columbus heard that one could sail west, and, assuming he could reach Asia by doing so, he persuaded the rulers of Spain to finance a trial voyage across the Atlantic in search of the Indies, the source of so many valuable spices. After the

first voyage in 1492, he made three more trips to the Americas before his death in 1506.

Unlike voyages the Vikings made to Newfoundland around 1000 and unlike Ming Chinese voyages to East Africa in the 1400s, the Spanish and Portuguese voyages had far-reaching consequences. After 1300, while the Aztec in Mexico and the Inca in Peru were creating powerful expansionist empires, on the opposite side of the Atlantic Europeans were learning about geography as part of their humanistic studies. Spanish and Portuguese explorers traveled farther and farther, first to the islands of the Mediterranean and the Atlantic, then to the west coast of Africa, and finally to the Americas. Wherever they landed, they claimed places as colonies for their monarchs. The Europeans transported plants, animals, and people (often against their will) to entirely new environments on the other side of the Atlantic. Within one hundred years of Columbus's first voyage, millions of Amerindians (the death toll reached 95 percent in some areas) had perished, victims of European diseases that no one understood.

FOCUS QUESTIONS

▶ How did the Aztec form their empire? How did the Inca form theirs? How did each hold their empire together, and what was each empire's major weakness?

▶ How did humanist scholarship encourage oceanic exploration? What motivated the Portuguese, particularly Prince Henry the Navigator, to explore West Africa?

▶ How did the Spanish and the Portuguese establish their empires in the Americas so quickly?

▶ What was the Columbian exchange? Which elements of the exchange had the greatest impact on the Americas? On Afro-Eurasia?

The Aztec Empire of Mexico, 1325–1519

Starting sometime around 1325, the Aztec, a people based in western Mexico, moved into central Mexico to Tenochtitlan (some 30 miles, or 50 km, northeast of modern-day Mexico City). The Aztec were one of many Nahua (NAH-wah) peoples who spoke the Nahuatl (NAH-waht) language. Like the Maya, the Nahua peoples had a complex calendrical system, built large stone monuments, and played a ritual ball game. The Aztec believed in a pantheon of gods headed by the sun that demanded blood sacrifices from their devotees. To sustain these gods, they continually went to war, gradually conquering many of the city-states in central Mexico to form the **Aztec Empire**.

The Aztec Settlement of Tenochtitlan

Though each people tells the story of its past differently, disparate accounts agree that around the 1200s various groups migrated to central Mexico. The heart of this area is the Valley of Mexico, 10,000 feet (3,000 m) above sea level and surrounded by volcanoes. The Valley of Mexico contains many shallow lakes and much fertile land.

The last Nahua groups to arrive referred to themselves as "Mexica" (meh-SHE-kah), the origin of the word *Mexico*; they came from a place called Aztlan, the origin of *Aztec,* a term no one at the time used but which this text will use despite its imperfections. Linguistic analysis of

the Nahuatl language indicates that its speakers originated somewhere in the southwest United States or northern Mexico.

By the 1300s, some fifty city-states, called **altepetl** (al-TEH-pe-tel), occupied central Mexico, each with its own leader, or "speaker," and its own government. Each altepetl had a palace for its ruler, a pyramid-shaped temple, and a market. The Aztec migrated to the region around the historic urban center of Teotihuacan, a large city with many lakes. Since this region was already home to several rival altepetl, the Aztec were forced to settle in a swampland called **Tenochtitlan** (teh-noch-TIT-lan).

Traditional accounts say the Aztec people arrived at Tenochtitlan in 1325, a date confirmed by archaeological excavation. The Aztec gradually reclaimed large areas of the swamps and on the drier, more stable areas erected stone buildings held together with mortar. They planted flowers everywhere and walked on planks or traveled by canoe from one reclaimed area to another.

Aztec Empire An empire based in Tenochtitlan (modern-day Mexico City) (see Map 15.1). Founded in 1325, the dynasty formed the Triple Alliance and began to expand its territory in 1428. At its peak it included 450 separate altepetl city-states in modern-day Mexico and Guatemala and ruled over a population of 4 to 6 million.

altepetl The 450 city-states of the Aztec Empire. Each altepetl had its own leader, or "speaker," its own government, a palace for its ruler, a pyramid-shaped temple, and a market.

Tenochtitlan Capital city of the Aztec, which they reclaimed from swampland. Housed a population of some 200,000 people.

Map 15.1 The Aztec Empire

Starting from their capital at Tenochtitlan (modern Mexico City), the Aztec conquered different neighboring peoples living between the Gulf of Mexico and the Pacific Ocean. Aztec rulers required the conquered peoples to pay taxes and submit tribute but gave few benefits in return. When Cortés landed on the coast of Mexico, he quickly found allies among the conquered peoples, particularly the Tlaxcalans. © Cengage Learning

Interactive Map

At its height, Tenochtitlan contained 60,000 dwellings, home to perhaps 200,000 people in an area of 5 square miles (13 sq km). The central marketplace offered cooked and uncooked food, slaves, tobacco products, and luxury goods made from gold, silver, and feathers. Consumers used cotton cloaks, cacao beans, and feather quills filled with gold dust as media of exchange, since the Aztec had no coins.

Nahua Religion and Society

The most important Nahua deity, the sun, controlled agriculture, and crops—primarily corn, beans, and peppers—were the main source of food. Engaged in a constant struggle with the forces of dark, the sun needed regular offerings of "precious water," the Nahuatl term for human blood. Ranking just under the sun-god were the gods of rain and agriculture. In addition, each altepetl had several deities associated with its native place. The Aztec believed that their patron god was Huitzilopochtli (wheat-zeel-oh-POSHT-lee), the hummingbird of the south. Another important god was Quetzalcoatl (kate-zahl-CO-ah-tal),

a creator god who was credited with devising the Nahuatl writing system.

The Nahua wrote on bark paper or deerskin covered with a thin white layer of limestone plaster. Their writing system functioned quite differently from Mayan. Nahuatl texts combine pictures with rebus writing, which uses images to represent something with the same sound; in English, for example, a picture of an eye functions as a rebus for the word *I*. The Nahua writing system served as a trigger to memory; people who had been trained to tell a certain story could look at a Nahua manuscript and be reminded of the details. But if one did not know the original story beforehand, it was impossible to make it out.

The leader of the Aztec, their Great Speaker, was in charge of all external matters, including war, the receipt of gifts, and relations with other altepetl. A group of nobles, priests, and successful warriors chose the new Great Speaker, and although they treated him as their ritual superior, they could depose him if they did not approve of his rule. All the top officials came from the royal family and had large private estates.

Nahua Writing   This Nahua manuscript depicts the main events that occurred during the life of a ruler. The circles near each figure are numbers. The red lines indicate the order of reading, starting from the top on the right-hand side and moving across the page to the left-hand side. The small crouching figure at the bottom of the red line on the upper left holds a club with obsidian blades, the Aztec weapon of choice.

Most of the Nahua were commoners, each of whom belonged to a "big house," a group who believed they were descended from a common ancestor. Ordinary people and slaves farmed the land and generated the surplus that underpinned the expansion of the Aztec alte-petl. The Nahua prepared the soil and planted seeds by hand. Because they had no draft animals, metal tools, or wheels, everything had to be carried and cultivated by hand.

Corn ripened in only fifty days, providing sufficient food for a family as well as a surplus. Grinding corn was exclusively women's work; for fear that they might antagonize the gods, men were forbidden to help. Ordinary people were required to pay tribute to their Aztec overlords by contributing a share of the crop, performing labor service for a certain time, paying other goods, and most onerous of all, providing victims for human sacrifice.

The Military and the Conquests of the Aztec

If successful in battle, warriors could rise in Aztec society to a high position. They then received lands of their own and were not required to pay taxes on them. Conversely, the best human sacrifice one could offer to the gods, the Nahua believed, was a warrior taken captive in battle. In their system of thirteen heavens and eight underworlds, the highest heaven, the Paradise of the Sun God, was for men who had killed the enemy in battle and for women who had died in childbirth, a type of battle in its own right.

The Aztec troops fitted their clubs, spears, and darts with blades made from obsidian, a volcanic glass that was sharp and easy to work but dulled easily. They protected themselves with thick cotton armor. Hand-to-hand combat was considered the most honorable form of warfare.

In 1428, the Aztec launched a series of conquests that led to the creation of an empire. By 1500, they had conquered 450 altepetl in modern Mexico, extending all the way to Guatemala, and ruled over a subject population estimated at 4 to 6 million (see Map 15.1).[2]

The Aztec conquered other peoples not simply to gain the wealth of subject peoples but also to feed their own deities. Conducting mass sacrifices at their temples, the Aztec killed tens of thousands of victims at a time and displayed their skulls on racks for all to see.

The Aztec Empire, though large and with a beautiful capital, had one major weakness. Once the Aztec conquered a given people, they demanded tribute and took sacrificial victims from them, yet they did nothing to incorporate them further into their empire.

The Inca Empire, 1400–1532

The **Inca Empire**, 2,500 miles (4,000 km) to the south in the highlands of the Andes, was structured differently. Each time the Inca conquered a new group, they integrated them into the empire, requiring them to perform labor and military service and resettling some groups to minimize the chances of revolt. Like the Aztec, the Inca worshiped deities that demanded human sacrifices, but never as many as in Mexico. Although the Inca successfully integrated subject peoples into their empire, they did not have an orderly system of succession. Each time their ruler died, everyone who hoped to succeed him plunged into full-time conflict until a new leader emerged victorious.

> **Inca Empire**   Founded in 1438 by Pachakuti (d. 1471), who launched a series of conquests outward from the capital at Cuzco. At its peak, the empire ruled over a population of 10 to 12 million.
>
> **ayllu**   Andean kin groups of the Inca Empire that worked the land in several adjacent ecological zones so they could maximize their yield should the crops in one zone fail.

Thunder gods. The Inca ruler, the Sapa Inca, or "Unique Inca," claimed descent from the sun-god. The priest of the sun-god was the second most powerful person in the Inca Empire.

Both the Sapa Inca and the sun-god priest belonged to the aristocracy, which was divided into three tiers: the close relatives of the ruler and previous rulers, more distant relatives, and then the leaders of the groups who had been conquered by the Inca. Although most Inca traced their ancestry through their father's line, the ruler's mother's family played a central role in court politics because the ruler took his wives from his mother's family.

The Inca had no orderly system of succession. Each time the Inca ruler died, all contestants for the position from among his male kin launched an all-out war until a single man emerged victorious, much like the system of tanistry prevalent among the Mongols (covered in Chapter 14 of Volume 1). During his reign the Sapa Inca lived as a deity among his subjects. Even so, he had to keep the support of the aristocracy, who could easily overthrow him at any time.

Like the ayllu ancestors, the ruler was believed to continue to live even after death. The Inca mummified the bodies of deceased rulers and other high-ranking family members. They organized the worship of local spirits who inhabited places in the landscape, ancestors of the rulers, and deities into a complex ritual calendar specifying which one was to be worshiped on a

Inca Religion and Andean Society

The ordinary people of the Andes lived in kin groups called **ayllu** (aye-YOU) that worked the land in several adjacent ecological zones. Most ayllu were divided into smaller subgroups, and men tended to marry women from another subgroup. All the people in a given ayllu recognized one person as a common ancestor.

The most important Inca deities were the Creator, the Creator's child the Sun, and the given day. Of 332 shrines in Cuzco, their capital city high in the Andes, 31 received human sacrifices, in many cases a young boy and a young girl, a symbolic married couple. Occasionally larger sacrifices occurred, such as when a ruler died, but the largest number of sacrificial victims killed at a single time was four thousand (as opposed to eighty thousand for the Aztec).

The Inca Expansion

As the Aztec believed their history began with their occupation of Tenochtitlan, the Inca traced their beginnings to their settlement in Cuzco. Archaeological evidence suggests that the Inca moved to Cuzco sometime around 1400. Although oral accounts conflict, most accept the date of 1438 as the year Pachakuti **(patch-ah-KOO-tee)** (d. 1471), the first great Inca ruler, launched military campaigns outward from Cuzco.

Much of Inca warfare consisted of storming enemy forts with a large infantry, often after cutting off access to food and water. For several days enemy forces traded insults and sang hostile songs such as this: "We will drink from the skull of the traitor, we will adorn ourselves with a necklace of his teeth, . . . we will beat the drum made from his skin, and thus we will dance." Attackers in quilted cotton launched arrows, stones from slingshots, and stone spears, and in hand-to-hand combat used clubs, some topped with bronze stars. Like other Andean peoples, the Inca knew how to extract metallic ore from rocks and how to heat different metals to form alloys. They made bronze and copper, but they did not develop their metallurgical expertise beyond making club heads, decorative masks, and ear spools for the nobility.

At its height, the Inca army could field as many as 100,000 men in a single battle, most of the rank-and-file drawn from subject peoples who were required to serve in the army. The rate of Inca expansion was breathtaking. Starting from a single location, Cuzco, by 1532 they ruled over a population estimated at 10 to 12 million inhabitants (see Map 15.2).

Inca Rule of Subject Populations

Unique among the Andean peoples, the Inca incorporated each conquered land and its occupants into their kingdom. Thousands of people

Map 15.2   The Inca Empire

In 1438, the Inca ruler Pachakuti took power in the capital at Cuzco and led his armies to conquer large chunks of territory along the Andes Mountains. Two north-south trunk routes, with subsidiary east-west routes, formed a system of over 25,000 miles (40,000 km) of roads. By 1532, the Inca ruled 10 to 12 million people in an empire of 1,500 square miles (4,000 sq km).
© Cengage Learning   **Interactive Map**

were forced to move to regions far from their original homes.

The Inca, like the Mongols, encouraged different peoples to submit to them by treating those who surrendered gently. They allowed local leaders to continue to serve but required everyone to swear loyalty to the Inca ruler, to grant him all rights to their lands, and to perform labor service as the Inca state required.

Inca officials also delegated power to indigenous leaders. Those of high birth could serve in the Inca government as long as they learned Quechua **(keh-chew-ah)**, the language of the

Inca. Each year Inca officials recorded the population in a census, not with a written script but by using a system of knotted strings, called **quipu** (key-POOH). Each town had a knot keeper who maintained and interpreted the knot records, which were updated annually.

📖 **Primary Source**

Chronicles *Learn how the Inca used the mysterious knotted ropes called quipu as record-keeping devices that helped them govern a vast and prosperous empire.*

To fulfill the Inca's main service tax, male household heads between twenty-five and fifty had to perform two to three months' labor each year. Once assigned a task, a man could get as much help as he liked from his children or wife, a practice that favored families with many children.

The Inca did not treat all subject peoples alike. From some resettled peoples they exacted months of labor, and many subject groups who possessed a specific skill, such as carving stones or making spears, performed that skill for the state. Others did far less. For example, many Inca looked down on a people they called Uru, literally meaning "worm," who lived on the southern edge of Lake Titicaca. The Uru were supposed to catch fish, gather grasses, and weave textiles, but they performed no other labor service. An even more despised group was required each year to submit a single basket filled with lice, not because the Inca wanted the lice, but because they hoped to teach this group the nature of its tax obligations.

quipu Inca system of record keeping that used knots on strings to record the population in a census and divide people into groups of 10, 50, 100, 500, 1,000, 5,000, and 10,000.

Each household also contributed certain goods, such as blankets, textiles, and tools, that were kept in thousands of storehouses throughout the empire. One Spaniard described a storehouse in Cuzco that particularly impressed him: "There is a house in which are kept more than 100,000 dried birds, for from their feathers articles of clothing are made."

One lasting product of the Inca labor system was over 25,000 miles (40,000 km) of magnificent roads (see Map 15.2). While some of these routes predated the Inca conquest, the Inca linked them together into an overall system. Since the Inca did not have the wheel, most of the traffic was by foot, and llamas could carry small loads. With no surveying instruments, the Inca constructed these roads across deserts, yawning chasms, and mountains over 16,000 feet (5,000 m) high. Individual messengers working in shifts could move at an estimated rate of 150 miles (240 km) per day, but troops moved much more slowly, covering perhaps 7 to 9 miles (12–15 km) per day.

Despite its extent, the Inca Empire appeared stronger than it was. Many of the subject peoples resented their heavy labor obligations, and each time an Inca ruler died, the ensuing succession disputes threatened to tear the empire apart.

Keeping Records with Knots The Inca kept all their records by using knotted strings, called quipu, attaching subsidiary cords, sometimes in several tiers, to a main cord. Different types of knots represented different numeric units; skipped knots indicated a zero; the color of the string indicated the item being counted.

Intellectual and Geographic Exploration in Europe, 1300–1500

Between 1300 and 1500, as the Aztec and Inca were expanding their empires overland in the Americas, Portuguese and Spanish ships colonized lands farther and farther away, ultimately reaching the Americas. European scholars extended their fields of study to include many new topics. Meanwhile, new printing technology made books more available and affordable, enabling people like Christopher Columbus to read and compare many different books. Columbus's own trips to the Americas extended the expeditions of earlier explorers.

The Rise of Humanism

Since the founding of universities in Europe around 1200, students had read Greek and Latin texts and the Bible. Instructors used an approach called scholasticism, in which the main goal was to reconcile the many differences among ancient authorities to form a logical system of thought.

Around 1350, a group of Italian scholars pioneered a new intellectual movement called **humanism**. Humanists studied many of the same texts as before, but they tried to impart a more general understanding of them to their students in the hope that students would improve morally and be able to help others do the same.

One of the earliest humanist writers was the Italian poet Petrarch (1304–1374). Scholasticism, Petrarch felt, was too abstract. It did not teach people how to live and how to obtain salvation. Although he composed much poetry in Latin, he is remembered for the poetry he composed in Italian, one of several European vernacular languages that came into written use in the fourteenth and fifteenth centuries.

The ideals of humanism do not lend themselves to easy summary. In 1487, a Venetian woman named Cassandra Fedele (fay-DAY-lay) (1465–1558) addressed the students and faculty of the University of Padua in a public oration that set out her own understanding of

Cameraphoto Arte, Venice / Art Resource, NY

The Art of Humanism In 1487, the scientist, artist, and engineer Leonardo da Vinci portrayed man, not God, as the center of the universe. Above and below the ink drawing, the left-handed Da Vinci wrote notes in mirror writing to explain that his drawing illustrated a text about proportions by the Roman architect Vitruvius (ca. 75–15 B.C.E.). Unlike earlier artists, da Vinci personally dissected corpses so that he could portray the structure of human muscles as accurately as possible.

humanism. Having studied Greek and Latin with a tutor, Fedele urged her audience to devote themselves to studying Cicero, Plato, and Aristotle because, she maintained, while wealth and physical strength cannot last, "those

humanism Intellectual movement begun around 1350 in Italy by scholars who opposed scholasticism. Humanists claimed expertise in the humanities, which included traditional liberal arts—like logic, grammar, arithmetic, and music—as well as fields of study like language, history, literature, and philosophy.

Henry the Navigator (1394–1460) Portuguese prince who supported Portuguese explorations across the Mediterranean to the Moroccan city of Ceuta, across the Atlantic to the Canary and Madeira Islands, and along the West African coast past Cape Bojador (in modern Mauritania).

things which are produced by virtue and intelligence are useful to those who follow." She continued: "Certainly for this reason this part of philosophy has laid claim for itself to the name of 'humanity,' since those who are rough by nature become by these studies more civil and mild-mannered." She eloquently expressed the major tenet of humanism: studying the humanities made students, whether from noble or low-born families, more refined and better people.[3]

Historians call this period of humanist revival the Renaissance, which means "rebirth," to contrast it with the earlier centuries, but many continuities linked the intellectual advances of the twelfth and thirteenth centuries with those of the humanist era.

The introduction of printing in Europe contributed greatly to the humanist movement because movable type made books cheaper. Johannes Gutenberg (ca. 1400–1468) printed the first European book, a Bible, using movable type sometime before 1454. This was not the first book in the world made using movable type; the Chinese knew about movable type as early as the eleventh century, and the world's earliest surviving book using movable type was made in Korea in 1403. We should remember, too, that Gutenberg could not have printed the Bible if paper, a Chinese invention, had not come into widespread use in Europe between 1250 and 1350.

Within fifty years of its introduction, printing had transformed the European book. Although European readers had once prized illuminated manuscripts prepared by hand, with beautiful illustrations and exquisite lettering, now typesetters streamlined texts so that they could be printed more easily. Some of the most popular books described marvels from around the world. The Latin translation of the Greek geographer Ptolemy and the travel account of Marco Polo, a Venetian who traveled in Asia, were both in Columbus's

personal library, and he carefully wrote long notes in the margins of the passages that interested him.

Early European Exploration in the Mediterranean and the Atlantic, 1350–1440

Widely read travel accounts whetted the appetite for trade and exploration. European merchants, primarily from the Italian city-states of Venice and Genoa, maintained settlements in certain locations far from Europe, such as Constantinople (see Map 15.3). These communities had walled enclosures called *factories* that held warehouses, a place for ships to refit, and houses for short- and long-term stays.

After around 1350, as European navigators began to sail past the Strait of Gibraltar into the Atlantic Ocean, cartographers began to show the various Atlantic islands, such as the Canary Islands and the Azores, off the coast of Africa on their maps. One motivation for exploring these unknown islands was religious. As the Catholic rulers of Spain and Portugal regained different Islamic cities in Iberia during the thirteenth and fourteenth centuries, in a campaign called the Reconquista, they hoped to expand Christian territory into North Africa. At the time, Spain itself contained several distinct kingdoms. In 1415, a Portuguese prince named Henry, now known as **Henry the Navigator** (1394–1460), led a force of several thousand men that captured the Moroccan fortress of Ceuta (say-OO-tuh). Using the rhetoric of the Crusades and armed with an order from the pope, his goal was to convert the inhabitants to Christianity.

Henry tried to take the Canary Islands for Christianity in 1424, but the inhabitants, armed only with stone tools, repelled the invaders; nevertheless, the Portuguese captured and enslaved Canary islanders on a regular basis. The Portuguese occupied the island of Madeira, and in 1454 they established plantations there, which soon exported large amounts of sugar.

Many navigators were afraid to venture past the Madeira Islands because of the dreaded torrid zone. Greek and Roman geographers had posited that the northern temperate zone, where people lived, was bordered by an uninhabitable frigid zone to the north and a torrid zone to the

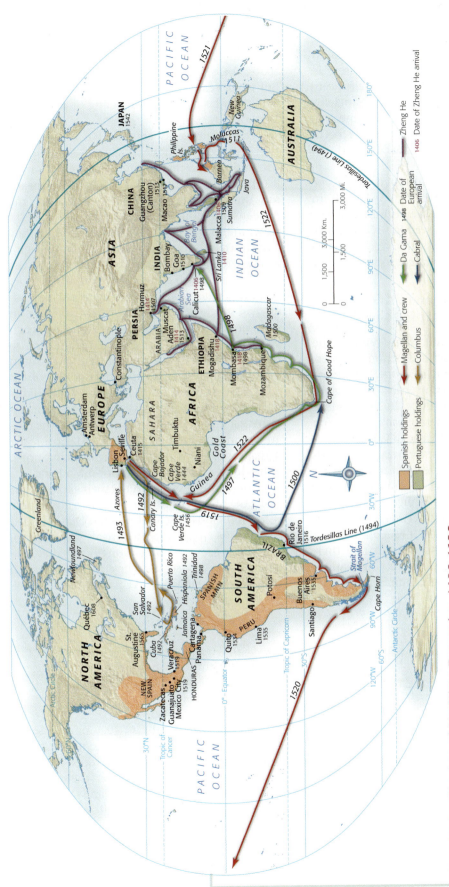

Map 15.3 The Age of Maritime Expansion, 1400–1600
Between 1400 and 1600, maritime explorers pioneered three major new routes: (1) across the Atlantic Ocean from Europe to the Americas, (2) across the Pacific from the Americas to Asia, and (3) south along the west coast of Africa to the Cape of Good Hope. Once the Portuguese Vasco da Gama rounded the Cape in 1498, he connected with the well-traveled hajj route linking East Africa with China that Zheng He's ships had taken in the early 1400s. © Cengage Learning

▶ **Interactive Map**

south, whose scorching heat made it impossible to cross. Following the revival of interest in Greek and Roman geography in the twelfth century, all informed people realized, as the ancients had, that the globe was round. (The American writer Washington Irving invented the myth that everyone before Columbus thought the world was flat.)

Many Europeans had assumed that Cape Bojador, just south of the Canary Islands in modern Morocco, marked the beginning of the impenetrable torrid zone (see Map 15.3). But in 1434 the Portuguese successfully sailed past the cape and reported that no torrid zone existed.

Portuguese Exploration of Africa and the Slave Trade After 1444

If there were no torrid zone, Henry realized, the Portuguese could transport slaves from the west coast of Africa and sell them in Europe. Portuguese vessels had already brought back thirty-eight African slaves from West Africa. In 1444, Henry dispatched six caravels to bring back slaves from the Arguin bank, south of Cape Bojador in modern-day Mauritania. The caravel was a small sailing ship, usually about 75 feet (23 m) long, that had two or three masts with square sails.

In 1444, Henry staged a huge public reception of the slaves for his subjects. The ships' captains presented one slave each to a church and to a Franciscan convent to demonstrate their intention to convert the slaves to Christianity. An eyewitness description captures the scene:

"These people, assembled together on that open space, were an astonishing sight to behold.... But what heart, however hardened it might be, could not be pierced by a feeling of pity at the sight of that company?"[4]

One could easily assume that this description is an early critique of slavery, but, in fact, the author, like many of his contemporaries, accepted the need for slavery. These Europeans saw the trade in slaves as a Christian act: the Africans, as non-Christians, were doomed to suffer in the afterlife, but if they converted, they could attain salvation. From its very beginnings, the European slave trade combined the profit motive with a missionary impulse.

Within ten years the Portuguese slave traders had reached agreements with two rulers in northern Senegal to trade horses for slaves each year. The price of a horse varied from nine to fourteen slaves. By the time of Henry's death in 1460, Portuguese ships had transported about 1,000 slaves a year, fewer than the 4,300 slaves who crossed the Sahara overland in Muslim caravans each year at the time. After 1460, the oceanic trade continued to grow. Many of the African slaves worked on sugar plantations, either in the Canary Islands or on Madeira.

The Portuguese continued their explorations along the African coast, and in 1487, a Portuguese ship commanded by Bartholomew Dias rounded the Cape of Good Hope at Africa's southern tip. The Portuguese became convinced that the quickest way to Asia and the riches of the spice trade was around Africa, as Chapter 16 will show.

The Iberian Conquest of Mexico, Peru, and Brazil, 1492–1580

Columbus's landfall in the Caribbean had immediate and long-lasting consequences. Representatives of the Spanish and Portuguese crowns conquered most of Mexico and Latin America with breathtaking speed. In 1517, the Spanish landed for the first time on the Aztec mainland; by 1540, they controlled all of Mexico, Central America, and the northern sections of South America. Portugal controlled Brazil by 1550. By 1580, Spain had subdued the

peoples of the southern regions of South America. Given that the residents of the Canary Islands, armed only with stone tools, managed to repel all attempts to conquer them for 150 years, how did the Spanish and Portuguese move into the Americas and conquer two sophisticated empires so quickly?

The subject peoples of the Aztec, who had not been incorporated into the empire, welcomed the Spanish as an ally who might help them overthrow their overlords. Moreover, the Spanish arrived in Peru just after the installation of a new Sapa Inca, whose opponents still hoped to wrest power from him. The Europeans also had other advantages, like guns and horses, which the Amerindians lacked. Finally, the Europeans were completely unaware of their most powerful weapon: the disease pools of Europe.

Columbus's First Voyage to the Americas, 1492

In 1479, Isabella (1451–1504) ascended to the throne of Castile and married Ferdinand of Aragon, unifying the two major kingdoms of Spain. Throughout the 1480s, Columbus approached both the Spanish and the Portuguese monarchs to request funds for a voyage to the Indies by sailing west from the Canary Islands.

In keeping with the scholastic and humanist traditions, Columbus cited several authorities in support of the new route he proposed. One passage in the Bible (II Esdras 6:42) stated that the world was six parts land, one part water. Columbus interpreted this to mean that the distance from the Iberian Peninsula to the western edge of Asia in Japan was only 2,700 miles (4,445 km). In actuality, the distance is over 6,000 miles (10,000 km), and the world is about 70 percent water and 30 percent land, but no one at the time knew this.

In rejecting his proposal, the scholars advising the Portuguese and Spanish monarchs held that the world was bigger than Columbus realized. The men on board a ship carrying its own provisions would die of starvation before reaching Asia. These scholars did not realize that any ship crossing the Atlantic would be able to stop in the Americas and obtain food.

Several developments occurred in 1492 that prompted Isabella and Ferdinand to overturn their earlier decision. Granada, the last Muslim outpost, fell in 1492, and all of Spain came under Catholic rule. In that same year the rulers of Aragon and Castile expelled all Jews from Spain, a measure that had been enacted by France and England centuries earlier. Delighted with these developments, Ferdinand and Isabella decided to fund Columbus, primarily because they did not want the Portuguese to do so, and also because he was asking for only a small amount of money, enough to host a foreign prince for a week.

Isabella and Ferdinand gave Columbus two titles: *admiral of the ocean sea* and *viceroy*. An admiral commanded a fleet, but *viceroy* was a new title indicating a representative of the monarch who would govern any lands to which he sailed. Columbus was entitled to one-tenth of any precious metals or spices he found, with the remaining nine-tenths going to Isabella and Ferdinand. No provision was made for his men.

Columbus departed with three ships from Granada on August 3, 1492, and on October 12 of the same year arrived in Hispaniola, a Caribbean island occupied by the modern nations of Haiti and the Dominican Republic. Although Europeans knew about Islamic astrolabes and sextants, Columbus did not use them. He sailed primarily by dead reckoning: he used a compass to stay on a westerly course and, with the help of a clock, estimated his speed and so the approximate distance he traveled in a day. Columbus always thought that he was in Japan; he had no idea that he was in the Americas.

His first encounter with the people on the island was peaceful: "In order to win their friendship," Columbus wrote in his logbook, "I gave some of them red caps and glass beads which they hung round their necks, and also other trifles. These things pleased them greatly and they became marvelously friendly to us." The two sides exchanged gifts and tried to make sense of each other's languages. The island's residents spoke **Arawak**. "They are the color of Canary Islanders (neither black nor white)," Columbus noted, an indication that he thought of the Arawak as potential slaves.

> **Primary Source: The Agreement with Columbus of April 17 and April 30, 1492** *Read the contract signed by Columbus and his royal patrons, and see what riches he hoped to gain from his expedition.*

> **Arawak**   General name for a family of languages spoken in the 1500s over a large region spanning modern Venezuela to Florida. The term also includes all the Arawak-speaking peoples, including those Columbus met on Hispaniola in 1492.

A Comparison of Columbus's and Zheng He's Voyages

Many people have wondered why the Spanish and the Portuguese, and not the Chinese of the Ming dynasty, established the first overseas empires. The Chinese, who first set off in 1405, had almost a century's head start on the

The Santa Maria Versus Chinese Treasure Ships: Is Bigger Always Better? Columbus and Zheng He made journeys of about the same length—5,000 miles (8,000 km)—but in very different vessels. The *Santa Maria* (*left*) measured 80 feet (24 m) long, while the treasure ships of Zheng He (*below*) were over twice that length. Chinese ships, with watertight compartments and movable rudders, were technologically much more sophisticated than European boats of the same period. Still, Columbus complained that his ships were too large to venture into unknown shallow waters (one of his original three ships ran aground during the first voyage), a reminder that smaller boats were better suited for exploration. (From The Ship, an Illustrated History by Bjorn Landstrom. Copyright 1961.)

Europeans. Their biggest ships extended a full 200 feet (61 m) in length, while Columbus's ships were two-fifths of that length. The full fleet of 317 Chinese treasure ships, led by Admiral Zheng He, carried 28,000 men; the doctors on board outnumbered Columbus's entire crew.

China was richer than either Spain or Portugal. It was arguably the richest country in the world in the early fifteenth century, while Spain and Portugal were far smaller. Yet their small size gave both the Portuguese and the Spanish powerful motivation to seek new lands.

Columbus's voyages differed from the Chinese voyages in another critical sense. The navigators on the Chinese treasure ships knew each destination because they followed the best-traveled oceanic route in the world before 1500. Muslim pilgrims from East Africa traveled up the East African coast to reach their holy city of Mecca, and Chinese pilgrims sailed around

Southeast Asia and India to reach the Arabian peninsula. The Zheng He voyages simply linked the two routes together. In contrast, when Columbus and other later explorers set off, they were consciously exploring, looking for new places to colonize and going where no one else (or at least no one else that anyone remembered) had gone before.

The Chinese, however, had no concept of a "colony"—no colonies comparable to the Madeira or Canary Islands. Rulers of earlier Chinese dynasties had sometimes conquered other peoples, but always in contiguous neighboring lands, never overseas.

The Ming government ordered an end to the voyages in 1433 because they brought no financial benefit to the Chinese. In contrast, the Spanish and Portuguese voyages brought their countries immediate returns in gold and slaves and the promise of long-term profits if settlers could establish enterprises such as sugar plantations.

Spanish Exploration After Columbus's First Voyage, 1493–1517

From the beginning Columbus did not exercise tight control over his ships. When he first reached the Americas, the ship *Niña* set off on its own to search for gold, and Columbus had no choice but to welcome it back. The *Santa Maria* had already run aground and been dismantled to make a fort, and Columbus needed both remaining ships to return home. With only two ships, he was forced to leave thirty-nine men behind in the fort, but when he returned on his second voyage in 1493, he found that all had been killed, presumably in disputes with the Arawak over women. Relations between the Arawak and the Spanish were never again as harmonious as they had been during the first voyage.

Once the Spanish realized that Columbus had discovered a new landmass, they negotiated the **Treaty of Tordesillas** (tor-duh-SEE-yuhs) with the Portuguese in 1494, while Columbus was away on his second voyage. The treaty established a dividing line: all newly discovered territory west of the line belonged to Castile, while all the lands to the east were reserved for Portugal. Lands already ruled by a Christian monarch were unaffected by the agreement. Although the pope, himself a Spaniard, supported the treaty, no other European power accepted its terms. Portugal

gained Africa, the route to India, and eventually Brazil.

Columbus never solved the problem of how to compensate his men. When recruiting sailors in Spain he spoke of great riches, but the agreement he had signed with Ferdinand and Isabella left no share of wealth for his men. On his first voyage, his men expected to sail with him to Asia and return, but on subsequent voyages many joined him expressly so that they could settle in the Americas, where they hoped to make fortunes. In 1497, the settlers revolted against Columbus, and he agreed to allow them to use Indians as agricultural laborers. Because Columbus was unpopular with the settlers, in 1499 the Crown removed him from office and replaced him with a new viceroy.

In 1503 the Spanish established the **encomienda system**. Under this system, the Spanish monarchs "entrusted" a specified number of Amerindians to a Spanish settler, who gained the right to extract labor, gold, or other goods from them in exchange for teaching them about Christianity. Although designed to protect the indigenous peoples, the encomienda system often resulted in further exploitation.

Spanish and Portuguese navigators continued to land in new places after 1503. The Spanish crossed 120 miles (193 km) from Cuba to the Yucatán Peninsula in 1508–1509 and reached Florida in 1510. In 1513, Vasco Núñez de Balboa (bal-BOH-uh) crossed through Panama to see the Pacific, and by 1522 the Portuguese navigator Magellan had circumnavigated the globe, although he died before his ship returned home.

The Conquest of Mexico, 1517–1540

One of the early Spanish **conquistadors**, Hernán Cortés (kor-TEZ), led the conquest of Mexico. While in Cuba, Cortés had heard rumors from the Maya peoples of the Yucatán about a larger, richer empire to the north. He sought to launch an

Treaty of Tordesillas Treaty signed by the Portuguese and the Spanish in 1494 that established a dividing line: all territory 1,185 miles (1,910 km) west of the line belonged to Castile, while all the islands to the east were reserved for Portugal.

encomienda system (Literally "entrusted") System established in 1503 by the Spanish in the hope of clarifying arrangements with the colonists and of ending the abuse of indigenous peoples of the Americas.

conquistadors (Literally "conquerors") The term for the Spaniards who conquered Mexico, Peru, and Central America in the 1500s. Many came from families of middling social influence and made their fortunes in the Americas.

Malinché   Nahua noble-woman who served as translator for and adviser to Cortés. Trilingual in Spanish, Nahuatl, and Mayan, she played a crucial role in the Spanish conquest of Mexico because she commanded the respect of the Nahua peoples.

expedition and within two weeks had recruited 530 men to travel with him.

When Cortés landed in the Yucatán in early 1519, he immediately met a woman who helped him penetrate the Spanish-Nahua language barrier: a Nahua noble-woman named **Malinché (mah-lin-HAY)** who had grown up among the Maya and could speak both Nahuatl and Mayan. Given to Cortés as a gift, Malinché learned Spanish quickly. The Spaniards called her Doña Marina. As adviser to Cortés, she played a crucial role in the Spanish conquest of Mexico, partially because she commanded the respect of the Nahua peoples.

Cortés landed on the coast of Mexico on April 20, 1519, and slightly over two years later the Aztec had surrendered their capital and their empire to him. Yet this outcome had been far from certain. The Spanish had only 1,500 men.

On their way to Tenochtitlan, the Spaniards fought a major battle lasting nearly three weeks with the people of Tlaxcala **(tlash-CAH-lah)**. After their defeat the Tlaxcalans became the Spaniards' most important allies against their own hated Aztec overlords. When, in November 1519, the Spaniards first arrived at the capital city of Tenochtitlan, the Great Speaker Moctezuma allowed them to come in unharmed. The Spaniards could not believe how beautiful the city was. According to a Spanish foot

Bibliothèque nationale de France/Snark/Art Resource, NY

Cortés's Interpreter, Malinché   This image dates to the 1500s and shows what Cortés's army looked like when it first landed in Mexico. The Spaniards, with their heavy armor and horse, contrast sharply with the local peoples, who use bands tied around their foreheads to bear the weight of food in containers as well as to carry a small child (*far left*). The army was a mixed force: Malinché, who was Cortés's mistress and interpreter, stands at the far right, with the bearded Cortés on her left.

soldier, "Gazing on such wonderful sights, we did not know what to say, or whether what appeared before us was real." The Aztec were comparably amazed by the Spaniards' guns, armor, and horses, an animal not native to the Americas, whose size greatly impressed the Aztec.

For one week the Spaniards and the Aztec coexisted uneasily, until the Spanish placed Moctezuma under house arrest. Then, in the spring of 1520, while Cortés was away, one of his subordinates ordered his men to massacre the city's inhabitants, and prolonged battles resulted. The Spaniards killed Moctezuma and, after suffering hundreds of casualties, retreated to Tlaxcala, the city of their allies. At this point, it seemed that the Aztec would win.

But by then smallpox had reached the Americas. The native peoples of America had little or no resistance to European smallpox, measles, malaria, sexually transmitted diseases, or even the common cold. Beginning in December 1518, disease ravaged Hispaniola, then Puerto Rico, Jamaica, and Cuba. By October 1520, smallpox had arrived in Tenochtitlan. Moctezuma's successor died of smallpox in early December, and the mass deaths threw the entire city into disarray.

Even so the Spaniards had great difficulty conquering the Aztec. It took eighty days of sustained fighting before Tenochtitlan surrendered in August of 1521. Spanish guns and cannon were not decisive. Some 100,000 troops and a portable fleet of boats supplied by the Tlaxcalans enabled the Spaniards to win.

In 1524, twelve Franciscan friars arrived in Mexico, where they were welcomed by Cortés. The Franciscans became the most important missionary order among the Nahuatl speakers. (See the feature "Movement of Ideas: *The Sacrifice of Isaac:* A Sixteenth-Century Nahuatl Play.") The Spanish gradually imposed a more regular administration over Mexico under the governance of a viceroy.

The Spanish Conquest of Peru, 1532–1550

The order of events in the Spanish conquest of Peru differed from that in Mexico, where Cortés had arrived before smallpox. The smallpox virus traveled overland from Mexico and, in 1528, caused an epidemic in which many Inca, including the Sapa Inca, died. War among the contenders to the throne broke out. In November 1532, when the Spanish forces arrived, led by Francisco Pizarro (pih-ZAHR-oh) (1475–1541), they happened upon the moment of greatest instability in the Inca kingdom. Atahualpa (ah-tuh-WAHL-puh; also spelled Atawallpa) had become ruler only after defeating his older half-brother, whom he still held in captivity. Atahualpa had taken severe countermeasures against his brother's supporters, many of whom sided immediately with the Spaniards.

When Pizarro and his 168 men arrived at Cajamarca, where Atahualpa was living, Atahualpa initially received the Spanish peacefully. Then, on their second day in Cajamarca, the Spanish attacked unexpectedly, gaining an initial advantage from their guns, armor, and horses. An estimated seven thousand Inca, yet not a single Spaniard, died in the carnage.

Pizarro himself captured Atahualpa, who offered to pay an enormous ransom for his release: the Inca filled a room 2,600 cubic feet (74 cubic m) half with gold and half with silver, which the Spaniards melted down and divided among Pizarro's troops. Those with horses received 90 pounds (41 kg), equivalent today to perhaps $500,000, and those on foot half that amount. Then the Spanish reneged on their agreement and killed Atahualpa.

It took twenty years for the Spanish to gain control of Peru. In 1551, they named the first viceroy for Peru and gradually established a more stable administration. The first Spanish census, taken in the 1570s, showed that half the population had died from European disease, with the toll in some places reaching as high as 95 percent.

The Portuguese Settlement of Brazil, 1500–1580

In 1500, Pedro Álvares Cabral (kah-BRAHL) (1467/68–1520) landed in Brazil. Although the Portuguese claimed Brazil following Cabral's voyage, few of them came to this resource-poor country. Most Portuguese sought their wealth in Asia, as discussed in the next chapter.

The Sacrifice of Isaac: A Sixteenth-Century Nahuatl Play

The members of the Catholic orders who lived in Mexico used different approaches to teach the Nahua peoples about Christianity. In addition to printing bilingual catechisms in Spanish and Nahuatl, they sponsored the composition of plays in Nahuatl on religious themes. Since these plays were not published but only circulated in hand-written manuscripts, very few survive. The short play *The Sacrifice of Isaac* recounts the story from the Hebrew Bible of Abraham and Isaac (see pages 38 and 184), which addresses a topic of great interest to the Nahua peoples: human sacrifice.

God the Father appears in the play to ask Abraham to sacrifice his son Isaac, but he later sends an angel to instruct Abraham to offer a lamb instead.

Abraham, his first wife, and Isaac all embody obedience, a virtue prized both by the ancient Hebrews and the Nahua peoples. Abraham's slave Hagar and her son Ishmael urge Isaac to disobey his father; both still worship the sun (not God), a sure clue to the audience that they are evil.

Corresponding faithfully to the version in the Hebrew Bible, the play shows an obedient Isaac offering himself for sacrifice until the moment the angel instructs Abraham to free him and sacrifice a lamb instead. The lively quality of the Nahuatl language suggests that it was written sometime after the Spanish conquest, probably by a native speaker who converted to Christianity.

The Devil, Ishmael, and Hagar Trick Isaac

(A demon enters, dressed either as an angel or as an old man.)

DEMON: What are you doing, young man? For I see your affliction is very great.

ISHMAEL: Most certainly my affliction is great! But how is it that you know if I have pain? Who told you this?

DEMON: Do you not see that I am a messenger from heaven? I was sent here from there in order to tell you what you are to do here on earth.

ISHMAEL: Then I wait to hear your command.

DEMON: Hear then why it is that you are troubled. Do I astound you? Truly it is because of the beloved child, Isaac! Because he is a person of a good life, and because he always has confidence in the commands of his father. So you contrive and wish with all your energy that he not be obedient to his father and mother. Most assuredly I can tell you what you must do to accomplish this.

ISHMAEL: Oh how you comfort me when I hear your advice. Nor do I merit your aid. You are most truly a dweller in heaven and my protector!

DEMON: Open your heart wide to my command! Look now—his father and mother have invited many others to a banquet; they are relaxing and greatly enjoying themselves. Now is the time to give Isaac bad advice so that he might forget his father and his mother and go with you to amuse himself in some other place. And if he should obey you, they will certainly punish their son for this, however well they love him.

ISHMAEL: I shall do just as you command.

DEMON: Then, indeed, I am going to return to heaven. For I came only to console you and tell you what you must do....

(Hagar the slave and her son Ishmael enter.)

HAGAR: Now while the great lord Abraham once again entertains many for the sake of his son whom he so greatly loves, we are only servants. He values us but little. And you, my son, merit nothing, are worthy of nothing. Oh that I might placate myself through you, and that you might calm all my torment upon earth! But so it is; your birth and its reward are eternal tears.

(Here they both weep—also the son.)

ISHMAEL: Oh you sun! You who are so high! Warm us even here with your great splendor as well as in every part of the world, and—in the way which you are able—prosper all the peoples of the earth! And to us, yes, even to us two poor ones—who merit nothing and who are worthy of nothing! Know now, oh my mother, what I shall do: later, when they are all feasting, perhaps I shall be able to lead Isaac away with some deceit, so that we might go to divert ourselves in some other quarter. With this action he will violate the precept of his father, who will not then love him with all of his heart.

HAGAR: What you are thinking is very good. Do it in that way.*

Abraham and Isaac on the Mountain

ABRAHAM: Now hear me, my beloved son! Truly this is what the almighty God has commanded me in order that His loving and divine precept might be fulfilled; and so that He might see whether we—the inhabitants of the earth—love Him and execute His Divine Will. For He is the Lord of the living and of the dead. Now with great humility, accept death! For assuredly He says this: "Truly I shall be able to raise the dead back to life, I who am the Life Eternal." Then let His will be done in every part of the earth.

(Here Abraham weeps. The Music of the "Misericordia" is heard.)

ISAAC: Do not weep, my beloved and honored father! For truly I accept death with great happiness. May the precious will of God be done as He has commanded you....

ANGEL: Abraham! Abraham!

(Here an angel appears and seizes Abraham's hand so that he is unable to kill his son.)

ABRAHAM: Who are you, you who speak to me?

ANGEL: Now know the following by the authority and word of God. For He has seen how much you love Him; that you fulfill His divine precept; that you do not infringe it; that you brought your cherished son—he whom you love so much—here to the peak of the mountain; and that you have come to offer him here as a burnt sacrifice to God the almighty Father. Now truly for all this, by His loving Will, I have come to tell you to desist, for your cherished son Isaac does not have to die.

ABRAHAM: May His adored will be done as He wishes it. Come here, oh my beloved son! Truly you have now been saved by death by His hand.

(Here he [Abraham or Isaac] unties the cloth with which he was blindfolded, and loosens the ropes with which his hands were bound.)

ANGEL: Then understand this: as a substitute for your beloved son, you shall prepare a lamb as God wishes it. Go, for I shall accompany you and leave you at your house.

Source: Excerpts from Marilyn Ekdahl Ravicz, *Early Colonial Religious Drama in Mexico: From Tzompantli to Golgotha,* The Catholic University of America Press, 1970, pp. 87–90 and 95–96. Reprinted with permission of The Catholic University of America Press.

QUESTIONS FOR ANALYSIS

▶ What information does the author include to make the audience think Ishmael is bad and Isaac good?

▶ What does the text propose as an appropriate substitute for human sacrifice?

In 1533 the Portuguese monarch John III (r. 1521–1557) made a systematic effort to encourage the settlement of Brazil by granting large territories to Portuguese nobles, many of them his courtiers.

Finding no significant amounts of gold, the Portuguese began to build sugar plantations. Since so many of the indigenous Amerindians had died, the plantation owners imported slaves from Africa.

In 1580 Philip II succeeded to the throne of both Spain and Portugal, and the two countries remained under a single king until 1640. The Portuguese and Spanish empires had evolved parallel structures independently. The highest colonial official, the viceroy, presided over a royal colony and governed in concert with an advisory council who could appeal any decisions to the king.

The social structure in the colonies was basically the same throughout Latin America. At the top of society were those born in Europe, who served as military leaders, royal officials, or high church figures. Below them were creoles, those with two European parents but born in the Americas. Those of mixed descent (mestizos in Spanish-speaking regions, memlucos in Brazil) ranked even lower, with only Amerindians and African slaves below them. By 1600, 100,000 Africans lived in Brazil, many working in the hundreds of sugar mills all over the colony.

The Columbian Exchange

At the same time that European diseases like smallpox devastated the peoples living in America, European animals like the horse, cow, and sheep came to the Americas and flourished. In the other direction came plant foods indigenous to the Americas like tomatoes, potatoes, peanuts, and chili peppers. This transfer is referred to as the **Columbian exchange**.

Of all the European imports, smallpox had the most devastating effect on the Americas. Only someone suffering an outbreak can transmit smallpox, which is contagious for about a month: after two weeks of incubation, fever and vomiting strike; the ill person's skin then breaks out with the pox, small pustules that dry up after about ten days. Either the victim dies during those ten days or survives, typically with a pock-marked face and body.

One Nahuatl description captures the extent of the suffering:

Columbian exchange All the plants, animals, goods, and diseases that crossed the Atlantic, and sometimes the Pacific, after 1492.

Sores erupted on our faces, our breasts, our bellies…. The sick were so utterly helpless that they could only lie on their beds like corpses, unable to move their limbs or even their heads…. If they did move their bodies, they screamed with pain.[5]

Although no plants or animals had an effect as immediate as smallpox, the long-term effects of the Columbian exchange in plants and animals indelibly altered the landscape, diets, and population histories of both the Americas and Europe. When Columbus landed on Hispaniola, he immediately realized how different the plants were: "All the trees were as different from ours as day from night, and so the fruits, the herbage, the rocks, and all things." He also remarked on the absence of livestock: "I saw neither sheep nor goats nor any other beast."[6]

On his second voyage in 1493, Columbus carried cuttings of European plants, including wheat, melons, sugar cane, and other fruits and vegetables. He also brought pigs, horses, chickens, sheep, goats, and cattle.

While smallpox traveled from Europe to the Americas, there is evidence that syphilis traveled in the other direction. The first well-documented outbreaks of syphilis in Europe occurred around 1495, and one physician claimed that Columbus's men brought it to Madrid soon after 1492. No European skeletons with signs of syphilis before 1500 have been found, but an Amerindian skeleton with syphilis has, suggesting that the disease did indeed move from the Americas to Europe. Causing genuine pain, syphilis could be passed to the next generation and was fatal for about one-quarter of those who contracted it, but it did not cause mass deaths.

Assessing the loss of Amerindian life due to smallpox and the other European diseases has caused much debate among historians because no population statistics exist for the Americas before 1492. Figures for the population of the entire Americas can be little more than guesswork. For the entire period of European colonization in all parts of the Americas, guesses at the total death toll from European diseases, based on controversial estimates of precontact populations, range from a low of 10 million to a high of over 100 million.

By 1600, two extremely successful agricultural enterprises had spread through the Americas. One was sugar, and the other was cattle raising. The Americas contained huge expanses of grasslands in Venezuela and Colombia, from Mexico north to Canada, and in Argentina and Uruguay. In each case the Spaniards began on the coastal edge of a grassland and followed their rapidly multiplying herds of cattle to the interior.

As European food crops transformed the diet of those living in the Americas, so too did American food crops transform the eating habits of people in Afro-Eurasia. American food crops moved into West Africa, particularly modern Nigeria, where even today people eat corn, peanuts, squash, manioc (cassava), and sweet potatoes.

Two crops in particular played an important role throughout Afro-Eurasia: corn and potatoes (including sweet potatoes). Both produced higher yields than wheat and grew in less desirable fields, such as on the slopes of hills. Although few people anywhere in the world preferred corn or potatoes to their original wheat-based or rice-based diet, if the main crop failed, hungry people gratefully ate the American transplants. By the eighteenth century corn and potatoes had reached as far as India and China, and the population in both places increased markedly.

Chapter Review and Learning Activities

Unlike the earlier Viking voyages to Newfoundland and Chinese expeditions to East Africa, Columbus's landfall in 1492 had lasting consequences. The major difference was that the arrival of the Spaniards and the Portuguese initiated the Columbian exchange, an unprecedented transfer of diseases, plants, and animals from one continent to another. The mass deaths of the Amerindians preceded the large-scale movement of Europeans and Africans to the Americas. The migrations in the first hundred years after Columbus's arrival in Hispaniola produced the mixed composition of the population of the Americas today. As we will see in the next chapter, the arrival of the Europeans had a very different impact on Asia.

How did the Aztec form their empire? How did the Inca form theirs? How did each hold their empire together, and what was each empire's major weakness?

The Aztec, based in modern Mexico, demanded much from their subject peoples, including grain and other goods, labor, and sacrificial victims, but they gave little in return. Living in their own communities, the subject peoples had little reason to be loyal to the Aztec and every reason to ally with any power against them.

The Inca Empire of the Andes was organized differently. Once the Inca conquered a locality, they incorporated its residents in their empire, sometimes even relocating them. Their weakness was that whenever the Sapa Inca died or became weak, all those desiring to succeed him engaged in a free-for-all struggle, which created great instability in the empire. When one leader emerged victorious, he took severe measures against all his rivals, who would readily ally with any enemy of the new Sapa Inca.

 How did humanist scholarship encourage oceanic exploration? What motivated the Portuguese, particularly Prince Henry the Navigator, to explore West Africa?

Benefiting from the lowered cost of printed books, the humanists emphasized the rigorous re-examination of the classics, preferably in the original Latin and Greek, including geographical works. Christopher Columbus owned copies of Ptolemy's geography and Marco Polo's travel account. Although ancient geographers posited the existence of a torrid zone that could not be crossed because it was scorchingly hot, Portuguese navigators, many sponsored by Prince Henry the Navigator, made their way down the coast of West Africa and realized that the zone did not exist. Hoping to make Portugal a wealthy slave-trading state, the Portuguese rulers professed a desire to convert the Africans they captured and brought them to Europe as slaves.

 How did the Spanish and the Portuguese establish their empires in the Americas so quickly?

The Spanish tapped the resentment of the subject peoples, including both the Tlaxcalans in Mexico and the Inca opponents of Atahualpa, against their rulers. European horses and guns frightened the Amerindians, but the most powerful European weapon was invisible: European smallpox and other diseases to which Amerindians had no resistance. The mass deaths made it possible for the Spanish and Portuguese to gain control over modern-day Mexico, Central America, and South America within one hundred years after Columbus's 1492 arrival in Hispaniola.

 What was the Columbian exchange? Which elements of the exchange had the greatest impact on the Americas? On Afro-Eurasia?

Of all the plants, animals, and microbes going between the Americas and Afro-Eurasia after 1492, disease had the greatest impact. The death toll from smallpox ranged between 50 and 90 percent, and estimates suggest that at least 10 million Amerindians died in the years after the first outbreak of smallpox in 1518. American food crops traveling in the other direction, particularly corn and potatoes, spread throughout Afro-Eurasia and enabled many to survive famines.

FOR FURTHER REFERENCE

Coe, Michael. *Mexico*. London: Thames and Hudson, 1984.

Cohen, J. M., trans. *The Four Voyages of Christopher Columbus*. New York: Penguin, 1969.

D'Altroy, Terence. *The Incas*. Malden, Mass.: Blackwell Publishing, 2002.

Flint, Valerie I. J. *The Imaginative Landscape of Christopher Columbus*. Princeton: Princeton University Press, 1992.

Grafton, Anthony, et al. *New Worlds, Ancient Texts: The Power of Tradition and the Shock of Discovery*. Cambridge: The Belknap Press of Harvard University Press, 1992.

Lockhart, James. *The Nahuas After the Conquest: A Social and Cultural History of the Indians of Central Mexico, Sixteenth Through Eighteenth Centuries*. Stanford: Stanford University Press, 1992.

Lockhart, James, and Stuart Schwartz. *Early Latin America: A History of Colonial Spanish America and Brazil*. New York: Cambridge University Press, 1983.

Russell, Peter. *Prince Henry "the Navigator": A Life*. New Haven: Yale University Press, 2000.

Schwartz, Stuart B. *The Iberian Mediterranean and Atlantic Traditions in the Formation of Columbus as a Colonizer*. Minneapolis: The Associates of the James Ford Bell Library, University of Minnesota, 1986.

Schwartz, Stuart B. *Victors and Vanquished: Spanish and Nahua Views of the Conquest of Mexico*. New York: Bedford/St. Martin's, 2000.

Smith, Michael E. *The Aztecs*. Malden, Mass.: Blackwell Publishing, 1996.

KEY TERMS

Christopher Columbus (324)

Aztec Empire (325)

altepetl (325)

Tenochtitlan (325)

Inca Empire (328)

ayllu (328)

quipu (330)

humanism (332)

Henry the Navigator (332)

Arawak (335)

Treaty of Tordesillas (337)

encomienda system (337)

conquistadors (337)

Malinché (338)

Columbian exchange (342)

VOYAGES ON THE WEB

Voyages: Christopher Columbus

"Voyages" is a real time excursion to historical sites in this chapter and includes interactive activities and study tools such as audio summaries, animated maps, and flashcards.

Visual Evidence: The Ten Stages of Inca Life According to Guamán Poma

"Visual Evidence" features artifacts, works of art, or photographs, along with a brief descriptive essay and discussion questions to guide your analysis of visual sources.

World History in Today's World: Miss Bolivia Speaks Out

"World History in Today's World" makes the connection between features of modern life and their origins in the periods in this chapter.

CourseMate

Go to the CourseMate website at *www.cengagebrain.com* for additional study tools and review materials—including audio and video clips—for this chapter.

Maritime Expansion in Afro-Eurasia, 1500–1700

Matteo Ricci (left) and Another Missionary (Private Collection/The Bridgeman Art Library)

The Italian priest **Matteo Ricci** (1552–1610) knew more about China than any other European of his time. Though frustrated by the small number of converts he made to Christianity during his two decades as a missionary, Ricci **(REE-chee)** described Chinese political and social life in positive terms. While Ricci was sometimes less complimentary, in the following passage his idealized view of China was meant as a criticism of his own society. Ricci was correct in his assessment that China was more populous, more prosperous, and more stable than Europe in the first decade of the seventeenth century:

It seems to be quite remarkable ... that in a kingdom of almost limitless expanse and innumerable population, and abounding in copious supplies of every description, though they have a well-equipped army and navy that could easily conquer the neighboring nations, neither the King nor his people ever think of waging a war of aggression.... In this respect they are much different from the people of Europe, who are frequently discontent with their own governments and covetous of what others enjoy.... Another remarkable fact and ... marking a difference from the West, is that the entire kingdom is administered by ... Philosophers. The responsibility for orderly management of the entire realm is wholly and completely committed to their charge and care.... Fighting and violence among the people are practically unheard of.... On the contrary, one who will not fight and restrains himself from returning a blow is praised for his prudence and bravery.[1]

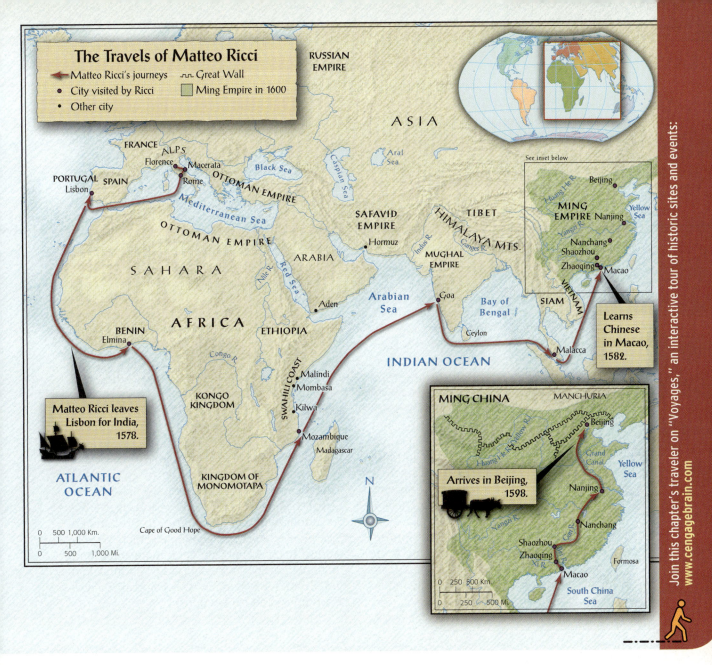

The Travels of Matteo Ricci

- → Matteo Ricci's journeys
- ● City visited by Ricci
- ● Other city
- ∿∿∿ Great Wall
- ▨ Ming Empire in 1600

Matteo Ricci leaves Lisbon for India, 1578.

Learns Chinese in Macao, 1582.

Arrives in Beijing, 1598.

RUSSIAN EMPIRE

ASIA

FRANCE
ALPS
Florence • Macerata
Rome
OTTOMAN EMPIRE

PORTUGAL SPAIN
Lisbon

Black Sea

Caspian Sea

Aral Sea

TIBET

HIMALAYA MTS.

Mediterranean Sea

OTTOMAN EMPIRE

SAHARA

SAFAVID EMPIRE

Hormuz

ARABIA

MUGHAL EMPIRE

AFRICA

Nile R.

Red Sea

Aden

ETHIOPIA

BENIN
Elmina

Congo R.

KONGO KINGDOM

SWAHILI COAST
Malindi
Mombasa
Kilwa

Mozambique

Madagascar

KINGDOM OF MONOMOTAPA

ATLANTIC OCEAN

Goa

Arabian Sea

Bay of Bengal

Ceylon

INDIAN OCEAN

SIAM

VIETNAM

Malacca

Cape of Good Hope

N

See inset below

MING EMPIRE
Beijing
Huang He R.
Nanjing
Yellow Sea
Yangzi R.
Nanchang
Shaozhou
Zhaoqing
Macao

MING CHINA
MANCHURIA
Huang He (Yellow R.)
Beijing
Grand Canal
Yellow Sea
Nanjing
Yangzi R.
Nanchang
Can R.
Shaozhou
Zhaoqing
Xi R.
Macao
Formosa
South China Sea

0   500 1,000 Km.
0   500 1,000 Mi.

0   250 500 Km.
0   250 500 Mi.

Join this chapter's traveler on "Voyages," an interactive tour of historic sites and events: www.cengagebrain.com

	1475	1500	1525	1550	1575	1600	1625	1650	1675

Lifetime of Matteo Ricci 1552 – 1610

EUROPE

Vasco da Gama sails for India 1497

Martin Luther sets off Protestant Reformation 1517

Dutch East India Company founded 1602

AFRICA

Reign of Kongo King Afonso Mvemba a Nzinga 1506 – 1543

Dutch at Cape Town 1652

SOUTH AND EAST ASIA

Ming dynasty — 1644

Reign of Akbar in Mughal India 1556 – 1605

Tokugawa Shogunate founded in Japan 1603

Matteo Ricci (1552–1610) Italian Jesuit missionary who traveled to China in the sixteenth century. Tried unsuccessfully to reconcile Christianity with Confucianism and convert Ming scholar-officials.

From Ricci's point of view, all that China lacked was religious truth. He understood that to communicate his Christian ideas he had to conform to the expectations of the "Philosophers," the scholar-officials who staffed the enormous imperial bureaucracy of Ming China. To this end, he learned Mandarin Chinese, studied Confucian texts, and dressed in silk garments to show a social status "equal of a Magistrate."

Italian by birth, Ricci joined the Jesuits, a Catholic religious order dedicated to "conversion of the Infidels." Because it was the Portuguese who pioneered the direct oceanic route from Europe to Asia, Ricci traveled from Rome to Lisbon to learn Portuguese and prepare for his mission. He then spent four years in India before traveling to China, where he lived from 1582 until his death in 1610. Meanwhile, other Jesuits were traveling to Japan, Brazil, Quebec, West Africa, and the Mississippi River Valley, taking advantage of the new maritime connections established in the sixteenth century by the navigators who pioneered direct routes from Europe to the Americas, West Africa, the Indian Ocean, and East Asia.

Primary Source:
Journals: Matteo Ricci
This story about Jesuit missionaries in China provides an interesting look at the link between religion and politics in the early seventeenth century.

While European mariners were a new presence in the Indian Ocean, they traveled on routes that had long been used by Asian and African merchants. In fact, the new maritime routes from Europe to Africa, the Indian Ocean, and East Asia first developed by Portuguese sailors were far less revolutionary than the connections between Europe, Africa, and the Americas that followed from the voyages of Christopher Columbus (see Chapter 15). The dominant powers in Asia remained land-based empires, such as Mughal (MOO-gahl) India and Ming China, rather than European overseas colonies. As Matteo Ricci's story shows, Europeans who traveled the maritime routes often operated on the margins of powerful Asian empires.

Still, the creation of more direct and sustained networks accelerated commercial and cultural interaction among Europe, Africa, and South and East Asia in the sixteenth and early seventeenth centuries, especially after the Dutch displaced the Portuguese as the main European players in the Indian Ocean. Following the maritime trade routes to China, Matteo Ricci became a key figure in the beginning of an ongoing "great encounter" between Europe and China.[2] Between 1400 and 1600, new and deepening economic linkages developed in the Indian Ocean, even as the Asian empires, such as India and China, became larger and more ambitious. In both Europe and Asia, major cultural and intellectual developments accompanied new encounters and connections.

FOCUS QUESTIONS

▸ What changes and continuities were associated with Portuguese and Dutch involvement in the Indian Ocean trade?

▸ What were the main political characteristics of the major South Asian and East Asian states? How was their development influenced by the new maritime connections of the sixteenth and early seventeenth centuries?

▸ How did religious and intellectual traditions of Eurasia change during this period, and what were the effects of encounters between them?

Maritime Trade Connections: Europe, the Indian Ocean, and Africa, 1500–1660

Unlike the Atlantic, the Indian Ocean had long served to connect rather than divide, facilitating trade among East Africa, the Persian Gulf, India, Southeast Asia, and China. The Portuguese added a new element to this network when their ships appeared in Indian Ocean waters in the early 1500s. Though their intention was to create an empire like that being constructed by Spain in the Americas, their political and military ambitions went largely unmet. The Dutch followed the Portuguese, stimulating the older oceanic trade networks while also building new ones.

Africa was connected to both the Atlantic and Indian Ocean systems. In East Africa the Portuguese encountered an existing commercial network. In West Africa, however, an entirely new oceanic trade began: the Atlantic slave trade.

Portugal's Entry into the Indian Ocean, 1498–1600

Henry the Navigator's exploration of the Atlantic Ocean culminated in 1488 when Bartholomew Dias and his crew rounded the southern tip of Africa at the Cape of Good Hope (see Chapter 15). These journeys had both economic and religious motives: in seeking an oceanic trade link with Asia, the Portuguese were trying to outflank Muslim intermediaries who controlled the land routes through western Asia and North Africa.

In 1497 the Portuguese explorer **Vasco da Gama** (1460–1524) sailed for India. Sailing up the East African coast, da Gama hired a local pilot who used Arabic-language charts and navigational guides to guide the Portuguese from Africa to western India. One of these books boasted of the superiority of Arab knowledge: "We possess scientific books that give stellar altitudes.... [Europeans] have no science and no books, only the compass.... They admit we have a better knowledge of the sea and navigation and the wisdom of the stars." The Portuguese

were sailing into well-charted waters, the same ones visited by Zheng He one hundred years earlier (see Chapter 15).

When they reached India, the Portuguese anchored their ships in well-established, cosmopolitan ports. India was at the center of the world's most extensive maritime trading system. In the western Indian Ocean, merchants transported East African gold, ivory, slaves, and timber to markets in southern Arabia, the Persian Gulf, and western India. Among the many goods exported from India along the same routes was highly valuable cotton cloth.

On the east coast of India another set of maritime networks connected the Bay of Bengal and the markets of Southeast Asia with Ming China. Muslim-ruled Malacca (**mah-LAK-eh**), which controlled trade through the straits between Sumatra and the Malaya Peninsula, had a population of over fifteen thousand traders from all over the Indian Ocean world. Here silk and sugar joined the long list of traded commodities. Cinnamon from the fabled "spice islands" was particularly precious. Whoever controlled the narrow straits at Malacca would profit handsomely from all this commercial activity.

Economically, the Portuguese had almost nothing to offer: the first Indian king with whom they negotiated was insulted by the poor quality of their gifts. But their ship-mounted cannon allowed them to destroy coastal defenses. Seizing important trading centers from East Africa to Malacca, the Portuguese controlled a huge area after 1582. Their aggressive behavior earned them a widespread reputation as rough, greedy, and uncivilized.

In some cases the Portuguese redirected trade to profit themselves at the expense of previous merchant groups. For example, for centuries the East African gold trade had been dominated by Swahili (**swah-HEE-lee**) merchants, African

Vasco da Gama (1460–1524) Portuguese explorer who in 1497–1498 led the first European naval expedition to reach India by sailing around the Cape of Good Hope, laying the foundation for the Portuguese presence in the Indian Ocean in the century.

**The [...]
1600 [...]**

Early [...]
Atlant [...]
chant: [...]
storm: [...]
cargo. [...]
stock [...]
prise [...]
owner [...]
a vent [...]
men a [...]
shares [...]

Th [...]
put the [...]
comme [...]
single [...]
more n [...]
reinves [...]
at the c [...]
with th [...]
Amster [...]
Europe [...]

Kongo kingdom West-central African kingdom whose king converted to Christianity in the early sixteenth century and established diplomatic relations with the Portuguese. Became an early source of slaves for the new Atlantic slave trade.

a monopoly on Dutch trade with Asia, overseen from company headquarters in Batavia in what became the Dutch East Indies (today's Indonesia). In the coming centuries other European powers would copy the Dutch model and use chartered companies to extend their own national interests.

The Dutch East India Company was a heavily armed corporate entity that maintained its monopoly through force. "Trade cannot be maintained without war," said one governor of the East India Company, "nor war without trade."[4] The Dutch thus repeated the Portuguese pattern of using military force in the Indian Ocean to secure commercial profit, while at the same time introducing modern business and administrative techniques that made them more efficient and effective.

In addition to their commercial innovations, the Dutch had made major advances in ship design and construction. In 1641 they took Malacca from the Portuguese, and in 1658 they took the island of Sri Lanka (south of India). The Dutch presence in Africa focused on Cape Town, established at the southern tip of the continent in 1652 to provision Dutch ships en route to the Indian Ocean. The Dutch East India Company made huge profits, especially from the spice trade. To do so, it sometimes violently intervened in local affairs to increase production, as on the Bandas Islands, where company men killed or exiled most of the local population and replaced them with slaves drawn from East Africa, Japan, and India to grow nutmeg.

At this time, the entire Indian Ocean economy was being stimulated by the introduction of large quantities of American silver being mined by the Spanish in South America. In fact, the increased flow of silver into China and the Indian Ocean trade networks probably had a greater effect on those economies than the activities of European merchants. Still, the Dutch, with their efficient business organization and shipping infrastructure, were in an ideal position to profit from this development.

Origins of the Atlantic Slave Trade, 1483–1660

Matteo Ricci's route to India led him down the coast of West Africa, where Portuguese ventures in slave trading had laid the foundation for what became the largest movement of people to that point in human history: the forced migration of Africans across the Atlantic Ocean. The Portuguese first used African slaves to grow sugar on islands off the West African coast. By the early seventeenth century sugar plantations in Brazil and the Caribbean were generating huge profits, relying on the labor of slaves that European merchants purchased in the markets of West Africa.

The **Kongo kingdom** was one of many African societies that were destabilized by the Atlantic slave trade. When the Portuguese arrived at the capital city of Mbanza Kongo in 1483, they found a prosperous, well-organized kingdom with extensive markets in cloth and iron goods. King Afonso Mvemba a Nzinga **(uh-fahn-so mm-VEM-bah ah nn-ZING-ah)** (r. 1506–1543) converted to Christianity, renamed his capital San Salvador, sent his son Enrique to study in Lisbon, and exchanged diplomatic envoys with both Portugal and the Vatican.

With Portuguese help, Afonso conducted wars to expand his kingdom, with the side effect of further stimulating the slave trade: Portuguese merchants were anxious to purchase war captives. As demand for slaves increased, therefore, so did the supply. King Afonso complained, without success, to his "brother king" in Portugal: "many of our people, keenly desirous as they are of the wares and things of your Kingdoms, … seize many of our people, freed and exempt men…. That is why we beg of your Highness to help and assist us in this matter … because it is our will that in these Kingdoms there should not be any trade of slaves nor outlet for them."[5] Foreign goods and foreign traders had distorted the traditional market in slaves, which had previously been a byproduct of warfare, into an economic activity in its own right.

As sugar production surged, the demand for slaves increased decade by decade. Not all parts of Africa were immediately affected. Yet over time the rise of the Atlantic slave trade would fundamentally alter the terms of Africans' interactions with the wider world (see Chapter 19).

The Politics of Empire in Southern and Eastern Asia, 1500–1660

In the course of Matteo Ricci's long journey he came in contact with a great variety of cultural and political systems. By far the largest and most powerful of these societies were Mughal India and Ming China.

Mughal India was a young and rising state in sixteenth-century South Asia with an economy stimulated by internal trade and expanding Indian Ocean commerce. Keeping the vast Mughal realms at peace, however, required India's Muslim rulers to maintain a stable political structure in the midst of great religious and ethnic diversity.

In the sixteenth century Ming China was the most populous and most productive society in the world. We have seen that Matteo Ricci was impressed with its order and good governance. But even while the Ming Dynasty earned Ricci's admiration in the early seventeenth century, it was about to begin a downward spiral that would end in 1644 in loss of power and a change of dynasty.

Since political leaders in the neighboring East Asian states of Vietnam and Korea had long emulated Chinese systems and philosophies of statecraft, Ming officials recognized these states as "civilized." Japan, while also influenced by China in many ways, was by Ming standards disordered and militaristic in this period, though it did achieve a more stable political system in the seventeenth century.

The Rise of Mughal India, 1526–1627

During Matteo Ricci's four-year stay in western India, the **Mughal dynasty**, the dominant power in South Asia, was at the height of its glory under its greatest leader, **Emperor Akbar** (r. 1556–1605). Building on the military achievements of his grandfather, who had swept into northern India from Afghanistan in the early sixteenth century, Akbar's armies controlled most of the Indian subcontinent. Ruling 100 million subjects from his northern capital of Delhi, the "Great Mughal" was one of the most powerful men in the world.

The Mughal state, well positioned to take advantage of expanding Indian Ocean trade, licensed imperial mints that struck hundreds of millions of gold, silver, and copper coins. The influx of silver from the Americas starting in the sixteenth century stimulated market exchanges. Dyed cotton textiles were a major export, along with sugar, pepper, diamonds, and other luxury goods.

State investment in roads helped traders move goods to market. The Mughals also supported movement of populations into previously underutilized lands by granting tax-exempt status to new settlements. The eastern half of Bengal (today's Bangladesh) was transformed from tropical forest land into a densely populated rice-producing region.

Agriculture was the ultimate basis of Mughal wealth and power, providing 90 percent of the tax income that paid for Mughal armies and the ceremonial pomp of the court at Delhi. The Mughals sent tax clerks out to the provinces, surveying the lands and diverting much of the revenue to Delhi. But they also ensured the loyalty of the old aristocracy by confirming its rights to 10 percent of the local revenue.

People may be conquered by the sword, but more stable forms of administration are usually necessary if conquest is to turn into long-term rule. A principal political challenge was that the Islamic faith of the Mughal rulers differed from the Hindu beliefs of most of their subjects. Akbar's policy was one of toleration and inclusion. He canceled the special tax that Islamic law allows Muslim rulers to collect from nonbelievers and granted Hindu communities the right to follow their own social and legal customs. Hindu *maharajahs* were

Mughal dynasty (1526–1857) During the height of their power in the sixteenth and seventeenth centuries, Mughal emperors controlled most of the Indian subcontinent from their capital at Delhi.

Emperor Akbar (r. 1556–1605) The most powerful of the Mughal emperors, Akbar pursued a policy of toleration toward the Hindu majority and presided over a cosmopolitan court.

📄 **Primary Source:**

Akbarnama *These selections from the history of the house of Akbar offer a glimpse inside the policies and religious outlook of the Mughal emperor.*

incorporated into the Mughal administrative system. Since Hindus were accustomed to a social system in which people paid little attention to matters outside their own caste groups, they could view the ruling Muslims as simply another caste with its own rituals and beliefs.

Akbar's policy of religious tolerance was continued by his successor Jahangir (r. 1605–1627) and his remarkable wife **Nur Jahan** (1577–1645). When Jahangir was faced with regional rebellions, Nur Jahan (noor ja-HAN), an intelligent and skilled politician, took charge and kept Mughal power intact. Since women could not appear at court in person, she issued government decrees through trusted family members, taking special interest in women's affairs. Originally from Iran, Nur Jahan patronized Persian-influenced art and architecture and built many of the most beautiful mosques and gardens in north India.

Nur Jahan was also interested in commerce and owned a fleet of ships. Even more than Akbar's, her policies facilitated both domestic and foreign trade and had a strong influence on the wider world. Indian merchants, sailors, bankers, and shipbuilders were important participants in Indian Ocean markets, and the cosmopolitan ports of Mughal India teemed with visitors from Europe, Africa, Arabia, and Southeast Asia (see Map 16.1). But there was little Chinese presence and no follow-through to the fifteenth-century voyages of Zheng He. Unlike the Mughal rulers of India, the leaders of Ming China saw maritime trade more as a threat than an opportunity.

The Apogee and Decline of Ming China, 1500–1644

By 1500 the **Ming dynasty** in China was at the height of its power and prestige. In 1368 the

Ming had replaced the Mongol Yuan dynasty, and the early Ming rulers were highly conscious of the need to restore Confucian virtue after years of what they saw as "barbarian" rule. Like earlier Chinese dynasties, the Ming defined their country as the "Middle Kingdom" and called the emperor the "Son of Heaven." China was at the center of the world, and the emperor ruled with the "Mandate of Heaven."

The emperor's residence in the Forbidden City in Beijing (bay-JING), constructed during the early Ming period and still standing today, was at the center of a Confucian social order based on strict hierarchical relationships. The emperor stood at the top of a social hierarchy in which the junior official owed obeisance to the senior one, the younger brother to the older one, the wife to the husband, and so on throughout society. Those empowered by such hierarchies, including the emperor himself, were required to show benevolence to their social inferiors. Hierarchy governed foreign relations as well. Ming officials respected those societies that had most successfully emulated Chinese models, such as Korea and Vietnam. Japan and the societies of Inner Asia were usually thought of as "inner barbarians," peoples touched by Chinese civilization but still uncouth. The rest of the world's peoples were regarded as "outer barbarians." From a Ming standpoint, the only conceivable relationship between any of these other kingdoms and China was a tributary one. Foreign kings were expected to send annual missions bearing tribute in acknowledgement of China's pre-eminent position.

Confucians believed that if such stable hierarchies of obeisance and benevolence were maintained, then the people would prosper. And in the early sixteenth century peace and prosperity were the norm in Ming China. The network of canals and irrigation works on which so much of the empire's trade and agriculture depended were refurbished and extended. Public granaries were maintained as a hedge against famine. New food crops, including maize, peanuts, and potatoes from the Americas, improved the health of the population, which had reached about 120 million people by the time of Matteo Ricci's arrival in 1582.

The **examination system**, based on the Confucian classics and requiring years of study, helped ensure that the extensive Ming

Nur Jahan (1577–1645) Mughal empress who dominated politics during the reign of her husband Jahangir. By patronizing the arts and architecture and by favoring Persian styles, she had a lasting cultural influence on north India.

Ming dynasty (1368–1644) Chinese imperial dynasty in power during the travels of Matteo Ricci. At its height during the fifteenth century, by 1610 the Ming dynasty was showing signs of the troubles that would lead to its overthrow.

examination system Chinese system for choosing officials for positions in the Ming imperial bureaucracy. Candidates needed to pass one or more examinations that increased in difficulty for higher positions.

Map 16.1 **Maritime Trade in the Eastern Indian Ocean and East Asia**
By 1630 the Dutch had overtaken the Portuguese in Indian Ocean trade, the French and English were becoming more active, and Spanish silver from American mines was stimulating trade across South, Southeast, and East Asia. Dutch ships passed through Cape Town in South Africa bearing Asian and African cargo, such as valuable spices, for European markets. Still, the dominant powers in Asia remained land-based empires such as the Mughal Empire in India and the Ming Empire in China. Traditional trade routes controlled by local sailors and merchants—between Japan and China, between the South China Sea and the Bay of Bengal, and between western India, the Persian Gulf, and East Africa—were also growing in volume in the seventeenth century. © Cengage Learning · **Interactive Map**

bureaucracy was staffed by competent officials at the local, county, and imperial levels. With a hierarchy of well-educated officials supervised by dynamic emperors, the early Ming efficiently carried out the basic tasks of government.

The elaborate and expensive Ming bureaucracy required an efficient system of tax collections. In 1571 Ming officials decided that only payments in silver would be acceptable, generating a surge in global demand for silver. While Japan was the traditional source of silver for China, its mines could not keep up with demand. The Spanish city of Manila in the Philippines became the destination for the

The Destitute of Ming China   While acknowledging the power of the Ming dynasty and other great kingdoms and empires of the past, we might also remember that even amidst wealth and luxury, poverty was the fate of many. These scenes of the poor of Suzhou were painted in 1516 by the artist Zhou Chen as "a warning and admonition to the world."   [(Zhou Chen (Chinese). *Beggars and Street Characters*, 1516. Handscroll; ink and light color on paper, 31.9 × 244.5 cm. © The Cleveland Museum of Art. John L Severance Fund 1964.94)]

Wanli Emperor   (r. 1573–1620) Ming emperor at the time of Matteo Ricci's mission to China. Vain and extravagant, he hastened the decline of the Ming dynasty through lack of attention to policy and the promotion of incompetent officials.

Manila Galleons, an annual shipment of silver from Mexico. Thus, silver was central to an emerging trans-Pacific trade, which was from the beginning connected to the Indian Ocean network, helping to lay the foundation of a global economy.

The efforts of Ming officials to control seaborne trade, which they saw as the unpredictable realm of "pirates" like the Japanese and Portuguese, met with only limited success because the momentum of foreign trade driven by the demand for silver had become too powerful. In this emerging world economy, reliance on foreign silver supplies made the Ming economy vulnerable to distant economic shocks. While the influx of silver stimulated Chinese economic growth, it also caused inflation. Even more severe was the effect of declining silver

supplies on the world market after 1620. By that date economic contraction was contributing to an accelerating crisis in Ming governance.

The decline of the Ming is associated with the **Wanli Emperor** (r. 1573–1620), whose apathetic attitude toward his duties allowed petty jealousies to influence the imperial court. Without imperial oversight, corruption increased, and local peasant uprisings became more common. When Matteo Ricci was finally granted permission to enter the Forbidden City and performed the ritual *kowtow*, prostrating himself with his forehead on the ground, he did so before a vacant Dragon Throne. The Wanli Emperor was inaccessible, remaining deep in the recesses of the Forbidden City.

Matteo Ricci, in his tribute to Ming governance cited in the chapter opening, appears to have failed to notice the decay that was setting in below the impressive façade of the Wanli Emperor's court. But in 1644 northern invaders from Manchuria breached the walls of Beijing and drove the Ming from power (see Chapter 20).

Tradition and Innovation: Korea, Vietnam, and Japan, 1500–1650

The societies most strongly connected to Chinese civilization in the early modern period were Korea, Vietnam, and, more loosely, Japan. The Chosŏn (choh-SAN) dynasty of Korea, who closely followed the Ming imperial model, established one of the world's most stable political systems, ruling the Korean peninsula from 1392 until the early twentieth century. The capital at Seoul (sole) was home to a Confucian academy where young men trained for examinations that led to social prominence and political power.

While early modern Korea was not as commercially dynamic as Ming China, it did benefit from a remarkable series of innovations undertaken by the **Emperor Sejong** (r. 418–1450). In 1446, Sejong (SAY-jung) brought together a group of scholars to devise a new phonetic script based on the Korean language. This distinctive *han'gul* (HAHN-goor) writing system, still in use today, enabled many more Koreans to read and write. Emperor Sejong supported projects to write the history of the country in the new Korean script and to translate key Buddhist texts. He also supported printers in producing large books more cheaply. As a result, Korea became one of the world's most literate societies.

Vietnamese leaders copied Chinese imperial models while at the same time jealously guarding their independence. After 1428, when the general who took power in Vietnam after defeating a Ming army gave his name to the new **Lê dynasty**, Confucian scholar-officials gained greater influence at court in traditionally Buddhist Vietnam. Military expeditions expanded the size and strength of the Vietnamese state, and agrarian reforms led to greater equality in landholding and greater productivity in agriculture.

Japan lay further outside the orbit of Chinese civilization than either Korea or Vietnam. Political power was decentralized during Japan's Ashikaga (ah-shee-KAH-gah) Shogunate (1336–1568), and the Japanese emperor, unlike his Chinese, Korean and Vietnamese counterparts, was a ritual figure with no real authority. The greatest political power was the *shogun,* a supreme military ruler who acted independently of the imperial court. But the Ashikaga shoguns themselves had little control over the *daimyo* (DIE-mee-oh), lords who ruled their own rural domains. As each daimyo had an army of *samurai* (SAH-moo-rye) military retainers, incessant warfare spread chaos through the islands.

Ashikaga Japan was a land of contrasts. While the daimyo lords engaged in violent competition for land and power, they also acted as benefactors of Buddhist monasteries. The samurai warriors, with their strict *bushido* code of honor and loyalty, were also practitioners of the Zen school of Buddhism, with its emphasis on mental discipline and acute awareness. Flower arranging and the tea ceremony were also highly developed, peaceful counterpoints to the ceaseless military competition of the daimyo.

In the late sixteenth century several Japanese lords aspired to replace the Ashikaga family, the most ambitious being **Toyotomi Hideyoshi** (r. 1585–1598). In 1592, as Matteo Ricci was journeying in southern China, Hideyoshi's forces attacked Korea with an army of 200,000 soldiers. A statue of Admiral Yi in central Seoul still commemorates his use of heavily fortified "turtle ships" to defend Korea against the Japanese attack.

In a power struggle following Hideyoshi's death, the Tokugawa (TOH-koo-GAH-wah) clan emerged victorious. After 1603, the **Tokugawa Shogunate** centralized power by forcing the daimyo to spend half the year in the shogun's new capital of Edo (today's Tokyo). Compared with the highly centralized imperial model of Korea, political power in Japan was still diffuse,

Emperor Sejong (r. 1418–1450) Korean emperor of the Chosŏn dynasty, credited with the creation of the *han'gul* script for the Korean language.

Lê dynasty (1428–1788) The longest-ruling Vietnamese dynasty. Drawing on Confucian principles, its rulers increased the size and strength of the Vietnamese state and promoted agricultural productivity.

Toyotomi Hideyoshi (r. 1585–1598) A *daimyo* (lord) who aspired to unify Japan under his own rule. His attempts to conquer Korea and China failed, and members of the competing Tokugawa family became shoguns and unified the islands.

Tokugawa Shogunate (1603–1868) The dynasty of shoguns, paramount military leaders of Japan. From their capital at Edo (now Tokyo), Tokugawa rulers brought political stability by restraining the power of the daimyo lords.

Himeji Castle   Incessant warfare during the Ashikaga period led the Japanese *daimyo* barons to build well-fortified stone castles. The introduction of cannon in the sixteenth century made the need for such fortifications even greater. Himeji Castle was begun in 1346; Toyotomi Hideyoshi greatly expanded and beautified it in the late sixteenth century. Now a UNESCO World Cultural and Heritage Site, Himeji is the best-preserved castle in all of Japan.

with many daimyo controlling their own domains. But the Tokugawa system brought a long-term stability that made possible economic and demographic growth (see Chapter 20).

Despite this increased unity, some daimyo formed diplomatic and trade alliances with Jesuit missionaries. Unlike in China, in Japan the missionaries attracted many converts, and the shoguns became deeply suspicious of both European and Japanese Christians. After 1614 they outlawed the religion; hundreds of Japanese Christians were killed, some by crucifixion, when they refused to recant their faith. From then on, apart from an annual Dutch trade mission confined to an island in the port of Nagasaki, no Christians were allowed to enter the country.

Eurasian Intellectual and Religious Encounters, 1500–1620

In the early modern Afro-Eurasian world, intellectual ferment was often associated with new religious ideas. In western Europe the Protestant Reformation divided Christians over basic matters of faith. Matteo Ricci himself was a representative of the Catholic Reformation, which sought to re-energize Roman Catholicism. In Mughal India, many people converted to Islam and the new faith of Sikhism was founded, while the emperor himself promoted his own

"Divine Faith" to reconcile diverse religious traditions. In China, Matteo Ricci attempted to convince Ming scholar-officials that Christianity was compatible with the oldest and purest versions of Confucianism.

Challenges to Catholicism, 1517–1620

While Renaissance humanism had led to significant artistic and intellectual achievement in western Europe (see Chapter 15), it coincided with increasing corruption in the Catholic Church. For example, popes and bishops raised money for prestigious building projects, such as Saint Peter's Basilica in Rome, by selling "indulgences," which church authorities said could liberate souls from purgatory and allow them to enter into heaven. Thus the cultural richness of the Roman Church was underwritten by practices that some European Christians viewed as corrupt and worldly.

One infuriated critic, a cleric named **Martin Luther** (1483–1546), argued that salvation could not be purchased; only God could determine the spiritual condition of a human soul. After Luther made his challenge public in 1517, he was excommunicated by the church and began to lead his own religious services, thus initiating the Protestant Reformation (see also Chapter 17). The Christian church, already divided since the eleventh century between its Eastern Orthodox and Roman Catholic branches, was now divided within western Europe itself (see Map 16.2). In the seventeenth century significant political violence erupted among some western European states led by Protestants and others led by Catholics. (See Chapter 17)

As a significant minority of sixteenth-century western Europeans left Catholicism, they developed a variety of alternative church structures, rituals, and beliefs. Taking advantage of increased literacy and the wider availability of printed Bibles after the fifteenth-century development of movable-type printing, Luther argued that individuals should read their own Bibles and not rely on priests to interpret God's word for them. He translated the Bible into the German language, making the scriptures available for the first time to the many who could read German but not Latin.

Although much of Europe, like the region of Matteo Ricci's hometown in central Italy, remained securely Catholic, the Reformation shook the Catholic Church, prompting it to launch a response known as the **Catholic Reformation**. A major focus of the Catholic Reformation was more rigorous training of priests to avoid the abuses that had left the church open to Protestant criticism. As a member of the Jesuit order, or Society of Jesus, Ricci was especially trained in the debating skills needed to fend off Protestant theological challenges. The Jesuits were one of several new Catholic orders developed to confront the Protestant challenge and, especially in the Jesuit case, to take advantage of the new maritime routes to spread their faith around the world.

Another challenge to Catholic belief that developed during Ricci's lifetime was the "new science" associated with his fellow Italian **Galileo Galilei** (1564–1642). Catholic theologians had reconciled faith and reason by incorporating classical Greek thinkers, especially Aristotle, into church teachings. Galileo (gal-uh-LAY-oh) struck at the heart of that intellectual system by challenging the authority of Aristotle. For example, pointing his telescope toward the heavens, Galileo affirmed the heliocentric theory first proposed in 1543 by the Polish astronomer Nicolaus Copernicus, which placed the sun rather than the earth at the center of the solar system. Further support for the Copernican system, a theory contrary

Martin Luther (1483–1546) German theologian who in 1517 launched the Protestant Reformation in reaction to corruption in the Catholic Church. His followers, called Lutherans, downplayed the priestly hierarchy, emphasizing that believers should themselves look for truth in the Bible.

Catholic Reformation Reform movement in the Catholic Church, also called the Counter Reformation, that developed in response to the Protestant Reformation. The church clarified church doctrines and instituted a program for better training of priests.

Galileo Galilei (1564–1642) Italian scientist who provided evidence to support the heliocentric theory, challenging church doctrine and the authority of Aristotle. He was forced to recant his position by the inquisition, but his theories were vindicated during the scientific revolution.

Primary Source: Table Talk *Read Martin Luther in his own words, speaking out forcefully and candidly—and sometimes with humor—against Catholic institutions.*

Primary Source: Letter to the Grand Duchess Christina *Read Galileo's passionate defense of his scientific research against those who would condemn it as un-Christian.*

Map 16.2   The Protestant Reformation

By the middle of the sixteenth century Protestant churches were dominant in England, Scotland, the Netherlands, Switzerland, and Scandinavia. German principalities were divided between Protestants and Catholics. Catholicism remained dominant across most of southern Europe, though Protestants formed a significant minority in France. The religious landscape was especially complex in southeastern Europe, where, under Ottoman authority, there were substantial communities of Catholics, Protestants, Orthodox Christians, and Muslims.   © Cengage Learning

Interactive Map

Predominant religion in 1555

- Lutheran
- Calvinist (Reformed)
- Church of England
- Roman Catholic
- Orthodox
- Muslim
- ➜ Spread of Calvinism
- ◄ Huguenot center
- ◯ Ottoman Empire, 1566

Black Sea

Mediterranean Sea

Adriatic Sea

Baltic Sea

North Sea

ATLANTIC OCEAN

OTTOMAN EMPIRE

BESSARABIA
MOLDAVIA
WALLACHIA
Danube R.
TRANSYLVANIA
BULGARIA
SERBIA
Belgrade
GREECE
Pest
Buda
HUNGARY
Vienna
AUSTRIA
MORAVIA
BOHEMIA
Prague
Jan Hus, 1369–1415

LITHUANIA
PRUSSIA
Riga
Helsinki
Warsaw
POLAND
BRANDENBURG
SAXONY
Leipzig
Erfurt
Eisleben 1483–1546
Birthplace of Martin Luther
Wittenberg Martin Luther
HOLY ROMAN EMPIRE
Hamburg
Nuremberg
Augsburg
Munich
Stuttgart
Speyer
Strasbourg
Edict of Worms, 1521
Worms
Marburg
Birthplace of John Calvin, 1509–1564
Basel
Zurich
Ulrich Zwingli 1484–1531
Geneva
John Calvin
Trent
Council of Trent 1545–1563

SWEDEN
Stockholm
Bergen
NORWAY 1536/1607
DENMARK
Copenhagen

NETHERLANDS
Amsterdam
Münster
Antwerp
Brussels
Noyon
Paris
Orléans
Rennes
FRANCE
Nantes
Edict of Nantes, 1598
La Rochelle
Bordeaux
Toulouse
Avignon
Marseilles

SCOTLAND 1560
Edinburgh
John Knox, 1505–1572
Penetration of Calvinism to England after 1558
ENGLAND 1536
Oxford
John Wyclif, 1320–1384
London
Plymouth
IRELAND
Dublin

ITALY
Venice
Milan
Pavia
Genoa
Pisa
Florence
Rome
Roman Inquisition established, 1542
Naples
Bari
Corsica
Sardinia
Sicily

SPAIN
Madrid
Toledo
Seville
Granada
Valencia
Barcelona
Balearic Is.
Loyola
Birthplace of Ignatius Loyola, 1491–1556

PORTUGAL
Lisbon

MOROCCO
ALGIERS   OTTOMAN EMPIRE
TUNIS

400 Mi.
400 Km.
200
200
0
0

N

10°W
0°
10°E
20°E
30°E

Akbar with Representatives of Various Religions at His Court For years, the Mughal emperor Akbar hosted weekly conversations among scholars and priests of numerous religions, including the Jesuits seen here on the left. Akbar also sponsored the translation of varied religious texts, including the Christian Bible, into Persian, even though he himself was illiterate. When criticized by some Muslim scholars for his patronage of Hindu arts and his openness to other religious traditions, Akbar is said to have replied, "God loves beauty."

to both classical tradition and church teachings, was offered by the German mathematician Johannes Kepler, who argued that elliptical rather than circular orbits best explained planetary motion. Church authorities argued that the heliocentric theory contradicted the book of Genesis by displacing the earth from its central place in God's creation. The inquisition, a church bureaucracy devoted to the suppression of heresy, tried Galileo and forced him to recant his support for the heliocentric theory.

The ferment of the new ideas arising from the Protestant Reformation and the "new science" helped sharpen Matteo Ricci's intellectual training and prepare him for his travels. In India he took part in lively religious and philosophical debates that were valuable preparation for his missionary work in China.

Islam, Sikhism, and Akbar's "Divine Faith," 1500–1605

In India, the Mughal ruler Akbar, in addition to bringing Hindus and Muslims together, attracted to his court scholars, artists, and officials from Iran, Afghanistan, and Central Asia, thus creating a fertile environment in which Persian, Turkish, and Indian artistic influences flowed together. The Taj Mahal, a "love poem in marble" built by Akbar's grandson as a memorial to his wife, is the best-known example of the Persian-influenced architecture inspired by Nur Jahan and other Mughal leaders.

Keenly interested in religion, Akbar also routinely invited leaders from various religious traditions to debate at his court. In 1579, the year after Ricci arrived at Goa, a diplomatic embassy arrived from the Great Mughal requesting that Catholic missionaries come to Delhi. "We hope for nothing less than the conversion of all India," wrote Ricci. Two missionaries went to Delhi, bringing a richly produced, lavishly illustrated, and very costly Bible as a gift for the emperor. Although the emperor did not convert, his interest in the Jesuit mission characterized his open-mindedness.

During this time Sufism was also attracting new converts. In addition to obeying the Muslim laws of submission, Sufis were mystics who used special rituals and prayers to approach closer to God. Some Muslim scholars, especially those who stressed the more legalistic aspects of Islam, looked with suspicion on the emotional Sufi forms of religious devotion. Akbar brought both the legal scholars and the Sufi mystics to his court and listened intently to their debates.

Akbar also brought Jews, Hindus, and representatives of other faiths, such as Sikhs, to Delhi. Sikhism was a new faith whose followers rejected the caste system while striving to reconcile Islamic and Hindu beliefs. Akbar extended to the Sikhs the same tolerance he had granted more established religions. Having encountered so many different spiritual traditions, he announced his own adherence to a "Divine Faith" that he said both included and transcended them all. However, Akbar's "Divine Faith" never spread beyond the Mughal court and disappeared after his own death.

Meanwhile, Hinduism was undergoing important changes and reforms. The epic story of the *Ramayana,* formerly read only by priests trained in the ancient Sanskrit language, was retold in 1575 by a prominent poet using the commonly spoken Hindi language, making this story of an ancient king, a manifestation of the god Vishnu, more accessible. This development reflected new forms of Hindu devotion that de-emphasized the role of Brahmin priests. Like the translation of the Bible into languages such as English and German and like the new availability of Buddhist texts in the Korean *han'gul* script, the Hindi *Ramayana* promoted religious inquiry at all levels of society, not just among kings, priests, and philosophers.

Ricci in China: Catholicism Meets Neo-Confucianism, 1582–1610

Ming China was less religiously diverse than Mughal India, with Buddhism as the empire's majority faith. In fact, when Ricci first arrived in Ming China, he adopted the dress of a Buddhist priest, with a shaved head, a beard, and flowing robes. Soon he came to understand, however, that affiliating himself with Buddhism would not carry much weight with the Confucian scholar-officials who manifested the power of the emperor. Many of these *literati* looked down on the poorly educated Buddhist clergy. Ricci subsequently changed his appearance and

habits to appeal to this prestigious class of individuals. His plan was to convert China from the top down.

Confucian scholars emphasized education as the main route to self-cultivation. While most of the emperor's subjects remained nonliterate peasant cultivators, children from more privileged households were taught to read from a young age. After they had mastered the basics, boys had to memorize the classic texts of Confucianism, collections of poems, and histories of past times that usually focused on the virtues of ancient sages.

In theory, any young man could take the annual examinations and, if successful, become an imperial official. In reality, only the elite could afford private tutors. Still, the Ming system was based on merit: wealth and status could not purchase high office, and even the privileged had to undergo years of intensive study.

Though women were barred from taking the examinations, the Ming emphasis on education did contribute to the spread of female literacy. Foreign observers noted how many girls were able to read and write. However, education for girls reinforced Confucian views of gender. Rather than reading histories of sages and virtuous officials, girls usually read stories about women who submitted to their parents when they were young, obeyed their husbands once they were married, and listened to their sons when they became widowed. Chinese girls were thereby indoctrinated into the Confucian ideal of strict gender hierarchy.

Matteo Ricci paid careful attention to debates among advocates of various schools of Confucianism as he built up an argument for the compatibility of Confucianism and Christianity. At this time the Neo-Confucian philosophy of Wang Yangming (1472–1529) was especially influential. While other Confucians had emphasized close observation of the external world, Wang stressed self-reflection, arguing that "everybody, from the infant in swaddling clothes to the old, is in full possession of ... innate knowledge." Ricci accused Wang's Neo-Confucian followers of distorting Confucianism. By returning to the original works of the ancient sages, Ricci said, the Chinese literati would discover that one could convert to Christianity while retaining the ethical and philosophical traditions of Confucius.

Once his language skills were sufficiently developed, Ricci took advantage of a favorite Ming pastime to share his views. Scholar-officials would often invite interesting speakers to a banquet and, after dinner, hold philosophical debates. For many in the audience, Ricci's well-known ability to instantly memorize and repeat long lists of information, and even repeat them backwards, would have been of greater interest than his views on Confucian philosophy and Christian theology. It was a highly relevant skill in a society where difficult exams were the main path to power and status. But while his hosts might have been entertained by his arguments, few were persuaded by them.

Ricci also impressed his hosts with examples of European art and technology, especially printed books, paintings, clocks, and maps. Ricci's world map, locating the "western barbarians" for the first time in relation to the "Middle Kingdom," was such a success that Chinese artisans were employed to print reproductions.

For Ricci, however, mnemonic tricks, maps, and clocks were only a means to convert his audience to Christianity. Criticizing both Buddhism and Neo-Confucianism, Ricci emphasized those aspects of the Western tradition that appealed most to Confucian intellectuals: its moral and ethical dimensions rather than its character as a revealed religion. For example, after learning that Chinese scholars were usually upset to hear about the suffering and death of Jesus, he largely avoided that central aspect of Christianity. (See the feature "Movement of Ideas: Christianity in China.")

Ricci's most influential work published in Chinese was *The True Meaning of the Lord of Heaven*. Composed with the aid of the small number of Chinese Christian converts, it is a dialogue between a "Chinese Scholar" and a "Western Scholar." In the following passage Ricci criticizes Buddhism and argues for the compatibility of Confucianism and Christianity:

> *Chinese Scholar: The Buddha taught that the visible world emerges from "voidness" and made "voidness" the end of all effort. The Confucians say: "In the processes of Yi there exists the Supreme Ultimate" and therefore make "existence" the basic principle [of all things] and "sincerity" the subject of the study of self-cultivation. I wonder who, in your revered view, is correct?*

> *Western Scholar: The "voidness" taught by the Buddha [is] totally at variance with the doctrine concerning the Lord of Heaven [i.e., Christianity], and it is therefore abundantly clear that [it does] not merit esteem. When it comes to the "existence" and "sincerity" of the Confucians, however … they would seem to be close to the truth.*[6]

Such arguments did not convince many, but at least the Jesuits in China, unlike their brethren in Japan, were accepted as representatives of a legitimate school of philosophy.

Some Jesuits and Vatican officials felt that *The True Meaning of the Lord of Heaven* and other attempts by Ricci to reconcile Christianity and Confucianism went too far. For example, Ricci argued that veneration of ancestors was compatible with Christianity and the biblical command to "honor your father and your mother." Less flexible church authorities felt that Chinese ancestor rites were pagan and should be rejected. Ricci knew that such a rigid interpretation of cultural practice would limit the appeal of Christianity among potential converts, who would be ostracized by family and friends if they abandoned their household shrines. Although Matteo Ricci made no more than a handful of converts, he played an important role in world history as the first major figure in the ongoing "great encounter" between Europe and China.

Christianity in China

Are Christianity and Confucianism compatible? Matteo Ricci thought so, though other Jesuits disagreed. How did Chinese officials and intellectuals address this question?

At first, Ming toleration of Christianity continued during the Qing dynasty (see Chapter 20), as an edict of the Emperor Kangxi in 1692 proclaimed: "The Europeans ... commit no crimes, and their doctrine has nothing in common with that of the false sects in the empire, nor has it any tendency to excite sedition." The emperor ordered that Christian churches be protected and open to worshipers. In 1715, however, the church reversed Ricci's policy by declaring that Confucian rites were incompatible with Christianity. Emperor Kangxi was furious: "To judge from this proclamation, their religion is no different from other small, bigoted sects of Buddhism." In 1721 he banned Christians from preaching in his empire.

Earlier, in the seventeenth century, Confucian intellectuals had given assessments of the Catholic faith, examples of which are given below.

Chinese Commentaries on Christianity

1) [The Jesuits] are extremely intelligent. Their studies concern astronomy, the calendar, medicine and mathematics; their customs are compounded of loyalty, good faith, constancy and integrity; their skill is wonderful. Truly they have the means to win minds.... The only trouble is that it is a pity that they speak of a Master of Heaven, an incorrect and distasteful term which leads them into nonsense.... Our Confucianism has never held that Heaven had a mother or a bodily form, and it has never spoken of events that are supposed to have occurred before and after his birth. Is it not true that herein lies the difference between our Confucianism and their doctrine?

2) Compared with the contents of the Buddhist books, what [the Christians] say is straightforward and full of substance. The principal idea comes down to respecting the Master of Heaven, leading a life that conforms with morality, controlling one's desires and studying with zeal.... Nevertheless ... what they say about paradise and hell appears to differ barely at all from what the Buddhists maintain and they go even further than the latter when it comes to extravagance and nonsense.

3) [The Jesuits] openly take issue with the false ideas of Buddhism.... Meanwhile, where they do take issue with Confucianism, they do not dare to open their mouths wide for they wish to use the cap and gown of the literate elite to introduce their doctrine even into Court, so as to spread their poison more effectively.

4) The superiority of Western teaching lies in their calculations; their inferiority lies in their veneration of a Master of Heaven of a kind to upset men's minds.... When they require people to consider the Master of Heaven as their closest relative and to abandon their fathers and mothers and place their sovereign [king] in second place, giving the direction of the state to those who spread the doctrine of the Master of Heaven, this entails an unprecedented infringement on the most constant rules. How could their doctrine possibly be admissible in China?

5) [The Ming emperor] sacrifices to Heaven and to Earth; the princes sacrifice to the mountains and rivers within the domains; holders of high office sacrifice to the ancestral temple of the founder of their lineage; gentlemen and ordinary individuals sacrifice to the tables of their own [immediate] ancestors.... In this way ... there is an order in the sacrifices that cannot be upset. To suggest that each person should revere a single Master of Heaven and represent Heaven by means of statues before which one prays each day ... is it not to profane Heaven by making unseemly requests?

6) In their kingdom they recognize two sovereigns. One is the political sovereign [the king] the other is the doctrinal sovereign [the pope].... The former reigns by right of succession and passes on his responsibilities to his descendents. He nevertheless depends upon the doctrinal sovereign, to whom he must offer gifts and tokens of tribute.... It comes down to having two suns in the sky, two masters in a single kingdom.... What audacity it is on the part of these calamitous Barbarians who would like to upset the [political and moral] unity of China by introducing the Barbarian concept of the two sovereigns!

7) We Confucians follow a level and unified path. Confucius used to say ... "To study realities of the most humble kind in order to raise oneself to the comprehension of the highest matters, what is that if not 'serving heaven?'" ... To abandon all this in order to rally to this Jesus who died nailed to a cross ... to prostrate oneself before him and pray with zeal, imploring his supernatural aid, that would be madness. And to go so far as to enter darkened halls, wash oneself with holy water and wear amulets about one's person, all that resembles the vicious practices of witchcraft.

8) In the case of Jesus there is not a single [miracle] that is comparable [to those of the ancient sages]. Healing the sick and raising the dead are things that can be done by great magicians, not actions worthy of one who is supposed to have created Heaven, Earth and the Ten Thousand Beings. If one considers those to be exploits, how is it that he did not arrange for people never to be sick again and never to die? That *would* have increased his merit.

9) Our father is the one who engendered us, our mother the one who raised us. Filial piety consists solely in loving our parents.... Even when one of our parents behaves in a tyrannical fashion, we must try to reason with him or her. Even if a sovereign behaves in an unjust way, we must try to get him to return to human sentiments. How could one justify criticizing one's parents or resisting one's sovereign on the grounds of filial piety toward the Master of Heaven?

Source: Jacques Gernet, *China and the Christian Impact: A Conflict of Cultures* (New York: Cambridge University Press, 1986), pp. 39–40, 53, 82, 107, 108, 120, 159, 161.

QUESTIONS FOR ANALYSIS

▶ In which documents is Christianity judged to be incompatible with China's social and political traditions? How is that incompatibility described?

▶ Matteo Ricci was critical toward Buddhism. In these documents, where and how do Chinese authors equate Christianity with Buddhism?

▶ Do these critiques seem to be based on a deep or superficial understanding of seventeenth-century Christianity?

Chapter Review and Learning Activities

The new maritime route from Europe to Asia that took Matteo Ricci from Europe through the Indian Ocean to Ming China, while not as revolutionary as the one that connected Europe with the Americas, stimulated important new economic, political, and cultural connections across early modern Afro-Eurasia. Among the important outcomes were the beginnings of the Atlantic slave trade, increased interaction between the great land-based Asian empires and European states, and competition among European states for dominance in Asian trade.

 ### What changes and continuities were associated with Portuguese and Dutch involvement in the Indian Ocean trade?

Even as the Portuguese and Dutch intruded on the Indian Ocean, there was significant continuity with earlier patterns of trade. While the Portuguese did manage to control strategic coastal locations, they did not create an overarching imperial structure for the Indian Ocean. Most Africans remained unaffected by Portuguese initiatives. During the seventeenth century, the Dutch East India Company brought deeper changes, especially in commerce. Significant quantities of goods, such as Indian textiles, Chinese porcelain, and Southeast Asian spices, were now carried to Europe, often purchased with American silver. In fact, the huge inflow of silver was a greater stimulus to the Asian economies ringing the Indian Ocean than European merchant activity itself.

While the Dutch were a formidable new military presence, their direct influence, like that of the Portuguese, was limited to the few islands and coastal fortifications under their control. African and Asian rulers were still the key to politics in places like the Swahili city-states of East Africa, the Persian Gulf and Bay of Bengal, and mainland Southeast Asia.

 ### What were the main political characteristics of the major South Asian and East Asian states? How was their development influenced by the new maritime connections of the sixteenth and early seventeenth centuries?

The dominant political players in East and South Asia were land-based empires with leaders who paid little attention to maritime affairs. Ming China, the most populous and most powerful, benefited from the increased tempo of maritime trade, but agriculture was the principal foundation supporting the complex Ming imperial bureaucracy. By the time of Matteo Ricci's arrival in Beijing late in the sixteenth century, however, political and economic crises were about to undermine the Ming dynasty, and in 1644 the Forbidden City fell to northern invaders.

Korea, Vietnam, and Japan derived at least part of their political culture from China. The Korean state modeled its imperial system most closely on Ming China, and Vietnam, even after fending off a Ming military incursion, emulated the Chinese imperial system and sent tribute to the Forbidden City. Sixteenth-century Japan, by contrast, was a disordered land with little central authority. In the seventeenth century, the Tokugawa Shogunate consolidated power and brought greater stability that produced a surge in commercial activity and artistic innovation.

Like Ming China, Mughal India benefited from increased Indian Ocean commerce even as its wealth and power were primarily derived from taxation on agriculture. Under Akbar, India possessed military might, economic productivity, and cultural creativity. With a Muslim ruling class, a Hindu majority, and a royal court that looked to Persia, Turkey, and Central Asia for artistic stimulation, the artistic and administrative achievements of the Mughal Empire reflected the culture of tolerance promoted by Akbar.

 ### How did religious and intellectual traditions of Eurasia change during this period, and what were the effects of encounters between them?

Akbar's exploration of various religious traditions characterized a Eurasian intellectual climate in which cultural encounters were becoming more frequent. His open-minded attitude was not universal, however. In western Europe differences between Protestants and Catholics increasingly led to violence and warfare (as we will see in the next chapter), and in India Akbar's policy of tolerance would be reversed by his successors. Most Chinese literati were ethnocentric in their belief that Chinese traditions such as Confucianism gave them all the guidance they needed, and Ricci gained few converts. European clocks, paintings, telescopes, and maps impressed them, but mostly as novelties. Nevertheless, Ricci was usually received in a respectful manner and helped lay the foundations for ongoing encounters between China and Europe.

FOR FURTHER REFERENCE

Brook, Timothy. *The Confusions of Pleasure: Commerce and Culture in Ming China*. Berkeley: University of California Press, 1998.

Chaudhuri, K. N. *Asia Before Europe: Economy and Civilization of the Indian Ocean from the Rise of Islam to 1750*. Cambridge: Cambridge University Press, 1990.

Dale, Stephen Frederick. *Indian Merchants and Eurasian Trade, 1600–1750*. Cambridge: Cambridge University Press, 1994.

Hilton, Anne. *The Kingdom of Kongo*. Oxford: Clarendon Press, 1985.

Pearson, Michael. *The Indian Ocean*. New York: Routledge, 2007.

Richards, John. *The Mughal Empire*. New York: Cambridge University Press, 1996.

Spence, Jonathan. *The Memory Palace of Matteo Ricci*. New York: Viking Penguin, 1984.

Subrahmanyam, Sanjay. *The Portuguese Empire in Asia, 1500–1700*. New York: Longman, 1993.

KEY TERMS

Matteo Ricci (348)

Vasco da Gama (349)

Dutch East India Company (351)

Kongo kingdom (352)

Mughal dynasty (353)

Emperor Akbar (353)

Nur Jahan (354)

Ming dynasty (354)

examination system (354)

Wanli Emperor (356)

Emperor Sejong (357)

Lê dynasty (357)

Toyotomi Hideyoshi (357)

Tokugawa Shogunate (357)

Martin Luther (359)

Catholic Reformation (359)

Galileo Galilei (359)

VOYAGES ON THE WEB

Voyages: Matteo Ricci

"Voyages" is a real time excursion to historical sites in this chapter and includes interactive activities and study tools such as audio summaries, animated maps, and flashcards.

Visual Evidence: An Ivory Mask from Benin, West Africa

"Visual Evidence" features artifacts, works of art, or photographs, along with a brief descriptive essay and discussion questions to guide your analysis of visual sources.

World History in Today's World: Conflict in Ayodhya

"World History in Today's World" makes the connection between features of modern life and their origins in the periods in this chapter.

CourseMate

Go to the CourseMate website at www.cengagebrain.com for additional study tools and review materials—including audio and video clips—for this chapter.

17

Religion, Politics, and the Balance of Power in Western Eurasia, 1500–1750

n de Chardin
te Collection/The Bridgeman
brary)

In 1673, the Frenchman **Jean de Chardin** (1643–1713) started on the second of his long journeys to Iran. On his first visit the shah had made a deal with Chardin to come back with European jewelry for the royal collection. But when Chardin returned with the jewels he found that the shah had died, and that he was expected to renegotiate the sale. Those negotiations led to frustration on both sides.

Cultural differences lay at the heart of this disagreement. Jean de Chardin (**JAHN duh shar-DAN**) expected his original contract to be honored, while his Iranian hosts saw haggling over price as an essential part of commercial life that helped to establish a personal relationship between buyer and seller. Even though Chardin had spent years in Persia (as Europeans called Iran) and spoke the language well, he still had difficulty adjusting to its business culture:

I shall not say anything of the deceits, tricks, wiles, disputes, threats and promises with which I was plagued for ten days … to make me lower the price. I was so weary of all the indirect means the nazir [minister] made use of that … I begged he would rather give back my jewels. … What provoked him the most, as he said, was that I kept firm to my first agreement without the least abatement. He had put himself in so violent a passion … that one would have thought he was going to devour me, and indeed I should have dreaded some bad consequences from so vehement an indignation if I had not been well acquainted with the

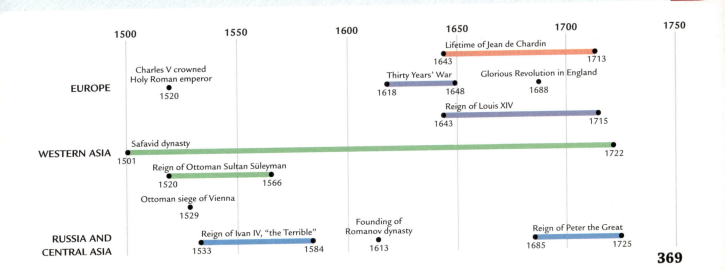

The Travels of Jean de Chardin

- → First journey to Persia
- → Second journey to Persia
- → Other journeys
- • City visited by Chardin
- • Other city
- — Boundaries, ca. 1680

Join this chapter's traveler on "Voyages," an interactive tour of historic sites and events: www.cengagebrain.com

ATLANTIC OCEAN

Chardin flees to England, 1681.

SWEDEN

DENMARK AND NORWAY

North Sea

RUSSIAN EMPIRE

Moscow

ENGLAND
London

Amsterdam
Cologne

EUROPE

PRUSSIA
Warsaw

POLAND-LITHUANIA

HOLY ROMAN EMPIRE

Paris

Vienna

HUNGARY

AUSTRIA

Pest

FRANCE

ALPS
Milan

Aral Sea

Urganch

Travels overland to Isfahan.

Caspian Sea

Kaffa

CAUCASUS MTS.

Tiflis

from Persia

Marseilles

Genoa

Venice
Florence

Adriatic Sea

Corsica

Rome

OTTOMAN EMPIRE

Danube R.

Black Sea

Constantinople

Yerevan

Nachivan
Tabriz

SAFAVID EMPIRE

Qum

ASIA

Sava
Kashan

to India

PORTUGAL

Madrid

SPAIN

Sardinia

Messina
Sicily

Athens

Smyrna

Antioch

Baghdad

Isfahan

Shiraz

to Europe via Cape of Good Hope

Ceuta

Jean de Chardin leaves France on his first voyage to Persia, 1664.

Tunis

Mediterranean Sea

Crete

Cyprus

Damascus

Persian Gulf

Fez

OTTOMAN EMPIRE

Alexandria

Nile R.

Red Sea

AFRICA

N

0   200   400 Km.
0   200   400 Mi.

	1500	1550	1600	1650	1700	1750
					Lifetime of Jean de Chardin	
					1643 — 1713	
EUROPE		Charles V crowned Holy Roman emperor 1520		Thirty Years' War 1618 — 1648	Glorious Revolution in England 1688	
					Reign of Louis XIV 1643 — 1715	
WESTERN ASIA	Safavid dynasty 1501 —				1722	
		Reign of Ottoman Sultan Süleyman 1520 — 1566				
		Ottoman siege of Vienna 1529				
RUSSIA AND CENTRAL ASIA		Reign of Ivan IV, "the Terrible" 1533 — 1584	Founding of Romanov dynasty 1613		Reign of Peter the Great 1685 — 1725	

Persians' manner of acting on like occasions. What I found most difficult to bear was the reproaches of the courtiers who … found it very strange that I should stick so stiffly to my first word; some of them ascribed it to my obstinacy and others to an over-greediness of excessive gain.*/1

[1]Excerpt from Sir John Chardin, *Travels in Persia, 1673–1677*, an abridged English verion of *Voyages du chevalier Chardin en Perse, et autres lieux de l'Orient*, Dover, 1988, pp. 8, 70. Reprinted with permission of Dover Publications, Inc.

Jean de Chardin
(1643–1713) French traveler and businessman who voyaged to Iran in 1665; learned the language and made a contract with the shah to return with jewelry. On a second trip in 1673, he reached Iran after passing through the Ottoman Empire.

On a positive note, Chardin complimented Persians for their warm generosity: "The most commendable property of the manners of the Persians is their kindness to strangers; the reception and protection they afford them and their universal hospitality." He also praised the Iranians' general "toleration in regard to religion," with the exception of the "the clergy of the country who, as in all other places, hate to a furious degree all those who differ from their own opinion."

Coming from a country where Protestants faced persecution from a Catholic king, Chardin had deep personal experience with religious intolerance. Himself a Protestant, he would eventually have to abandon his native France to settle in Protestant-governed Britain. As in Shi'ite-governed Iran, where Sunni Muslims were a persecuted minority, religion and politics were closely connected in early modern Europe. In both Christian and Islamic lands, religious fervor fueled competition for wealth and power at a time when the refinement of gunpowder technologies was making warfare more lethal.

Chardin's experiences were also characteristic of this period's global interconnections. The previous two chapters traced increasing political, economic, biological, and cultural interactions in the Atlantic and Indian Ocean worlds. This chapter focuses on the complex interplay between religion and politics within and between Christian and Muslim societies and on the shifting balance of power between major states in western Eurasia and the Mediterranean.

Three Muslim-ruled states were on the rise in sixteenth-century Eurasia. One was the Safavid (SAH-fah-vihd) Empire in Iran visited by Chardin. To reach its capital of Isfahan, Chardin traveled across the even more powerful Ottoman Empire. Already well established by 1500, the Ottomans continued to expand their power westward across North Africa and northward into Europe. The antagonism between the Ottomans and the Safavids was reinforced by their rulers' adherence to different branches of Islam. Together with Mughal India, the Ottomans and Safavids represented a sixteenth-century Islamic resurgence.

Powerful states were also emerging in sixteenth-century Europe. While the Orthodox Christian rulers of Russia were consolidating and extending their power, Spanish kings were attempting to unite Christendom against Protestant resistance. By the mid-eighteenth century, Spanish power was fading, and Catholic France and the Protestant nations of Great Britain and Prussia were on the rise.

Meanwhile, the Safavid Empire had collapsed entirely and the Ottoman Empire, while still powerful, had lost the initiative to the rising European states. By the mid-eighteenth century the ability to maintain and extend military power had come to depend on the efficient use of gunpowder weapons. The balance of power in western Eurasia now favored France, Britain, Austria, Prussia, and Russia, and national competition had largely replaced religious rivalry.

FOCUS QUESTIONS

▶ When, where, and how were religion and politics most closely intertwined in western Eurasian societies? When and why did religion come to play a less prominent political role?

▶ How did the balance of power between the dominant states of western Eurasia shift during this period?

▶ What do Jean de Chardin's travel writings tell us, both about Safavid Iran and about his own culture and values?

Land Empires of Western Eurasia and North Africa, 1500–1685

Unlike the maritime empires described in the last two chapters, the Ottoman, Safavid, and Russian Empires were land-based, created by the overland expansion of political and military power into neighboring territories. Since their core areas had earlier been conquered and administered by the Mongols, the origins of these land-based empires lay in the relationship between steppe nomads and settled agricultural peoples.

The rulers of the Ottoman Empire, whose power had been magnified by their seizure of Constantinople in 1453, were the most successful of the Turkic-speaking peoples who had migrated westward from the steppes to conquer sedentary agricultural societies. The Safavids were also Turkic-speaking and nomadic in origin. Both societies inherited Islamic law and tradition, although the Sunni (SOO-nee) Ottomans and the Shi'ite (shee-ite) Safavids had different, often conflicting, interpretations of Islam.

The rulers of Russia, by contrast, were products of a settled agrarian society, though their southern frontier had long had contact with steppe nomads. Starting in the mid-fifteenth century, the Russians turned the tables on the Mongols and conquered parts of the steppe that had once been ruled by the Golden Horde.

By the mid-seventeenth century, under the Romanov dynasty, the Russian Empire was moving westward toward Poland, eastward into Siberia, and southward toward the edges of Ottoman and Safavid power. The influence of the Russian Orthodox Church spread along with the empire.

The Ottoman Empire, 1500–1650

The legendary splendor of the Sublime Porte, center of Ottoman power in Constantinople, reflected the success of the Ottoman military elite in governing their sprawling and productive domains. In the sixteenth century those lands expanded to include Palestine, Syria, Arabia, Iraq, and much of Hungary. Ottoman fleets came to dominate the Black Sea and the eastern and southern shores of the Mediterranean, and the Ottoman navy challenged Christian fleets in the Red Sea, Persian Gulf, and Indian Ocean. From southeastern Europe Ottoman armies marched into the German-speaking lands of central Europe. The Ottomans also ruled Greece and conquered all of the Mediterranean coast of North Africa except Morocco, which remained the only significant Arab-ruled kingdom. In Egypt, Arabia, and

Janissaries An elite corps of slaves trained as professional soldiers in the Ottoman military. Janissary soldiers were Christian youths from the Balkans who were pressed into service and forced to convert to Islam.

Süleyman (r. 1520–1566) Credited with the development of literature, art, architecture, and law and for inclusive policies toward religious minorities, Süleyman extended the Ottoman Empire while maintaining economic and political stability.

Syria, Arabs were ruled by Turkish-speaking Ottoman administrators.

Early Ottoman expansion was driven by soldiers known as *ghazis* (GAH-zeez), horsemen of nomadic origin who were ambitious to conquer the Christian infidels of Byzantium for Islam. But the increasing scale of Ottoman military operations and the organization necessary to use gunpowder weapons such as muskets and cannon led to greater military professionalism. As ghazis were given land grants in conquered territories with responsibilities for maintaining order and collecting taxes, they became administrators rather than fighters. In order to meet their ever-increasing manpower needs, the Ottomans began to rely on **Janissaries**. As the need for such soldiers increased, the Ottomans regularly enslaved Christian youths in the Balkan and Caucasus Mountains.

Even if the concept of "elite slaves" sounds strange, relying on slaves as soldiers and administrators was an old tradition. A sultan might not be able to trust his own brothers or sons because they were vying for power of their own, but the loyalty of a slave general was absolute. If he disobeyed he could simply be killed: he had no family ties to protect him. By the sixteenth century, Janissaries played a central role in administration as well as in the military. Even the sultan's chief minister was a slave.

After conquering Arabia and Palestine, the Ottomans controlled Mecca, Medina, and Jerusalem, the three holiest cities for Muslims. While the Ottomans therefore emphasized their role as guardians of Islam, their empire also had to incorporate dozens of different communities with diverse religious and legal traditions.

The master strategist who reconciled central authority with local autonomy was Sultan **Süleyman** (r. 1520–1566). A strong military leader who greatly expanded the empire, Süleyman (soo-lay-MAHN) also devised an administrative system that regularized relations between the government and its population.

His court reflected the ethnic diversity of his empire. Turkish was the language of administration and military command, Arabic the language of theology and philosophy, and Persian the language of poetry and the arts. Europeans called him "Süleyman the Magnificent" for the dazzling opulence and splendor of his court. But within the empire he became known as "Süleyman the Lawgiver" for bringing peace and stability to the realm. The sultan's officials gained power through merit rather than family lineage. As one European ambassador reported: "Those who are dishonest, lazy and slothful never attain to distinction, but remain in obscurity and contempt. That is why they succeed in all they attempt … and daily extend the bounds of their rule."[2]

Süleyman centralized religious authority and sponsored the building of mosques and religious schools, partly to combat the intermixture of pagan practices with Islam. For that reason, Süleyman sent religious experts to rural Anatolia to promote Islamic orthodoxy among Muslim peasants who still embraced folk beliefs, deities, and rituals.

Nevertheless, the Ottomans did not impose a single legal system on existing cultural and religious traditions. Instead, they allowed local Christian and Jewish populations to govern their own affairs and maintain their own courts as long as they remained loyal to the sultan and paid their taxes promptly.

Many of the Iberian Jews who were driven from Catholic Spain in 1492 found safe haven in Morocco and Ottoman-ruled North Africa, where as a Ladino-speaking minority, with a language derived from medieval Spanish, they made significant contributions to intellectual and commercial life. Jean de Chardin himself enjoyed the empire's tolerance, passing unmolested through Ottoman lands even though the empire was at war with various European states. His journey was a testament to the safety, security, and stability bequeathed by Süleyman the Lawgiver.

Although the Ottomans were a substantial threat to central Europe in Süleyman's day, the Ottoman siege of Vienna in 1529 was turned back by the city's defenders, and in the Mediterranean a combined European fleet under Spanish command defeated the Ottoman navy

Süleyman the Magnificent   This portrait of Süleyman the Magnificent shows the influence of Persian miniature painting on the arts of the Ottoman Empire. Though most Muslim scholars rejected the practice of representing the human form in paintings and illuminated book manuscripts, fearing the sin of idol worship, the Ottomans borrowed these old artistic practices from their Iranian rivals.

Art Resource, NY

in the Battle of Lepanto in 1571. Even so, the Ottomans rebuilt their navy and stayed on the offensive in southeastern Europe into the later seventeenth century. (See the feature "Movement of Ideas: The Travels of Evliya Çelebi.")

Against the persistent Ottoman threat, the Europeans sought an ally in the Persian shah of Safavid Iran. For all their religious and cultural divergences, the Europeans and the Safavids found that mutual antipathy to the Ottomans gave them a starting point for cooperation.

Foundations of Safavid Iran, 1500–1629

Iran is a rich and productive land with a long history of influence in western and southern Asia. With Mesopotamia and the Mediterranean to the west and the Indus Valley and India to the south and east, Persian civilization benefited from contacts with other civilizations. Its agricultural wealth and its location as a commercial crossroads also attracted invaders. In the early sixteenth century, some of these invaders founded the **Safavid dynasty** (1501–1722) and challenged the power of the Ottoman Empire.

The Safavid invaders, known as *kizilbash* ("redheads") because of the color of their turbans, swept down from Azerbaijan to conquer Iran. Behind their leader **Ismail** (r. 1501–1524) the "redheads" conquered the Persian-speaking lands and drove west, capturing the important cities of Baghdad and Basra. In the process they adopted the Shi'ite interpretation of Islam and imposed it on their new subjects.

Shi'ites believe that when Muhammad died religious and political authority should have passed though the line of his son-in-law Ali. Sunni Muslims, by contrast, argue that any

rightly-guided man could succeed the Prophet's as *caliph*. In the seventh century the two sides came to blows. First Ali was killed, and then his son Hussein fell to the Sunni caliph. Safavid Shi'ites cursed the names of the Sunni caliphs, and every year held an elaborate festival of mourning to commemorate the death of Hussein.

Before the Safavids most people in Iran had been Sunni Muslims living alongside many small Sufi brotherhoods. Under Ismail,

---

Safavid dynasty (1501–1722) Dynasty that established Shi'ite Islam as the state religion in Iran and challenged the powerful Ottoman Empire. The Safavids fell to invaders from Central Asia in the early eighteenth century.

Ismail (r. 1501–1524) Founder of the Safavid dynasty in Iran who forced his subjects to adopt Shi'ite Islam. Came into military and religious conflict with the Ottoman Empire, which was Sunni.

The Travels of Evliya Çelebi

In the Turkish language, you say of someone who feels a constant urge for travel, "Evliya Çelebi gibi": "He is like Evliya Çelebi." Evliya Çelebi (1610–1683) was one of the great travelers of the seventeenth century. Son of an Ottoman official, he was raised in the sultan's palace in Constantinople. Guided, he wrote, by a dream that assured him the Prophet's blessing on his voyages, his journeys encompassed all of the Ottoman lands, including Greece, Syria, Egypt, Baghdad, Bosnia, Jerusalem, and Armenia. He also traveled beyond the sultan's domain to Vienna, Poland, and Russia.

The passages below are from Çelebi's descriptions of Europe and Europeans. In the first, he shares with his Ottoman readers his impressions of Austrian Catholics, Hungarian Protestants, and Jews. In the second he records his impressions of a surgical procedure he witnessed in Vienna.

Descriptions of Hungarian Protestants, Austrian Catholics, and Jews

The Hungarians are Lutherans while the Germans [or Austrians] are Catholics. Therefore these two infidel groups are opposed to one another, despite their both being Christians.... They communicate at the point of a spear.... The Hungarian state is quite puny ever since the time of Sultan Süleyman when … 300 walled towns were lost to the Ottomans. After that happened the Austrians prevailed over the Hungarians and made them into their subjects.

Still, compared to the Hungarians the Austrians are like the Jews: they have no stomach for a fight and are not swordsmen and horsemen. Their infantry musketeers, to be sure, are real fireshooters; but … they can't shoot from the shoulder as Ottoman soldiers do. Also, they shut their eyes and shoot at random....

The Hungarians, on the other hand, though they have lost their power, still have fine tables, are hospitable to guests, and are capable cultivators of their fertile land. And they are true warriors.... Indeed, they look just like our frontier soldiers, wearing the same dress as they and riding the same thoroughbred horses. They are clean in their ways and in their eating, and honor their guests. They do not torture their prisoners as the Austrians do. They practice sword play like the Ottomans. In short, though both of them are unbelievers without faith, the Hungarians are the more honorable and cleaner infidels.

The Jews never accept food and drink from other people. Indeed, they do not mingle with others—if they join your company it is an artificial companionship. All their deeds are calculated to treachery and the killing of Muslims, especially anyone named Muhammad. Even wine they refuse to buy from other people.

Source: Robert Dankoff and Robert Elsie, eds., *Evliya Çelebi in Albania and Adjacent Regions* (Boston: Brill, 2000), pp. 65–66, 68.

Observation of a Surgical Procedure in Vienna

Since there are many doctors in the hospital [of St. Stephan] the likes of Plato [and] Hippocrates ... the king himself comes to it when ill. These doctors wear pure white [gowns] and on their heads a type of linen skull cap of Russian leather.... Upon taking the patient's pulse, they immediately know the disease and accordingly know the [proper] treatment for it. So when a close relative of the king's was wounded ... by a bullet that penetrated deeply and was lodged in the side of his skull near his ear [he was brought to this hospital].

... I came to the Chief Surgeon and introduced myself [asking to be allowed to witness the operation]. Thereupon he had the wounded infidel brought in.... [He was] given a cup of liquid resembling saffron to drink, and passed out. The chief surgeon ... cut the skin of his forehead from ear to ear and flayed the skin effortlessly from the side of his right ear. The skull-bone appeared pure white. Not a drop of blood flowed. Then the surgeon lightly pierced the wounded fellow's skull from his ear to the temple. After this he inserted an iron clamp. When the handle of the clamp was turned, the skull began to rise up from where the fellow's scalp had been cut. The wounded man made a light movement at that moment.

When the clamp was turned again ... the top of the fellow's head was opened.... Inside his head the brains were visible.... Then he quickly took the bullet from the man's brain with a pair of forceps. With a sponge he wiped away the hard, dry blood from the spot where the bullet had been lodged all this time....

[A] giant ant was taken from [a] box with iron tongs. It was placed on the fellow's head where the skin had been cut. When the hungry ant bit the two edges of the skin, the surgeon cut the ant at the waist with scissors, leaving the head still biting the edges of the skin.... Eighty ants were made to bite the skin of the wounded fellow's head from ear to ear.... Gauze was inserted into the bullet hole in his skull and this was smeared with salve and bandaged.

Foul smelling incense was burned inside the room. Wine of a forty or fifty year-old vintage was poured in the wounded man's nose, and clay was smeared over [his entire body].... I remained there seven complete days observing the [convalescence]. On the eighth day the pleasant fellow had recovered, and began to move around the hospital with ease....

In the city of Vienna there are perfect masters of surgery ... and scholars of such wisdom and skill the equal of Ibn Sinā and Pythagoras together.

Source: J. W. Livingstone, "Evliya Çelebi on Surgical Operations in Vienna," *Al-Abath* (1970), vol. 23, pp. 230–232; translation modified.

QUESTIONS FOR ANALYSIS

▶ What does Çelebi criticize and what does he admire about various Europeans?

▶ Are there passages where he expresses prejudices and stereotypes about them?

Abbas I (r. 1587–1629) Safavid ruler who created a long and stable reign, beautified the capital city of Isfahan, promoted foreign trade, and repelled Ottoman invaders.

the Shi'ite version of Islam became the state religion, and Sunnis who would not agree to curse the early caliphs were driven into exile. Shi'ites, long a suppressed minority, now controlled a major Islamic state. Later the Ottoman army retook the Tigris-Euphrates River Valley, including Baghdad and Basra, where the cultural boundary between Arabic-and Persian-speaking populations and the religious boundary between Sunni and Shi'ite majorities were located.

Although the shift toward Shi'ism in Iran was permanent, over time the religious passions that drove initial Safavid policies died down. The greatest Safavid ruler, Shah **Abbas I** (r. 1587–1629), built a new capital at Isfahan (**is-fah-HAHN**), a city of half a million residents by the time Jean de Chardin commented on "the great number of magnificent palaces, the agreeable and pleasant houses … the really fine bazaars, the water channels and the streets of which the sides were covered with tall plane trees."[3] The gardens of Isfahan were legendary, and under Abbas Persian culture spread both east and west. Persian verse was widely admired, influencing Swahili poets in East Africa as well as Urdu poets in India. Isfahan, a showcase for Persian architecture and engineering, influenced the graceful silhouette of the Taj Mahal in India. In addition to creating beautiful abstract patterns on rich carpets, Persian artists were famous for miniature paintings depicting scenes from everyday life.

The economy also blossomed under Abbas's long and stable rule, with new irrigation works supporting agriculture, new markets for handicrafts, and a pilgrim trade bringing visitors to the holy sites of Shi'ite Islam. Iranian silks, carpets, and ceramics were traded overland and by sea to both the east and west, most especially by the Armenian merchant community.

In politics, the antagonism of the shah's chief minister to all things European was offset by the Safavid need to cultivate European alliances against the Ottomans in Constantinople. Following the dictum that "the enemy of my enemy is my friend," Shah Abbas invited diverse European merchants and diplomatic representatives to Isfahan,

anxious as he was to acquire guns, cannon, and military training assistance.

When Chardin observed the jockeying for position among the Europeans at the Safavid court, he noted that the Russian ambassador was given precedence and was told by the grand vizier: "The Muscovite [Russian] is our neighbor and our friend, and the commerce has been a long time settled between us, and without interruption. We send ambassadors to each other reciprocally almost every year, but we hardly know the other [Europeans]." As the Russian Empire expanded to the south, relations between the two powers intensified.

Origins of the Russian Empire, 1500–1685

Before the sixteenth century, the Slavic-speaking Russian people had been deeply influenced by Greek-speaking Byzantium. Medieval Russian princes and merchants cultivated relations with Constantinople, and the Russian city of Kiev became a central point for the diffusion of literacy and Orthodox Christianity. The monastic tradition of Orthodox Christianity took deep root.

The early consolidation of a Russian state is largely the story of two Ivans, Ivan III (r. 1440–1505) and Ivan IV (r. 1533–1584). Ivan III ruled Muscovy from his capital at Moscow. After the Ottoman seizure of Constantinople in 1453, Ivan drove the weakened Mongols out of the other Russian states and asserted his authority. He made an explicit connection between his own power and the Byzantine legacy, calling himself "tsar" ("caesar") and declaring that Russia would defend the Orthodox Christian heritage. Ivan's strategy of maintaining a large territorial buffer around the core Russian lands to protect them from invasion would become a perennial element of Russian imperial policy.

His successor Tsar Ivan IV centralized royal authority even further and extended Russian power to the west, east, and south, earning the nickname "Ivan the Terrible" for the random cruelty of his later years. To the west, his armies engaged Catholic Poland and Protestant Sweden. To the south they conquered Muslim populations in rich steppe grasslands and began to drive into the Caucasus Mountains between the Black and Caspian Seas. To the east, across the Ural Mountains, lay the forbidding lands of Siberia. The quest for animal furs lured the first Russian frontiersmen to these lands, and state power followed later (see Chapter 20). Defense and expansion of the Orthodox faith inspired Ivan's conquests.

Following the death of Ivan the Terrible came a "time of troubles" with no clear successor to the title of tsar. That period of uncertainty ended in 1613 when the Russian nobles offered royal power to Mikhail Romanov. The Romanov dynasty (1613–1917) continued imperial expansion (see Chapters 20 and 27). Like the sultans of the Ottoman Empire, the Romanov tsars remained in power into the early twentieth century.

The main sources of revenue for the tsars and the nobility were agricultural surpluses. Village-based farming was the foundation of all of the land-based empires, not only Russia but also the Ottoman and Safavid Empires, Mughal India, and Ming China (see Chapter 16). What was distinctive about Russia was the persistence of serfdom. Russian peasants were tightly bound to their villages, and the tsars and aristocracy increasingly saw these "souls," as they called the peasants, as property that could be bought and sold. The oppressive conditions of serfdom in Russia contrasted with developments in western Europe, where serfdom had either disappeared altogether or where peasant obligations were becoming less burdensome.

The Struggle for Stability in Western Europe, 1500–1653

The sixteenth century and the first half of the seventeenth century were a time of turmoil in western Europe. Warfare ensued wherever religious divisions became entangled with the ambitions of emperors, kings, and princes. Urbanization and commercialization heightened tensions, and attempts at political centralization were often met with resistance.

The Habsburgs were the most powerful family in Europe at the beginning of this period. Originally from central Europe, through marriages and diplomatic maneuvers the **Habsburg dynasty** aspired to control a pan-European Catholic empire. Conflict with the Ottoman Empire, including the need to protect Vienna from Ottoman attack, was one check on Habsburg power. Another was the rising power of England and France. Beginning with the reign of Queen Elizabeth I (r. 1558–1603), England's Tudor monarchs were solidly Protestant and stridently anti-Spanish, while the Catholic monarchs of France competed with the Spanish Habsburgs for power and influence.

The rebellious provinces of the Netherlands were another major distraction and expense.

By the mid-seventeenth century Habsburg power had started to fade, while religious and dynastic conflict brought civil war to England and France. Violence was greatest in central Europe, where thirty years of religiously driven warfare devastated the countryside.

> **Habsburg dynasty** Powerful ruling house that expanded from Austria to Spain, the Netherlands, and the Spanish Empire, as well as throughout the German-speaking world when Charles V (r. 1516–1555) was elected Holy Roman Emperor.

The Rise and Decline of Habsburg Power, 1519–1648

The greatest of the Habsburg monarchs was Charles I, who ruled Spain from 1516 to 1556. Educated in the Netherlands, he inherited both the Spanish crown at Madrid and the Habsburg domains in central Europe. His Dutch experience tied him to one of the most dynamic commercial

HIP/Art Resource, NY

Martin Luther Preaching Martin Luther was known as a powerful preacher, as seen in this contemporary depiction. The rapid spread of his Protestant ideas, however, resulted from the printing press as well. In 1455 the first metal movable type outside of Asia was invented by a German goldsmith; a hundred years later that invention allowed Martin Luther's ideas to spread far and wide.

prestigious position, and, having been crowned emperor by the pope, Charles became the principal defender of the Catholic faith.

With extensive territorial possessions in Europe and all the wealth of the Americas at their disposal, it seemed that the Habsburgs might be able to create a political unity in western Europe. But for all of the military campaigns undertaken by Charles V during his long reign, it was not to be. The French were too powerful a rival in the west, while the Ottoman Turks challenged Habsburg supremacy in eastern Europe and the Mediterranean. Equally significant were the violent repercussions from the Protestant Reformation that began to appear in the mid-sixteenth century.

Charles V became Holy Roman Emperor just as Martin Luther was challenging church authority (see Chapter 16). In 1521 Charles V presided over a meeting intended to bring Luther back under papal authority. Luther refused to back down and was declared an outlaw. The German princes chose sides, some declaring themselves "Lutherans," others remaining loyal to the pope and Holy Roman Emperor. Decades of inconclusive warfare followed, and religious division became a permanent part of the western European scene. Exhausted, in 1555 Charles agreed to a peace that recognized the principle that princes could impose either Catholicism or Lutheranism within their own territories. He then abdicated his throne and split his inheritance between his brother Ferdinand, who took control of the Habsburg's central European domains, and his son Philip, who became king of Spain.

Philip II (r. 1556–1598) ruled over a magnificent court at Madrid, and during his reign the Philippines (named for Philip himself) were brought under Spanish control. However, even with the vast riches of New Spain, wars severely strained the treasury, and increased taxes led to

Philip II (r. 1556–1598) Son of Charles V and king of Spain. Considering himself a defender of Catholicism, Philip launched attacks on Protestants in England and the Netherlands.

economies in the world, the central European territories dominated from Vienna were crucial in the European military balance, and his Spanish possessions included all the riches of the Americas. His family connections also made him king of Naples, controlling the southern part of Italy.

In 1520, Charles was crowned Holy Roman Emperor under the title Charles V, having defeated the French king to win that title. By the sixteenth century, the "emperor," elected by seven of the many kings, princes, and archbishops who ruled over German-speaking lands, had little real power. However, it was a unrest. Philip's militancy in attempting to impose Catholic orthodoxy on his subjects made religious divisions even more acute.

One example is the rebellion of the Spanish *Moriscos* (mohr-EES-kos) in 1568, Arabic-speaking Iberians who stayed in Spain after 1492. Though forced to convert to Christianity, many Morisco families continued to practice Islam in private. When the church tried to impose Catholic orthodoxy on them, the resulting rebellion took two years to suppress; Philip later ordered the expulsion of all remaining Iberian Muslims.

Philip also struggled with the Calvinists in his Dutch provinces. John Calvin was a Protestant theologian whose Reformed Church emphasized the absolute power of God over weak and sinful humanity. The possibility of salvation for human souls lay entirely with God, Calvin argued: "eternal life is foreordained for some, eternal damnation for others."

Philip regarded these Calvinists as heretics, and when he tried to seize their property they armed themselves in self-defense. Attempts to put down the rebellion only stiffened Dutch resistance. This constant warfare was a drain on the Spanish treasury. The struggle was never resolved in Philip's lifetime, but in 1609 a treaty was signed that led to the effective independence of the Dutch United Provinces.

England was another constant source of concern to Philip. Its Protestant rulers harassed the Spanish at every turn, even supporting the privateers who plundered Spanish treasure ships in the Caribbean. In 1588, Philip's attempt to assert his dominance over England failed when poor weather combined with clever English naval strategy to defeat Spain's great naval Armada.

By the early seventeenth century, the Habsburg Empire was falling apart from religious divisions and the expense of warfare on so many fronts. At this same time, silver imports from the New World began to decline. By midcentury, even their Catholic lands in Italy were in revolt.

Things were no better in the eastern Habsburg domains. The peace of 1555 had broken down, and warfare continued to rock central Europe. Unrest between Catholic and Lutheran rulers finally led to the catastrophic **Thirty Years' War** (1618–1648). As armies rampaged through the countryside, as much as 30 percent of the rural population died from famine and disease, a loss of population almost as great as that brought by the Black Death three hundred years earlier. Finally the Peace of Westphalia (1648) recognized a permanent division between Catholic and Protestant Germany. The ideal of a single overarching imperial structure was gone, replaced by the concept of a multiplicity of kingdoms and smaller principalities that recognized one another's sovereignty. By 1648, the Holy Roman Empire was shattered, and the era of Habsburg dominance in western European history was over.

Religious and Political Conflict in France and England, 1500–1653

France and England had the most to gain from the decline of Habsburg power. But both societies also had their own religious divisions and political conflicts.

While Protestants were always a minority in French society, they had an influence on French life and politics beyond their numbers. Many French Calvinists, known as Huguenots (HEW-guh-noh), followed John Calvin into exile in Switzerland; those who remained faced increasing persecution. In 1572, ten years of simmering religious tension exploded with the St. Bartholomew's Day Massacre, when the French king ordered the assassination of Protestant leaders. As news of the killing hit the streets of Paris, Catholic mobs began to slaughter Huguenots in a frenzy of violence that spread to other French cities.

The heir to the throne, Henry of Navarre, was a member of the Protestant Bourbon family. When he became king as Henry IV in 1589, facing a largely hostile Catholic population, he publicly converted to Catholicism and then, in 1598, issued the Edict of Nantes granting limited toleration of Protestant worship. Still, Catholic/Protestant tensions persisted.

The dominant French political figure of the time was **Cardinal Richelieu** (1585–1642). Although Richelieu (RISH-el-yeuh) was a church official, his

Thirty Years' War (1618–1648) Series of wars fought by various European powers on German-speaking lands. Began as a competition between Catholic and Lutheran rulers and was complicated by the dynastic and strategic interests of Europe's major powers.

Cardinal Richelieu (1585–1642) Influential adviser to French kings who centralized the administrative system of the French state and positioned the Bourbon rulers of France to replace the Habsburgs as the dominant Catholic force in Europe.

policies were guided by the interests of the French monarchy rather than by religious affiliation. He was willing, for example, to ally France with German Protestants against the Spanish Habsburgs, whom he saw as the main rivals to French power. French power grew, but so did social unrest following an increase in taxes and the attempts by Richelieu to tame the prerogatives of the aristocracy and amass greater power for the king and his ministers.

When Cardinal Richelieu and the king he had loyally served both died within a few months of each other and a child-king, **Louis XIV** (r. 1643–1715), came to the throne, revolts broke out. From 1648 to 1653, France was racked by civil war between the monarchy and those who were fed up with high taxes and the centralization of authority at court. But the

French monarchy survived, and, as we will see the long reign of Louis would mark a high point in French prestige and power.

English society entered the seventeenth century in relative tranquility under Queen Elizabeth. The "Elizabethan Age" was a time of increasing national confidence, as reflected in these verses of William Shakespeare (1564–1616):

> This royal throne of kings, this sceptred isle …
> This happy breed of men, this little world,
> This precious stone set in the silver sea …
> This blessed plot, this earth, this realm, this
>   England.[4]

But the peace did not last.

In religious matters, Elizabeth followed the Anglican Church tradition established by her father, King Henry VIII. Although Catholicism was made illegal, Henry had actually retained many Catholic rites and traditions, including a hierarchy of powerful bishops. Many English

Réunion des Musées Nationaux/Art Resource, NY

Louis XIV at Court   King Louis XIV was an active patron of the new science. It was his finance minister, Jean-Baptiste Colbert, who suggested that the king form the Royal Academy of Sciences in 1666. Here Colbert is shown presenting members of the Academy to the king; two globes and a large map indicate that the French monarch saw the development of science as a means of expanding his empire.

Protestants wanted further reform to purge Catholic influences like the emphasis on saints, statues, and elaborate rituals.

Protestant reformers known as **Puritans** grew discontented with the Stuart kings who came to power after Elizabeth. They scorned the opulence of court life and the culture of luxury of Anglican bishops. Increased taxes and assertions of centralized royal power were additional causes of complaint.

Under King **Charles I** (r. 1625–1649), tensions exploded. Charles pursued war with Spain and supported Huguenot rebels in France, but (unlike French kings) he could not raise taxes to finance his policies without the approval of Parliament. In 1628, when Parliament presented a petition of protest against the king, he disbanded it and did not call another for eleven years. By then Charles was so desperate for money that he had no choice but to reconvene Parliament. Reformers then tried to use the occasion to compel the abolition of the Anglican bishop hierarchy in favor of a more decentralized church organization. When Charles reacted by arresting several parliamentary leaders on charges of treason, the people of London reacted with violence. The king fled London, and the English Civil War (1642–1649) began.

Opposition to the king's forces was organized by the Puritan leader Oliver Cromwell (1599–1658).

Puritan soldiers showed their disdain by stabling their horses inside Anglican churches, smashing statues, and knocking out stained-glass windows. After seven years of fighting Cromwell prevailed, and the king was captured. Though the majority in Parliament favored negotiations, radicals insisted on summary justice. In 1649, King Charles was beheaded.

Oliver Cromwell became Lord Protectorate of the English Commonwealth and instituted a series of radical reforms. But the Commonwealth was held together by little other than his own will and his control of the army, and some of his policies were highly unpopular. Puritan suppression of the theaters, for example, while in keeping with strict Calvinist ideals, was resented by many. When Cromwell died in 1658, the Commonwealth went with him, and in 1660 Parliament invited Charles's son home from exile to re-establish the monarchy. The English had not yet found a way to balance monarchical and parliamentary power.

> **Puritans** Seventeenth-century reformers of the Church of England who attempted to purge the church of all Catholic influences. They were Calvinists who emphasized Bible reading, simplicity and modesty, and the rejection of priestly authority and elaborate rituals.
>
> **Charles I** (r. 1625–1649) King of England whose attempts to centralize royal power led to conflict with Parliament, where some members also resented the influence of his Catholic wife. His execution marked the end of the English Civil War.

The Shifting Balance of Power in Western Eurasia and the Mediterranean, 1650–1750

Religious divisions inflamed Europe during the sixteenth and early seventeenth centuries. By the middle of the eighteenth century, however, the situation stabilized as Catholic and Protestant rulers increasingly pursued policies on the basis of dynastic and national interests rather than religious ones.

New powers were emerging to displace old empires. In the later seventeenth century, Russia, England, and France each arose as great powers and were joined by Austria, still ruled by the Habsburg family, and Prussia, now the dominant kingdom amongst the many German principalities. As these five great powers jockeyed for advantage, others saw their power decline. Formerly powerful Poland was divided. Safavid Iran was invaded and conquered. The Ottomans remained powerful, but by the eighteenth century their days of expansion were over.

Between 1650 and 1750, power shifted north and west. Even the rulers of imperial Russia, whose empire continued to expand to the south and east, looked to western Europe as a source of power and innovation.

Safavid Collapse and Ottoman Stasis, 1650–1750

In 1722, Afghan invaders descended on Isfahan and left it in ruins. By 1747, the cultural and political achievements of the Safavid Empire were diminished.

Jean de Chardin's portrait of the Persian court suggests that corruption and poor leadership were already weakening the Safavids in the late seventeenth century. Shah Abbas had neglected to groom a successor. The next shah, pampered in the seclusion of the royal harem his whole life, had little education and no experience of government or administration. With the exception of the grand vizier, almost everyone seemed to follow the new shah's example of debauchery and corruption. Shi'ite clerics, who had been principal supporters of the Safavid dynasty in its earliest days, were appalled.

The last Safavid shah attempted to reverse these trends and regain the support of the clergy by imposing harsh conditions of public morality. He banned music, coffee, and (like the Puritans in England) public entertainments, restricted women to the home, and even destroyed the imperial wine cellar. Though popular with clerics, such actions were insufficient to revive the empire.

Weakness at the top was a recipe for disaster. Lacking strong direction, the bureaucracy became a drain on productivity. Bribery was constant, and provincial governors raised taxes on their own without forward revenue to Isfahan. The Safavids were easy pickings when Afghan invaders descended on the empire in 1722.

The Ottoman story is less dramatic, one of stasis rather than collapse. Although Ottoman armies laid siege to Vienna once again in 1683, threatening to expand even further into central Europe—and even as late as 1739 the Austrians ceded Balkan territory to Constantinople—such events were now the exception. In general, eighteenth-century Ottoman leaders were focused on maintaining and defending existing territories.

As the "gunpowder revolution" continued to make warfare more deadly, it also made defending an empire with expansive frontiers more expensive. While Ottoman agricultural and commercial production had been increasing during the time of Süleyman, by the early seventeenth century economic expansion was no longer keeping up with population growth. When hunger and hardship resulted, the Ottoman government attempted to control prices and restrict grain exports. Changes in global economics limited their success, however.

The vast influx of American silver into western Europe was creating steep inflation. While high prices in Europe facilitated the sale of Ottoman commodities to the west, the Ottoman elite spent silver at an even greater rate to purchase luxury goods, furs from Russia, and porcelain and silk from Iran and China. Attempts to control imports and exports only encouraged smuggling. Moreover, goods formerly transported across the Ottoman realm, and taxed in transit, were now shipped to Europe by sea. To offset the loss in trade revenues, Ottoman rulers raised taxes. But the debilitating effects of inflation and corruption were now straining relations between the Ottomans and their subject peoples.

As with the Safavids, the Ottoman Empire's problems represented opportunities for people chafing under Ottoman rule and for aspiring empires like Russia, which envied the warm water ports of the Black Sea. But unlike the Safavids, the Ottomans' empire persisted into the twentieth century.

Political Consolidation and the Changing Balance of Power in Europe, 1650–1750

In the latter part of the seventeenth century, stability returned to Europe. With the Habsburgs' failure to create a united Catholic empire, permanent political and religious divisions in western and central Europe became accepted. The rulers of France, England, Prussia, Austria, and Russia each consolidated their power internally while competing for national advantage.

In France, the Bourbon king Louis XIV created a court of legendary power, with his Versailles Palace rivaling Constantinople's Sublime Porte in splendor and luxury. Louis XIV tamed the independent power of the nobility and, while he asserted the Catholic identity of the French monarchy, pursued alliances even with Protestant powers when they served French national interests.

When Louis XIV came to the French throne, the nobles still dominated the countryside, and they remained jealous of their prerogatives.

Both lords and peasants lived in a world where local affiliations and obligations were more important than national ones. As during medieval times, peasants labored on their lords' estates and were subject to manorial courts. They spoke local dialects and lived by local customs; the royal court seemed distant indeed. Roads were poor, trade was hampered by local tolls, and even weights and measures varied in different parts of the country.

To assert his power, Louis increased the use of *intendants*, crown officials who were often from the middle class or the lower ranks of the nobility. Intendants depended on royal patronage and owed their loyalty to the king. Dispatched across the country, they enforced royal edicts that cut into the power of the landed nobility. As nobles lost local power, they too sought royal patronage and gravitated toward the lavish banquets, plays, operas, and ballets the court provided for their entertainment at Versailles.

In 1685, Louis formally revoked the Edict of Nantes, realigning the French state with Catholicism. Soon hundreds of thousands of French Protestants, including Jean de Chardin, fled to England, Switzerland, and the Netherlands. Some went to join the Dutch East India Company settlement at Cape Town in South Africa. Louis was determined to weaken Spain and Austria and position France as the world's dominant Catholic power. His motto was: "One King, One Law, One Faith."

In 1713, after years of conflict with Spain, the Netherlands, and the Austrian Habsburgs, a settlement was finally reached that brought order to the dynastic politics of Europe. Faced with the possibility that the Habsburgs might reunify Madrid and Vienna under a single ruler, the European powers supported a plan to put a Bourbon relation of Louis XIV on the Spanish throne, with the stipulation that the French and Spanish crowns could never be united. Now Louis and his successors could put even more energy into challenging England in a global competition for power (see Map 17.1).

The struggle between France and England had economic and military components. In the seventeenth century both countries had adopted **mercantilism**, a policy that put national economic interests at the forefront of foreign policy. Through the use of monopolistic chartered companies, Louis XIV's government sought to control foreign trade by directing colonial resources for the sole benefit of the motherland while restricting the access of others to French colonial markets.

Louis XIV's form of government has been termed "royal absolutism." "I am the state," he said, implying that all of public life should be directed by his own will. The French "Sun King" was the envy of all who aspired to absolute power.

In England, by contrast, when Charles II returned in 1660 to re-establish the Stuart monarchy after civil war and Puritan rule, absolute power was not an option. Charles preferred relatively tolerant policies, and although Puritan rule under Cromwell had given Calvinists something of a bad reputation, Charles welcomed Huguenot refugees from France, appointing Jean de Chardin as his royal jeweler. Nevertheless, Parliament imposed restrictions on Catholics and on Protestant "dissenters" who rejected the Anglican Church in favor of a more thoroughly reformed Protestantism: only Anglicans were allowed to hold public office.

With the death of Charles, religious tension rose to the point of crisis when his Catholic brother came to the throne as King James II (r. 1685–1689). While James II did not try to impose Catholicism on the largely Protestant kingdom, he did seek greater tolerance for his own faith. To prevent a Catholic succession, Parliament invited Charles's reliably Protestant daughter Mary, together with her Dutch husband William of Orange, to take the throne. James II went into exile and assembled an army to restore himself to power, but in 1690 he was defeated by Protestant forces led by William at the Battle of the Boyne in Ireland. William's victory made permanent the Protestant character of the British monarchy and furthered Protestant ascendency over the Catholics of Northern Ireland.

The so-called Glorious Revolution of 1689 was neither very glorious nor very revolutionary, but it did come with a constitutional innovation that would eventually have global repercussions. Since they had been invited to rule by Parliament, William and Mary were required to accept the

mercantilism Dominant economic theory in seventeenth- and eighteenth-century Europe that emphasized the role of international economics in interstate competition. Under mercantilism, restrictive tariffs were placed on imports to raise their prices, maximize the country's exports, and build up supplies of gold and silver bullion for military investment.

Map 17.1   Western Eurasia in 1715

By the early eighteenth century the Habsburg attempt to unify western Europe had failed, and the continent was permanently divided between Catholic and Protestant powers. In 1715 the dominant powers in the west were France, Great Britain, Austria, and Prussia. The Russian and Ottoman Empires to the east were formidable military powers, but the golden age of Spain had ended.   © Cengage Learning

 Interactive Map

Legend:
- French Bourbon lands
- Spanish Bourbon lands
- Austrian Habsburg lands
- Prussian lands
- Great Britain
- Boundary of the Holy Roman Empire
- Russian Empire
- Russian gains, by 1725
- Ottoman Empire, 1722

principle of annual parliamentary meetings. They also approved a **Bill of Rights**. While restrictions on individual liberty remained and most people had no real voice in governance, the English Bill of Rights established important precedents such as Parliametnary freedom of speech and the independence of the judiciary from royal interference.

English commerce thrived, both domestically and across the world, and the British navy was on its way toward global predominance, leading to persistent conflict with the French. Britain's constitutional balance between monarchical and parliamentary authority was exceptional among the great powers: Austria, Prussia, and Russia all followed the French model of royal absolutism.

The Ottomans remained formidable in southeastern Europe, while the Habsburgs still controlled an expansive empire from their capital at Vienna and were secure in their core territories after the second Ottoman siege of Vienna was lifted. The Austrian Habsburgs ruled over an ethnically and religiously heterogeneous population. Facing the same challenge as the Ottomans—how to assert a single royal authority over a diverse population—the Habsburgs generally pursued a similar policy: as long as the authority of the king was acknowledged and taxes were paid, local autonomy would be accepted. Thus after a Hungarian rebellion was suppressed, the privileges of the Hungarian nobility and many traditional Hungarian legal customs were retained.

In Protestant-dominated northern Germany, Prussia was the rising power in the aftermath of the Thirty Years' War. Although the German-speaking lands were still divided into numerous territories, with some princes ruling very small states, Prussia, from its capital at Berlin, emerged as the strongest German kingdom. Under Frederick William I (r. 1713–1740), Prussia became a pioneer in military technology and organization, using the latest cannon and muskets and developing a professional standing army of well-trained and disciplined troops. Many features of modern military life, such as precision marching, were pioneered under Frederick William. The Prussian middle class had little political influence. Instead, it was the Junkers (**YUNG-kurz**), the traditional rural aristocracy, who were the bedrock of royal absolutism. Their cooperation in taxing and controlling the peasants gave Frederick William and his successors resources to expand the military and make Prussia a force to be reckoned with.

Russian culture and the Russian state had developed in interaction not with western Europe but with steppe nomads, Byzantine Christians, and Asian powers such as the Safavid Empire, where Jean de Chardin had noted the prominence of Russian diplomats. However, a major shift came with Tsar **Peter the Great** (r. 1685–1725). After visiting the Netherlands as a young man, Peter came back urgently aware of Russia's backwardness and undertook reforms designed to put Russia on par with the rising Western states. He built the new city of St. Petersburg on the Baltic Sea as Russia's "window on the west." Its elegant baroque buildings, emulating those of Rome and Vienna, stood in contrast to the churches and palaces of Moscow, which reflected Central Asian architecture. Peter also tightened the dependence of the nobility on the Russian state. In a move that symbolized his desire to bring the country in line with Western models, he ordered Russian nobles to shave off their luxurious beards. From now on they would follow the latest European fashions.

Peter's ultimate goal, however, was power, and that meant focusing on the military. He established a regular standing army that was larger than any in Europe and bought the latest military technology from the West while working toward Russian self-sufficiency in the production of modern guns, cannon, and ships for his Baltic fleet. He also sponsored a new educational system to train more efficient civilian and military bureaucracies. But the middle class remained small, weak, and dependent on state patronage. The situation of the serfs was worse than ever. It was their heavy taxes that paid for the grandeur of St. Petersburg and the power of the Russian military, and it was their sons who fought Peter's wars.

Peter won victories against Poland, Sweden, and the Ottoman Empire, pushing the imperial frontiers from the Baltic Sea in the north to the

Bill of Rights In 1689, King William and Queen Mary of England recognized a Bill of Rights that protected their subjects against arbitrary seizure of person or property and that required annual meetings of Parliament.

Peter the Great (r. 1685–1725) Powerful Romanov tsar who built a new Russian capital at St. Petersburg, emulated Western advances in military technology, and extended the Russian Empire further into Asia.

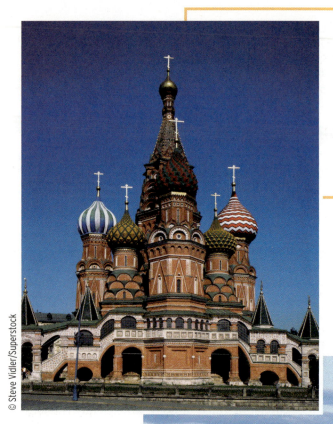

© Steve Vidler/Superstock

© Peter Christopher/Masterfile

St. Basil's Church and the Winter
Palace Architecture demonstrates Russia's diverse cultural influences. St. Basil's Cathedral (*left*) in Moscow highlights the impact of Byzantine and Persian traditions on Orthodox church architecture, while Peter the Great's Winter Palace (*below*), today part of the Hermitage Museum complex, testifies to the tsar's emulation of Western models in the construction of his new capital at St. Petersburg.

Primary Source: Edicts and Decrees *Read a selection of Peter the Great's decrees and find out how he wished to modernize, and Westernize, Russia.*

Black Sea in the south. The Siberian and Central Asian frontiers of the Russian Empire also continued to expand, in the latter case bringing more Muslims under Russian rule. Pragmatism dictated that there would be no systematic attempt to convert subject peoples to Orthodox Christianity.

Thus, by 1750, the roster of great powers that would dominate competition for European, and eventually global predominance had emerged: Britain, France, Austria, Prussia, and Russia, with the Ottomans still important as rulers of their vast domains.

Bourgeois Values and Chardin's View of the "Orient"

When reading travel accounts, we often learn as much about the traveler as about the places that he or she has visited. That is certainly true of Chardin's *Travels in Persia*. As we saw at the beginning of the chapter, Chardin's ideas about negotiation differed from those of his Iranian counterparts: he thought they were duplicitous, while they thought he was rude. Throughout the book Chardin contrasts the values of his own society with those of the "oriental" societies through which he moves.

Chardin was not close-minded. He admired Iranian medicine and astronomy, saying that "the Persian genius lies in the direction of the sciences more than toward any other profession." He enjoyed Persian poetry: "The number of figures of speech… is almost limitless. Nevertheless all of them are sublime." He praised Iranian architecture, describing the shah's residence as "one of the most imposing palaces that can be seen in any capital city."

Even regarding gender relations, Chardin kept an open mind. He understood that the tradition of veiling women was older than Islam, "the most ancient of anything their histories speak of," more of a social custom than a religious mandate. He even wondered if the custom of gender segregation might be preferable: "When [the men] do not see another man's wife," he wrote, they will not lose "the affection which they have, or ought to have, for their own." Of course, Chardin himself never entered the women's quarters of a palace, so he had no direct knowledge of the degree to which a woman might wield influence even while remaining secluded.

Still, Chardin frequently reveals his own values while pointing out their supposed absence in his Iranian hosts. Each of the following critiques of their behavior expresses a key element of Chardin's own middle class, Protestant value system:

- "They love to enjoy the present, and deny themselves nothing that they are able to procure, taking no thoughts for the morrow and relying wholly on providence, and their own fate they firmly believe to be sure and unalterable."

- "They cannot conceive that there should be such a country where people will do their duty from a motive of virtue only, without any other recompense."

- "They are not desirous of new inventions and discoveries [but] rest contented, choosing rather to buy goods from strangers than to learn the art of making them."*

These statements should probably not be taken as an accurate record of Iranian behavior, but they certainly do reveal Chardin's own priorities.

Thrift, foresight, plainspeaking, hard work, and detached curiosity: these values were characteristic of Chardin's own social group, the urban middle class of northwestern Europe. Like Chardin, middle-class members of the bourgeoisie did not have the advantages of the nobility, such as aristocratic titles, landed estates, and exemption from taxes. But they did possess property, education, and ambition, and they believed in the superiority of their own code of conduct over both foreigners and other social groups in their own countries.

The counting and measuring of time is an example. Whereas peasants marked time by the changing of the seasons and religious authorities by a ritual calendar, the bourgeoisie increasingly saw time not as slow cycles but as something akin to money, to be saved and invested. The development of ever smaller and more accurate timepieces reinforced this attitude. To Safavid officials, Chardin's close observance of minutes and hours must have seemed an irrational obsession. But such perspectives were rarely, if ever, represented in Western texts.

As more members of Europe's middle class traveled abroad in the eighteenth and nineteenth centuries, stereotypes of "exotic" societies began to multiply. Prejudices, such as the assumption that "oriental" societies were static

---

*Excerpts from Sir John Chardin, *Travels in Persia, 1673–1677,* an abridged English verion of *Voyages du chevalier Chardin en Perse, et autres lieux de I'Orient,* Dover, 1988, pp. 8, 70. Reprinted with permission of Dover Publications, Inc.

and unchanging, became engrained. Though Chardin himself, with his knowledge of Iranian language and culture, was less guilty than many of inflating the virtues of his own society by denigrating others, his *Travels in Persia* provides a preview of what was to come.

After leaving France to avoid religious persecution from Catholic authorities, Chardin achieved even greater wealth and prestige after he was appointed court jeweler to the British king. He then took employment with the British East India Company and moved to Holland. In Amsterdam his Calvinist beliefs and bourgeois values fit right in. As the eighteenth century progressed, Europe's urban middle class also began to contrast their own emphasis on thrift, foresight, plainspeaking, and hard work with the luxury and privilege enjoyed by their social superiors. As we will see, by the end of the eighteenth century bourgeois critiques of the European aristocracy had revolutionary implications.

Chapter Review and Learning Activities

The early modern period was a time of heightened competition between the empires and states of western Eurasia and, as the travels of Jean de Chardin show, also of increased commercial and cultural interaction. Religious divisions heightened political and military competition both in western Europe, divided between Catholics and Protestants, and in western Asia, where the Sunni-dominated Ottoman Empire struggled to assert its domination over the Shi'ite rulers of Safavid Iran.

When, where, and how were religion and politics most closely intertwined in western Eurasian societies? When and why did religion come to play a less prominent political role?

In the seventeenth and early eighteenth centuries, religion and politics became closely intertwined across western Eurasia. Ruling dynasties usually saw themselves as defenders of the faith, whether it was Orthodox Christianity for the Russian tsars, Roman Catholicism for the Habsburg emperors, Protestantism for the kings and queens of England, Sunni Islam for the Ottoman sultans, or Shi'ism for the Safavid shahs. Religious conflicts often fueled political and military competition, as in the Ottoman/Safavid competition for territory and influence, or in the Thirty Years' War that ravaged central Europe. Rulers differed, however, in how they responded to religious diversity *within* their domains. The Spanish, French, and British dynasties were the least tolerant of religious diversity.

The Safavids also imposed a single faith from the top down, but they tolerated Christian and Jewish minorities who played important commercial roles. The Ottomans, following the tradition established by Süleyman the Lawgiver, were more tolerant of religious diversity, recognizing that their vast empire could not be effectively ruled without the acquiescence of subject peoples.

By the eighteenth century, religion had become less central to politics. With the fall of the Safavid dynasty, Shi'ite Islam no longer had a powerful imperial patron. In Europe, rulers and dynasties were no longer as interested in religious affiliations as in power and profit.

How did the balance of power between the dominant states of western Eurasia shift during this period?

In the early eighteenth century the balance of power between states and empires in western Eurasia began to shift. At the beginning of the sixteenth century the Ottoman, Safavid, and Spanish Habsburg empires were each in an expansive phase. Two hundred years later the situation was quite different. The Safavid dynasty was gone. Madrid and Constantinople were still important capitals, but they had lost the initiative to other powers. Instead it was France, England, Austria, Prussia, and the quickly growing Russian Empire that dominated political and military competition in early eighteenth-century western Eurasia.

What do Jean de Chardin's travel writings tell us, both about Safavid Iran and about his own culture and values?

Jean de Chardin viewed Safavid culture through the lens of his own experiences. While he provides insights into seventeenth-century Iranian life, nevertheless, we must be careful not to take his assessments at face value. His criticisms of his Iranian hosts often arise from cultural differences. As a French Protestant from an urban background, Chardin embodied the ideas and ideals of the rising middle class of northern Europe. Literate, commercially oriented, and increasingly impatient with political and cultural customs that did not suit their interests, bourgeois men like Chardin would play an increasingly prominent role in world history.

KEY TERMS

Jean de Chardin (370)

Janissaries (372)

Süleyman (372)

Safavid dynasty (373)

Ismail (373)

Abbas I (376)

Habsburg dynasty (377)

Philip II (378)

Thirty Years' War (379)

Cardinal Richelieu (379)

Louis XIV (380)

Puritans (381)

Charles I (381)

mercantilism (383)

Bill of Rights (385)

Peter the Great (385)

FOR FURTHER REFERENCE

Beik, William. *Louis XIV and Absolutism: A Brief Study with Documents*. New York: Bedford/St. Martin's, 2000.

Bergin, Joseph. *The Seventeenth Century: Europe 1598–1715*. New York: Oxford University Press, 2001.

Braudel, Fernand. *The Mediterranean and the Mediterranean World in the Age of Philip II*. Sian Reynolds, trans. New York: Harper and Row, 1972.

Chardin, Jean de. *A Journey to Persia: Jean Chardin's Portrait of a Seventeenth Century Empire*. Ronald W. Ferrier, trans. and ed. London: I. B. Tauris, 1996.

Clot, Andre. *Suleiman the Magnificent*. London: Saqi Books, 2004.

Coward, Barry. *The Stuart Age: England, 1603–1714*. 3d ed. New York: Longman, 2003.

Faroghi, Suraiya. *The Ottoman Empire and the World Around It*. London: I. B. Tauris, 2006.

Fichtner, Paula Sutter. *Terror and Toleration: The Habsburg Empire Confronts Islam, 1526–1850*. New York: Reaktion Books, 2008.

Hughes, Lindsay. *Russia in the Age of Peter the Great*. New Haven: Yale University Press, 2000.

Savory, Roger. *Iran Under the Safavids*. New York: Cambridge University Press, 2007.

VOYAGES ON THE WEB

Voyages: Jean de Chardin

"Voyages" is a real time excursion to historical sites in this chapter and includes interactive activities and study tools such as audio summaries, animated maps, and flashcards.

Visual Evidence: Portrait of the Sajavid Court

"Visual Evidence" features artifacts, works of art, or photographs, along with a brief descriptive essay and discussion questions to guide your analysis of visual sources.

World History in Today's World: The Coffeehouse in World History

"World History in Today's World" makes the connection between features of modern life and their origins in the periods in this chapter.

CourseMate

Go to the CourseMate website at www.cengagebrain.com for additional study tools and review materials—including audio and video clips—for this chapter.

18

Empires, Colonies, and Peoples of the Americas, 1600–1750

tenant Nun
nant Nun by Catalina de
Translation copyright © 1996
ele Stepto and Gabriel
Reprinted by permission of
Press, Boston)

By the early 1600s, the Spanish had conquered the once-mighty Aztec and Inca and secured an American empire. But in some areas that had not been completely subdued, Amerindian peoples held on to their independence. A battle-hardened young soldier, **Catalina de Erauso** (1585–1650), described an encounter with one such group in South America:

On the third day we came to an Indian village whose inhabitants immediately laid hold of their weapons, and as we drew nearer scattered at the sound of our guns, leaving behind some dead. …
[A soldier] took off his helmet to mop his brow, and a devil of a boy about twelve years old fired an arrow at him from where he was perched in a tree beside the road. … The arrow lodged in the [soldier's] eye. … We carved the boy into a thousand pieces. Meanwhile, the Indians had returned to the village more than ten thousand strong. We fell at them again with such spirit, and butchered so many of them, that blood ran like a river across the plaza. … The men had found more than sixty thousand pesos' worth of gold dust in the huts of the village, and an infinity more of it along the banks of the river, and they filled their helmets with it.*/1

---

*Excerpt from *Catalina de Erauso, Lieutenant Nun: Memoir of a Basque Transvestite in the New World,* trans. Michele Stepto and Gabriel Stepto. Reprinted by permission of Beacon Press, Boston 1996.

The Map

VICEROYALTY OF NEW SPAIN

Caribbean Sea

Historical record of Catalina ends in Mexico, 1650.

Cartagena
Barranquilla
Caracas
Panama
Santa Fé de Bogotá
Quito

ANDES MOUNTAINS

AMAZON BASIN

Paita
Trujillo
Piscobamba

VICEROYALTY OF PERU

Lima
Guancavélica
Guamanga
Andahuailas
Cuzco

La Paz
Cochabamba
Mizque
Potosí

Disguised as a man, Catalina fights in the Spanish army.

PACIFIC OCEAN

ATACAMA DESERT
ALTIPLANO
ANDES MOUNTAINS
GRAN CHACO
PAMPAS

Tucumán

DUTCH BRAZIL
Recife

BRAZILIAN HIGHLANDS

Bahia

VICEROYALTY OF BRAZIL

CAMPOS

ATLANTIC OCEAN

São Paulo
Rio de Janeiro

N

La Plata

Concepción
Paicabi
Nacimiento
Valdivia

Promoted to rank of lieutenant.

Europe Inset

EUROPE   ATLANTIC OCEAN   FRANCE   Turin   REP. OF VENICE   OTTOMAN EMPIRE

San Sebastián
Bilbao
Valladolid
Pamplona
Toulouse
Marseilles
Genoa
PAPAL STATES
Rome
NAPLES
Naples

PORTUGAL
Madrid
Barcelona
Mediterranean Sea
Sardinia

Lisbon
Seville
Sanlúcar
Cádiz

Catalina de Erauso leaves the convent for Panama, 1603.

to Spain
Sicily

to Mexico

0 150 300 Km.
0 150 300 Mi.

Legend

The Travels of Catalina de Erauso

➤ Catalina de Erauso's journeys
● City visited by Catalina
● Other city
■ Spanish territory, ca. 1650
■ Portuguese territory, ca. 1650

0 300 600 Km.
0 300 600 Mi.

Join this chapter's traveler on "Voyages," an interactive tour of historic sites and events: www.cengagebrain.com

Timeline

1500   1550   1600   1650   1700   1750

Lifetime of Catalina de Erauso
1585   1650

NORTH AMERICA

Samuel de Champlain founds New France
1608

Huron population is decimated by disease
1640s

First African slaves in Virginia
1619

MEXICO AND THE CARIBBEAN

Viceroyalty of New Spain founded
1535

Lifetime of Sor Juana Ines de la Cruz
1648   1695

CENTRAL AND SOUTH AMERICA

Discovery of silver at Potosí
1545

Discovery of gold in Brazil
1695

Kingdom of Palmares
1630   1694

Catalina de Erauso
(1585–1650) Female Basque/Spanish explorer who, dressed as a man, lived the life of a soldier and adventurer in the Spanish viceroyalties of the colonial Americas.

Surprisingly, Catalina de Erauso (kat-ah-LEE-nah day eh-rah-OO-so), the soldier who painted this matter-of-fact picture of slaughter, was a woman.

Erauso, born in northeastern Spain, was placed in a convent by her family at the age of four. At the age of fifteen, when she was about to take the permanent vows that would confine her for a lifetime, she stole the keys and escaped: "I shook off my veil and went out into a street I had never seen. … I holed up for three days, planning and re-planning and cutting myself out a suit of clothes. … I cut my hair and set off without knowing where I was going."

Disguised as a boy, Erauso found employment as a personal assistant for a local nobleman, but she left when he "finally went so far as to lay hands on me." She stole some money, boarded a ship for Panama, and joined the Spanish army. For the next twenty years, Erauso traveled in the Spanish Americas, disguised as a man. A member of Spain's ethnically distinct Basque (bask) community, Erauso often teamed up with fellow Basques as she soldiered her way across Panama, Peru, Chile, Bolivia, and Argentina. According to her own story, her violent streak kept getting her into trouble. Card games often ended with insults and drawn swords, and more than once she had to run from the law after killing a man.

Erauso's exploits have become part of Latin American folklore, where she is known as *la monja alférez* (la mon-ha al-FAIR-ez), "the lieutenant nun." Her story is exceptional. But her deception was made easier by the frontier conditions. New arrivals from Europe and Africa increased decade by decade, interacting with indigenous inhabitants in a fluidly changing cultural landscape. It was literally a "new world"—new for European officials, settlers, and adventurers, new for African slaves who did most of the brute work, and new for America's indigenous peoples, who saw their ways of life undermined as they came under the control of Spain, Portugal, France, and England. The interaction of peoples from Europe, Africa, and the Americas was the foundation upon which new American societies would be built.

This chapter examines the political, economic, social, and cultural life of colonial America in the seventeenth and early eighteenth centuries, focusing especially on gender and race relations, the role of the Americas in the global economy, and the differences between the various European colonial ventures.

FOCUS QUESTIONS

▶ What were the principal forms of political and economic organization in the Americas in this period?

▶ What were the key demographic and cultural outcomes of the interaction of European, African, and Amerindian peoples in various regions of the Americas?

▶ What connections and comparisons can we draw between the different European colonial ventures in the Americas?

The Spanish Empire in the Americas, 1600–1700

The Spanish laid waste to the Aztec and Inca Empires in a remarkably short time. To rule their vast new territories, they immediately set up a highly centralized government that relied on close cooperation between crown and church. It was a strictly hierarchical power structure, with officials from Spain and locally born Spaniards at the top, the increasing number of people of mixed descent in the middle, and Indians and African slaves at the bottom. However, the farther one went from centers of authority the more fluid relations of gender and race became, enabling new possibilities in life.

From Conquest to Control

When Erauso arrived in Panama in 1603, the Spanish Empire was the most powerful European colonial venture in the Americas. True, a Spanish Armada had been repulsed by England in 1588, and the Dutch, still under Spanish rule, were laying the foundations for their own global enterprise. But Philip II of Spain could always count on American silver to replenish his treasury.

During the sixteenth century, the Spanish Habsburgs asserted increasing authority through a centralized bureaucracy headed by the Council of the Indies. In 1535, they sent the first viceroy to Mexico City, and in 1542 a second was dispatched to Lima. From that time forward, the emperor in Madrid sent officials to America as representatives of royal power. Eventually four **viceroyalties** were created: New Spain (with a capital at Mexico City), New Granada (Bogotá), Peru (Lima), and La Plata (Buenos Aires; see Map 18.1). Below the viceroys were presidencies, captaincy-generals, governors, and municipal authorities.

The other great institution of Spanish rule was the Catholic Church. The pope granted the Spanish crown the right to exercise power over the church in the Americas in all but purely spiritual affairs. Civil authorities appointed and dismissed bishops, while church leaders often served as top government officials. In the early colonial period, bishops sent directly from Spain occupied the higher church positions. In frontier areas, where missionaries brought Catholicism, they also brought Spanish rule.

American-born Spaniards known as *criollos* **(kree-OY-os)** grew in number, and by the seventeenth century, they were participating in government. While the top positions continued to be held by officials from Spain, criollos became a social and economic elite, often by seizing Amerindian land and exploiting Amerindian labor.

Although lust for gold had been a principal motive of the early conquistadors, it was silver that filled the Spanish treasury and transformed the world economy. In 1545, shortly after silver deposits were found in Mexico, the Spanish found a whole mountain of silver in the Andes at **Potosí** **(poh-toh-SEE)**. Andean silver enabled European trade with Asia, and much of the silver extracted from Potosí ended up in China.

Silver mining generated huge profits, but not for the workers who dug open the mountain. Conditions were so brutal that force was needed to get workers for the mines. Though the Crown had placed restrictions on *encomienda* **(in-coh-mee-EN-dah)** holders (see Chapter 15), a new legal system called the *repartimiento* **(reh-par-TEE-me-en-toh)** gave Spaniards the right to coerce Amerindian labor for specific tasks. Although the intent of reforming the encomienda system had been to limit abuses, most Spaniards assumed they still had a right to enslave Amerindians. Erauso, for example, commented that during one of her trading ventures a civic leader "gave me ten thousand head of llama to drive and a hundred-some-odd Indians." Apparently, these Amerindians had no say in the matter.

> **Primary Source**
> **Complaint of the Indians of Tecama Against Their Encomendero, Juan Ponce de León** *Read the testimony of several Indians on the conditions of Indian labor in New Spain, as reported by a notary.*

> **viceroyalties** Seats of power of the Spanish officials representing the king.
>
> **Potosí** Location high in the Andes in modern Bolivia where the Spanish found huge quantities of silver. Silver exports from Potosí and other American mines helped finance development of the early modern world economy.

Map 18.1 **The Spanish Empire in the Americas**

This map of the early-eighteenth-century Americas shows the territorial dominance of the Spanish Empire and its four viceroyalties. Though Portuguese Brazil was also large and rich, British and French colonial possessions were small and poor in resources by comparison. We should remember that this map shows European *claims* to territory. Some Amerindian societies remained autonomous and unconquered, especially in more remote regions of mountains, forests, and deserts. © Cengage Learning

Interactive Map

The Granger Collection

The Silver Mine at Potosí   The silver mines of Spanish America, of which Potosí was the greatest, enriched the Spanish treasury and facilitated the expansion of global trade. As this engraving from 1590 shows, however, it was the heavy toil of Amerindian workers on Potosí's mountain of silver that made it all possible. Spanish mine operators used the mercury amalgamation process to increase the yield of silver from ore, resulting in the frequently lethal mercury poisoning of workers such as those seen here.

Although the Spanish called their Andean labor system *mita* (**mee-tah**)—the same name used by the Inca for their system of labor tribute—the Spanish mita differed greatly from the Inca one. Under the Inca, mita required every household to contribute labor for tasks such as military service, road construction, and the maintenance of irrigation works. Exemptions were granted for families in difficult circumstances, and workers were fed, clothed, and well treated. By contrast, the Spanish paid scant attention to the well-being of laborers or their communities. Every adult male had to spend one full year out

of every seven working in the mines at wages that were not sufficient for his own support, let alone for his family. The use of poisonous mercury to separate silver from ore often led to sickness and death. Moreover, villagers had to work harder to compensate for the absence of adult males from their communities.

By 1600, Potosí was a major market with a population over 100,000. When Erauso set off with her llamas and one hundred Indians, she intended to exploit this market: "[The official] also gave me a great deal of money to buy wheat in the Cochabamba plains. My job was to grind it and get it to Potosí, where the scarcity of wheat made for high prices. I went and bought eight thousand bushels ... hauled them by llama to the mills ... and took them to Potosí. I then sold them all ... and brought the cash back to my master."* The llamas were indigenous, but the wheat grew from European seed, an example of the ongoing Columbian exchange (see Chapter 15).

Expanding markets accompanied the growth of administrative centers such as Mexico City, Lima, and Buenos Aires. In colonial Latin America, market-based agriculture was based on **haciendas** (ha-cee-EN-das).

> **haciendas** Large agrarian estates characteristic of colonial agriculture in Latin America.

While Amerindian communities remained largely self-sufficient, farming small village plots, the Spanish hacienda owners focused on meeting rising demand for agricultural produce. In addition to growing crops for sale, many grazed vast herds of cattle.

Within the boundaries of their own large estates, hacienda owners had almost total control, governing their lands and the people who lived on them without reference to outside authority. They used debt peonage as a way to control labor, by making loans to "their" Indians that were to be repaid in labor. But wages were never enough to repay the debt. Often, descendents of the original borrowers inherited these debts and became permanently bound to a single estate. Prevented by law from leaving the hacienda, Amerindians were unable to seek higher wages or better working conditions, and they remained desperately poor and ill educated across the generations.

> **Primary Source**
> **The Problem of the Indian and the Problem of the Land** *Read a Marxist's analysis of the oppression of Peru's Indians and his prescription for political change.*

Spain's main goal was to extract wealth from the Americas. While such goods as dyes, cotton, and leather hides were produced, no product came close in value to the tons of silver bullion sent in two annual shipments to Spain. Taking much, but investing little, Spain failed to lay the foundations for long-term prosperity; while other European nations were innovating in commerce and shipping (see Chapter 17), the Spanish stagnated in their mineral plunder. As a consequence, the Dutch, English, and French displaced Spain's pre-eminence during the seventeenth and eighteenth centuries.

By 1750, the patterns of life in Spanish-speaking America were set. The subjugation of indigenous peoples was well advanced. Large-scale haciendas and mining operations provided the economic foundation. Officials from Spain dominated the upper ranks of both church and state, while criollos became local officials, hacienda landowners, and merchants.

Colonial Society: Gender and Race on the Margins of Empire

Between the small Spanish elite and the Amerindians who continued to practice ancient cultural traditions, there existed a complex mix of peoples and cultures. European immigration, the importation of African slaves, and the continued loss of indigenous populations due to disease and deprivation were ingredients of this mix.

The Spanish elite brought an outlook concerned with enforcing strict hierarchies of caste, gender, and religious and ethnic identity. The Spanish fixation with "purity of blood" went back to the Reconquista (see Chapter 15), when reserving public office for men of pure Spanish descent was instituted to keep converted Jews and Muslims out of positions of power. This policy was transferred to the Americas: subjects of non-Spanish and non-Catholic origin were expected to defer to their social superiors.

Maintaining elitist hierarchies in the courts, schools, and urban spaces of Mexico City, Lima, and other centers of Spanish authority was easy enough. Outside the cities, however, conditions were more fluid. Spanish men rarely brought their wives and families to the Americas. Liaisons between Spanish men and indigenous women made "purity of blood" impossible to maintain: by the seventeenth century, a distinct *mestizo* (mes-TEE-zoh), or racially mixed Spanish/ Amerindian, category had emerged, a blending that came to characterize Mexican society.

Also difficult to maintain under frontier conditions was the power of the Catholic Church to

---

*Excerpt from *Catalina de Erauso, Lieutenant Nun: Memoir of a Basque Transvestite in the New World*, trans. Michele Stepto and Gabriel Stepto. Reprinted by permission of Beacon Press, Boston 1996.

impose orthodox religious ideas. In Spain itself, the inquisition strictly monitored the beliefs and behavior of the population. Families of *conversos* and *moriscos* (**mohr-EES-koz**), who had been forcibly converted from Judaism and Islam, were subjected to special scrutiny. On the colonial frontier, however, such groups sometimes were able to retain elements of their old faith.

Converted Amerindians were the largest group of Catholics deviating from church doctrine. During the sixteenth century, missionaries in Mexico and Peru baptized numerous indigenous worshipers who blended their cosmologies and rituals into Catholicism. While some church leaders campaigned against the continuation of "idol worship" among baptized Amerindians, more often Spanish missionaries tolerated such practices. Amerindian populations stabilized after the great losses of the sixteenth century, and where they formed a majority, as in the Andes, missionaries had little choice but to work through Amerindian cultures.

This process of **syncretism** is a theme in world history also seen, for example, when Islam spread to Africa and Buddhism to China. A thousand years before the conquest of the Americas, European converts to Christianity had adapted some of their pagan ideas to the new faith. For both ancient Europeans and colonized Amerindians, former gods reappeared as Christian saints. And while the Christian God might be male, worship of Mary as the Virgin Mother afforded spiritual space to the Aztec, for example, who previously worshiped the fertility goddess Tonantzin. In Mexico, the cult of the **Virgin of Guadalupe** epitomized the process of religious syncretism.

Erauso's story illustrates the fluidity of race and gender in frontier Spanish America. Once in Peru, she deserted the army and wandered alone into the mountains, where she nearly died but was rescued by two men who took her to their mistress's ranch:

The lady was a half-breed, the daughter of a Spaniard and an Indian woman, a widow and a good woman. ... The next morning she fed me well, and seeing that I was so entirely destitute she gave me a decent cloth suit. ... The lady was well-off, with a good deal of livestock and cattle, and it seems that, since Spaniards were scarce in those parts, she began to fancy me as a

husband for her daughter ... a girl as black and ugly as the devil himself, quite the opposite of my taste, which has always run to pretty faces. *

Never intending to marry the girl but merely to receive the widow's gifts, Erauso went along with this plan. She then writes, "In the two months I was putting off the Indian woman, I struck up a friendship with the Bishop's secretary," who introduced Erauso to his niece with the indication that they might get married. Again, Erauso accepted gifts from this potential in-law, but then "saddled up and vanished."

We cannot know how much of this story is embellished. But, apart from the twist of wooing other women in the guise of a man, it suggests how Iberian men (as Erauso presented herself to be) might be highly desirable marriage partners for families wishing to sustain or improve their social status. Marriage to a Spaniard could "improve" the family bloodline. Spanish men were in such short supply that Erauso could, by her own account at least, contract multiple engagements with ease. Of course, Spanish women were even less available as marriage partners. Most Spanish men could not afford to "import" wives from Iberia, and thus often fathered mixed-race children.

Erauso's narrative illustrates the two fundamental racial realities of the Spanish Americas. On the one hand, racial mixing was accepted as a part of life. On the other hand, whiteness conferred status. Even where **mestizos** or mulattos (of mixed Spanish/African descent) formed the majority, the ideal was Spanish "pure blood." A fair complexion was an indication of wealth and "good breeding." The tension between

> **syncretism** The fusion of cultural elements from more than one tradition. In colonial Latin America religious syncretism was common, with both Amerindians and Africans blending their existing beliefs and rituals with Catholicism.
>
> **Virgin of Guadalupe** An apparition of the Virgin Mary, with a dark complexion, said to have appeared to a Mexican peasant named Juan Diego in 1531. The cult of the Virgin of Guadalupe exerted a powerful attraction to Mesoamerica's surviving Amerindians. She remains a symbol of Mexican identity.
>
> **mestizo** Offspring of an Amerindian and Spanish union. Cultural and biological blending became characteristic of Mexican society.

*Excerpt from *Catalina de Erauso, Lieutenant Nun: Memoir of a Basque Transvestite in the New World*, trans. Michele Stepto and Gabriel Stepto. Reprinted by permission of Beacon Press, Boston 1996.

casta system A complex racial hierarchy devised in Spanish America to describe the dozens of possible outcomes of mixture between Europeans, Amerindians, and Africans.

Sor Juana Inés de la Cruz One of the great literary figures of colonial New Spain. Wrote poetry, prose, and philosophy despite having been denied a university education. Best known for her defense of the intellectual equality of men and women.

the ideal of racial purity and the reality of widespread racial mixing was encoded in the ***casta system***.

Gender relations and the social roles of women varied by social class. As in many societies, including the North African ones that had so strongly influenced Spanish culture, elite Spanish men demonstrated their wealth and status by keeping women out of the public realm. Elite parents, preoccupied with protecting the family honor, arranged unions for adolescent daughters who would, upon marriage, lead restricted lives. Those for whom no acceptable marriage could be found were sent to convents. Poorer families in which women played vital economic roles as farmers and artisans could not imitate such behavior.

Women sometimes had access to education, and those in convents also might rise to power within the confines of their all-female community. **Sor Juana Inés de la Cruz** (1648–1695) was the most famous of such women. Born into a

modest family, she was a child prodigy who learned to read Latin before the age of ten. She became a lady-in-waiting for the viceroy's wife in Mexico City and a popular figure at court. But after her application to the University of Mexico was denied, she entered the convent. In contrast to Catalina de Erauso, who saw convent life as a prison, Sor Juana accepted restricting herself to an all-women's community to develop her remarkable literary and intellectual skills.

Sor Juana's writings cover many topics, and her poetry is still taught to Mexican schoolchildren. She is best known for her belief in the equality of women with men: "There is no obstacle to love / in gender or in absence, / for souls, as you are well aware, / transcend both sex and distance."[2] After years of correspondence and debate with church leaders who denounced her work, she saw the futility of trying to change their minds and stopped publishing altogether. In 1694, church officials forced her to sell her library of four thousand books, and the next year she died of plague.

Sor Juana's story illustrates the degree to which New Spain duplicated the Spanish social order. But Erauso's narrative reminds us that the "New World" could also mean new possibilities.

Brazil, the Dutch, New France, and England's Mainland Colonies

Throughout the sixteenth century and into the seventeenth century, Spain remained the dominant imperial force in the Americas. But it was not the only European kingdom exploiting American resources. Portugal, though it placed a greater emphasis on its Asian empire, controlled Brazil, with its vast economic potential. Likewise the Dutch, while also focused on Asia, nevertheless harried the Spanish and Portuguese in the Western Hemisphere during the seventeenth century. The French and English were latecomers to the American colonial game, starting their settlements in North America only after the Spanish had created their great empire to the south. As in the Spanish colonies, the interactions of Europeans, Africans, and indigenous

Amerindians engendered diverse cultural patterns, and the further one moved into the frontier, the more fluid were the interactions among these peoples.

The Portuguese and Brazil

In the sixteenth century, Portugal's overseas efforts focused on the Indian Ocean (see Chapter 16). Discovered by accident and acquired by treaty, Brazil was an afterthought. Brazil had no large cities to conquer and no empires to plunder. Portuguese settlement was initially limited to the coast, and apart from a lucrative trade in tropical hardwood, Brazil initially offered little promise.

This situation changed dramatically in the later sixteenth century with the expansion of sugar plantations in northeastern Brazil. By the end of the seventeenth century, 150,000 African slaves comprised about half of the population. Meanwhile, Portuguese adventurers pushed into the interior seeking slaves, gold, and exotic goods such as brightly colored feathers from the Amazon. In 1695, gold was discovered in the southern interior in a region that thereby gained the name *Minas Gerais,* "General Mines." European prospectors brought African slaves to exploit the gold deposits, displacing the local Amerindians in the process. By the early eighteenth century, profits from sugar and gold had turned Brazil into Portugal's most important overseas colony.

In Brazil, missionaries were powerful players. Jesuits operated large cattle ranches and sugar mills to raise funds for church construction and missions to the interior. Missionaries often sought to protect Indian interests, but even so, they unwittingly introduced epidemic diseases and helped extend imperial policies that undercut indigenous life.

As soon as the sugar plantation economy was established in the northeast, slaves began to run away into the interior. Some of the runaways, called maroons, assimilated into Amerindian groups. Others formed their own runaway communities known as *quilombos.* Since the members of a quilombos were born and raised in different African societies, their political and religious practices often combined various African traditions and gods.

The quilombos community of **Palmares (pal-MAHR-es)** was founded in the early seventeenth century. The people at Palmares adapted the Central African institution of *kilombo,* a merit-based league of warriors that cut across family ties, ruled by their elected *Ganga Zumba* (Great Lord). Their religious life combined traditions of the Kongo kingdom with other African traditions and Catholicism. Numbering in the tens of thousands, Palmares defended itself against decades of Portuguese military assaults until it was finally defeated in 1694. However, the adaptation of African religion and culture to the American environment continued long after.

By 1750, Brazil had an exceptionally diverse culture. The Brazilian elite remained white,

dominating laborers who were primarily African rather than Amerindian. As in Spanish America, a large mixed-race group emerged along with a similarly complex hierarchy. Brazilian Catholicism, infused with African deities and beliefs, underwent a process of religious syncretism parallel to that of New Spain.

In Brazil, "black" and "African" were associated with slavery, the lowest condition of all. But like the Spanish casta system, the social and racial hierarchy in Brazil was flexible enough so that individuals or families might try to improve their standing. Dress, speech, education, marriage, and, above all, economic success were means by which Brazilians of mixed descent might gain status. Still, the basic polarities remained clear: white at the top, black at the bottom.

The Dutch in the Americas

Like the Portuguese, the Dutch were initially focused on Indian Ocean trade. However, from 1630 to 1654, the Protestant Dutch seized control of the northeastern coast of Brazil as part of their larger global offensive against the Catholic empires of Spain and Portugal.

In 1619, the Protestant Dutch, after an extremely violent conflict, had won their independence from Catholic Spain, which at that time also ruled over Portugal, and therefore Brazil. Following the model of the successful Dutch East India Company, a group of merchants formed the Dutch West India Company in 1621 to penetrate markets and challenge the Spanish in the Americas. They sought commercial advantage by constantly reinvesting their profits in faster ships and larger ventures. In Brazil, the most important of these were the sugar plantations, to which the Dutch brought more capital investment and a larger supply of slaves.

Palmares The largest and most powerful maroon community (1630–1694) established by escaped slaves in the colonial Americas. Using military and diplomatic means, their leaders retained autonomy from Portuguese Brazil for over half a century.

Ousted from Brazil by the Portuguese in 1654, some Dutch planters transferred their business techniques and more advanced sugar-processing technology to the Caribbean. Spanish-ruled islands like Cuba and Puerto Rico, as well as English ones like Jamaica and Barbados,

métis In colonial New France, the offspring of a European and Amerindian union.

Huron A matriarchal, Iroquoian-speaking Amerindian group in the St. Lawrence region that was devastated by the smallpox brought by French fur traders and missionaries in the mid-seventeenth century.

were transformed by the subsequent explosion of sugar production in the Caribbean, with dramatic consequences for Africa and the world economy (see Chapter 19).

Farther north, the Dutch West India Company founded the colony of New Netherland in 1624. They traded up the Hudson River Valley, allying with the powerful Iroquois Confederacy to tap into the lucrative fur trade. A small number of Dutch immigrants came as settlers to farm these rich and well-watered lands. But overall, Dutch commercial goals were still focused on Southeast Asia. In 1664, the Dutch surrendered New Netherland to the English without a fight. Their largest outpost, New Amsterdam, was renamed New York, and henceforth, only the French and English would compete for dominance in North America.

New France, 1608–1754

Since the days of Columbus, European navigators had sought a western route to Asia. In the second half of the sixteenth century, French mariners sailed up the St. Lawrence River looking for a "northwest passage" to Chinese markets. What they found instead was the world's largest concentration of fresh water lakes and a land teeming with wildlife. In 1608, Samuel de Champlain founded the colony of New France with its capital at Québec (kwa-BEC).

Even prior to the establishment of Québec, French fur traders had made their way up the St. Lawrence and into the Great Lakes. Like the Russians, who were expanding fur markets into Siberia at the same time, French fur traders were driven by lucrative European, Ottoman, and Safavid markets. Their indigenous trading partners did the actual work of trapping beaver and bringing the pelts to accessible trade posts. The yield of the Amerindian trappers increased with the use of iron tools from Europe, driving the quest for fur ever deeper into the interior.

Living far from other Europeans, French fur traders adapted to the customs of the First Nations peoples (as they are called in Canada). For example, tobacco smoking was an important

ritual that cemented trade and diplomatic alliances. Sometimes traders assimilated into First Nations communities and bore children who were Amerindian in language and culture. More often French trappers and traders visited only seasonally; their children, known in French as **métis** (may-TEE), learned both French and indigenous languages such as Cree and served as intermediaries between First Nations and European societies.

The fur trade had environmental and political effects. Once their traditional hunting grounds were exhausted, Amerindians had to venture farther to lay their traps. The competition for beaver pelts put them increasingly in conflict, while the guns for which furs were traded made conflict more lethal. New technologies and the desire for new commodities (iron tools and alcohol, as well as firearms) affected indigenous life well beyond the areas of European colonial control. On the Great Plains, for example, the introduction of firearms from New France and of horses from New Spain enabled a new style of buffalo hunting and mobile warfare among groups like the Sioux.

In the St. Lawrence region, the French were allied with the **Huron** people, who were receptive to Jesuit missionaries who came up the river. French traders established residence in Huron country and negotiated with local chiefs to supply them with furs. Division of labor by gender facilitated the process. Since Huron men worked in agriculture only when clearing fields in early spring, they were available for hunting and trading parties during the rest of the year, while the women stayed behind to tend the fields. The political power and economic resources that came from the fur trade therefore went mainly to men, and the traditional power of Huron women was undercut: male chiefs became more powerful at the expense of the matriarchs chosen by their clans to represent them on the Huron confederacy council.

While some Huron benefited from fur trading, the overall effects of contact with the French were disastrous. By 1641, half of the Huron population had been killed by disease. Many Huron sought baptism, praying that the priests' holy water would save them from the smallpox that the missionaries themselves had unwittingly introduced.

Museum of Fine Arts, Boston/Laurie Platt Winfrey/The Art Archive

French Fur Trader   French traders ventured far beyond the borders of European colonial society in their quest for valuable furs such as beaver pelts. They frequently adopted the technologies, languages, and customs of Amerindian peoples, and they sometimes married into Amerindian societies. At the same time, on the other side of the world, the global fur market was also driving Russian traders deep into the forests of Siberia.

Meanwhile, French settlers were attracted to the farmlands surrounding the city of **Québec**, where some fifty thousand French men and women lived by 1750. While fur traders and missionaries sought to integrate themselves into indigenous societies in their search for pelts to sell or souls to save, settlers were driven by the search for cheap land and lumber. In later years, as their numbers swelled and the frontier advanced, settlers would increasingly displace First Nations peoples.

In the first half of the eighteenth century, however, the most valuable French possessions in the Americas were not vast North American territories but relatively small Caribbean islands. Using African slave labor, French plantations in the West Indies made huge profits producing sugar for European markets. The same was true for England.

Mainland English Colonies in North America

For the English, as for the French, the Caribbean was the economic focal point of their American venture, especially after they began their own sugar plantations there in the later seventeenth century. Like the French, the English were relative newcomers, settling initially in Virginia and Massachusetts during the first half of the seventeenth century.

Though the first English settlement of **Virginia**, in 1607, was nearly wiped out, by the 1630s the colony was thriving. The soil was

Québec (est. 1608) Founded by Samuel de Champlain in 1608 as the capital of New France (in modern Canada), Québec became a hub for the French fur trade and the center from which French settlement in the Americas first began to expand.

Virginia (est. 1607) English colony in North America with an export economy based on tobacco production. The use of European indentured servants gave way to dependence on slave labor.

rich, and the Virginia colonists planted tobacco. Long used by Amerindian peoples for social and ritual purposes, tobacco became the foundation of Virginia's prosperity and generated a strong demand for labor.

English attitudes excluded Amerindians from participation in the evolving economy of Virginia, even as laborers. Unlike the French, who often cooperated with Amerindian societies, the English drove indigenous peoples out, replacing them with "civilized" English farmers. Sir Walter Raleigh, a major investor in the Virginia settlement, had taken this approach when sent to put down a late-sixteenth-century Irish rebellion and sought to displace the Irish with English settlers. In Virginia, the "savages" were Amerindian rather than Irish, but Raleigh's strategy remained the same. But plantations required more work than free settlers could provide. One solution was indentured labor. In this system, employers paid for the transportation costs of poor English and Irish peasants in return for four to seven years of work, after which time they received either a return passage or a small plot of land. Cheap as this labor was, tobacco planters preferred a more servile labor force. In 1619, the first shipment of slaves arrived, and by the late seventeenth century planters were buying larger numbers of African slaves in Virginia markets.

Virginia's population developed, therefore, through exclusion of Amerindian peoples, free immigration of English settlers, and forced immigration of African slaves. Colonial authorities worried about contact between white settlers and African slaves; as early as 1630, one Hugh Davis was whipped "for abusing himself to the dishonor of God and the shame of Christians, by defiling his body in lying with a Negro."[3] By the later seventeenth century, Virginia law prohibited interracial unions. Such liaisons nevertheless continued, but their *mulatto* offspring were discriminated against both legally and socially.

Even as slavery increased, Virginia evolved toward a system of governance in which free, propertied white men had a voice. In 1624 it became a royal colony, with a governor-general appointed by the king. But the Civil War that raged in England from 1642 to 1649 made imposing colonial rule from London difficult. By the 1660s, Virginia's assembly, the House of Burgesses, increasingly acted as an independent deliberative body, and by the eighteenth century, Virginia's ruling class of planters were accustomed to running their own affairs.

Farther south, the English colony of **Carolina** resembled the colonies of the West Indies, especially on the coast and the coastal islands. Carolina's plantations were generally much larger than Virginia's. Because Africans greatly outnumbered the few English settlers, they retained more of their own culture. West African words, language patterns, stories, and crafts persisted among African Americans along Carolina's coast and on offshore islands into the twentieth century.

Slavery was less important in the middle colonies, where New York City and Philadelphia emerged as vibrant political and economic centers. The twenty thousand German settlers who had arrived in Pennsylvania by 1700 added an ethnic variable, but the European immigrant population was still primarily English and Scottish.

The settlement of **New England** began with the arrival in the 1620s and 1630s of religious dissenters from the established Church of England. Soon more English settlers came for economic reasons: land was cheap, and wages were relatively high. Entire families migrated to New England intending to recreate the best features of the rural life they knew in England and combine them with American economic opportunity.

New England farming communities were self-sufficient both economically and demographically. Whereas elsewhere European men outnumbered European immigrant women, in New England the numbers were equally balanced, making cultural and racial mixture much less common. Since families did their own farmwork, there was little call for slave labor. Regarding indigenous peoples as competitors, settlers drove them out, beyond the colonial boundaries.

Boston was the commercial center of New England, its merchants oriented not to the farming settlements of the interior but to the maritime trade of the Atlantic. The cod fisheries of the North Atlantic provided the original foundation of Boston's wealth. Dried and salted, cod was an important source of protein and improved

Carolina (est. 1663) English colony that modeled West Indian social and economic patterns, with large plantations growing rice and indigo (used to produce a rich blue dye) with slave labor. Unlike in Virginia, Africans were a majority of the seventeenth-century population.

New England Beginning with the arrival of English Calvinists in 1620s, colonial New England was characterized by homogeneous, self-sufficient farming communities.

health throughout the Atlantic region. The highest-quality fish was consumed locally or exported to Europe. Cheaper, lower-quality fish was sent to the Caribbean for plantation slaves.

The colonial population of New England was troublesome for English authorities almost from the start. Because most of the early settlers were dissenting Protestants, the Church of England could not bolster royal authority as effectively as the Catholic Church did in the Spanish colonies. And, as in Virginia, the Civil War in England disrupted imperial oversight of colonial affairs during the middle of the seventeenth century. When British monarchs in the eighteenth century tried to impose a more centralized administrative system, they found that New Englanders would not give up their say in their own affairs (see Chapter 22).

In the seventeenth and early eighteenth centuries, Britain's mainland colonies were of limited economic and strategic importance. The silver of New Spain and the sugar of the West Indies generated profits on a much greater scale than Carolina's rice, Virginia's tobacco, or New England's grain. Faced with a hostile alliance of French and Indian societies to the north and west, the potential for expansion beyond the Atlantic seaboard seemed uncertain. These tensions were not confined to North America. By 1750, England and France were poised to battle for control of such diverse colonial territories as the Ohio River Valley, plantation colonies in the Caribbean, and trade settlements in South Asia. By that time the significance of Britain's mainland American colonies had grown substantially.

Connections and Comparisons Across the Colonial Americas

By 1750, Europe's impact on the Americas was profound. While different geographical conditions led to diverse economic and demographic outcomes, the various political, religious, and cultural traditions of the European colonial powers also left deep marks.

Throughout the Americas, one common feature was the continuing effects of the Columbian exchange (see Chapter 15). Horses and cattle, both introduced by the Spanish, flourished on the grasses of the wide-open American plains and supplied an export industry in hides. In Virginia, hogs brought from Europe thrived. European food crops like wheat and barley were planted along with native American crops like maize, potatoes, squash, and tomatoes to increase agricultural productivity.

However, few Amerindians shared in the bounty. By the middle of the eighteenth century, only Amerindian peoples in remote areas remained unaffected by contagions that Europeans introduced. The decimation of Amerindian populations transformed the landscape as well. In Mexico, Amerindian farmlands were converted to grazing for European livestock; in the Chesapeake, tobacco plantations displaced Amerindian agricultural and hunting lands.

All European powers exploited their colonies according to mercantilist principles, plundering American resources to augment the wealth of regimes at home. Actual imperial control of commerce was never as great in practice as it was in theory, however. In the seventeenth century, smuggling and piracy were common, and colonists were frequently able to evade laws that required them to trade only with their mother countries. In the middle and late eighteenth century, when European states attempted to assert control over their American holdings more strictly, tensions with colonists resulted (see Chapter 22).

Within the various colonies, quite different economic regimes took hold. Some enterprises were merely extractive: mines in Spanish America, or furs in New France, for instance. Here indigenous people formed the workforce (usually by compulsion in New Spain, and often voluntarily in Canada). In New Spain, large mining operations and expanding urban centers offered growing markets for hacienda owners, exceptionally powerful men whose large estates demanded the labor and obedience of dependent work-forces, usually Indians or mixed-race mestizos.

Lacking minerals to exploit, the economies of the English colonies all relied on agriculture (and, in New England, fishing), though their agricultural regimes and settlement patterns differed. In temperate New England, independent farmers worked small but productive plots, largely with family labor, and provided most of their own sustenance. In contrast, large plantations were the characteristic form of landholding in colonial Carolina. In the coastal lowlands and offshore islands, Carolina resembled the West Indian pattern of settlement, exploiting African slave labor forces to produce high-value commodities for export. In Virginia, a mixed pattern emerged. Slave labor was central to the Virginian economy, but the scale of plantation was much smaller than in Carolina. Some European settlers worked relatively small Virginia farms using a few slaves to supplement family labor.

Religious traditions shaped the development of all the colonial American cultures. Not surprisingly, the religious rivalries of the Reformation were imported to the Americas. The Catholic kings of France, Portugal, and Spain, seeing themselves as defenders of a single universal church, incorporated church officials in the administration of their territories. The politics of the Reformation magnified territorial and commercial

Catholic and Protestant Churches in the Americas   There is a sharp contrast between the interior of the Spanish colonial church of Santa Maria Tonantzintla (*left*) in Puebla, Mexico, and that of the Old Whaler's Church (*right*) in Martha's Vineyard, Massachusetts. The Spanish church embodies the Catholic preference for richly embellished church interiors associated with elaborate rituals and also incorporates indigenous Amerindian themes. The New England church reflects the asceticism and simplicity of the Calvinist tradition and bears no trace of Amerindian influence.
(left: © Robert Frerck/Odyssey Productions, Inc.; right: © David Lyons/Alamy)

competition between the Catholic Spanish and Protestant English, as well as between Catholic Portugal and the Protestant Dutch. These politics also affected French settlement. After 1627 the French monarchy, doubtful of Huguenot loyalty, banned Protestant emigration to New France.

In some English colonies, specific Protestant groups were dominant. The Church of England was the established church of Virginia and Carolina, while the Congregationalist Church was dominant in Massachusetts and Connecticut. Rhode Island, Maryland, and Pennsylvania were the only colonies that guaranteed freedom of religious worship.

As part of the religious divide of the early modern period, the English developed a strongly negative view of the Spanish and their empire. Associating Spain with religious intolerance and violent treatment of native peoples, the "black legend" of Spanish barbarism and cruelty infused English literature and philosophy. In the twentieth century the Mexican poet Octavio Paz turned the "black legend" on its head, arguing that the English were exceptionally harsh in their exclusion of Amerindians from colonial life, while the Spanish church at least allowed them "to form a part of one social order and one religion." The chance to be an accepted part of colonial society, "even if it was at the bottom of the social pyramid," Paz wrote, "was cruelly denied to the Indians by the Protestants of New England."[4] (See the feature "Movement of Ideas: Prospero and Caliban.")

Paz underestimated the missionary impulse among Protestant settlers in North America, some of whom made a strong effort toward conversion. He was correct, however, in pointing out the difference between the casta hierarchy of the Spanish Empire and the harsher form of racial discrimination that developed in British North America. The Spanish system, though based on hierarchy and inequality, was flexible, allowing for gradations of identification and classification between people of mixed European, African, and Amerindian backgrounds. The English system of racial classification was more sharply segregated. Though there was substantial intermixing between the races in the early colonial period, English authorities made little accommodation for mixed-race identities.

Gender identities were strongly fixed in every colonial society. In Europe, at that time, even modes of dress were regulated by law: no one was allowed to dress above his or her station, and mixing of clothing by gender was not permitted. However, as we have seen, social realities could be more fluid on the frontier. Catalina de Erauso was, of course, highly exceptional.

Badly wounded in a fight, and thinking she had better confess her sins before she died, Erauso told a priest about her deception. He did not believe her, but the nuns sent to confirm her claim, confirmed that she was, in fact, a woman. After she recovered, Erauso went to Spain to seek a pension from the king for her service as a soldier, and to Rome to meet the pope. News of her strange story spread across Europe, and as Erauso journeyed by horseback across France on her way to Italy, people came out to the road to see the famous woman warrior in a man's uniform. During her papal audience at the Vatican, she was admonished to restrain herself from violent behavior, but then the pope gave her formal permission to dress as a man for the rest of her life.

While in Rome, Erauso narrated her story to an unknown scribe, ending with the following anecdote:

> And one day in Naples, as I was strolling about the wharves, I was struck by the tittering laughter of two ladies, who leaned against a wall making conversation with two young men. They looked at me, and I looked at them, and one said, "Señora Catalina, where are you going all by your lonesome?" "My dear harlots," I replied, "I have come to deliver one hundred strokes to your pretty little necks, and a hundred gashes with this blade to the fool who would defend your honor." The women fell dead silent, and they hurried off.*

How did Erauso see herself? Did she resent having to act as a man in order to live her own life as she pleased? Or was her cross-dressing more than a masquerade? History provides no additional evidence.

It seems that Erauso preferred the life of the colonial frontier. According to legend, she returned to Mexico, disappeared into the mountains with a pack of burros, and was never heard from again. She was one of many European immigrants for whom the Americas represented new possibilities.

---

*Excerpt from *Catalina de Erauso, Lieutenant Nun: Memoir of a Basque Transvestite in the New World*, trans. Michele Stepto and Gabriel Stepto. Reprinted by permission of Beacon Press, Boston 1996.

Prospero and Caliban

When Catalina de Erauso arrived in New Spain, William Shakespeare was the leading play-wright in the English-speaking world. Shakespeare's imagination, like that of many Europeans in the early seventeenth century, was stimulated by tales of exotic adventure in what one of Shakespeare's characters referred to as "this brave new world." That line comes from *The Tempest* (1611), a drama that reflects European fascination with new discoveries in the Americas. Shakespeare used reports from Virginia settlers who had survived a shipwreck to weave a fantastic tale of magic, revenge, and the triumph of justice.

Stranded on an island is the great magician named Prospero and his daughter, Miranda. In the scene below, Prospero speaks with a misshapen monster named Caliban, the only native inhabitant of the island. From Prospero's perspective, Caliban deserves harsh treatment. In spite of the kindness shown by the magician, the monster attempted to rape Miranda. Things look very different from Caliban's viewpoint. The powers he inherited from his mother, Sycorax, cannot counter Prospero's magic, and he has no choice but to serve as the magician's slave while plotting his vengeance. Their unequal positions are even reflected in their names, which might be translated as "Prosperity" and "Cannibal." Though Shakespeare presents Prospero as having justice on his side, he also allows Caliban to voice his complaints as an abused native imprisoned by a colonial master.

The Tempest, Act 1, Scene 2

PROSPERO:
> Thou poisonous slave, got• by the devil
>   himself
> Upon thy wicked dam•, come forth!

CALIBAN:
> As wicked dew as e'er my mother brush'd
> With raven's feather from unwholesome fen
> Drop on you! a south-west blow on ye
> And blister you all o'er!

PROSPERO:
> For this, be sure, tonight thou shalt have
>   cramps,
> Side-stitches that shall pen thy breath up;
>   urchins•
> Shall, for that vast of night that they may work,
> All exercise on thee•; thou shalt be pinch'd
> As thick as honeycomb, each pinch more
>   stinging
> Than bees that made 'em.

CALIBAN:
> This island's mine, by Sycorax my mother,
> Which thou takest from me. When thou
>   camest first,
> Thou strokedst me and madest much of me,
>   wouldst give me
> Water with berries in't, and teach me how
> To name the bigger light, and how the less,
> That burn by day and night•: and then I loved
>   thee
> And show'd thee all the qualities o' the isle,
> The fresh springs, brine-pits, barren place and
>   fertile:
> Cursed be I that did so! All the charms
> Of Sycorax, toads, beetles, bats, light on
>   you!
> For I am all the subjects that you have,
> Which first was mine own king: and here you
>   sty• me

•**got** begotten

•**dam** mother.

•**urchins** goblins.

•**exercise on thee** torment you.

•**day and night** the sun and moon.

•**sty** imprison.

In this hard rock, whiles you do keep from me
The rest o' the island.

PROSPERO:
Thou most lying slave,
Whom stripes may move, not kindness! I have
used• thee,
Filth as thou art, with human care, and lodged
thee
In mine own cell, till thou didst seek to
violate
The honour of my child.

CALIBAN:
O ho, O ho! would't had been done!
Thou didst prevent me; I had peopled else•
This isle with Calibans.

PROSPERO:
Abhorred slave,
Which any print of goodness wilt not take,
Being capable of all ill! I pitied thee,
Took pains to make thee speak, taught thee
each hour
One thing or other: when thou didst not,
savage,
Know thine own meaning, but wouldst gabble
like
A thing most brutish, I endow'd thy purposes
With words that made them known. But thy
vile race,
Though thou didst learn, had that in't which
good natures

Could not abide to be with; therefore wast
thou
Deservedly confined into this rock,
Who hadst deserved more than a prison.

CALIBAN:
You taught me language; and my profit on't
Is, I know how to curse. The red plague rid you
For learning me your language!

PROSPERO:
Hag-seed•, hence!
Fetch us in fuel; and be quick, thou'rt best,
To answer other business. Shrug'st thou,
malice?
If thou neglect'st or dost unwillingly
What I command, I'll rack thee with old
cramps,
Fill all thy bones with aches, make thee roar
That beasts shall tremble at thy din.

CALIBAN:
No, pray thee.
Aside
I must obey: his art is of such power,
It would control my dam's god, Setebos, and
make a vassal of him.

PROSPERO:
So, slave; hence!

•**Hag-seed** child of a witch.

Source: The text is adapted from the following website:
http://the-tech.mit.edu/ Shakespeare/tempest/index.
html. The glossary is original.

•**used** treated.
•**else** otherwise.

QUESTIONS FOR ANALYSIS

▶ **To what extent does Shakespeare encourage us to empathize with Caliban? Is Caliban's situation in any way analogous to that of conquered Amerindian peoples?**

Chapter Review and Learning Activities

The Spanish were the dominant power in the colonial Americas, controlling the largest territories and populations while extracting considerable wealth, especially in silver, from New World mines. The Portuguese colony of Brazil, with large sugar plantations and profitable gold mines, was also significant. By the eighteenth century the French and English were also profiting substantially from sugar production in the West Indies, while their frontiers of settlement in North America expanded at the expense of Amerindian peoples.

🐎 What were the principal forms of political and economic organization in the Americas in this period?

In the sixteenth and early seventeenth centuries the Spanish were the dominant colonial power in the Americas. The flow of gold and silver from American mines, supplemented by other commodities extracted from the American environment through the mobilization of Amerindian labor, financed the splendor of the royal court and provided the wherewithal for increased European trade with Asia. At first it was Spaniards sent from Iberia who dominated colonial society, but by the seventeenth century American-born criollos were becoming more prominent, for example, through their control of large haciendas.

In Portuguese Brazil, large landholdings were also characteristic of colonial society. Main exports included sugar from coastal plantations and gold from mines in the south. Like all the European colonial powers, Portugal pursued mercantilist policies that emphasized extraction of colonial resources for the benefit of the court at Lisbon, with slaves providing much of the labor. The Dutch ruled Brazil (and New Netherland to the north) only briefly, but they had a significant impact on the sugar industry, improving methods of production and helping to transfer sugar production from Brazil to the Caribbean.

The economy of New France was driven by the highly lucrative fur trade. Since the French relied on Amerindian hunters and political leaders for their supply of pelts, diplomacy and alliances were central to their colonial policy, even as a colony of European settlement grew up around Québec.

The mainland colonies of England were diverse in political structure and economic orientation. Virginia and the Chesapeake specialized in the export of tobacco and imported slaves as a workforce. However, they also attracted many settlers. Further south in Carolina, plantations were larger and Africans were in the majority. The immigrant farmers of New England pursued a different strategy of agricultural self-sufficiency, though cod fisheries represented another means by which the bounty of the Americas was exported to Europe and beyond. The settlers of Virginia and New England developed a relatively strong expectation of being involved in government.

🐎 What were the key demographic and cultural outcomes of the interaction of European, African, and Amerindian peoples in various regions of the Americas?

Cultural developments in the Americas were related to demographic ones, especially the changing balance of population between European settlers, Amerindian survivors, and African slaves. In some regions Amerindian peoples remained a majority. In Mesoamerica and the higher Andes, for example, Amerindian populations stabilized after the huge losses of the sixteenth century. Indigenous languages and cultures remained strong, even while labor systems such as the mita in the Andes and the appearance of large Spanish-owned haciendas subordinated Amerindian peoples to European power.

In other, more remote parts of the Americas, Amerindian peoples who were far from the frontiers of European power retained not only their own languages and cultures but also political autonomy. The other extreme was found in areas such as New England, where European settlers almost completely displaced the original inhabitants. This pattern was exceptional, however; across much of the colonial Americas the more common pattern was demographic and cultural mixture. Both the mestizo population of New Spain and the métis of New France are examples of important mixed European/Amerindian groups in the colonial period. In Brazil, Africans were a larger part of the population, and European/African mixture became a defining feature of Brazilian life.

What connections and comparisons can we draw between the different European colonial ventures in the Americas?

Religion is one important area where comparisons can be drawn. In Iberia, the Catholic Reformation had led to a firm church policy of monitoring and enforcing religious orthodoxy. In the frontier conditions of the Americas, however, the failure to stamp out alternative beliefs and practices is shown by the infusion of Amerindian beliefs into Christianity in New Spain and New France, and of African ones in Brazil. While Protestants in North America also tried to convert Amerindians to Christianity, their congregational and theological traditions made it much more difficult for religious syncretism to take place. In religion as in social life more generally, English colonists were less tolerant of syncretism than Spanish colonists.

Whatever political, economic, or religious rules and regulations colonial governments put in place, the fact remained that, outside the major centers of European control, life on the American frontiers remained fluid as European, Amerindian, and African peoples created new societies with new cultural traditions. The story of Catalina de Erauso and of millions of other people in the colonial Americas could not otherwise have taken place.

FOR FURTHER REFERENCE

Benton, Lauren A. *Law and Colonial Cultures: Legal Regimes in World History, 1400–1900.* New York: Cambridge University Press, 2002.

Burkholder, Mark, and Lyman Johnson. *Colonial Latin America.* 6th ed. New York: Oxford University Press, 2007.

Eccles, William J. *The French in North America, 1500–1783.* Rev. ed. Lansing: Michigan State University Press, 1998.

Erauso, Catalina de. *Lieutenant Nun: Memoir of a Basque Transvestite in the New World.* Translated by Michele Stepto and Gabriel Stepto. Boston: Beacon Press, 1996.

Fernandez-Armesto, Felipe. *The Americas: The History of a Hemisphere.* London: George Weidenfeld and Nicholson, 2003.

Kamen, Henry. *Empire: How Spain Became a World Power, 1492–1763.* New York: HarperCollins, 2003.

Lavrin, Asunción. *Sexuality and Marriage in Colonial Latin America.* Lincoln: University of Nebraska, 1992.

Nash, Gary. *Red, White and Black: The Peoples of Early North America.* 5th ed. New York: Prentice Hall, 2005.

Paz, Octavio. *Sor Juana.* Translated by Margaret Sayers Peden. Cambridge: Harvard University Press, 1988.

Sweet, James H. *Recreating Africa: Culture, Kinship, and Religion in the African-Portuguese World, 1441–1770.* Durham: University of North Carolina Press, 2006.

Taylor, William. *Magistrates of the Sacred: Priests and Parishioners in Eighteenth Century Mexico.* Stanford, Calif.: Stanford University Press, 1996.

KEY TERMS

Catalina de Erauso (392)	Palmares (399)
viceroyalties (393)	métis (400)
Potosí (393)	Huron (400)
haciendas (396)	Québec (401)
syncretism (397)	Virginia (401)
Virgin of Guadalupe (397)	Carolina (402)
mestizo (397)	New England (402)
casta system (398)	
Sor Juana Inés de la Cruz (398)	

VOYAGES ON THE WEB

Voyages: Catalina de Erauso

"Voyages" is a real time excursion to historical sites in this chapter and includes interactive activities and study tools such as audio summaries, animated maps, and flashcards.

Visual Evidence: Representing the *Casta* System

"Visual Evidence" features artifacts, works of art, or photographs, along with a brief descriptive essay and discussion questions to guide your analysis of visual sources.

World History in Today's World: Thanksgiving and the Mashpee Wampanoag

"World History in Today's World" makes the connection between features of modern life and their origins in the periods in this chapter.

CourseMate

Go to the CourseMate website at www.cengagebrain.com for additional study tools and review materials—including audio and video clips—for this chapter.

19

The Atlantic System: Africa, the Americas, and Europe, 1550–1807

Olaudah Equiano
(British Library/The Bridgeman
Art Library)

In 1789, members of England's growing abolitionist movement, campaigning against the slave trade, provided an eager audience for a new publication, *The Interesting Narrative of the Life of Olaudah Equiano, or Gustavus Vassa, the African*. For many, it was the first time they heard an African voice narrate the horrors of slavery. The story of **Olaudah Equiano** (ca. 1745–1797) shows how he suffered as a slave, but also how he beat the odds. Equiano's readers learned of the horrors of the infamous Middle Passage across the Atlantic:

The first object which saluted my eyes when I arrived on the coast was the sea, and a slave-ship.... These filled me with astonishment, which was soon converted into terror.... I was now persuaded that I had gotten into a world of bad spirits, and that they were going to kill me.... [T]hey made ready with many fearful noises, and we were all put under deck ... now that the whole ship's cargo was confined together [the stench of the hold] was absolutely pestilential. The closeness of the place, and the heat of the climate, added to the number in the ship, which was so crowded that each had scarcely room to turn himself, almost suffocated us.... This wretched situation was again aggravated by the galling of the chains, now become insupportable; and the filth of the [latrines], into which the children often fell, and were almost suffocated. The shrieks of the women, and the groans of the dying, rendered the whole a scene of horror almost inconceivable.[1]

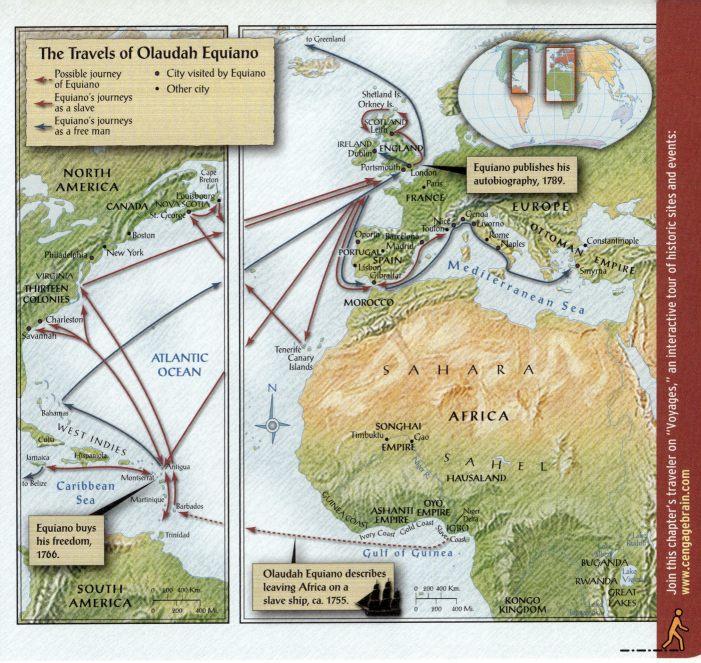

The Travels of Olaudah Equiano

Legend:
- Possible journey of Equiano
- Equiano's journeys as a slave
- Equiano's journeys as a free man
- City visited by Equiano
- Other city

Equiano publishes his autobiography, 1789.

Equiano buys his freedom, 1766.

Oulaudah Equiano describes leaving Africa on a slave ship, ca. 1755.

**Map labels:**
NORTH AMERICA, CANADA, Cape Breton I., Louisbourg, NOVA SCOTIA, St. George, Boston, Philadelphia, New York, VIRGINIA, THIRTEEN COLONIES, Charleston, Savannah, ATLANTIC OCEAN, Bahamas, WEST INDIES, Cuba, Jamaica, Hispaniola, Antigua, Montserrat, to Belize, Caribbean Sea, Martinique, Barbados, Trinidad, SOUTH AMERICA

to Greenland, Shetland Is., Orkney Is., SCOTLAND, Leith, IRELAND, Dublin, ENGLAND, Portsmouth, London, Paris, FRANCE, EUROPE, Genoa, Livorno, Nice, Toulon, Rome, Naples, OTTOMAN EMPIRE, Constantinople, Oporto, Barcelona, Madrid, PORTUGAL, SPAIN, Smyrna, Lisbon, Gibraltar, MOROCCO, Mediterranean Sea, Tenerife, Canary Islands, SAHARA, AFRICA, SAHEL, SONGHAI EMPIRE, Timbuktu, Gao, HAUSALAND, Niger R., GUINEA COAST, ASHANTI EMPIRE, OYO EMPIRE, Niger Delta, Ivory Coast, Gold Coast, Slave Coast, IGBO, Gulf of Guinea, KONGO KINGDOM, BUGANDA, RWANDA, GREAT LAKES, Lake Rudolf, Lake Albert, Lake Victoria, Lake Tanganyika

Join this chapter's traveler on "Voyages," an interactive tour of historic sites and events: www.cengagebrain.com

Timeline:

	1600	1650	1700	1750	1800	1850

Lifetime of Oulaudah Equiano — 1745 – 1797

AMERICAS
- British take Jamaica 1655
- Peak of slave imports 1715 – 1780

AFRICA
- Fall of Songhai Empire 1591
- Lifetime of Kimpa Vita/Dona Beatriz 1680 – 1706
- Omani Arabs evict the Portuguese from Fort Jesus in Mombasa 1696
- Height of Asante and Dahomey 1700 – 1800

EUROPE
- Seven Years' War 1756 – 1763
- British abolition of the slave trade 1807

411

Olaudah Equiano (1745–1797) Afro-British author and abolitionist who told of his enslavement as a child in Africa, his purchase of his own freedom in the West Indies, his move to England, and his wide travels as a sailor.

At least 12 million Africans had similar experiences between the sixteenth and nineteenth centuries, and unknown numbers perished in Africa even before they reached the coast.

The historical importance of Equiano's *Interesting Narrative* has been established, though some scholars question the authenticity of its earliest passages. Disputed evidence suggests that the author was born in the Americas and created his account of Africa and the voyage across the Atlantic by retelling other slaves' stories. Whether Olaudah Equiano (oh-lah-OO-dah ek-wee-AHN-oh) actually experienced the terror he reports in the passage above or based the story on other accounts, few other sources bring us closer to the reality faced by millions of Africans in this period or offer a more eloquent critique of slavery.

By 1745, when Equiano's life began, the Atlantic slave trade was at its height. Hundreds of thousands of Africans crossed the Atlantic every year. They lived in diverse environments—the Brazilian tropics, the temperate lands of Virginia, the rocky shores of Nova Scotia—and performed a great variety of tasks. Most were sent to the sugar plantations of the

Primary Source: The Interesting Narrative of Olaudah Equiano and Written by Himself *Read selections from an ex-slave's autobiography, one of the most influential abolitionist books published in England.*

West Indies. Sugar was the foundation of the Atlantic economy and a source of immense profit and suffering.

The interconnection of Africa, America, and Europe characterized the Atlantic system. The so-called triangular trade sent Africans to the Americas as slaves; sugar, tobacco, and natural resources from the Americas to Europe; and manufactured goods from Europe to both Africa and the Americas. Africans labored on American plantations whose profits enriched Europe, while in those parts of Africa affected by the Atlantic slave trade, life became much less secure.

The Atlantic system fostered political competition. Warfare among West Africans increased, while European powers vied for Atlantic supremacy; Equiano himself participated in naval clashes between the French and English. The slave trade also had cultural repercussions. Africans arrived not merely as slaves but also as carriers of traditions that were to profoundly influence the development of American society.

Finally, the abolition of slavery was itself a complex process involving actors from different parts of the Atlantic, including plantation slaves who resisted bondage and Europeans who grew uncomfortable with the contradiction between Christianity and slavery. It was to his readership of fellow Christians that Olaudah Equiano especially appealed.

FOCUS QUESTIONS

▶ How were existing African economic and political systems integrated into the Atlantic plantation system? What were the effects of this interaction on Africans and African societies?

▶ What were the major social and economic features of the plantation complex in the West Indies and on the American mainland? What cultural patterns were associated with forced African migration to the Americas?

▶ How did the plantation complex affect political and economic developments in Europe in the eighteenth century?

African History and Afro-Eurasian Connections, 1550–1700

The impact of the Atlantic slave trade on African history cannot be judged outside of Africa's cultural and geographic context. Contrary to common assumptions, Africa was not an isolated continent; it had ancient connections to Europe and Asia across the Mediterranean, the Red Sea, and the Indian Ocean.

Africa's diverse deserts, grasslands, and rainforests produced a variety of political systems. Some Africans lived in small bands of hunter-gatherers, while others were subjects of powerful monarchs. Equiano describes the Igbo-speaking villages in the Niger Delta region of West Africa as productive communities where yam-based agriculture supported a dense population. Other nearby societies had more centralized and hierarchical political structures, but in Igbo (ee-BWOH) society, men and women accumulated titles and authority on the basis of achievements rather than birth. As was nearly universal in Africa, clan elders made community decisions. Even when owing tribute or obeisance to more distant potentates, African villages retained their own mechanisms for keeping peace and administering justice.

In the **Great Lakes region** of east-central Africa migration led to cultural interactions between Africans of different backgrounds. For example, Bantu-speaking migrants from the west brought knowledge of grain agriculture, as well as their sophisticated iron technology. In return, these farmers gained access to cattle from their pastoralist neighbors. Although tillage provided the bulk of calories and was the focus of work, cattle represented wealth and prestige. No proper marriage contract could be negotiated unless the groom's family gave cattle to the family of his intended. Agriculture in the Great Lakes was also stimulated by the introduction of plantains (bananas), a Southeast Asian fruit from across the Indian Ocean. Supported by agricultural surpluses and dominated by clans wealthy in cattle, a number of powerful kingdoms such as Rwanda and Buganda emerged in the Great Lakes region.

While these societies developed without direct contact beyond the continent, other African societies had formative contacts with external political systems, commercial markets, and religious traditions. For example, Ethiopia, Kongo, and South Africa all had connections to the wider Christian world. The Ethiopian Church was the oldest, already over a thousand years old when the Portuguese attempted a military alliance in the sixteenth century.

Great Lakes region   A temperate highland region in and around the Great Rift Valley in east-central Africa. Characterized by agriculture and cattle pastoralism, a substantial iron industry, and dense populations.

Kimpa Vita (ca. 1680–1706) Christian reformer in the Kongo kingdom, also known as Dona Beatriz. She preached that Jesus Christ was an African. Was executed as a heretic by forces loyal to the Kongo king.

Sahel Arid region south of the Sahara Desert that played an important historic role as a West African center of trade and urbanization. Islam traveled with the caravans across the Sahara, making the Sahel a diffusion point for Islam in West Africa.

Songhai Empire (1464–1591) Important Islamic empire with a prosperity based on both interregional and trans-Saharan trade. Stretched from the Atlantic into present-day Nigeria, reaching its height in the sixteenth century before being invaded from Morocco.

In the Kongo kingdom, civil war and invasion by outside forces led to disintegration and the abandonment of the Kongo capital of San Salvador in the seventeenth century. Into this political vacuum stepped **Kimpa Vita** (ca. 1680–1706), who declared that she had been visited by St. Anthony. It was said that she died each Friday, only to arise each Sunday after having conversed with God, who told her that the people of Kongo must unite under a new king. She taught that Christ and the apostles were black men who had lived and died in Kongo. Portuguese missionaries regarded her beliefs as heresy. Nevertheless, her doctrine was popular, and her followers repopulated the old capital city. She was captured by rivals, tried for witchcraft and heresy, and burned at the stake. But the Kongo tradition of depicting Jesus as an African endured.

The ascetic Calvinist version of Christianity was brought to South Africa by Dutch and French Huguenot immigrants in the late seventeenth century. Calvinism was worlds apart from the mystical Ethiopian faith or religious syncretism in Kongo. In the very southeastern tip of Africa, where Cape Town was founded in 1652, the indigenous Khoisan (KOI-sahn)-speaking peoples were few in number, had no metal weapons, and, most fatally, no resistance to diseases such as smallpox. Within a hundred years white settlers had enslaved them or driven them beyond the expanding colonial border.

Islam provided another avenue for Africa's global interconnection. On the East African coast, African Muslims had long plied maritime trade routes in the eastern Indian Ocean. The sultan of Oman (oh-maan), at the entrance to the Persian Gulf, wrested control of the

Swahili coast from the Portuguese and evicted them from Fort Jesus in Mombasa in 1696. Thereafter, Swahili princes and aristocrats ruled over their own local affairs, while generally acknowledging the Omani sultan as their overlord.

The other center of African Islam was the **Sahel**. Here urban civilization developed from trade between the grassland savanna and the rainforest further south. Fishermen drew in the resources of the great Niger River. Flowing from the mountains of the west, through the savanna to the desert edge, and on through the rainforests of the Niger Delta—where Equiano placed his childhood home—the river was a highway of trade; West Africa's most important cities clustered on its banks. Stimulated as well by the trans-Saharan trade, cities like Timbuktu were also southern destinations for camel caravans from North Africa.

The **Songhai Empire**, with its capital at Gao along the Niger River, arose from a thousand-year-old tradition of large-scale states in this region (see Map 19.1). In addition to leading armies of conquest, the *askias* (emperors) of Songhai (song-GAH-ee) were patrons of Islamic arts and sciences. The Sankore Mosque in Timbuktu, with its impressive library, became a center of intellectual debate. Timbuktu was famous for its gold trade as well as its book market, where finely bound editions were eagerly sought by Muslim scholars, both Arab and African. When rulers, traders, and intellectuals from Songhai went on the *hajj* (pilgrimage) to Arabia, they amplified the empire's connections with the broader world.

Even within the mighty Songhai Empire, however, most Africans lived in small agricultural villages where Islam spread slowly. Here older gods and ritual practices endured, sometimes incorporated with elements of Islam. Even in cities like Timbuktu and at the court of powerful Songhai kings, syncretism was characteristic of West African Islam.

The success of the askias (AH-skee-as) of Songhai attracted attention from neighbors to the north. Morocco's leaders had remained independent of the Ottoman Empire and had

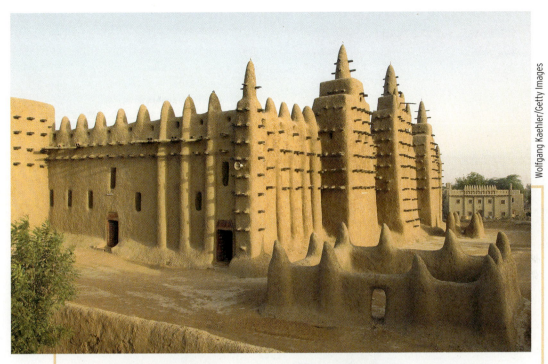

The Great Mosque at Jenne   The city of Jenne (Djenné) is an ancient West African trade site on the upper Niger River. Jenne's merchants benefited from trans-Saharan trade, and in the thirteenth century, when the original mosque on this site was built, the city's people embraced the Islamic faith. This mosque, a World Heritage Site, is the largest mud-brick structure in the world and shows how Islamic architecture was influenced by the use of local materials and by West African aesthetic principles. The current structure is over one hundred years old.

successfully driven off the Portuguese. Envious of Songhai's gold and salt mines, the Moroccan sultan decided on conquest, and in 1591 the army he sent out from Marrakesh conquered Songhai. The once mighty Songhai Empire splintered into numerous smaller kingdoms, chiefdoms, and sultanates. Never again would a large-scale African state rise to such dominance in the Sahel.

While Songhai was at its height in the sixteenth century, Europeans were constructing fortifications along the West African coast. Though the major centers of population and prosperity lay in the African interior, the Portuguese, French, English, and others were finding a way to redirect West African trade to the coast, focusing on the commodity in which they were soon most interested: slaves. The economic geography of West Africa slowly moved from the interior toward the coast. While the process was gradual, and while connections across the Sahara Desert and the Indian Ocean continued, Africa's international connection was now shifting toward the Atlantic Ocean and, beyond, to the Americas.

Map 19.1   West African States and Trade, ca. 1500

In 1500 Africa's primary global connections were across the Sahara Desert, up the Nile, across the Red Sea, and into the Indian Ocean. Large kingdoms and empires such as those of Songhai in the west and Ethiopia in the northeast benefited from participation in world trade, as did the Swahili city-states in the east. The arrival of Europeans added a new set of interconnections along the West African coast, but only in South Africa did Europeans come as settlers. Large states were the exception in Africa; societies smaller in scale populated vast regions of the continent.   © Cengage Learning

Interactive Map

Africa and the Americas: The Plantation Complex

European occupation of the Americas, the continuing decline of Amerindian populations, and new trade links with West Africa set the stage for the rise of the **Atlantic plantation system**. Slavery formed its basis. Millions of Africans were transported to the Americas and enslaved on plantations by Europeans who reaped huge fortunes. In the Americas, plantation regions were completely transformed. Imported plants and animals replaced indigenous ones, and Africans became a predominant population, as planters systematized the production of sugar and related products like molasses and rum on an industrial scale.

As Equiano's story describes, Africans were more than passive victims of the Atlantic slave trade and plantation system. Many resisted. And though mortality rates were high and survivors were often deprived of their own languages, many managed to keep much of their culture and contribute it to new societies arising in the New World. Meanwhile, societies on the continent of Africa were disrupted by their integration into the Atlantic system.

The Ecology and Economics of Plantation Production

When the Spanish conquered the Caribbean islands, they first tried to exploit Amerindians, who refused to cooperate and soon fell victim to the deadly diseases the Europeans brought with them. Later, European indentured servants were imported, but they were vulnerable to the tropical diseases such as yellow fever and malaria that had been brought from Africa. When sugar became the sole focus of West Indian agriculture, neither European nor Amerindian labor proved sufficient.

Enslaved Africans filled the void. They were expensive, but they could survive the Caribbean environment. As natives of the Old World, they had developed resistance to the same diseases as Europeans, and as natives of the tropics, they were also more resistant to tropical diseases. Tragically, their ability to survive enhanced their value as slaves.

Throughout history many societies have allowed for slavery; such "societies with slaves" were common in the Islamic world and in Africa itself. Equiano described a mild form of servitude in the Niger Delta region, where the slaves had a lower place in society but retained legal rights. "Societies with slaves" developed in the Americas as well, such as in Pennsylvania and Mexico. In fact, only 5 percent of the Africans who crossed the Atlantic during the era of the Atlantic slave trade came to British North America.

However, in real "slave societies" such as those created by the plantation system, slaveholding is the heart of social and economic existence. The genuine "slave societies" of Brazil and the Caribbean consumed 80 percent of slave imports.

On a typical Caribbean plantation, the owner and his family occupied a "great house." As absentee ownership became more common, the work of overseeing slave labor was performed by lower-status European immigrants, legendary for their harshness, or by men of mixed race (though mulattos did not automatically have higher status on a plantation). Equiano told of a French sugar planter on Martinique with "many mulattoes working in the fields [who] *were all the produce of his own loins!*"

Slaves performed all the backbreaking work of planting, weeding, harvesting, and turning the raw cane into a semiprocessed product for

> **Atlantic plantation system**
> The focal point in the new set of interchanges between Africa, Europe, and the Americas that peaked in the eighteenth century. Utilized African slave labor to produce large quantities of agricultural products, particularly sugar, for international markets.

From William Clark, *Ten Views in the Islands of Antigua*, 1823, British Library
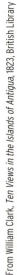

Caribbean Sugar Mill   Sugar production was an industrial as well as agricultural enterprise. Here wind power is used to crush the sugarcane; the rising smoke indicates the intense heat of the furnaces used to boil down the juice. The slaves' work was hard, dangerous, and unceasing: such machinery was usually operated six days a week year-round.

export. Because raw sugar is bulky, the juice was squeezed out of the cane and boiled down for shipment. Sugar production was organized like a factory assembly line that is always rolling, with raw materials always at hand. Sugarcane was planted year-round so that it could be cut and processed year-round, with full-time use of the machinery that crushed the juice from the cane and the large copper kettles that boiled down the juice. The entire process was physically strenuous, and the kettles sometimes exploded, taking lives in the process.

Under such harsh conditions many Africans were worked to death. Barbados is representative. In 1680 there were 50,000 African slaves on the island. Over the next forty years another 50,000 slaves were imported, but the total black population actually *dropped* to 45,000. Slave populations were not self-sustaining. The mortality rate was high, and the birthrate was low. As Equiano noted, the overseers, "human butchers" left in charge by their absentee masters, "pay no regard to the situation of pregnant women. The neglect certainly conspires with many others to cause a decrease in the births, as well as in the lives of the grown negroes." Equiano calculated that Barbados, not the worst island in terms of African mortality, required a thousand fresh imports annually just to maintain a level population.

Equiano himself escaped the harsh fate of working on a Caribbean sugar plantation. While still a boy he was sold to a British naval officer; he spent much of his early life aboard ships and developed a lifelong fondness for London, where he was baptized as a teenager. He was then sold to a Philadelphia merchant with business interests in the West Indies. Literate in English, and with a good head for numbers, Equiano was well treated while tending to his master's business, which sometimes included trading in slaves. He witnessed many cruelties:

> It was very common in several of the islands, particularly in St. Kitt's, for the slaves to be branded with the initial letters of their master's name, and a load of heavy iron hooks hung around their necks.... I have seen a negro beaten till some of his bones were broken, for only letting a pot boil over. It is not uncommon, after a flogging, to make slaves go on their knees and thank their owners and ... say "God Bless You."

Equiano was keenly aware of the even worse fate he could have faced as a field slave.

Of course, sugar was not the only plantation crop in the Americas. Slaves also tended the tobacco plantations of Virginia and the indigo plantations of Carolina. But while Carolina plantations were organized much like those of the West Indies, the British colonies of the Chesapeake were further at the margins of the plantation complex. Here male and female slaves were more balanced in numbers. Better diet and higher fertility made the slave population self-reproducing in British North America by 1720, a sharp contrast to conditions in the Caribbean.

African Culture and Resistance to Slavery

Previously some historians argued that the process of being uprooted and enslaved overwhelmed Africans, who—deprived of any connection with home—became psychologically dependent on their masters and lost their will to resist. More recent historical research has revealed the inaccuracy of this image of passivity. Resistance to slavery was widespread.

Slaves were constantly looking for ways to escape their bondage and, failing that, to resist their captivity in large or small ways. Slave traders, owners, and overseers were ever vigilant, and the penalties for insubordination were gruesome. Slaves often found safer, more subtle ways to assert their humanity and express their defiance. Songs and stories derived from African cultural traditions might be used to ridicule a master using words he could not understand. Religious rites—African, Christian, or a synthesis of multiple belief systems and rituals—might serve as assertions of dignity and spiritual resilience. Expressions of deference to the slave master might be deceiving.

Resistance to slavery sometimes began even before the slave ships arrived in America. Equiano describes the nets that were used to keep Africans from jumping overboard and relates that "one day ... two of my wearied countrymen, who were chained together ... preferring death to such a life of misery, somehow made through the nettings and jumped into the sea." Insurrections aboard slave ships were also common, as this dramatic description from 1673 attests:

> A master of a ship ... did not, as the manner is, shackle [the slaves] one to another ... and they being double the number of those in the ship found their advantages, got weapons in their hands, and fell upon the sailors, knocking them on the heads, and cutting their throats so fast as the master found they were all lost ... and so went down into the hold and blew up all with himself.[2]

Equiano tells of a slave trader who had once cut off the leg of a slave for running away. When Equiano asked how such an action could be squared with the man's Christian conscience, he was simply told "that his scheme had the desired effect—it cured that man and some others of running away."

Some Africans were freed by their masters, but many others simply escaped. Yet, if an individual or a small group escaped, where would they go, and how would they live? Options for escaped slaves included joining pirate communities in the Caribbean (which in spite of their reputation for brutality were relatively egalitarian), forming autonomous communities of runaway slaves, or settling among Amerindian populations.

Already in the sixteenth century Africans were banding together to form **maroon communities**. Perhaps the best known was Palmares in northeastern Brazil (see Chapter 18).

maroon communities Self-governing communities of escaped slaves common in the early modern Caribbean and in coastal areas of Central and South America.

Palmares was unique in scale, but smaller maroon communities were common in the Caribbean. Some of the islands were too small for maroons to successfully avoid recapture, but the interior mountains of Jamaica were perfect for that purpose.

When the Spanish fled Jamaica in 1655 during a British attack, they left behind hundreds of African slaves who headed for the hills. Free, these maroons farmed, fished, and occasionally pillaged British sugar plantations on the coasts. Their threat to the British came not so much from raiding but from the sanctuary that they could provide to other escaped slaves. After several slave uprisings in the early eighteenth century, the British increased their attacks on the maroons. The British and maroons fought to a stalemate, leading to a treaty that allowed the maroons autonomy in exchange for the promise that they would hunt, capture, and return future runaways.

In some places runaway slaves might seek sanctuary in an Amerindian village and become a part of that society. Sometimes larger-scale cooperation between maroons and Amerindians occurred. In Florida, Africans who escaped from slavery in Carolina and Georgia formed an alliance with Creek Indians, and the cultural interaction between the two groups led the "Black Seminoles" to adopt many elements of Creek culture.

Of course, slaves who escaped could be recaptured and face terrible punishments, or they could find survival in an unknown environment to be extremely difficult. Even when Africans had to resign themselves to being plantation slaves, covert resistance was possible. Slowing down and subverting the work process was a common form of defiance, even where the risk of the whip was ever present.

Religion is perhaps the area where Africans could best resist enslavement without risking flight or outright rebellion. Where Africans were great in number, their religious practices showed the greatest continuity. In both Brazil and Cuba, for example, Africans merged their existing beliefs with Christianity, transforming the *orisas* (or-EE-shahs), gods of the Yoruba people (of present-day western Nigeria), into Catholic

A Coromantyn Free Negro, or Ranger, armed.

A Jamaican Maroon   In Jamaica and elsewhere in the Caribbean, escaped slaves banded together to form maroon communities. This man's gun and sword show that the maroons organized themselves to protect their independence from European colonialists. While some joined maroon communities, other escaped slaves joined Amerindian societies or the crews of pirate ships.

Private Collection/The Bridgeman Art Library

saints. Xangó, the Yoruba deity of thunder and lightning, is still venerated today in the Cuban and Brazilian syntheses of Catholicism and African religion called *Santeria* (san-ta-REE-ah) and *Candomblé* (can-dome-blay). (See the feature "Movement of Ideas: Afro-Brazilian Religion.")

In areas where Africans were a smaller percentage of the population, as in most of British North America, European cultural influences were more dominant. But religion allowed for self-assertion here as well. While white Christians preached obedience now and rewards in the afterlife, slaves sung hymns of liberation and told Bible stories such as Moses leading his people to freedom.

Equiano's life story illustrates an unusual strategy of escape from slavery: working within the system. His freedom came about through a combination of good fortune and business acumen. He was fortunate that his final owner was Quaker, a member of the Society of Friends who had strong doubts about whether Christians should own slaves. This master agreed that if Equiano could repay the money he had spent on him, Equiano would have his freedom, and he allowed Equiano to trade on his own account in his spare time. In this way the young man saved enough money to buy his own freedom. He returned to England, which he regarded as his home, where he worked as a hairdresser for the London elite and learned to play the French horn. But he frequently went back to sea, working as a sailor in the Atlantic and the Mediterranean and even joining an unsuccessful voyage to the North Pole..

In some places, **manumission** was encouraged as an act of Christian charity. Of course, those most likely to be freed were women, children, and the elderly: adult male Africans had little chance of attaining freedom through a simple act of charity. In colonial Latin America, persons were free *unless* proven otherwise; black men who escaped their masters and moved far enough away might "pass" as free men. In British North America, however, manumission was uncommon and legal codes made little or no distinction between free blacks and slaves, as this story from Equiano's stay in Georgia attests:

> After our arrival we went up to the town of Savannah; and the same evening I went to a friend's house ... a black man. We were very happy at meeting each other ... after supper ... the watch or patrol came by, and, discerning a light in the house ... came in and sat down, and drank some punch with us.... A little after this they told me I must go to the watch-house

> with them; this surprised me a good deal after our kindness to them, and I asked them "Why so?" They said, that all Negroes who had a light in their houses after nine o'clock were to be taken into custody, and either pay some dollars or be flogged.

This was not an isolated incident: on other occasions Equiano's trade goods were confiscated for no reason other than his vulnerability as a black man, and several times he was nearly re-enslaved in spite of possessing a document attesting to his freedom. Thereafter he avoided such places altogether.

Effects of the Atlantic Slave Trade on West Africa

The Atlantic slave trade had profound reverberations in West African societies such as the Kongo kingdom, where Portuguese traders originally found that they could buy slaves. The slaves for purchase were often war captives. As the demand from American plantations for slaves increased, however, traditional sources of supply were insufficient, and the slave trade began to transform African social, economic, and military institutions.

> **manumission** The voluntary freeing of slaves by their masters.
>
> **Asante kingdom** (ca. 1700–1896) A rising state in eighteenth-century West Africa, with its capital at Kumasi in the rainforest region of what is now Ghana. Asante's wars of expansion produced prisoners who were often sold into the Atlantic slave circuit.

The **Asante kingdom** was an expanding power in West Africa. As the ruling kings, the *Asantehenes*, pursued their ambitions for greater power through military expansion, they took many prisoners. Before the rise of the Atlantic slave trade, these war captives might be traded in prisoner exchanges, redeemed for ransom, or kept as household servants. But now a more profitable fourth option developed: sale to Europeans and transport across the ocean. Where war captives had once been a mere byproduct of traditional warfare, now Asante (uh-SHAN-tee) generals had a new motive for military expansion: the Atlantic

Afro-Brazilian Religion

The strong African element in the religious life of Brazil is not surprising given that more people of African descent live in Brazil than in any other country outside of Africa. Africans infused their beliefs into Roman Catholicism during the age of colonialism and slavery. Although Catholics were supposed to receive the sacraments and religious instruction from ordained priests, many slaves did not have access to regular church services. Instead they elevated their own spiritual leaders and devised their own rituals, infusing their faith with African elements.

In Roman Catholicism only men could be priests, but in many African societies from which Brazilian slaves originated, women played important roles as seers, prophets, and healers. Such women prophets would sometimes enter a trance as if possessed by spirits and deities; a Christian might say they were possessed by the Holy Spirit or by a saint, and her utterances might be described as "speaking in tongues." This tradition, in which women were intermediaries between humans and powerful deities and spirits, was carried to the Americas and continues in Brazil today in the heavily African form of spirituality called *Candomblé*.

In the eighteenth century, leaders of the Catholic Church worried that this process of religious syncretism was leading to heretical ideas. Sometimes they would use ecclesiastical courts (church courts) to try to suppress what they saw as unacceptable beliefs and rituals. For example, they sometimes saw drums and dancing as satanic. The two eighteenth-century documents below, which describe African elements in Brazilian Catholicism, are both taken from court documents at which African priestesses were on trial for heresy.

Document 1

Most conspicuous in the … diabolic dance was one Negress Caetana … and in the occasion of the dance she would preach to the others and say that she was God who made the sky and earth, the waters and the stones. To join in this dance they would first build a doll which they made with the appearance in imitation of the devil, and place him on an iron lance and with a cape of white cloth…. They would put him in the middle of the house, on a small rug, on top of some crosses, and around them they would place pots, some with cooked herbs…. After having arranged this effigy, all would begin dancing and saying their sayings, that that was the saint of their homeland, and in this way worshipped the dummy. In the same dance the priestess would feign death and fall to the ground, and others would lift her and take her into a room, and after this dance one named Quitéria would emerge from the room and would climb to the top of the house, and would begin preaching in her tongue saying that she was God and daughter of Our Lady of the Rosary and of Saint Anthony [also a Catholic patron saint of slaves]…. And after this practice, she would leave the [temple] and a Negress would bring in a dead chicken and another a small cauldron [from which] with a bundle of leaves she would sprinkle holy water.

Document 2

[Luzia was] dressed as the angel ... with a saber in her hand, with a wide ribbon tied to her head.... [She was attended by] two Negresses, also Angolan, and one black man playing ... a little drum ... and playing and signing for the space of one or two hours, [Luzia] would become as if out of her own judgment, saying things that no one understood, and the people would lie on the ground that she would cure, and she would reach over them various times, and on these occasions say that she had the winds of prophecy.

Source: Paulo Simões, *Tupã, olorum, Jesus and the Holy Spirit: An Analysis of the Cultural and Ideological Implications of Religious Change in Brazil*, M.A. thesis, California State University Long Beach, 1999, pp. 55–56.

QUESTIONS FOR ANALYSIS

▶ How do the African slaves described in these documents seem to be combining African rituals and Catholic beliefs?

▶ What similarities and differences are there between the rituals ascribed to Caetana and those of Luzia? What was the principal spiritual role of each of these women?

📺 **Primary Source: A Voyage to New Calabar River in the Year 1699** *Learn about the slave trade in West Africa, from a Frenchman on an English slave-trading expedition.*

Dahomey (ca. 1650–1894) African kingdom in present-day southern Benin, reaching its height of influence in the eighteenth century. Its leaders sought regional power by raiding for slaves in other kingdoms and selling them for firearms and European goods.

slave trade. British slave traders sailed to Cape Coast Castle, one of many coastal fortifications built to facilitate the slave trade, to pay with currency, rum, cloth, and guns for these unfortunate captives.

The kingdom of **Dahomey** (dah-HOH-mee) focused on the capture of slaves, trading them for guns to build a military advantage over their neighbors. As the prices for slaves rose during the eighteenth century, more and more guns were imported into West Africa. Faced with aggressive neighbors like Dahomey, other African rulers found they too needed to enter the slaves-for-guns trade, out of self-defense. Keeping your own people from being enslaved sometimes meant selling people from neighboring societies. It was a vicious cycle.

Indigenous African slavery was transformed by the Atlantic slave trade. Before the Atlantic system developed, an African parent in difficult circumstances might "pawn" a child to someone with sufficient resources to keep him or her alive. It was a desperate move, but sometimes necessary. A child thus enslaved was not viewed as mere property of his or her master. Rather, the chances were good that an enslaved child would be incorporated into the new master's society. This

Mary Evans Picture Library

A Slave Sacrifice at Dahomey   The Atlantic slave trade cheapened life in Africa as well as in the Americas. The kings of Dahomey based their power on slave raiding and trade with the Europeans. Here members of the Dahomean royal family, and two European observers, await the sacrifice of slaves about to be thrown from the heights in honor of the king. The umbrella is a symbol of monarchy in parts of West Africa.

process of incorporation sometimes took the form of "fictive kinship." Descendants of captive outsiders (such as pawned children or war captives) would come to be identified with local lineages. Though the stigma of slave origins might never be completely forgotten, their descendants would gradually become recognized as members of the community. In patrilineal societies, where descent is traced through the father's line, children of a free man and a slave woman had rights in their father's lineage.

African slave raiders profited from the complementary preference of African masters for female slaves and European plantation owners for male ones. Male slaves could be exported, while female captives were more likely to be sold within West Africa's own slave markets. The fates of their children were likely to be quite different, however. In Africa the women's offspring would often be assimilated into the host community; in the Americas assimilation into European society was hardly an option.

As an abolitionist, Equiano perhaps had an interest in downplaying the negative aspects of indigenous slavery. But the transformation of West African systems of slavery under the impact of the Atlantic trade is suggested by a passage from the *Interesting Narrative* where Equiano, being taken to the coast, is purchased by an African master:

> *A wealthy widow ... saw me; and having taken a fancy to me, I was bought off the merchant, and went home with them. Her house and premises ... were the finest I ever saw in Africa: they were very extensive, and she had a number of slaves to attend her. The next day I was washed and perfumed, and when mealtime came, I was led into the presence of my mistress, and ate and drank before her with her son. That filled me with astonishment; and I could scarcely avoid expressing my surprise that the young gentleman should suffer me, who was bound, to eat with him who was free.... Indeed everything here, and their treatment of me, made me forget that I was a slave. The language of these people resembled ours so nearly, that we understood each other perfectly. They had*

> *also the very same customs as we.... In this resemblance to my former happy state, I passed about two months; and now I began to think I was to be adopted into the family....*

Equiano first sketches the traditional practice of incorporating outsiders. However, by this time traditional systems had been transformed under the influence of the Atlantic trade. His new mistress now had the option of selling him for cash; in Equiano's account she sold him back into the slave export channel that led to the coast.

In such ways, on scales large and small, traditional institutions were transformed by the Atlantic market. Warfare increased, and the climate of insecurity often led to more centralized political structures. Those who traded in slaves gained power and status. By the later eighteenth century, some African "societies with slaves" started to become "slave societies," wherein conditions of servitude became essential to the functioning of state and society. While the power of a few Africans was enhanced, by far the biggest political and economic advantages went to European slave traders and plantation owners.

Some historians have warned that we should not exaggerate the impact of the Atlantic slave trade on continental Africa. It is true that many African societies had no connection with external slave markets and that others had slave markets of long standing. Farming and herding remained the principal economic activities in Africa. But in a continent where land was plentiful but people were scarce, the loss of population through the export of slaves harmed economic growth. Europe and Asia experienced surges in population during the eighteenth century, due in large part to the introduction of productive new food crops from the Americas. While such crops were introduced in Africa as well, nevertheless the total population of the African continent remained stagnant. It is hard not to conclude that the Atlantic slave trade had sharply negative effects, not only for those taken captive and shipped to the Americas but also for the continent they were forced to leave behind.

Europe and the Atlantic World, 1650–1807

By the eighteenth century the Atlantic Ocean was awash with people, goods, plants, animals, diseases, religious and political ideas, and cultural forms such as music and storytelling traditions, circulating freely between Europe, Africa, and the Americas. Meanwhile, Britain and France—now surpassing the Spanish, Portuguese, and Dutch as the world's dominant naval powers—were locked in nearly constant conflict. War costs strained both countries. Mercantilist policies, intended to generate the funds to fight these wars, created incentives for smuggling by respectable New England merchants as well as less reputable pirates of the Caribbean. As a result, the Atlantic world emerged as a transcultural zone where enterprising adventurers, sometimes even former slaves like Olaudah Equiano, sought their fortunes.

Economic and Military Competition in the Atlantic Ocean, 1650–1763

The economic exchange between Europe, Africa, and the Americas is often called the **triangular trade**, which refers to the movement of manufactured goods from Europe to Africa, of African humanity to the Americas, and of colonial products, such as sugar, tobacco, and timber, back to Europe.

> **triangular trade** The network of interchange between Europe, Africa, and the colonial Americas. Consisted of raw materials and agricultural produce sent from the Americas to Europe; manufactures sent to Africa and used for the purchase of slaves; and slaves exported from Africa to the Americas.

The image of triangular trade is convenient, but it simplifies the realities of world trade in this period. For example, Indian Ocean trade networks connected to Atlantic ones whenever they brought cotton textiles from India to West African consumers (see Map 19.2). Paid for in American silver, Indian textiles were then exported to Africa, Europe, and the Americas. Cowrie shells, harvested from the Indian Ocean and used as currency in West Africa, were imported in huge quantities by European traders during this era. Global trade links were not simply triangular but interoceanic; the Atlantic system was part of an emerging global economy.

European mercantilist policies that sought to monopolize colonial markets in both the Indian and Atlantic Oceans resulted in political and military conflict. While the Portuguese, Spanish, and Dutch still profited from their American and Asian possessions, none of them could compete with the growing military strength of France and England. The War of Jenkins's Ear (1739–1742) was emblematic of events. The Spanish, after asserting that only their own ships could trade among their American colonies, apprehended the English Captain Robert Jenkins smuggling goods to and from their territory. When he got back to England, Jenkins claimed the Spaniards had tortured him and cut off his ear; it was even held aloft by a member of Parliament demanding revenge!

The outbreak of the War of Jenkins's Ear between the British and the Spanish in the Caribbean was paralleled by competition and conflict in Europe. When the Prussian army invaded Austrian territory, resulting in the War of the Austrian Succession (1740–1748), France allied with Prussia, and Britain with Austria. While the British dominated the French in naval battles, the French were dominant on the continent, producing stalemate in Europe with no immediate effect on possessions in the Americas.

However, these conflicts focused British and French attention on the economic and strategic value of their American colonies. In 1745 the English Parliament considered raising the tax on sugar imports to finance the war. A lobbyist for the sugar planters argued against the bill, claiming that it would harm the very industry on which Britain relied for its economic strength. If increased taxation meant that "our sugar colonies should decline, those of our neighbors, our enemies and rivals in trade and navigation, would advance."[3] The lobbyist was probably thinking of Saint-Domingue (san doh-MANGH), the western half of the island of Hispaniola that the French had taken from

From 1518 to 1850 approximately 11,000,000 slaves were shipped from Africa to the Western Hemisphere; of these about 500,000, or 5 percent, were imported into areas now part of the United States.

Main sources of African slaves
Main slave-trade routes from Africa
Main areas of slave importation in the Western Hemisphere

Map 19.2   The Atlantic Slave Trade
The Middle Passage from Africa to the Americas was the greatest forced migration in human history. The vast majority of the Africans who lived through it were put to work on Caribbean islands or coastal plantations. The Arab trade in African slaves, across the Sahara Desert and the Indian Ocean, was much older, but at no time matched the scale of the Atlantic trade.   © Cengage Learning   Interactive Map

Spain in 1697, which produced more sugar than any other West Indian colony.

The French and British were soon back at war. Skirmishes in the Ohio River Valley in North America led to the outbreak of the **Seven Years' War** (1756–1763), a tri-continental conflict that may be thought of as the first "world war." In 1758, while still the property of a Royal Navy officer, Olaudah Equiano saw action as a combatant at the British siege of Louisbourg:

The engagement now commenced with great fury on both sides: [the French ship] immediately returned our fire and we continued engaged with each other for some time; during which I was frequently stunned with the thundering of the great guns, whose dreadful contents burned many of my companions into eternity.

The British victory in this engagement at the gateway to the St. Lawrence River soon led to the conquest of Québec and New France. At the same time, the British were scoring victories over the French in India (see Chapter 20).

British mercantilist policies were never entirely able to control trade in North America and the Caribbean. For example, the sugar and molasses produced on islands in the British West Indies were supposed to be sent directly to England. However, New England merchants defied such strictures and traded directly with the Caribbean, exchanging North American products such as timber, cattle, horses, and

Seven Years' War (1756–1763) Fought simultaneously in Europe, the West Indies, North America, and South Asia, this war shifted the balance of power between Britain and France in favor of the British, making their influence paramount in India and Canada.

foodstuffs for sugar. They then refined the sugar into molasses or rum to trade directly for slaves on the West African coast, contrary to mercantilist regulations.

Although American merchants found ways to evade mercantilist restrictions on trade, they deeply resented them. The anger of colonial traders was strongest in commercial cities such as Boston, Philadelphia, and New York. The Seven Years' War added to the tensions between the British crown and its American colonies. Having spent a huge sum to defend the American colonies from France, the British thought it fair that Americans help pay for their own protection. But new taxes and restrictions on trade soon prompted colonists to rally to the slogan "no taxation without representation." The Boston Tea Party (1773), during which merchants dressed as Amerindians threw bricks of tea into Boston Harbor, arose from resentment at the monopoly on tea imports granted to the British East India Company. Such were the increasing tensions between the European powers and their colonies (see Chapter 22).

Life on the Eighteenth-Century Atlantic Ocean

Olaudah Equiano, who spent almost half his life aboard ship, was familiar with the turbulent mass of humanity that made its living from the sea: slave traders, cod fishermen, pirates, and officers and crew fighting for king and country.

Violence was common. Press gangs stalked the banks of the English coast looking for a chance to seize the able-bodied and force them onto ships, a situation that Equiano and many others saw as akin to slavery. English peasants, driven from the countryside by land enclosures that favored the landed gentry, often ended up at sea, as did Irishmen forced off their lands by English settlement. The sea was often a refuge for the desperate.

Grand Banks Fishing area located south and southeast of present-day Newfoundland, Canada. Noted for its immense quantities of cod, a source of protein for the residents in and around the Atlantic and of large profits for British colonial traders.

Life aboard ship was rough. Sailors had no privacy and were closely controlled. Captains had to be alert or they might lose command of their crews. Sometimes disgruntled sailors felt they had nothing more to lose and risked their lives in mutiny.

The great lexicographer Samuel Johnson commented: "A ship is worse than a jail. There is, in a jail, better air, better company, better convenience of every kind; and a ship has the additional disadvantage of being in danger."[4]

Johnson went on to say that once men became accustomed to life at sea they no longer could adjust to any other. That seemed to fit Equiano, who "being still of a roving disposition" after he gained his liberty, never went for more than a few years on dry land. Life at sea offered opportunity for an ambitious soul from a poor background. Military prowess, acumen in trade, seamanship—all required competence. Life at sea rewarded ability, in contrast to most of British life, where ancestry and social class held sway.

Even as a young slave, Equiano was able to earn a promotion to the rank of "able seaman" for his service during the Seven Years' War. He equated that promotion with status as a freeman, and it made him eligible for a payment from the Crown at war's end. He was bitterly disappointed when his owner, who was also his commanding officer, not only pocketed his pension but also sold him to a new master. Still, life at sea gave Equiano his greatest opportunities.

The Atlantic Ocean also represented opportunities for fishermen. Enormous quantities of cod were pulled from the **Grand Banks**, off the coast of Newfoundland. Basque fisherman had first discovered this area in medieval times, and salted cod became a staple of the Mediterranean diet. By the eighteenth century ships from England, Spain, France, Iceland, Portugal, and Massachusetts were exploiting this fish, which once cured was easily stored and transported.

In New England, the codfish became a symbol of prosperity. In the early eighteenth century the Boston Town Hall had a gilded cod hanging from its ceiling. The fishing communities of the North Atlantic provided an alternative to the slave-based plantation model of the south:

New Englanders were becoming a commercial people, independent and prosperous and resentful of monopolies. While the West Indies sugar planters were thriving on their protected markets, New Englanders were growing rich on free-trade capitalism.… Even the fishermen were independent entrepreneurs, working not on salary but, as they still do in much of the world, for a share of the catch.[5]

Some participants of the Boston Tea Party were involved in trading salt cod to the West Indies for molasses to be refined and sold in Africa for slaves. Thus, while cod fishing might instill an independent spirit in New England, it also provided a cheap means to feed captives in the West Indies. In the Atlantic world, slavery and freedom were two sides of the same coin.

Abolition of the British Slave Trade, 1772–1807

In 1775 Olaudah Equiano worked as a plantation supervisor on the Central American coast. Equiano did not seem to mind, and even congratulated himself on a job well done: "All my poor countrymen, the slaves, when they heard of my leaving them were very sorry, as I had always treated them with care and affection, and did everything I could to comfort the poor creatures."

Over the next decade, however, Equiano, like many others, came to believe that slavery was inherently evil and needed to be abolished. His change in thinking was partly an outcome of deepening religious conviction. After surviving a shipwreck, Equiano joined the Methodist movement, whose founder had argued that slavery was incompatible with Christian morality. Equiano wrote, "O, ye nominal Christians! Might not an African ask you, 'learned you this from your God, who says unto you, Do unto all men as you would men should do unto you,?" Throughout the 1780s more and more British Christians raised their voices in opposition to slavery. Though the slave owners and slave traders formed a powerful lobby in the British Parliament, public opinion was turning against them.

Apart from Christian conscience, other factors aided the **abolitionist** cause. In 1772 a judge had ruled that no slave, once he or she reached England, could be compelled to return to a colony where slavery was practiced. Essentially, this meant that the condition of slavery had no legal basis in British law. Britons were proud of their tradition of "liberty," constitutionally guaranteed by the Bill of Rights of 1689. But the British constitution was also based on the protection of rights of property. Which rights were paramount: those of slaves to their own liberty, or those of slave owners to their property?

British abolitionists decried the link between British sugar consumption, by far the highest in the world, and the evils of slavery. In his poem "Poor Africans," William Cowper wrote:

> I pity them greatly, but I must be mum,
> For how could we do without sugar and rum?
> Especially sugar, so needful we see,
> What, give up our desserts, our coffee and tea?

Abolitionist boycotts won the debate at the breakfast table, as more Britons saw slavery not as something distant and abstract, but as an evil in which they personally participated by consuming sugar.

Equiano intended his *Interesting Narrative* to be part of the accelerating abolitionist campaign. Like many authors at this time, he advertised for subscribers who would pay in advance and receive their copies once the book was written and printed. Subscriptions were a way for people to support causes they believed in; subscribers to Equiano's book included Thomas Clarkson, Josiah Wedgewood, and William Wilberforce. Clarkson had written a university essay on the theme "Is enslaving others against their will ever justified?" He decided the answer was "no" and became a leading antislavery organizer. Wedgwood, a highly successful ceramics entrepreneur, made a plate featuring the image of an African in chains saying "Am I Not a Man and a Brother?" that was sold across the country. And Wilberforce, a member of Parliament, took the abolitionist cause to the House of Commons.

After the publication of the *Interesting Narrative* in 1789, Equiano spent three years touring England, Scotland, and Ireland speaking at antislavery meetings. Book royalties made him the wealthiest black man in England, and he married an English wife in 1792.

abolitionist A man or woman who advocated an end to the practice of slavery. In the late eighteenth century a powerful abolitionist movement was created in England.

As he began an English family, Equiano remained politically active. Wilberforce had decided to press only for the abolition of the slave trade, not of the condition of slavery itself. Not interfering in existing property relations, even when the property consisted of human beings, had a better chance in Parliament. Even with this more limited agenda, the abolition of the slave trade took much longer than its proponents had hoped. The convulsions of the French Revolution made progressive reforms deeply suspect. (In fact, Equiano even deleted the names of his more radical subscribers to avoid trouble.) When Equiano passed away in 1797, he was still waiting.

It was not until 1807 that Parliament finally passed the **Act for the Abolition of the Slave Trade**. Another whole generation of Africans had to wait before slavery itself was abolished in the British Empire, an advance that did not help slaves in non-British territories such as Cuba, Brazil, and the southern United States. Meanwhile, the British government, with the full backing of public opinion, pursued a global campaign to eliminate slave markets. That was a significant turnabout, considering that Britain had perhaps benefited more than any other nation from four centuries of the Atlantic slave trade.

Act for the Abolition of the Slave Trade   Law passed in 1807 by the English Parliament ending the trade in slaves among British subjects. The British government then used the Royal Navy to suppress the slave trade internationally.

Chapter Review and Learning Activities

The Atlantic system as it developed in the seventeenth and eighteenth century encompassed a broad range of economic, environmental, cultural, and political interactions. Olaudah Equiano experienced many different facets of Atlantic life, but his story points most clearly to the centrality of slavery. By remaking himself as a free man and an abolitionist, Equiano played a pioneering role in purging slavery from the human story. The *Interesting Narrative of the Life of Olaudah Equiano, or Gustavus Vassa, the African* was a substantial contribution to that cause, guaranteeing the author's place in history.

 How were existing African economic and political systems integrated into the Atlantic plantation system? What were the effects of this interaction on Africans and African societies?

On the eve of the Atlantic slave trade, African history was unfolding in diverse ways. Most Africans lived in small societies where they farmed, tended their livestock, raised their children, and managed their own affairs through discussion and consensus. Large African states also arose from the cultural and economic interchange between African groups, as in the Great Lakes, or from trade across ecological frontiers, as in the Sahel. When African states were in direct contact with Asia and Europe, as were the Songhai Empire and the Swahili city-states, it was most often through Muslim routes of trade and pilgrimage. The rise of the Atlantic slave system transformed those African societies, especially in West Africa, into suppliers or sources of slaves for American plantations. While wealth and power went to those Africans who seized the opportunity to benefit from slavery and the slave trade, participation in the Atlantic system left much of Africa more violent, insecure, and less productive than before.

 What were the major social and economic features of the plantation complex in the West Indies and on the American mainland? What cultural patterns were associated with forced African migration to the Americas?

The plantation complex of the Atlantic world, especially the sugar plantations of the West Indies, represented something new in world history: an agro-industrial enterprise geared specifically for commercial export markets. Sugar planters imported most of their labor, food, and equipment and focused on producing a single crop for distant markets. As a result, sugar became an essential part of the European diet. The cultural outcomes of the plantation system were complex. As in the mainland colonies, new societies emerged from the mixture of African, Amerindian, and European cultural and biological elements (see Chapter 18). Maroon communities were one form of resistance; persistence of African cultural traditions was another means by which slaves could assert their dignity and humanity. Meanwhile, out on the ocean, sailors, fishermen, pirates, and even a slave like Olaudah Equiano sometimes found greater opportunities than were available on land.

 How did the plantation complex affect political and economic developments in Europe in the eighteenth century?

Events in the Atlantic reinforced the shifting balance of power in Europe. Buoyed by the profits of sugar plantations, the French and British became the key players in the European power struggle by the late seventeenth century. Economic competition in the age of mercantilism set them into a conflict that culminated in the Seven Years' War (1756–1763), fought not only in the Atlantic but also in North America, continental Europe, and South Asia. British victory led to a British mastery of the seas of which Olaudah Equiano, having fought in the war, was quite proud.

FOR FURTHER REFERENCE

Anstey, Roger. *The Atlantic Slave Trade and British Abolition, 1760–1810*. New York: Macmillan, 1975.

Carretta, Vincent. *Equiano, the African: Biography of a Self-Made Man*. New York: Penguin Books, 2007.

Curtin, Philip. *Africa Remembered: Narratives by West Africans from the Era of the Slave Trade*. 2d ed. Long Grove, Ill.: Waveland Press, 1997.

Curtin, Philip. *The Rise and Fall of the Plantation Complex: Essays in Atlantic History*. 2d ed. New York: Cambridge University Press, 1998.

Eltis, David. *Economic Growth and the Ending of the Trans-Atlantic Slave Trade*. New York: Oxford University Press, 1987.

Equiano, Olaudah. *The Interesting Narrative of the Life of Olaudah Equiano, or Gustavus Vassa, the African*. Edited by Vincent Carretta. 2d ed. New York: Penguin Putnam, 2003.

Lovejoy, Paul. *Transformations in Slavery: A History of Slavery in Africa*. 2d ed. New York: Cambridge University Press, 2000.

Mintz, Sidney. *Sweetness and Power: The Place of Sugar in Modern History*. New York: Penguin Books, 1985.

Northrup, David. *Africa's Discovery of Europe, 1450–1850*. New York: Oxford University Press, 2002.

Patterson, Orlando. *Slavery and Social Death: A Comparative Study*. Cambridge: Harvard University Press, 1985.

Rediker, Marcus. *The Slave Ship: A Human History*. New York: Viking, 2007.

Thornton, John. *Africa and Africans in the Making of the Atlantic World, 1400–1800*. 2d ed. New York: Cambridge University Press, 1998.

VOYAGES ON THE WEB

Voyages: Olaudah Equiano

"Voyages" is a real time excursion to historical sites in this chapter and includes interactive activities and study tools such as audio summaries, animated maps, and flashcards.

Visual Evidence: The Horrors of the Middle Passage

"Visual Evidence" features artifacts, works of art, or photographs, along with a brief descriptive essay and discussion questions to guide your analysis of visual sources.

World History in Today's World: The World's Sweet Tooth

"World History in Today's World" makes the connection between features of modern life and their origins in the periods in this chapter.

KEY TERMS

Olaudah Equiano (412)

Great Lakes region (413)

Kimpa Vita (414)

Sahel (414)

Songhai Empire (414)

Atlantic plantation system (417)

maroon communities (419)

manumission (421)

Asante kingdom (421)

Dahomey (424)

triangular trade (426)

Seven Years' War (427)

Grand Banks (428)

abolitionist (429)

Act for the Abolition of the Slave Trade (430)

▶ CourseMate

20

Empires in Early Modern Asia, 1650–1818

...ern Chinese
...in Local
..., 1800s
(...Vind Picture Archives)

The British were just consolidating their power in northeastern India in the late 1780s when a young Chinese sailor named **Xie Qinggao** (1765?–1821) visited Calcutta, India. Xie had been born in the Guangdong province of south China, a region with a long history of commercial interaction with foreign ships. His life was transformed when, at the age of eighteen, he was involved in a shipwreck and rescued by a Portuguese vessel. His subsequent travels extended beyond coastal China, the Japanese islands, the Korean peninsula, and Southeast Asia to include the entire Indian Ocean commercial world and Europe itself. Years later, he recalled his impressions of British rule in India:

Bengal is governed by the British. The military governor, who is named "La" ["Lord"] rules from Calcutta. There is a small walled city inside of which live officials and the military while merchants reside outside the wall in the surrounding district…. The buildings and towers form cloud-like clusters, the gardens and pavilions are strange and beautiful…. More than 10,000 English live there with fifty to sixty thousand soldiers from the local people…. When the top officials go out on parade it is particularly impressive. In the front are six men on horseback … all wearing big red robes. The two men on the left and the right are dressed just like the "La," but his chest is covered with strange embroidery that looks like a fortunetelling sign…. The local people are of several types.

The Travels of Xie Qinggao

- ➤ Xie Qinggao's possible routes
- • City mentioned by Xie
- • Other city

European territories, ca. 1800
- British
- Dutch
- Portuguese
- Spanish

MANCHURIA

GOBI

QING EMPIRE

Beijing

KOREA

Sea of Japan

JAPAN
Kyoto
Edo

Huang He R.

Nanjing

Shanghai

Yellow Sea

Nagasaki

Fuzhou

East China Sea

Guangzhou (Canton)

Macao (Port.)

Xi R.

Formosa

Delhi

HIMALAYA MTS.

Ganges R.

Xie visits British India, ca. 1787.

Calcutta

Chittagong

MARATHA INDIA

Cuttack

Ganges Delta

BURMA

Hanoi

Hainan

Xie Qinggao leaves Guangzhou on a Portuguese ship, ca. 1783.

Bombay

Poona

BRITISH INDIA

Bay of Bengal

Rangoon

SIAM

Bangkok

Hue

VIETNAM

Arabian Sea

Goa (Port.)

Malabar Coast

Masulipatam

Coromandel Coast

Madras

Pondicherry (Fr.)

Karikal (Fr.)

CAMBODIA

Phnom Penh

Gulf of Siam

Saigon

South China Sea

Manila

Philippine Is.

Philippines Sea

PACIFIC OCEAN

Calicut

Cochin

Trivandrum

Cape Comorin

Colombo

Ceylon

Andaman Is.

Andaman Sea

Phuket

Songkhla

Pattani

Malay Peninsula

Cebu

to Europe via Cape of Good Hope

Achin

Alor Setar

Penang

Kota Baharu

Kuantan

Brunei

Davao

Celebes Sea

INDIAN OCEAN

Selangor

Malacca

Johor Baharu

Borneo

Celebes

Moluccas

New Guinea

Padang

Sumatra

Bengkulu

Batavia

Java

Sunda Is.

Java Sea

DUTCH EAST INDIES

Banda Sea

Timor

Arafura Sea

N

0   400   800 Km.
0   400   800 Mi.

Join this chapter's traveler on "Voyages," an interactive tour of historic sites and events:
www.cengagebrain.com

	1600	1650	1700	1750	1800	1850

Lifetime of Xie Qinggao
1765 — 1821

CHINA

Qing dynasty
1644

Reign of Emperor Kangxi
1662–1722

Reign of Qianlong
1735–1795

(to 1911)

Treaty of Nerchinsk
1689

Macartney Mission
1792–1793

SOUTH AND SOUTHEAST ASIA

Mughal India
(from 1526)

(to 1857)

Reign of Emperor Aurangzeb
1658   1707

Battle of Plassey
1757

JAPAN

Tokugawa Shogunate
1603

(to 1868)

Reign of Yoshimune
1716–1745

433

The Bengalis are relatively numerous, and the Brahmin caste is particularly well off…. The rich among them have clothing, food and dwellings like those of the English that are beautiful and impressive. The poor are almost naked … taking cloth several inches wide to wrap around their waists to cover their lower halves.[1]

Xie Qinggao (1765?–1821) Sailor from southern China who traveled across the Indian Ocean and throughout Europe. After becoming blind, Xie retired from sailing and dictated his story, published as *Hai-Lu,* or *Record of Sea Journeys.*

Xie Qinggao (shee-ay ching-GOW) was living in the Portuguese settlement of Macao, working as a translator because blindness had ended his career as a sailor, when a visitor from a neighboring Chinese province, fascinated by Xie's stories of his adventurous sailor's life, decided to record them. If not for the visitor's curiosity, Xie's story, like that of most ordinary people throughout history, would never have been recorded. By 1820, when Xie recorded this story in his *Record of Sea Journeys,* the British had conquered all of South Asia.

Xie's presence in Calcutta was part of an age-old trading network that connected the South China Sea with ports in Southeast Asia, India, the Persian Gulf, and East Africa. That network existed before the arrival of Portuguese ships in the sixteenth century and continued to exist even as the Dutch, British, and French developed more aggressive and heavily armed commercial organizations (see Chapter 16). But the officials of the British East India Company described by Xie Qinggao (called "Company men") were representative of an important new phase of this history. In their conquest of Bengal the British were striking at the authority of the Mughal Empire and so, for the first time, directly challenging one of the major Asian land-based empires.

Indeed, the creation and maintenance of empire were a consistent political theme in early modern South and East Asia. The Manchu emperors of the Qing (ching) dynasty, ruling not just China but also extensive Central Asian territories, controlled the greatest land-based empire of the age. As Qing armies and diplomats extended their influence to the west, they came into increasing contact with emissaries of the Russian Empire, which was expanding into Central Asia from the west. Meanwhile, the British were moving to supplant the Mughals as the major power of South Asia. Taken together, the expansion of the British and Russian Empires showed the increasing influence of Europe in Asian affairs. Japanese rulers, however, resisted these eighteenth-century trends, consolidating power on their own islands rather than seeking further territory, and rejecting European influence as a matter of state policy.

This chapter focuses on the expansion of empires in the late seventeenth and eighteenth centuries in East, South, and Central Asia. In the process we will see how imperial leaders had to contend with factors such as changing military technologies, commercial growth, increasing social and religious interactions, and population growth and ecological change, all of which might affect the success or failure of their policies.

FOCUS QUESTIONS

▶ How did the Qing emperors build and maintain their empire in East and Central Asia?

▶ What factors drove Russian imperial expansion in the eighteenth century?

▶ What were the principal causes of the decline of Mughal power, and how were the British able to replace the Mughals as the dominant power in South Asia?

▶ In comparison with the Qing, Russian, and British Empires, what were some unique features of early modern Japanese history?

The Power of the Qing Dynasty, 1644–1796

In 1644 armies from Manchuria overran Beijing, deposed the Ming dynasty, and established the Qing dynasty. From 1683 to 1796, just three long-ruling emperors ruled Qing China. It was a time of political stability, explosive population growth, economic expansion, and intellectual and artistic dynamism. China's empire expanded to encompass parts of Central Asia, Tibet, and the island of Taiwan. Qing emperors ruled China until 1911.

Establishment of Qing Rule, 1636–1661

The Manchu had been nomads who lived on the steppe beyond the Great Wall (see Map 20.1). By the sixteenth century the Chinese had brought farming to this frontier, and by the late Ming period Chinese culture had spread among the Manchu.

To maintain cordial relations, earlier Ming officials bestowed favors on Manchu leaders, such as the right to wear elaborate dragon-patterned robes of silk. The Manchu in turn emulated Chinese-style governance, while maintaining their own language and nomadic traditions such as fighting on horseback and a love of hunting. In the 1590s Ming generals called on the Manchu to help resist a Japanese invasion. Unfortunately for the Ming, Manchu armies united under a ruler who declared himself leader of the **Qing dynasty** and organized his fighters into eight "banners," named for the color of the flags that the different regiments carried in battle. As the Manchu strengthened and the Ming declined, Mongol and Chinese generals allied with the Qing, while maintaining their units under their own regimental banners.

After one of China's own rebel armies stormed the capital and the last Ming emperor committed suicide, the Manchu established their power in the north. However, Ming holdouts waged fierce battles against Qing forces in the south for four decades. The Qing used diplomacy as well as force in dealing with the resistance: adversaries who surrendered were well treated and were incorporated into the Qing military under the banner system.

Qing rulers retained Confucianism as the official state ideology to attract Chinese scholar-officials into the imperial bureaucracy. They also kept the examination system and the Chinese

> **Qing dynasty** (1644–1911) Sometimes called the Manchu dynasty after the Manchurian origins of its rulers. Qing (meaning "brilliant") rule extended from Beijing as far as Mongolia and Tibet.

Emperor Kangxi
(r. 1662–1722) One of the most powerful and long-ruling emperors in Chinese imperial history, Kangxi extended the Qing Empire, expanded the economy, and cultivated an image as a Confucian scholar and sage.

system of ministries, assigning one Chinese and one Manchu official to each. The Chinese scholar-officials had the requisite knowledge and experience, but the Manchu officials, thought to be more loyal, were there to supervise the work.

Qing rulers carefully guarded their Manchu culture and identity. Intermarriage between Manchu and Han Chinese was forbidden, and the Manchu elite continued to speak their own language and to practice their own form of Buddhism. Qing emperors spent their summers at the great

palace of Chengde (**chung-deh**), beyond the Great Wall, where horsemanship, hunting, and camping were reminders of nomadic life.

While the Manchu made few efforts to impose their culture on Chinese subjects, the Qing did decree that all men had to cut their hair in the Manchu style, called a *queue* (**kyoo**), with a shaved forehead and a single long braid in back. Chinese men reluctantly complied, saying it was either "lose your hair or lose your head."

The Age of Three Emperors, 1661–1799

When **Emperor Kangxi** (r. 1662–1722) ascended the Dragon Throne in 1662, the fate of the Qing

Map 20.1 The Qing Empire, 1644-1783

Beginning from their homeland in the north, the Manchu rulers of the Qing dynasty not only conquered China but also built an empire stretching far into Central Asia, matching the contemporary expansion of the Russian Empire. The Qing Empire grew to more than twice the size of its Ming predecessor. Tibetans, Mongols, and other subject peoples were ruled indirectly through local authorities loyal to the Qing emperors. © Cengage Learning   Interactive Map

Palace Museum, Beijing

cities of Beijing, Nanjing (nahn-JING), and Guangzhou (gwahng-jo) each grew to over a million residents. By Confucian standards, Qing China was prosperous indeed.

The emperor Yongzheng (r. 1723–1735) continued his predecessor's Confucian policies. He ordered a detailed census and compiled an 800,000-page encyclopedia to guide administrators across his vast and complex empire. By basing rural taxation on updated land registers, Yongzheng both increased state revenue through more efficient tax collection and spread the tax burden more equitably between commoners and gentry.

During the reign of Qianlong (r. 1736–1795) the power of Qing China reached its height. Coming to the throne as a young man, **Qianlong (chee-YEN-loong)** ruled for sixty years before abdicating: true to Confucian ideals of filial piety, he did not want his reign to exceed that of his grandfather, Kangxi. During these six decades the commercial economy became even more dynamic. Mainstays of production were luxury goods for export, especially silk and porcelain. Vast quantities of silver from Japan and Spanish America continued to flow into Qing China, financing public works as well as private investment. Some Chinese farmers found that tobacco, another American crop, was a profitable addition to their fields. Artisans and small-scale entrepreneurs expanded the glass-making, brewing, and coal-mining industries. Thus eighteenth-century China retained its long-established position as the largest industrial economy in the world.

Qianlong (r. 1736– 1795) Qing emperor who ruled during the empire's greatest territorial expansion and prosperity. Late in his reign, corruption began to infect the state bureaucracy. Rejected an English attempt to establish diplomatic relations.

was still in doubt. However, by 1683, he had successfully suppressed Ming resistance and annexed their last redoubt, the island of Taiwan. Six decades of Kangxi's rule established the Qing as masters of one of the greatest empires the world had ever known.

Kangxi (kang-shee) aspired to be a "sage ruler." He studied the Confucian classics closely, and official portraits often depict him in scholarly poses. Because the Manchu were "barbarians," Kangxi sought to assure his Chinese subjects that his rule was soundly based on Confucian principles.

Confucians believed that agriculture is the source of wealth and that a large population is a sign of prosperity. As farmers improved agricultural productivity by planting American crops like peanuts, sweet potatoes, and maize in previously marginal areas, China's population boomed, growing from about 100 million in 1500 to about 250 million by 1750. The

Women's Work in Qing China

Cotton textile production emerged as a major commercial industry around the city of Nanjing in

Yangzi River Valley
Agriculturally productive region with the important urban center of Nanjing. The Yangzi River delta was the site of strong industrial and commercial growth in the eighteenth century.

the lower **Yangzi River Valley**. Unlike silk, cotton cloth was inexpensive, affordable to all but the poorest Chinese consumers, and had the advantages of being comfortable, durable, and easy to clean. Traditionally, women produced textiles in China; the cotton industry reinforced those traditions.

All Chinese women were expected to work with their hands. Wealthy women prided themselves on the opulence of their handiwork. For rural women, tending silkworms and spinning silk thread were admired as accomplishments that had the additional virtue of providing income. The division of labor was summed up in the expression "Men plow, women weave."[2] Spinning and weaving cotton within the household meshed neatly with such traditions, and in commercialized regions such as the Yangzi (yang-zuh) delta, these activities drove economic growth.

Upon marriage young women left their own families to join their husband's household, where they were often at the mercy of demanding mothers-in-law. As the economy became more commercialized, young women spent more time indoors spinning and weaving cloth. But while contributing to the income of their husband's family, they did not necessarily gain much benefit for themselves.

In fact, these activities might have made women's situation worse, since more time working at home may have increased the occasion of footbinding, whereby young girls' feet were disfigured into small points. Originally bound feet were a distinction signifying wealth and leisure, but the fashion spread. Young girls' feet were broken and compressed into 3-inch balls by binding the four smaller toes under the sole of the foot and forcing the big toe and heel together. With bound feet, women suffered constant pain, limited mobility, and frequent infections.

Qing officials were disgusted by the practice, and Manchu women never bound their daughters' feet. But the practice was so well established among the Chinese that Qing officials did not try to abolish it.

There were some more positive notes. For example, female infanticide declined during this period, perhaps due to the improved financial prospects of women in textile production. Also,

elite women had opportunities for education and artistic expression. Educated to be sensitive and refined, these women wrote many of the greatest poems from Qing times.

Why didn't the dynamic commercial economy of eighteenth-century China initiate a full-fledged industrial revolution? Some historians point to the Confucian outlook that emphasized order over innovation and that regarded commerce as a low-status occupation. Others suggest that the availability of cheap labor suppressed incentives to invest in new laborsaving methods. Spinners and weavers, finishers and dyers, all worked for little pay. Human labor thus remained the engine of Chinese textile production.

The Qing Empire and Its Borderlands

By both force and diplomacy, territorial expansion was one of the greatest Qing achievements. The advances of the "gunpowder revolution" were complemented by the use of the banner system to incorporate frontier peoples into the empire.

During the century after the Manchu secured southern China and Taiwan, the Qing Empire doubled in size. The Manchu then had to deal with the age-old Chinese problem of bringing stability to their empire. That meant asserting their control over Mongolian nomads and Turkish-speaking Muslim peoples to their west, stationing soldiers as far away as Tibet, and contending with the challenge of the Russian Empire as it expanded into Central Asia.

The main threat came from the Zunghars, Central Asian Mongols devoted to Tibetan Buddhism. The spiritual leader of the Tibetans and of the Zunghar Mongols was the Dalai Lama (DAH-lie LAH-mah). The Manchu used both force and subterfuge against the Zunghars, sending an army to Tibet but also supporting one of the rival contenders for the title of Dalai Lama. With Tibet paying tribute to Beijing, the Zunghars were weakened. Finally in 1757, Qianlong issued a genocide order: the men were slaughtered (a few survived by crossing into Russian territory), the women and children enslaved, and the lands repopulated with sedentary minorities, such as the Muslims still found in today's Xinjiang (shin-jyahng)

The Weaving of Flower'd Silks, two Women at Work.

Stapleton Collection/ The Bridgeman Art Library

Silk Weaving Silk weaving was a highly profitable enterprise in eighteenth-century China. Women played a central role in all stages of silk production, operating large and complex looms such as the one pictured here. The spinning of cotton thread and weaving of cotton cloth were also increasingly important at this time, and women dominated production in the cotton industry as well.

province. After 1757, a Chinese dynasty was never again threatened by steppe nomads.

Elsewhere Qing officials relied on diplomacy, exacting tribute from societies outside their direct control. Annual tribute missions to Beijing symbolized the fealty even of powerful leaders, like the emperors of Korea and Vietnam who preserved their autonomy through ritual recognition of the Qing as overlords. Tribute was also sent by non-Han peoples living on the margins of Chinese society, in the hills, jungles, and steppes.

Though Tibet and western Xinjiang had been brought under Qing rule, these areas were not, like Chinese provinces, administered directly. Rather, local political authorities were allowed to continue under Manchu supervision as long as taxes were paid, order was kept, and loyalty to the Qing was maintained. For example, the Qing appointed a Tibetan official to report on Tibetan affairs but otherwise did nothing to supplant the influence of Buddhist monks. Tibetan and Mongol emissaries were often received at Chengde, the Manchu summer palace, rather than in the Forbidden City in Beijing.

Unlike the Ming, the Qing were not interested in asserting cultural superiority over tributary societies. The Ming had actively assimilated linguistically and culturally foreign peoples into Han Chinese language and culture. But the Qing viewed China as just one part of a wider Manchu empire. Eighteenth-century Qing maps had Chinese labels for Chinese provinces and Manchu labels for non-Chinese areas, illustrating how Qianlong saw himself as a Manchu emperor.

Trade and Foreign Relations

Not all of the Qing Empire's external relations were encompassed within the tributary system. Though the Qing treated the Russians on equal terms, they were reluctant to grant diplomatic equality to other European powers.

As the Russian Empire expanded eastward, Kangxi was concerned that they might ally with the steppe nomads. After some skirmishes, the Russians and the Chinese agreed to the **Treaty of Nerchinsk** in 1689, according to which the Qing recognized Russian claims west of Mongolia, while the Russians agreed to disband settlements to the east. Yongzheng and Qianlong continued this policy through treaties that fixed the boundary between the two empires.

Treaty of Nerchinsk The 1689 treaty between Romanov Russia and Qing China that fixed their Central Asian frontier.

Macartney Mission The 1792–1793 mission in which Lord Macartney was sent by King George III of England to establish permanent diplomatic relations with the Qing Empire. Because he could not accept the British king as his equal, the Qianlong emperor politely refused.

While the Russians came overland, other Europeans came by sea. European trade focused on south China, especially Guangzhou (called Canton by the Europeans), which had remained loyal to the Ming after the fall of Beijing. Like their Ming predecessors, Qing emperors regarded oceanic trade with suspicion. They associated Guangzhou with "greedy" traders rather than sober scholar-officials, and with adventurous sailors like Xie Qinggao (who was born and raised in this area) rather than dependable village-bound farmers. Accordingly, the Qing restricted European trade to this single port and required European traders to deal only with state-approved firms known as *cohongs*. Since cohong merchants had a monopoly on trade with Europeans, they found it easy to fix prices and amass huge profits.

The British in particular were frustrated with the structure of the China trade. Having little to trade for Chinese goods but silver, they

Primary Source: Edict on Trade with Great Britain *Emperor Qianlong declines Britain's request for increased trade in China.*

saw the continued outflow of money toward Asia as a fiscal problem. As conflicts between British merchants and sailors and Chinese officials and residents of Guangzhou increased, tensions mounted.

Finally the British sought to establish formal diplomatic relations. In 1792 King George III sent the **Macartney Mission** to negotiate an exchange of ambassadors. Granted passage from Guangzhou to Beijing, Macartney refused to perform the ritual *kowtow* of full prostration before the emperor, consenting only to drop to one knee, as he would before his own king. He asked that more ports be opened to foreign trade and that restrictions on trade be removed. Qianlong's response to King George III was unequivocal: "We have never valued ingenious articles, nor do we have the slightest need of your country's manufactures. Therefore, O King, as regards your request to send someone to remain at the capital, while it is not in harmony with the regulations of the Celestial Empire we also feel very much that it is of no advantage to your country."[3] Qianlong saw China as the center of the civilized world, and he insisted that the British should appear before him only if bearing tribute in recognition of his superior position.

Qianlong's attitude was understandable. The Qing controlled the largest and wealthiest empire on earth and had no need to look beyond their borders for resources. But all was not well. Inefficiency and corruption were creeping into the system. As Qianlong grew old, the power of eunuchs increased at court at the expense of the well-trained scholar officials. Meanwhile, the absence of technological improvements in farming put pressure on the food supply. As more marginal lands were cleared for cultivation, deforestation, the silting up of rivers, and floods resulted. Peasant rebels saw the non-Chinese Manchu as illegitimate and dreamed of restoring the Ming dynasty.

When Qianlong abdicated in 1796, the gravity of these internal challenges was not yet clear. Nor could he foresee how powerful the British would be in fifty years when they returned to impose their demands by force. Qing officials still believed that the old ways sufficed. But the threat to imperial China no longer came by land; in the nineteenth century no Great Wall could keep out the new invaders from the sea.

The Russian Empire, 1725–1800

Like the Chinese, the Russian people had long experience with steppe nomads. The Russian state had been founded as part of the dissolution of the Mongol Empire, and Russian leaders viewed control of the steppe as necessary for the security of their heartland. Peter the Great had pushed Russia's borders further west, east, and south, making Russia a great power on two continents. Yet, for all the splendor of the Romanov court, conditions for the majority of Russians remained grim.

Russian Imperial Expansion, 1725–1800

In the west, Russia dominated the Baltic Sea region after defeating the Swedes in 1721. When the Polish kingdom collapsed after the 1770s, Russia, along with Prussia and Austria, shared in its partition. Russian power thrust to the south as well, largely at the expense of the Ottoman Empire. The great prize was the Crimean peninsula, annexed by Russia in 1783 (see Map 20.2). A major trade emporium since ancient times, the Crimea brought both strategic and economic benefits. Russia made its first inroads into the Caucasus Mountains at this time as well.

Eastward, Russians expanded across Siberia, extending their fur-trapping frontier. Their initial penetration was carried out not by imperial forces but by mercenary soldiers called **Cossacks** (from the Turkish word *kazakh*, meaning "free man") hired by wealthy traders. The Cossacks originated as fiercely independent horsemen, Slavic-speakers who had assimilated the ways of their nomadic Mongol and Turkish neighbors on the steppes. The Cossack code of honor was based on marksmanship, horsemanship, and group spirit. Russian soldiers and administrators subsequently followed the fur traders' Cossacks into the Siberian frontier, taking formal control to make sure the tsars got their share.

The fur trade exploited the expertise and labor of indigenous Siberians, whom the Russians called the "small people of the north." If a community did not deliver its quota of furs, Cossacks might attack, carrying women and children off into slavery. Though trappers and traders might profit, Russian merchants and the Russian treasury reaped the lion's share. Once the fur-bearing animals of a given area had been depleted, the frontier moved on to virgin terrain. Thus the eastern frontier extended to Alaska, which the Bering Expedition claimed for the tsar in 1741 (see Map 20.2).

The Russians also established influence over parts of Asia south of Siberia, hoping to establish trade links with India. Peter the Great maintained armed control over the steppes on Russia's borders, while pursuing a diplomatic strategy on the further Central Asian frontier. He ordered that young men be taught Mongolian, Turkish, and Persian languages and sent them to the many small principalities of Central Asia as diplomatic representatives. Meanwhile, as we have seen, skirmishes between Russian and Manchu soldiers led to the Treaty of Nerchinsk.

Reform and Repression, 1750–1796

Much of the new imperial territory was acquired during the reign of **Catherine the Great** (r. 1762–1796), one of the dominating figures of eighteenth-century Eurasian politics. Catherine brought cultural and intellectual influences from western Europe to the tsarist court at St. Petersburg, even as exciting new ideas were energizing reform and revolution in the West. However, while Catherine brought the latest in art, architecture, and fashion to Russia, she adamantly ruled out political reform. Instead, she consolidated ever more power to herself.

The Russian nobility benefited from her authoritarianism. In return for their loyalty and service, Catherine gave the nobles more power over the serfs who farmed their estates. At the same time, the profitable market for grain in western Europe gave them an incentive to make increasingly harsh demands on their serfs. In their elegant townhouses and country estates, the Russian aristocracy saw Western luxuries as essential to their lifestyle and thought nothing of those who toiled for them like slaves.

As the situation of the serfs deteriorated, unrest led to rebellion. In the 1770s a Cossack chieftain named Yemelyan Pugachev gained a huge following after claiming that he was the legitimate tsar. Pugachev promised the abolition of serfdom and an end to taxation and military conscription. After several years of rebellion, Pugachev was captured, brought back to Moscow, and sliced to pieces in a public square. Catherine became even less tolerant of talk of reform.

Catherine's policies were pragmatic. A convert herself, she restrained the

Cossacks Horsemen of the steppe who helped Russian rulers protect and extend their frontier into Central Asia and Siberia.

Catherine the Great (r. 1762–1796) German princess who married into the Romanov family and became empress of Russia. Brought western European cultural and intellectual influences to the Russian elite. Her troops crushed a major peasant uprising.

The Russian Empire
- Russia in 1533
- Added by 1598
- Added by 1721
- Added by 1796
- ✕ Fort

PACIFIC OCEAN

BRITISH NORTH AMERICA (CANADA)

Novo Arkhangelsk (Sitka)
TLINGIT

Border set in 1826

RUSSIAN AMERICA (ALASKA)

ALEUTS

INUIT

INUIT

Bering Strait

60°N

70°N

Bering Sea

50°N

INUIT

CHUKCHI

KORYAKS

Petropavlovsk
ALEUTS

Kamchatka Peninsula

Kolyma R.

GREENLAND

ARCTIC OCEAN

100°W
120°W
140°W
160°W
80°N
180°
160°E
140°E
120°E
100°E
80°E
60°E
40°E
20°E

60°W
40°W
20°W

80°N

Iceland

70°N

Arctic Circle

Sea of Okhotsk

Okhotsk

Yana R.

Zashiversk

Sakhalin I.

Zhigansk

Yakutsk

Lena R.

Olenek R.

S I B E R I A

EVENKI

YAKUTS

LAMUTS

Khatanga R.

Viluy R.

Amur R.

MANCHURIA

Kara Sea

Barents Sea

Lower Tunguska R.

TUNGUSY

EVENKI

Nerchinsk

Obdorsk

SAMOYEDS

Taz R.

OSTYAKS

Yenisey R.

Bratsk

GREAT BRITAIN

SWEDEN

NORWAY

Arkhangelsk

FINLAND

OSTYAKS

Ob R.

Surgut

TARTARS

Kem R.

Krasnoyarsk

Irkutsk

Baltic Sea

St. Petersburg

Novgorod

Verkhoturye

URAL MOUNTAINS

Tula R.

Omsk

Biysk

MONGOLIA

HOLY ROMAN EMPIRE

Riga

Tobol R.

Ishim R.

Irtysh R.

PRUSSIA

Moscow

Smolensk

Nizhni Novgorod

Kama R.

POLAND

Samara

AUSTRIA

Kiev

UKRAINIANS

Saratov

COSSACKS

Ural R.

KAZAKS

QING EMPIRE

HUNGARY

Dnieper R.

Dniester R.

COSSACKS

Volga R.

Black Sea

GEORGIA

Caspian Sea

Aral Sea

OTTOMAN EMPIRE

IRAN

AFGHANISTAN

TIBET

NEPAL

BHUTAN

BURMA

INDIA

Map 20.2   The Expansion of Russia, 1500–1800

By the end of the eighteenth century the Russian Empire extended westward into Europe, southward toward the Black Sea and Caspian Sea, and, most dramatically, eastward into Central Asia, Siberia, and the Americas. © Cengage Learning

🖱 Interactive Map

Catherine the Great   Equestrian portraits of monarchs on white horses were common in eighteenth-century Europe, though rarely were women represented this way. Catherine, a German princess who married into the Russian royal family, removed her husband from the throne in 1762 in a bloodless coup. Tough and brilliant, she ruled under her own authority for over three decades.

Erich Lessing/Art Resource, NY

Orthodox church from attempting to convert non-Russian peoples. In the case of Siberia, the reason was financial: converts to Orthodoxy had tax protections that indigenous people lacked. In the cases of the steppe and the Central Asian frontier, Catherine saw that working with local Muslim leaders was the best way to maintain stability. In the Crimea, for example, she protected the rights of the local Muslim nobility: "It is Our desire that without regard to his nationality or faith, each [nobleman] shall have the personal right to these lands and any advantages that will accrue from their use." (See the feature "Movement of Ideas: Petitioning Catherine the Great.")

Thus while conditions for Russian serfs might deteriorate, and force might prevail on the Siberian frontier, imperial Russian interactions with Asian societies were flexible.

Primary Source: Catherine the Great's Grand Instruction to the Legislative Commission *Catherine the Great gives instructions to the commissioners charged with developing a new code of laws for the Russian Empire.*

India: From Mughal Empire to British Rule, 1650–1800

In the later seventeenth century the Mughal Empire was at its zenith when the emperor Aurangzeb (ow-rang-ZEB) extended his power throughout south India and took the title Alamgir, "World Seizer." A hundred years later, however, Mughal power was in retreat as the British East India Company established its dominance.

Petitioning Catherine the Great

It was common in tsarist Russia for communities to petition the tsar or tsarina for redress of grievances. Often people felt that oppression resulted from the misuse of power by local and provincial officials: if only the tsarina herself knew of these abuses, surely she would correct them. Catherine the Great encouraged this attitude and invited her subjects (other than the serfs, who had no right to address her) to submit their petitions to her.

The first of the two petitions below was submitted by a group of Tartar nobles, that is, by the Muslim, Turkish-speaking elite of an area incorporated into the Russian Empire. The Kazan Tartars had ruled the Volga River region in the fourteenth century, but in the fifteenth century this region was conquered by the Russian tsar Ivan the Terrible. Ivan slaughtered much of the Muslim population

and forcibly converted many of the survivors to Orthodox Christianity. Not until the reign of Catherine did the tsars allow new mosques to be built again in Kazan.

The second petition to Catherine was submitted by a group of Jewish leaders in Belarus. The majority of the population of Belarus (meaning "white Russia") consisted of Slavic speakers closely related to Russians in language and culture. Belarus was ruled from Poland/Lithuania until the eighteenth century, after which it was incorporated into the Russian Empire. The Jews of this region were known as *Ashkenazim*. Their liturgical language was a form of Hebrew, but their everyday language was Yiddish, a dialect of German infused with Hebrew vocabulary that was unintelligible to Russian speakers. To the greatest extent possible, the Ashkenazim took care of their own community affairs.

Petition from Tatar Nobles in Kazan Province, 1767

12. We the under-signed believe that nothing is more offensive to a person, regardless of his faith and rank, than to suffer disrespect and insults toward his religion. This makes one extremely agitated and provokes unnecessary words of abuse. But it often happens that people of various ranks say extremely contemptuous things about our religion and our Prophet … and this is a great affront for us. Therefore we request a law that anyone who curses our religion be held legally accountable… . [We further ask that] we Tatars and nobles not be forced to convert to Orthodoxy, but that only those who so wish … be baptized… .

15. If any of our people are voluntarily baptized into the faith of the Greek confession [i.e., into the Orthodox Church] they should be ordered to move to settlements with Russians the very same year in which the conversion takes place… . We ask that, under no circumstances, are converts to be permitted to sell their houses, garden plots, and pastures to Russians or people of other ranks, but are to sell only to us Tatars; they must sell either to unconverted kinsmen or other Tatars… . Also, without a special personal order from Her Imperial Majesty, no churches should be built in our localities and thereby put pressure upon us… .

Petition from Belarussian Jews, 1784

1. Some [Belarussian Jews] who live in towns engage in trade and, especially, in the distillation of spirits, beer and mead [honey beer], which they sell wholesale and retail. This privilege was extended to them when Belarus joined the Russian Empire. Hence everyone active in this business used all their resources to construct buildings suitable for distillation... . After the Belarussian region joined the Russian Empire, the Jews in some towns constructed more of these in the same fashion and at great expense. The imperial monarchical decree [on Jews] emboldens them to request tearfully some monarchical mercy.

2. According to an ancient custom, when the squires built a new village, they summoned the Jews to reside there and gave them certain privileges for several years and the permanent liberty to distill spirits, brew beer and mead, and sell these drinks. On this basis the Jews built houses and distillation plants at considerable expense. The squires, at their own volition, farmed out the inns to the Jews, with the freedom to distill and sell liquor... . But a decree of the governor-general of Belarus has now forbidden the squires to farm our distillation in their villages to Jews, even if the squires want to do this. As a result [these] poor Jews [have been left] completely impoverished... . They therefore request an imperial decree authorizing the squire, if he wishes, to farm out distillation to Jews in rural areas.

3. ...Jews have no one to defend them in courts and find themselves in a desperate situation—given their fear, and ignorance of Russian—in case of misfortune, even if innocent... . To consummate all the good already bestowed, Jews dare to petition that ... in matters involving Jews and non-Jews ... a representative from the Jewish community ... be present to accompany Jews in court and attend the interrogation of Jews. But cases involving only Jews ... should be handled solely in Jewish courts, because Jews assume obligations among themselves, make agreements and conclude all kinds of deals in the Jewish language and in accordance with Jewish rites and law (which are not known to others). Moreover, those who transgress their laws and order should be judged in Jewish courts. Similarly, preserve intact all their customs and holidays in the spirit of their faith, as is mercifully assured in the imperial manifesto... .

Source: Excerpts from Gregory L. Freeze, *From Supplication to Revolution: A Documentary Social History of Imperial Russia*, Oxford University Press, 1988. Reprinted by permission.

QUESTIONS FOR ANALYSIS

▸ What attitude did the writers of these petitions express toward Catherine's imperial authority?

▸ What do these documents tell us about the relationship of religion to empire in eighteenth-century Russia?

Aurangzeb (r. 1658– 1707) Mughal emperor who used military force to extend his power but whose constant campaigns drained the treasury and whose policy of favoring Islam at the expense of India's other religions generated social and political tensions.

Maratha kingdoms Loosely bound, west-central Indian confederacy that established its autonomy from Mughal rule in the eighteenth century and challenged the invading British in the nineteenth.

Nader Shah (1688– 1747) Iranian ruler who invaded India from the north in 1739, defeating the Mughal army and capturing the Mughal emperor, who handed over the keys to his treasury, and even the fabled Peacock Throne, before Nader Shah agreed to withdraw. Mughal power went into permanent decline.

Even during **Aurangzeb's** long rule (1658–1707), regional leaders resisted the central power of Delhi. And after his death, the Mughal Empire began to fragment, leading to invasions from Iran and Afghanistan and the emergence of autonomous regional states. As in the past, the wealth of empire attracted invaders from the mountains and steppes who were strong enough to destabilize the existing order, but not to replace it. Arriving by sea, however, the British represented something different. Starting from their base in Bengal, they would fill the vacuum left by Mughal decline.

Aurangzeb and the Decline of Mughal Authority, 1658–1757

Aurangzeb was an energetic, capable, and determined ruler who presided over a stable and prosperous realm. The wealth he controlled was staggering. Some came from territorial conquests that brought treasure flowing back to Delhi. But agriculture, trade, and industry were the true foundations of his wealth.

Mughal officials encouraged the commercial farming of sugarcane, indigo, and cotton to enhance the tax base, and many peasants benefited from the focus on marketable crops. American crops like maize and tobacco were another stimulus to growth. The population did not increase as rapidly as China's in the same period: disease and famine kept mortality rates high. Still, the population of India rose from about 150 million in 1600 to about 200 million in 1800. As in other land-based empires, taxes on agriculture were the principal source of government revenue.

The stability of the Mughal heartland in north India was good for trade and industry. Participation in the expanding Indian Ocean economy brought in gold and silver. Silk and opium were produced for Southeast Asian markets, but the principal source of prosperity was the textile sector. Consumers in the Netherlands, France, and England found Indian cotton cloth cheaper, more comfortable, and more easily washed than domestic woolens or linens. South Asians were among the most powerful commercial agents in the world, using the silver that flowed in through Indian Ocean trade to pay cash advances to weavers, who then contracted lower-caste women to spin cotton yarn.

For Mughal rulers, commercial wealth was a mixed blessing, however. Prosperity afforded provincial leaders the cash and incentive to build up their own military forces. Aurangzeb's constant military campaigns were largely driven by the need to quell such restive provinces.

In the process Aurangzeb reversed Akbar's earlier policy of religious tolerance (see Chapter 16). While many Muslims lived in the empire, most Mughal subjects were Hindus. Whereas Akbar had courted allies among Hindus, Sikhs, and other communities, Aurangzeb imposed an additional tax on all non-Muslims, causing great resentment.

Hindus trying to wrest free of central control, such as in the **Maratha kingdoms**, were now motivated by religious resentments as well as political and economic ambitions. Maratha leaders used guerilla tactics, well suited to the region's tough terrain, to keep the Mughal armies at bay. From 1695 to 1700, Aurangzeb left Delhi to live in military encampments. Vast sums were spent on his campaigns, and as the emperor was preoccupied with military affairs, corruption and incompetence crept into the government.

By the time of his death in 1707, Aurangzeb was full of despair. From his deathbed he wrote his son: "I have not done well to the country or to the people, and of the future there is no hope." A prolonged succession struggle ensued, regional leaders ignored Delhi, tax collectors withheld government funds, and the empire became vulnerable.

The main threat came from Iran. After the fall of the Safavid dynasty, **Nader Shah** (1688–1747) rallied Iranian forces to defend the country from Afghan invaders. His invasion of India marked the end of Mughal authority. The Marathas tried to march on Delhi, but they were decisively defeated by Afghani invaders in 1761. With Maratha expansion checked, India seemed ready to break apart. Instead, the British took the mantle of Mughal imperial power.

The Tomb of Aurangzeb   The Mughal emperor Aurangzeb was a deeply spiritual man, but his advocacy of Islam in multireligious India weakened the empire. His simple grave contrasts with the ornate magnificence of most Mughal architecture.

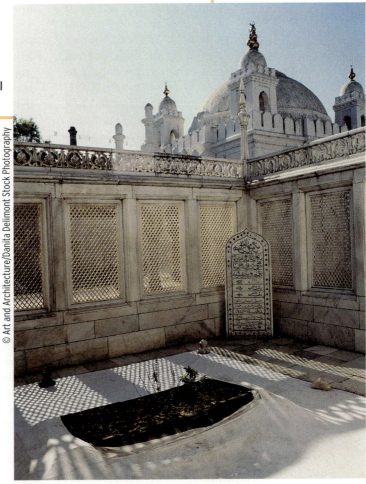

© Art and Architecture/Danita Delimont Stock Photography

Foundations of British Rule, 1739–1818

The seaborne European empires in Asia were originally geared toward commercial exploitation rather than territorial control. Mughal rulers paid little attention to the Dutch, English, and French East India Companies operating on the fringes of their empire. In Amsterdam, Paris, and London, Company home offices handled shipping schedules, insurance, and warehousing. In Asia, Company agents identified profitable opportunities and negotiated with locals. The usual pattern was for Europeans to directly control only their own "factories," fortified outposts where they lived and kept their trade goods, and perhaps a bit of adjacent territory.

Cotton cloth was a major trade item, as were opium (first destined for Indonesian markets, and later for China), raw silk (exported to both Europe and Japan), and pepper. Saltpeter, a key ingredient in gunpowder, was another important European import from Asia. European rulers, following the theory of mercantilism, believed that their own economies were damaged by the high silver exports needed to finance this trade. But the commerce was so profitable that silver exports continued.

With the decline of Mughal power, some Company agents seized the opportunity to expand the autonomy of their enterprises, thus laying the foundations for European empire in Asia. One of the first and most brilliant of these was **Joseph Francois Dupleix** (1697–1764). During the 1740s he seized the British factory at Madras, only to be attacked in turn by a local Indian ruler. Although Dupleix (doo-PLAY)

Joseph Francois Dupleix (1697–1764) Governor-general in charge of all French establishments in India. Dupleix used diplomacy to forge alliances with local rulers and with their help defeated a much larger British force in the 1740s.

commanded just 230 French troops plus some 700 Indian recruits, or *sepoys* (SEE-poyz), superior French firepower and organization enabled him to defeat a force of nearly 10,000 men, and Dupleix seized rule from his Indian enemy. For diplomatic reasons, Paris ordered Dupleix to return Madras to the British, but Dupleix's example would be followed with more lasting effect.

Further north, the British East India Company factory at Calcutta tapped into the rich trade of the populous Mughal province of Bengal. The nawab (ruler) of Bengal, Siraj ud-Daulah (suh-raj uhd–duh-oo-lah), saw the British as a threat, and in 1756 his soldiers seized Calcutta. But Robert Clive, a British soldier of fortune, outmaneuvered him. First, Clive secured backing from Hindu commercial and banking interests in Bengal who preferred to deal with the commercially minded British. Second, Clive made an alliance with the nawab's own uncle, who hoped to become nawab himself. In 1757, at the **Battle of Plassey**, the nawab's 50,000 troops faced only 800 Englishmen, plus about 2,000 sepoys. But some of Siraj ud-Daulah's troops had been secretly paid not to fight by Clive's Hindu friends, while the forces controlled by his uncle switched to the British side. Afterwards, Siraj's uncle was duly installed as nawab, but the English plundered his treasury, as Company officials drained fortunes from north India to build stately London residences and palatial country houses in England.

From Bengal, the British could have marched on Delhi and ended the Mughal era once and for all. But Clive decided on a more subtle policy of recognizing the weakened Mughal emperor while insinuating the Company into existing Mughal institutions. The East India Company became the official revenue collector of the rich northeastern provinces of Bengal, Bihar (bee-HAHR), and Oudh (OW-ad), while extorting alliances from various nawabs, maharajahs, and sultans by offering them "protection."

In Parliament, some doubted whether Clive and the Company were serving England's interests. They were also horrified by the famine

following the failure of the monsoon rains in 1769, during which one-third of the Bengal's population perished. Although the Company fed its own employees and soldiers, it did nothing for Bengalis while continuing to extract its revenue. One member of Parliament complained: "We have outdone the Spaniards in Peru. They were at least butchers on a religious principle, however diabolical their zeal. We have murdered, deposed, plundered, usurped—nay, what think you of the famine in Bengal being caused by a monopoly of the servants of the East India Company?"[4]

The India Act in 1784 attempted to redress such abuses. **Lord Charles Cornwallis** was dispatched as governor-general and commander of British forces in India. Unlike Clive (who committed suicide in disgrace), Cornwallis was an aristocrat and a member of the British establishment. His assignment was to enforce a policy whereby Company employees might serve as either officials or traders, but not as both. Cornwallis believed that British colonial rule was justifiable. As his successor declared: "No greater benefit can be bestowed on the inhabitants of India than the extension of British authority."[5] That idea would long endure.

British influence spread. Provincial rulers looked to the British as patrons and protectors in the anarchy that accompanied Mughal decline. The British also absorbed Indian influences, learning Indian languages and adopting Mughal styles of dress and behavior. Because there were no English women in India, Company employees frequently consorted with local women, who provided a bridge to Indian society and culture.

Xie Qinggao's account of a Company court proceeding at Calcutta provides a snapshot of British influence:

The head judge sits, and ten guest judges [the jury] sit on his side. The head guest judge is the elder of the guest merchants… . On the day they consider the suit and then decide the outcome, if one of the guest judges does not agree they must hear the case again. Even if this happens two or three times, no one views this as inconvenient.[6]

But while the Company used British-style jurisprudence among themselves, they did not choose to displace South Asian legal traditions. Instead, Indian litigants could pursue their

Werner Forman / Art Resource, NY

A British East India Company Official   Eighteenth-century Englishmen adopted many features of Mughal court life: dressing in Mughal fashion, smoking from a hookah, enjoying the entertainment of Indian musicians and dancers, and taking up the Mughal sport of polo. Many of these Mughal cultural practices, including the game of polo, had themselves been imported from Persia. This portrait bears comparison with that of the Safavid Shah Sulayman II.

cases in local courts or in British ones. They might choose British courts because of corruption in the Mughal ones; however, they would still expect their own customs to be respected. The British East India Company therefore employed Muslim and Hindu legal advisers to help implement a multilayered intercultural judicial system.

In the 1770s the top Company official declared: "The dominion of all India is what I never wish to see." But Indian challenges to British authority required action if existing interests were to be defended. In the west, for example, when Maratha armies threatened the British East India Company's factory at Bombay, the British engaged in a series of alliances and interventions in that region. Finally, in 1818 they defeated the Marathas in battle and were on the way to establishing their control over all of South Asia.

Tokugawa Japan, 1630–1790

After Hideyoshi's adventurous attempt to invade China at the end of the sixteenth century (see Chapter 16), early modern Japan remained largely aloof from the world. Unlike Korea and Vietnam, Japan did not pay tribute to the Chinese emperor. Unlike islands like the Spanish Philippines, the Dutch East Indies, or Qing-controlled Taiwan, it was subject to no foreign power. Instead, Japan followed its own distinctive political, economic, and cultural dynamic. It was a period of tremendous vitality. The Tokugawa (toe-koo-GAH-wah) shoguns and *daimyo* lords ruled over a rapidly growing society with a flourishing economy and major accomplishments in fields such as poetry, theater, and architecture.

The story of early modern Japan divides roughly into two periods. From 1630 to 1710, the Tokugawa system was at its height. But from 1710 to 1800, financial and environmental problems stymied the Tokugawa. Population growth stalled, and a widening gap between rich and poor led to social tension.

Tokugawa Japan, 1630–1710

While the Japanese emperor remained a shadowy figure, real political power rested with the Tokugawa shoguns, the generals who constrained the autonomy of Japan's provincial lords, the daimyo. With stability enforced, seventeenth-century Japan reaped the fruits of peace.

The nation brought back into production valuable resources that had been neglected during the violence and insecurity of the sixteenth century. Farmers improved irrigation, replacing dry field agriculture with rice paddies, and proceeded to clear forests and terrace hillsides, while fishermen took greater advantage of the bounty of the surrounding seas.

The shoguns and daimyo tapped into this productive wealth through an efficient tax system based on precise surveys of land and population. Farmers, no longer subject to arbitrary taxes, had an incentive to boost production knowing that they could keep the surpluses. Mining was stimulated by the Chinese demand for silver and copper. Some of the new wealth was siphoned off by the administrative elite, but some of it also went toward the improvement of roads and irrigation works, further stimulating economic growth. An increase in coinage made possible a truly national economy.

The expansion of Japanese cities was most notable. Many castle towns, originally civil war strongholds, developed into cultural and commercial centers. The most spectacular example was the capital of Edo (ED-doe), which grew from a small village to a city of more than a million people by 1720.

A pressing social question of the early Tokugawa period was to define a peacetime role for the *samurai* warrior. Accordingly, the samurai code, or *bushido* ("the way of the warrior"), instructed samurai to cultivate both the military and civil arts, and in times of peace to emphasize the latter: "Within his heart [the samurai] keeps to the ways of peace, but … keeps his weapons ready for use. The … common people make him their teacher and respect him… . Herein lies the Way of the *samurai,* the means by which he earns his clothing, food and shelter."[7] Samurai were thus seen as intellectual and cultural leaders. They established schools, wrote Confucian treatises, and patronized the arts. But they maintained absolute allegiance to their daimyo lords, for whom they were ever ready to die.

The dynamism of the times tested boundaries. Regulations requiring rural families to be self-sufficient were widely ignored as farm families increasingly geared their production toward urban markets. Confucian strictures on women were sometimes contradicted. Elite women wrote literature, and women of other social classes also had some mobility. While women in samurai households were subject to tight patriarchal control, urban merchant and artisan families were less restrictive. Thus women participated as performers as well as audience members in new forms of dance and theater.

Tokugawa Japan and the Outside World

In foreign policy, the Tokugawa shoguns showed their conservatism by promulgating **Seclusion Edicts** that limited European contact. After the 1630s only a single annual Dutch trading mission was allowed. Bibles and Christian texts were proscribed, and Japanese were forbidden to practice Christianity or even to risk exposure to that religion through travel overseas.

But these policies of isolation were sometimes contradicted by reality. For one thing, Japanese seclusion applied only to Europeans. Trade with Chinese and Korean merchants grew even as that with the Europeans declined, and as a result Japanese foreign trade increased. Xie

Seclusion Edicts Series of edicts issued by the Tokugawa shoguns that, beginning in the 1630s, outlawed Christianity and strictly limited Japanese contact with Europeans.

Qinggao, who visited Nagasaki as a sailor, noted the high volume of Japanese exports in silver, porcelain, paper and brushes, flower vases, and dying stamps, much of it destined for Chinese markets. And while contact with Europeans was limited, the scientific and philosophical books that reached Japan through the annual Dutch trade missions—called **Dutch learning**—found an eager audience, especially among samurai.

While Dutch learning was new and exotic, Chinese influence on Japanese intellectual life was deep and well established. Xie noted that "the king wears Chinese clothes" and that "the country uses Chinese writing." Tokugawa thinkers, many of them samurai, downplayed China's influence, exalting Japan's indigenous *Shinto* religion and its emphasis on the spiritual forces of the natural and ancestral worlds. Buddhism, some argued, led to empty abstract thoughts, while Shinto connected to a tangible spirit of shared national feeling. Others further argued that Japan, not China, should be regarded as the "Middle Kingdom" because of the greater purity of its Confucian traditions.

This competitiveness was not connected to empire building. The only territorial expansion of the Tokugawa Shogunate was to the lightly populated northern islands, especially Hokkaido (ho-KIE-do), whose indigenous Ainu people lived by hunting, gathering, and fishing and were no match for Japanese weapons. After losing several battles, the Ainu were gradually disenfranchised by Japanese settlers and fishermen. Still, Hokkaido was very remote, and barely an exception to the Tokugawa policy of isolation. In contrast to Qing, Russian, and British activities in Asia, Japan simply opted out of empire building.

Challenges, Reform, and Decline, 1710–1800

In 1710 Japan was rich, populous, and united. But the eighteenth century brought new challenges. The main problem was ecological. During the seventeenth century the population of Japan had doubled to over 30 million people. Farms became smaller and smaller, and without improvements in technology or sources of energy, Japan had nearly reached its limit in food production. As in China, irrigation had led to silting up of rivers and increased danger of floods. In addition, economic growth had

depleted Japan's timber resources. Wood became more expensive, and excessive logging led to soil erosion.

In the 1720s and 1730s **Yoshimune** (r. 1716–1745), one of the greatest Tokugawa shoguns, launched a program of reform, urging frugality and curtailment of unnecessary consumption. He told the samurai to give up the ease of urban life and return to the countryside. True to the Confucian tradition, Yoshimune interpreted social problems as resulting from moral lapses. But his edicts could not change people's behavior.

Nevertheless, Yoshimune did sponsor some successful reforms. Most importantly, he reformed tax collections to eliminate local corruption, and he set strict limits on interest rates to relieve increasingly hard-pressed farmers. He also sponsored the cultivation of sugar and ginseng to replace imports from Korea and Southeast Asia while promoting the use of sweet potatoes on marginal land to increase the food supply. Support for increased fishing resulted in greater supplies of seafood and soil fertilizer.

Yoshimune also sought to bring merchants under greater government control. Increased government involvement in commerce especially suited larger trading houses that were anxious to secure government-backed monopolies. But these policies tended to undermine entrepreneurialism, and gradually they made Japanese business more regulated and monopolistic and less dynamic and inventive.

For all his effort and energy, Yoshimune's reforms only amounted to "struggling to stand still."[7] After 1750, incidents of rural unrest nearly doubled. Peasants particularly resented policies forcing them to toil on public works projects without pay. Tensions also grew in rural communities where water and timber were becoming scarcer. However, such crises did not lead to a breakdown of order, as was occurring in Mughal India. The political, economic, and cultural legacies of the Tokugawa endured far into the nineteenth century, until outside powers finally dispelled Japan's isolation and awakened its ambitions for empire (see Chapter 24).

Dutch learning Traditional Japanese title for Western knowledge. Knowledge of Dutch in Tokugawa Japan was a sign of worldliness and sophistication.

Yoshimune (1738–1795) Eighth Tokugawa ruler to hold the title of shogun. A conservative but capable leader under whose rule Japan saw advances in agricultural productivity.

Chapter Review and Learning Activities

Xie Qinggao's travels took him along the margins of great Asian empires. The Qing dynasty and the Russian Empire were extending their power further into Central Asia during Xie's lifetime, while the British East India Company was expanding its power in South Asia at the expense of the declining Mughal Empire. Japan alone retained a largely nonexpansionist policy, its dynamic, urbanizing society protected from direct contact with Europeans by its conservative rulers.

In spite of Qing, Russian, and British imperial expansion in eighteenth-century Asia, many people still lived outside the control of large states and empires, and many boundaries between states were unclear. That would change in the later nineteenth century when even more powerful and aggressive imperial forces—western European, Russian, and Japanese—would encompass the globe with empires. The stage was set for more dramatic confrontations between the powers in Asia.

How did the Qing emperors build and maintain their empire in East and Central Asia?

The Kangxi emperor and his successors were careful to emulate Chinese models of good governance to bolster their legitimacy with Han Chinese officials. Manchu rulers cultivated their image as Confucian sages while using the well-established examination system to staff the imperial bureaucracy. At the same time, the Manchu identity of the Qing emperors helped them control an immense domain and accommodate many diverse peoples besides their Han Chinese subjects. Tibetans, Mongols, and the Turkic-speaking Muslims of Xinjiang paid tribute to the Qing emperors.

What factors drove Russian imperial expansion in the eighteenth century?

In the later eighteenth century Russian leaders continued the momentum they inherited from Peter the Great. Participation in the great power politics of Europe brought Baltic regions and Poland into the empire. Continuing aggression against the Ottoman Empire resulted in new territories being added to Russian control in the Caucasus Mountains and around the Black Sea. Most dramatically, the empire grew across Siberia to the Pacific, acquiring rich resources and vast economic potential. Like the Chinese, the Russians had often been invaded by Central Asian peoples, and their expansion in that direction was at least partially a pre-emptive strike. But at least two further motivations came into play: the profitability of the Siberian fur trade and ambitions to establish the Russian state as a great power in both Europe and Asia.

What were the principal causes of the decline of Mughal power, and how were the British able to replace the Mughals as the dominant power in South Asia?

Like the Qing, the rulers of the Mughal Empire governed a diverse population, but their Islamic religion set them apart from the majority of their subjects. Aurangzeb, the last powerful Mughal emperor, deviated from the policies of his predecessors by forcefully advocating Islam, thus provoking regional resistance to Mughal authority. At the same time, ambitious local rulers, benefiting from the economic expansion that came with increased regional and global trade, were asserting their autonomy. Aurangzeb was largely successful in keeping such forces in check, but his successors, distracted by succession struggles and foreign invasions, saw power slip from their hands.

The British East Indian Company was the main beneficiary of Mughal decline. Robert Clive manipulated local Indian politics to score a seemingly implausible victory at the Battle of Plassey. Then, taking advantage of Mughal weakness, Company officials redirected part of the vast wealth of north India to their own accounts. Amid accusations of corruption, the British Parliament intervened to regularize the administration of British India by separating it from the commercial activities of the British East India Company. Thus the British government, responding to events rather than implementing a proactive program of imperial expansion, had become deeply embroiled in the political and military affairs of India. The land-based empire of the Mughals was becoming part of the sea-based empire of the British.

In comparison with the Qing, Russian, and British Empires, what were some unique features of early modern Japanese history?

The isolationism of the shoguns of Tokugawa Japan was a major exception to the rule of expanding empires in eighteenth-century Asia. Their Seclusion Edicts ran parallel to their domestic policies: in each case they intended to reinforce order, stability, and hierarchy. Still, Tokugawa society was exceptionally dynamic, characterized by economic and demographic growth, urbanization, and cultural creativity.

FOR FURTHER REFERENCE

Bayly, C. A. *Indian Society and the Making of the British Empire*. New York: Cambridge University Press, 1990.

Brower, Daniel R., and Edward J. Lazzarini. *Russia's Orient: Imperial Borderlands and Peoples, 1700–1917*. Bloomington: Indiana University Press, 1997.

Crossley, Pamela. *The Manchus*. Oxford: Blackwell Publishers, 2002.

Kappeler, Andreas. *The Russian Empire: A Multiethnic History*. Harlow, U.K.: Longman, 2001.

Keay, John. *The Honourable Company: A History of the English East India Company*. London: HarperCollins, 1991.

Matsunosuke, Nishiyama. *Edo Culture: Daily Life and Diversions in Urban Japan, 1600–1868*. Honolulu: University of Hawaii Press, 1997.

Perdue, Peter C. *China Marches West: The Qing Conquest of Central Eurasia*. Cambridge: Harvard University Press, 2005.

Richards, John. *The Mughal Empire*. New York: Cambridge University Press, 1996.

Spence, Jonathan. *Emperor of China: Self Portrait of K'ang Hsi*. New York: Knopf, 1974.

Totman, Conrad. *Early Modern Japan*. Berkeley: University of California Press, 1993.

KEY TERMS

Xie Qinggao (434)

Qing dynasty (435)

Emperor Kangxi (436)

Qianlong (437)

Yangzi River Valley (438)

Treaty of Nerchinsk (439)

Macartney Mission (440)

Cossacks (441)

Catherine the Great (441)

Aurangzeb (446)

Maratha kingdoms (446)

Nader Shah (446)

Joseph Francois Dupleix (447)

Battle of Plassey (448)

Lord Charles Cornwallis (448)

Seclusion Edicts (450)

Dutch learning (451)

Yoshimune (451)

VOYAGES ON THE WEB

Voyages: Xie Qinggao

"Voyages" is a real time excursion to historical sites in this chapter and includes interactive activities and study tools such as audio summaries, animated maps, and flashcards.

Visual Evidence: The "Floating World" of Tokugawa Japan

"Visual Evidence" features artifacts, works of art, or photographs, along with a brief descriptive essay and discussion questions to guide your analysis of visual sources.

World History in Today's World: The Train to Tibet

"World History in Today's World" makes the connection between features of modern life and their origins in the periods in this chapter.

Go to the CourseMate website at www.cengagebrain.com for additional study tools and review materials—including audio and video clips—for this chapter.

21

European Science and the Foundations of Modern Imperialism, 1600–1820

Joseph Banks
(Private Collection/The Bridgeman Art Library)

When the young British botanist **Joseph Banks** (1743–1820) sailed on the first European expedition to cross the Pacific Ocean in 1769–1771, on the ship *Endeavor* commanded by Captain Cook, his interest went beyond flora and fauna to include the people he encountered on the voyage. From the Amerindians of Tierra del Fuego (the southern tip of South America), to the Polynesians of the Pacific, to the Aboriginal peoples of Australia, Banks kept careful notes of his interactions with peoples of whom Europeans had little previous knowledge. His concern with these cultures went beyond mere curiosity. He was interested in understanding the relationships *between* societies. For example, when Banks learned that Tahitians understood the speech of the Maori **(MAO-ree)** of New Zealand, he recognized that there was a family connection between the two peoples. Banks was a pioneer of *ethnography*, the study of the linguistic and cultural relationships between peoples. Banks was also mystified by the behavior of the Polynesian people he and his shipmates met when they stepped ashore on the island of Tahiti:

Though at first they hardly dared approach us, after a little time they became very familiar. The first who approached us came crawling almost on his hands and knees and gave us a green bough.... This we received and immediately each of us gathered a green bough and carried it in our hands. They marched with us about ½ a mile and then made a general stop and, scraping the ground clean ... every one of them threw

Joseph Banks explores Newfoundland, 1766.

Banks leaves England on the Endeavor, 1768.

Death of Cook, 1779.

RUSSIAN EMPIRE

EUROPE

ASIA

NORTH AMERICA

Banks I.

ALASKA

RUPERT'S LAND

CANADA

THIRTEEN COLONIES

ATLANTIC OCEAN

OTTOMAN EMPIRE

AFRICA

PERSIA

ARABIA

Senegal R.

Niger R.

Nile R.

Segu

DAHOMEY

Cape Coast Castle

Mombasa

HIMALAYAS

Mt. Everest

Calcutta

Bombay

Goa

INDIA

Madras

Ceylon

QING EMPIRE

JAPAN

Manila

Philippine Is.

Batavia

EAST INDIES

Great Barrier Reef

NEW HOLLAND (AUSTRALIA)

Botany Bay

PACIFIC OCEAN

Sandwich (Hawaiian) Is.

Tahiti

VICEROYALTY OF NEW SPAIN

V. OF NEW GRANADA

VICEROYALTY OF BRAZIL

V. OF PERU

SOUTH AMERICA

V. OF RIO DE LA PLATA

Rio de Janeiro

Cape Town

INDIAN OCEAN

North I.

New Zealand

South I.

Tierra del Fuego

Cape Horn

0 1,000 2,000 Km.
0   1,000   2,000 Mi.

ANTARCTICA

The Travels of Joseph Banks

- → Joseph Banks's journeys
- → Later journeys by Cook
- • City visited by Banks
- • Other city

European territories, ca. 1770
- British
- Dutch
- French
- Portuguese
- Russian
- Spanish

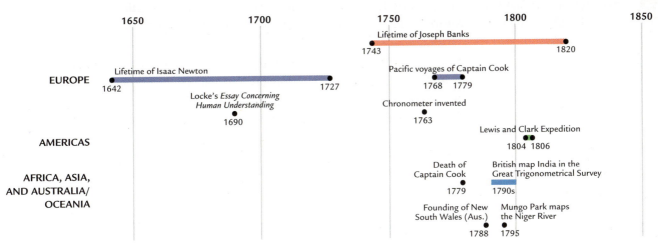

Timeline:

1650   1700   1750   1800   1850

EUROPE

Lifetime of Isaac Newton
1642 — 1727

Locke's *Essay Concerning Human Understanding*
1690

Lifetime of Joseph Banks
1743 — 1820

Pacific voyages of Captain Cook
1768 — 1779

Chronometer invented
1763

AMERICAS

Lewis and Clark Expedition
1804 1806

AFRICA, ASIA, AND AUSTRALIA/ OCEANIA

Death of Captain Cook
1779

British map India in the Great Trigonometrical Survey
1790s

Founding of New South Wales (Aus.)
1788

Mungo Park maps the Niger River
1795

Join this chapter's traveler on "Voyages," an interactive tour of historic sites and events: www.cengagebrain.com

455

his bough down upon the bare place and made signs that we should do the same…. Each of us dropped a bough upon those that the Indians had laid down, we all followed their example and thus peace was concluded.[1]

Joseph Banks (1743–1820) English botanist on Captain James Cook's first voyage in the Pacific who categorized different species of plants and brought them back to England. Also established the Royal Botanic Gardens at Kew.

Such ceremonies became a bit less mysterious to Banks after he began to learn the Tahitian language and made friends with a high priest who helped him understand Polynesian customs. Still, even after years of contact, the cultural gulf between the Tahitians and the Englishmen remained immense.

Banks returned to England in 1771 after a three-year journey. The crewmen who had survived the *Endeavour*'s three years at sea were among the few who had ever sailed around the entire world. Captain Cook became an instant celebrity. He had accomplished his mission of charting the Pacific Ocean, thus facilitating future European voyages to such places as Hawai'i, New Zealand, and Australia. He had also carried out important astronomical observations.

In fact, scientific inquiry was central to the *Endeavour*'s mission. The drawings and specimens of plant and animal life Banks brought back greatly expanded European knowledge of the natural world. He was interested not merely in collecting exotic flora and fauna but also in systematically classifying and cataloging his findings. While Cook was using his mathematical and navigational skills to chart the oceans, Banks was developing a system for naming and describing natural phenomena in order to clarify familial relationships in nature.

Why was Banks taken on board the *Endeavour* in the first place? There was no immediate, tangible benefit from his work. But science now enjoyed considerable social and political support. Especially in Britain and France, leaders understood the connection between science and empire. Banks's reconnaissance of the natural world, like that of the physical world undertaken by Cook, was a prelude to the more assertive European imperialism of the nineteenth century. While Polynesians were struggling to understand what they saw as the strange behavior of their British visitors, Cook was claiming their islands "for the use of his Brittanick majesty." Banks came home dreaming of "future dominions," becoming an influential advocate of British settlement in Australia.[2] Science and empire would remain companions throughout the nineteenth century.

After the return of the *Endeavour* Banks never again traveled outside Europe. But from 1778 to 1820, as president of the Royal Society, the most prestigious scientific establishment in Europe, he focused on fields such as "economic botany," which linked science to technological and economic development. At the same time, men and women more philosophically inclined than Banks were extending the scientific model of inquiry, with its emphasis on reason, to human society, creating what is called the European Enlightenment.

FOCUS QUESTIONS

▶ When and how did Europe's Scientific Revolution begin to have practical applications?

▶ How did Enlightenment thought derive from the Scientific Revolution, and how did it differ from previous European thought systems?

▶ How did systematic classification and measurement support European imperialism in the late eighteenth and early nineteenth centuries?

▶ How did the societies of Oceania and Australia experience encounters with Europeans in this period?

From Scientific Revolution to Practical Science, 1600–1800

Joseph Banks was heir to a tradition that stretched back to the sixteenth century, when Nicolaus Copernicus first published his theory of a heliocentric solar system and Galileo Galilei upset church authorities by providing strong evidence that the earth rotates around the sun (see Chapter 16). Although for most Europeans the Christian faith still held most of the answers to basic questions, by the eighteenth century, men and women who embraced rational inquiry were becoming increasingly prominent in Europe. Often with the aid of royal patronage, they began to pursue the "new science."

The development of science was important not only from a purely intellectual standpoint. Science became "revolutionary" as its practical applications enhanced the political and military power of Europe on the world stage. In his own research and as a national leader in science, Joseph Banks contributed to developments linking scientific progress to real-world applications and economic purposes.

The Development of the Scientific Method

In seventeenth-century western Europe, thinkers divided into two camps: the "ancients" and the "moderns." The "ancients" emphasized the authority of Aristotle and other classical authors as the foundation on which knowledge in fields such as medicine, mathematics, and astronomy should be built. The "moderns" had a bolder idea.

Rejecting the infallibility of both classical authority and Christian theology, the "moderns" argued that human reason provided the key to knowledge. Their viewpoint contradicted the Christian idea of humanity as "fallen," tainted by original sin, and capable of salvation only through God's mercy. The "moderns" believed instead that humankind was endowed by God with reason and could, through that reason, apprehend the truth. "All our knowledge begins with the senses, proceeds then to understanding, and ends with reason. There is nothing higher than

René Descartes (1596–1650) French scientist, mathematician, and philosopher who developed the deductive method of reasoning, moving from general principles to particular facts.

Sir Francis Bacon (1561–1626) English politician, essayist, and philosopher. Known for his *Novum Organum* (1620), in which he argues for inductive reasoning and the rejection of *a priori* hypotheses. His science was based on close observation of natural phenomena.

Isaac Newton (1642–1727) Skilled theoretical and experimental scientist who did more than anyone to create a new, systematic architecture for science: the universal law of gravitation. One of the inventors of differential calculus, he also undertook extensive experiments with optics.

📟 **Primary Source**
Sir Isaac Newton Lays Down the Ground Rules for the Scientific Method *Newton provides four detailed rules that define the principles of the Scientific Method.*

reason," wrote the eighteenth-century German philosopher Immanuel Kant.[3]

One seventeenth-century thinker who used a *deductive* approach to truth was the Frenchman **René Descartes** (1596–1650). Descartes (**DAY-cart**) argued that the axioms of true philosophy had to be grounded in human reason. He associated rationality with mathematics and thought that logic could produce truth. Upholding doubt as the key to knowledge, he began by questioning even his own existence. His deduction, "I think, therefore I am," expresses his faith that reason is at the core of existence. Descartes also had to doubt the existence of God before he could prove to his own satisfaction that God did, in fact, exist. That proof, too, derived from rational thought rather than accepted truths or sacred texts.

Descartes is considered a philosopher and not a scientist because his works were based on introspection rather than observation of the objective world. At the same time, others were laying the foundations for modern science based on experimentation and the observation of nature. The Englishman **Sir Francis Bacon** (1561–1626) was one of the main proponents of an *inductive* approach to science: working from modest, carefully controlled observations toward larger truths. Like Descartes, Bacon believed that doubt produced knowledge. "If a man will begin with certainties," he wrote, "he shall end in doubts; but if he will be content to begin with doubts he shall end in certainties."[4] Both Descartes and Bacon contributed to an intellectual trend in western Europe that emphasized belief in the ability of human reason to strive

toward God's truth on the basis of science. (See the feature "Movement of Ideas: A Japanese View of European Science.")

The Englishman **Isaac Newton** (1642–1727) was a gifted experimentalist in Bacon's inductive tradition. His work in optics, for example, led to important improvements in telescopes. But he was pre-eminently a theorist who followed Descartes' lead in using deductive reasoning to establish general principles. To achieve the mathematical rigor necessary to describe the acceleration and deceleration of bodies in motion, Newton invented a differential calculus. Using the calculus to analyze observations of planetary motion, he arrived at the conclusion that all matter exerts gravitational attraction, proportional to its mass and the distance between it and another object. Newton's universal law of gravitation was a breakthrough in human understanding of the natural world.

Whereas the new science had earlier caused anxiety by calling faith into question, by the early eighteenth century an English poet could write: "Nature and Nature's laws lay hid in night; God said Let Newton Be! and all was light."[5] Newton himself was a devout Christian. While many Christians continued to believe that God actively intervened in nature, those who adopted Newton's outlook tended to see the universe as a self-functioning outcome of God's perfect act of creation. God was a clock maker who, having set his machine in motion, interfered no further.

Newton confidently declared that he could use mathematics to "demonstrate the frame of the system of the world." Joseph Banks inherited not only Newton's optimism but also his position as president of the Royal Society, an assembly of leading thinkers. Starting with Newton and continuing with Banks, the Royal Society served as a nerve center for European science.

Practical Science: Economic Botany, Agriculture, and Empire

Studying plant life is characteristic of all cultures. Reliant on their surroundings for medicine as well as for food, people have always

Bildarchiv Preussischer Kulturbesitz/Art Resource, NY

Advances in Astronomy   Apart from Galileo and Newton, many other European scientists were involved in the quest for astronomical knowledge. Here the Danish astronomer Tycho Brahe is depicted in the observatory from which he made the most detailed stellar observations since ancient Greek times. The German mathematician Johannes Kepler used Brahe's data to support the Copernican view of a sun-centered universe.

sought an intimate knowledge of their natural environment. With the rise of modern botany, scientists began to collect and catalogue the world's flora systematically.

Carl Linnaeus (1707–1778) was the pioneering figure in this area. As a medical student, Linnaeus studied plants for their medicinal properties, but as his enthusiasm for plant collecting grew, he enlarged his focus. He traveled across Sweden gathering plant specimens, restored the botanical gardens at his university, and eventually sent nineteen of his students around the world to gather specimens for study. Two of Linnaeus's students were aboard the *Endeavour* with Joseph Banks.

Carl Linnaeus (1707–1778) Swedish founder of the modern systems of botany and zoology. The basic parameters of his classification systems are still in use.

A Japanese View of European Science

In the history of modern science, a common pattern has been repeated around the world. Those who generated new ideas, such as Galileo, were often attacked for their assault on tradition, but later their innovations were absorbed into the European status quo. When Europeans then took the new science to other continents, once again these ideas and approaches challenged established tradition. Here we have an example from anatomy, with a Japanese observation of the dissection of a human corpse.

For medieval Europeans the main authority in anatomy was the ancient Greek physician Galen, who, though he dissected many birds and animals, had theories about the inner workings of the human body that were based largely on speculation. Then, in 1543, a Belgian physician published a new scheme of human anatomy based on actual dissection of human cadavers. Adherents of Galen's view were upset, as were those many Christians who saw the violation of dead bodies as sacrilegious. Over the next two hundred years, however, dissection became a routine process.

In the eighteenth century, the Tokugawa shoguns had severely limited Japanese contacts with Europeans. But through the annual Dutch trade mission to Nagasaki a few books entered the country, and some curious Japanese scholars learned Dutch so they could read them (see Chapter 20). Below, a physician named Sugita Gempaku (1733–1817) describes how, having looked at a Dutch anatomy text, he was astonished to see how accurate it was when he witnessed the dissection of a human body.

A Dutch Lesson in Anatomy

Somehow, miraculously I obtained a [Dutch] book on anatomy. [Then] I received a letter from … the Town Commissioner: "A post-mortem examination of the body of a condemned criminal by a resident physician will be held tomorrow…. You are welcome to witness it if you so desire."

The next day, when we arrived at the location … Ryotaku reached under his kimono to produce a Dutch book and showed it to us. "This is a Dutch book of anatomy called *Tabulae Anatomicae*. I bought this a few years ago when I went to Nagasaki, and kept it." As I examined it, it was the same book I had and was of the same edition. We held each other's hands and exclaimed: "What a coincidence!" Ryotaku continued by saying, "When I went to Nagasaki, I learned and heard," and opened this book. "These are called *long* in Dutch, they are the lungs," he taught us. "This is *hart,* or the heart." … However, they did not look like the heart given in the Chinese medical books, and none of us were sure until we could actually see the dissection.

Thereafter we went together to the place that was especially set aside us to observe the dissection…. That day, the butcher pointed to this and that organ. After the heart, liver, gall bladder and stomach were identified, he pointed to other parts for which there were no names. "I don't know their names. But I have dissected quite a few bodies from my youthful days…. Every time I had a dissection, I pointed out to those physicians many of these parts, but not a single one of them questioned 'What was this,' or 'What was that?'" We compared the body as dissected against the charts both Ryotaku and I had, and could not find a single variance from the charts. The Chinese *Book of Medicine* says that the lungs are like the eight petals of the lotus flower, with three petals hanging in front, three in back, and two petals forming like two ears.... There were no such divisions, and the position and shapes of intestines and gastric organs were all different from those taught by the old theories. The official physicians ... had witnessed dissection seven or eight times. Whenever they witnessed the dissection, they found that the old theories contradicted reality. Each time they were perplexed and could not resolve their doubts. Every time they wrote down what they thought was strange. They wrote in their books, "The more we think of it, there must be fundamental differences in the bodies of Chinese and of the eastern barbarians." I could see why they wrote this way....

We decided that we should also examine the shape of the skeletons left exposed on the execution ground. We collected the bones, and examined a number of them. Again, we were struck by the fact that they all differed from the old theories while conforming to the Dutch charts....

On the way home we spoke to each other and felt the same way. "How marvelous was our actual experience today. It is a shame that we were ignorant of these things until now. As physicians ... we performed our duties in complete ignorance of the true form of the human body." ... Then I spoke to my companion, "Somehow if we can translate anew this book called *Tabulae Anatomicae*, we can get a clear notion of the human body inside out. It will have great benefit in the treatment of our patients. Let us do our best to read it and understand it without the help of translators." ...

The next day, we assembled at the house of Ryotaku and recalled the happenings of the previous day. When we faced the *Tabulae Anatomicae* we felt as if we were setting sail on a great ocean in a ship without oars or a rudder. With the magnitude of the work before us, we were dumbfounded by our own ignorance.... At that time I did not know the twenty-five letters of the Dutch alphabet. I decided to study the language with firm determination, but I had to acquaint myself with letters and words gradually.

Source: From David J. Lu, editor and translator, *Japan: A Documentary History,* M.E. Sharpe, 1997, pp. 264–266. Reprinted with permission of David Lu.

QUESTIONS FOR ANALYSIS

▶ **What was the basis of earlier Japanese views of anatomy, and how were they contradicted by the Dutch textbook?**

▶ **How does Gempaku's experience compare with that of "The Travels of Evliya Çelebi" (see Chapter 17)?**

In 1735 Linnaeus published his classification of living things, *Systema Naturae*. His system classified species using hierarchal categories: genus/order/class/kingdom. Thus, any new plant from anywhere in the world could be classified in a way that, to Linnaeus, revealed the divine order of God's creation.

Linnaeus also developed a "binomial" ("two name") system for giving organisms consistent Latin names, the first name indicating the genus and the second the species. Now, as new species were discovered, they received names that made them part of a single knowledge system.

Linnaeus knew of Banks, and after the return of the *Endeavour* he sent Banks a letter of congratulations. Linnaeus's attempts to acclimatize valuable foreign plants to grow in Sweden's cold climate were largely unsuccessful. But economic botany was an area in which Banks excelled.

Banks was a leading figure in the drive for "improvement," which in agriculture meant using scientific methods to increase the productivity of existing land and bring new land under cultivation. Since the seventeenth century, English farmers had learned to improve the soil by sowing clover and turnips in fields that had previously been left fallow. They also practiced selective breeding of livestock to boost the production of wool, meat, and milk.

The Dutch pioneered a technique of reclaiming low-lying land by using windmills to pump water from marshes impounded within dikes. Joseph Banks was among the "gentleman farmers" in England who could afford to invest in this technology to drain farmland for production. Banks's estate exemplified all the measures that were improving agricultural productivity in eighteenth-century England: the draining of marshes, experiments with crop rotations, and crossbreeding of farm animals. The net effect was an "agricultural revolution."

Since draining land was expensive, farmland in Holland remained scarce. Nevertheless, land distribution was fairly egalitarian. In England, by contrast, the agricultural revolution caused inequality. As the rural gentry consolidated larger, more efficient farms, poorer rural families were driven off the land.

Like peasant societies elsewhere, English village society was oriented toward stability and security. For example, farm families shared common access to pastures and woodlands. But in the seventeenth and eighteenth centuries, as members of the English gentry, like the Banks family, accumulated landholdings, new laws allowed them to "enclose" common lands as private property, in what is called the enclosure movement.

Having lost access to the commons, rural families were forced to either work for the gentry or move elsewhere. One person's "improvement," therefore, could be another's ticket to unemployment. Banks himself received numerous protests from displaced farmers, and his London house was once attacked by protesters of a trade law that benefited landholders like Banks while raising the price of bread for the poor. The interests of "gentlemen" were represented in Parliament, but those of average Londoners were not.

Joseph Banks played a pivotal role in globalizing the practical application of science through his advocacy of "economic botany." To this end he developed a pioneering experimental facility at Kew Gardens, "a great botanical exchange house for the empire."[6] New plant specimens from around the world were brought to Kew to be examined, catalogued, and cultivated, and the benefits of this "economic botany" were then disseminated both within Britain and throughout the expanding British Empire. In such places as the West Indies, South Africa, and India, botanical gardens were established by British governors and commercial concerns as part of the effort to achieve "improvement" on a global scale. Unlike the haphazard Columbian exchange, this was biological diffusion aided by science. For example, when the British navy needed secure supplies of timber from tall trees for ship construction, English botanists identified South Asian mahogany as a possible supplement to British and North American oak and shipped seeds from India to botanical gardens in the British West Indies for study. Another example is the story of merino sheep, which Banks imported from Spain for crossbreeding purposes to improve British wool. While this experiment was not successful in England, merino sheep formed the basis of the early colonial economy of British Australia.

Botany and Art Most scientific expeditions, starting with Banks's own journey to the Pacific and Australia, employed artists to catalogue in fine detail the new flora they encountered. This exquisite rendering of a Corypha Elata plant, native to northern Australia, was produced by an anonymous Indian artist employed by the British.

The emphasis on science and "improvement" also served to justify the dominance of the English elite at home and abroad. Advocates of the enclosure movement argued that those who were thrust aside would ultimately benefit from scientifically rational agriculture. The same attitude applied across the empire. Aboriginal Australians might not understand the necessity of fencing off vast land holdings for sheep—thus barring them from their ancestral lands—but no one, the "improvers" said, should stand in the way of progress.

Francis Bacon, the great proponent of experimental science, had first applied the idea of bringing improvement to colonized peoples to Ireland:

> [We shall] reclaim them from their barbarous manners … populate, plant and make civil all the provinces of that kingdom … as we are persuaded that it is one of the chief causes for which God hath brought us to the imperial crown of these Kingdoms.[7]

By Banks's day the emphasis on God's will had lessened; the stress was now on the fulfillment of the earth's potential in accordance with a beneficent natural order. But the message was the same: we must "reclaim" land from "barbarous" people to make it more productive. Banks wrote, after the founding of a botanical garden in Calcutta, that economic botany "would help to banish famine in India and win the love of the Asiatics for their British conquerors."[8] The connection between science and empire was explicit.

The European Enlightenment, 1700–1800

Optimism about science influenced views on society as well. During the eighteenth century, **Enlightenment** thinkers argued that the same capacity that allows scientists to unlock the secrets of nature could also be applied to social, political, and economic questions. Just as the inner workings of nature could be understood by human reason and described with mathematical precision, so Enlightenment philosophers saw reason as the best means of understanding and improving society. By the late eighteenth century, progress in human affairs seemed not only possible, but inevitable.

For lofty ideals to find application in society, they need to influence those in power, and Enlightenment philosophy did impress Europe's kings, queens, and aristocracies. But there were limits to how far "enlightened" rulers would follow through on reform. Few rulers were willing to undermine the traditions that gave them power.

"Enlightened" Ideas: Politics, Economics, and Society

The contrast between two English political philosophers, Thomas Hobbes (1588–1679) and John Locke (1632–1704), demonstrates the growing optimism of the Enlightenment. A friend of René Descartes, Hobbes, applied deductive reasoning to the question of how best to sustain political order in human society. In the state of nature, he observed, anarchy prevails, and life is "nasty, brutish, and short."[9] Social and political order, he argued, becomes possible only when individuals relinquish their autonomy to a ruler. Hobbes rejected the "divine right of kings," however, and based his advocacy for absolute monarchy on reasoned arguments instead.

While Hobbes had used Descartes' method of deductive reasoning starting from axiomatic principles, **John Locke** (1632–1704) was a medical doctor who preferred Bacon's inductive approach, starting with experience and observation. His conclusions could not have been more different. In his *Essay Concerning Human Understanding* (1690), Locke argued that political order derives from a contract in which individuals receive protection of their basic rights, "life, liberty and property," while they voluntarily give up some of their autonomy to the state, which was itself balanced between executive and legislative authorities. What Locke described was not full democracy: in his view only propertied males were capable of participating in government. But the rights of all would be protected regardless of gender or social class.

Hobbes's pessimism derived from witnessing the anarchy of the English Civil War, while Locke's optimism was connected to the role he played as an adviser to King William and Queen Mary during the Glorious Revolution (see Chapter 17). The balance between the powers of king and Parliament, and the protection of individual liberties through a Bill of Rights, were real-world applications of Locke's theories.

A French thinker who was influenced by English constitutional thought was the Baron de Montesquieu (1689–1755), who traveled to England to observe its very different constitutional system. His book *The Spirit of the Laws* (1748) argues for limitations on the power of government and a rational distribution of power between different social classes. Montesquieu (maw-tuh-SKYOO) believed that, as societies became more advanced, their political systems would become more liberal and their people more free. Following Locke, who argued that executive and legislative powers should be separate and balanced, Montesquieu maintained that judicial functions should also be protected from executive interference.

The most original economic thinker of the Enlightenment was Adam Smith, whose *Wealth of Nations* (1776) emphasizes the self-regulating power of markets. Smith argued for the encouragement of free markets and unfettered economic interchange within and between nations. The French term *laissez faire* (lay-say fair) has often been applied to Smith's vision of free-market capitalism. He argued that economic productivity is based on a division of labor. If a work process is subdivided among workers, each specializing in one aspect of production, Smith argued, more can be produced in a day. He applied the same principle to international trade. If each nation specializes in the production of what it is best fit to produce, and trades with other nations specializing in products best fitted to their economic

Enlightenment European philosophical movement of the late seventeenth and eighteenth centuries that stressed the use of reason rather than the authority of ancient philosophers or religious leaders in descriptions of society and the natural world.

John Locke (1632–1704) Philosopher who applied Bacon's inductive reasoning to the study of politics and argued that a stable social order is based on a contract between rulers and ruled and requires the safeguarding of "life, liberty and property."

laissez faire (French, "leave to do") Economic philosophy attributed to Scottish Enlightenment thinker Adam Smith, who argued that businesses and nations benefit from a free market where each party seeks to maximize its comparative economic advantage.

potential, everyone gains. Smith was opposed to slavery because he thought that labor contracts negotiated in a free market lead to more efficient production. He believed that the "invisible hand" of the market functioned like Isaac Newton's laws of gravitational attraction, maintaining balance and harmony in economic affairs. Like Locke, he believed that protection of private property was a core function of government.

Smith's advocacy of the free market contradicted existing European policies based on monopoly and mercantilism. Like other Enlightenment thinkers, Smith was using reason to challenge existing assumptions. And whereas mercantilism had been based on a zero-sum view of economics, in which one nation could advance only at another's expense, Smith held the more optimistic view that freer international trade would lead to more wealth for all.

While philosophers across Europe aspired to the title "enlightened," it was through Paris that the intellectual currents of the Western world flowed. Indeed, we still use the French word for philosophers, *philosophes* (fill-uh-SOHF), to describe these intellectuals today. The most important of them was François-Marie Arouet, better known as Voltaire (1694–1778). Voltaire (vawl-TARE) was famous as a satirist who used his reason to spotlight the superstitions, prejudices, and follies of eighteenth-century European society. In his novel *Candide* (1759), he mocked the corruption and injustice of the world around him. He believed that reason makes all phenomena and situations intelligible, and that seeing yourself in a wider context is a necessary component of enlightened thinking, since understanding others is a precondition for self-knowledge. Voltaire incurred the displeasure of religious authorities by arguing that organized religion is always and everywhere a hindrance to free and rational inquiry.

Enlightenment ideas were discussed passionately in the *salons* (drawing rooms) of Paris. Often hosted by women of means and education, these salons brought philosophical and artistic discussions into the homes of the elite; Voltaire and other notable philosophers were highly sought after guests. But though women often organized and participated in these gatherings, few

Enlightenment thinkers were ready to recognize that the restrictions on the role of women in society were a matter of custom, not reason.

Some women protested their exclusion. A seventeenth-century English scientist, Margaret Cavendish, noted that restrictions on women's roles resulted from nothing more than "the over-weening conceit men have of themselves."[10] Another Englishwoman, Mary Astell, challenged John Locke's idea that absolute authority, while unacceptable in the state, was appropriate within the family. Late in the eighteenth century Mary Wollenstonecraft went even further in her *Vindication of the Rights of Women* (1792). Only through equal access to education, full citizenship, and financial autonomy, Wollenstonecraft said, could women's full potential as individuals and as wives and mothers be achieved.

For the elite who attended salons, arguing about daring ideas was mostly a matter of fashion. At the other end of society, Enlightenment ideas were of little concern to tradesmen and farmers, people whom Voltaire and most other philosophes considered irrational and tradition-bound. Of all the classes, Enlightenment thought had the greatest impact on the *bourgeoisie,* or middle class.

The French bourgeoisie were economically successful but lacked the social status and political rights of aristocrats. Skepticism toward authority thus came naturally to them. Expanding literacy meant that even those who did not travel in the refined circles, and who might never be invited to a salon, nevertheless had access to these ideas. The most important publishing project of the age was the *Encyclopedia*, or *Rational Dictionary of the Arts, Sciences and Crafts,* initially compiled under the direction of Denis Diderot. More than any other work, this encyclopedia made the case for a new form of universal knowledge based on reason and critical intelligence.

Primary Source: Treatise on Toleration *Voltaire makes a powerful argument for cultural and religious tolerance.*

philosophes French intellectuals who promoted Enlightenment principles.

Encyclopedia A collection of the works of all the great Enlightenment thinkers. Compiled in Paris between 1751 and 1776, it promoted a new form of universal knowledge based on reason and the critical use of human intellect.

Division of Rare Books & Manuscripts Collection, Cornell University

The *Encyclopedia*   Denis Diderot, the leading figure behind the *Encyclopedia*, aspired to collect all scientific and philosophical information in one publication. Essays numbering 70,000 were accompanied by 3,000 illustrations, including "The Print Shop" shown here. The original essays were widely translated, spreading Enlightenment ideas across Europe.

The growth of the publishing industry facilitated the dissemination of the *Encyclopedia,* and translation into English, Spanish, and German gave it international impact.

The German philosopher Immanuel Kant (1724–1804) emphasized that cowardice stood in the way of enlightenment. Unquestioned tradition, "man's inability to make use of his understanding without direction from another," hinders our progress. "Have courage to use your own reason," Kant concluded; "that is the motto of enlightenment."[11] But translating that motto into political reality meant confronting powerful vested interests, with radical, and ultimately revolutionary, implications.

enlightened despots
Eighteenth-century European rulers who sought to systematically apply Enlightenment ideals to the administration of government.

"Enlightened Despots" in Eighteenth-Century Europe

Most philosophes thought that if society were to become enlightened, the change would have to come from above. That provided some monarchs, so-called **enlightened despots**, a new rationale for absolute power. Rather than simply claiming "divine right," they portrayed themselves as bringing order, harmony, and reason to their domains. In the late seventeenth century, Louis XIV is supposed to have said, "I am the state." Now in the eighteenth century, Frederick the Great of Prussia (r. 1740–1786) defined himself as "first servant of the state," a crucial difference.

Frederick was perhaps the most "enlightened" of the great monarchs of the eighteenth century. He studied music and literature as a young man and became a first-rate flute player. His patronage made Prussia, previously considered only a military power, a center for the arts. Frederick absorbed French literature and the ideas of the philosophes. After meeting in 1750, he and Voltaire maintained a correspondence, trading philosophical ideas. He reformed the Prussian legal system, advocated freedom of conscience, and allowed some freedom of the press. However, Prussia's military ethic continued, and it remained a tightly regimented society. Prussian territory doubled in size as its army became one of the largest and strongest in Europe.

Enlightenment influenced monarchs elsewhere. The Austrian Empress Maria Theresa (r. 1740–1780) undertook significant reforms. She put strict limits on landlords' power and was also the first European monarch to call for compulsory public education. Maria Theresa's son, Joseph II (r. 1780–1790), carried reform forward, abolishing serfdom and liberalizing restrictions on the press and religion. Some Austrians did not approve of Joseph's autocratic methods, but public approval was not Joseph's concern, nor a concern of any other "enlightened despot."

In Russia, Catherine the Great also took an interest in Enlightenment philosophy and corresponded with Voltaire. She found Enlightenment ideals enticing in theory, but not in her political practice. Under Catherine's rule the power of the Russian aristocracy over their serfs became greater than ever. Russia remained the least open and least liberal of the European great powers.

In France, King Louis XV (r. 1715–1774) had inherited not only great power from his great-grandfather Louis XIV, but also difficult challenges. Louis XV was only five years old when he came to the throne and did not take command until the 1740s. While his mistress entertained philosophes, Louis contended with such matters of state as the loss of the Seven Years' War to England (see Chapter 19). Wishing to reform his country's finances, he was blocked by vested interests: the French nobility refused to pay any taxes at all.

In Britain, the constitutional balance of power established in 1689 prevented any kind of despotism, enlightened or otherwise. The Scottish and English thrones were peacefully united to form Great Britain in 1707, and parliamentary factions developed into organized political parties. In 1714 a reliably Protestant German prince was crowned King George I. Speaking little English, George I accepted the powers of Parliament and hence the limitations on his own power. Some challenges went unmet: restrictions on the civil rights of British Catholics remained, and attempts to reform the House of Commons to increase the representation of merchants and professionals such as doctors and lawyers failed. Nevertheless, as the century progressed, constitutional and parliamentary government in Britain evolved. Elsewhere in Europe, however, the eventual failure of "enlightened despots" to substantially reform their societies would lead to conflict and revolution (see Chapter 22).

Measuring and Mapping: Exploration and Imperialism in Africa, India, and the Americas, 1763–1820

Enlightenment thinkers sought to apply science's mathematical outlook to all things. In an age of expanding European empires, this quest for quantification had global implications. In the late eighteenth and early nineteenth centuries, the measurement of time and the mapping of space forged permanent links between science and empire.

Global control required detailed knowledge of world geography, and Europeans developed procedures and technologies to acquire that knowledge. For navigators the main challenge was the "problem of longitude," the need to find a way to accurately establish a ship's position on an east/west axis. As European expeditions gathered geographical information across Africa, India, and the Americas, and communicated that knowledge through scientific societies back home, the power of Europe expanded. The "future dominions" of which Joseph Banks dreamed at the time of the *Endeavour*'s journey were, by the early 1800s, becoming a reality.

Practical Science, the Royal Society, and the Quest for Longitude

As a natural scientist, Banks was most competent in the field of living organisms. Within the Royal Society over which he presided from 1778 to 1820, many saw mathematics and astronomy as the superior sciences. Whether dealing with flora and fauna or with calculus and planetary orbits, however, all scientists were interested in practical applications of their theories. For a nation in ascendance on the basis of its maritime prowess, the most important applications of mathematics and astronomy concerned navigation. The **problem of longitude** occupied the best minds of the time.

The basic problem had puzzled mariners for much of human history. The best way to describe the location of any given point is with a set of imaginary intersecting lines that we know as latitude and longitude. Lines of latitude, determining position along a north/south axis, are easy to fix by observing natural phenomena, such as the height of the sun or familiar stars above the horizon. In the Middle Ages, Arab sailors introduced the quadrant and astrolabe (**AS-truh-labe**), navigational tools that gave captains a way to chart latitude.

More difficult was to determine longitude, the relative position of a point on an east/west axis. Distance traveled in this direction could be determined if the time at any two points could be accurately compared. Until the late eighteenth century, ships' captains had no better solution than setting a log adrift and charting its motion to roughly calculate the speed and distance traveled. By this system captains often miscalculated their position by hundreds of miles, and the toll in shipwrecks, lost lives, and cargo

problem of longitude   The lack of an accurate means of determining a ship's position on an east/west axis. The problem was solved with the invention of an accurate shipboard chronometer by English cabinetmaker John Harrison.

was great. Equally tragic was the suffering, including loss of life from dehydration and scurvy, that resulted when ships wandered endlessly looking for land, unsure how far away it was or whether it lay to the east or to the west.

The regular, clocklike cosmos described by scientists from Galileo to Newton offered hope. Longitude could be accurately fixed if a captain knew exactly what time it was on board relative to any other fixed location on earth. Observing that the motion of the heavens could be described mathematically, European scientists set out to find a way to translate celestial time into local time on board a ship. To do so, they would have to strictly predict the positions of two known heavenly points—the sun, the moon, or a star—for one location on earth and then compared those with their actual position on a ship.

The problem was that very few celestial events could be predicted with any certainty. Lunar and solar eclipses could be used this way, but they occurred too rarely to be useful. Galileo had shown that the moons of Jupiter eclipsed on a regular and predictable basis. If the timing of these eclipses could be charted, a ship's captain could compare the known time of the eclipse at a fixed location (such as his port of departure) and the actual observation of the eclipse at sea to determine his longitude. The system worked well on land, but at sea the method was impractical. The movement of the ship made it nearly impossible to keep the moons of Jupiter in telescopic vision while the calculations were made.

For a maritime power like England, the "problem of longitude" became a matter of public policy. So valuable was a solution to this problem that in 1714 the British Parliament offered a cash prize to anyone who could solve it, but for decades none were worthy of serious consideration. In popular speech, "discovering the longitude" came to mean "attempting the impossible."

But the astronomers in the Royal Society were persistent. The key to the problem, Isaac Newton believed, was to determine the "lunar distance" by finding a way to accurately measure the position of the moon relative to the sun by day, and to the stars by night. All that were needed were sky charts by which the future locations of these heavenly bodies could be accurately predicted. Astronomers spent hundreds of thousands of hours working on these charts. The problem was made even more complicated because a separate star chart would be needed for the entirely different night sky of the Southern Hemisphere.

By the 1760s the astronomers and mathematicians in the Royal Society were close to a solution. The role of the *Endeavour,* which set out in 1769, was to observe the movement of Venus across the face of the sun, an event that occurred every eight years. By making identical observations in a wide variety of geographic locations, of which Cook's was by far the farthest from the Royal Observatory at Greenwich, astronomers would be able to predict much more accurately the future path of Venus. The solar, lunar, and stellar charts available to Cook on this journey were already much better than any other captain had ever used in the Pacific.

Meanwhile, there was another, potentially simpler solution: using a clock that accurately showed the current time at the point of departure, or any known location. A captain could calculate the time at his present location, compare it with the time kept by the clock, and calculate longitude. The problem was that eighteenth-century clocks were not accurate enough. Relying on a shipboard clock that was gaining or losing fifteen seconds a day could send a ship hundreds of miles off course.

English cabinetmaker John Harrison took on the challenge of perfecting a timepiece that would be reliable enough to be carried to sea and maintain its accuracy despite the constant motion from the waves, excessive humidity, and changes in temperature. Harrison began work on his first "chronometer," as these timepieces came to be known, in 1727. It became his life's work: the last of his four versions was not finished until 1763, when he completed a compact chronometer that was accurate within one second per day.

Harrison's challenges were not only technical. Many astronomers in the Royal Society looked down on a mere "cabinetmaker" like Harrison, and were unwilling to give his prototypes the kind of trials that might lead to the prize. They believed that only mathematics could provide a solution.

As it turned out, both Harrison and the astronomers were on the right track. On Cook's first voyage, he used the latest astronomical charts with great success. On his second voyage Cook also took a chronometer and was very impressed, reporting that "it exceeded the expectations of its most zealous advocate and … has been our faithful guide through all vicissitudes of climate."[12] By the early nineteenth century Harrison's chronometer was standard equipment.

Mariners needed to set a fixed point from which the 360 degrees of longitude could be established. That "prime meridian" was set at Greenwich, the site of the Royal Observatory. Even the French, who first used Paris as the zero point, eventually accepted the British standard. As a legacy of those days of British maritime dominance, longitude is still measured from Greenwich to this day.

John Harrison's work, along with that of British astronomers, helped establish Greenwich as the "center of the world." Nearby, Banks developed Kew Gardens as the world center of botany. In both cases "practical science," the ability to apply the scientific outlook, propelled the increasing power of Britain in particular, and Europe in general, across the globe.

Mapping Central Asia, Africa, India, and the Americas

While the maritime empires of western Europe were growing, the Qing Empire was also expanding to include parts of Central Asia. Matteo Ricci had earlier introduced modern maps to China (see Chapter 16), and in the eighteenth century Qing officials refined their mapmaking skills and applied them to their empire: "the Qing court," notes one scholar, "like other early modern states, chose to adopt these cutting-edge technologies for state building."[13] Still, the Enlightenment remained a primarily European phenomenon. Whereas Qing maps dealt only with a single empire, European maps encompassed the entire globe. European explorers from various nations contributed to a single, expanding network of knowledge.

Courtesy National Maritime Museum, London

Harrison's Chronometer John Harrison solved the "problem of longitude," greatly increasing the safety and efficiency of oceanic navigation, when he perfected his chronometer in 1763. An elegant piece of craftsmanship, Harrison's chronometer was a sophisticated and durable timepiece that kept accurate time even on rough seas and in high humidity, exemplifying the British tradition of "practical science."

Joseph Banks and the Royal Society founded and funded the **African Association** (primarily in response to French competition). Until this time, Europeans had restricted themselves to small coastal settlements connected with the Atlantic slave trade. But the French seemed positioned to expand inland from their long-established outpost at the mouth of the Senegal River, a gateway to the predominantly Muslim Sahel.

The founders of the African Association knew that even more than the Senegal River, the key geographic feature of West Africa was the Niger River, but they knew little of its origins and path. Discovering the course of the Niger would add to geographic, botanical, and ethnographic knowledge and also promote British imperial expansion. Recruiting a young Scottish doctor named Mungo Park, whom Banks had earlier recommended as surgeon on a ship bound for Southeast Asia, the African Association sponsored a voyage of exploration to West Africa in 1795.

Park's voyage was difficult. The West African interior had been destabilized by the Atlantic slave trade, and his mission depended on the hospitality of Africans he met en route. He made it safely to Segu, an important political and economic center ever since the empire of Songhai (see Chapter 19), and got a clearer picture of how people and goods moved along the river and into North Africa and Egypt, while confirming that the Niger flowed west to east. But illness drove Park back to the coast before he could determine whether the river flowed into the forested delta (in today's southern Nigeria) where British slave traders had long been active.

At the same time, the British were pursuing an even more elaborate project in India. The English East India Company ruled rich territories from its bases at Calcutta in the northeast and Madras in the south, supplanting the Mughal Empire not only with guns and diplomacy but also with maps.

African Association (f. 1788) Society founded by Joseph Banks to sponsor geographical expeditions into Africa and chart the course of the Niger River, a feat achieved by Mungo Park.

Beginning in the 1790s, the **Great Trigonometrical Survey** undertook to map the Indian subcontinent. From a baseline meridian of longitude established in the south of India, precise triangulations were made between two other points and the first known location. Once three locations could be precisely defined in terms of longitude and latitude, the survey could proceed with further triangular measurements.

Eventually the Great Trigonometrical Survey drove straight across India to the Himalayas. The highest mountain peak in the world, called Chomolungma, "Mother of the Universe," by the Tibetans, was renamed by the British

"Mount Everest" after George Everest, the British surveyor-general. Such renam -ing occurred all over the world in this period.

The purposes of the Great Trigonometrical Survey were in keeping with the principles of the Enlighten-ment. Europeans had seen the Mughal Empire as an exotic and mystical land. The survey transformed the strange and unknow- able "Hindustan" of earlier maps into "India," a coherent world region. The process of mapping expressed imperial control, even over areas that

Great Trigonometrical Survey Beginning in the late 1790s, the British conducted this survey to plot the entire Indian subcontinent on a mathematically precise grid. The survey was a prelude to the expansion of Britain's Indian empire.

Matthew H. Edney, *Mapping an Empire*, University of Chicago Press, 1997, pg. 20

The Great Trigonometrical Survey Beginning in southern India in the 1790s, British surveyors undertook a painstaking mapping project that by 1843 had reached the Himalayas. Accurate maps were a key source of British imperial power.

Map 21.1 The Exploration of Western North America

While Captain George Vancouver followed James Cook's Pacific expeditions and traced the Pacific coastline of North America, in the 1790s Alexander Mackenzie traced routes from the Pacific and Arctic Oceans into the frigid interior of British North America. A decade later Meriwether Lewis and William Clark investigated a transcontinental route from St. Louis to the Oregon coast. U.S. Army Captain Zebulon Pike led expeditions up the Mississippi River and explored the southern and western regions of the Louisiana Purchase, turning south from the Colorado Mountains into New Spain. Geographic exploration went hand-in-hand with expanding state frontiers across North America, as in the wider world. © Cengage Learning

Interactive Map

had not yet been conquered. As one historian has written, "Imperialism and mapmaking intersect in the most basic manner. Both are fundamentally concerned with territory and knowledge."[14]

In the Americas, Captain Cook's Pacific journeys helped determine the size of North America; then in the 1790s Captain George Vancouver and his crew charted its western coasts as far north as Alaska. These maritime expeditions inspired transcontinental ones. After a first failed attempt to cross Canada on foot and canoe, the Scottish fur trader Alexander Mackenzie traveled from Montreal to London to equip himself with the latest technology: a sophisticated compass, sextant, chronometer, and telescope. Returning to Canada, and relying on the knowledge of indigenous First Nations people, Mackenzie and his party of nine became the first persons known to have crossed the entire American continent from east to west (see Map 21.1).

A parallel expedition took place in the new United States of America: the **Lewis and Clark Expedition** from the Mississippi River to the Pacific coast (1804–1806). One motivation for the government sponsors of Meriwether Lewis and William Clark, including President Thomas Jefferson, was to assess the potential for an American outlet to the Pacific Ocean to facilitate trade with Asia. Their reports, however, made clear the huge size and vast economic potential of the American interior itself. Like Banks and his protégés, Lewis and Clark carefully noted the flora and fauna on their journey, bringing the natural world of the American West into the orbit of scientific knowledge. Also like Banks, they noted the customs of indigenous peoples, while speculating on their possible origins and the linguistic and cultural relationships between them. They carried surveying equipment with them and created maps that settlers would later use to help them occupy the land. In the American West we see another example of the close relationship between science and empire.

Whether it was a new plant species, the height of a mountain, or the location of a harbor, any new fact could be related to a centralized system of classification organized along hierarchical and mathematical lines. Control of knowledge radically increased the power of empire in the nineteenth century.

Lewis and Clark Expedition (1804–1806) Government-sponsored team led by Meriwether Lewis and William Clark to open up a route through Native American territory to the Pacific. The expedition also collected new plant species and evaluated the potential for trade with Asia.

Oceania and Australia, 1770–1820

The three journeys of Captain **James Cook** consolidated the role of science in advancing the expansion of the British Empire. As we have seen, his first expedition, accompanied by Joseph Banks aboard the *Endeavour*, returned to England in 1771 with significant astronomical, botanical, geographic, and cultural information. On his second and third journeys, Cook sailed near the coast of Antarctica and north to the Arctic Ocean; he also added the Hawaiian Islands to Europe's map of the Pacific.

Joseph Banks did not accompany Cook's later journeys. But from England he played a major role in the settlement of Australia. By 1820 the foundation had been laid for a British colony on a continent that had been virtually unknown to Europeans before Cook's voyage.

James Cook (1728–1779) British sea captain whose three voyages to the Pacific Ocean greatly expanded European knowledge of the region. Captain Cook, regarded as a great national hero by the British public, was killed in an altercation with Hawaiian islanders in 1779.

Captain Cook in Polynesia, 1769–1779

On the first voyage, Cook and Banks were aided by a Tahitian high priest named Tupaia (too-PUH-ee-uh). Tupaia understood several Polynesian languages and, coming from a family of navigators, was able to supplement Cook's instruments and charts with a local understanding of winds and currents. He also helped Banks understand Polynesian cultural practices, such as the meaning of the peace ritual that had so mystified the Englishman when he first set foot on the island.

In spite of Tupaia's help, miscommunications persisted. In his journals, Banks noted with frustration "how much these people are given to thieving." "All are of the opinion," he writes, "that if they can once get possession of anything it immediately becomes their own."[15] Usually it was small items that went missing, but when some of their important astronomical devices disappeared, Cook was worried. Banks, with his developing knowledge of Tahitian society, was able to get the equipment back.

Theft among the English was a problem as well. Sailors kept stealing nails from the ship to trade with the islanders, for whom iron was new and valuable. However, one day when a Tahitian woman refused to sell her stone axe for an iron nail, a sailor took it anyway, and Cook decided to make an example of him. He ordered a flogging for the man and invited some Tahitian chiefs to witness the punishment:

> [The chiefs] stood quietly and saw him stripped and fastened to the rigging, but as soon as the first blow was given they interfered with many tears, begging the punishment might cease, a request which the Captain would not comply with.[16]

The Tahitians' views of property and punishment differed from those of the English; they were much less focused on exclusive ownership of material goods, and would not use corporal punishment in a simple case of theft. Unlike Banks, who made a genuine attempt to understand the people of the island and to mediate such disputes, Cook's attitude was strictly utilitarian: he wanted to make his astronomical and navigational observations, get fresh supplies of food and water, and move on.

Misunderstanding led to the death of Captain Cook on a Hawaiian beach in 1779. When Cook and his men first arrived, they received a joyous reception. Nevertheless, there were tensions. His men were exhausted from a futile trip to the Arctic in search of a "northwest passage" linking Asia and Europe, and they resented Cook's attempts to stop them from their usual practice of trading iron nails for sex. Cook was trying to protect the Hawaiians from the venereal disease rampant aboard ship. After departing Hawai'i, storm damage forced Cook to return, but there was no joyous greeting. Instead, an argument ensued, and islanders stabbed Cook to death.

For all the power of modern science, the death of Captain Cook shows the limitations of reason in governing human interactions. There were no chronometers, no astronomical sightings, no surveys or charts with which to safely navigate the waters of cross-cultural communication. New economic relations, new technologies, and new belief systems undermined the existing order of societies drawn into the European-dominated global system.

Joseph Banks and the Settlement of Australia

The impact of Joseph Banks on the history of Australia is inscribed on one of its most famous geographic features, Botany Bay, where Banks undertook an intensive reconnaissance of eastern Australia's unique plant life. He is sometimes called "the Father of Australia" for the role he played in the foundation of the colony of New South Wales in 1788 with its capital at Sydney.

New South Wales began as a penal colony, its overwhelmingly male population consisting of prisoners, many of them Irish, who had little to lose from taking a chance on resettlement halfway around the world. The colony got off to a rocky start. Few of the convicts knew how to survive in this foreign terrain. Nor could they rely on the aboriginal population, which either kept its distance or attacked.

The colonial economy of New South Wales strengthened with the introduction of merino sheep in 1805, descendants of the same sheep that Joseph Banks had imported from Spain to Kew Gardens for the king's flock. The grasslands of New South Wales proved ideal grazing, and wool exports financed the development of colonial society. By the early nineteenth century most settlers were free immigrants rather than convicts, the cities of Sydney and Melbourne were on paths to prosperity, and new British colonies were founded across the continent. After 1817, the name *Australia* was used to refer to this collection of colonies.

Joseph Banks regarded those developments as "improvement," another successful outcome of the application of practical science. But British settlement had a devastating impact on the original inhabitants of the continent. Aboriginal Australians had rich and complex traditions, as well as keen knowledge of the local environment from which, as hunter-gatherers whose ancestors had lived on the continent for tens of thousands of years, they derived all the necessities of life. But they had no metal tools, little political organization, and no immunity to Afro-Eurasian diseases like smallpox. As in the Americas in previous centuries, the Aborigines experienced the European territorial advance as a plague: more than half died in the nineteenth century. The survivors either fled to remote areas, worked for Europeans on their commercial ranches, or moved to cities, a disenfranchised subclass.

Chapter Review and Learning Activities

Joseph Banks lived in an atmosphere of great optimism. As president of the Royal Society, he saw tremendous advances in scientific inquiry, not merely in the accumulation of data but also in the development of increasingly advanced systems of scientific classification. Banks was typical of many products of the Scientific Revolution and Enlightenment in his strong belief in progress, and he never seems to have worried that "progress" could have losers as well as winners. Yet the application of science to agriculture in England led to many farming families being dispossessed of their land. And, as we will see in future chapters, European imperial expansion, facilitated by the development of practical science, would lead to conflict all across the nineteenth-century world.

🛳 When and how did Europe's Scientific Revolution begin to have practical applications?

The calm confidence inspired by Sir Isaac Newton's description of an orderly, rational universe that could be described through the elegance of mathematics presented eighteenth-century European thinkers with a world that seemed full of promise. Science, it seemed, could not only accurately *describe* the natural world, but also through practical applications enhance nature for human purposes. In the field of botany, for example, Linnaeus's system of classification was the foundation for the "practical science" of Joseph Banks's agricultural and botanical studies on his own estates and at Kew Gardens. Likewise, the development of a more refined system of measuring time and mapping both nautical and terrestrial space drew on scientific developments in astronomy and mathematics but also found real-world applications, most notably in the expansion of European empires.

🛳 How did Enlightenment thought derive from the Scientific Revolution, and how did it differ from previous European thought systems?

The Scientific Revolution in Europe introduced the idea of a well-ordered universe that could be understood through close observation and the application of human reason. Enlightenment philosophers extended this belief in a rational, ordered universe to develop an optimistic view of human society in which political and economic affairs might also be governed by human reason. They rejected the pessimism of earlier Christian beliefs, which had focused on sin and human fallibility, and instead proposed that reason could show the way to reform and improve human societies. Most philosophes imagined that societal enlightenment would come from the actions of enlightened rulers applying reason to the problems of governance; however, "enlightened despots" were unable to fulfill the highest aspirations of the Enlightenment.

🛳 How did systematic classification and measurement support European imperialism in the late eighteenth and early nineteenth centuries?

The link between "practical science" and the expansion of European empires gave the Scientific Revolution a global dimension. More than simple curiosity drove the mapping projects and surveying expeditions sent to Africa, India, and the Americas in this period. While the accumulation of scientific knowledge for its own sake was certainly one factor motivating explorers like Park, Mackenzie, and Cook, they all realized that British imperial ambitions were strengthened through the increase of geographic knowledge, the charting and mapping of space, and the accumulation of cultural information about indigenous societies.

🛳 How did the societies of Oceania and Australia experience encounters with Europeans in this period?

The peoples of Oceania and Australia experienced their encounters with Europeans as a shock and a challenge. Tahitians, Hawaiians, and others were as baffled by the strange behavior of the Europeans as Joseph Banks was by his initial experiences with Polynesian culture. Soon at least some Europeans learned Polynesian languages and vice versa, and the cultural gap was narrowed. Still, as the death of Captain Cook demonstrates, there were severe limitations on cross-cultural communications. Soon the Europeans would be in a position to impose their own technologies and economic systems on Oceanic societies. The same was true to an even greater extent in Australia, where the indigenous Aborigines were even less able to resist European advances and Afro-Eurasian diseases.

FOR FURTHER REFERENCE

Crosby, Alfred. *The Measure of Reality: Quantification in Western Europe, 1250–1600.* Cambridge: Cambridge University Press, 1997.

Drayton, Richard. *Nature's Government: Science, Imperial Britain, and the "Improvement" of the World.* New Haven: Yale University Press, 2000.

Edney, Matthew H. *Mapping an Empire: The Geographical Construction of British India, 1765–1843.* Chicago: University of Chicago Press, 1990.

Fara, Patricia. *Sex, Botany and Empire: The Story of Carl Linnaeus and Joseph Banks.* New York: Columbia University Press, 2004.

Fernandez-Armesto, Felipe. *Pathfinders: A Global History of Exploration.* New York: W.W. Norton, 2007.

Gascoigne, John. *Joseph Banks and the English Enlightenment: Useful Knowledge and Polite Culture.* New York: Cambridge University Press, 2003.

Henry, John. *The Scientific Revolution and the Origins of Modern Science.* 3d ed. New York: Palgrave, 2008.

Israel, Jonathan. *Radical Enlightenment: Philosophy and the Making of Modernity, 1650–1750.* New York: Oxford University Press, 2002.

Jacob, Margaret. *The Cultural Meaning of the Scientific Revolution.* New York: McGraw-Hill, 1988.

Salmond, Anne. *The Trial of the Cannibal Dog: The Remarkable Story of Captain Cook's Encounter in the South Seas.* New Haven: Yale University Press, 2003.

Sorbel, Dava, and William J. H. Andrews. *The Illustrated Longitude: The True Story of a Lone Genius Who Solved the Greatest Scientific Problem of His Time.* New York: Walker & Co., 1998.

KEY TERMS

Joseph Banks (456)
René Descartes (458)
Sir Francis Bacon (458)
Isaac Newton (458)
Carl Linnaeus (459)
Enlightenment (464)
John Locke (464)
laissez faire (464)
philosophes (465)
Encyclopedia (465)
enlightened despots (466)
problem of longitude (468)
African Association (470)
Great Trigonometrical Survey (471)
Lewis and Clark Expedition (473)
James Cook (473)

VOYAGES ON THE WEB

Voyages: Joseph Banks

"Voyages" is a real time excursion to historical sites in this chapter and includes interactive activities and study tools such as audio summaries, animated maps, and flashcards.

Visual Evidence: The Death of Captain Cook

"Visual Evidence" features artifacts, works of art, or photographs, along with a brief descriptive essay and discussion questions to guide your analysis of visual sources.

World History in Today's World: A New Northwest Passage

"World History in Today's World" makes the connection between features of modern life and their origins in the periods in this chapter.

Go to the CourseMate website at www.cengagebrain.com for additional study tools and review materials—including audio and video clips—for this chapter.

22 Revolutions in the West, 1750–1830

Simón Bolívar
(Mirelle Vautier)

In August of 1805 a young South American climbed one of the hills outside Rome to gain a panoramic view of the "eternal city." For **Simón Bolívar** (1783–1830) the history of Rome summed up all that was great and all that was tragic in history. Over the next two decades he led the drive for the independence of Spain's South American colonies.

Greatness was what Bolívar sought for Spain's American colonies as he dedicated himself to achieving their independence:

Here every manner of grandeur has had its type, all miseries their cradle....

[Rome] has examples for everything, except the cause of humanity: ... heroic warriors, rapacious consuls ... golden virtues, and foul crimes; but for the emancipation of the spirit ... the exaltation of man, and the final perfectibility of reason, little or nothing.... The resolution of the great problem of man set free seems to have been something ... that would only be made clear in the New World.... I swear before you, I swear by the God of my fathers, I swear on their graves, I swear by my Country that I will not rest body or soul until I have broken the chains binding us to the will of Spanish might![*][1]

---

*Excerpt from Simón Bolívar "Oath Taken at Rome, 15 August 1805" translated by Frederick H. Fornoff. From David Bushnessl, ed., *El Libertador: Writings of Simon Bolivar*. Copyright © 2003. Reprinted by permission of Oxford University Press.

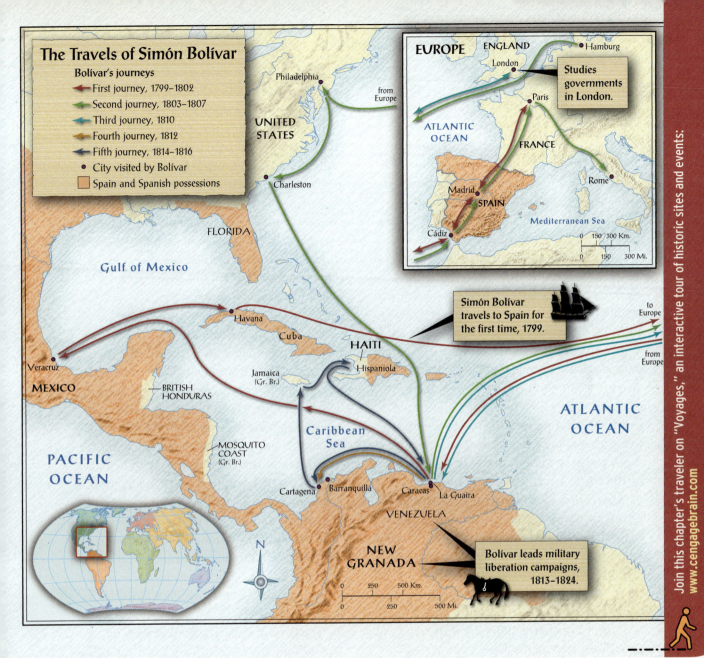

The Travels of Simón Bolívar

Bolívar's journeys
- ◆—— First journey, 1799–1802
- ◆—— Second journey, 1803–1807
- ◆—— Third journey, 1810
- ◆—— Fourth journey, 1812
- ◆—— Fifth journey, 1814–1816
- • City visited by Bolívar
- ▨ Spain and Spanish possessions

EUROPE

ENGLAND
Hamburg
London

Studies governments in London.

ATLANTIC OCEAN

Paris

FRANCE

Madrid

SPAIN

Rome

Cádiz

Mediterranean Sea

0   150   300 Km.
0   150   300 Mi.

Philadelphia

from Europe

UNITED STATES

Charleston

FLORIDA

Gulf of Mexico

Havana

Cuba

HAITI

Hispaniola

Simón Bolívar travels to Spain for the first time, 1799.

to Europe

from Europe

ATLANTIC OCEAN

Veracruz

MEXICO

BRITISH HONDURAS

Jamaica (Gr. Br.)

MOSQUITO COAST (Gr. Br.)

Caribbean Sea

PACIFIC OCEAN

Cartagena   Barranquilla   Caracas   La Guaira

VENEZUELA

NEW GRANADA

Bolívar leads military liberation campaigns, 1813–1824.

0   250   500 Km.
0   250   500 Mi.

N

Join this chapter's traveler on "Voyages," an interactive tour of historic sites and events:
www.cengagebrain.com

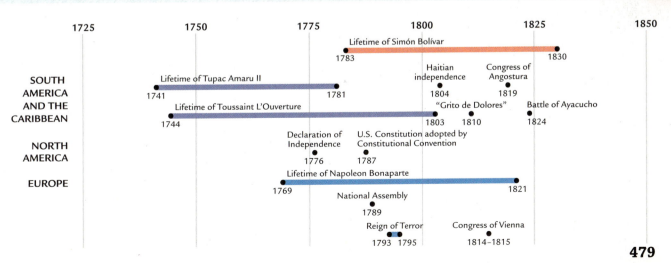

	1725	1750	1775	1800	1825	1850

SOUTH AMERICA AND THE CARIBBEAN

Lifetime of Simón Bolívar
1783 — 1830

Lifetime of Tupac Amaru II
1741 — 1781

Haitian independence
1804

Congress of Angostura
1819

Lifetime of Toussaint L'Ouverture
1744 — 1803

"Grito de Dolores"
1810

Battle of Ayacucho
1824

NORTH AMERICA

Declaration of Independence
1776

U.S. Constitution adopted by Constitutional Convention
1787

EUROPE

Lifetime of Napoleon Bonaparte
1769 — 1821

National Assembly
1789

Reign of Terror
1793 1795

Congress of Vienna
1814–1815

479

Simón Bolívar (1783–1830) Revolutionary who was born in Venezuela and led military forces throughout present-day Ecuador, Colombia, Bolivia, and Peru, becoming the most important military leader in the struggle for independence in South America. In Latin America he is known simply as *El Libertador* (el lee-bir-TAH-door), "the Liberator."

Simón Bolívar's (see-MOAN bow-LEE-varh) oath changed not only his own life but also the course of Latin American history.

Growing up in one of the richest households in Venezuela, Bolívar had studied the great thinkers of the Enlightenment. He first went to Europe in 1799, when he was only sixteen, to visit an uncle in Madrid. There he spent his money freely while enjoying the life of the Spanish court. He fell in love and, in spite of his youth, married and returned with his bride to Caracas. Sadly, she died just eight months later. Now in his early twenties, inspired by the examples of revolution in North America and France, he returned to Europe to visit a former teacher, a revolutionary who had been driven out of Venezuela by the Spanish authorities.

Apart from visiting Rome, he spent most of this trip in Paris, the intellectual center of the Enlightenment and the political center of revolution. In the previous decade the French monarchy had been overthrown and replaced by a republic. Now the republic was being superseded by the dictatorship of Napoleon Bonaparte. Bolívar's worldview was greatly affected by his experience of post-revolutionary French politics. The French Revolution, like ancient Rome, had brought forth both "golden virtues" and "sordid crimes." Only in the Americas, thought Bolívar, could the full liberation of the human spirit be achieved.

Bolívar proved himself a brilliant military leader. Between 1813, when he entered his native Caracas at the head of a liberation army, and 1824, when he drove the Spanish army from Peru, he fulfilled the oath he had taken in Rome. Like other revolutionaries of the late eighteenth and early nineteenth centuries, Bolívar started out with high hopes founded in Enlightenment optimism. But turning independence from Spanish rule into true liberty for the people of South America proved difficult. By the time of Bolívar's death in 1830, many South Americans had become concerned about his dictatorial tendencies. His story, as one biographer has emphasized, is one of "liberation and disappointment."[2]

Elsewhere in Latin America and the Caribbean, and in North America and France, other revolutionaries also believed that prejudice and tradition would give way to rationality and enlightenment and that new political and social systems would both guarantee liberty and provide order and security. In 1776, Britain's North American colonists had broken free and founded a democratic republic that seemed to combine liberty with moderation. A more volatile historical precedent was the French Revolution, which swung violently from constitutional monarchy to radical republic to military dictatorship. In the Caribbean, the Republic of Haiti was created following one of the largest slave uprisings in world history.

The issue of slavery was very much on Bolívar's mind. Like his North American counterpart George Washington, Bolívar was a slave owner. Could the dream of liberty be compatible with the reality of slavery? Such discrepancies between dreams and harsher realities were, in fact, a central theme of the age. Reconciling the twin mandates of liberty and equality, and securing both within a stable and well-ordered state, was a tremendous challenge for revolutionaries across North and South America, the Caribbean, and France.

FOCUS QUESTIONS

▶ What political compromises were made in establishing the new United States of America?

▶ What were the major phases of the French Revolution?

▶ How were the revolutions in Latin America and the Caribbean influenced by the history of colonialism?

▶ How much did the outcomes of these revolutions in western Europe and the Americas represent a thorough transformation of existing political and social structures?

The American War of Independence, 1763–1791

On April 19, 1775, British regulars marched on the town of Concord to seize and destroy arms secretly stockpiled there by the Massachusetts militia. At Concord's North Bridge, they and militiamen exchanged gunfire. Surprised by the colonials' steadfast resistance and confused by their irregular tactics, the British beat a retreat, harassed along their flanks all the way back to Boston (see Map 22.1).

To say the gunfire at Concord was "heard 'round the world" may be an exaggeration. Yet that day's skirmish at a rural bridge began an "American Revolution" that would fundamentally change the world over time. The Declaration of Independence (1776), justifying the rebellion, is one of the most influential political statements in world history, while the Constitution of the United States of America (1787) has provided a model of limited yet effective government ever since. The founding of the United States was a powerful testament to the principles of the Enlightenment. Nevertheless, the Enlightenment's highest aspirations, of universal liberty and equality, were undermined by compromises made during the nation-building process, especially bargains about slavery.

Revolution and War, 1763–1783

A key turning point in the relations between Britain and the colonists was the British victory in the French and Indian War. That North American conflict was only one theater of the Seven Years' War (1756–1763) that pitted British against French. The British victory opened up new possibilities for expansion on the western frontier. Many colonists were excited about opportunities that lay in the Ohio River Valley and other areas west of the Appalachian Mountains. But British leaders were cautious. No sooner had they defeated the French than they were faced with a Native American uprising. European settlements on the frontier would generate more conflict, inevitably requiring more British troops and resources. For these reasons, the Proclamation of 1763 established a fixed westward limit to colonial expansion, much to the disgust of colonists.

Primary Source: The United States Declaration of Independence *Read a selection from Jefferson's famous text, which lays out the Enlightenment principles on which the United States was founded.*

Map 22.1   The American Revolutionary War
In terms of military firepower the British Empire far outmatched the American Continental Army. The British could deploy an almost unlimited number of well-armed professional soldiers, and their navy was able to enforce a blockade of American ports. As would happen so often in modern world history, however, fighters who were highly motivated to throw off the imperial yoke managed to overcome the odds and win their independence.   © Cengage Learning

Interactive Map

Not only were the British restraining colonial expansion, but they were also determined that the colonists should bear the costs of their own defense. But the new taxes, such as the Stamp Act of 1765, were bitterly resented. Along with attempts to restrict colonial trade with the West Indies, New England merchants were aggrieved by the monopoly granted to the East India Company for the supply of tea to the colonies. Resistance to that law took the form of

illegal smuggling, and more dramatically of the Boston Tea Party, where colonists dressed as Amerindians tossed a boatload of East India Company tea into Boston harbor. Lacking representation in Parliament, colonials had no direct way to influence British government policy. "No taxation without representation!" became their rallying cry.

British policies led many settlers to conclude that their rights as freeborn British subjects were

Protesting the Stamp Act Needing additional resources to control its expanded American frontier after victory in the Seven Years' War, the British Parliament imposed a Stamp Act on the North American colonies in 1765. In this engraving colonists angry at the new tax have strung up one of the king's officials on a "liberty pole," and they prepare to tar and feather another. Tarring and feathering, which often left the victim permanently disfigured, was an exceptionally violent form of vigilante justice.

The TORY'S Day of JUDGMENT.

The Granger Collection

being assailed. The final straw was suspending the charter of the Massachusetts Bay Company in 1775, disbanding the colonial legislature, and imposing a British governor. By this time the colonists had formed militias for self-defense, and the scene was set for confrontation.

A Continental Congress was held in 1775 that brought together representatives from each of the thirteen colonies. **George Washington** (1732–1799) was appointed commander of its army. Washington, a Virginian, had served as an officer during British military campaigns in the Ohio River Valley.

On July 4, 1776, Congress approved Thomas Jefferson's **Declaration of Independence**, which not only detailed grievances but also made a stirring announcement:

> We hold these truths to be self-evident: That all men are created equal; that they are endowed by their creator with certain inalienable rights; that among these are life, liberty and the pursuit of happiness; that, to secure these rights, governments are instituted among men, deriving their just powers from the consent of the governed.

The phrase "consent of the governed" built on John Locke's theory of government as based on a contract in which individuals receive protection of their basic rights by voluntarily submitting to a legitimate government. But Jefferson went further: when the "consent of the governed" was lacking, rebellion was justified: "When a long train of abuses and usurpations … evinces a design to reduce them under absolute Despotism, it is their right, it is their duty, to throw off such Government and to provide new Guards for their future security."

The British had some advantages in the fight. The tens of thousands of "redcoat" soldiers in North America were well equipped and well trained. Moreover, many Loyalists in the colonies argued against rebellion. For Benjamin Franklin this was a family affair. Franklin himself was reluctant to exchange his British identity for an American one, and his son William, the royally appointed governor of New Jersey, refused to do so. Many free blacks, aware that slavery had already been eliminated in England and that prominent leaders

George Washington
(1732–1799) Commander of the Continental Army in the American War of Independence from Britain; also first president of the United States of America.

Declaration of Independence
(1776) Document written by Thomas Jefferson justifying the separation of Britain's North American colonies, declaring them free and independent states.

Joseph Brant (1742–1807)
Mohawk leader who supported the British during the American War of Independence.

of the rebellion included slave owners like Washington and Jefferson, were Loyalist as well.

A key British ally was the Mohawk nation under their leader **Joseph Brant** (Mohawk name Thayendanegea) (1742–1807). Brant's sister had married an Irish fur trader. Thereafter, the Brants were important mediators in the Iroquois/British alliance against the French. Brant had traveled to London to meet King George III (for later developments in Brant's family, see Chapter 25).

In 1777 colonists defeated a British force at Saratoga in New York. Not only did that surprise victory give the colonists a forward base against the Mohawk, but it also persuaded the French that the American rebellion might succeed. Early in 1778 a Franco-American treaty was signed. The French supplied the rebel army with weapons and harried the British fleet in the Atlantic and Caribbean.

Apart from the French alliance, the rebellious colonists had several advantages. The rural population supported the Continental Army with supplies, information on British movements, and knowledge of the local terrain. Women played a notable role. They did extra work, including blacksmithing and other "male" jobs, in the absence of their soldier-husbands, and they also produced shoes, clothes, and munitions for the Continental Army. Finally, since British soldiers were reluctant to search them, women made excellent spies and carriers of communication.

Another advantage was the leadership ability of General Washington, who managed to maintain the morale of his troops through the harsh winter at Valley Forge in 1777–1778 and to outmaneuver the British commander Lord Cornwallis at the culminating battle at Yorktown in 1781. After British troops had been surrounded by Washington's army, French ships cut off their retreat, and the war was over. In the Treaty of Paris (1783), the British government acknowledged the independence of the new United States of America.

Creating a Nation, 1783–1791

An early motto of the new republic was *Novus Ordo Secolorum:* "A New Order of the Ages." The

founders saw the birth of their nation as an event that would usher in a new era, "an epoch," as Washington put it, "when the rights of mankind were better understood and more clearly defined, than at any former period."

But separation from the British did not by itself bring about revolutionary change. Many conditions remained the same, as would be true in other revolutions to follow. For example, under British rule each of the thirteen colonies had developed a distinct political culture. In spite of another new motto, *E Pluribus Unum,* "Out of Many, One," representatives of the individual states proved reluctant to sacrifice local sovereignty to create a more unified nation. The first constitution, the Articles of Confederation, required that the federal government request funds from the individual states. Lacking its own tax-raising power, the Confederation government had no army and therefore no effective power.

Under the Articles of Confederation, the states were responsible for debts remaining from the war, and they levied taxes to meet those obligations. These taxes forced poorer farmers, who lived primarily through barter, to sell land to raise the necessary cash. Such farmers also stood to lose their right to vote, which was accorded only to property owners. Incensed that land speculators were profiting at their expense in this way, Massachusetts war veterans rose up in an armed rebellion led by Daniel Shays. While Shay's Rebellion (1786–1787) was suppressed by the state militia, the crisis nevertheless bolstered those who argued for a stronger federal government with powers of taxation and the ability to assume war debts.

Mercy Otis Warren, one of the most prolific writers of her time, put it this way: "Our situation is truly delicate and critical. On the one hand we are in need of a strong federal government founded on principles that will support the prosperity and union of the colonies. On the other we have struggled for liberty … [and will not relinquish] the rights of man for the dignity of government." Delegates from the thirteen states met at the Constitutional Convention in 1787 to face the central issue of how to rebalance the relative power of the state and federal governments.

Compromise was the hallmark of the new **Constitution of the United States of America** (1787). While granting to the federal government the powers of taxation, judicial oversight, banking, international diplomacy, and national defense, it left specific powers, such as determining the voting franchise, to the states. A system of checks and balances, as earlier proposed by the French *philosophe* Montesquieu, ensured the separation of executive, legislative, and judicial authority. A balance was struck between the interests of large and small states by a two-house legislature with a House of Representatives in which each state was allocated a number of seats based on its population, and a Senate in which each state was equally represented by two senators.

Equally important was the balance struck between the power of majorities and the rights of minorities. Congress amended the Constitution in 1791 with a Bill of Rights to ensure that specific civil liberties would be guaranteed even in the face of majority opinion. For example, the Bill of Rights made the establishment of a state church impossible, protecting the rights of religious minorities. It also guaranteed freedom of the press, freedom of assembly, the right to bear arms, and other fundamental freedoms.

Most states restricted the vote to property owners, women were not enfranchised, and the president and senators were elected indirectly rather than by popular vote. No political agency was given to Native Americans, slaves, or even most free blacks. Nevertheless, the Constitution has endured, possessing both fixed principles as well as the flexibility to meet new challenges.

George Washington was the unanimous choice of the state electors as president in 1789. He served two terms and then retired. Washington, like Simón Bolívar on his European sojourn, looked to ancient Rome for inspiration. His model was the general Cincinnatus, who, after leading Roman armies to victory, left the political stage to live as a simple citizen. In 1796, after two terms as president, Washington refused a third term and retired to his plantation. The example he set was one of public service rather than personal aggrandizement.

The Constitutional Convention, for all its achievements, failed to resolve the dichotomy between liberty and slavery. Southern delegates had no intention of liberating the 40 percent of southerners who were slaves. Though the abolitionist movement was gaining momentum, plantation owners prevailed: the Constitution defined each slave as three-fifths of a person for calculating the size of congressional delegations and allowed the states to define slaves as nonpersons for other purposes.

In this critical way Enlightenment ideals of liberty were unmet in the United States of America.

> **Constitution of the United States of America** (1787) Agreement that created more unified national structure for the United States, providing for a bicameral national legislature and independent executive and judicial authority, and incorporating a Bill of Rights.

The French Revolution, 1789–1815

If the founders of the United States found it difficult to fully implement Enlightenment ideals, French revolutionaries had an even more difficult time. Resistance came not only from the monarchy and aristocracy but also from the Catholic Church and other European leaders who feared that revolt would spread to their countries as well. In France, compromise would prove impossible.

The Revolution moved through three stages. The first focused on the relatively moderate goal of constitutional monarchy. The second phase was led by the Jacobins, who sought a radical transformation of French society. But Jacobin rule soon degenerated into a bloody Reign of Terror. Finally, amidst the turmoil emerged a military genius who not only restored order but also extended French power across Europe: Napoleon Bonaparte.

Louis XVI and the Early Revolution, 1789–1792

Ruling over 24 million subjects from a fabulous palace at Versailles, **Louis XVI** (r. 1774–1793) was one of the wealthiest and most powerful people in the world. But the foundations of the French Bourbon dynasty were rotting. When he took the throne, the French treasury was empty and public debt was out of control. The loss of the Seven Years' War (1756–1763) had cost the French territory in the Americas and in Asia, and left a pile of debt. The common people were crushed by taxes, while the nobility paid none at all.

In 1789, Louis decided he had no choice but to convene an Estates-General in Paris to which each of the three Orders of French society would send representatives. The First Estate consisted of the Catholic Church, the Second Estate consisted of the nobility, and the Third Estate comprised everyone else, that is, the vast majority of French men and women. It was an extreme measure; no French king had called a meeting of the Estates-General since 1614.

In the provinces elections were held for **Third Estate** delegates, many of whom were lawyers, merchants, and other members of the middle class stifled by the monarchy and nobility. Inspired by the American Revolution, they demanded fundamental reforms, such as the creation of a representative legislative body. They collected notebooks of grievances to bring to Paris a catalogue of complaints and ideas for change.

Many members of the First Estate were also members of the nobility, and the Catholic Church, by far the biggest landowner in France, was, like the aristocratic members of the Second Estate, exempted from direct taxation. Since each estate had only one vote, Louis anticipated that the privileged members of the First and Second Estates would vote together, canceling out proposals that came from the Third Estate.

Rather than accept this situation, delegates from the Third Estate took matters into their own hands. They declared themselves to be a **National Assembly** and took an oath that they would not disband until a constitutional monarchy had been established. In fear, Louis XVI summoned troops to defend his palace at Versailles, 12 miles (19.3 km) outside of Paris. It was the summer of 1789, and the French Revolution had begun.

Thus far the contest was between the nobles and the relatively well-off representatives of the Third Estate, who *aspired* to power and influence. But events were pushed in a new direction by the actions of the common people. Parisians stormed the Bastille (**bass-TEEL**), a building that served as both a jail and an armory. They freed prisoners, armed themselves from the arsenal's stockpile, and killed the mayor of Paris.

Louis decided he had better compromise with the Third Estate after all. He recognized the National Assembly, which promptly declared the principle of equality before the law, eliminated the special prerogatives of the nobility, and abolished serfdom and all the remaining feudal obligations of the peasantry. In the "Declaration of the Rights of Man and the Citizen," the National Assembly declared that "men are born and remain free and equal in rights," that "the natural and inalienable rights of man" are "liberty, property, security, and resistance to oppression," that all citizens are eligible for government positions "without other distinctions than that of virtues and talents," and that necessary taxation "must be assessed equally on all citizens in proportion to their means." Freedom of thought and religion were established, and mandatory payments to the Catholic Church were eliminated. The ideas of the philosophes were thus articulated as political principles.

In spite of this radical agenda, the National Assembly was otherwise quite conservative. For example, no rights were extended to women.

Louis XVI (r. 1774–1793) King of France whose inability to adequately reform the French fiscal system laid the foundation for the French Revolution. After showing reluctance to rule as a constitutional monarch, Louis was arrested and beheaded by republican revolutionaries.

Third Estate Before the Revolution, the order of French society that included most common people (the First Estate was aristocracy, the Second clergy, and the Third everyone else).

National Assembly (1789) Revolutionary assembly formed by members of the Third Estate after the failure of the Estates-General. They agreed on the "Declaration of the Rights of Man and of the Citizen," forcing the king to sign the assembly's constitution.

Primary Source: The Declaration of the Rights of Man and of the Citizen *This document, drafted by the National Assembly of France, is an Enlightenment cousin of Jefferson's Declaration.*

In her *Declaration of the Rights of Women,* the author Olympe de Gouges (oh-lamp duh GOOJ) protested: "The exercise of the natural rights of women has only been limited by the perpetual tyranny that man opposes to them; these limits should be reformed by the laws of nature and reason."[3] Such appeals were ignored by the men who seized power.

Within the National Assembly revolutionary zeal was secondary to establishing a new constitutional monarchy. But neither the king nor the assembly could control the pace of change. In the fall of 1789, the poor took action. Angered by the high price of bread and distrustful of the intentions of the king, twenty thousand Parisians marched to Versailles in what was called the "March of the Women" because of the preponderance of women in its ranks. The marchers forced the king to return to his palace in the heart of Paris, where they could keep a closer eye on him.

Despite the centrality of Paris, the vast majority of French men and women were still rural peasants who resented the privileges the nobles still had over them. "Justice" came from courts presided over by their lord, they had to donate free labor to cultivating his estates, and they were often forced to grind their wheat into flour at the lord's mill, where lack of competition allowed him to charge whatever he liked. While the National Assembly deliberated, peasants took matters into their own hands, sometimes burning only the manorial rolls that listed their feudal obligations, and sometimes burning the estates themselves to the ground.

In this tense atmosphere the National Assembly organized a Legislative Assembly to draft a written constitution in which power would

The Granger Collection

Parisian Women March to Versailles   Women played a distinctive role in the French Revolution. Elite women sponsored the gatherings that spread Enlightenment and revolutionary ideals in their *salons,* while the common women engaged in direct action, as here in 1789 where they are shown marching to Versailles to force the king to return to Paris.

be shared between the king and representatives of the people. In the summer of 1791, Louis tried to escape from France, but he was captured and made prisoner in his palace. Meanwhile, many members of the nobility had fled to other capitals, hoping to convince Europe's kings and aristocrats to help overthrow the Revolution.

By the summer of 1792 French forces had lost to Habsburg regiments in the Netherlands, and there were fears of an Austrian invasion. As a severe shortage of grain increased tensions, the people of Paris staged demonstrations and then attacked the royal palace. Hundreds of citizens and soldiers died.

The time when compromise was possible was at an end. While some in the Legislative Assembly were disappointed that the king and his followers refused to play by the new rules of constitutional monarchy, others were happy that the experiment had not worked. They were republicans, who believed that any form of monarchy undermined liberty.

The Jacobins and the Reign of Terror, 1793–1795

Under pressure from the people of Paris, the Legislative Assembly declared a republic and instituted universal manhood suffrage. The National Assembly dissolved itself in favor of a National Convention, which immediately declared the end of the monarchy and began writing a republican constitution for France. They found Louis XVI guilty of treason and beheaded him in January 1793.

Under the **Jacobins**, led by Maximilien Robespierre (ROBES-pee-air), the French Revolution passed through its most idealist and most violent phase. Robespierre had been deeply influenced by the philosophy of Jean-Jacques Rousseau, who had argued that a legitimate state expressed the "general will" of the people. Rousseau envisioned a form of direct democracy practiced by enlightened citizens, but he rejected the checks on government power proposed by Montesquieu and implemented in the Constitution of the United States. Instead Rousseau talked of constructing a "Republic of Virtue."

In the name of "liberty, equality, and fraternity," the Republic confiscated lands belonging to the church and to the nobility, and slavery in the French Empire was abolished. Everyone, rich and poor alike, was addressed as "Citizen." The year 1793 became Year One, marking the victory of reason over the old Christian faith. The months were divided into three weeks of ten days each, following the logic of the new metric system. The old names of the days of the week, irrationally based on pagan traditions, were replaced. Time itself would have a revolutionary new beginning.

But no fresh start was really possible; the past could not be so easily erased. Catholics resented Jacobin attacks on the church, and the bourgeoisie were shocked by the Jacobins' seizure of property. Meanwhile, the kings of Prussia and Austria declared war on France, determined to end the Revolution and restore the monarchy.

Robespierre imposed a harsh dictatorship. Not for the last time in world history, a revolutionary leader declared that in order to save the revolution, liberty would have to be sacrificed. A dictatorial Committee of Public Safety replaced democratic institutions. The committee quashed its enemies with a so-called Reign of Terror in which forty thousand people were beheaded. The symbol of the Revolution now became the guillotine (gee-yuh-TEEN), in which the condemned placed their head on a block before having it removed by the swift fall of a sharp, heavy blade. The fact that the guillotine became a symbol of revolutionary violence is ironic. The philosophes were horrified by public executions in which several swings of a heavy axe were often needed to fully decapitate the condemned, or in which screaming victims were slowly burnt to death at the stake. Dr. Joseph Guillotin had intended his invention as an enlightened means of execution, clean and swift. Now his attempt at humane reform had been transformed into a means of terror.

Nevertheless, the Jacobins were successful in securing the Republic against Austrian and Prussian invaders. They fielded an enormous

Jacobins Most radical republican faction in the National Convention. They organized a military force that saved the republic, but their leader Maximilien Robespierre, head of the Committee of Public Safety, ruled by decree and set in motion the Reign of Terror.

Primary Source: Rousseau Espouses Popular Sovereignty and the General Will *Modern political philosophy owes much to the ideas of this French philosopher.*

army of conscripts, mostly peasants who had never before traveled far from home. Once trained for defense of the Republic, many developed a stronger sense of French national identity.

Military success, however, emboldened the Jacobins' domestic enemies. People in the provinces were angry at the radicalism they associated with Paris, and many members of the middle class favored a more moderate republic. A further irony was added to the story of the guillotine: those who had used it to execute their enemies often ended with their own heads in a basket. Robespierre himself was beheaded before the end of 1794.

The Age of Napoleon, 1795–1815

The National Convention reasserted power and created a new constitution with a more limited electorate and a separation of powers. From 1795 to 1799, however, the country remained sharply divided. The Directory, which formed the executive of the new government, faced conspiracies both by the Jacobins trying to return to power and by monarchists trying to restore the Bourbon dynasty. Meanwhile, the French armies continued to gain victories as a young general named **Napoleon Bonaparte** (1769–1821) took northern Italy from the Austrians. In 1799 two members of the Directory plotted with Napoleon to launch a *coup d'état* and form a new government.

Like George Washington, Napoleon looked to ancient Rome for inspiration. But unlike the American general, Napoleon followed Rome's imperial example, transforming a republic into an empire. In 1804 he crowned himself Emperor Napoleon I. But first he secured the approval of the legislature and had the move ratified by national referendum. In fact, Napoleon was quite popular. Tired of fractious politics, the nation sought "enlightened dictatorship."

Indeed, by the orderliness and rationality of his administration, Napoleon seemed to fulfill the hopes of the eighteenth-century philosophes. In 1801 he reached a compromise with the pope that allowed Catholic worship and restored government support for the clergy. The Bank of France was created to stabilize finances, and a new legal system, the Napoleonic Code, recognized the equality of all French citizens. Napoleon neutralized political opposition by bringing monarchists into his administration and by tapping into the spirit of nationalism that had developed during the Revolution. The French were now citizens of a nation rather than subjects of a king, and Napoleon cultivated their patriotism, promising not liberty but glory.

French nationalism was stimulated by Napoleon's military achievements. Though the emperor's planned invasion of England was stymied in 1805 by the victory of Lord Nelson's fleet at Trafalgar, Napoleon's forces were unstoppable on the continent. In some cases the French were greeted as liberators. The German composer Ludwig von Beethoven, for example, initially dedicated his "Heroic" symphony to Napoleon. When he realized that personal ambition and the quest for French glory were the emperor's true motivations, he scratched that dedication from the title page. Simón Bolívar was likewise disappointed by Napoleon's imperial pretensions, but like others, he still admired Bonaparte's skills.

French armies swept through Iberia and Italy and asserted control over the Netherlands, Poland, and the western half of Germany. The Austrians and Prussians suffered embarrassing losses to the French armies, who were commanded by the greatest general of the age and by a new breed of military officers chosen for their talent rather than their aristocratic connections.

But Napoleon's ambition caused him to overreach and bring about his own downfall. In 1812 he mounted a massive attack on Russia. The Russian army could in no way prevent this assault, but they used their vast spaces to military advantage. When Napoleon reached Moscow, he found that the city had been abandoned and largely burned to the ground by its own people. Napoleon had nothing to claim as a prize. The French army, retreating through the Russian winter, was decimated. Of the 700,000 troops that had invaded Russia, fewer than 100,000 returned.

A broad coalition of anti-French forces then went on the offensive, invaded France, forced

Napoleon Bonaparte (1769–1821) Military commander who gained control of France after the French Revolution. Declared himself emperor in 1804 and attempted to expand French territory, but failed to defeat Great Britain and abdicated in 1814. Died in exile after a brief return to power in 1815.

Napoleon to abdicate in 1814, and restored the Bourbon monarchy by placing Louis XVIII (r. 1814–1824) on the throne. Dramatically, Napoleon then escaped his exile, returned to Paris, and reformed his army before finally being defeated by British and Prussian forces at the Battle of Waterloo in 1815. He died in exile on a remote South Atlantic island.

By this roundabout route France finally became a constitutional monarchy. Still, Napoleon's impact was substantial. French conquests stimulated nationalism all across Europe and even, through Napoleon's invasion of Egypt, in North Africa (see Chapter 23). Napoleon's conquest of Spain created conditions favorable to the ambitions of Latin American revolutionaries like Simón Bolívar. And within France's overseas empire, the most dramatic developments took place on the Caribbean island of Saint-Domingue (san doe-MANG).

The Haitian Revolution, 1791–1804

The colony of Saint-Domingue was by far France's richest overseas possession. Occupying the western half of the island of Hispaniola, Saint-Domingue accounted for as much as a third of French foreign trade. Half a million African slaves toiled there under conditions so harsh that the planters had to keep constantly importing more and more Africans to replenish those who were worked to death.

The reaction of white planters in Saint-Domingue to the events of the French Revolution was conflicted. Some were inspired and dreamed of forming their own independent republic. But abolishing slavery and establishing true equality in Saint-Domingue would have brought the entire plantation economy to a halt. In fact, white planters could not even conceive of liberating their slaves. The slaves themselves had little way of knowing what was happening in Paris. Initially, therefore, the central conflict was between the whites and the *gens de couleur* (zhahn deh koo-LUHR), free men and women, mostly of mixed race, who about equaled the whites in number. They were artisans and small farmers who supplied the large plantations; some were even prosperous enough to own slaves themselves. Many were literate, and having followed the events of the American and French Revolutions, they demanded liberty and equality for themselves. By 1791, civil war broke out between the planters and the gens de couleur.

This civil war made an opening for a vast slave uprising organized by a *Voudun* (voh-doon) priest called Boukman (because he was literate). Voudun beliefs and rituals derived from West and Central Africa, and as a religious leader Boukman had great authority among African slaves, while his position as a field manager and coach driver for his master gave him wide-ranging connections in the slave community. He secretly organized thousands of slaves to rise up at his signal. When they did so, in the summer of 1791, they were spontaneously joined by tens of thousands of other slaves from across the island, as well as by maroons, runaway slaves who lived in the mountains.

Just as French peasants had burned the manor houses of their aristocratic overlords, now Boukman's slave army attacked the planters' estates in Saint-Domingue. Forty thousand marched on the city of Le Cap, where whites and gens de couleur had taken refuge. The slaughter lasted for weeks. When planter forces finally captured and executed the rebel leader, they fixed his head to a pole with a sign that read: "This is the head of Boukman, chief of the rebels."

In 1792 the French government sent an army to restore order. But then a new commander emerged. François-Dominique Toussaint was born a slave but had been educated by a priest and had worked in his master's house rather than in the fields. The name by which he is remembered, **Toussaint L'Ouverture**

Toussaint L'Ouverture
(1744–1803) Leader of the Haitian revolution. Under his military and political leadership, Haiti gained independence and abolished slavery, becoming the first black-ruled republic in the Americas. He died in exile in France.

(1744–1803), reflects his military skill: *l'ouverture* refers to the "opening" he would make in the enemy lines. Like Olaudah Equiano (see Chapter 19), Toussaint L'Ouverture (too-SAN loo-ver-CHUR) bridged the worlds of slave and master. He could organize the slaves to fight while forging alliances with whites, gens de couleur, and the foreign forces that intervened in the conflict. By 1801 his army controlled most of the island. Toussaint supported the creation of a new constitution that granted equality to all and that declared him governor-general for life.

Initially revolutionaries in France supported the rebels, but Napoleon had other ideas, and in 1802 he sent an expedition to crush Toussaint's new state. Although Toussaint was open to compromise as long as slavery would not be restored, he was arrested and sent to France, where, harshly treated, he died in prison in 1803.

Meanwhile, as Haitian rebels kept up the fight, Napoleon's soldiers, lacking immunity to tropical diseases, succumbed to yellow fever. Just as the Russian winter would later spoil Napoleon's plan, the West Indies climate also undid his forces. His troops withdrew, and in 1804 the independent nation of Haiti was born.

The independence of Haiti had ramifications throughout the Atlantic world. Slave owners in the United States were terrified by Haiti's example. Some plantations stepped up security measures, such as by placing even tighter limits on slaves' movements, while the U.S. government at first refused to grant Haiti diplomatic

Toussaint L'Ouverture   In this contemporary engraving the Haitian revolutionary leader Toussaint L'Ouverture is shown in an equestrian pose associated with civil and military power. Toussaint brought Enlightenment ideals to the elemental struggle of Haiti's slaves for liberation. His leadership was sorely missed in Haiti after he was tricked into negotiations with France and died in a French prison.

recognition. Venezuela was even more directly affected. In 1795 a Venezuelan who returned from Haiti, a free *zombo* (of mixed African/Amerindian ancestry), led a rebellion of slaves and free persons of color, sending the elite of Caracas into a panic. Simón Bolívar was just twelve at that time, but later he would seek the support of the Haitian government in his own fight for freedom and would argue for the abolition of slavery.

The Latin American Wars of Independence, 1800–1824

Simón Bolívar and other Latin American revolutionaries looked to the ideals of the Enlightenment and the examples of the United States, France, and Haiti in charting their own wars of independence. In Latin America, relations between *criollos* (American-born Spaniards) and people of African, Amerindian, or mixed descent shaped the course of revolution. Beyond widespread agreement on the need to expel the Spanish, the divergent interests of these groups made it difficult to establish common political ground.

In Mexico as in South America, a major question was whether the revolutionaries would be content fighting for independence from Spain or would also want more substantial social and economic reforms. Frightened by the bloodshed in France and the slave uprising in Haiti, elites were cautious. But in Mexico, Bolivia, Venezuela, and elsewhere, Amerindians and slaves sought a complete transformation of society.

Simón Bolívar and South American Independence

The conditions for Latin American independence were closely connected to events in Europe. In 1808 Napoleon put his own brother on the Spanish throne, forcing the Spanish king to abdicate. (The king of Portugal, by contrast, fled to Brazil, which was ruled as a monarchy throughout this period.) In the Spanish-speaking Americas, loyalty to the king meant opposition to the French-imposed regime in Madrid, and local elites created *juntas* (ruling groups) to assert local rule. But were these juntas (HUN-tah) temporary organizations to be disbanded when the legitimate king returned to power, or precursors of a permanent transfer of power from Madrid to the Americas? Loyalists made the former

argument, while Republicans like Bolívar and his Argentinean counterpart José de San Martín (1778–1850) saw the chance to win complete independence. This division of opinion meant that they would have to fight against powerful local loyalists as well as Spanish troops.

A principal grievance was the power of the direct representatives of royal authority in Spanish America. These *peninsulares* dominated the affairs of church and state, much to the frustration of ambitious criollos, who felt that the existing system was an impediment to their rightful place as leading members of their communities. Criollo merchants, for example, were continually frustrated by restrictions on trade imposed by the peninsulares.

But the struggle involved more than just imperial representatives and local elites. In most places, building a popular base of support for independence required appealing to Indians, Africans, *mestizos,* and other people of mixed descent, who together comprised the vast majority of the population.

For example, Bolívar's home city of Caracas, facing the sea, was culturally and economically connected to the Caribbean. Slave plantations were an important part of its economy, and Bolívar spent part of his childhood on a plantation worked by slaves. In addition, Caracas had a large community of *pardos,* free men and women of mixed African-Spanish-Native American ancestry. As in Haiti, unity across lines of class and race was hard to achieve.

In the Venezuelan interior Bolívar would need the cooperation of *llaneros* (yah-neyr-ohs), tough frontier cowboys of mixed Spanish/Amerindian descent (like the *gauchos* of Argentina and the *vaqueros* of Mexico). Farther south, Bolívar's armies eventually entered the

Viceroyalty of Peru, where the social divide was between the Spanish-speaking colonists of the coastal areas and the still considerable Amerindian population of the Andes. Bolívar was constantly tested by the necessity of forging alliances among such disparate groups.

As elsewhere in Spanish America, a junta took power in Caracas following Napoleon's removal of the Spanish king. These leaders saw their power as temporary until the rightful monarchy was restored. The junta sent the well-traveled Bolívar on diplomatic missions to London and Washington in 1810, but Bolívar lobbied the British to support his plan for independence instead. Upon his return, he attended the first Congress of Venezuela, which on July 3, 1811, became the first such body in Latin America to declare independence from Spain.

Racial, ethnic, and regional divisions inhibited any strong sense of "Venezuelan" identity upon which a new nation could be founded. The constitution restricted voting rights to a small minority of overwhelmingly white property owners and did nothing to abolish slavery. In addition, the llaneros of the interior felt threatened by a constitutional provision that extended private property ownership to the previously uncharted plains. If the lands where they herded wild cattle were fenced off by wealthy ranchers, the cowboys feared for their livelihoods.

A huge earthquake in the spring of 1812 compounded the instability of the new Venezuelan republic. Soon forces loyal to Spain were on the offensive. The young republic collapsed, and Bolívar set out on the military path he would pursue for the next twelve years, proclaiming a "war to the death" (see Map 22.2). Captured Spaniards would be executed, he declared, while American-born Spanish loyalists would be given a chance to mend their ways.

In the summer of 1813 Bolívar's army entered Caracas, but the divisions within society worked against him. To broaden his movement's appeal, Bolívar had forged alliances with groups that had been excluded from the first congress and constitution. He sought out the cooperation of the llaneros and promised abolition of slavery. But criollos in the capital regarded the cowboys as bandits and reacted with suspicion.

In addition to such internal dissension, the cause of independence suffered a setback in 1815 after Napoleon's defeat at Waterloo and the restoration of the Spanish monarchy. The Madrid government dispatched fifty ships and over ten thousand soldiers to restore imperial authority in South America. Bolívar retreated to the island of Jamaica, where he once again sought British help. (See the feature "Movement of Ideas: Simón Bolívar's Jamaica Letter.") He also traveled to Haiti, asking for support from its government with a pledge to seek "the absolute liberty of the slaves who have groaned beneath the Spanish yoke in the past three centuries."[4] Most importantly from a military standpoint, he recruited battle-hardened British mercenaries to serve as his elite force.

Returning to Venezuela in 1817, Bolívar established himself in the interior and was recognized as the supreme commander of the various patriotic forces that were contesting Spain's effort to re-establish control. To slaves who joined his army he offered freedom, and he revived his alliance with the llaneros of the plains. Bolívar's toughness in battle and his willingness to share the privations of his men—once spending a whole night immersed in a lake to avoid Spanish forces—won him their loyalty.

In 1819, even while the Spanish still held Caracas, delegates to the **Congress of Angostura** planned for the resuscitation of independent Venezuela. Bolívar argued for a strong central government with effective executive powers, fearing that a federal system with a strong legislature would lead to division and instability. Rather than stay to see these plans carried out, however, Bolívar went south and west to confront imperial forces in the Spanish stronghold of Bogotá. Seeking a broader foundation for Latin American liberty, he began his fight for *Gran Colombia,* a political union he envisioned would encompass today's Venezuela, Colombia, Panama, Ecuador, and Peru.

Bolívar and his troops suffered greatly on their campaign into the frigid Andean mountains. But they attracted local recruits to their cause, including many from the area's Indian population. The demoralized Spanish forces, led by generals who could not match Bolívar's strategic brilliance, quickly gave way, first in Bogotá and then in Ecuador. Meanwhile, further south,

Congress of Angostura (1819) Congress that declared Venezuelan independence after Simón Bolívar gave an opening address arguing for a strong central government with effective executive powers.

Map 22.2 Independence in Latin America

Paraguay led the way toward Latin American independence in 1811, followed by rebels in Buenos Aires who declared the independence of the United Provinces of Rio de la Plata (the core of today's Argentina) in 1816. The next year forces led by José de San Martín crossed the Andes, linked with the rebel army of Bernardo O'Higgins, and secured Chilean independence. The Chilean rebels then traveled north by sea to attack Spanish positions at Lima, with inconclusive results. By that time, however, Simón Bolívar had secured the independence of Venezuela and Ecuador, uniting them into the independent state of Gran Colombia. Combined Chilean and Colombian forces defeated the Spanish at Ayachuco in 1824, finalizing the independence of Spanish Latin America.
© Cengage Learning **Interactive Map**

Liberation campaigns
- Bolívar 1817–1818
- San Martín 1817–1818
- O'Higgins 1817–1818
- Bolívar 1819
- San Martín 1819–1821
- Bolívar 1821
- Bolívar 1822
- San Martín 1822
- Bolívar 1823–1824
- Bolívar 1825
- ★ Major battle
- **1811** Date of independence
- — Boundaries as of 1830

other liberators were scoring equivalent successes. José de San Martín (hoe-SAY deh san mar-TEEN) took the region of Rio de la Plata (today's Argentina), while Chile's successful republican forces were led by Bernardo O'Higgins (the Spanish-speaking son of an Irish immigrant). Together San Martín and O'Higgins had occupied the coastal regions of Peru, leaving only its Andean region in loyalist hands.

The situation in the Andes had been tense since an Amerindian uprising in 1780 led by **Tupac Amaru II** (1741–1781) (TOO-pack ah-MAR-oo). Tupac had been educated by Jesuit priests and for a time served the Spanish government. But the poverty, illiteracy, and oppression faced by his own people caused him first to petition for reform and then, when his pleas were ignored, to change his name, adopt indigenous dress, and organize a rebellion.

Tupac Amaru's revolt was savagely suppressed. He was forced to witness the torture and death of his own wife and family members before his own execution. The Spanish government

Tupac Amaru II (1741–1781) José Gabriel Condorcanqui Noguera, a descendant of the last Inca ruler; called himself Tupac Amaru II while leading a large-scale rebellion in the Andes against Spanish rule. He was defeated and executed.

then banned the wearing of indigenous cloth and the use of the indigenous Quechua **(KEH-chwah)** language. Henceforth, local Amerindians avoided contact with Spanish officials whenever they could. Though highland Amerindians were potential allies of Bolívar, they remained aloof, more concerned with their own autonomy.

Nevertheless, Bolívar's troops engaged the Spanish in the Andes in 1824 at the Battle of Ayacucho. Their victory was complete, and South America was free from Spanish control. Still unanswered, however, was how independence from Spain would translate into liberty for the diverse peoples of South America.

Mexico and Brazil, 1810–1831

Mexico's path to independence had a different starting point. Whereas leadership in the initial struggle in Venezuela was led by socially conservative criollos, in Mexico the deposition of the Spanish king quickly led to a popular uprising of mestizos and Indians. Parish priest **Miguel de Hidalgo y Costilla** (1753–1811) rallied the poor in the name of justice for the oppressed, issuing his famous *Grito* ("cry"): "Long live Our Lady of Guadalupe! Long live the Americas and death to the corrupt government!" His appeal to the Virgin of Guadalupe, a dark-skinned representation of the Virgin Mary as she had appeared to a lowly peasant, symbolized Hidalgo's appeal to Indians and mestizos. Hidalgo called for the creation of a Mexican nation with the words *"¡Mexicanos, Viva México!"*

Shocking to Spanish officials, Hidalgo's call also alarmed Mexico's criollos, who flocked to the loyalist banner. His forces scattered, and Hidalgo was excommunicated and executed. As late as 1820, Spanish authority seemed secure.

When independence did come in 1821, it resulted not from a popular insurgency but from a conservative backlash against changes emanating from Madrid. Threatened by liberal reforms in Spain, these elite conservatives supported Mexican military officers who turned on their former Spanish allies. Contrary to Father Hildago's vision, Mexican independence brought neither social nor economic reform. Nevertheless, Hidalgo still symbolizes Mexican independence, and the anniversary of the *Grito de Dolores,* September 16, is celebrated as Mexico's national day.

Brazil followed an entirely different path. In 1808 the Portuguese royal family fled Napoleon's invasion, seeking refuge in Brazil. In 1821 the king returned to Portugal, leaving his son Pedro behind as his representative. Pedro, however, declared himself sympathetic to the cause of independence, and in 1824

> **Miguel de Hidalgo y Costilla** (1753–1811) Mexican priest who launched the first stage of the Mexican war for independence. Hidalgo appealed to Indians and mestizos and was thus viewed with suspicion by Mexican criollos. In 1811, he was captured and executed. The Spanish publicly displayed his severed and mutilated head in Guanajuato as a warning to other rebels.

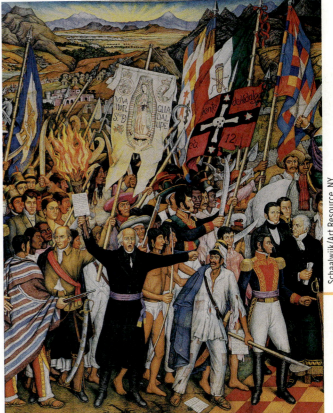

Schaalwijk/Art Resource, NY

Padre Hildalgo In 1810 Padre Hidalgo rallied the common people of Mexico, especially mestizos and Indians, under the banner of the Virgin of Guadalupe, for independence from Spain. Mexican elites opposed him, however, and cooperated with Spanish authorities to crush the uprising. Hidalgo was executed. When Mexican independence was achieved in 1821, the criollo elite was firmly in charge of the new nation.

Simón Bolívar's Jamaica Letter

An important starting point for Simón Bolívar's political philosophy was the work of the great Enlightenment thinker the Baron de Montesquieu. In his *Spirit of the Laws* (1748), Montesquieu had argued that there was no universal template for human governance; rather, any given society is best governed by a political and legal system suited to its own culture and traditions. Bolívar argued that the institutions of independent Latin America must mesh with its own traditions rather than merely copy models imported from the outside. In this statement from 1815, written before the major experiments with republican independence had taken place in Latin America, Bolívar assesses the background to the postindependence constitutional order.

Bolívar's Jamaica Letter

In my opinion, this is the image of our situation. We are a small segment of the human race; we possess a world apart, surrounded by vast seas, new in almost every art and science.... [We are] moreover neither Indians nor Europeans, but a race halfway between the legitimate owners of the land and the Spanish usurpers—in short, being Americans by birth and endowed with rights from Europe—find ourselves forced to defend these rights against the natives while maintaining our position in the land against the intrusion of the invaders....

The posture of those who dwell in the American hemisphere has been over the centuries purely passive. We were at a level even lower than servitude, and by that very reason hindered from elevating ourselves to the enjoyment of freedom.... From the beginning we were plagued by a practice that in addition to depriving us of the rights to which we were entitled left us in a kind of permanent infancy with respect to public affairs. If we had been allowed to manage even the domestic aspects of our internal administration, we would understand the processes and mechanisms of public affairs....

The Americans, within the Spanish system still in force, and perhaps now more than ever, occupy no other place in society other than that of servants suited for work, or, at best, that of simple consumers, and even this role is limited by appalling restrictions.... We were ... lost, or worse, absent from the universe in all things relative to the science of government and the administration of the state. We were never viceroys, never governors ... hardly ever bishops or archbishops; never diplomats; soldiers, only in lower ranks.... In short, we were never leaders, never financiers, hardly even merchants....

The Americans have made their debut on the world stage suddenly and without prior knowledge ... having to enact the eminent roles of legislators, magistrates, ministers of the treasury, diplomats, generals, and all the other supreme and subordinate authorities that make up the hierarchy of a well-organized state....

Perfectly representative institutions are not appropriate to our character, our customs, and our current level of knowledge and experience.... Until our compatriots acquire the political skills and virtues that distinguish our brothers to the north, entirely popular systems, far from being favorable to us, will, I greatly fear, lead to our ruin....

The people of South America have manifested the inclination to establish liberal and even perfect institutions, an effect, no doubt, of the instinct all men share of aspiring to the highest possible degree of happiness, which is invariably achieved in civil societies founded on the principles of justice, freedom and equality.... More than anyone, I would like to see America become the greatest nation on earth, regarded not so much for its size and wealth as for its freedom and glory. Although I aspire to a perfect government for my country, I can't persuade myself that the New World is ready at this time to be governed by a grand republic.... The American states need the stewardship of paternalistic governments to cure the wounds and ravages of despotism and war....

The idea of merging the entire New World into a single nation with a single unifying principle to provide coherence to the parts and to the whole is both grandiose and impractical. Because it has a common origin, a common language, similar customs, and one religion, we might conclude that it should be possible for a single government to oversee a federation of the different states eventually to emerge. However, this is not possible, because America is divided by remote climates, diverse geographies, conflicting interests, and dissimilar characteristics....

When success is uncertain, when the state is weak ... all men vacillate; opinions are divided, inflamed by passion and by the enemy, which seeks to win easy victory in this way. When we are at last strong, under the auspices of a liberal nation that lends us its protection, then we will cultivate in harmony the virtues and talents that lead to glory; then we will follow the majestic path toward abundant prosperity marked out by destiny for South America; then the arts and sciences that were born in the Orient and that brought Enlightenment to Europe will fly to a free Colombia, which will nurture and shelter them.

Source: Excerpts from Simón Bolívar "Oath Taken at Rome, 15 August 1805" translated by Frederick H. Fornoff. From David Bushnessl, ed., *El Libertador: Writings of Simon Bolivar* (pp. *12-30*). Copyright © 2003. Reprinted by permission of Oxford University Press.

QUESTIONS FOR ANALYSIS

▶ What forces does Bolívar think must be taken into account when planning Latin America's future?

▶ What limits does he feel those forces place on the continent's political aspirations?

▶ What comparisons does he draw between North and South America?

Pedro I (r. 1824–1831) became the constitutional monarch of an independent Brazil. Although unpopular with some people, such as sugar planters who disapproved of an 1830 treaty with Britain to abolish the slave trade, the constitutional monarchy lasted until 1889.

Revolutionary Outcomes and Comparisons, to 1830

In the first half of the nineteenth century the United States of America established itself as a vigorous republic. By 1830 there were twenty-four states; settlers moved to new territories; and high wages and cheap land attracted swelling numbers of European immigrants.

Americans pursued what they considered their "manifest destiny," a clear and divinely approved mission to settle the continent. Lewis and Clark's expedition pointed the way west, and the vast Louisiana Purchase (purchased from Napoleon in 1803) gave the new republic room to grow. These lands were not, however, empty. Over the course of the nineteenth century, western expansion would be marked by blood and violence. And since the issue of slavery remained unresolved, regional tensions increased. As new states entered the Union, would they be free or would they be slave? It would take a violent civil war to solve that question.

In Europe, conservative elites used the defeat of Napoleon to suppress reform. The Bourbon dynasty was restored, and Prince Metternich of Austria orchestrated the **Congress of Vienna** (1815), which reinstated a balance of power among Britain, France, Austria, Prussia, and Russia (see Map 22.3). Aristocrats once again flouted their wealth in the capitals of Europe, no longer afraid of revolutionary violence.

The spread of nationalism and the association of that idea with progressive reform proved, however, a constant challenge to European rulers. When Greek nationalists won their independence from the Ottoman Empire in 1829, the event did not at first appear to threaten the European status quo. But it was not long before ethnic minorities in the Austrian and Russian Empires began organizing along national lines, while the idea of a single, powerful German nation began to spread as well. Other ideals of the French Revolution also remained alive, such as the idea that equality could only be achieved through a more equitable distribution of wealth. A rising generation of revolutionaries would soon try once again to overturn Europe's status quo.

In Haiti, the transition from slave colony to free republic proved difficult. As freed slaves established their own farms on small plots of land, a massive decline in production resulted. The sharp decline in plantation exports robbed the new government of its tax base. The political transition to independence proved equally difficult. The personal ambitions of early Haitian rulers, fueled by tensions between the mixed-race gens de couleur and Haitians of African/slave descent, created a long-standing culture of corruption and dictatorship in Haitian politics.

In Latin America, Simón Bolívar's vision of a state of *Gran Colombia* was never achieved. Military commanders preferred to take power as presidents of their own separate republics, and South America became a patchwork of separate, often squabbling nations. Lacking strong traditions of local governance, these new republics were dominated by a small number of wealthy landowners. Concentrated wealth provided no foundation on which to build democracy, and, as Bolívar foresaw, the fragmentation of *Gran Colombia* left South America vulnerable to external powers such as Great Britain and the United States.

One of Bolívar's top commanders, José Antonio Páez, declared Venezuela a separate republic in 1830, repudiating the connection with *Gran Colombia* and establishing an authoritarian style of

Congress of Vienna   (1815) Conference at which the balance of power of European states was restored after the defeat of Napoleon Bonaparte.

Map 22.3   Europe in 1815

After the disruptions to the political map of Europe caused by the French Revolution and the expansion of Napoleon's empire, in 1815 European diplomats restored earlier boundaries and established a conservative status quo at the Congress of Vienna. One important change was the appearance of the Prussian-led German Confederation, a tariff union that helped lay the foundation for the later unification of Germany (see Chapter 23).   © Cengage Learning   **▶ Interactive Map**

rule that would have ominous implications for all of Latin America. He was one of the *caudillos*, dictatorial rulers who looked after their own interests and those of the military above all else. If Napoleon had been something of an "enlightened despot," the same could rarely be said of caudillos who seized power in many of the new South American nations.

Although Africans, Amerindians, and people of mixed descent played important roles in the Latin American wars of independence, their efforts were not to be rewarded with power or privilege, even where slavery was abolished. Benefiting most from independence were the criollos, who consolidated their political and economic dominance by assuming positions of authority vacated by departing peninsulares. As for the church, while individual priests might side with the downtrodden, the Catholic hierarchy allied itself with the wealthy and powerful.

caudillos   Latin American military men who gained power through violence during the early nineteenth and twentieth centuries.

Chapter Review and Learning Activities

Simón Bolívar had a forceful personality, and in his impatience with the feuding and squabbling that jeopardized his great project he sometimes resorted to dictatorial means. But in the end he resisted the allure of dictatorship and resigned as leader of *Gran Colombia*. He died in sad exile, experiencing neither the might of Napoleon Bonaparte in power nor the peace of George Washington in retirement. A recent biographer admits that Bolívar "never found the ideal balance between order and freedom" and that he was "better at analyzing the ills of Latin America than in devising remedies." But the fact remains that virtually all South Americans, whatever their differences of political ideology, social class, or ethnic or racial identity, take Simón Bolívar as their starting point for discussions of who they are and what they might be. That legacy makes him one of the great figures of nineteenth-century world history.

 ### What political compromises were made in establishing the new United States of America?

The founders of the United States of America created an effective set of institutions by compromising on issues such as the influence of larger and smaller states on the federal government and on the balance between executive, judicial, and legislative power. One compromise that came out of the constitutional negotiations, however, both contradicted the noblest aspirations of the Enlightenment and laid the groundwork for future conflict. The persistence of slavery in the United States, and the expansion of slavery through the admission of new slave states to the Union, highlighted the contradiction between a status quo inherited from the colonial era and the United States' self-definition as the "land of the free." The War of Independence set the country on a new path, but it did not completely overcome such legacies of the past.

 ### What were the major phases of the French Revolution?

In the first phase, representatives of the Third Estate tried to create a constitutional monarchy. But the storming of the Bastille and attacks on the manor houses of the nobility created a more confrontational environment. Rather than compromise, Louis XVI and the nobility sought help from other European rulers to restore their power. In the next, most radical phase of the Revolution, the Jacobins under Maximilien Robespierre mobilized mass armies to fight off the invaders and instituted a harsh security regime: the Reign of Terror. It was not long before the Jacobins were swallowed up by the violence they had unleashed. The rise of Napoleon Bonaparte represented the final phase of the Revolution. Now it was national glory rather than individual liberty that inspired Napoleon's troops and the French nation. Though he instituted many social and political reforms in the tradition of Enlightenment rationality, Napoleon's imperial project contradicted the Revolution's early emphasis on individual rights.

 ### How were the revolutions in Latin America and the Caribbean influenced by the history of colonialism?

In Latin America and the Caribbean, as in the United States and France, the possibilities of revolution were conditioned by continuities with the past. The French island colony of Saint-Domingue, one the world's largest producers of sugar, had a sharply divided social system with French planters at the top, mixed-race gens de couleur below, and, at the very bottom, a large population of African slaves. Toussaint L'Overture brought not just military leadership to the slave revolt but also an ability to connect the raw power of the slave rebellion with Enlightenment ideals. His attempt to reconcile those two realities was, however, frustrated by French treachery. Simón Bolívar did at least have an opportunity to put his dreams into reality, but here again history and tradition seemed to work against the fulfillment of his vision. The stark differences in wealth between the large landowners and the majority of the population, and the related cultural divide between the Spanish-descended elite and the mestizos (Indian and African majorities), meant that there was but a weak middle class of shopkeepers and small independent farmers as a foundation on which to build democratic republics. And, in spite of the example of Father Hidalgo in Mexico, the Catholic Church remained aligned with powerful Spanish elites.

How much did the outcomes of these revolutions in western Europe and the Americas represent a thorough transformation of existing political and social structures?

In each case, the persistence of the past blocked the full realization of the revolutionary intentions. In the United States, slavery persisted in spite of a rhetorical commitment to "liberty and equality." In France, revolutionary excesses led from a vision of democracy to the reality of Napoleonic dictatorship. In Latin America and the Caribbean, continuing social inequality undermined efforts to establish stable republican governments. And nowhere were women fully included in the agenda of equality. A French revolutionary argued in 1792 that "the perfectibility of man is unlimited," not just possible, but inevitable. Study of the political processes examined in this chapter leads to a more cautious conclusion. Even in the wake of revolution, societies are not blank slates ready for entirely fresh characters to be written. Reconciling the twin mandates of "liberty" and "equality" remained a challenge for every postrevolutionary society.

FOR FURTHER REFERENCE

Bailyn, Bernard. *The Ideological Origins of the American Revolution*. Cambridge, Mass.: Belknap, 1992.

Bell, Madison Smartt. *Toussaint Louverture: A Biography*. New York: Pantheon, 2007.

Bushnell, David. *Simón Bolívar: Liberation and Disappointment*. New York: Pearson Longman, 2004.

Bushnell, David, and Neill MacAuley. *The Emergence of Latin America in the Nineteenth Century*. New York: Oxford University Press, 1994.

Doyle, William. *Origins of the French Revolution*. New York: Oxford University Press, 1999.

Englund, Steven. *Napoleon: A Political Life*. New York: Scribner's, 2004.

Geggus, David P. *The Impact of the Haitian Revolution in the Atlantic World*. Columbia: University of South Carolina Press, 2002.

Rowe, Michael (ed.). *Collaboration and Resistance in Napoleonic Europe: State Formation in an Age of Upheaval*. New York: Palgrave Macmillan, 2003.

Van Young, Eric. *The Other Rebellion: Popular Violence, Ideology, and the Mexican Struggle for Independence, 1810–1821*. Stanford: Stanford University Press, 2001.

Wood, Gordon S. *The American Revolution*. New York: Modern Library, 2002.

KEY TERMS

Simón Bolívar (480)

George Washington (483)

Declaration of Independence (483)

Joseph Brant (484)

Constitution of the United States of America (485)

Louis XVI (486)

Third Estate (486)

National Assembly (486)

Jacobins (488)

Napoleon Bonaparte (489)

Toussaint L'Ouverture (490)

Congress of Angostura (493)

Tupac Amaru II (494)

Miguel de Hidalgo y Costilla (495)

Congress of Vienna (498)

caudillos (499)

VOYAGES ON THE WEB

Voyages: Simón Bolívar

"Voyages" is a real time excursion to historical sites in this chapter and includes interactive activities and study tools such as audio summaries, animated maps, and flashcards.

Visual Evidence: Portraits of Power: George Washington and Napoleon Bonaparte

"Visual Evidence" features artifacts, works of art, or photographs, along with a brief descriptive essay and discussion questions to guide your analysis of visual sources.

World History in Today's World: Bolivian Politics

"World History in Today's World" makes the connection between features of modern life and their origins in the periods in this chapter.

 CourseMate

Go to the CourseMate website at www.cengagebrain.com for additional study tools and review materials—including audio and video clips—for this chapter.

23

The Industrial Revolution and European Politics, 1780–1880

Alexander Herzen
(© RIA Novosti/Alamy)

Driven into exile by the Russian government, the socialist thinker **Alexander Herzen** (1812–1870) took his family and fled west; their "covered sledge crunched through the snow" as they set off in the bitter Russian winter. Friends and servants accompanied them to the border: "There for the last time we clinked glasses and parted, sobbing."[1] In early 1848 they were enjoying the relative warmth of Italy when news came of revolution in Paris. "The name of the city," Herzen wrote, "is bound up with all the loftiest aspirations, with all the greatest hopes of contemporary man—I entered it with a trembling heart, with reverence, as men used to enter Jerusalem and Rome."[2]

Like Simón Bolívar four decades earlier, Herzen was seeking revolutionary inspiration in hopes of transforming his native land. In the spring of 1848 revolution spread from Paris across western Europe, but by summer conservative authorities were re-establishing control. Herzen was bitterly disappointed. After 1848 he saw the West as decadent and corrupt; he argued that the Russians, though suffering from political repression and economic backwardness, had the greatest potential for bringing socialism to the world:

What a blessing it is for Russia that the rural commune has never been broken up, that private property has never replaced the property of the commune: how fortunate it is for the Russian people that they have remained … outside European civilization, which would undoubtedly have sapped the life of the commune…. The future of Russia lies with the peasant.[3]

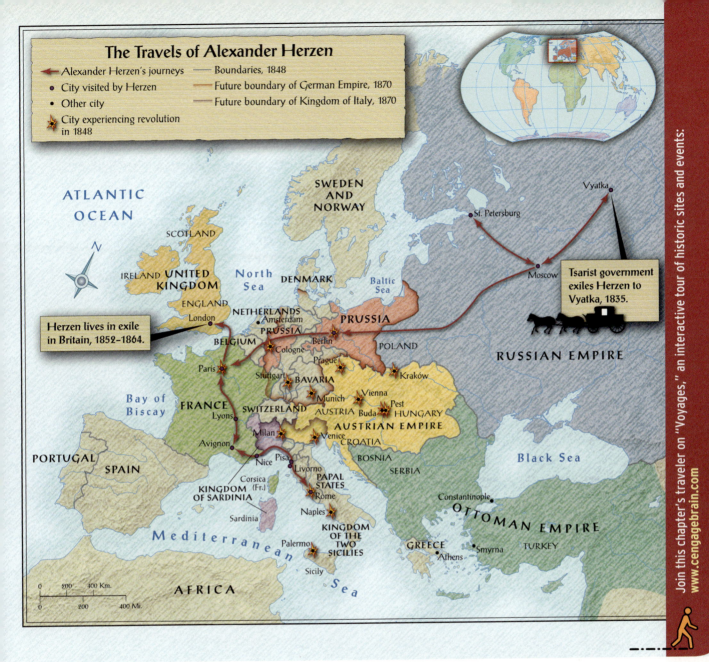

The Travels of Alexander Herzen

Legend:
- ← Alexander Herzen's journeys
- ● City visited by Herzen
- ● Other city
- ✹ City experiencing revolution in 1848
- —— Boundaries, 1848
- —— Future boundary of German Empire, 1870
- —— Future boundary of Kingdom of Italy, 1870

ATLANTIC OCEAN

SWEDEN AND NORWAY

SCOTLAND

IRELAND   UNITED KINGDOM

North Sea

DENMARK

Baltic Sea

St. Petersburg

Vyatka

Moscow

Tsarist government exiles Herzen to Vyatka, 1835.

RUSSIAN EMPIRE

ENGLAND

London

NETHERLANDS
Amsterdam

PRUSSIA

PRUSSIA

Cologne   Berlin

POLAND

Herzen lives in exile in Britain, 1852–1864.

BELGIUM

Paris

Prague

Kraków

FRANCE

Stuttgart   BAVARIA

Munich   Vienna

Pest

Lyons

SWITZERLAND

AUSTRIA   Buda   HUNGARY

Bay of Biscay

Milan   Venice

AUSTRIAN EMPIRE

CROATIA

Avignon

Nice   Pisa

Livorno

BOSNIA

SERBIA

Black Sea

PORTUGAL   SPAIN

Corsica (Fr.)

KINGDOM OF SARDINIA

Sardinia

PAPAL STATES

Rome

Naples

Constantinople

OTTOMAN EMPIRE

KINGDOM OF THE TWO SICILIES

GREECE

Smyrna   TURKEY

Palermo

Mediterranean Sea

Athens

Sicily

AFRICA

0   200   400 Km.
0   200   400 Mi.

Join this chapter's traveler on "Voyages," an interactive tour of historic sites and events:
www.cengagebrain.com

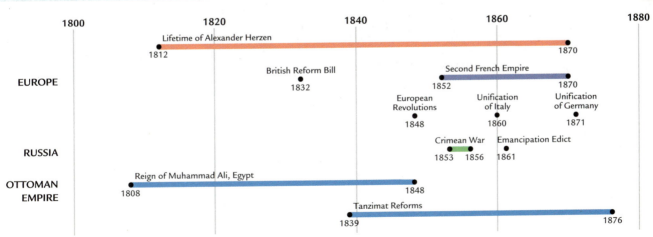

Timeline:

1800 — 1820 — 1840 — 1860 — 1880

Lifetime of Alexander Herzen 1812 – 1870

EUROPE
- British Reform Bill 1832
- Second French Empire 1852 – 1870
- European Revolutions 1848
- Unification of Italy 1860
- Unification of Germany 1871

RUSSIA
- Crimean War 1853 – 1856
- Emancipation Edict 1861

OTTOMAN EMPIRE
- Reign of Muhammad Ali, Egypt 1808 – 1848
- Tanzimat Reforms 1839 – 1876

Alexander Herzen (1812–1870) Russian socialist and revolutionary thinker who published journals smuggled into Russia that influenced radical opinion toward reform and emancipation of the serfs. His philosophy combined socialism with fierce commitment to individual liberty.

In this passage Herzen combines two of the most powerful ideas of his age, socialism and nationalism, in his argument that the collectivist tradition of the Russian peasantry, modernized for the industrial age, would show the way toward a more equitable world.

Alexander Herzen lived through one of the most eventful periods of human history: the Industrial Revolution. Coal-driven steam engines unleashed the power of fossil fuels in the industrializing economies of western Europe and the United States, driving the machinery of new factories and propelling steamships and locomotives. More efficient transportation bound the entire world's people more tightly in networks of trade and communication. The sleigh that took Herzen's family to the West would soon be replaced by a railroad, and some of those peasants he celebrated would leave their rural communes to work in mines and factories.

The Industrial Revolution not only transformed methods of production and transportation but also stimulated new social conditions and political ideologies. More people moved to cities, where many lived in squalid conditions. Rapid social change stimulated debates among reformers and revolutionaries. Alexander Herzen absorbed the sometimes conflicting ideals of liberals, who emphasized individual liberty; socialists, who stressed the collective good; and nationalists, who gave more thought to the advancement of their own group and less to the fate of humanity as a whole.

Debates in social theory were sparked by the writings of the German socialist Karl Marx and the English evolutionary biologist Charles Darwin, each of whom, in different ways, contributed to the widespread belief that the industrial age was a time of progress. But the Industrial Revolution posed particular challenges to the Russian and Ottoman Empires. Political elites in these old land-based empires, now on the fringe of industrializing Europe, were torn between policies of reform, including the adaptation to Western models of law and governance, and conservative policies that stressed continuity over change.

FOCUS QUESTIONS

▶ What were the most important outcomes of the Industrial Revolution?

▶ What were the main features of European political development during and after the revolutions of 1848?

▶ Why were the ideas of Karl Marx and Charles Darwin of such great significance for world history?

▶ How did the leaders of the Russian and Ottoman Empires respond to the challenge of an industrializing western Europe?

The Industrial Revolution: Origins and Global Consequences, 1780–1870

Innovations—new forms of energy, new inventions, new ways of organizing human labor—were the foundation of the **Industrial Revolution**. By burning coal to drive steam engines, applying those steam engines to power machinery, and organizing mechanical processes in factories to centralize and rationalize the division of labor, industrial societies achieved unprecedented economic growth.

Britain took the lead, soon followed by continental Europe and the United States. By the middle of the nineteenth century industrialized societies were poised to translate economic power into military and political predominance on the world stage.

The Industrial Revolution was a global process. Improvements in transportation and communications—the steamship, railroad, and telegraph—created a global market for raw materials. At the same time, as industrial production outstripped domestic demand, industrialists sought world markets to expand production even further.

Origins of the Industrial Revolution, 1780–1850

In England, the agricultural revolution of Joseph Banks and other "improving farmers," while increasing food production, also drove many rural people off the land (see Chapter 21). In search for new work, these people moved to cities, mines, and emerging factory towns. While previously their work had been governed by the seasons and the constraints of muscle power, now their lives became dominated by the relentless power of steam and the factory clock. People who had once known virtually everyone around them now found themselves living in the anonymity of industrial cities.

The fluidity of the British elite was a spur to economic innovation. Whereas elsewhere in Europe the titled nobility remained aloof from commerce, in England lines were less firmly drawn between aristocrats, members of the gentry, and merchant families. And while continental European philosophers usually concerned themselves with pure science over practical applications, "the English genius," Herzen remarked, "finds repellent an abstract generalization."[4] The "practical science" promoted by Joseph Banks during his long tenure as president of the Royal Society demonstrated Herzen's point.

> **Industrial Revolution** Changes that began in late eighteenth-century Britain and transformed the global economy by creating new markets for raw materials and finished goods. Accompanied by technological changes that revolutionized production processes, living and working conditions, and the environment.

The British economy was stimulated by its empire. Timber and furs from Canada, sugar from the Caribbean, cotton textiles from India, and tea from China were part of a global trade network dominated by British shipping. Previously, the banks, stock exchanges, and insurance houses of London were primarily directed toward trade. In the late eighteenth and nineteenth century, their investments expanded to include industrial production as well. Industrial capitalism was born.

The Industrial Revolution was unleashed by improvements in the production of iron. Iron smelters worldwide had long used wood charcoal to fuel their furnaces, but production amounts were limited to small batches, and increased demand for iron drove wood prices ever higher. While coal was plentiful in Britain, much of it contained too many impurities to burn at the high temperatures necessary for iron production. Then in the early eighteenth century an English inventor discovered a means of purifying coal to make a more concentrated product called coke. In the 1760s, after a way was devised to remove impurities from the coke-iron product, coal could be used to make low-cost, high-quality iron in plentiful amounts.

The full potential of this energy revolution was realized with the development of the steam engine. Building on earlier crude designs, James

Watt developed an efficient steam engine in 1764, and for the first time it became possible to turn coal into cheap power.

Meanwhile, other entrepreneurs were focusing on the social organization of production. In his *Wealth of Nations,* Adam Smith had argued that division of labor was a key to increased productivity. Smith used the example of pins. A single person making a pin from start to finish, Smith explained, would be much less productive than a group of artisans who each focused on a single step in the process. The division of labor was key to the development of the factory system of production.

In the 1760s entrepreneur and abolitionist Josiah Wedgwood began to experiment with a more complex division of labor in his ceramics factory. By breaking the production process down into specialized tasks, his factory produced greater quantities of uniform dinnerware at less expense. Wedgwood advanced the factory system of production even further when, in 1782, he was the first to install a steam engine, combining Smith's division of labor and Watt's steam power. The age of mass production had begun.

But it was in the textile industry where division of labor and steam power combined to full potential. At that time, India was by far the world's largest producer of cotton textiles, and Indian calico cloth flooded the British market. Unhappy with the competition, British wool producers convinced Parliament to impose high tariffs on Indian calicoes, making them less affordable.

However, the tariffs did not apply to raw cotton. At first British entrepreneurs used a decentralized "putting-out" system of providing raw materials to a rural family, who would manufacture the cloth. The family used a traditional gender division of labor, the women first spinning the cotton into thread that the men then wove into cloth. Since spinning took more time than weaving, men were frequently idled while they waited for their wives catch up.

The problem was solved when British inventors found ways to mechanize the spinning process, making it possible to produce much greater quantities of high-quality cotton thread. But with spinning now more efficient, it was the old methods of weaving that held back production, giving industrialists an incentive to mechanize the entire process. Experiments with steam-driven power looms took several decades, but by the 1830s the manufacture of cloth had been mechanized and consolidated into factories.

Growth in textile production increased the demand for raw cotton. After 1793 supplies from India were augmented by new production in the United States. In that year, American inventor Eli Whitney invented the cotton gin, which efficiently separated seeds from cotton. Whitney's machine stimulated cotton production in the United States, which soon became the world's biggest supplier.

By the mid-nineteenth century, virtually every field of manufacture was transformed by the social organization of the factory and the energy revolution of coal and steam. Britain's early lead in industrialization combined with its strength in international commerce to make it a dominant global power, soon copied by others. Coal-rich Belgium was the first to develop a substantial network of steam-fired factories, followed by France and Germany. Industrial production was also increasing in the United States, particularly in northern states like Massachusetts.

Global Dimensions of the Industrial Revolution, 1820–1880

The Industrial Revolution was a global process. Railroads, steamships, and the telegraph dramatically increased the pace of global interactions, and people around the world consumed inexpensive factory-produced goods. By the later nineteenth century most of humankind participated in the global commodity markets of industrial capitalism.

Early industrial Britain had benefited from its transportation network. The country's coastal shipping, combined with river and canal transport, stimulated domestic markets. Water transport had always been more efficient than transport by land, but as the price of iron dropped railroads became a viable alternative. At first railroad cars were horse drawn, but by 1829 the industrial cities of Manchester and

Liverpool in northern England were connected by steam locomotive.

By midcentury a dense network of railroads covered western Europe (see Map 23.1), increasing both urbanization and mobility. Railroads were not only an efficient and inexpensive means of transporting freight, but they could also transport people more cheaply and comfortably than by stagecoach. In North America, transcontinental railroads in the United States and Canada speeded European settlers west. By 1880 railroad construction had also begun in Russia, British India, and Mexico.

Steamships were another product of "the age of steam and iron." By 1850 steamships had improved transportation in industrial nations, especially in the United States, where large

waterways like the Mississippi River conveyed people and goods over large distances. The international influence of steamships was even more revolutionary. The first steam-powered crossing of the Atlantic took place in 1838 and of the Pacific in 1853. Though sailing ships remained common, by the 1870s steamships were dramatically reducing transportation times and shipping costs, as well as enhancing the military advantage of Western nations around the world. The completion of the Suez Canal in 1869 (linking the Mediterranean and Red Seas), combined with the power of steamships, cut transportation time from Europe to South Asia from months to weeks. Such advances enabled the expansion of European imperialism in Africa and Southeast Asia and

Map 23.1 Continental Industrialization, ca. 1850

Ease of access to iron and coal spurred industrialization in parts of Europe, such as northeastern France, Belgium, and northwestern regions of the German Confederation. By 1850 railroad connections supplemented rivers and canals as means of transport with an efficiency that lowered the cost of both raw materials and finished products. By the end of the century every nation in Europe was tightly integrated by rail, facilitating as well the movement of people and goods across the continent. © Cengage Learning **Interactive Map**

the tightening of control over existing colonies, like British India.

The invention of the telegraph enabled information to move even more quickly than people and goods. The first long-range telegraph message was sent in 1844. In 1869 a submarine cable was laid beneath the Atlantic Ocean, allowing for instantaneous transcontinental communication. Shipping companies used the telegraph to lower the cost of shipping and increase global trade. Military officers with telegraphic information had a powerful tactical advantage, as well.

Industrialization expanded the need for raw materials, especially cotton. After the British gained control of India, the export of finished cloth was replaced by the export of raw cotton. Partly because of the lower cost of factory-made textiles, and partly because of tariffs aiding British industry, India actually suffered a process of deindustrialization during the early mid-nineteenth century, as unemployed Indian spinners, weavers, and dyers fled to the countryside.

Another supplier of cotton was Egypt. After Napoleon's invasion of Egypt, an ambitious Ottoman military commander, **Muhammad Ali** (r. 1808–1848), seized power. Muhammad Ali **(moo-HAH-muhd AH-lee)** had witnessed firsthand the superiority of European weaponry and

Muhammad Ali
(r. 1808–1848) Egyptian ruler who attempted to modernize his country's economy by promoting cotton cultivation and textile manufacturing and by sending young Egyptians to study in Europe.

knew that his regime needed to keep up with the latest advances. He therefore encouraged cotton production to pay for railroads, factories, and guns, while sending science and engineering students to study in France. Egyptian peasants, however, saw little benefit from global markets. That was even truer for slaves picking cotton in the United States. For many in India, Egypt, and North America, the Industrial Revolution's appetite for cotton was a curse, not a blessing.

Commodities from around the world were drawn into the web of industry. Palm oil and peanuts from West Africa helped lubricate industrial machinery. Hides from the *pampas* **(PAHM-pahs)** grasslands of Argentina spurred a proliferation of leather goods, and sisal from Mexico was exported for making rope. Africans and Latin Americans participated in the Industrial Revolution primarily as suppliers of raw materials.

As we will see in the following three chapters, ways of life in the Americas, Africa, Asia, and the Pacific were challenged by the Industrial Revolution. In fact, similar challenges faced the peoples of Europe. In England, for example, skilled artisans known as Luddites broke into factories and smashed the machinery, seeing mechanization as a threat to their livelihoods. Kings, aristocrats, and religious leaders often saw growing cities as breeding grounds for moral decay and social disorder. But there were many Europeans, Alexander Herzen among them, who emphasized the possibilities of the new age.

Reform and Revolution in Nineteenth-Century Europe, 1815–1880

In 1815 the great powers of Europe banded together to quell the fires of the French Revolution and its aftermath. Their success did not last long. Monarchy and aristocratic prerogative no longer sat well with the rising urban middle class and the new industrial working class of Europe.

The rising social classes strove for greater liberty, augmenting the ideals they inherited from the Enlightenment and French Revolution with new ideologies. Liberals, most influential in Britain, emphasized the freedom of the individual and the sanctity of private property. Socialists, growing in numbers and influence, stressed their belief in collective organization for the betterment of society. The romantic movement, especially strong among Germans, increasingly emphasized depth of feeling over the cool rationality of the Enlightenment. The passion of romanticism became linked with nationalism, the most powerful of the ideologies swirling through industrializing Europe.

Tensions rising from industrial change came to a crescendo in 1848, when revolution spread across Europe. In Paris, Berlin, Vienna, Budapest, Rome, and other European cities, it seemed that the old order was being swept away. But the fire of revolution soon died down. Revolutionaries like Alexander Herzen were shocked and disappointed when conservative, authoritarian leaders re-established control.

Nineteenth-Century Ideologies: Liberalism, Socialism, Romanticism, and Nationalism

Alexander Herzen embodied the new sensibilities. His writings exhibit four different, sometimes contradictory, ideas: liberalism, socialism, romanticism, and nationalism.

Liberalism implied open-mindedness and the need for social and political reform. In the nineteenth century, Britain was most strongly associated with liberal tendencies, while European monarchs and their supporters resisted reform. Liberals favored freedom of conscience, freedom of trade, the protection of property rights, and limitations on the political power of religious authorities. While liberals approved of the extension of voting rights to men with property and education, only late in the century did liberalism become associated with universal male suffrage.

Socialism was better developed in France and Germany. Some socialists favored the overthrow of the state as a precondition for the collectivization of property and the realization of social equality. Other socialists thought their cause could be advanced by working within existing institutions, while advocates of yet another strand of socialism created utopian communities outside the state. In liberal Britain,

democracy and socialism developed together, while in Russia, with its more authoritarian government, the revolutionary strand of socialism predominated.

Romanticism prioritized emotional intensity and authenticity over the rationalism and formality of the Enlightenment. "You can no more bridle passions with logic than you can justify them in the law courts," Herzen wrote, even as a series of love affairs tore his marriage apart.[5] Starting with Ludwig von Beethoven, German composers developed themes of musical romanticism culminating in the long, complex, and powerful operas of Richard Wagner (1813–1883).

Romanticism was strongly connected to *nationalism,* the most powerful political ideology of the industrial age. Nationalists, like Wagner, sought to develop cultural and historical pedigrees for peoples who did not yet have nation states to represent them. Some nationalists worked to bring together members of language groups, such as Germans and Italians, who were divided by political boundaries. Others sought to separate their group from multinational empires: Poles from Russia, Greeks from the Ottoman Empire, and Hungarians from Austria. Unlike the concern showed by liberals and socialists for humanity as a whole, nationalists focused on the interests of their particular group.

Victorian Britain, 1815–1867

In 1815 Britain was dominated by conservative elites, such as the landed classes who dominated Parliament imposed tariffs on imported grain, raising the price of bread. Unemployment was high among returning soldiers, and the enclosure movement and the new factory system were driving many out of villages and into urban slums.

Conditions in cities were appalling. Wages were low, and many employers preferred children, especially girls, as factory workers because they were nimble, could fit into tight spaces, and were easy to control. Industrial cities were unhealthy places. The lack of sanitation was noted by Friedrich Engels, a German socialist leader, during his visit to Manchester in 1844:

V&A Images, London/Art Resource, NY

The Crystal Palace   The Crystal Palace, one of the great feats of Victorian engineering, was completed in 1851 as the centerpiece of Britain's Great Exhibition. The designers of this imposing structure, made entirely of iron and glass, intended it as a monument to industrial, technological, and commercial progress.

Right and left a multitude of covered passages lead from the main street into numerous courts, and he who turns in thither gets into a filth and disgusting grime, the equal of which is not to be found…. Inhabitants can pass into and out of the court only by passing through foul pools of stagnant urine and excrement…. At the bottom flows, or rather stagnates, the Irk, a narrow, coal-black, foul-smelling stream, full of debris and refuse, which it deposits on the shallower right bank. In dry weather, a long string of the most disgusting, blackish-green, slime pools are left standing on this bank, from the depths of which bubbles of miasmatic gas constantly arise and give forth a stench unendurable even on the bridge forty or fifty feet above the surface of the stream./6

*From *The Marx-Engels Reader*, Second Edition, by Karl Marx and Friedrich Engels, edited by Richard C. Tucker. Copyright 1978, 1972 by W.W. Norton & Company, Inc. Used by permission of W.W. Norton & Company, Inc.

Disease spread rapidly in such neighborhoods, becoming even more deadly after increased contact with India brought cholera to England. In London, thousands died from infected water supplies.

Wealthier families moved to pleasant suburbs, isolated from filth, disease, and the pollution spewed by what poet William Blake called England's "dark, satanic mills." The prevailing view of the upper class was that the poor were responsible for their own fate, an attitude satirized by novelist Charles Dickens in *A Christmas Carol* when Ebenezer Scrooge says that if people are so poor that they are likely to die, "they should do so and decrease the surplus population."

The British middle and lower classes had no right to vote and thus no direct means of influencing policy. Attempts by industrial workers to form unions were outlawed by Parliament as dangerous "combinations." Factory workers might find solidarity in churches: Methodism's

egalitarian ethos allowed workers to assert spiritual, if not social and political, equality. Others sought solace in gin and opium.

By the time of Queen Victoria (r. 1837–1901), however, the reform impulse animated British politics. Charitable organizations grew in size, their leaders arguing that the poor could improve their lot if only they would adopt middle-class values like thrift and sobriety. Many saw that the government also had a role to play, especially in improving health and sanitation.

Early Victorian reform was guided by a philosophy called *utilitarianism*. Jeremy Bentham, utilitarianism's leading proponent, argued that political and social policies needed to be judged by their utility in light of present-day circumstances. In 1840 the government built a model prison based on Bentham's designs in which each prisoner had a separate cell with more light and air than in the notoriously dark and dank prisons of the previous age. Following utilitarian philosophy, the number of crimes for which the death penalty could be applied was radically reduced.

Animated by British "practical science," the government sponsored scientific studies to improve urban planning, water supplies, and hygiene. Investigations of child labor led to public outcry and legislation that regulated abhorrent labor conditions. Restrictions on the activities of Catholics were also lifted. And by the 1850s wages increased: even less skilled workers were beginning to benefit from British pre-eminence in industry and trade.

The conservatism of the post-Napoleonic period was giving way to a more liberal political environment. Middle-class liberals, believers in free trade and individual autonomy, were frustrated by their lack of political representation and by policies that favored landed interests over urban ones. Most did not, however, believe in full democracy: education and property were still preconditions for political participation.

The Reform Bill of 1832 brought Parliament into closer accord with the social changes brought on by industrialization. First, seats in Parliament were redistributed to take account of the growth of cities. Second, the property requirements for voting were lowered so that better-off members of the middle class, such as male shopkeepers, could vote. This new Parliament better reflected the interests of industrialists and the urban middle class.

Economic policies began to shift toward free trade. As improvements in transportation made grain from the Americas and eastern Europe less expensive, factory owners lobbied for an end to agricultural tariffs, arguing that cheaper bread would help keep wages down. In 1846 Parliament opened British markets to foreign grain, showing the new power of urban interests versus the interests of the rural gentry.

A powerful voice of British liberalism, praised by Alexander Herzen, was **John Stuart Mill** (1806–1873). In his book *On Liberty* (1859), Mill argued that liberty involved freedom not only from arbitrary government interference but also from "the tendency of society to impose … its own ideas and practices as rules of conduct …."[7] His emphasis on freedom from both political oppression and social conformity led Mill to conclusions that were radical for the time: he thought the vote should be extended not only to working men but also to women.

By the 1860s, social change again necessitated political reform. The Reform Bill of 1867 nearly doubled the number of voters, though women and those without property were still excluded. But the easing of restrictions on trade unions increased their power, and at the end of the 1880s another reform bill gave most British men the vote. Thus the unwritten British constitution evolved to reflect changing social dynamics.

The Reform Bill of 1832 Bill that significantly reformed the English House of Commons by lowering property qualifications for the vote. Still, only wealthier middle-class men were enfranchised.

John Stuart Mill (1806–1873) English philosopher and economist who argued for the importance of individual liberty.

France: Revolution, Republic, and Empire

In 1815, diplomats at the Congress of Vienna restored the Bourbon dynasty to power in France. After the revolutionary and Napoleonic years, however, it was impossible to return to the past, and in 1830 the unpopular Bourbon monarch was overthrown.

Some of those who organized street protests against the king clamored for a return to republican government. Many middle-class liberals, however, feared that a republic would favor working-class opinion at the expense of private property. Their leaders advocated a constitutional monarchy and invited Louis Philippe, a nobleman with moderate views, to take the throne. More interested in business than in royal protocol, King Louis Philippe was called the "bourgeois king."

Although Louis Philippe's regime was certainly more open than that of the Bourbons, voting was restricted to a small minority of property-owning men, and republicans despised him. In early 1848, after police in Paris fired on a crowd of demonstrators, 1,500 barricades went up around the city. Louis Philippe abdicated and fled the country. Herzen rushed to Paris after hearing the news. For the first time in fifty years France was a republic in which the people themselves were sovereign. The change was so sudden that men meeting in a newspaper office to plan the country's future were divided on how to proceed. An influential socialist, **Louis Blanc** (loo-EE blawnk) (1811–1882), argued that private ownership of industry was inefficient, leaving many unemployed, and unfair, giving workers no say in how the factories were run. He called for cooperative workshops to be set up by the government and run by the workers. Employment would be guaranteed for all.

Although Blanc was popular, his plan was strongly opposed by defenders of property rights, and the republic implemented only a weakened version of Blanc's plan. Employment was provided on public works projects, such as the planting of trees, and those who could not find work were guaranteed enough money to live on. Almost all this money was spent in Paris, a fact resented by the rural majority, who backed the presidential candidacy of **Louis Napoleon** (1808–1873).

Louis Napoleon represented, in his own words, "order, authority, religion, popular welfare at home, national dignity abroad." His candidacy was supported not only by liberals fearful of Blanc's radicalism but also by the many French peasants who resented Paris while recalling the glorious days of Napoleon Bonaparte. After being elected president, Louis Napoleon declared himself Napoleon III, emperor of France. As before, France went swiftly from constitutional monarchy, to republic, to empire.

One Paris evening in the summer of 1848, Alexander Herzen heard a crowd marching past his window. They were, he wrote, "clumsy, rascally fellows, half peasants, half shopkeepers, somewhat drunk … they moved rapidly but in disorder, with shouts of '*Vive Louis-Napoleon!*' … [I] shouted at the top of my voice: '*Vive la République!*' Those who were near the windows shook their fists at me and an officer muttered some abuse, threatening me with his sword."[8] As conservatives gained strength, Herzen's revolutionary vision evaporated.

Napoleon III presided over the Second Empire (1852–1870), a period of stability, prosperity, and expanding French power. As president Louis Napoleon eliminated Blanc's socialist program and sought to stimulate the economy by selling government bonds to finance railway construction and by backing semipublic financial institutions to provide capital for commerce and industry. Although Napoleon III was authoritarian, he respected the rule of law and basic civil liberties. Like Napoleon Bonaparte, he gained support by appealing to French nationalism and by expanding the French Empire.

Eventually, however, Napoleon III was unable to cope with the rising threat of Prussia. In 1870 German armies invaded France and drove him from power, to be replaced in 1871 by the Third Republic.

The Habsburg Monarchy, 1848–1870

News of the 1848 uprising in Paris spread like wildfire across Europe. The dominant power in central Europe was the Austrian Empire, still ruled by the Habsburg family. Protestors, university

Louis Blanc (1811–1882) French socialist who advocated the use of the state to rectify problems of unemployment and exploitation in the workplace. His ideas were briefly put into practice during the revolution of 1848 in Paris.

Louis Napoleon (1808–1873) Conservative nephew of Napoleon Bonaparte who was elected president of the Second Republic before declaring himself emperor in 1852. Was forced to abdicate in 1871 after losing the Franco-Prussian War.

students prominent among them, took to the streets of Vienna in early 1848 demanding new rights. The befuddled emperor reportedly asked, "Are they allowed to do that?" Prince Metternich, the architect of the Congress of Vienna, resigned his position as chancellor and fled to England.

Another challenge to the Habsburgs' empire was the demand from their Italian and Hungarian subjects for national rights. In Budapest a Hungarian assembly created a new constitution ratifying religious freedom, equality before the law, and an end to the privileges of the old feudal nobility. Revolution also swept Austria's northern Italian possessions, its Czech-speaking provinces, and Balkan territories like Croatia.

The young Emperor Franz Joseph II (r. 1848–1916) sought the support of the rural majority. As in France, peasants were shocked by the radicalism of university students and urban workers, and their support helped Habsburg authorities re-establish control within their German-speaking territories. But Franz Joseph's success was far from complete. By 1859 Italian rebels won independence from Austria, and in 1866 Prussian forces defeated the Habsburg army. The discontent of subject nationalities continued. With crises looming, the emperor proclaimed the Dual Monarchy in 1867, creating a federal structure for the empire. He would be simultaneously emperor of Austria and king of Hungary, allowing each state its separate institutions.

Through this compromise Austria retained its great power status and settled the long struggle between German rulers and Hungarian subjects. However, it did nothing to address the grievances of Czechs or Croats. Failure to resolve the empire's regional, ethnic, and class divisions would help spark world war in the next century.

The Unification of Italy, 1848–1870

In 1848 Italian liberals dreamt of a new political order based on ties of language, culture, and history. But they would have to overcome significant regional differences and the long-standing division of the Italian peninsula into numerous states. The north was subject to the same forces of industrialization and urbanization as western Europe, while the south was still largely peasant and traditional in its Catholicism. Differences in dialect made it difficult for Italians from different parts of the peninsula to understand one another. Such divisions had enabled conservatives to stifle liberal reforms and attempts at unification.

Like other Italian idealists of the time, **Giuseppe Garibaldi** (jew-SEP-pay gar-uh-BOWL-dee) (1807–1882) believed in the need for a *risorgimento*, a political and cultural renewal of Italy that would restore its historic greatness. Condemned to death for leading an uprising in Genoa, he fled to South America, where he took part in a Brazilian uprising. In 1848 he returned to Italy and fought in the northern wars against Austria.

> **Giuseppe Garibaldi** (1807–1882) Italian nationalist revolutionary who unified Italy in 1860 by conquering Sicily and Naples.

Then in 1860 a rebellion broke out in southern Italy. With the kingdom of Naples tottering, Garibaldi landed on the island of Sicily with a thousand poorly trained troops, overthrew its corrupt ruler, and crossed to the mainland. Joined by other enthusiastic rebels, his army marched north, bringing Naples and Sicily into a new, united Italy.

Garibaldi sought to establish an Italian republic, but he was outmaneuvered by royalists, who established the new Italy as a constitutional monarchy. By 1870 the Papal States were incorporated into the kingdom, and the process of unification was complete, adding Italy to the list of great powers in Europe with an eye toward empire.

Germany: Nationalism and Unification, 1848–1871

Before 1848 German speakers were divided among over thirty different states, from small kingdoms to powerful ones like Austria and Prussia. Realizing that these political divisions could hamper economic growth, the Prussian government had begun organizing a customs union. But those Germans suspicious of Prussian conservatism and militarism did not welcome its leadership.

Frankfurt Assembly
Assembly held in 1848 to create a constitution for a united German confederation. Elected Frederick William IV as constitutional monarch, but William refused the offer on the principle that people did not have the right to choose their own king.

When the revolutionary impulse of 1848 hit Berlin, Friedrich Wilhelm IV of Prussia (r. 1840–1857) took a hard line, using military force to crush demonstrators who stormed an arsenal and seized a royal palace. Although the king did grant Prussia a constitution whereby a representative assembly was elected through universal manhood suffrage, he and his ministers remained free to ignore it and rule as they liked. Friedrich William saw the constitution as an expression of royal beneficence, not as a matter of rights.

The Prussian government, like that of Austria, did not support German political unification in 1848, fearing that its power would be undermined. In other German states, however, there was significant support for the idea of a unified Germany under a liberal constitution. A committee of prominent liberals organized an election, and in 1848 the **Frankfurt Assembly** met to write a constitution. The delegates drafted a Declaration of Fundamental Rights that embodied the best of liberal political principles, including freedom of assembly and freedom of speech. Seeking a symbol of unity, they offered the crown to Friedrich Wilhelm as constitutional monarch of a democratic German state. But the Prussian king refused to accept what he called "a crown from the gutter," rejecting the principle of popular sovereignty upon which the proposed constitution was based.

Ullstein/The Granger Collection

German Industrialization   The Krupp family had been important innovators and manufacturers of armaments since the period of the Thirty Years' War (1630–1648). In the nineteenth century, with the foundations of the Krupp Steelworks, they became the most important of German industrialists, their field cannon playing an important role in securing victory in the Franco-Prussian War (1870–1871). Here the sprawling Krupp steel factory in the town of Essen shows that fields and factories could still be found close together in late-nineteenth-century Europe.

Friedrich Wilhelm's refusal killed any hope of unifying Germany under a liberal constitution. But the forces of industrialization, the building of railroads, and rapid urbanization were creating conditions in which a unified Germany seemed more desirable than ever. In the 1860s, under the initiative of its chancellor, **Otto von Bismarck** (1815–1898), Prussia started to create a new German nation.

Bismarck, Prussia's "iron chancellor," was of aristocratic background. A strict conservative, he told a committee of the German Confederation in 1862: "Not through speeches and majority decisions are the great questions of the day decided—that was the mistake of 1848— but by iron and blood."[9] Bismarck's policy of militarization led to victories over Denmark and Austria, sparking German national pride even outside of Prussia. In the wake of 1848 some Germans had grown cynical about representative government, associating it with the petty quarrels of politicians. Now they were inspired by a romantic vision of a grand German state fulfilling the people's destiny as a great world power.

Napoleon III's opposition to Prussian expansion led to the Franco-Prussian War of 1870–1871, during which the French emperor was captured by German forces. The unification of Germany in 1871, accomplished in the wake of victory over France, was to have profound implications. The rise of a unified Germany with the fastest-growing industrial economy in the world helped propel a scramble for colonies that set the stage for two world wars.

Otto von Bismarck (1815–1898) Statesman who unified Germany in 1871 and became its first chancellor. Previously, as chancellor of Prussia, had led his state to victories against Austria and France.

New Paradigms of the Industrial Age: Marx and Darwin

Europeans in this era believed that science could reveal the secrets of the natural world and that human society could be improved through rational inquiry. Of the many scientists and social theorists of Europe's industrial age, Karl Marx and Charles Darwin stand out. Marx, in his dissection of capitalism and explanation of the inevitability of socialist revolution, developed a systematic framework for the analysis of human history. Darwin, in describing how natural selection drives the process of evolution, developed a new framework for understanding natural history. Both developed new ways of ordering knowledge that substantially altered previous modes of thought.

The Communists … openly declare that their ends can only be attained by the forceful overthrow of all existing social conditions. Let the ruling classes tremble at a Communistic revolution. The proletarians have nothing to lose but their chains. They have a world to win. WORKING MEN OF ALL COUNTRIES UNITE![*/10]

In spite of conservatives retaking control after 1849, Marx believed that socialist revolution in Europe was not only possible but also inevitable.

Karl Marx (1818–1883) German author and philosopher who founded the Marxist branch of socialism; wrote *The Communist Manifesto* (1848) and *Das Kapital*.

Karl Marx, Socialism, and Communism

The Manifesto of the Communist Party, published in 1848 by **Karl Marx** (1818–1883) and Friedrich Engels, directly challenged the status quo:

*Excerpt from *The Marx-Engels Reader,* Second Edition, edited by Robert C. Tucker. Copyright © 1978, 1972 by W.W. Norton & Company, Inc. Used by permission of W.W. Norton & Company, Inc.

🖥 **Primary Source:**

"Working Men of All Countries, Unite!" *Read these excerpts from The Manifesto of the Communist Party and find out why "the proletarians have nothing to lose but their chains."*

Marx was a brilliant student who had earned a doctoral degree in philosophy. He absorbed from the works of Hegel a philosophy that the human mind progresses through stages toward absolute knowledge. While accepting this theory of progress, he rejected the idea that it takes place primarily at the level of consciousness. Marx instead developed a materialist view that saw history as propelled by changes in "modes of production." To greatly simplify Marx's concept of scientific materialism, he held that economic forces—the way things are produced—generate the social, political, and ideological characteristics of a given society.

Hegel's dialectic described a process in which a dominant idea, called a thesis, generates a contending idea called an antithesis. These two ideas come into conflict until they generate a new, superior idea called a synthesis. Marx interpreted the dialectic in terms of material relations rather than abstract ideas. Changing modes of production produce antagonistic social classes. These social classes come into conflict in the political arena, generating ideologies that match their class interests.

As Marx analyzed the original French Revolution, for example, he explained that the rise of capitalism challenged the old feudal system of production, leading to the rise of the bourgeoisie (the propertied middle class that stood between the aristocracy and mass of French society) and its overthrow of the monarchy and aristocracy. Whereas the aristocracy had promoted an ideology of power that emphasized family lineage, the bourgeoisie emphasized rights of property. The liberalism of Mill and Herzen, Marx argued, was simply the self-interested philosophy of the property-owning bourgeoisie.

Marx recognized that the bourgeoisie, "during its rule of scarce one hundred years, has created more massive and more colossal productive forces than have all preceding generations together."[11] But he felt that capitalism contains a fatal flaw. The very efficiency of capitalism causes recurrent crises when more goods are produced than the market can absorb. Wages are slashed and factories are closed. Then the economy recovers, but with each crash the division between the property owners and the workers increases: "Society as a whole," Marx wrote, "is more and more splitting up into two great hostile camps, into two classes directly facing each other: Bourgeoisie and Proletariat."[12] The struggle between these two classes, the propertied middle class and the industrial working class, was made inevitable by the capitalist mode of production, and the victory of the working class, Marx argued, would lead to the realization of socialism. The full establishment of socialism, though it might take a long time, would be the *final* stage in human progress, after which there would be no further class conflict.

From a global perspective, Marx explained the link between industrial capitalism and European imperialism:

> The need of constantly expanding market for its products chases the bourgeoisie over the whole surface of the globe…. It has drawn from under the feet of industry the national ground on which it stood…. In place of the old local and national seclusion and self-sufficiency, we have intercourse in every direction, universal interdependence of nations…. The bourgeoisie, by the rapid improvement of all instruments of production and by the immensely facilitated means of communication draws all … nations into civilization.*[13]

Global expansion, however, can only delay the collapse of capitalism, not prevent it.

Marx's internationalist philosophy challenged the idea of nationalism. Nationalists argued that bonds of culture and history unified a people across lines of social class. To them, a German was a German, whether she was a princess or a chambermaid, whether she lived in

*Excerpt from *The Marx-Engels Reader,* Second Edition, edited by Robert C. Tucker. Copyright © 1978, 1972 by W.W. Norton & Company, Inc. Used by permission of W.W. Norton & Company, Inc.

Prussia or in Austria. To Marx such romanticized notions merely distracted proletarians from recognizing that their true interests lay not with the rich and powerful who spoke the same language, but with workers across the world. The Socialist International, which Marx helped to organize, was dedicated to fostering such working-class solidarity. But despite Marx's arguments, nationalism exerted an increasingly powerful influence among all social classes.

Marx spent the rest of his life refining his theories. Though by the time of his death in 1883 there had been no socialist revolutions, his ideas were spreading and his followers increasing.

Charles Darwin, Evolution, and Social Darwinism

Prior to publishing his groundbreaking book *On the Origin of the Species by Means of Natural Selection* in 1859, the British scientist **Charles Darwin** (1809–1882) had spent many years gathering evidence. Geologists had already determined that the earth was millions of years old and that its surface features had changed greatly over time. Darwin believed that long-term biological change, evolution, also characterized natural history. His search was for the mechanism of the evolutionary process.

In the Galapagos Islands off the coast of South America, Darwin observed that finches and turtles differed from those on the mainland and even in other areas of the islands. He theorized that the variations resulted from the adaptation of species to different environments. His principal contribution was the idea that natural selection drove this process.

Darwin explained the origins of all life on earth as resulting from competition for survival. Organisms with traits that gave them a better chance of survival passed those traits along to their offspring. Over time, the accumulation of diverse traits led to the appearance of new species, while failure in the struggle for existence led to the extinction of unsuccessful ones. Like Newton's theory of gravitation, Darwin's

evolutionary theory was elegant, universally applicable, and a substantial advance in understanding.

In *The Descent of Man* (1871), Darwin made it clear that human beings had also undergone natural selection in their evolution as a species, an idea that generated considerable controversy by contradicting the biblical account of man's creation. Religious leaders denounced his work as an example of the materialism and immorality of modern life and thought. (See the feature "Movement of Ideas: Religious Leaders Comment on Science and Progress.") Darwin's insights were, however, accepted by virtually all natural scientists.

Darwin's ideas reflected broader intellectual trends beyond the domain of natural science. The great upsurge in economic productivity was inspiring a belief that human history is a story of progress. Karl Marx had absorbed this idea as a student and saw Darwin's theory of evolution as reinforcing his own view that human history proceeds through stages (feudalism, capitalism, socialism). Marx was just one of many observers who thought that Darwin's work supported an optimistic view of human history.

Charles Darwin (1809–1882) English natural historian, geologist, and proponent of the theory of evolution.

But Darwin's concept of a "survival of the fittest" in the natural world had less positive implications when applied to human society. *Social Darwinism* was the idea that differences in wealth and power could be explained by the superiority of some and the inferiority of others. Social Darwinists argued that riches were a proper consequence of superior talent. The poor were those with inferior traits. Analogies from nature were thus used to justify social inequality. Social Darwinism was also used to explain Europe's increasing global dominance: European imperialism was simply natural selection at work. "Inferior peoples" would be displaced as part of an inevitable natural process. Darwin himself, however, never drew such corollaries from his work.

Religious Leaders Comment on Science and Progress

While the nineteenth century saw the rise of secular ideologies such as liberalism, socialism, and nationalism, religion continued to shape the views of most people around the world. The excerpts below illustrate the implications of modern industrial ideologies for religious faith as interpreted by a Sunni Muslim scholar and a Roman Catholic pope.

The first selection comes from Sayyid Jamāl ad-dīn al-Afghani (1838–1897). He was educated in Islamic schools in Afghanistan and Iran and then spent twenty years in British-ruled India, also traveling to western Europe and the Ottoman Empire.

Al-Afghani saw Pan-Islamic unity as necessary for effective resistance to European dominance and worked to heal divisions between the Sunni and Shi'ite Muslim communities.

The second passage is by Pope Pius IX (r. 1846–1878), who became a staunch conservative when Roman revolutionaries forced him to temporarily flee the Vatican in 1848. Pius IX greatly increased papal authority when he proclaimed the doctrine of papal infallibility, which stated that the pope's statements on central issues of faith were to be regarded as coming directly from God and could not be challenged.

Sayyid Jamāl ad-dīn al-Afghani

1. "Lecture on Teaching and Learning" (1882)

If someone looks deeply into the question, he will see that science rules the world. There was, is, and will be no other ruler in the world but science.... In reality, sovereignty has never left the abode of science. However, this true ruler, which is science, is continually changing capitals. Sometimes it has moved from East to West, and other times from West to East.... The acquisitions of men for themselves and their governments are proportional to their science. Thus, every government for its own benefit must strive to lay the foundation of the sciences and to disseminate knowledge....

The strangest thing of all is that our *ulama* [scholarly community] these days have divided science into two parts. One they call Muslim science, and one European science. Because of this they forbid others to teach some of the useful sciences. They have not understood that science is that noble thing that has no connection with any nation, and is not distinguished by anything but itself. Rather, everything that is known is known by science, and every nation that becomes renowned becomes renowned through science....

How very strange it is that the Muslims study those sciences that are ascribed to Aristotle with the greatest delight, as if Aristotle were one of the pillars of the Muslims. However, if the discussion relates to Galileo, Newton and Kepler, they consider them infidels. The father and mother of science is proof, and proof is neither Aristotle nor Galileo. The truth is where there is proof, and those who forbid science and knowledge in the belief that they are safeguarding the Islamic religion are really enemies of that religion. The Islamic religion is the closest of religions to science and knowledge, and there is no incompatibility between science and knowledge and the foundation of the Islamic faith....

2. "Answer of Jamal al-Din to Renan" (1883)

All religions are intolerant, each one in its way. The Christian religion, I mean the society that follows its inspirations and its teachings ... seems to advance rapidly on the road of progress and science, whereas Muslim society has not yet freed itself from the tutelage of religion.... I cannot keep from hoping that Muslim society will succeed someday in breaking its bonds and marching resolutely in the path of civilization after the manner of Western society.... No I cannot admit that this hope be denied to Islam.

Source: Excerpt by Sayyid Jamāˉl ad-dīˉn al-Afghani from *An Islamic Response to Imperialism,* edited and translated by Nikki Keddie, Berkeley, Calif., University of California Press, pp. 161, 186. Reprinted with permission of the author.

Pope Pius IX

Quanta Cura (Condemning Current Errors), 1864

For well you know, my brothers, that at this time there are many men who applying to civil society the impious and absurd principle of "naturalism," dare to teach that "the best constitution of public society ... requires that human society be conducted and governed without regard being had to religion any more than if it did not exist; or, at least, without any distinction between true religion and false one." From which false idea ... they foster the erroneous opinion ... that "liberty of conscience and worship is each man's personal right, which ought to be legally proclaimed and asserted in every rightly constituted society; and that a right resides in the citizens to an absolute liberty, which should be restrained by no authority whether ecclesiastical or civil, whereby they may be able openly and publicly to manifest and declare any of their ideas whatever, either by word of mouth, by the press, or in any other way." Whereas we know, from the very teaching of our Lord Jesus Christ, how carefully Christian faith and wisdom should avoid this most injurious babbling.

And, since where religion has been removed from civil society, and the doctrine and authority of divine revelation repudiated, the genuine notion itself of justice and human right is darkened and lost, and the place of true justice and legitimate right is supplied by material force.... [Then] human society, when set loose from the bonds of religion and true justice, can have, in truth, no other end than the purpose of obtaining and amassing wealth, and ... follows no other law ... except ... ministering to its own pleasure and interests.

Amidst, therefore, such great perversity of depraved opinions ... and (solicitous also) for the welfare of human society itself, [we] have thought it right again to raise up our Apostolic voice.

Source: Excerpt from Pope Pius IX, *Quanta Cura* (Condemning Current Errors), from www.ewtn.com. Reprinted by permission.

QUESTIONS FOR ANALYSIS

▶ How do Pius IX and al-Afghani differ in their views of the relationship between religion and the ideas and ideals of industrial modernity?

▶ Are there any connections between these nineteenth-century debates and current controversies concerning science and faith in the Christian and Islamic worlds?

Reform and Reaction: Russia and the Ottoman Empire, 1825–1881

In 1798 Napoleon invaded Ottoman Egypt. Then in 1812 he marched on Moscow. Though the French retreated in both cases, both Russians and Ottomans were put on notice: the West was advancing. For both empires, the question became: was it better to emulate the legal, educational, social, and political reforms of western Europe, or to follow conservative policies that emphasized continuity with the past?

Emancipation and Reaction in Russia

Alexander Herzen was from a generation of educated Russians inspired by the revolutionary changes that had taken place to the west. He saw Russia as a backward place, "coarse and unpolished" compared with western European society, but thought Russia could be reinvigorated if it joined the European mainstream.[14] Westernizers like Herzen were inspired by the Decembrist Revolt of 1825, a failed uprising of Russian officers desiring constitutional government. They were opposed by Slavophiles who believed that Russia should stand by her Slavic traditions, Orthodox Christianity, and the tsarist state.

After 1815, Russian tsars commanded the world's largest army and an empire that spread from Poland to Alaska. But their imperial power was not reflected in social conditions. Russia was overwhelmingly rural. It had a powerful aristocracy but a weak middle class and almost no modern industry. With neither a strong bourgeoisie nor a growing proletariat, Russian society was divided between a landowning nobility and serfs so poor, illiterate, and lacking in rights that they could be won or lost in a game of cards.

The nobility profited from this system, as did the government, which depended on serf conscripts for its huge army. Change was not likely to come from above. After the Decembrist revolt, the new tsar, Nicholas I (r. 1825–1855), established a secret police that would send Alexander Herzen and other dissenters into exile.

With the advent of modern industry, the gap between Russia and the other great powers widened, as demonstrated by the **Crimean War** (1853–1856). Having taken control of the Crimean peninsula on the northern shore of the Black Sea in the late eighteenth century, the Russians sought to expand even further along the Ottoman frontier. They attacked in the 1850s on the pretext of protecting Orthodox Christians from Ottoman mistreatment. Fearing the Russian expansion would upset the balance of power in Europe, the British and the French came to the Ottomans' defense. Poorly trained Russian conscripts were given badly outdated rifles, while modern British and French naval vessels dominated the Black Sea. Unable to make up in numbers what they lacked in equipment and organization, the Russians were defeated. The lesson was clear: modern wars could not be won without an industrial foundation.

Tsar Alexander II (r. 1855–1881), who succeeded to the throne near the end of the Crimean conflict, recognized that Russia's social structure, based on serfdom, could not support a powerful modern state. In 1861 Alexander II issued his **Emancipation Edict**. Increased labor mobility was one rationale for emancipation, since industrial development would require the movement of peasants into cities. However, to avoid antagonizing the nobility, the edict required that serfs pay for their own emancipation. Moreover, the communal organization of the peasant villages, where collective decisions were made about

Crimean War (1853–1856) War fought in the Crimean peninsula between the Russian and Ottoman Empires. France and Britain sent troops to aid the Ottomans and prevent Russian expansion.

Tsar Alexander II (r. 1855–1881) Also known as Alexander the Liberator, best known for his emancipation of the serfs.

Emancipation Edict 1861 edict by Tsar Alexander II that freed the Russian serfs. However, serfs had to pay their former owners for their freedom, and the land they were allocated was often insufficient to produce the money needed to meet that cost for freedom.

what and when to plant, impeded improvements in agriculture through capital investment and scientific principles.

Alexander Herzen saw the Emancipation Edict as a wasted opportunity for more meaningful reform. After 1848 he had become disillusioned with the West, but he imagined that Russia's very lack of development presented a fresh opportunity. As he explained in his periodical *The Bell*, published in London, Herzen thought that a liberal state could be created that guaranteed individual freedoms, while the communal organization of the Russian peasantry could be used to build a new social order. Though banned by the tsar's censors, *The Bell* was smuggled into Russia and widely read, even by top officials.

Nevertheless, after the Emancipation Edict, the agenda of the Slavophiles, who wished for as little change as possible, predominated, while Westernizers became targets of the secret police whose job it was to identify "troublemakers" and exile them, often to harsh labor camps in Siberia.

At the same time, the tsar's government began taking action in support of industrialization. During the 1870s government support led to a boom in railroad construction, stimulating the coal and iron industries. High tariffs on foreign goods promoted the development of Russian factories, although they continued to lag well behind the pace of western European growth. While by 1880 English, French, and German workers were enjoying some benefits of increased productivity, such as better clothing and housing, Russian workers were still suffering from the dangerous and squalid conditions that had marked the first phase of industrialization in the West.

Another challenge for Alexander's government was the question of nationalities. In Germany, nationalism might overcome regional

Adoc-Photos/Art Resource, NY

Emancipated Serfs   As with freed slaves in the U.S. South during the late nineteenth century, living conditions for most Russian serfs were not immediately transformed by emancipation in 1861. Most were illiterate and, like the wheat threshers shown here, had to rely on their own labor power. Even so, Alexander Herzen, admiring their collective village institutions, saw the peasants as the foundation of Russia's socialist future.

Turkish Factory   Nineteenth-century industrialization was a global process, with many world regions tied to industrial processes solely as suppliers of raw materials and consumers of finished products. Here we see that in the western Ottoman Empire, factory production itself became a part of economic life. In this factory girls and women are weaving silk thread into cloth; the factory supervisor, however, is a man. In Japan as well (see Chapter 24), early textile production relied primarily on women's labor.

and class differences to serve as the ideological foundation of a modern state. In multiethnic Russia such use of nationalism was impossible because over half the people in the empire were not Russian. The tsars harshly suppressed nationalist uprisings, such as an 1863 rebellion in Poland. Observing from London, Herzen was distraught, having hoped that Polish success would pave the way for reform in Russia.

By that time Herzen's generation was losing influence to a younger group of Russian revolutionaries with little patience for philosophical debate. The tsarist police were everywhere, forcing Russian rebels to conspire in secret. Anarchists among them thought that freedom could be achieved only through the abolition of the state,

its bureaucracy, and its army. Some accepted the need for violence and even terrorism to achieve their ends: a bomb killed Tsar Alexander II in 1881, causing a further crackdown on dissidence. Herzen died in exile, his dream of Russia showing the way to a better future unfulfilled.

Reform and Reaction in the Ottoman Empire

Though large and powerful, the Ottoman Empire was under increasing pressure in the early nineteenth century. Having lost control of Egypt to the independent regime of Muhammad Ali, Greece to an independence movement in 1829, and Algeria to French invaders in 1830, the Ottomans were also slipping in the Balkans, the mountainous region of southeastern Europe they had controlled since the days of Süleyman the Magnificent.

After the loss of Greece, Sultan Mahmud II (r. 1808–1839) attempted reform. After his death, his initiatives were expanded during the era of the **Tanzimat reforms**, through which Ottoman bureaucrats sought to break the power of the elite Janissary corps in order to reorganize the army along modern lines. The Ottoman government established new types of schools within the empire, such as colleges of military science and medicine, and sponsored student travel and study in western Europe. A new system of primary and secondary schools following a European-style curriculum supplemented the existing *madrasas,* or religious schools. The urban elite began to travel more widely and to read French, Armenian, and Turkish newspapers, and European-style buildings were erected in Istanbul to modernize the capital. The legal system was also revamped so that the same civil code applied to everyone, Muslim and non-Muslim alike, with full equality before the law. Finally, to facilitate trade with the West, the Tanzimat (TAHNZ-ee-MAT) reformers introduced a new commercial code modeled on European rather than Islamic principles.

Some Muslim religious leaders worried that by borrowing so many ideas from the West the government was undercutting the traditional religious and cultural foundations of their society. They resented their loss of control over the educational and legal systems that had been a principal source of their power and prestige. On the other hand, progressive Ottoman officials were dissatisfied with the centralized and bureaucratic nature of the Tanzimat program and argued for a constitutional monarchy guided by the principles of liberalism.

When Sultan Abd al-Hamid (AHB-dahl-ha-med) III came to power in 1876, he at first agreed to create a representative government. With the backing of conservatives, however, he suspended the constitution a year after its creation and ruled as dictator. Vacillating between reform and reaction, Ottoman authorities proved unable to strike a stable balance. As in Russia, reactionary policies replaced reformist ones.

Primary Source: Imperial Rescript *In this proclamation, Abdul Mejid announces plans to reform and modernize the Ottoman Empire, while protecting the rights of non-Muslims.*

Tanzimat reforms (1839–1876) Restructuring of the Ottoman Empire. Control over civil law was taken away from religious authorities, while the military and government bureaucracies were reorganized to gain efficiency.

Chapter Review and Learning Activities

Alexander Herzen's outlook was transformed by the disappointments of 1848, but he never gave up his belief that socialism and individual liberty would one day be achieved, with Russia showing the way. In 1870, the very year that Herzen died,

Vladimir Ilyich Lenin was born. It was Lenin who would bring socialism to Russia in the form of Marxian communism (see Chapter 27); Herzen's dream of liberty for the Russian people would be long deferred.

What were the most important outcomes of the Industrial Revolution?

The Industrial Revolution transformed the world. More energy was available for human use than ever before once technological breakthroughs unleashed the power of coal. Steam engines drove the factories, ships, and railways of the industrial era. The more centralized organization of the factory system increased productivity, even as early industrial workers suffered from poor living conditions. On a global level, improved transportation and communication stimulated global commodity markets as industrialists sought out raw materials for their factories and markets for their finished goods.

What were the main features of European political development during and after the revolutions of 1848?

In 1815, European leaders thought they had finally contained the disruption to older patterns of authority represented by the French Revolution and the Napoleonic era. At that very time, however, the shift toward industrial factories was starting to undermine traditional social and economic relationships. Across Europe conservative leaders struggled to contain the new ideologies of liberalism, socialism, and nationalism. In early 1848 it seemed that the reformers and revolutionaries would be able to sweep away the old power structures in the name of freedom. But in the end their achievements were negligible. France and Austria were empires, the new Italy was a monarchy, and the kaiser who ruled a newly unified Germany after 1871 was a conservative Prussian. Britain was the exception to the European rule of revolutionary enthusiasm followed by conservative response. Victorian Britain was characterized instead by an evolutionary process of liberal reform that gradually enfranchised more of the queen's subjects.

Why were the ideas of Karl Marx and Charles Darwin of such great significance for world history?

Two European thinkers of the industrial era whose ideas would have a powerful global influence were Karl Marx and Charles Darwin. Marx analyzed the economic and historical foundations of industrial civilization, concluding that socialist revolution was the inevitable outcome of capitalist development. Marx's combination of idealism and scientific analysis was appealing to many who sought a blueprint for revolutionary change, not only in Europe but also around the world. The power of Charles Darwin's identification of natural selection as the mechanism of evolutionary change lay in its simplicity and universality. Darwin reinforced the growing faith of the industrial age in the explanatory power of science. At the same time, Social Darwinists applied his insights to political and economic conditions in ways that emphasized struggle and conflict.

How did the leaders of the Russian and Ottoman Empires respond to the challenge of an industrializing western Europe?

Many within Europe were disturbed by the new social and political conditions of the Industrial Revolution and the ideas that came with them. The challenge of adapting to the industrial age was also faced by the Russians and the Ottomans, two empires located on the margins of European industrial development. In both cases conservatives and reformers vied for influence. In the Ottoman Empire, reformers instituted significant changes in educational, legal, and military structures during the Tanzimat period, before losing ground to conservatives later in the century. In spite of the emancipation of the serfs in 1861, the Russian tsars became even more conservative. While sponsoring railroad construction and industrial development, the Romanov tsars opposed all moves toward liberalism.

FOR FURTHER REFERENCE

Anderson, Benedict. *Imagined Communities: Reflections on the Origin and Spread of Nationalism.* London: Verso, 1991.

Auerbach, Jeffrey. *The Great Exhibition of 1851: A Nation on Display.* New Haven: Yale University Press, 1999.

Berlin, Isaiah. *Russian Thinkers.* New York: Viking, 1978.

Goodwin, Jason. *Lords of the Horizons: A History of the Ottoman Empire.* New York: Picador, 2003.

Herzen, Alexander. *My Past and Thoughts. Translated by Constance Garnett.* Berkeley: University of California Press, 1982.

Hobsbawm, Eric. *The Age of Capital, 1848–1875.* New York: Simon and Schuster, 1975.

Mayr, Ernst. *One Long Argument: Charles Darwin and the Genesis of Modern Evolutionary Thought.* Cambridge, Mass.: Harvard University Press, 1993.

Mokyr, Joel. *The Lever of Riches: Technological Creativity and Economic Progress.* New York: Oxford University Press, 1992.

Tilly, Louise. *Industrialization and Gender Inequality.* Washington, D.C.: American Historical Association, 1993.

Wheen, Francis. *Karl Marx: A Life.* New York: W.W. Norton, 2000.

KEY TERMS

Alexander Herzen (504)

Industrial Revolution (505)

Muhammad Ali (508)

The Reform Bill of 1832 (511)

John Stuart Mill (511)

Louis Blanc (512)

Louis Napoleon (512)

Giuseppe Garibaldi (513)

Frankfurt Assembly (514)

Otto von Bismarck (515)

Karl Marx (515)

Charles Darwin (517)

Crimean War (520)

Tsar Alexander II (520)

Emancipation Edict (520)

Tanzimat reforms (523)

VOYAGES ON THE WEB

Voyages: Alexander Herzen

"Voyages" is a real time excursion to historical sites in this chapter and includes interactive activities and study tools such as audio summaries, animated maps, and flashcards.

Visual Evidence: The Beehive of Victorian Britain

"Visual Evidence" features artifacts, works of art, or photographs, along with a brief descriptive essay and discussion questions to guide your analysis of visual sources.

World History in Today's World: Turkey and the European Union

"World History in Today's World" makes the connection between features of modern life and their origins in the periods in this chapter.

Go to the CourseMate website at www.cengagebrain.com for additional study tools and review materials—including audio and video clips—for this chapter.

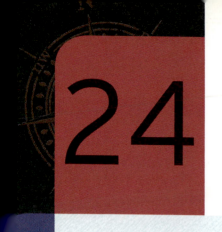

24 China, Japan, and India Confront the Modern World, 1800–1910

Fukuzawa Yûkichi
(Fukuzawa Memorial Center Keio University)

In 1859 the government of Japan sent its first delegation to visit the United States. On the crossing **Fukuzawa Yûkichi** (foo-koo-ZAH-wah yoo-KII-chi) (1835–1901), a twenty-four-year-old samurai, studied *Webster's Dictionary*, but it did not prepare him very well for his experiences in San Francisco. "There were many confusing and embarrassing moments," he later wrote, "for we were quite ignorant of the customs of American life." At his hotel he was amazed when his hosts walked across expensive carpets with their shoes on. Fukuzawa attended a dance wearing the outfit of a samurai, with two swords and hemp sandals:

To our dismay we could not make out what they were doing. The ladies and gentlemen seemed to be hopping around the room together. As funny as it was, we knew it would be rude to laugh, and we controlled our expressions with difficulty as the dancing went on.... Things social, political, and economic proved most inexplicable.... I asked a gentleman where the descendants of George Washington might be.... His answer was so very casual that it shocked me. Of course, I know that America is a republic with a new president every four years, but I could not help feeling that the family

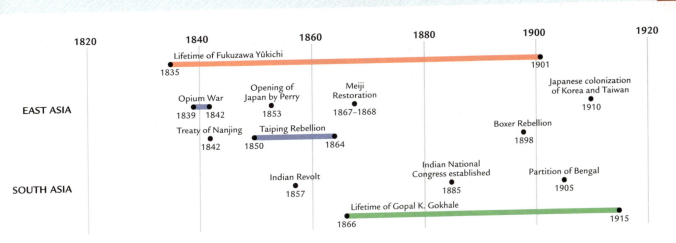

The Travels of Fukuzawa Yûkichi

→ Fukuzawa Yûkichi's journeys
⟶ Possible route of Fukuzawa
• City visited by Fukuzawa
• Other city
☐ British Empire, 1870

Fukuzawa Yûkichi joins delegation to San Francisco, 1860.

JAPAN, CA. 1860

Fukuzawa walks from Nagasaki to Osaka.

Join this chapter's traveler on "Voyages," an interactive tour of historic sites and events: www.cengagebrain.com

Timeline

	1820	1840	1860	1880	1900	1920
		Lifetime of Fukuzawa Yûkichi 1835 — 1901				
EAST ASIA		Opium War 1839–1842	Opening of Japan by Perry 1853	Meiji Restoration 1867–1868		Japanese colonization of Korea and Taiwan 1910
		Treaty of Nanjing 1842	Taiping Rebellion 1850–1864		Boxer Rebellion 1898	
SOUTH ASIA			Indian Revolt 1857	Indian National Congress established 1885	Partition of Bengal 1905	
			Lifetime of Gopal K. Gokhale 1866 — 1915			

527

of Washington would be revered above all other families. My reasoning was based on the reverence in Japan for the founders of the great lines of rulers—like that for Ieyasu of the Tokugawa family of Shoguns.*

*From *The Autobiography of Yukichi Fukuzawa*, by Eiichi Kiyooka, 1960, pp. 112–116, 277, 18, 164, 210, 190. Copyright © 1960 Columbia University Press. Reprinted with permission of the pubisher.

Fukuzawa Yûkichi (1835–1901) Japanese writer, teacher, political theorist, and founder of Keio University. His ideas about learning, government, and society greatly influenced the Meiji Restoration. Considered one of the founders of modern Japan.

Though he was much more knowledgeable about the Western world than most Japanese, Fukuzawa said of himself and his American hosts, "neither of us really knew much about the other at all."[1]

Fukuzawa had grown up in a low-ranking samurai family who were expected to give unconditional support and service to their lord, but he was an ambitious nonconformist. As a young man he dedicated himself to "Dutch learning," and becoming convinced of the merits of Western science, he developed a philosophy that emphasized independence over subservience and science over tradition.

Fukuzawa's lifetime was one of remarkable change. All across the world societies struggled to adapt to the new industrial age with its advances in transportation and communications technologies, the spread of new religious and secular ideologies, and the dynamics of a changing global economy. In western Europe rulers, reformers, and rebels all struggled for control over the direction of change. Russian and Ottoman elites debated whether to emulate Western models (see Chapter 23). In East Asia, Japanese, Chinese, and Koreans were also divided when faced with increasingly aggressive Western powers. While Japanese reformers like Fukuzawa embraced change along Western lines as a means of empowerment, conservatives here and elsewhere in East Asia saw Europe and the United States as hostile threats to their established social, political, and economic systems.

Fukuzawa was a leader of the Westernizing faction that came to dominate Japan after the Tokugawa Shogunate was overthrown in 1868. The new Japanese government was able to resist the Western powers and, with military victories over China and Russia, expand its own empire. The leaders of Qing China, by contrast, proved incapable of reforming their society quickly or thoroughly enough to turn aside the Western challenge. By the late nineteenth century, China had been carved into spheres of influence by Britain, France, Germany, Japan, and the United States. Korean leaders were also slow to adapt to the industrial age, and the Korean peninsula was incorporated into the Japanese Empire.

South Asians also had to adapt to the industrial age, as well as balance their own traditions with powerful new economic forces and cultural influences. A major rebellion in 1857 signaled how deeply many Indians resented British rule. The failure of that revolt stimulated Indian intellectuals and political leaders to develop new ideas and organizations to achieve self-government. Indian nationalists, like those in Japan and China, struggled with the question of how to deal with the power of Western models in everything from clothing to house design to political philosophy.

This chapter focuses on the various strategies of resistance and accommodation used by the peoples of China, Japan, and British India in their attempts to come to terms with the industrial age. All these societies had to respond to the rising challenge from the West. Fukuzawa Yûkichi's proposal that Japan should emulate the West to become strengthened and modernized was just one of the solutions put forward in nineteenth-century East and South Asia.

FOCUS QUESTIONS

▶ What were the main forces that undermined the power of the Qing dynasty in the nineteenth century?

▶ What made it possible for Japan to be transformed from a relatively isolated society to a major world power in less than half a century?

▶ What were the principal ways that British-ruled Indians responded to imperialism?

China's World Inverted, 1800–1906

Four decades after China's emperor dismissed England's diplomatic advances (see Chapter 20), the British returned to force China open. Suddenly faced with Europe's industrial might, Qing officials agreed to a series of unequal treaties. But rebellion shook China. While some officials humiliated by the decline in imperial prestige entertained reform, they were outmaneuvered by conservatives who opposed adopting Western political, educational, and economic models. By the end of the nineteenth century, soldiers from Britain, France, the United States, and Japan had occupied the Forbidden City, as the great powers proceeded to divide China into their own "spheres of influence."

The conservatives' policies were a disaster. Fukuzawa Yûkichi, who had implemented Western-styled reform in Japan, observed in 1899: "I am sure that it is impossible to lead [the Chinese] people to civilization so long as the old government is left to stand as it is."[2] Seven years later the last Manchu emperor abdicated, and China's dominant role in East Asia was usurped by Japan.

Qing China Confronts the Industrial World, 1800–1850

In the late eighteenth century the British East India Company faced an old problem for Western traders in China: apart from silver, they had no goods that were of much value in Chinese markets. Their solution was to develop poppy plantations in South Asia, refine the poppy seeds into opium, and smuggle the narcotic into China. The strategy was commercially brilliant, but ethically problematic. As Victorian reformers earnestly sought to stamp out opium addiction in Britain, the East India Company hypocritically promoted opium smuggling to China.

Highly addictive, opium is a strong painkiller that also induces lethargy and a sense of hopelessness. Addicts neglect their own health and even the care of their own children and parents. Opium smugglers conducted their illegal trade in open disregard for Chinese governmental authority. Moreover, the lucrative opium trade drained silver out of China, thus jeopardizing China's silver-based fiscal system and undermining its national economy.

Primary Source: Letter to Queen Victoria, 1839 *On behalf of the emperor, Lin Zezu implores Queen Victoria to halt the British opium trade in China.*

By 1839 Sino-British relations were in crisis. The Qing government declared that drug traders would be beheaded and sent a scholar-official named Lin Zezu (**lin say-shoe**) to Guangzhou to suppress the opium trade. In a letter to Queen Victoria, Lin made his government's position clear:

> [By] introducing opium by stealth [the British] have seduced our Chinese people, and caused every province in the land to overflow with that poison. They know merely how to advantage themselves; they care not about injuring others! … Therefore those foreigners who now import opium into the Central Land are condemned to be beheaded and strangled.[3]

To the British government, however, the issue was not opium but free trade. According to liberal economic theory, free trade is always and everywhere best for everyone. If the Chinese could not understand this simple idea, then they would have to be *forced* to understand. The British responded to Lin's appeal with war.

The Opium War (1839–1842) was a severe shock to the Qing government. The British used their iron-clad gunboats to blockade the Chinese coast and bombard coastal cities such as Guangzhou and Shanghai. Being so easily defeated by "western barbarians," many Qing commanders committed suicide in disgrace.

Treaty of Nanjing (1842) One-sided treaty that concluded the Opium War. Britain was allowed to trade in additional Chinese ports and took control of Hong Kong. The provision for extraterritoriality meant that Britons were subject to British rather than Chinese law.

Taiping Rebellion (1850–1864) Massive rebellion against the Qing led by Hong Xiuquan, who claimed to be the younger brother of Jesus Christ come to earth to create a "Heavenly Kingdom of Great Peace." The imperial system was greatly weakened as a result of the uprising.

With no bargaining power, the Qing felt compelled to agree to the humiliating terms of the **Treaty of Nanjing**, the first of a series of unequal treaties that eroded Chinese sovereignty in the coming decades. The agreement opened five "treaty ports" to unrestricted foreign trade and gave possession of Hong Kong, upriver from the great port of Guangzhou, to the British. The treaty's provision of extraterritoriality, whereby British subjects in China were subject to British rather than Chinese law, was a particular injury to Chinese pride. The Treaty of Nanjing left the British and other European nations eager for even greater power over China. Using supposed Qing violations of the Nanjing treaty as a pretext, in 1856 the British and French invaded and marched toward Beijing. They burned to the ground Qianlong's magnificent summer palace and briefly occupied the Forbidden City. In 1860, the Qing agreed to another, even more unequal treaty that opened more ports to Western trade and allowed "international settlements" in key Chinese cities such as Shanghai and Guangzhou. These settlements, where only Europeans were allowed to live, were foreign enclaves on Chinese soil. The British also mandated that imperial documents were no longer to use the Chinese character for "barbarian" to describe the British.

The Taiping Rebellion, 1850–1864

The Opium War and the unequal treaties that followed caused some Chinese to conclude that the Manchu had lost the "Mandate of Heaven." The population had grown by over 100 million between 1800 and 1850. Amidst the political chaos, the peasantry was suffering from neglect, misrule, and hunger. Farmers brought more marginal lands into production; agricultural yields declined; villages were repeatedly flooded. Although imperial governments had long been responsible for flood control and famine relief, the Qing had raised taxes for its military in the midst of the people's suffering.

In the mid-nineteenth century China was shaken by revolts, including a major Muslim uprising in the northwest. The situation was especially desperate in Guangdong province, where the **Taiping Rebellion** (1850–1864) began,

School of Oriental and African Studies/The Art Archive

The Taiping Rebellion   This contemporary print shows the defense of Shanghai by Qing forces in 1860. Though the Taiping controlled China's "southern capital" of Nanjing, the support given to the Qing military by Western powers, fearful of the anarchy that might accompany the loss of Manchu control, kept Shanghai under Manchu authority. Nanjing fell to the imperial army in 1864.

sending the empire into chaos. The leader of the Taiping **(tie-PING)** was Hong Xiuquan (1813–1864). After traveling to Guangzhou and failing the imperial examinations several times, Hong Xiuquan **(hoong shee-OH-chew-an)** studied with some Western missionaries, adding his own interpretation to their message.

Mixing Christianity with peasant yearnings for fairness and justice, Hong gained hundreds of thousands of followers to his vision of reform. In their Heavenly Kingdom, the Taiping proclaimed, "inequality [will not] exist, and [everyone will] be well fed and clothed."[4]

At the core of the Taiping movement were committed followers who practiced severe self-discipline. Many of these initiates were, like Hong, from the Hakka ethnic group. The Hakka were only brought under imperial control during Ming times and had never fully assimilated. Women had relatively independent roles, and their feet were never bound. Hong's "long-haired rebels" refused to wear the long, braided ponytail, or queue, mandated by Manchu authorities as a sign of subservience. "Ever since the Manchus poisoned China," he said, "the influence of demons has distressed the empire while the Chinese with bowed heads and dejected spirits willingly became subjects and servants."[5]

Hong and his original converts attracted a mass following. In late 1850 some twenty thousand Taiping rebels defeated an imperial army sent to crush them; they then went on the offensive and began a long northward march that ended in 1853 with an invasion of Nanjing. Of the tens of thousands of Manchu living within the city walls, those who did not die in battle were systematically slaughtered. Hong moved into a former Ming imperial palace and declared Nanjing the capital of his Heavenly Kingdom of Great Peace.

After 1853, however, the Taiping rebels gained no more great victories. Their rhetoric of equality alienated the educated elite, and influential members of the gentry organized militias to fight the Taiping. As the Taiping movement grew in wealth and power, some leaders indulged in expensive clothing, fine food, and elaborate rituals. In addition, the Taiping were unable to recruit experienced administrators because their religious beliefs were at odds with the Confucian ideals of scholar-officials. Perhaps most important, Taiping leaders did nothing to form foreign alliances that might have altered the balance of power in their favor.

In the early 1860s the British and French, who had done so much to undercut the Qing, now rallied to the dynasty's defense. From their base at Nanjing, the Taiping threatened Shanghai and the European interests that were rapidly developing there. In 1864, Qing forces, supported by European soldiers and armaments, stormed Nanjing. A Manchu official reported: "Not one of the 100,000 rebels in Nanjing surrendered themselves when the city was taken but in many cases gathered together and burned themselves and passed away without repentance."[6] By that time as many as 30 million people had been killed, and China's rulers were more beholden to European powers than ever before.

"Self-Strengthening" and the Boxer Rebellion, 1842–1901

In the wake of the Opium War, some educated Chinese began arguing that only fundamental change would enable the empire to meet the rising Western challenge. Those calls became louder after the debacle of the Taiping Rebellion. The drug trade was no longer the issue. Now representatives of industrial capitalism arrived by steamship looking for markets and cheap labor, while an increasing number of missionaries sought the salvation of Chinese souls. The educated reform faction joined the **Self-Strengthening Movement**. China, these reformers said, could acquire modern technology, and the scientific knowledge underlying it, without sacrificing the merits of its Confucian tradition. As one of their leaders stated: "What we have to learn from the barbarians is only one thing, solid ships and effective guns."[7]

The reformers established government institutions for the translation of Western scientific texts, the first since the days of Jesuit influence in the seventeenth century. Members of the gentry established new educational institutions that merged the study of Confucian classics with coursework in geography and science. And for the first time some young Manchu and Chinese men ventured to Europe and the United States to study Western achievements firsthand.

Conservatives scoffed at their efforts. A prominent Neo-Confucian commented that since the most ancient times no one "could use mathematics to raise a nation from a state of decline or to strengthen it in times of weakness."[8] Chinese scholar-officials derived their power and prestige from their mastery of the Confucian classics. To accept foreign principles in education would undercut the influence of the scholarly elite, and to emphasize military over scholarly pursuits would have gone against Confucianism. "One does not waste good sons by making them soldiers," went an old saying.

Conservative attitudes coalesced at the top of the imperial hierarchy. During the reign of two child emperors, real power lay in the hands of a conservative regent, the **Empress Ci Xi** (1835–1908), an imperial concubine who came to dominate the highest reaches of the Qing bureaucracy. Conservatives rallied around Ci Xi (**kee shee**). She discouraged talk of reform and diverted funds for modernization, such as

---

Self-Strengthening Movement Nineteenth-century Chinese reform movement with the motto "Confucian ethics, Western science." Advocates of self-strengthening helped to find a way to reconcile Western and Chinese systems of thought.

Empress Ci Xi (1835–1908) The "Dowager Empress" who dominated Qing politics in the late nineteenth century, ruling as regent for the Emperor Guangxi. She blocked the Hundred Days' Reforms and other "self-strengthening" measures.

programs to build railways and warships, to prestige projects, such as rebuilding the ruined summer palace.

Ci Xi's power was checked by the unequal treaties with Western nations, whose arrogance toward the Celestial Empire infuriated the "Dowager Empress." In spite of limited beginnings of industrialization and the acquisition of some modern armaments, the Qing military was no match for its rivals. In 1884, during a dispute over rights to Vietnam, French gunboats obliterated the Qing southern fleet within an hour. Southeast Asia, no longer tributary to the Qing, would now belong to France.

The European powers were not the only ones threatening the integrity of the Qing Empire; by this time Japan was also aggressively pursuing a policy of industrialization and militarization. Japan and Qing China came into conflict in Korea, where an uprising against the Chosôn dynasty brought both Japanese and Chinese military forces, resulting in the Sino-Japanese War of 1894–1895. The Qing, having lost their southern fleet to France, now lost almost their entire northern fleet to Japan. The treaty that ended the war gave Japan possession not only of Korea but also of the island of Taiwan.

On this occasion, reformers sought the support of the young Guangxu (gwahng-shoo) emperor (r. 1875–1908), who issued a series of edicts in the summer of 1898 that came to be called the Hundred Days' Reforms. Guangxu was inspired by a group of young scholars who had traveled to Beijing to present a petition urging the founding of a state bank, the raising of government bonds for large-scale building of railroads, and the creation of a modern postal system. The most fundamental of the Hundred Days' Reforms concerned education. Expertise in poetry and calligraphy would no longer be required. Instead, the examination essays would focus on practical issues of governance and administration. Beijing College was to add a medical school, and all the Confucian academies were to add Western learning to their curricula.

Ci Xi ended the Hundred Days' Reforms by proclaiming that Guangxu had asked her to rule in his name and confining him, along with his most progressive advisers, in the palace. Some advocates of self-strengthening were charged with conspiracy and executed; others left the country or lapsed into silence.

Meanwhile the aggression of external powers intensified. Germans seized the port city of Qingdao (ching-dow) and claimed mineral and railway rights on the Shandong peninsula; the British expanded their holdings from Hong Kong; and the Russians increased their presence in Manchuria (see Map 24.1). Public anger grew, directed at the Manchu for letting the empire slip so dramatically.

During the nineteenth century, many Chinese sought security by joining secret societies. One of these, the "Society of Righteous and Harmonious Fists," also known as the Boxers because of their emphasis on martial arts, now rose to prominence. Virulently antiforeign, in 1898 they attacked European missionaries and Chinese Christian converts, thus beginning the **Boxer Rebellion**. Empress Ci Xi, having resisted progressive reforms, decided to side with the rebels and declared the Boxers a patriotic group: "The foreigners have been aggressive towards us, infringed upon our territorial integrity, trampled our people under their feet.... They oppress our people and blaspheme our gods."[9]

> **Boxer Rebellion** (1898) Chinese uprising triggered by a secret society called the Society of Righteous and Harmonious Fists, a fiercely anti-Western group. Intended to drive out Westerners, it resulted instead in foreign occupation of Beijing.

But imperial support for the Boxers was another disaster. In the summer of 1900, twenty thousand foreign troops from over a dozen different nations marched on Beijing and occupied the Forbidden City. Another humiliating treaty followed. The Qing were required to pay 450 million ounces of silver (twice the country's annual revenue) to the occupying forces. Like the Taiping, the Boxer Rebellion left China weaker and more beholden to foreigners than ever before.

Finally, after the disaster of the Boxer Rebellion, Ci Xi's government implemented the Hundred Days' Reforms, abolishing the examination system and making plans for a constitutional order with some degree of popular representation. But it was too late. In 1911 the first revolution of twentieth-century China thrust the Qing dynasty into historical oblivion.

Map 24.1 Asia in 1910

By 1910, empire was the status quo across Asia. In addition to the established British, French, and Dutch possessions, the United States (Philippines) and Japan (Korea and Taiwan) were new imperial players. The Russian Empire was also a powerful presence, expanding at the expense of Iran, though its defeat by Japan in 1905 showed the limits of its influence in East Asia. Qing China was still technically a sovereign state; however, the "concessions" controlled by Western powers after the imposition of unequal treaties meant that important coastal regions were under de facto European colonial control. © Cengage Learning ▶ Interactive Map

Territories held by
Western powers

Great Britain
France
Netherlands
United States
Russian Empire

Japan and its territories
Independent Asian states
Ottoman Empire
Major railroads

The Rise of Modern Japan, 1830–1905

When Fukuzawa Yûkichi wrote that China could never move forward under Qing leadership, he was in a good position to judge. He had been instrumental in Japan's own transformation from weakness and isolation to industrialization, centralized state power, and imperialism. After the Meiji **(MAY-jee)** Restoration of 1868 Japan looked to the West not just for its technology but also for its principles of education, economic organization, and state building. Yet socially, culturally, and spiritually, the Japanese retained their ancient traditions. By borrowing foreign ideas and adapting them to Japanese culture, Japanese society actually achieved the "self-strengthening" that had been desired by Chinese reformers.

The turning point came in 1853. After the arrival of a U.S. fleet, isolation from the West was no longer possible. Having observed the consequences of the Opium War for China, Fukuzawa and others advocated radical reform based on the rapid acquisition of Western knowledge and technology. As elsewhere, reform was opposed by defenders of the status quo. But in Meiji Japan, reformers took charge of imperial policy, laying the foundations of military and industrial modernization. Military victories over China in 1895 and Russia in 1905 confirmed their success and fulfilled Fukuzawa's dream that his country would be recognized as equal to the Europeans and Americans in Asian affairs.

Late Tokugawa Society, 1830–1867

Growing up in the busy commercial center of Osaka, where his father had been sent to look after his *daimyo* lord's affairs, Fukuzawa was highly conscious of the gap between his family's samurai status and its low income. Samurai were not supposed to deal with mundane affairs such as shopping and handling money. But since they could not afford servants, lower samurai like the Fukuzawa family had no choice but to do so. Fukuzawa remembered how they would

do their shopping at night, with towels over their faces to hide their shame. Even worse was the scornful treatment they met when they returned to their home village: "Children of lower samurai families like ours were obliged to use a respectful manner of address in speaking to the children of high samurai families, while these children invariably used an arrogant form of address to us. Then what fun was there in playing together?"[10] Although Fukuzawa's father was an educated man and well versed in the Chinese classics, no achievement on his part could raise his family's status.

While at the bottom of the samurai hierarchy, the Fukuzawa family had higher status than most people. Below them were the farmers, then the artisans, then the merchants, and lowest of all the outcasts who performed such unsavory tasks as working in leather and handling the bodies of executed criminals.

The young Fukuzawa longed to escape the social strictures that limited his ambitions. Education proved the key. Fukuzawa received no formal education until he was fourteen, and then it was the traditional curriculum of Confucian classics taught in Chinese. Frustrated, he sought his family's permission to travel to the port city of Nagasaki, the site of the annual Dutch trade mission. This was the only opening the Tokugawa government allowed to Europeans, and it was therefore also the center of "Dutch learning" (see Chapter 20). Begun in 1853, Fukuzawa's study of Western medical and scientific texts convinced him of the superiority of Western over Chinese styles of education.

Just a few months earlier American **Commodore Matthew Perry** (1794–1858) had sailed from the United States into Edo harbor, his steam-powered "black ships" sending shock waves through Japanese society. Perry's mission was to impress on the Tokugawa government the power of Western military technology and force it to establish diplomatic relations with the United States and open Japanese ports to foreign trade. Fearing that the Americans and Europeans might unleash a destructive barrage to open Japan to the outside world, the Tokugawa government submitted and, in 1858, signed an unequal treaty with the United States and five European powers granting access to treaty ports and rights of extraterritoriality.

Among those who accused the shogun of having humiliated the nation by signing this treaty were some daimyo who hoped to use the crisis to increase their independent power. Some even acquired modern weapons to fire at passing European ships. In the early 1860s it was not clear whether the Tokugawa government still possessed enough authority to enforce its edicts. Seeking some breathing space, in 1862 the shogun sent a delegation to Europe hoping to delay further unequal treaties. Fukuzawa, who was part of this delegation, later published his observations of European life in a widely read book called *Western Ways.*

By the time of his return in 1863, things were becoming more and more dangerous. Apart from the rebellious lords, another rising source of anti-Tokugawa pressure was coming from a group of *rônin* **(ROH-neen)**, samurai without

Commodore Perry's Arrival in Japan   This Japanese print shows the arrival of Commodore Matthew Perry's steam-powered "black ships" near Edo (modern Tokyo) in 1853. After Perry's return to Japan in 1854, demanding that Japan be opened to Western trade, Japanese leaders debated how best to respond. The 1859 Tokugawa mission to San Francisco on which Fukuzawa Yûkichi served was an attempt to discover more about the U.S. government and its motives in East Asia.

masters. The rônin were a floating population of proud men of limited means, many of whom were nostalgic for a glorious past when their military skills were highly prized. "The whole spirit," Fukuzawa said, "was one of war and worship of ancient warriors."[11] These rônin were stridently antiforeign. Fukuzawa, who had now learned English and was working as a government translator, was a potential target for their anger. For years he never left his home at night, fearful of being assaulted by anti-Western thugs.

The Meiji Restoration, 1867–1890

The challenge of the West required a coordinated national response, and neither the weakened Tokugawa government nor the rebellious daimyo could provide one. But there was another possible source of national unity: the imperial court at Kyoto. Some rebels against Tokugawa rule flocked to the banner of the child emperor under the slogan: "Revere the Emperor! Expel the Barbarians!"

In 1867 supporters of the emperor clashed with the shogun's forces. Fukuzawa was now a teacher, and when the fighting came to Edo he was lecturing on economics from an American textbook: "Once in a while … my pupils would amuse themselves by bringing out a ladder and climbing up on the roof to gaze at the smoke overhanging the attack."[12] He remained neutral, for his own safety and that of his students, fearing antiforeign sentiments on both sides.

The armies of the imperial party were successful. In 1868 the **Meiji Restoration** brought a new government to power at Edo, now renamed Tokyo. Fukuzawa was delighted to discover that the administration of the newly restored Meiji ("enlightened") emperor, then only a child, was dominated by reformers who began to utterly transform the closed, conservative society that Fukuzawa had known as a child. Most were, like Fukuzawa himself, men from middle and lower samurai families that placed a strong emphasis on scholarship.

The Meiji reforms replaced the feudal daimyo domains with regional prefectures under the control of the central government. Tax collection was centralized to solidify the government's economic control. For the first time commoners were allowed to carry arms, and a national conscript army was formed, equipped with the latest weapons and led by officers trained in modern military organization. All the old distinctions between samurai and commoners were erased: "The samurai abandoned their swords," Fukuzawa noted, and "non-samurai were allowed to have surnames and ride horses."[13] The rice allowances on which samurai families had lived were replaced by modest cash stipends. Many former samurai had to face the indignity of looking for work.

Fukuzawa coined two of the Meiji reform's most popular slogans: "Civilization and Enlightenment" and "Rich Nation, Strong Army." Viewing education as the key to progress, the government set up a national system of compulsory schooling and invited Fukuzawa to head the Education Ministry. He preferred to keep his independence, founding both a university and a newspaper.

The policy of the Meiji oligarchs was to strengthen Japan so it could resist Western intrusion and engage the world as an equal by adopting Western methods. Delegates sent to Europe in 1873 were stunned by the West's industrial and technological development. They were particularly impressed with the newly unified Germany and the politics of its chancellor, Otto von Bismarck, finding these to be a model combination of nationalism and military-industrial power.

Many at home, however, were critical of this new direction. Some samurai took up arms against the Meiji regime, most notably the forty-two thousand who participated in the Satsuma Rebellion of 1877. Their leader, Saigō Takamori, ritually disemboweled himself when the battle turned against his men, and he later became a hero to the conservatives. But the Meiji reformers countered by creating their own cult of Saigō and turning him into a romantic hero, using appeals to tradition to support their policies of change.

> **Meiji Restoration** (1868) A dramatic revolution in Japan that overthrew the Tokugawa, restored national authority to the emperor, and put the country on a path of political and economic reform under the slogans "Revere the Emperor" and "Expel the Barbarians." Meiji industrialization turned Japan into a major world power.

As in Europe, the rewards of increased industrial productivity were unequally distributed in Meiji Japan. Landowners benefited most from advances in agriculture such as the importation of new seeds and fertilizer and the government creation of agricultural colleges to improve methods of cultivation. Rice output increased 30 percent between 1870 and 1895, but peasants often paid half their crop in land rent and had to pay taxes now as well. To make ends meet, rural families sent their daughters to work in factories the government was setting up. Poorly paid and strictly supervised, their dexterity and docility were exploited for the benefit of others.

Meiji Japan went further than the Germans in giving the state control of industrial development. The government constructed railroads, harbors, and telegraph lines and made direct investments in industry. Viewing economic planning as more conducive to social harmony than market competition, Meiji ministers and the oligarchs behind them did not leave economic development to market forces. Hence, the industrial economy was based on a tight connection between state and industry that continued even after the government sold its industrial assets to private interests. After 1880, Japanese industry was controlled by *zaibatsu* (zye-BOT-soo), large industrial cartels that collaborated closely with the civil service. Some of the nineteenth-century zaibatsu, like Mitsubishi, still exist today.

Political liberalism was also part of late-nineteenth-century Japanese life. Fukuzawa had helped plant the liberal seed with an influential essay on John Stuart Mill's *On Liberty* (see Chapter 23). Like Mill, Fukuzawa addressed issues of gender, writing that "the position of women must be raised at once" and that education should be the first step toward greater gender equality.[14] A twenty-year-old woman named Toshiko Kishida (toe-she-ko KEE-she-dah) went even further, speaking eloquently for women's rights in meetings across the country, even adding a little humor: "If it is true that men are better than women because they are stronger, why aren't our sumo wrestlers in the government?"[15]

One of Fukuzawa's greatest contributions in resolving the strains of the early Meiji period was in creating a space for "public opinion" in Japanese politics. Even if he disagreed with what Toshiko said, when she traveled the country arguing for women's rights she embodied Fukuzawa's principle of *enzetsu*, a word he created to describe something that had never existed in Japan before: "public speaking." In becoming a modern nation, Japan was also becoming a mass society where rulers had to take account of popular feelings and opinions. As a newspaper editor Fukuzawa's views were widely discussed, and as a writer and publisher he was the principal source of the Japanese public's view of the Western world. In fact, *all* Western books in Japan came to be known as *Fukuzawa-bon.*

Fukuzawa was particularly proud of his part in using public opinion to pressure the Meiji oligarchs for a formal constitution that provided for a popularly elected legislature. After years of debate, in 1889 Japan became a constitutional empire, with a legislature elected by propertied male voters. The Japanese constitution was based on the German one, where the emperor rather than elected representatives controlled the real levers of power. Like Germany under Bismarck, Meiji Japan achieved unification through conservative nationalism rather than a broader liberalism based on individual rights. The slogan "for the sake of the country" encapsulated the idea that individuals were to sacrifice for the larger good. And like Germany, Japanese militarism combined with nationalism to make the country more aggressively imperialistic.

Japanese Imperialism, 1890–1910

The idea that Japanese national prestige required the acquisition of an empire was reinforced by the imperialistic activity of the Europeans and the United States around the world. Doctrines of Social Darwinism were increasingly popular, portraying international relations as a "struggle for existence." Fukuzawa, too, adopted this harder-edged attitude, saying: "There are only two ways in international relations: to destroy, or to be destroyed."[16] His opinion mattered, not only because of his books and his newspaper, but also because graduates of his own Keio Academy were now rising to power in the Meiji bureaucracy.

Peace Negotiations This print by Kiyochika Kobayashi shows Japanese and Chinese negotiations at the end of the Sino-Japanese War. By terms of the Treaty of Shimonoseki (1895), the Qing Empire ceded the island of Taiwan to Japan, recognized Japanese rights over Korea, and agreed to make substantial reparations payments. The Qing and Meiji diplomats in this portrait are clearly differentiated by their clothing.

Japan flexed its imperial muscles first in Korea, where its forces confronted those of China while both were responding to an uprising in 1894. Japanese victory in the consequent **Sino-Japanese War** (1894–1895) caused a wave of national pride. In addition to acquiring control over Korea and Taiwan, the Meiji government forced Qing China to grant it access to treaty ports and rights of extraterritoriality similar to those enjoyed by European powers. At the same time, Japan renegotiated its own treaties with Europe, this time on a basis of equality.

The Japanese pressured Korea to adopt reforms that paralleled their own of the early Meiji period. At first the Korean king allied himself with the Japanese, but in 1896 he sought protection from the Russians. For the next eight years Korean reformers allied themselves with Japan while the king and other conservatives promoted Russian interests on the peninsula. Meanwhile, Meiji rulers saw the Russians as a direct threat to their own sphere of influence in northeastern Asia.

The result was the **Russo-Japanese War** of 1904–1905. Just as the Japanese navy had decimated the northern Qing fleet ten years earlier, now it scored a major naval victory over Russia. The Japanese navy, led by its impressive flagship the *Mikasa*, destroyed or disabled most of Russia's Pacific fleet. While the United States brokered peace negotiations, the Japanese government posted advisers to all the important Korean ministries. In 1910, after

Sino-Japanese War (1894–1895) A war caused by a rivalry over the Korean peninsula; ended with a one-sided treaty that favored Japan, which obtained treaty rights in China as well as control of Korea and Taiwan.

Russo-Japanese War (1904–1905) War caused by territorial disputes in Manchuria and Korea. Japan's defeat of Russia was the first victory by an Asian military power over a European one in the industrial age.

a Korean nationalist assassinated the Japanese prime minister, Japan annexed Korea.

Japan's victory in the Russo-Japanese war had global consequences. Russia was a European great power, with the world's largest military. The defeat of a European power by an Asian one inspired nationalists across Africa and Asia: European superiority was not inevitable after all.

As Japanese imperial ambitions grew in Asia and the Pacific, the Germans, French, and English were also expanding their presence in the region, while the United States annexed Hawai'i and took over the Philippines. The world was becoming a smaller place, and imperial aspirations would become a touchstone of conflict in the twentieth century.

British India, 1818–1905

By the early nineteenth century the British were the "new Mughals," the dominant political force on the Indian subcontinent. Even under foreign rule, however, South Asians carried on the same type of debate that could be heard in China and Japan, as well as in Russia and the Ottoman Empire: whether to adjust to the new circumstances by rejecting Western cultural models, by embracing them, or by finding a way to balance them with indigenous cultural traditions. A major rebellion in 1857 was inspired by the first of those choices, but after the British had suppressed the revolt and consolidated their rule even further, the option of holding on to the past was no longer viable. Indian nationalists then began developing new ideas and organizations in response to the problem of British rule, and by the beginning of the twentieth century the foundations of modern Indian nationalism had been laid.

India Under Company Rule, 1800–1857

There was no exact date on which the British took control of India. The Battle of Plassey in 1757 laid open Bengal. The defeat of the Maratha confederacy in 1818 added the rich and populous territories in the hinterland of Bombay (today's Mumbai). By the time the Sikhs of the Punjab succumbed in 1849, the British East India Company controlled virtually the entire subcontinent. By 1850 the British "Raj" was one of the great empires of world history.

Britain could not control so much territory and so many people without the participation of indigenous allies. Much of the subcontinent was ruled through a "princely state" system whereby traditional rulers were kept in nominal charge with the guidance of British advisers. These princely rulers became part of the British East India Company's administrative machinery, helping them in such crucial areas as tax collection while maintaining an appearance of continuity with the past.

Whereas early Mughal rulers had stimulated the South Asian commercial economy by promoting its connection with Indian Ocean markets, the British yoked the Indian economy to British interests, causing a loss of industry. By 1830, unemployment among India's textile workers was reaching a critical level, leaving India "to fall backward in time … losing most of its artisan manufacturing abilities, forcing millions of unemployed craftsmen to return to the soil to scratch meager livelihoods directly from crowded land."[17] In India, the rural-to-urban migration of the European Industrial Revolution was reversed.

Technological and social changes caused shifts in Anglo-Indian social and cultural interactions as well. In the eighteenth century, almost all the Europeans in India had been men.

Rammohun Roy   Rammohun Roy was the
leading thinker of the Bengal Renaissance, striving
to reconcile liberal ideas from the West with
Bengali, Persian, Mughal, and Hindu cultural and
intellectual traditions. Himself a Hindu, Roy
advocated reform of the caste system and
restrictions on child marriage, while promoting
the idea that Hinduism could be reformed from
within by returning to the original principles of its
ancient sacred texts.

© Bristol City Museum and Art Gallery, U.K./The Bridgeman Art Library

They often spoke Indian languages, wore Indian
clothing, established relationships with Indian
women, and played Mughal games like polo.
But in the age of steamships and the telegraph,
British officials were more likely to bring their
families and live in segregated communities,
speaking English and gradually growing distant
and aloof from the Indians among whom
they lived.

Now it was Indians who tried to adjust to
English language and culture. In the northeastern city of Calcutta, Britain's main commercial
center, young Indians like **Rammohun Roy**
(1772–1833) explored ways to assimilate
European cultural influences. A native speaker
of Bengali, Roy studied Sanskrit so he could
read ancient Vedic texts in their original language, and he also wrote in Arabic, Persian, and
English. Businessman as well as scholar, Roy
gleaned liberal ideas from contact with British
traders and officials. He used those ideas to promote a reformed Hinduism that combined
both a return to the religion's most ancient
philosophical principles and a series of reforms
in the liberal spirit, such as an end to child
marriage.

Roy became the leader of an intellectual
movement called the Bengal Renaissance, an
important influence on later Indians who
absorbed Western culture and thought into
their own traditions. He was also politically
active, lobbying the British government for
changes to policies that favored English business interests at the expense of Indian ones.

The British believed that they could show
India the path to progress. In the 1830s one East
India Company official declared that British
education should create a "class of persons
Indian in blood and color, but English in taste,

in opinions, in morals, and in intellect," defining progress as the replacement of Indian culture
by British culture. Roy and his successors rejected
that approach, believing instead that they could
use European ideas to reinvigorate Indian traditions. However, by the mid-nineteenth century
the increase in British missionaries traveling to
India created a wider concern that the British
were seeking to overturn Indians' cultural traditions and convert them to a foreign religion.
When combined with a
loss of support from some
of India's elites for the
British presence and the
economic strains that were
appearing in the country-
side, the missionary presence created a volatile
situation.

Rammohun Roy (1772–1833)
Bengali reformer and religious
philosopher who opposed the
caste system, polygamy, the
prohibition of widow remarriage, the lack of education for
common people, and discrimination against women.

The Indian Revolt of 1857 and Its Aftermath

The **Indian Revolt of 1857** began with a mutiny among the *sepoys* (SEE-poyz), the 200,000 Indian soldiers commanded by British officers. The sepoys were essential to British rule, and their revolt sent shock waves across north India.

Indian Revolt of 1857 Revolt of Indian soldiers against British officers when they were required to use greased ammunition cartridges they suspected were being used to pollute them and cause them to convert to Christianity. The revolt spread across north India.

The immediate cause of the Indian Revolt was the introduction of a new, faster-loading rifle. The loading procedure required soldiers to bite off the ends of the guns' ammunition cartridge casings, which were greased. The rumor spread among Muslim troops that the cartridge had been greased with pig fat; many Hindus believed that fat from cattle had been used. Both groups suspected that the British were trying to pollute them, since contact with pork was forbidden to Muslims and cattle were sacred to Hindus. The rebellious soldiers saw the new cartridges as part of a plot to convert them to Christianity. (See the feature "Movement of Ideas: Religion and Rebellion: India in 1858.")

Outraged that some sepoys had been imprisoned for refusing to use the greased cartridges, a group of soldiers killed their British officers, marched to Delhi, and rallied support for the restoration of the aging Mughal emperor. The revolt quickly spread across northern and western India. The rani (queen) of Jhansi (jan-see), one of the Maratha kingdoms, rallied her troops and rode into battle. Violence was terrible on both sides, the rebels sometimes killing English women and children, and the British strapping rebels to cannon and blowing them to pieces. Even after order was restored, bitterness remained.

British observers believed that the cause of the rebellion was simply the backwardness of the Indian people. Prior to 1857, many had held the liberal belief that Indians were perfectly capable of "becoming English" through education and assimilation. After 1857, racial stereotypes became much more powerful, with many in Britain believing that Indians (like Africans) were naturally and permanently inferior. Social Darwinism reinforced this emerging belief in race as the physical manifestation of not just cultural but also biological inferiority.

The Indian rebels knew what they were fighting against, but were less unified about what they were fighting for. Loyalty to an aged and obscure Mughal emperor was insufficient. In South Asia the cultural, linguistic, and religious landscape was exceptionally diverse, making it all the more necessary to develop a sense of identity embracing all the peoples under British rule. The lack of coordination among regional rebellions made it easy for the British to retake control.

By 1858 the revolt was over, and the British government responded by disbanding the East India Company and abolishing the last vestiges of Mughal authority. In 1876, Queen Victoria added "Empress of India" to her titles. Direct control was extended over many of the princely states. Still, alliances were maintained with many traditional rulers, who were pampered financially even if they had no real political power. The British colonial administration was centralized and given enhanced fiscal responsibilities. At the top of that system stood the Indian Civil Service, elite government officials selected on the basis of a rigorous examination. In theory, anyone who passed the examination could join the Indian Civil Service. Since the exams were only administered in England, however, Indian candidates did not have a realistic chance.

The general trend was toward a much harsher racial division in colonial society. When a British viceroy ruled that an Indian could testify against a British subject in court, he was widely attacked by the British community. Westernized Indians were disheartened when the British turned to the remnants of the old aristocracy for allies, and dismayed when the British mocked them for trying to assimilate into English culture. In 1885 they organized a new political movement called the Indian National Congress.

The Origins of Indian Nationalism, 1885–1906

Amidst all the political and social tensions, the Indian economy grew. As in Europe, railroads played a major role (see Map 24.2). Tracks

Map 24.2 **Indian Railroads, 1893**
After provoking the Indian Revolt of 1857 by seizing the lands of an Indian ruler, the British learned to treat traditional rulers with greater respect. Some of the princely states were very extensive and their rulers, such as the Nizams of Hyderabad, quite wealthy. Even in the princely states, however, the British clearly predominated. After 1857 they built an extensive railroad and telegraph network to further tighten their control. However, improved transport and communications had the unintended consequence of helping bring Indians together from across the subcontinent, fueling the growth of Indian nationalism. © Cengage Learning   **Interactive Map**

British India, 1895
Areas under direct British control
Dependent princely states
Railroads

and engines were imported from England, creating profits for English manufacturers and employment for English workers, while Indian taxpayers financed the 50,000 miles (80,500 km) of rail constructed under British rule. But there were benefits as well. The railroads, along with telegraphs and postal service, created a communications infrastructure that put India's diverse peoples and regions in closer contact with one another than ever before.

India's emerging middle class, often educated in India in the English language following a British school curriculum, had the

Religion and Rebellion: India in 1858

The following passage was written in the Urdu language in 1858 by an Indian Muslim, Maulvi Syed Kutb Shah Sahib. Maulvi Syed saw the rebellion as a chance to drive the British out of India. In this letter to Hindu leaders, he urged Hindu/Muslim cooperation to accomplish that goal, arguing that the British were consciously defiling both religions in an attempt to force conversions to Christianity.

One of the grievances Maulvi Syed mentions are British laws concerning widows. Islamic law encourages the remarriage of widows, following the example of Muhammad, whose wife Khadijah was a widow. Among Hindus, however, patriarchal beliefs dictated that a wife's life was essentially over once her husband died. The custom of *sati* encouraged widows to throw themselves on the fire when their husbands were cremated to demonstrate their devotion and to allow them to be reunited in the next life. In fact, relatively few Hindu women, usually from the highest castes, actually did so. The Hindu reformer Rammohun Roy had argued that Hindus should give up the practice of sati, and in 1829 the British abolished it by law. They also issued another order that widows should be allowed to remarry.

Another controversy to which the author refers is the "doctrine of lapse," a colonial ruling that if an Indian prince died without a male heir, direct control over his territory would go to the British. In 1856 the city of Lucknow and the rich province of Oudh had been taken over by the British through this device. The author's references to food pollution may refer to the widespread suspicion that the British were forcing Indians under their control (such as sepoys and prisoners) into contact with forbidden animal fats.

Maulvi Syed on British Christians

The English are people who overthrow all religions. You should understand well the object of destroying the religions of Hindustan [India]; they have for a long time been causing books to be written and circulated throughout the country by the hands of their priests, and, exercising their authority, have brought out numbers of preachers to spread their own tenets....

Consider, then, what systematic contrivances they have adopted to destroy our religions. For instance, first, when a woman became a widow they ordered her to make a second marriage. Secondly, the self-immolation of wives [sati] on the funeral pyres of their deceased husbands was an ancient religious custom; the English ... enacted their own regulations prohibiting it. Thirdly, they told people it was their wish that they ... should adopt their faith, promising that if they did so they would be respected by Government; and further required them to attend churches, and hear the tenets preached there.

Moreover, they decided and told the rajahs that such only as were born of their wives would inherit the government and property, and that adopted heirs would not be allowed to succeed, although, according to your [Hindu] Scriptures, ten different sorts of heirs are allowed to share in the inheritance. By this contrivance they will rob you of your governments and possessions, as they have already done with Nagpur and Lucknow.

Consider now another of their designing plans: they resolved on compelling prisoners, with the forcible exercise of their authority, to eat their bread. Numbers died of starvation, but did not eat it, others ate it, and sacrificed their faith. They now perceived that this expedient did not succeed well, and accordingly determined on having bones ground and mixed with flour and sugar, so that people might unsuspectingly eat them in this way. They had, moreover, bones and flesh broken small and mixed with rice, which they caused to be placed in the markets for sale, and tried, besides, every other possible plan to destroy our religions.

They accordingly now ordered the Brahmins and others of their army to bite cartridges, in the making of which fat had been used. The Muslim soldiers perceived that by this expedient the religion of the Brahmans and Hindus only was in danger, but nevertheless they also refused to bite them. On this the British resolved on ruining the faith of both, and [lashed to the cannons] all those soldiers who persisted in their refusal [and blew them to pieces]. Seeing this excessive tyranny, the soldiery now, in self-preservation, began killing the English, and slew them wherever they were found, and are now considering means for slaying the few still alive here and there. It is now my firm conviction that if these English continue in Hindustan they will kill everyone in the country, and will utterly overthrow our religions; but there are some of my countrymen who have joined the English, and are fighting on their side....

Under these circumstances, I would ask, what course have you decided on to protect your lives and faith? Were your views and mine the same we might destroy them entirely with a very little trouble; and if we do so, we shall protect our religions and save the country....

All you Hindus are hereby solemnly adjured, by your faith in Ganges; and all you Muslims, by your belief in God and the Koran, as these English are the common enemy of both, to unite in considering their slaughter extremely expedient, for by this alone will the lives and faith of both be saved....

The slaughter of cows is regarded by the Hindus as a great insult to their religion. To prevent this a solemn compact and agreement has been entered into by all the Muslim chiefs of Hindustan, binding themselves, that if the Hindus will come forward to slay the English, the Muslims will from that very day put a stop to the slaughter of cows, and those of them who will not do so will be considered to have abjured the Koran, and such of them as will eat beef will be regarded as though they had eaten pork....

The English are always deceitful. Once their ends are gained they will infringe their engagements, for deception has ever been habitual with them, and the treachery they have always practiced on the people of Hindustan is known to rich and poor. Do not therefore give heed to what they say. Be well assured you will never have such an opportunity again. We all know that writing a letter is an advance halfway towards fellowship. I trust you will all write letters approving of what has been proposed herein.

Source: Records of the Government of the Punjab and Its Dependencies, New Series, No. VII (Lahore: Punjab Printing Company, 1870), pp. 173–175.

QUESTIONS FOR ANALYSIS

▶ What reasons does Maulvi Syed give to justify the rebellion? Which of those reasons does he feel are most important?

▶ What actions does he think are necessary for the rebellion to succeed? Given what you know about Indian history, what might have prevented such actions from being taken?

Indian National Congress (1885) Organization formed by wealthy, Western-educated Indians to advance the cause of Indian involvement in their own governance. In the twentieth century, it would become the vehicle for India's independence under the leadership of Mohandas K. Gandhi.

Gopal K. Gokhale (1866–1915) Indian political leader, social reformer, and advocate of Indian self-government to be achieved through negotiation.

Bal Gangadhar Tilak (1856–1920) Indian nationalist who demanded immediate independence from Britain, mobilizing Hindu religious symbolism to develop a mass following and arguing that violence was an acceptable tactic for anticolonial partisans.

Partition of Bengal (1905) A British partition of the wealthy northeastern Indian province of Bengal for administrative expediency; became a touchpoint of anticolonial agitation.

clearest vision of "India" as a single political space that, under proper leadership, could come together and speak with one voice. In the beginning, however, the **Indian National Congress** was composed of relatively advantaged men who cared most about the interests of their own social class. For example, it campaigned to have the examination for the elite Indian Civil Service (ICS) administered in India so that Indians would have a better opportunity to compete.

Since they were in closer personal contact with whites than most Indians, the congress members were sensitive to the racism that permeated British India. Every British outpost had a "club" where British officials and merchants gathered to socialize. Indians, no matter how accomplished, were excluded from clubs—except as servants.

Following in the tradition of Rammohun Roy, young congress members like **Gopal K. Gokhale** (1866–1915) tried to reconcile the British and Indian values they had absorbed through upbringing and education. They challenged their rulers to live up to the high ideal enunciated by Queen Victoria in 1858: "And it is our further will that, so far as may be, our subjects, of whatever race or creed, be freely and impartially admitted to offices in our service, the duties of which they may be qualified, by their education, ability and integrity." At the beginning, Gokhale (go-KAHL-ee) and the Indian National Congress were fighting not to change the system but to find a place within it, believing that slow reform was better than revolutionary change. They did not seek independence, but self-rule for India within the British Empire. And self-rule could not be achieved, they acknowledged, until its people learned to respect one another more fully across lines of religion, caste, language, and gender.

Other Indian nationalists, such as **Bal Gangadhar Tilak** (1856–1920), took a more confrontational approach. They questioned why the British had any right to be in India at all. Tilak (tih-lak) declared: "*Swaraj* ("self-rule") is my birthright, and I must have it!"[18] Tilak's appeal was more emotional, and his plan much simpler than that of the congress: organize the masses to pressure the British, and they will leave. Tilak's radicalism was both a threat to the British and a challenge to the Indian National Congress. Because he used Hindu symbols to rally support, his movement also alarmed the country's large Muslim minority. While Indian nationalists accused the British of using "divide and rule" tactics, the British claimed that among the subcontinent's diverse factions only they were neutral.

The British promise of "good government" was tested during the failure of the monsoon rains in 1896–1897. With its command of railroads and telegraphs, the British government could be expected to move food from regions with a surplus to those in need. Instead it left matters to the market: grain prices climbed, merchants stockpiled food, and millions starved to death. The supposed competency of British officials was called into question.

The government meanwhile continued to use spectacular public rituals to display its power and legitimize its rule. The most impressive was the "durbar" procession, a combination of circus, parade, and political theater held at Delhi in 1903. Organized to celebrate the coronation of the new British king, it featured *maharajahs* in ceremonial garb, hundreds of parading elephants, tens of thousands of marching soldiers, and elaborate salutes to India's new emperor.

Conflict arose in 1905 when British bureaucrats decided to split the northeastern province of Bengal in two. No Indians were consulted about the **Partition of Bengal**, which created a predominantly Muslim province in the east.

Delhi Durbar of 1903 The British rulers of India used lavish political ceremonies to awe their subjects. Never was the pomp and circumstance greater than at the durbar held in Delhi in 1903 to celebrate the coronation of King Edward VII as emperor of India. Representing the absent king was his viceroy, Lord Curzon, who accepted the congratulations of the Indian princes seen here in procession before the Mughalera Red Fort riding on magnificently outfitted elephants.

© Christie's Images/Corbis

Nationalists again accused the British of using "divide and rule" tactics to reinforce their power by dividing Hindus from Muslims.

In protest, the Indian National Congress organized a boycott of British goods. Bengali activists made huge bonfires of English cloth across the province. Conditions were now ripe for bringing together the Western-educated elite of the congress and the millions of urban and rural Indians struggling toward a better future.

In 1906, the same year of the anti-Partition protests, the man who would be most responsible for forging that alliance between leaders and people returned to India. Mohandas K. Gandhi (1869–1948) was then a little-known lawyer coming home from South Africa, where he had led that country's Indian community in protests against racial discrimination. Gandhi (GAHN-dee) would come to symbolize a new India in the twentieth century.

Chapter Review and Learning Activities

Fukuzawa Yûkichi was just one voice in a global debate over appropriate responses to the disruptive influences of modern industrialism and Western imperialism. The decisiveness and success of the Meiji reformers stood in sharp contrast to the conservative response of the Manchu rulers of China, and while Japan became an imperial power China was carved up into spheres of influence. Nationalism, an ideology initially derived from Western historical experience, was now being used by Asians to critique the European-dominated global order of the industrial age. In Japan, national feeling was reinforced by military victory. In China, modern ideas of nationalism were central to the movement to overthrow imperial rule and create a modern state. In India nationalists struggled to create a unified nationalist movement in response to British rule. In the late-nineteenth-century world, it seemed that societies could be competitive only if they achieved a strong sense of national purpose.

 What were the main forces that undermined the power of the Qing dynasty in the nineteenth century?

Corruption was one factor that undermined Qing power, but the real problem was the inability of Manchu and Chinese elites to find an adequate response to rising external pressure. The opium trade was the main focus of Chinese anger with the West, and in 1839 the industrial age burst in upon the Qing Empire with the British victory in the Opium War. Internal rebellions, especially the Taiping uprising, compounded the problem for Qing officials. Attempts at reform based on principles of "self-strengthening" were rejected by conservative opponents of change. The Qing Empire's lack of dynamic leadership culminated in imperial support for the Boxer rebels, with their virulent antiforeign ideology and lack of any vision on which a modern, industrial China could be built. China entered the twentieth century in an unprecedented position of weakness.

 What made it possible for Japan to be transformed from a relatively isolated society to a major world power in less than half a century?

The challenges facing the Tokugawa shoguns were similar to those facing China, but the outcome was very different. Having witnessed the devastating effect of modern weapons in China, Tokugawa officials had no real choice but to open to the West after the arrival of Admiral Perry in 1853, even if doing so badly tarnished their domestic reputation. Japan entered a period of unrest as officials oscillated between the conservative desire to fend off the noxious foreigners and the reformist program embraced by Fukuzawa Yûkichi. Shortly after the shogun was removed and the emperor returned to power during the Meiji Restoration of 1868, it became clear that the new regime had embraced and even exceeded the reformers' agenda. The modernization of the Japanese economy and military was accomplished with astonishing rapidity. While at first there was some resistance, and even outright rebellion, from former samurai and peasants, military victories over China and Russia consolidated support for the Meiji regime. Japan entered the twentieth century as a major industrial power and a player in the game of imperialism in East Asia.

 What were the principal ways that British-ruled Indians responded to imperialism?

Under Company rule, some Indian intellectuals, such as Rammohun Roy, sought to create an intellectual synthesis that would bridge British and Indian culture, much as Mughal culture had once been synthesized with north Indian elements. Anglo/Indian relations deteriorated, however, in the wake of the Indian Revolt of 1857. After suppressing the rebellion, the British began a more direct form of administration. South Asian resistance to British rule then moved in the direction of mass nationalism. Moderates like Gokhale argued that compromise and accommodation with the British were the best path for

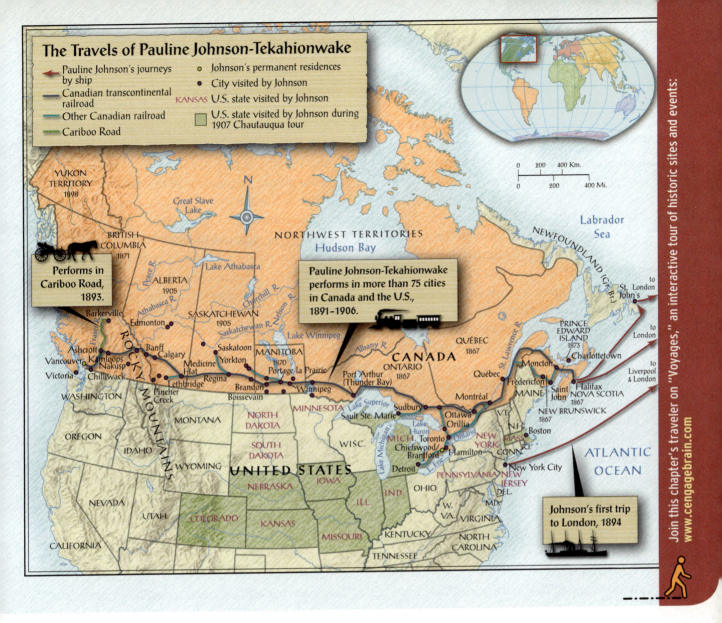

The Travels of Pauline Johnson-Tekahionwake

Legend:
- → Pauline Johnson's journeys by ship
- Canadian transcontinental railroad
- Other Canadian railroad
- Cariboo Road
- ○ Johnson's permanent residences
- ● City visited by Johnson
- KANSAS U.S. state visited by Johnson
- ▢ U.S. state visited by Johnson during 1907 Chautauqua tour

Performs in Cariboo Road, 1893.

Pauline Johnson-Tekahionwake performs in more than 75 cities in Canada and the U.S., 1891–1906.

Johnson's first trip to London, 1894

YUKON TERRITORY 1898

BRITISH COLUMBIA 1871

ALBERTA 1905

SASKATCHEWAN 1905

MANITOBA 1870

NORTHWEST TERRITORIES

Hudson Bay

Great Slave Lake

Lake Athabasca

Lake Winnipeg

ONTARIO 1867

QUÉBEC 1867

CANADA

NEWFOUNDLAND (Gr. Br.)

Labrador Sea

PRINCE EDWARD ISLAND 1873

NOVA SCOTIA 1867

NEW BRUNSWICK 1867

MAINE

ATLANTIC OCEAN

UNITED STATES

WASHINGTON, OREGON, MONTANA, IDAHO, WYOMING, NEVADA, UTAH, CALIFORNIA, NORTH DAKOTA, SOUTH DAKOTA, NEBRASKA, COLORADO, KANSAS, MINNESOTA, IOWA, MISSOURI, WISC., ILL., IND., OHIO, KENTUCKY, TENNESSEE, W. VA., VIRGINIA, NORTH CAROLINA, PENNSYLVANIA, NEW YORK, NEW JERSEY, MD., DEL., MICH., MASS., CONN., R.I., N.H., VT.

Cities: Barkerville, Edmonton, Ashcroft, Vancouver, Nakusp, Kamloops, Victoria, Chilliwack, Banff, Calgary, Medicine Hat, Pincher Creek, Lethbridge, Regina, Saskatoon, Yorkton, Portage la Prairie, Brandon, Boissevain, Winnipeg, Port Arthur (Thunder Bay), Sault Ste. Marie, Sudbury, Orillia, Toronto, Chiefswood/Brantford, Hamilton, Detroit, Ottawa, Montréal, Québec, Fredericton, Saint John, Moncton, Halifax, Charlottetown, Boston, New York City, St. John's, London, Liverpool & London

ROCKY MOUNTAINS

Peace R., Fraser R., Athabasca R., Saskatchewan R., Churchill R., Nelson R., Albany R., St. Lawrence R.

Lake Superior, Lake Huron, Lake Michigan, Lake Ontario, Lake Erie

Join this chapter's traveler on "Voyages," an interactive tour of historic sites and events: www.cengagebrain.com

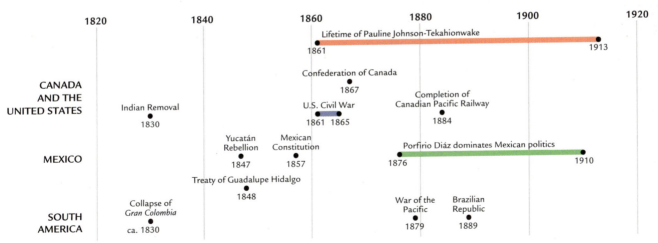

Timeline:

	1820	1840	1860	1880	1900	1920

Lifetime of Pauline Johnson-Tekahionwake: 1861–1913

CANADA AND THE UNITED STATES
- Indian Removal 1830
- U.S. Civil War 1861–1865
- Confederation of Canada 1867
- Completion of Canadian Pacific Railway 1884

MEXICO
- Yucatán Rebellion 1847
- Mexican Constitution 1857
- Treaty of Guadalupe Hidalgo 1848
- Porfirio Díaz dominates Mexican politics 1876–1910

SOUTH AMERICA
- Collapse of *Gran Colombia* ca. 1830
- War of the Pacific 1879
- Brazilian Republic 1889

Patriotic Canadians might have heard these as dissonant words; nevertheless; they gave Johnson's powerful performance loud applause.

"A Cry from an Indian Wife" reflected Johnson's own mixed ancestry. Her father's family was Mohawk, an Iroquois (ir-UH-kwoi) band that had established a close alliance with the British during the colonial period. As a child Pauline would listen to Mohawk legends and tales of a family history that included Joseph Brant, the Mohawk leader who had fought with the British in the American War of Independence (see Chapter 22). The British family connection was deepened when Pauline's father married an Englishwoman. Their wedding photograph shows optimism toward this cultural mixture: the groom wears both British medals and an Iroquois wampum belt, while the English bride's stiff Victorian attire is offset by the ceremonial tomahawk she holds in her lap.

Her father balanced two worlds, serving as both a Canadian government employee and a respected member of the Six Nations Band Council. Her mother instilled strict Victorian values in her children on the Six Nations Reserve in Ontario. Johnson-Tekahionwake (da-geh-eeon-wa-geh) would have a lifelong challenge trying to balance her Mohawk with her English ancestry. Though she grew up on the Iroquois reserve, she spoke only English, and though fascinated by Mohawk tales, she was most influenced by British literature. She was a loyal and patriotic Canadian, yet she spoke out against her country's policies toward indigenous First Nations societies.

As an adult, Pauline Johnson began to use her father's Mohawk family name

Pauline Johnson-Tekahionwake (1861–1913) Canadian poet of mixed British and Mohawk ancestry.

Tekahionwake ("double life") in advertisements for a new career: traveling across Canada performing her poetry. Before radio and movies, there was a big audience for traveling artists, and Pauline Johnson-Tekahionwake became one of the nation's best-known entertainers. Her performances drew attention to her dual heritage. She appeared on stage in a dramatic buckskin outfit to perform poems such as "A Cry from an Indian Wife," after intermission reappearing in a Victorian evening gown to recite poems of nature and love. Having found a way to earn a living through her art—a challenge for a woman of her time—Johnson-Tekahionwake crossed Canada nineteen times, often performing in the United States as well, before retiring to Vancouver on the Pacific coast, where she collected native stories.

But the late nineteenth century was a difficult time for a mixed-race person. Racial divisions were becoming more and more sharply drawn in Canada, where the white majority thought that Amerindian peoples were doomed to disappear in the face of industrial and commercial progress. The engine of progress, symbolized by the very railroad that Johnson used to reach her audience, threatened to overrun anyone who stood in its way.

Indeed, the nineteenth century was a time of relentless change across the Western Hemisphere. In 1830, much of North and South America still lay outside the control of European-derived governments. By 1895, revolutionary changes in transportation and communication technologies, along with the arrival of many new European immigrants, had changed the balance of power. The frontiers of modern nations expanded at the expense of indigenous peoples. Industrialization, mining, and commercial forestry and agriculture became the keys to wealth and power in the Americas.

Perhaps the most striking feature of this period was the rise of the United States as both the dominant hemispheric power and a global force. Canada was also a growing economic power, where many shared in rising prosperity. In Latin America, by contrast, only the privileged elites enjoyed the benefits of state building.

Telegraphs, steamships and railroads, massive new cities, and enormous industrial fortunes posed challenges to many older ways of life. Social readjustments in the nineteenth-century Americas included the abolition of slavery, the arrival of new immigrants, changing gender relations, and, as Johnson-Tekahionwake's story indicates, difficult times for indigenous peoples.

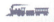

FOCUS QUESTIONS

▶ What challenges did Canada and the United States need to overcome in establishing themselves as transcontinental powers?

▶ What factors help explain conditions of inequality in nineteenth-century Latin America?

▶ Across the Americas, did nineteenth-century developments represent progress for indigenous peoples, ethnic and racial minorities, and women?

Political Consolidation in Canada and the United States

Consolidation of state power was a major feature of the nineteenth century in North America. Canada overcame deep regional divisions to become a nation, while the United States emerged from the Civil War with a more powerful and ambitious federal government than ever before. In both cases, governments extended their authority more deeply into society and more broadly across expanded territories as increased immigration from Europe brought the Great Plains and the Pacific coast under the control of Ottawa and Washington.

Confederation in Canada

Canada was a product of slow evolution rather than revolutionary transformation. In 1830 British North America consisted of more than half a dozen disconnected colonies. Yet by 1892, when Pauline Johnson-Tekahionwake made her debut on a

responsible government
Nineteenth-century constitutional arrangement in North America that allowed colonies to achieve dominion status within the British Empire and elect parliaments responsible for internal affairs. The British appointed governors as their sovereign's representative and retained control of foreign policy.

Confederation of Canada
(1867) Confederation of former British colonies united under a single federal constitution. Recognized under the British North America Act, the confederation was a dominion within the British Empire.

Toronto stage, Canadians possessed a national identity even while affiliating themselves with the British Empire. Like many, Johnson-Tekahionwake was proud of being both Canadian and British: "And we, the men of Canada, can face the world and brag/That we were born in Canada beneath the British flag."*

In 1830, British North America contained a diversity of peoples and landscapes. Upper Canada, with its capital at Toronto on the northern shore of Lake Ontario, was the fastest-growing region, where cheap land attracted English, Irish, and Scottish immigrants. Lower Canada, the lands along the St. Lawrence River now known as Québec, retained its French-speaking Catholic majority, the *Québecois* **(kay-bek-kwah)**. The Atlantic colonies were primarily populated by seafaring people dependent on the bounty of the Atlantic Ocean. And at the opposite end was British Columbia, its Pacific capital of Victoria more accessible to San Francisco than to Toronto. Far from the main population lay trading posts that brought commercial opportunity to the frontier, but also guns, alcohol, and violence to indigenous communities.

Several First Nations, such as the Cree, Ojibwa **(oh-jib-wuh)**, Sioux **(soo)**, and Squamish **(skwaw-mish)**, remained independent in the early nineteenth century. Mingled among them were communities of French-speaking *métis* **(may-TEE)**, frontiersmen of mixed European/Amerindian descent. Farther from the main areas of European settlement and British control were the Inuit hunters of the far north.

Having learned from the American War of Independence, the British government first offered Britons who emigrated to British North America (or to Australia, New Zealand, or South Africa) limited participation in government, while still appointing a governor from London

*Excerpt from *Flint and Feather: The Complete Poems of E. Pauline Johnson (Tekahionwake)*. Copyright © 1969 Hodder and Stoughton.

to watch out for British imperial interests. By 1830, however, this compromise had not achieved stability. British North Americans called for **responsible government**, an elected parliamentary government in which the leader of the majority party would become prime minister. Lack of British action led to uprisings, but they were easily suppressed. No one emerged to lead Canada to independence, and most British North Americans, English as well as French speaking, seemed to think that progress was best achieved gradually through negotiation.

During the 1840s, as the climate for reform increased in Britain, an official report recommended responsible government for Canada. New policies cut British tariffs on North American goods to British markets, such as timber, fish, and grain. Before, the economic security of British North America had come at the expense of economic growth. Though some feared the loss of guaranteed British markets, in fact the removal of mercantilist restrictions led to a boom in Canadian trade, especially with the United States.

In this atmosphere of reform, even French Canadians favored continued association with the British Empire. As far back as 1763 the British Parliament had guaranteed equal rights for French-speaking Catholics. Though the influx of British settlers alarmed the Québecois, most trusted that British constitutional models would protect their linguistic, religious, and cultural traditions. Likewise, many First Nations peoples in east and west Canada favored empire. For the Johnson family, whose ancestors had fought alongside the British for generations, their beneficence was unquestioned.

By the 1860s the British Parliament had granted responsible government to most British North American colonies. A bigger challenge was bringing them under a single constitution. No colony wished to relinquish control over its own internal affairs. Shared concerns about the United States, however, soon moved the colonies to work together. The U.S. government distrusted the British colonies to the north, and border tensions ran high after Confederate guerillas raided Vermont from Québec in 1864.

In 1867 the British Parliament passed the British North America Act, creating the **Confederation of Canada** with a federal capital

Library and Archive of Canada, acc. 1973-84-1

A Métis Man and His Wives   The métis of the Canadian frontier were culturally and biologically mixed descendants of French traders and First Nations women. Protective of their independence, many métis resisted incorporation into the Canadian confederation, often in alliance with First Nations communities. These rebellions were defeated by Canadian forces in 1869 and 1885.

at Ottawa. Though only four of the current Canadian provinces were included in the original confederation, a legal framework for later expansion was put in place. Canada was now a "dominion" within the British Empire. Local affairs were in the hands of the Canadian and provincial governments. However, Queen Victoria appointed a governor-general to represent the Crown, and Britain continued to control Canada's foreign relations.

The confederation's first prime minister was the Scottish-born leader of the Conservative Party, **Sir John A. MacDonald** (1815–1891). Leading Canada for most of its first twenty-five years, MacDonald compromised ably with both Britain and the provinces while building a central government in Ottawa. He was fortunate to do so during a time of rapid economic growth.

The building of the Canadian Pacific Railway (1869–1884) was of central importance to both political consolidation and economic growth, facilitating the incorporation of Manitoba and the Northwestern Territories into the Canadian confederation. British Columbia, which entered the confederation in 1871, was effectively tied to the rest of Canada only with the completion of this railway.

Canada's Great Plains were transformed. With the advent of cheap steel plows, grain production boomed. Canadian wheat exports rose from 10 million bushels in 1896 to 145 million bushels in 1914. Over a million farmers and their

Sir John A. MacDonald
(1815–1891) Dominant political figure of the Confederation of Canada whose Conservative Party dominated Canadian politics from 1867 until his death. A stable constitutional order and the Canadian Pacific Railway were two of his most important legacies.

families took advantage of free land and the cheap agricultural implements churned out by the new industrial plants to move out onto the prairie. They were the audience for Pauline Johnson-Tekahionwake as she took her act to the town halls and opera houses springing up in farming centers and mining camps. Two new western provinces, Alberta and Saskatchewan (sa-SKACH-uh-won), entered the confederation in 1905.

Economic growth was promoted by a stable and effective federal government. The dominance of the Conservatives ended after MacDonald's death in 1891, but stability continued when, starting in 1896, the Liberal Party won four consecutive elections based on a strong centrist base. The Liberals emphasized "race fusion," acknowledging Canada as a bicultural land where English and French, Protestant and Catholic, could live in peace, forging a Canadian identity based on mutual tolerance. Canadians did not always live up to that ideal: Amerindians and non-European immigrants were subject to brutal racism. Still, a unique nationalism accommodating Canada's affiliation with the British Empire was taking shape.

**Primary Source:
A New Model: Democracy in America** *Read de Tocqueville's statement that in a democratic nation, although citizens can attain equality of conditions, they will never be content with their equality.*

Sectionalism and Civil War in the United States

Unlike Canada, the United States entered the nineteenth century with a strong constitution and a lively sense of national identity. (See the feature "Movement of Ideas: Alexis de Tocqueville's *Democracy in America*.") The Louisiana Purchase gave the young country a sense of unbounded opportunity. The way was open as never before for the westward expansion of the United States

(see Map 25.1). But westward expansion also provoked crisis. As new states entered the Union, would they be slave or free? Could balance between North and South be maintained in the scramble for new territory?

In 1820 Congress adopted the Missouri Compromise, which established the rules for admission of new western states. Tensions then resurfaced during the presidency of **Andrew Jackson** (r. 1829–1837). Unlike previous American presidents, Jackson presented himself as representing the common man. During his campaign, his supporters emphasized his humble southern roots and his military leadership in defeating a British invasion at New Orleans in 1814. He invited one and all to the White House for his inaugural ball, and a riot nearly broke out.

As president, Jackson oversaw the forced migration of Amerindians stipulated by the **Indian Removal Act** passed by Congress in 1830. Ironically, before the act the Cherokee had tried to preserve their sovereignty by adopting a constitution that melded traditional Cherokee ways with the American political model. But U.S. policies, driven by the discovery of gold in Georgia and the hunger for land on which to grow cotton, ended those experiments. A forced march to Oklahoma killed over four thousand on what the Cherokee call the *Nunna daul Tsuny,* the "Trail Where They Cried."

The Industrial Revolution provided both the means and further motives for the expansion west. Steam-powered riverboats lowered the cost of transport and connected western territories to national and global markets. The completion of the Transcontinental Railway in 1869 and the simultaneous extension of telegraph lines further aided that process. Even ignoring the price paid by Amerindians for American political and economic growth (as did most American settlers), there was one big problem: western expansion increased conflicts between northern and southern states. Huge territories—Texas, California, the Great Plains, the desert Southwest, and the Rocky Mountains—were added after 1848. Would those vast spaces be settled by free white homesteaders or by plantation owners and black slaves?

The Democratic Party declared that the issue should be decided by "popular sovereignty," meaning by the voters within the new states. **Abraham Lincoln** (1809–1865), a leader of the new Republican Party founded by antislavery activists in 1854, disagreed. To put the issue in the hands of territorial voters, Lincoln declared, would be little more than "the liberty of making a slave of other people." Lincoln stressed the moral dimension of the question. He was opposed to the westward spread of slavery "because of the monstrous injustice of slavery itself."[2] Other Republicans opposed the westward extension of slavery not because it was wrong but because they thought that slavery was incompatible with the spread of the free, independent farmers they saw as the bedrock of society.

Lincoln can also be understood in a global context, as the revolutionary movements of 1848 in Europe had shown the connection between the spread of liberty and the need for national consciousness to rise above

Abraham Lincoln (1809–1865) Sixteenth president of the United States and the country's first Republican president. His election on an antislavery platform led eleven states to secede from the Union, plunging the country into the Civil War.

Map 25.1 U.S. Expansion, 1783-1867

The United States expanded dramatically during the decades after independence. Vast territories were purchased from France (the Louisiana Purchase) and Russia (Alaska), acquired by treaty with Great Britain (the Pacific Northwest) and Spain (Florida), and annexed from Mexico after its defeat in the Mexican-American War. Contemporary observers regarded the growth of the United States into a transcontinental power as such an inevitability they called the process one of "manifest destiny." © Cengage Learning **Interactive Map**

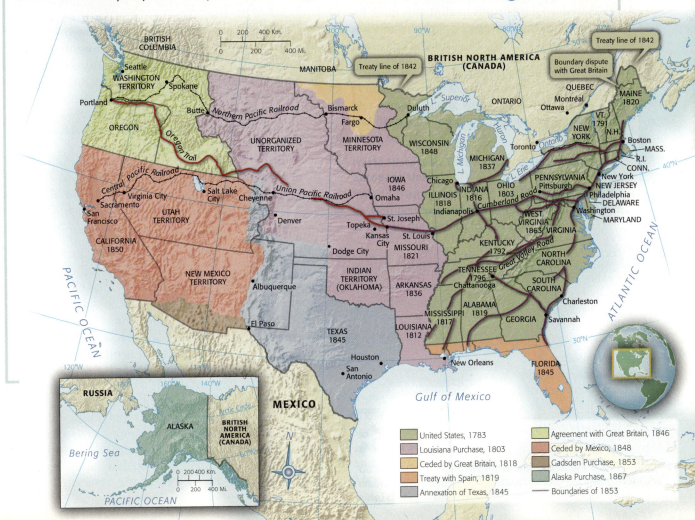

Alexis de Tocqueville's *Democracy in America*

The French historian Alexis de Tocqueville first traveled to the United States in 1831 at the age of twenty-six, and at age thirty he published the original French version of *Democracy in America*. Later, as a deputy in the French National Assembly, he was a political moderate and opposed both the Socialists and Louis Napoleon (see Chapter 23). Based on extensive travels and personal observations, *Democracy in America* is still regarded as one of the most insightful analyses of the "American character" ever written.

Author's Introduction

Among the novel objects that attracted my attention during my stay in the United States, nothing struck me more forcibly than the general equality of condition among the people.... The more I advanced in the study of American society, the more I perceived that this equality of condition is the fundamental fact from which all others seem to be derived and the central point at which all my observations constantly terminated.

On Patriotism

As the American participates in all that is done in his country, he thinks himself obliged to defend whatever may be censured in it; for it is not only his country that is then attacked, it is himself.... Nothing is more embarrassing in the ordinary intercourse of life than this irritable patriotism of the Americans. A stranger may be well inclined to praise many of the institutions of their country, but he begs permission to blame some things in it, a permission that is inexorably refused.

Geography and Democracy

The chief circumstance which has favored the establishment and the maintenance of a democratic republic in the United States is the nature of the territory that the Americans inhabit. Their ancestors gave them the love of equality and of freedom; but God himself gave them the means of remaining equal and free, by placing them upon a boundless continent. General prosperity is favorable to the stability of all governments, but more particularly of a democratic one, which depends upon the will of the majority, and especially upon the will of that portion of the community which is most exposed to want.... In the United States not only is legislation democratic, but Nature herself favors the cause of the people.

In what part of human history can be found anything similar to what is passing before our eyes in North America? The celebrated communities of antiquity were all founded in the midst of hostile nations, which they were obliged to subjugate before they could flourish in their place. Even the moderns have found, in some parts of South America, vast regions inhabited by a people of inferior civilization, who nevertheless had already occupied and cultivated the soil. To found their new states it was necessary to extirpate or subdue a numerous population.... But North America was inhabited only by wandering tribes, who had no thought of profiting by the natural riches of the soil; that vast country was still, properly speaking, an empty continent, a desert land awaiting its inhabitants....

Three or four thousand soldiers drive before them the wandering races of the aborigines; these are followed by the pioneers, who pierce the woods, scare off the beasts of prey, explore the courses of the inland streams, and make ready the triumphal march of civilization across the desert.... Millions of men are marching at once towards the same horizon; their language, their religion, their manners differ; their object is the same. Fortune has been promised to them somewhere in the West, and to the West they go to find it....

Religion and Democracy

The Americans combine the notions of Christianity and of liberty so intimately in their minds that it is impossible to make them conceive the one without the other....

In France I had almost always seen the spirit of religion and the spirit of freedom marching in opposite directions.... [American Catholics] attributed the peaceful dominion of religion in their country mainly to the separation of church and state. I do not hesitate to affirm that during my stay in America I did not meet a single individual, of the clergy or the laity, who was not of the same opinion on this point....

Associations and Civil Society

In no country in the world has the principle of association been more successfully used or applied to a greater multitude of objects than in America.... The citizen of the United States is taught from infancy to rely upon his own exertions in order to resist the evils and the difficulties of life; he looks upon the social authority with an eye of mistrust and anxiety, and he claims its assistance only when he is unable to do without it.... If some public pleasure is concerned, an association is formed to give more splendor and regularity to the entertainment. Societies are formed to resist evils that are exclusively of a moral nature.... In the United States associations are established to promote the public safety, commerce, industry, morality, and religion. There is no end which the human will despairs of attaining through the combined power of individuals united into a society.

Tyranny of the Majority

I know of no country in which there is so little independence of mind and real freedom of discussion as in America. In any constitutional state in Europe every sort of religious and political theory may be freely preached and disseminated.... In America the majority raises formidable barriers around the liberty of opinion; within these barriers an author may write what he pleases, but woe to him if he goes beyond them.

Source: Excerpts from Alexis de Tocqueville, *Democracy in America.* Edited by J.P. Mayer and Max Lerner. Translated by George Lawrence. English translation copyright © 1965 by Harper & Row, Publishers, Inc. Reprinted by permission of HarperCollins Publisher Inc.

QUESTIONS FOR ANALYSIS

▶ What does de Tocqueville see as the most essential features of American civilization, and what does he identify as its strengths and weaknesses?

▶ Are the Frenchman's observations still relevant to an understanding of the United States today?

Reconstruction (1865–1877)
Period immediately after the American Civil War during which the federal government took control of the former Confederate States and oversaw enforcement of constitutional provisions guaranteeing civil rights for freed slaves.

local interests. Like his contemporary Alexander Herzen, Lincoln held a romanticized vision of nationalism, but unlike Herzen, he rejected socialism (see Chapter 23). The Republicans believed firmly in the autonomy of individuals in social and economic life.

For many white southerners, Lincoln and the Republican Party were a threat to freedoms long protected by the sovereignty of the states. To them, Republicans represented a hard-edged industrialism that contrasted with the gracious southern way of life based on virtues like valor and honor. After all, some argued, sick or elderly slaves were cared for by their masters, while industrial workers injured on the job were thrown into the street.

After Lincoln's election in 1860, these divisions could no longer be bridged: "A house divided against itself," he said, "cannot stand." Eleven southern states declared their independence as the Confederate States of America, plunging the country into civil war (1861–1865). Accurate weapons and powerful explosives, combined with tactics that threw masses of uniformed soldiers in waves upon each other, led to suffering on an unimagined scale. Over 600,000 people died, the most in any American armed conflict. The North had a clear superiority in industrial infrastructure: railroads for moving men and materiel, iron foundries to produce guns and munitions, and textile factories to produce uniforms. The Confederates had several less tangible advantages: superior military leadership and soldiers who believed deeply in their cause and were fighting to defend their homes. However, the South's export-oriented agricultural economy left it vulnerable to a Union naval blockade. The Confederate States were highly dependent on British markets for tobacco and cotton and British factories for arms and ammunition. Unable to match the productivity of northern farms and factories, by 1865 southern resistance was overwhelmed.

Primary Source: Four Score and Seven Years Ago ... *Read an excerpt from Lincoln's Gettysburg Address.*

In 1863 Lincoln had issued the Emancipation Proclamation, making the abolition of slavery rather than the mere preservation of the Union a goal of the war. After the Union victory in 1865, the federal government was in a position to finally settle the question that had been left unresolved at the Constitutional Convention: how could the principle of liberty be reconciled with the reality of slavery? The assassination of Abraham Lincoln in 1865 meant that the most able American politician would not be able to help resolve such issues.

Federal troops occupied the South to ensure that federal law was observed as part of a process known as **Reconstruction**. White southerners resented occupation and the assertions of Republicans that the South should be remade in a northern image. In spite of new constitutional amendments intended to protect the civil and voting rights of freed slaves, southern politicians in the Democratic Party sought to end Reconstruction and restore a race-based system of governance.

The presidential election of 1876 was a major turning point. The Democratic candidate won a narrow majority of the popular vote, but the results in several states were disputed. An electoral commission gave all the disputed states to the Republican candidate, Rutherford B. Hayes. Southern Democrats were convinced to accept this outcome when Hayes agreed to withdraw federal troops from the former Confederacy, and to put an end to Reconstruction.

In the view of some, Reconstruction magnified the power of the federal government too much and violated "states' rights." But for southern blacks, "states' rights" was a disaster. Vigilante violence against blacks increased dramatically, and southern state legislatures enacted segregationist policies that came to be known as Jim Crow. Like Russian serfs, who were emancipated at about the same time (see Chapter 23), freed American slaves discovered that their freedom was far from complete.

The Gilded Age

After the Union victory the United States experienced a spurt in population growth and productivity. As in Canada, the opening of the Great Plains brought huge economic dividends. As the price of steel fell, the spread of railroads and steamships lowered transport costs and made commercial agriculture possible in more regions. Increased agricultural production led to falling grain prices in the cities, where industrial employment surged.

During the last two decades of the nineteenth century, electricity and steel supplemented steam and iron , as giant American steel and oil corporations exceeded any level of economic organization the world had ever seen. This period is often called the **Gilded Age**. (A gilded object is covered with gold on the outside, concealing base metal within.) Yet beyond the fortunes of the most privileged were a host of problems: grinding rural poverty across the South; an urban working class crammed into dirty and unsafe tenements in the industrial North; and political favors for sale to the highest bidder. By 1890 less than 1 percent of the U.S. population controlled 90 percent of the nation's wealth.

In reaction to the inequalities of the Gilded Age, farmers in the Midwest and Plains states organized a movement against corporate interests that controlled the storing and shipping of grain. At the same time, industrial workers began to form unions to fight for better pay and working conditions. Some Americans advocated socialism, thinking that capitalism would never serve the greater good. But they remained a minority. When most Americans demanded equality, what they really meant was opportunity.

In 1893 the nation celebrated its self-confidence at the Great Columbian Exposition held in Chicago, designed to surpass the world's fair held the previous year in Paris. Chicago was the most rapidly growing city in the Americas; wealthy

Gilded Age Period of economic prosperity in the last two decades of the nineteenth century. The opulence displayed by the wealthy masked the poverty, political corruption, and unsafe living and occupational conditions for the working class during this period.

Chicago Historical Society, ICHH-02554

The Columbian Exposition   The Columbian Exposition, held in Chicago in 1893, was a self-congratulatory celebration of the "triumph of science and civilization" four hundred years after the voyage of Christopher Columbus. The illuminated exhibits were the first experience most of the awestruck visitors had ever had of electrical power. Walt Disney's father was a construction worker at the Exposition, and its architectural influence was obvious in Disney's theme parks in the United States, France, Japan, and Hong Kong.

from grain trading, stockyards, and industry, the "city of broad shoulders" sponsored the construction of a dazzling model city, featuring the world's first Ferris Wheel as a response to the Eiffel Tower of Paris. The Columbian Exposition was a monument to "progress."

Attending the fair was Frederick Jackson Turner, a historian from the University of Wisconsin and author of the paper "The Significance of the Frontier in American History." Turner noted that the United States' development had been predicated on the availability of an open frontier. The lack of class enmity in American life, compared with social conflict in Europe, was due to the frontier mentality. American democracy itself was a product of the frontier, Turner argued (ignoring the people who had lived there prior to white settlement). Now, however, the frontier was closing.

Indeed, American society was in trouble. Economic boom turned to bust as overproduction led to a business slump. Thousands lost their jobs; farmers could not sell their grain or milk. The crisis was temporary, but at century's end the United States was clearly no longer a frontier society but a modern industrial state. It had become the world's leading industrial *and* agricultural producer. Now the country would trade continental frontiers for global ones and make its influence felt among all the world's peoples.

Reform and Reaction in Latin America

Consolidation of power was also characteristic of nation states in Latin America. As in Canada and the United States, Latin Americans had to overcome regional and sectional differences to develop effective national institutions. They also faced external challenges. In the middle of the nineteenth century Mexico lost northern territory to the United States and then suffered a decade of French occupation. Domination by Europe and the United States skewed Latin American economic production toward foreign markets: overreliance on exports of agricultural produce and natural resources and imports of industrial goods and technologies hindered the development of integrated national economies.

Conservatives, Liberals, and the Struggle for Stability in Mexico

Mexico won its independence from Spain under conservative ideas and leaders (see Chapter 22). Thereafter, the government fell into the hands of ineffective military leaders, the *caudillos* (kouh-DEE-yohs), of whom General Antonio Lopez de Santa Ana (1794–1876) was the most notorious. After independence, authorities proved incapable of dealing with the challenges that lay before them.

Traditionally, Mexico's wealth in people, resources, settled agriculture, and culture was in its central and southern parts. Its northern state of Texas, by contrast, was an untamed frontier with only a few officials and missionaries mixed in with the *vaquero* (vah-KAIR-oh) cowboys, Amerindians such as Apache and Comanche, and the occasional American adventurer. None paid much attention to Mexican authorities.

In the 1820s Mexico attempted to stabilize this distant frontier by inviting English-speaking settlers into Texas. Most were Americans who planned to use slave labor to produce cotton. But since Mexico had already abolished slavery, the importation of slaves was illegal. President Santa Ana would either have to enforce that law or allow the Texans to flaunt his authority.

By 1836, when Santa Ana came north with his troops, there were thirty thousand American settlers in Texas. Unhappy with Mexican rule, these settlers allied with discontented Spanish-speaking Texans to fight for independence. Despite his victory at the Alamo, Santa Ana lost Texas. Initially the rebels declared a republic, but a referendum in 1845 prepared the way for the annexation of Texas by the United States.

Mexico's loss of territory to the United States did not stop there. President James Polk, a southern Democrat, pursued an aggressive policy toward Mexico, provoking war in 1846. U.S. forces penetrated to Mexico City, and the Treaty of Guadalupe Hidalgo (1848) gave the United States the northern half of Mexico. Alta California entered the Union in 1850 as the state of California, adding its rich resources to the United States. Mexico's "*Norte*" had become the American Southwest.

Responding to this humiliating loss and inspired by the European revolutions of 1848, **Benito Juárez (beh-NEE-toh WAH-rez)** (1806–1872) and other middle-class Mexicans supported *La Reforma,* a movement to get rid of caudillo rule and create a more progressive Mexican nation. A Zapotec Amerindian, Juárez had struggled to advance in a society monopolized by the *criollo* elite. He worked his way through law school and in 1848 was elected governor of the southern state of Oaxaca.

In 1855 conservatives removed Santa Ana in a coup d'état, but they were immediately challenged by an army led by Juárez and the liberals. The success of *La Reforma* was enshrined in the Mexican Constitution of 1857. The new constitution restricted the privileges of the Catholic clergy and the military, both seen as impediments to progress. It contained a Bill of Rights and established a strong unicameral legislature to offset executive power. The old caste system was eliminated: everyone was now equal before the law.

Conservatives, however, reacted angrily to such reforms, especially limitations on the church's power and the seizure of its land. While some in the church followed the example of Father Hidalgo in supporting the rights of the majority (see Chapter 22), most priests allied with the conservative elites.

Contention between liberals and conservatives created an opening for the French emperor Napoleon III, who sent troops to Mexico in 1861. His stated intention was to force payments of Mexican debt, but his real motive was to resurrect a French empire in the Americas. The liberal government fought back. In 1862, on the fifth of May (*Cinco de Mayo*), a small army of Mexicans defeated a much larger French force at the Battle of Puebla. But Mexico lost the war after conservatives helped the French invaders take Mexico City. While pressure from Europe and the United States eventually forced the French to withdraw, the struggle between liberals and conservatives for control of Mexico continued until the death of Juárez in 1872.

The coming to power of **Porfirio Díaz** (1830–1915) in 1876 altered the balance in Mexican politics, since he himself was a political conservative but an economic liberal. Like the old caudillos, he ruled as dictator, and during his long tenure as president (1876–1880 and 1884–1911) he ignored the ideals of *La Reforma,* such as freedom of speech and assembly. He was, however, a firm believer in free trade and foreign investment, and Mexico actively sought capital from Britain and the United States to help stimulate its economy. Economic development had political implications: the power of the state expanded, for example, as improved rail transportation gave government greater access to the entire country.

Apart from railroads and mining, most new investment was in agriculture. In the colonial era these large estates, known as *haciendas,* were only weakly connected to international markets; now, in response to the expansion of those markets, their owners intensively planted export crops like cotton, sugar, and hemp. Commercial agriculture brought great wealth to Mexico's landowners, its urban commercial class, and foreign investors. Peasants, however, were driven by poverty to work on these plantations for very low wages.

Nineteenth-century liberals believed that social, political, and economic freedoms all progressed as part of the same package. But the late-nineteenth-century Mexican economy showed the limitations of that theory. The Díaz regime demonstrated to the world that the open markets espoused by classical liberalism could be combined with authoritarian political rule.

Benito Juárez (1806–1872) Mexican statesman and politician who was intermittently president of Mexico during the 1860s and 1870s and leader of *La Reforma.* His liberal principles were enshrined in the Constitution of 1857.

Porfirio Díaz (1830–1915) President of Mexico during much of the last half of the nineteenth century and during the first decade of the twentieth century. While he ignored Mexican civil liberties, Díaz developed infrastructure and provided much needed stability.

Porfirio Diáz During his long rule Porfirio Diáz improved Mexico's transportation infrastructure and invited foreign investment. He did nothing, however, to address the country's deep social and economic inequalities, or to respond to the demands of liberal Mexicans for democratic reforms. Like many dictators in world history, he was fond of bestowing medals and honors on himself.

Spanish-Speaking South America

By the 1830s there were nine separate nations where the Spanish Empire in South America had once been, and, as in Mexico, their economies were geared toward exporting raw materials for industrial processes completed elsewhere and then importing the finished products. Plantation owners, commercial intermediaries, political elites, and foreign investors all prospered, but farmers and laborers were left behind.

The story of Venezuela was fairly typical. The president, José Antonio Páez (1790–1873), was a self-made military leader for whom the liberation campaigns had been a personal opportunity as well as a political cause. Páez (PAH-ays) consolidated his power in typical caudillo fashion by forging an alliance with the old criollo aristocracy. While the president was a man of rough manners, fond of attending cockfights, the snobbish oligarchs were willing to overlook such behavior because Páez was able to control the common people.

Nevertheless, in the 1860s, after a brief civil war, Venezuelan reformers took charge and established a more liberal regime. Slavery was finally abolished, and the government borrowed money to build railroads and expand school facilities. Still, little changed: the export-oriented agricultural sector was controlled by an economic oligarchy with close ties to foreign investors.

Argentina was more economically successful. Railroads made it easier to get Argentine cattle to market, and the development of refrigerated steamship compartments in the 1860s brought European consumers Argentine beef. As the economy boomed, the capital, Buenos Aires, became one of the world's great cities. Cosmopolitan politicians, merchants, and lawyers enjoyed the city's broad boulevards, elegant plazas, and pleasant cafés. A growing working class, many of them recent immigrants from Italy, worked in meatpacking plants and other export-oriented industries. From their neighborhood cafes arose the sensual *tango*, Argentina's gift to musical culture.

Apart from Argentina, the most successful South American republic was Chile. As elsewhere in Latin America, conservatives and liberals, centralizers and believers in provincial autonomy squared off, but here a conservative consensus emerged early on. The Catholic Church was especially powerful.

Political consensus may have been easier to achieve in Chile because of its success in competing with its neighbors, Peru and Bolivia. Starting in the 1840s, the three countries greatly benefited from *guano* (GWA-noh), or bird droppings, along the Pacific coast: guano makes an excellent fertilizer, and the expansion of commercial agriculture created a worldwide demand, steamships providing low-cost transport. Of course, shoveling guano was not pleasant. Tens of thousands of Chinese laborers were transported to South America to do the job.

Buenos Aires The Argentine capital of Buenos Aires was an exceptionally prosperous city entering the twentieth century. As in Paris, New York, and Berlin, automobiles were beginning to compete with horse-drawn carriages along its spacious boulevards.

Library of Congress Prints and Photographs Division Washington, D.C. 20540 USA

As guano deposits declined, these countries began to develop nitrate mines, but intensifying competition for resources led to the **War of the Pacific**. Chile's victory enhanced its reputation: its political institutions strengthened, its economic situation improved, and Chileans developed a stronger sense of national identity. The war was disastrous for Bolivia, which lost its access to the sea (see Map 25.2).

From Empire to Republic in Brazil

Brazil followed a unique path, hardly surprising given its vast size, distinct ecology, and relationship to Portugal. Brazil became independent in 1822, with Pedro I, heir to the Portuguese

throne, its first emperor. He was succeeded by his son, and Brazil remained a monarchy until 1889.

Despite being a constitutional monarchy, Brazil's principal political tensions were quite similar to those of its republican neighbors. Brazilian liberals, including its urban middle class, responded to progressive European trends, such as free trade and the protection of civil liberties, while the country's conservatives, large estate owners and military men, stressed traditional values such as the authority of the Catholic Church. The abolition of slavery, a

War of the Pacific (1879) War among Bolivia, Peru, and Chile over natural resources of the Pacific coast. Chile emerged victorious, gaining international prestige, while Bolivia's loss made it a poor, landlocked country.

Map 25.2 Latin America, ca. 1895

By 1895 all of the nations of South America and Central America were independent except for British, French, and Dutch Guyana. Bolivia became landlocked after losing the War of the Pacific in 1879 and ceding coastal territory to Chile. Panama seceded from Colombia in 1903 with military backing from the United States, which was anxious to protect its canal zone interests. Many Caribbean islands remained British, French, and Dutch colonies. However, Cuba was freed from Spanish rule in 1898, the same year the United States took control over Puerto Rico. Dense railroad networks were a sign of foreign investment in exports like minerals and livestock products, as seen here in Mexico, Chile, Argentina, Uruguay, and southern Brazil. © Cengage Learning

🖱 Interactive Map

major liberal priority, was not achieved until 1888, later than anywhere else in the Americas.

In fact, slavery had become even more widespread when coffee replaced sugar as the country's primary export. Coffee plantations expanded inland from initial bases in the south, and by 1880 Brazil was the world's largest coffee producer, supplying the expanding urban populations of the United States and western Europe.

A Brazilian export closely tied to industrialization was rubber. The Brazilian government stimulated a rubber boom by granting gigantic land concessions, and improved transportation and communication technologies allowed Brazilian entrepreneurs, backed by foreign capital, to exploit the Amazon basin on a large scale.

The rubber boom went bust, however, when production spread to Central Africa and Southeast Asia, while overexploitation led to declines in Amazonian yields. The rubber bust was matched by a sharp decline in coffee exports during a global economic slump in the 1890s. Brazil found itself in the same dependency trap as other South American nations, too reliant on exports of agricultural products and raw materials and on imports of industrial goods and technologies from Europe.

Meanwhile, in the second half of the nineteenth century Brazil's northeastern plantation regions were becoming less important as coffee, cattle, and grain production surged in the south, with European immigrants rather than Afro-Brazilian slaves providing most of the labor. Abolitionist sentiment grew, and the monarchy lost its credibility. In 1889 the emperor was deposed, Brazil became a republic, and slavery was finally purged from the Western Hemisphere.

Connections and Comparisons in the Nineteenth-Century Americas

Throughout the Americas, changes resulted from the integration into global markets and the consolidation of state power. One general result was the elimination of Amerindian sovereignty. In 1830 many indigenous societies still governed their own affairs; by 1895 such independence was found only in the most remote regions. As ever larger numbers of European immigrants crossed the Atlantic, and slavery ended, racial demographics changed in diverse ways. Just as important were changes in gender roles. Pauline Johnson-Tekahionwake was not the only woman seeking greater autonomy in late-nineteenth-century society.

The Fates of Indigenous Societies

The nineteenth century was decisive for America's indigenous peoples. Before the Industrial Revolution, Amerindian societies in regions as diverse as the Andes, the Arctic, Amazonia, and the Great Plains retained control over their own political, social, and cultural lives. Some, like the Johnson family and other Iroquois on the Six Nations Reserve, maintained connections with settler societies while balancing old traditions and new influences. But by the end of the century Amerindian sovereignty had disappeared.

Take Mexico, for example. After Mexican independence in 1821 Mayan-speaking villagers on the Yucatán (yoo-kah-THAN) peninsula continued to live much as before, with little reference to Spanish-speaking government officials. They grew maize, beans, and other staple crops, in communities deeply rooted in the pre-Columbian past. Although Christians, their Catholicism was a mixture of local and imported beliefs. Now part of a wider network as both producers and consumers, nevertheless their self-sufficiency allowed them to choose their own terms of contact with the outside world.

Yucatán Rebellion (1847)
Maya uprising on Mexico's Yucatán peninsula, challenging the authority of the Mexican government and local landowners. Some Maya communities defended their sovereignty into the 1890s.

Sitting Bull (ca. 1831–1890)
Sioux chieftain who led Amerindian resistance to settlement of the Black Hills. After defeating the U.S. cavalry and General George Custer at the Battle of Little Bighorn in 1876, he was killed in 1890 for promoting the Ghost Dance Movement.

By the 1840s commercial agriculture in the Yucatán was booming. At first, planters of sugar and henequen could not attract Amerindian workers at the wages they were willing to offer. Just at this time, however, Mexican tax collectors were becoming more assertive because of the expensive wars with Texas. Forced to produce cash to pay their taxes, peasants resorted to debt peonage (see Chapter 18). Formerly independent peasants became entrapped laborers on large estates.

Meanwhile, the Spanish-speaking elite of the Yucatán revolted against the authority of Mexico City and declared the peninsula's independence. Taking advantage of the disarray, a small group of Maya militants began a guerilla campaign in 1847, known as the **Yucatán Rebellion**, attacking both Mexican government officials and local oligarchs. Since the Mexican army was engaged in war with the United States, the rebels soon controlled over half the Yucatán peninsula. Once the war in the north was over, however, Mexican officials redeployed their forces against the Maya rebels.

Mexican liberals, under the Zapotec leader Benito Juárez, saw the Maya as primitive folk standing in the way of "progress." Nation building and market economics were engines of progress, and the Yucatán rebels were attacking both. Although government authority had been reasserted in most places by the 1850s, scattered fighting continued until 1895. By then the economic autonomy of the Yucatán Maya had been broken: the need for cash to pay their taxes had driven them to low-wage peonage on plantations producing for export.

The indigenous communities of the Great Plains could hardly have been more different from the Maya. The Maya were farmers living in densely settled permanent villages, while Plains Amerindians lived in mobile bands and depended on buffalo hunting for both food and a source of trade goods. But both groups' ways

of life proved incompatible with the industrial nation-state.

The ancient buffalo-hunting culture of the Plains was given impetus by the arrival of horses in the sixteenth and seventeenth centuries. Formerly agricultural people like the Lakota (luh-KOH-tuh) Sioux and the Cheyenne moved to the Plains using horses and rifles to develop an efficient hunting culture. After 1846, when Great Britain ceded Oregon to the United States, large numbers of settlers sought their fortune on the "Oregon Trail." By the time of the Civil War, Dakota Territory was strung with a series of forts to protect settlers against Amerindians.

For a time it seemed that negotiations between the Sioux and the U.S. government might preserve stability. An 1868 treaty, for example, forbade white settlement in the Black Hills, sacred to the Sioux and other Plains societies. Four years later, however, gold was discovered, and waves of white prospectors descended on mining camps in the heart of sacred Sioux land. To Sioux leaders like **Sitting Bull** (ca. 1831–1890) treaties with the U.S. government seemed worthless.

The Sioux prepared for war, and in the summer of 1876 they massacred Lieutenant Colonel George Custer and the Seventh United States Cavalry at the Battle of Little Big Horn. In the American press, Custer's demise was portrayed as a heroic "last stand" against savages. Amid calls for swift vengeance, some advocated the total annihilation of Amerindians.

Starting in the 1870s, European immigrants and American settlers began arriving in the Dakota Territory as permanent homesteaders by rail. In 1890 the U.S. government abrogated its treaty with the Sioux to open lands for these settlers. The whole Lakota way of life, which depended on open grazing lands for buffalo, was now imperiled.

Despairing, some Plains Amerindians were attracted to the teachings of a mystic named Wovoka (wuh-VOH-kuh), leader of the Ghost Dance Movement. Wovoka's followers believed that he was a messiah sent to liberate them and that by dancing the Ghost Dance they would hasten a millennium in which earthquakes would

Sitting Bull and Buffalo Bill Cody   In the 1880s, before his death in 1890, the great Sioux war chieftain performed in Buffalo Bill Cody's Wild West Show, an indicator of how far his people had fallen in the decade since his defeat of George Custer at the Little Big Horn. As Native American resistance to white encroachment was overcome, patronizing notions of Amerindians as "noble savages" developed alongside the persistent Euro-American image of "blood-thirsty Indians."

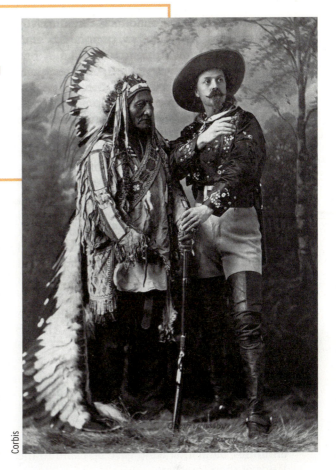

Corbis

drive the invaders from the earth and leave the native peoples in peace and prosperity.

The U.S. government regarded the Ghost Dance Movement as subversive and ordered the arrest of Sitting Bull in the belief that he led the movement. Soon, Sitting Bull was killed in a skirmish; two weeks later, at Wounded Knee, the Seventh Cavalry executed their Sioux captives, killing at least 150 people, nearly half of whom were women and children. An editorial writer at a South Dakota newspaper had this to say:

The Whites, by law of conquest, by justice of civilization, are masters of the American continent, and the best safety of the frontier settlements will be secured by the total annihilation of the few remaining Indians. Why not annihilation? Their glory has fled, their spirit broken, their manhood effaced; better that they die than live the miserable wretches that they are.[3]

Such support of a policy of genocide was not uncommon. (The author of this editorial was L. Frank Baum, who ten years later would write *The Wonderful Wizard of Oz.*)

Rather than annihilation, the federal Bureau of Indian Affairs separated Amerindian children from their parents to prevent them from learning the language, culture, and rituals of their own people. The Ghost Dance and other ceremonies were forbidden and could be practiced only in secret. Amerindian armed resistance was over. The frontier wars persisted only in entertainment, courtesy of Buffalo Bill Cody's popular Wild West shows.

When she began to travel across Canada in the 1890s, Pauline Johnson-Tekahionwake saw firsthand the tragedy of the Plains Amerindians. She witnessed the sad spectacle of "a sort of miniature Buffalo Bill's Wild West" in which Blackfoot warriors caricatured their old war maneuvers. Some might have been veterans of the **Métis Rebellions**, the uprisings of mixed-race and First Nations peoples that had inspired Johnson to write "A Cry from an Indian Wife."

The Métis settlement in the Red River Valley of what is now the Canadian province of Manitoba represented the older form of European/First Nations interaction. During the heyday of the fur trade, mixed-race families were not uncommon. Sometimes Europeans were absorbed

Métis Rebellions   (1867 and 1885) Rebellions by the Métis of the Red River Settlement in Manitoba, a group with mixed French/Amerindian ancestry who resisted incorporation into the Canadian Confederation. In 1885 their leader Louis Riel again led them in rebellion against Canadian authority.

into indigenous communities, and sometimes the offspring of mixed unions established their own communities.

The first of two Métis Rebellions came immediately after Canadian Confederation in 1867. London had transferred authority over the territories of the Hudson's Bay Company to the Canadian government without consulting the people who lived there. The Métis leader Louis Riel organized his community to resist incorporation, which they feared would lead to loss of their lands and the erosion of their French language. Riel declared a provisional government and soon secured guarantees that Canada would protect the language and Catholic religion of the Métis. Negotiations led to the incorporation of Manitoba into Canada in 1870.

At the same time, Canadian policies assumed that First Nations peoples would disappear as a distinct population. Plains dwellers were increasingly desperate. The buffalo were dwindling; alcohol was becoming a scourge. The railroad brought settlers and commerce, but their hunting traditions and lack of capital made a transition to farming almost impossible. In exchange for exclusive reserves and small annuities, band after band gave up claim to the lands of their forebears.

The Indian Act of 1876 asserted the authority of the Canadian state over First Nations communities. Children were separated from their families and sent to "industrial schools," given English names, and forbidden to speak their own languages. Canadian officials banned traditional rituals, such as the *potlatch*, a feast during which the host makes an overwhelming display of prestige by ceremoniously giving away his wealth to others in the community. The idea of giving away all your wealth could not have stood in greater contrast to the ethos of capitalism on which Canada was being built.

Meanwhile, government surveyors were dividing the prairie into 640-acre lots. The arrival of a flood of settlers would make the Métis a minority in their own land, and Louis Riel once again organized a resistance, this time forging alliances with disaffected Cree,

Assiniboine, and other First Nations peoples. In 1885, Métis partisans attacked a government outpost as Riel's indigenous allies burned down white homesteads. But they were no match for three thousand troops sent west on the Canadian Pacific Railway. Riel was arrested, convicted of high treason, and hanged. When Pauline Johnson-Tekahionwake recited "A Cry from an Indian Wife" in 1892, these events were still fresh in the minds of her audience.

If we compare the Yucatán Rebellion, the struggles of the Lakota Sioux, and the Métis Rebellions, we might first be struck by this difference: whereas the Mexican government and economic oligarchy wanted to incorporate the Maya peasantry as laborers in the commercial plantation system, the United States and Canada had no use for Amerindians even as workers.

But the three cases have much in common. In the Yucatán, the Black Hills, and Manitoba, people rose up to defend their cultures against intrusion. In all three places, indigenous and imported ideas had already merged: Maya beliefs and Catholicism, Sioux traditions with horse-based buffalo hunting, French and First Nations cultures in the days of the fur trade. But these adaptations had taken place in a preindustrial age. Now the Maya, Sioux and Métis were unable to fend off the intrusion of industrialized, capitalistic, nation building.

Abolition, Immigration, and Race

Race was a major issue across the Americas during Pauline Johnson-Tekahionwake's lifetime. During her childhood the lines were fairly simple: British (mostly Protestants), French and Irish (mostly Catholics), First Nations peoples (themselves quite diverse), and mixtures between them such as the Métis. By the time of her adult travels, that picture had been complicated by the arrival of new immigrants: Chinese, Italians, Russians, and others. Early in the twentieth century, half of the population on the prairies was born outside of Canada. The same was true throughout the Americas. The United States was the most favored destination, but Argentina and Brazil also attracted many European immigrants.

In Brazil and the Caribbean, the abolition of slavery was connected to immigration patterns and policies. Slavery was abolished in the British West Indies in 1833 and on the French islands fifteen years later. Unable to keep the former slaves as poorly paid wage earners, landowners turned to indentured workers. In the English-speaking Caribbean, indentured laborers came largely from British India, part of a broader South Asian diaspora (scattering) that also took contract workers to South Africa, Malaya, and Fiji. In Cuba, where slavery was not abolished until 1878, the sugar plantations required so much labor that over a hundred thousand Chinese workers came to the island as indentured workers to supplement slave labor.

Like Cuba, Brazil was bringing in new migrants even before slavery was abolished in 1888. Brazilian employers brought contract laborers from Japan to work on coffee farms. In fact, the largest group of Japanese-descended persons outside Japan is found in Brazil. Much larger, and more influential in Brazilian culture, however, was the Afro-Brazilian population with its origins in the old sugar plantation system. Brazilian art, music, dance, and religious worship all show a deep African influence.

The rulers of republican Brazil were embarrassed by the country's African heritage. Their mottos were "order" and "progress," and in their minds black people represented neither. To "improve" the country racially, the government recruited immigrants from Europe. Germans, Italians, and others were given incentives to relocate and became an important presence in the economically dynamic southern part of the country. The northeast, site of the old plantation system, remained more African in population and culture.

Racism was also evident in immigration to the United States. The Anglo-Protestant majority portrayed Irish Catholics as drunk, violent, and lazy. Demeaning stereotypes also greeted new immigrants from southern and eastern Europe, such as Italian Catholics and Russian Jews. Prejudice against Chinese and Japanese immigrants on the west coast was even more intense, and Congress banned Chinese immigration altogether in 1882. Still, in 1890 fully 14.8 percent of the population had been born outside the United States, and some doubted whether these new arrivals could ever be assimilated.

Racism continued to drive policy toward Americans of African descent. In 1896 the Supreme Court upheld the legality of racial segregation in the South. In northern cities recent immigrants, in spite of prejudices against them, often fared better than African Americans; many Irish Americans, for example, found good work as police officers and firemen, jobs that were closed to blacks. African Americans, on whose backs the republic had been built, now watched as new arrivals from Europe leaped ahead of them.

Harsh racial rhetoric and even harsher racial realities pervaded throughout the Americas. Encounters among Amerindians, Africans, Asians, and Europeans seemed decisively in favor of the latter. For all the variation among the nations of North and South America, they had one thing in common: light-skinned men were in charge.

Gender and Women's Rights

In 1848, the Seneca Falls Convention was held in upstate New York. Sometimes seen as the beginning of the modern women's movement, the meeting was inspired by the abolitionist movement and the revolutions of Europe. The women met to proclaim universal freedom and gender equality, declaring: "Now, in view of this entire disfranchisement of one-half the people of this country, their social and religious degradation ... and because women do feel themselves aggrieved, oppressed, and fraudulently deprived of their most sacred rights, we insist that they have immediate admission to all the rights and privileges which belong to them as citizens of these United States."

Such proclamations would eventually transform gender relations in the United States, Canada, and the world. In the short

Bicycle Advertisement This advertisement from 1896 associates the bicycle with the newfound mobility and independence of the "new woman." In the poems of Pauline Johnson-Tekahionwake, it was often a canoe that allowed women to "be content."

run, however, most women, like Pauline Johnson-Tekahionwake, had to explore their own possibilities without much external support. Just as she investigated her own complex identity through life and art, her public performances also explored her identity as a woman. The costume change she made halfway through her recitals—from buckskin to evening gown, from Tekahionwake to Pauline Johnson—transformed her from a passionate and even erotic persona to a distant and ethereal one.

For middle-class women in the United States and Canada, the bicycle became a symbol of a new mobility and new kind of freedom. For Pauline Johnson-Tekahionwake the canoe played this role. Some of her nature poems, such as "The Song My Paddle Sings," derived from canoe trips she took as a young woman on the Six Nations Reserve:

… *The river rolls in its rocky bed;*
My paddle is plying its way ahead …
And up on the hills against the sky,
A fir tree rocking its lullaby,
Swings, swings,
Its emerald wings,
*Swelling the song that my paddle sings.**

In her canoe poems Johnson-Tekahionwake is always in control, even when, as is often the case, she has a male companion. The independence asserted in her poetry was reflected in her personal life as well. She had several significant relationships but no marriage, and though money was a constant worry, she was financially

---

*Excerpt from *Flint and Feather: The Complete Poems of E. Pauline Johnson (Tekahionwake)*. Copyright © 1969 Hodder and Stoughton.

independent. Perhaps Johnson-Tekahionwake's autonomy arose from her mixed heritage, deriving from both the matriarchal tradition of the Mohawk as well as the new possibilities for women proclaimed at Seneca Falls.

How exceptional were Pauline Johnson-Tekahionwake's attitudes and experiences? Middle-class women in major commercial cities like Toronto, Chicago, or Buenos Aires had much in common. Some were politically active, seeking legal equality and the vote for women. Some organized campaigns for social improvement, working to limit abuses of child labor, to improve sanitary conditions, or to fight the evils of alcohol. Some took advantage of new educational opportunities. There were few women doctors, lawyers, and university professors in the Americas by the end of the nineteenth century, but there were many new openings for schoolteachers and nurses. The invention of the typewriter and the emergence of large corporations also created a vast new job market for secretaries.

Often young women from the lower or middle classes took positions as teachers, nurses, or secretaries until they married. Such behavior was consistent with the "cult of true womanhood." A woman's role was in a "separate sphere": women were to maintain a refined home environment as sanctuary from the brutal and competitive "men's world" of business and industry. Even though women like Johnson-Tekahionwake might reject the "cult of true womanhood," many women who aspired to be middle class embraced the idea.

The experiences of women varied tremendously according to their nation, culture, race, and social class. A middle-class homemaker in Buenos Aires had a more comfortable life than a Swedish pioneer getting her family through winter on the Canadian prairie. Likewise, an Irish nun teaching immigrant children in Chicago would be difficult to compare with a Maya mother sending her sons off to work on a Yucatán plantation. For her part, Pauline Johnson-Tekahionwake possessed a life of mobility and autonomy that would have been unimaginable to her foremothers.

Chapter Review and Learning Activities

Earlier in the twentieth century, Pauline Johnson-Tekahionwake was routinely included in anthologies of Canadian poetry, and children learned "A Cry from an Indian Wife" and "The Song My Paddle Sings" by heart. Now her flowery, romantic poems have gone out of fashion. Still, she remains an important figure in Canadian literary history. In 1906, while on a voyage to London, she met and befriended the Squamish chief Joseph Capilano, who had journeyed to the imperial capital to protest violations of the treaty between his people and the Canadian government. When Pauline Johnson retired from the stage, she moved to the Pacific coast and spent the rest of her life collecting the Squamish tales, which were published as *The Legends of Vancouver*. In her quest to reconcile her own multiple identities, Johnson-Tekahionwake helped lay the literary foundations for what would later become a larger national dialogue about honoring the rich cultural heritage and protecting the rights of Canada's First Nations.

What challenges did Canada and the United States need to overcome in establishing themselves as transcontinental powers?

Unlike the thirteen British colonies that broke away to form the United States of America, Canadians built their confederation by gaining responsible government within the framework of the British Empire. The challenge was to find common constitutional ground on which to unite diverse regions and peoples. The Métis Rebellions showed how sharp the differences could be, but political compromise under strong but moderate leadership prevailed, while after 1867 the Canadian Pacific Railway and the extension of the telegraph provided the communications infrastructure for the new nation. The establishment of the United States as a transcontinental power was a substantially more violent process, as displayed in both the Mexican-American War, fought to wrench vast territories from Mexico, and in the American Civil War, when disputes over western expansion led to conflict between free and slave states. Once that war was over, the status of the United States as a continental power was ensured.

What factors help explain conditions of inequality in nineteenth-century Latin America?

The colonial inheritance in Latin America was one of sharp social and economic inequality. The criollo elites whose domination continued after independence gained even more power with the expansion of global markets, enriching themselves by allying with foreign investors and bringing more and more land into production for external markets. The vast majority of people saw little benefit from investments in land and transportation facilities. In fact, many people, such as Amerindian villagers, lost their autonomy as they became low-wage workers producing goods for distant markets.

Across the Americas, did nineteenth-century developments represent progress for indigenous peoples, ethnic and racial minorities, and women?

The powerful and the privileged in nineteenth-century America had a strong belief in progress, reinforced by rapid industrial growth and technological development. For indigenous peoples whose ancestors suffered and sometimes died at the hands of expanding national states, the word *progress* is a cruel misrepresentation of a bitter historical record. The experiences of ethnic and racial minorities were mixed. By 1888, slavery had finally been abolished across the Americas, a major step forward for peoples of African descent. As the histories of countries like Brazil, the United States, and Cuba demonstrate, however, even legal equality proved difficult or impossible to achieve, while the idea that blacks might achieve social and economic equality with dominant national groups was hardly even considered. Immigrants from Europe, while often facing initial prejudice, largely used the expansive opportunities offered in the Americas; Asian immigrants, by contrast, faced deeper, long-term restrictions on their mobility. The experience of women in the industrial age differed depending on nationality and social status. Amerindian women whose communities lost their lands to settlers and plantation owners lost both status and security. Urban middle-class women had more material comforts but were usually confined to the domestic sphere. By the 1890s, however, some educated women were organizing to fight for equal rights; in the twentieth century that struggle would become a global one.

FOR FURTHER REFERENCE

Bender, Thomas. *A Nation Among Nations: America's Place in World History*. New York: Hill and Wang, 2006.

Bushnell, David, and Neill Macauley. *The Emergence of Latin America in the Nineteenth Century*. 2d ed. New York: Oxford University Press, 1994.

Cronon, William. *Nature's Metropolis: Chicago and the Great West*. New York: W.W. Norton, 1992.

Dickason, Olive Patricia. *Canada's First Nations*. 3d ed. New York: Oxford University Press, 2001.

Fernández-Armesto, Felipe. *The Americas: A Hemispheric History*. New York: Modern Library, 2003.

Frazier, Donald S. *The United States and Mexico at War*. New York: Macmillan, 1998.

Gray, Charlotte. *Flint and Feather: The Life and Times of E. Pauline Johnson, (Tekahionwake)*. Toronto: HarperCollins, 2002.

Levine, Robert M. *The History of Brazil*. New York: Palgrave Macmillan, 2006.

Nelles, H. V. *A Little History of Canada*. New York: Oxford University Press, 2004.

Niven, John. *The Coming of the Civil War, 1837–1861*. Arlington Heights, Ill.: Harlan Davidson, 1990.

Wasserman, Mark. *Everyday Life and Politics in Nineteenth Century Mexico*. Albuquerque: University of New Mexico Press, 2000.

KEY TERMS

Pauline Johnson-Tekahionwake (552)

responsible government (554)

Confederation of Canada (554)

Sir John A. MacDonald (555)

Andrew Jackson (556)

Indian Removal Act (556)

Abraham Lincoln (557)

Reconstruction (560)

Gilded Age (561)

Benito Juárez (563)

Porfirio Diáz (563)

War of the Pacific (565)

Yucatán Rebellion (568)

Sitting Bull (568)

Métis Rebellions (569)

VOYAGES ON THE WEB

Voyages: Pauline Johnson-Tekahionwake

"Voyages" is a real time excursion to historical sites in this chapter and includes interactive activities and study tools such as audio summaries, animated maps, and flashcards.

Visual Evidence: The Residential School System for First Nations Children

"Visual Evidence" features artifacts, works of art, or photographs, along with a brief descriptive essay and discussion questions to guide your analysis of visual sources.

World History in Today's World: Pharmaceutical Riches in Amazonia

"World History in Today's World" makes the connection between features of modern life and their origins in the periods in this chapter.

CourseMate

Go to the CourseMate website at www.cengagebrain.com for additional study tools and review materials—including audio and video clips—for this chapter.

26

The New Imperialism in Africa and Southeast Asia, 1830–1914

King Khama III
(Photo courtesy of Neil Parsons from The Botswana National Archives & Records Service)

In the short space of twenty years, between 1870 and 1890, European powers drew colonial boundaries on their maps of Africa, without the consent, and in most cases without even the knowledge, of those they planned to rule. In many places Africans mounted spirited resistance, but the Europeans' technological superiority proved impossible to overcome. As the British poet Hilaire Belloc observed: "Whatever else happens, we have got the Maxim gun, and they have not." During his lifetime, **King Khama III** (ca. 1837–1923) of the Bangwato **(bahn-GWA-toe)** people of southern Africa witnessed the great changes that came with the advance of the European empires. As a child, he was familiar with the occasional European hunter or missionary crossing the kingdom; as a king, he was forced to take drastic action to prevent the complete subjugation of his society:

At first we saw the white people pass, and we said, "They are going to hunt for elephant-tusks and ostrich-feathers, and then they will return where they came from." … But now when we see the white men we say "Jah! Jah!" ("Oh Dear!"). And now we think of the white people like rain, for they come down as a flood. When it rains too much, it puts a stop to us all.… It is not good for the black people that there should be a multitude of white men.[1]

King Khama III (ca. 1837–1923) King of the Bangwato, a Tswana-speaking southern African group. His successful diplomacy helped establish the Bechuanaland Protectorate, putting the Bangwato and other kingdoms under British rather than South African rule.

In 1895, King Khama (**KAH-ma**) and two neighboring kings began a long diplomatic mission, journeying by ox-cart, railroad, and steamship from their homes in what is now the nation of Botswana, across South Africa, and all the way to London. They were in a difficult position. The frontier of white settlement already established in South Africa was moving northward, and the discovery of diamonds and gold had added further momentum to European expansion. The kings' goal was to have the British government declare a protectorate that would allow their people to retain their farming and grazing lands and at least some control over their own affairs. The British public responded positively to their appeals, the colonial secretary argued in their favor, and they even had an audience with Queen Victoria. Thanks in great part to their effort and skill, the people of Botswana were later spared the agonies of *apartheid* ("separateness") as practiced in twentieth-century South Africa (see Chapter 30).

Still, Khama's success was only partial. Individual African societies might make better or worse deals with the forces of imperialism, but none could escape them. The late nineteenth century was the time of the New Imperialism, when powerful industrial nations vied for control of colonial territories and resources all across the globe. In Southeast Asia as well, Europeans were competing for colonies, while American, French, German, and British flags went up over scattered Polynesian islands, Meiji Japan took control over Korea and Taiwan, and the last sovereign Amerindian societies were defeated in the United States and Canada (see Chapters 24 and 25).

Applied science and industrial productivity generated the technological, military, and economic advances that powered the New Imperialism. Those societies in possession of the tools of empire—modern firearms, telegraphs, and steamships—were able to assert their power as never before. In Africa and Southeast Asia, local leaders were able to resist only by manipulating European rivalries for their own ends. Even such independent states as Siam and Ethiopia were incorporated into the unequal global system based on empire. Indigenous leaders around the world could relate to King Khama's predicament.

FOCUS QUESTIONS

▶ What were the main causes of the New Imperialism?

▶ In what different ways did Africans respond to European imperialism?

▶ What were the main outcomes of the New Imperialism in Southeast Asia?

▶ What connections and comparisons can be made between Africa and Southeast Asia in the late nineteenth century?

The New Imperialism

Europeans and Africans had interacted long before the Industrial Revolution. After the sixteenth century European engagement was largely limited to collecting slaves from the west coast of Africa. Until the late nineteenth century, only small groups of European settlers and a few intrepid explorers had ventured into the African interior.

The Industrial Revolution altered this. The export of slaves was replaced by the export of African products to Western markets, while African imports of industrial manufactures increased. For most of the nineteenth century, African merchants and African political authorities facilitated the new trade connections. Then something dramatic happened. As King Khama noted, suddenly after 1870 Africans confronted "a multitude of white men." The era of **New Imperialism** had begun. Heightened competition among industrial states for African raw materials and markets was one motive for European colonial expansion; personal ambition and religious conviction were others. Modern technology made possible rapid partition and conquest during the "scramble for Africa."

Political and Economic Motives

Germany was the fastest-growing industrial economy in the second half of the nineteenth century. Having defeated the French in 1871, the Germans wanted to show that they were the equals of the British by acquiring an empire of their own. There was also a domestic logic to German imperialism. The German leader Otto von Bismarck recognized that rapid industrialization and urbanization were having destabilizing social effects and that the working class was becoming organized. From Bismarck's standpoint, if the public's attention could be focused on military glory and imperial expansion, then nationalism would strengthen German unity and weaken the appeal of socialism.

For the French as well, international prestige, national glory, and domestic politics were important in stimulating imperial expansion. French politicians needed to restore their country's international standing after the humiliating defeat by the Germans. Imperial expansion in Africa and Southeast Asia accomplished that goal and gave legitimacy to the government of the Third Republic (see Chapter 23).

Britain already presided over a vast overseas empire. Britain's centuries-old focus on maritime affairs, its early industrial lead, and its domination of global finance had brought resource-rich territories such as India and South Africa under its control, even while Victorian liberals, with their belief in free trade, had tried to limit imperial expansion.

The rise of Germany caused Britain to more actively pursue imperial power. The Conservative Party (also called the Tories) had traditionally been the party of the rural gentry. But in the 1870s a new generation of Tory leaders, led by Benjamin Disraeli (1804–1881), sought to broaden their base of support by becoming the party of empire. After the Reform Act of 1884 a majority of the country's male population could vote, and Disraeli found that appeals to patriotism and national glory helped win elections. As in Germany and France, domestic politics fueled imperial policy. The Liberal Party under W. E. Gladstone (1809–1898), always concerned that British taxpayers would have to bear the costs of colonial wars, tried unsuccessfully to resist this trend. The security needs of existing colonies caused the British Empire to expand even during periods of Liberal rule.

Economic factors intensified the national competition that characterized the New Imperialism. Large corporations investing huge sums of money in the chemical and metals industries needed access to natural resources like tin, oil,

> **New Imperialism** An increase in European imperial activity during the late nineteenth century, caused primarily by increased competition between industrial states for raw materials and markets and by the rise of a unified Germany as a threat to the British Empire.

and rubber from around the world. As long as Britain was the dominant power and enforced global free trade, such resources were available to anyone with the ability to buy them. But as competition increased among the great powers, faith in the free market began to wane.

The New Imperialism therefore brought a return to mercantilist policies. Countries desired exclusive power over empires from which they could extract resources for the benefit of the home economy. Chartered companies such as those that had dominated Europe's eighteenth-century colonial enterprises came back. The imperial powers also had two other interests. First, they needed markets for the goods they were producing. Second, they needed new investment opportunities. By the 1890s imperial expansion was closely tied to industrial capitalism. As a result, the free-market preferences of economic liberals became less central to European policymakers.

Ideology and Personal Ambition

The New Imperialism was associated with challenges to the social ideals of liberalism. Social Darwinism, the idea that races and nations were locked in a "struggle for existence," had now become the dominant ideology in Europe. Most white people saw themselves as sitting atop an unchangeable hierarchy of races, a belief that justified colonial expansion as part of the natural order of things. Some predicted that the world's weaker peoples would gradually die out; others argued that it was the duty of "advanced" races to "civilize" the "inferior" ones.

In the early nineteenth century, missionaries inspired by the abolitionist movement dedicated themselves to the salvation of African souls and the redemption of the continent from primitive superstition. In the 1820s, the London Missionary Society established stations in South Africa. **David Livingstone** (1813–1873) spent the better part of his life in Africa, and most of his later years beyond the borders of European control. Livingstone saw Africans as fully capable in every way;

his dream was eventually to have African Christians in positions of church leadership. In pursuit of this goal he spent time among the Bangwato, serving as a tutor to one of the kings who accompanied Khama to London.

Livingstone's goal was achieved by Samuel Ajayi Crowther. Born in what is now western Nigeria, Crowther was sold into slavery in 1821. By then the British were committed to abolition, and the Royal Navy seized the Portuguese ship on which he was held captive along with his mother and brother. The British dropped the twelve-year-old off at Freetown in Sierra Leone, established as a home for such "re-captives." After education in Sierra Leone and England, and having served on a mission to the Niger River, Crowther was ordained as an Anglican priest. One of his enduring contributions to African Christianity was his translation of the Christian texts into his own native Yoruba and other African languages.

In 1864, Crowther became the Anglican bishop of West Africa. But he was disappointed to find that some white missionaries resented his appointment and refused to follow his directives. Unlike Livingstone, they viewed blacks as permanent children, incapable of handling high office. Crowther was forced into retirement and replaced with an English bishop. (See the feature "Movement of Ideas: Bishop Turner's View of Africa.")

David Livingstone's story was well known in England (even if Samuel Ajayi Crowther's was not). When Khama and his friends visited England, they found that by using the name *Livingstone* they could always get a cheer from the crowd. Many in the audience knew the dramatic story of how a young American journalist, Henry Morton Stanley (1841–1904), had located Livingstone in Central Africa when he was feared lost. Stanley exemplified the spirit of the New Imperialism, regarding Africans as savages and treating them as such.

Unlike Livingstone's expeditions, Stanley's explorations were made for his own benefit. Having traced the great Congo River from its source deep in Central Africa to its outlet on the Atlantic, Stanley formed an alliance with **King Leopold II of Belgium** (r. 1865–1909) to profit from his discoveries.

David Livingstone (1813–1873) Scottish missionary and explorer idolized in Britain for his commitment to the spiritual and moral salvation of Africans.

King Leopold II of Belgium (r. 1865–1909) Ignited a "scramble for Africa" when he claimed the large area of Central Africa he called the Congo Free State. The ruthless exploitation of Congolese rubber by Leopold's agents led to millions of deaths.

Samuel Ajayi Crowther   A thoughtful theologian and talented linguist, Samuel Ajayi Crowther became the first Anglican bishop of West Africa in 1864. Increasing British racism undercut his authority, however. After Crowther, the Anglican Church did not appoint another African bishop in West Africa for over fifty years.

Belgium was a small kingdom that had become independent from the Netherlands only in 1830. Leopold envied European monarchs with claims to imperial territory, declaring, "I must have my share of this magnificent African cake!" He hired Stanley to organize a military expedition to stake a claim to the vast region surrounding the Congo River. The other European powers became alarmed. If Africa really were a vast source of wealth, they could not afford to miss out. In the 1880s all the other factors associated with the New Imperialism—political, strategic, economic, and ideological—came together in a rapid scramble for African territory.

Concerned that Leopold might destabilize the balance of power in Europe, Otto von Bismarck brought together representatives of the European colonial powers at the **Berlin Conference** in 1884 to establish rules for the partition of Africa. No Africans were present. The European delegates declared that the boundaries of the French, British, Belgian, German, Portuguese, Italian, and Spanish possessions in Africa would be recognized only where those powers established "effective occupation." For Africans, this meant twenty years of constant warfare and instability as European governments scrambled to secure the "effective occupation" of the territories they claimed.

Berlin Conference (1884) Conference organized by the German chancellor Otto von Bismarck in which representatives of the major European states divided Africa among themselves.

Africa and the New Imperialism

As late as 1878, Europe's colonial presence was almost entirely restricted to the African coast (see Map 26.1 on page 585). The all-out scramble for control of African territory was therefore something new. Suddenly, Africans were confronted by a European onslaught equipped with machine guns, field cannon, telegraphs, and steamships. Should they fight back? Seek diplomatic options? Ally themselves with the new intruders? African leaders tried all of these options, with little success.

Although Europeans viewed Africa in simplistic stereotypical terms, in

Primary Source: Parable of the Eagle, Limbo, Prayer for Peace, Vultures *The literature of four African writers expresses the traumatic effects of colonialism.*

Bishop Turner's View of Africa

While the "scramble for Africa" was taking place, some people of African descent in the Americas began to develop a "Pan-African" perspective that stressed the common circumstances and aspirations of black people around the world. One strand of Pan-Africanism focused on the possible emigration of American blacks back to Africa. Here a major figure was Henry McNeal Turner (1834–1915). Born free but poor in South Carolina, Turner learned to read and write while working as a janitor at a law firm. After becoming a preacher, in 1857 he joined the African Methodist Episcopal Church (AME), an entirely black-run denomination, and during the Civil War served as the first black chaplain in the United States Army. After the war he was elected to the Georgia assembly but was prevented from taking his seat on racial grounds. The fact that he was of mixed race and fair skinned made no difference.

The failure of Reconstruction (see Chapter 25) to bring true liberty to black Americans left Turner bitter. As lynching and legalized segregation became the norm, he argued that it was foolish to suppose that blacks would ever be allowed to prosper in the United States, and he became a strong advocate for emigration to Africa. His first interest was Liberia, an independent nation founded by freed African Americans. He then became aware of South Africa, where black Christians were interested in affiliating themselves with the AME Church to escape the control of white missionaries. In the 1890s he traveled to both countries and ordained a number of South African bishops.

1883

There is no more doubt in my mind that we have ultimately to return to Africa than there is of the existence of a God; and the sooner we begin to recognize that fact and prepare for it, the better it will be for us as a people. We have there a country unsurpassed in productive and mineral resources, and we have some two hundred millions of our kindred there in moral and spiritual blindness. The four millions of us in this country are at school, learning the doctrines of Christianity and the elements of civil government. As soon as we are educated sufficiently to assume control of our vast ancestral domain, we will hear the voice of a mysterious Providence, saying, *"Return to the land of your fathers...."*

Nothing less than nationality will bring large prosperity and acknowledged manhood to us as a people. How can we do this? Not by constantly complaining of bad treatment; by holding conventions and passing resolutions; by voting for white men for office; by serving as caterers and barbers, and by having our wives and daughters continue as washerwomen and servants to the whites. No—a government and nationality of our own can alone cure the evils under which we now labor, and are likely yet the more to suffer in this country.

It may be asked, where can we build up a respectable government? Certainly not in the United States.... I am sure there is no region so full of promise and where the probabilities of success are so great as the land of our ancestors. The continent appears to be kept by Providence in reserve for the Negro. There everything seems ready to raise him to deserved distinction, comfort and wealth.... And the time is near when the American people of color will ... erect the UNITED STATES OF AFRICA.

The murders and outrages perpetrated upon our people ... since 1867 [are] ... an orgy of blood and death.... I know we are Americans to all intents and purposes. We were born here, raised here, fought, bled and died here, and have a thousand times more right here than hundreds of thousands of those who help to snub, proscribe and persecute us, and that is one of the reasons I almost despise the land of my birth....

1891

You can ridicule it if you like, but Africa will be the thermometer that will determine the status of the Negro the world over.... The elevation of the Negro in this and all other countries is indissolubably connected with the enlightenment of Africa....

1893

These black [Muslim] priests ... walking around here with so much dignity, majesty and consciousness of their worth are driving me into respect for them. Some come from hundreds of miles from the country—out of the bush—better scholars than any in America. What fools we are to suppose these Africans are fools! ... Since I reached here, I see native Africans running engines, manning oar and steamboats, and ... two black ocean pilots and another black man measuring the depth of the ocean and guiding the ship amid the dangerous points. Poor black man, how the world tells lies about you!....

I have found out another thing since I have come to Africa, gone scores of miles through the interior and noted the tact, taste, genius and manly bearing of the higher grade of the natives.... Those who think the receding forehead, the flat nose, the proboscidated mouth and the big flat-bottom foot are natural to the African are mistaken. There are heads here by the millions, as vertical or perpendicular as any white man's head God ever made....

I have long ago learned that the rich Negro, the ignorant Negro ... and the would-be white Negro care nothing for African redemption, or the honor and dignity of the race ... I have never advocated all the colored people going to Africa, for I am well aware that the bulk of them are lacking in common sense and are too fond of worshiping white gods.... [E]very man who has a drop of African blood in his veins should be interested in the civilization, if not the salvation, of her millions, and how any black man can speak in contemptuous language of that great continent and her millions, when they gave him existence ... is a mystery to me.

Source: From Edwin S. Redkey, *Respect Black: The Writings and Speeches of Henry McNeal Turner* (New York: Arno Press), pp. 42–44, 52–55, 83, 143–144. Copyright © 1971.

QUESTIONS FOR ANALYSIS

▶ How did Turner think Africa could be useful to African Americans, and vice versa?

▶ How were his ideas about Africans in particular, and race issues in general, similar to or different from those of Social Darwinists?

reality Africa was an immense continent of complex cultural and geographic variety. Africa's own historical dynamics, including the rise of Muslim states in West Africa and the creation of the Zulu Empire in the far south, are essential for understanding Europe's partition of the continent.

Western Africa

After the abolition of the transatlantic slave trade, European merchants still frequented the African coast to acquire raw materials for rapidly expanding industries. While Egypt became a major source of raw cotton for British industry, the most important product coming from sub-Saharan Africa was palm oil, for use as an industrial lubricant. Starting in the 1820s, African farmers planted and processed oil products for the export market, and many West Africans became wealthy in this trade.

The "legitimate trade" in agricultural products did not bring an end to slavery in Africa. The long-standing Indian Ocean trade in slaves to Arabia and the Persian Gulf increased, and the use of slaves *within* West Africa actually increased after abolition: privileged Africans used slave labor on palm oil plantations in West Africa, and Arab plantation owners used slaves to grow cloves and other spices on the East African island of Zanzibar.

Initially, as West African economies became more integrated into world markets, political power remained with African kingdoms and chiefdoms. In an influential essay in 1868, a British-educated African surgeon named John Africanus Horton called for African kingdoms to reform themselves by incorporating Western constitutional practices. But Horton's call for merging African traditions with Western models was never successfully implemented. Europe's "scramble for Africa" came too suddenly for such reforms to be carried out.

In 1874, with the pro-imperial Conservative Party of Benjamin Disraeli in power,

Asante kingdom Dominant power in the West African forest in the eighteenth and early nineteenth centuries. The Asante capital was sacked by British forces in 1874 and again in 1896. In 1900, Yaa Asantewa's War represented a final attempt to expel the British.

Britain reversed its policy of noninvolvement in Africa's interior by attacking the **Asante kingdom**, which was badly outgunned. Besides being technologically inferior, the Asante (uh-SHAN-tee) state was too small compared to the British Empire to fight on equal terms. Moreover, some Asante chiefdoms allied with the British to escape Asante royal control. As in Mesoamerica in the 1520s, indigenous rivalries facilitated European conquest.

The limited yet long-standing French presence in West Africa expanded dramatically in the last three decades of the nineteenth century. Most of the African societies the French encountered were Muslim. After the demise of the Songhai empire (see Chapter 19), a string of new states formed by Islamic reformers spread across the West African interior in the early 1800s.

The seeds of Islamic reform were planted in West Africa by Sufi brotherhoods whose initiates practiced a mystical form of Islam by mastering complex prayers and rituals. Members of these brotherhoods were loyal to each other and devoted to their religious teachers. They moved to remote areas to escape the corruption and impiety of cities such as Timbuktu, in hopes of reviving the purity of early Islam. The origins of the *jihad* movements of nineteenth-century West Africa lay in their criticism of political leaders who tolerated the mixing of Islamic and traditional African practices and beliefs.

One of the most important West African jihad leaders was Usuman dan Fodio (1754–1817). In what is now northern Nigeria, dan Fodio called for the local emir to put his government in line with Islamic law. When the emir tried to assassinate him, Usuman dan Fodio (OO-soo-mahn dahn FOH-dee-oh) and his followers went on the offensive. They built a large army and consolidated several small emirates into the new Sokoto (SOH-kuh-toh) Caliphate. From here the jihadist impulse spread both east and west. Throughout the nineteenth century, West African Muslim populations became stricter in their practice, and Islam gained large numbers of new adherents.

At first, the leaders of Sokoto and other jihadist movements focused on reforming their own Muslim societies and paid little attention to Europeans. In the 1870s, however, as the French

Map 26.1 Africa, 1878 and 1914

The dramatic expansion of European imperialism in Africa is seen in the comparison of maps from 1878 and 1914. Before the "scramble for Africa" the European colonial presence was largely limited to small coastal enclaves. At that time frontiers of European settlement were found only in Algeria and in the Cape Colony. By 1914 Europeans dominated the entire continent, with only Liberia and Ethiopia retaining their independence. The British were the main power in eastern and southern Africa, the French in West and North Africa, and the Belgians in Central Africa.   © Cengage Learning

▣ Interactive Map

began to move up the Senegal River, conflict ensued. The West African Muslim who organized the most sustained resistance to French incursion was **Samori Toure** (ca. 1830–1900).

Samori Toure (**sam-or-ee too-RAY**), from a relatively humble merchant background, built a new state on the upper Niger by training soldiers to use imported rifles. At first his ambitions were merely political, but in 1884 he declared himself to be "commander of the faithful," leader of a jihad against lax Muslims and unbelievers. Even then, Samori avoided confronting the French, focusing instead on controlling trade routes in slaves, salt, and gold. But once the French had conquered his neighbors, they turned their attention to Samori.

Unable to prevail in conventional warfare, in 1891 Samori retreated to the east with his army and launched a guerilla campaign. Cut off from access to imported ammunition and gunpowder, Samori's soldiers learned to manufacture their own from local materials. But they could not hold out for long. Because his soldiers oppressed the local people, he had no local base of support, and the French were relentless in their attacks. After Samori was captured and exiled in 1893, the French were masters from the Senegal to the Niger Rivers.

The French march to the east threatened British control of Egypt and the Nile Valley. To head off the French advance, British forces moved to stake a claim of "effective occupation" over the savanna region still dominated by the Sokoto Caliphate. After Usuman dan Fodio's death, the caliphate became decentralized, with individual emirs controlling walled city-states and the surrounding countryside. Thus the British did not face the combined armies of a unified caliphate and attacked each city-state separately. The traditional tactics of savanna warfare, where peasants retreated into walled cities while warriors mounted cavalry charges, were no match for rifles and machine guns; British field cannon easily blew breeches in the city walls. Some emirs fought, some fled, and some surrendered, as British forces took control of what is now northern Nigeria.

The lack of alliances among African peoples facilitated the process of European imperialism. Lacking organizational or ideological foundations for a broader unity, African leaders dealt only with the local manifestations of the scramble for Africa. Even as they vied with one another, the Europeans possessed a broader overview of African developments, and they used their superior communications technology and geographical knowledge to great advantage.

Southern Africa

In southern Africa as well, the dynamics of African history facilitated European imperialism. Long before the Dutch established their settlement at Cape Town (see Chapter 16), the ancestors of King Khama and his people, Bantu-speaking farmers, herders, and ironmakers, had populated the land. In the drier highland areas, they lived in centralized chiefdoms near permanent sources of water. In the moister region between the Drakensberg Mountains and the Indian Ocean, population density was historically lower, and the clan chiefs who presided over councils of elders had little autonomous power.

In the late eighteenth century, drought led small chiefdoms to band together to secure permanent water sources. The most successful of the new states was the Zulu Empire. Its leader, **Shaka** (r.?1820–1828), formed a standing army of soldiers from different clans, emphasizing their loyalty to him and to the Zulu state rather than to their own chiefdoms, and chose his generals on the basis of merit rather than chiefly status. Young women were organized into agricultural regiments, and no one was allowed to marry without Shaka's permission.

The conquests of Shaka's armies were known as the *mfecane* (**mm-fuh-KAHN-ay**), "the crushing." Many chiefdoms were violently absorbed into the Zulu Empire, though some neighboring chiefs submitted voluntarily. In either case, conquered peoples were taken into Zulu society and became Zulu. The mfecane set in motion a chain reaction as other leaders copied Zulu military tactics and carried the

Samori Toure (ca. 1830–1900) Founder of a major state in West Africa who adopted the pose of a jihadist leader in competition with neighboring kingdoms. After being forced into confrontation by the French, he launched a long but unsuccessful guerilla campaign against them.

Shaka (r. 1820–1828) Founder and ruler of the Zulu Empire. Zulu military tactics revolutionized warfare in southern Africa. Through the *mfecane*, or "crushing," Shaka violently absorbed many surrounding societies into his empire.

frontier of warfare a thousand miles north. The Bangwato and other societies in the interior fled, abandoning much of their land.

Shaka had several English advisers. He was particularly interested in their guns, but he never gave up his reliance on spears to equip his army. The British were a new factor in southern Africa, having taken Cape Town from the Dutch during the Napoleonic Wars. Coveting the strategic value of the Cape, at first they had no interest in securing the interior. But in 1820 English settlers moved inland, occupying lands vacated by Africans fleeing to escape Zulu armies. However, sending English settlers into these areas angered the Boer descendants of the original Dutch colonists who had established Cape Town in 1652 and moved into the African interior in the eighteenth century (see Chapter 19). On their Great Trek of 1834–1836, some Boer farmers moved even further inland.

Boer settlement and British firepower overwhelmed African communities already weakened by the mfecane. The Xhosa (KOH-suh) chiefdoms, for example, lost rich grazing lands to the colonists. Neither negotiation nor military resistance could stem the European tide. Contact with colonial society created divisions within Xhosa society: some Xhosa converted to Christianity and grew crops for colonial markets, but traditionalist Xhosa saw them as abandoning their own people.

Then another disaster struck. A fatal disease wiped out large numbers of Xhosa cattle, key to their social and political as well as economic life. Facing starvation as well as invasion, some Xhosa turned to the prophecies of a young woman, Nongqawuse (nawng-ka-WOO-say) (ca. 1840–1898), who said the ancestors told her that if the people slaughtered their remaining cattle, departed warriors would return to defeat the whites and Xhosa traitors. The result was the tragic **Xhosa Cattle Killing**.

Belief in the power of ancestors was traditional to the Xhosa, and women often had the power to communicate with them. But the idea that the raising of the dead would accompany a new era of peace was borrowed from Methodist missionaries. Nongqawuse's message was a combination of indigenous beliefs with the Christian concept of the "millennium," a period

of perfect peace that awaits believers at the end of time. Seeing no other way out of their predicament, many Xhosa followed Nongqawuse's prophecy and killed their cattle. When the departed failed to return and hunger spread throughout the land, British conquest became inevitable. Over a hundred thousand lives were lost, and the remaining Xhosa were incorporated into Britain's Cape Colony. The British exiled Nongqawuse to Robben Island off the Cape coast (where, a century later, Nelson Mandela was also incarcerated).

Finally, mineral discoveries, diamonds in 1868 and gold in 1884, motivated the British to aggressive conquest of the South African interior. The Boers, proud of their independence, sought a German alliance to protect themselves against British imperialism. Africans in the interior, like Khama's Bangwato, found themselves facing the full brunt of European military technology for the first time.

In 1879, British authorities issued an ultimatum demanding that the Zulu king Cetshwayo disband his regiments. Cetshwayo refused to comply. Zulu warriors did defeat the British at the major Battle of Isandhlwana, but this defeat only made the invaders more determined. Zulu warriors were trained to rush the enemy in dense regimental ranks, an ineffectual strategy against machine guns. In 1880 the British sacked the Zulu capital and sent Cetshwayo into exile.

The main figure of the New Imperialism in southern Africa was **Cecil Rhodes** (1853–1902), a mining magnate (and founder of the DeBeers diamond syndicate) who advocated a British empire "from Cape to Cairo." His British South Africa Company (BSAC) was a chartered company with its own army and ambitions for conquest. It was to avoid annexation by the BSAC that Khama traveled to London, even as Rhodes was planning an invasion of the Boer republics, on whose land the great gold strikes were located.

Xhosa Cattle Killing (1856–1857) A large cattle die-off in Africa caused by a European disease. Some Xhosa accepted the Nongqawuse prophecies that if the people cleansed themselves and killed their cattle their ancestors would return and bring peace and prosperity. The result was famine and Xhosa subjection to the British.

Cecil Rhodes (1853–1902) British entrepreneur, mining magnate, head of the British South Africa Company, and prime minister of the Cape Colony. Rhodes played a major role in the expansion of British territory in southern Africa.

THE RHODES COLOSSUS
STRIDING FROM CAPE TOWN TO CAIRO.

Cecil Rhodes   The most important of Victorian imperialists, Cecil Rhodes dreamed of British imperial control of eastern and southern Africa "from Cape Town to Cairo." Combining political and economic clout, Rhodes was prime minister of the Cape Colony, founder of the DeBeers diamond syndicate, owner of some of the world's richest gold mines, and head of the British South African Company. He later endowed the Rhodes Scholarship program to bring elite Americans of British descent to Oxford University in England so that the United States might share Britain's imperial purpose.

After the failure of a BSAC invasion, the British government resorted to war. The South African War (1899–1902) that followed was a preview of twentieth-century warfare. The British had no trouble taking control of the towns and railway lines, but they were frustrated by the tactics of the Boer combatants, who blended into the civilian population and launched guerilla attacks in the countryside. To separate civilians from soldiers, the British put Boer women and children into "concentration camps" (the first use of that term). Over twenty thousand Boer civilians, many of them women and children, died of illness. Though the South African War was between the British and the Boers, some twenty thousand Africans, enlisted to fight by both sides, were also killed.

The British won the war but then compromised with their defeated foes. The **Union of South Africa** (1910) was created by joining British colonies with former Boer republics under a single constitution. The union has been called "an alliance of gold and maize," combining British mining and Boer agriculture. Both needed African labor. In 1913 the Native Land Act, passed by the new, all-white South African parliament, limited Africans to "native reserves" that included only a tiny proportion of their traditional landholdings. The goal was to drive Africans to work in mines and on white farms at the lowest possible pay, laying the economic foundations for what would later be called apartheid.

Because of King Khama's negotiations with the British government, his people were not part of this new South Africa and were ruled instead by the British Colonial Office. The Zulu and the Xhosa, meanwhile, like other Africans incorporated into the Union of South Africa, experienced the harshest form of colonial racism. As mineworkers and low-wage laborers on settler farms, they struggled at the lowest level of the global economy.

Conquest and Resistance

Between 1880 and 1900, European powers occupied and partitioned Africa. France and Britain held the largest African empires; Portugal and Germany each had substantial territories in the east and south; Italy and Spain were relatively minor players; and King Leopold of Belgium claimed the vast Congo in the center of the continent.

The technological advantages enjoyed by the Europeans made victory over Africans all but inevitable. The "tools of empire" included more than just rifles and machine guns. Steamships

Union of South Africa
Self-governing dominion with the British Empire created in 1910 from a number of British colonies and Boer republics after the South African War. This compromise protected both British mining and Boer agriculture at the expense of African interests.

and telegraphs shrunk the distance between European centers of command and European officials on the ground, allowing for quicker coordination. Because African rivers drop sharply from highlands to the sea, sailing ships could not penetrate far inland. But steam-powered ships could readily penetrate the continent's interior. And beginning in the 1890s, railroads too conveyed troops and colonial administrators.

Advances in medical technology further facilitated European conquest. One reason that Europeans had rarely ventured inland during the era of the slave trade was the danger of contracting malaria, against which they had no resistance. By the time of the "scramble for Africa" scientists had discovered that quinine, derived from the bark of a South American tree, was an effective defense against the disease.

In spite of European technological superiority, Africans fought back. The Nile Valley was one arena of resistance to British imperialism. Its strategic value increased with the construction of the **Suez Canal**. Built by a French engineer and financed by French and English capital, the canal became the main shipping route between Europe and Asia.

The Egyptian king, or khedive, supported the construction of the canal, thinking it would generate revenue that would allow Egypt to maintain its independence. But a fall in the cotton prices after 1865, when the end of the American Civil War brought U.S. cotton back onto the world market, reduced Egyptian government revenues. Unable to pay the country's mounting debts, the khedive was forced to sell Egypt's shares in the Suez Canal to the British and to accept European oversight of government finances. European officers were imposed on the Egyptian military, which was reorganized as an Anglo-Egyptian force.

In 1882, Egyptian military officers rebelled against the khedive and his European backers, but they were quickly suppressed by the British, who then foisted a governor-general on the Egyptian government. The British thus came to dominate Egypt, much as they dominated the "princely states" in India, keeping real power in their own hands while granting indigenous rulers titles and luxurious lifestyles.

Once in control of Egypt, the British needed to secure the Upper Nile Valley as well. Here they faced resistance from a jihadist state in Sudan, where a cleric named **Muhammad Ahmad** (1844–1885) proclaimed himself to be **The Mahdi** (MAH-dee). In 1881, Muhammad Ahmad declared a holy war against Egypt. The Mahdi's forces took the city of Khartoum from the British in 1884, while killing the British commander. When Muhammad Ahmad died of typhus a few months later, however, his movement lost impetus.

The jihadist movement was reinvigorated in the 1890s by the *khalifa* ("successor") to the Mahdi. To counter French and German colonial claims, the British had become intent on establishing "effective occupation" over the entire Nile Valley. The Battle of Omdurman (1898), between British and Mahdist armies, was the bloodiest battle between European and African forces during the entire period. Though outnumbered two-to-one, Anglo-Egyptian forces used their Maxim guns to terrible effect, killing ten thousand Mahdist soldiers. British soldiers are reported to have killed Sudanese soldiers as they lay wounded, in retribution for the siege of Khartoum.

Elsewhere African resistance to colonial occupation was on a smaller scale, as in the Asante kingdom. The British had sacked the Asante capital of Kumasi in 1874, but then withdrew. In the 1890s, however, with the Germans and French now active in the region, British forces once again moved toward Kumasi. The Asante reluctantly accepted a British protectorate but rebelled after the new British governor demanded that the "golden stool" be brought before him. The golden stool was the sacred symbol of Asante kingship; according to legend, it had descended from the heavens to confirm the sovereignty of the first Asante king. The governor's request was intolerable.

As they prepared for war, some Asante doubted whether they could succeed. A queen mother from one of the confederated chiefdoms, Yaa Asantewa (YAH ah-san-TAY-wuh), stood forward and spoke: "[If] you the men of

> **Suez Canal**   (1869) French-designed canal built between the Mediterranean and the Red Sea that greatly shortened shipping times between Europe and Asia. The Suez Canal Company was dominated by European economic interests.
>
> **The Mahdi, Muhammad Ahmad**   (1844–1885) *Mahdi* is the term some Muslims use for the "guided one" expected to appear before the end of days. Muhammad Ahmad took this title in the Sudan and called for a jihad against British-dominated Egypt.

Asante will not go forward, then we will. We the women will. I shall call upon my fellow women. We will fight the white men. We will fight till the last of us falls in the battlefields." The Yaa Asantewa War of 1900 was a military defeat for the Asante, but it caused later British governors to treat the Asante royal family with respect and to acknowledge Asante legal traditions when codifying colonial laws.

Coordinating resistance was even more difficult in regions where traditional political organization was less centralized. The Maji Maji (MAH-jee MAH-jee) Revolt in German East Africa was led by a religious prophet, Kinjekitile, who attempted to forge an alliance between numerous small chiefdoms. In the 1890s German military conquest had met little opposition. By 1905, however, people in the region were angered after the Germans forced them to grow cotton. African farmers had little time to tend their own food crops while enduring the hard labor of planting, weeding, and harvesting cotton. The payment they received was barely enough to pay colonial taxes, and cotton robbed their fields of fertility.

Maji Maji meant "powerful water," a reference to a sacred pool that attracted pilgrims from across a wide area. Kinjekitile used this sacred shrine as a rallying point, promising his followers that bathing in the sacred stream would make them immune to German bullets. Of course, this did not happen, and the Germans suppressed the Maji Maji revolt ruthlessly. But they also learned not to press their advantage too far, and they no longer enforced mandatory cotton growing.

Thus, the Africans' willingness to fight could force the Europeans to adjust their policies. Throughout the colonial period, Africans also used milder forms of resistance, such as songs and dances that criticized their European rulers, as a way to preserve their culture and express their humanity.

Africans were, nonetheless, consistently demeaned by the imperial powers. A new fad at Western expositions was to display "natives" as a curiosity for the amusement of Western audiences. King Khama and his colleagues were themselves taken to see a "Somali village" on display at London's Crystal Palace. The worst excess came in 1906, when a Central African named Ota Benga was displayed in a cage at the Bronx Zoo in New York. He later committed suicide. The disrespect and cruelty fostered by racist ideas endured into the twentieth century.

The New Imperialism in Southeast Asia

Europeans had long competed for access to trade in Southeast Asia and had established some imperial bases. And in the late nineteenth century the New Imperialism led to nearly complete Western domination. In mainland Southeast Asia, the French allied with Vietnamese emperors to extend their power over what became French Indochina. The British expanded from India into Burma and used the commercial city of Singapore to extend their empire into Malaya. On the thousands of islands that make up insular Southeast Asia, the Dutch were the dominant Western power; the United States joined the imperial club when it took the Philippines from Spain (see Map 26.2).

Mainland Southeast Asia

Vietnam's imperial structure was declining in the late eighteenth century. With the country wracked by rebellion, the Nguyen (NWIN) family allied with French missionaries and in 1802 established a new dynasty, with Catholic missionaries representing French influence at the Nguyen court.

Map 26.2   The New Imperialism in Southeast Asia, 1910
European nations had controlled parts of Southeast Asia, such as the Dutch East Indies and the Spanish Philippines, since the sixteenth and seventeenth centuries. The New Imperialism of the nineteenth century strengthened European control over those societies while bringing the entire region (with the exception of Siam, or Thailand) under Western colonial rule. In remote regions, such as the highlands of central Borneo, the process of conquest was not complete until the early twentieth century.   © Cengage Learning   ⬛ Interactive Map

The French moved from indirect influence to direct imperial control when Emperor Napoleon III sent an army of occupation to Vietnam in 1858. In 1862 the Nguyen ruler ceded control of the Mekong (MAY-kong) Delta and the commercial center of Saigon to France, opened three "treaty ports" to European trade, and gave the French free passage up the Mekong River. By 1884 the French were in control of all

of Vietnam but still faced guerilla resistance. The French army of conquest killed thousands of rebels and civilians before establishing firm control. Ironically, French authorities called the violence inflicted on the Vietnamese a campaign of "pacification."

By then French forces had conquered the neighboring kingdom of Cambodia and had taken Laos by agreement with the kingdom of

Federation of Indochina
(1897) Federation created
by the French after having
conquered Vietnam,
Cambodia, and Laos. Was
an administrative conve-
nience, as societies that
made up the federation
had little in common.

Siam (see below). In 1897, they combined these territories into the **Federation of Indochina**, or simply French Indochina. French colonial authorities took over vast estates on which to grow rubber and turned rice into a major export crop. The profits went almost entirely to French traders and planters.

Burma was likewise incorporated into the British Empire in stages. By the 1870s, Britain controlled the south, while in the north a reformist Burmese king attempted to modernize the country under indigenous rule. British representatives had no patience for these experiments. They refused to take off their shoes in the king's presence, a terrible affront to court protocol. Finally in 1886 British forces invaded from India and took the capital of Mandalay.

While suppressing a number of regional rebellions, they brought administrators from India and began building railroads to the rich timber resources of the Burmese jungles.

The trading city of Singapore had been Britain's most valuable possession in Southeast Asia since 1819. It attracted many Chinese immigrants and became the center of the Chinese merchant diaspora in the region. Initially, the British were content to control the main ports and grow rich on the trade between the Indian Ocean and the South China Sea, leaving politics to the dozens of Muslim sultanates of Malaya. But the 1870s introduced a more active imperialism. The completion of the Suez Canal in 1869 shortened the shipping routes from Europe to the Indian Ocean, and British merchants were particularly anxious to exploit the rich tin resources of the Malay Peninsula, for which the Second Industrial Revolution had dramatically increased demand.

© Roger Viollet/The Image Works

French Colonialism in Indochina Like other European colonialists, the French argued that they were developing their imperial territories for the good of their subjects through both a "civilizing" cultural mission and economic development projects such as road building. As this photograph from Southeast Asia indicates, however, it was the "natives" who did most of the work and their colonial overlords who grabbed the lion's share of profit.

As in Africa, local rivalries facilitated a policy of "divide and conquer." British "residents" gave local rulers "advice" on the governance of their sultanates; if the sultan refused, they would simply recognize another ambitious man as ruler and work through him. As in Egypt and the princely states of India, indigenous rulers were left in place but power was squarely in the hands of Europeans. The British prided themselves on having brought efficient administration to yet another corner of the globe. Meanwhile, they expanded plantations of commercial crops such as pepper, palm oil, and rubber.

Insular Southeast Asia

The Dutch had been the dominant European presence in the islands of Southeast Asia since the seventeenth century (see Chapter 16). After the Dutch East India Company was disbanded in 1799, colonial authorities imposed new constraints on the Dutch East Indies. In 1830, for example, Dutch authorities forced rice farmers on the island of Java to convert to sugar production. One Dutch official declared that "they must be taught to work, and if they were unwilling out of ignorance, they must be ordered to work." Through coercion the Dutch could buy sugar at low prices and then sell it for a great profit on world markets.

Fueled by greed, Dutch authorities asserted more and more formal administrative control over Java and Sumatra, where individual sultans had previously been left in charge of local affairs. At the same time, the increasing presence of other European powers motivated the Dutch to seek control of hundreds of other islands. Those who resisted, such as rebels on the Hindu-ruled island of Bali, were slaughtered. The New Imperialism significantly deepened Dutch power over the Indonesian archipelago.

The United States was the new presence in Asia and the Pacific. The arrival of Admiral Perry in Japan in 1853 (see Chapter 24) significantly expanded American influence in Asia, and the United States claimed a direct territorial stake in the Pacific when it annexed the Hawaiian Islands in 1898.

The extension of American imperialism to the Philippines came as a result of the Spanish-American War of 1898–1900. In the 1880s Filipino nationalists began resisting Spanish authority, and in 1896 they revolted to gain independence. In 1899, the Spanish handed the islands over to the Americans by secret treaty. Some Americans protested that it was contrary to American principles to become a colonial power. The writer Mark Twain, for example, joined the Anti-Imperialist League, declaring that American motives in the Philippines were no more pure than those of European imperialists.

The Filipino revolutionaries continued to struggle for independence, now against an American occupation. Four years of fighting left five thousand U.S. soldiers and over sixteen thousand Filipino combatants dead. Thousands of civilians perished in concentration camps used to separate them from the guerillas. While the Anti-Imperialist League continued its protests, President McKinley declared that "it is our duty to uplift and civilize and Christianize" the Filipinos, making Social Darwinism a driving idea in U.S. foreign policy.

Observing the debate in American public opinion, British poet Rudyard Kipling urged Americans to take on imperial responsibilities:

Take up the White Man's burden—
Send forth the best ye breed—
Go bind your sons to exile
To serve your captives' need;
To wait in heavy harness,
On fluttered folk and wild—
Your new-caught, sullen peoples,
Half-devil and half-child.*

Kipling worried that the British Empire was in decline and that only an imperialistic United States could save the world for Anglo-Saxon civilization: Americans needed to "take up the White Man's burden," Kipling argued, for the benefit of the Filipinos themselves.

Taking the opposite view, African American writer W. E. B. Du Bois (doo boyz), noted that the New Imperialism led to white domination across the world, and predicted in 1903 that "the problem of the twentieth century is the problem of the color-line."[2] His statement was as true for Southeast Asia as it was for Africa or the United States.

*Verse from "The White Man's Burden" by Rudyard Kipling, from *Rudyard Kipling's Verse Definitive Edition* by Rudyard Kipling, 1920, Doubleday.

Imperial Connections and Comparisons

The New Imperialism was driven by the desire to control resources while maintaining a strategic military presence at the global level. The history of rubber shows how industrial and technological developments led to imperialism. The abilities of the rulers of Siam (Thailand) and Ethiopia to retain their independence despite the New Imperialism are exceptional examples that nevertheless prove the rule of Western dominance.

A Case Study of the New Imperialism: Rubber

In the first half of the nineteenth century, inventors found new applications for rubber in such products as waterproof clothing and factory conveyor belts. The spread of telephones, electrical lines, and bicycles generated a booming trade in rubber. At first the only source was the Brazilian Amazon.

But Brazil's extensive rubber reserves were not enough to meet demand. To maintain its monopoly, Brazilians tried to prevent the export of rubber seeds, but a British agent managed to smuggle some to a nursery near London at Kew Gardens. From there, rubber seedlings were sent to British colonies in Asia. After plantings in Singapore were successful, rubber spread to Malaya, Thailand, Vietnam, and the Dutch East Indies. As in Brazil, great fortunes were made at the expense of local farmers, and rainforests were felled to make room for large rubber plantations. European traders secured access to an essential commodity and reaped the lion's share of profits. Meanwhile, colonial taxation drove local peasants to work for low wages under harsh conditions.

The most notorious abuses took place in the Congo Free State, the personal domain of Leopold II. The Belgian king ordered his agents to use whatever means necessary to maximize the harvest. His agents, paid bonuses based on the amount of rubber they delivered, demanded impossible quotas. Sometimes they kept women in cages, promising to release them only after their husbands had delivered enough rubber. African farmers went hungry as their own fields went untended.

Torture in King Leopold's Congo Here two victims of Leopold's policies, Mola and Yoka, display their mutilated limbs. The hands of Mola were eaten by gangrene after his hands were tied too tightly by Leopold's agents. Yoka's right hand was cut off by soldiers who planned to receive a bounty at headquarters by using the hand as proof of a kill. Once the world learned about this extreme violence, humanitarian voices were raised against King Leopold. (Anti-Slavery International)

When the quotas were still not met, the killing began. Free State soldiers under the command of Belgian officers and agents were instructed to bring back the hands of those they killed. To increase their bounties, these soldiers would sometimes chop off the hands of the living and bring them back to the Belgian trade stations for a cash reward. Eventually 10 million people died, mostly from hunger.

Leopold claimed to be a great humanitarian, but by the late 1890s stories of violence from the Congo began to reach home. A clerk in Brussels noticed that the ships that were arriving full of rubber and ivory were returning to the Congo with only guns and ammunition in their holds. His further investigation revealed the full horror of Leopold's crimes, and he helped form the Congo Reform Association to demand that they be ended. Finally, in 1908 King Leopold sold his African empire to the Belgian government, reaping a huge profit on the sale. A heritage of violence still affects the Congo today, while Brussels is filled with the many grand monuments that Leopold built with the fortune he made in the rubber trade.

Enduring Monarchies: Ethiopia and Siam

Given the overwhelming strength of European domination in the age of the New Imperialism, it seems surprising that Ethiopia and Siam (present-day Thailand) managed to retain their independence.

The ancient Christian kingdom of Ethiopia first met modern European firepower in 1868 when a British relief column was sent to rescue an Englishman held hostage by the Ethiopian king. The British easily crushed the African army they encountered. When **Menelik II** (r. 1889–1913) became emperor, he was determined to strengthen his state against further assault. Ethiopia had long had a decentralized political structure in which rural lords, commanding their own armies, were more powerful than the emperor himself. Menelik (men-uh-lik) consolidated power at the imperial court and created his own standing army, equipped with the latest repeating rifles. Finally, he used his credentials as a Christian to enhance his

diplomatic influence in Europe, where his ambassadors played the European powers against one another to Ethiopia's advantage.

Menelik was also fortunate that the European assault of Ethiopia came from Italy, the weakest of the European imperial powers. At the Battle of Adowa (1896) the Ethiopians were victorious, though Italy did take the strategically important region of Eritrea on the Red Sea. Britain, the dominant power in northeastern Africa, was convinced that Menelik would be able to maintain security on the Egyptian frontier and allow European traders free access to his kingdom. Since this was cheaper than occupying the country by force, the British sponsored the development of modern infrastructure, such as banks and railroads, during Menelik's reign. The benefits, as usual, went to Ethiopian elites and European investors. The Ethiopian majority continued to scratch a meager existence.

In the second half of the nineteenth century the kings of Siam also faced absorption into European empires, with the British expanding from India in the west and the French threatening from Indochina in the east. Two long-ruling kings, Mongkut (r. 1851–1868) and Chulalongkorn (r. 1868–1910), transformed the ancient kingdom into a sovereign nation. Both used internal reform and diplomatic engagement to deal with the threats of New Imperialism.

> **Menelik II** (r. 1889–1913) Emperor who used diplomacy and military reorganization to retain Ethiopian independence, defeating an Italian army of invasion at Adowa in 1896.

As a young man Mongkut (mang-koot) lived in a Buddhist monastery. When he emerged to become king in 1851, he found that his monastic experience, where he had interacted with men from all social classes, prepared him to become a popular leader. Having learned English, mathematics, and astronomy from Western missionaries, he could interact with Europeans as well.

Observing China's fate after the Opium Wars, Mongkut was determined to meet the Western challenge. Conservatives at court opposed his reforms as undermining Buddhist traditions. Nevertheless, Mongkut invited Western emissaries to his capital, installed them as advisers, and exempted them from the usual

Chulalongkorn (r. 1868–1910) King of Siam (Thailand) who modernized his country through legal and constitutional reforms. Through successful diplomacy he ensured Siam's continued independence while neighboring societies were absorbed into European empires.

court protocols, such as crawling on their knees before the king. Though Mongkut favored the British, he balanced their influence with French and Dutch advisers. He also opened Siam to foreign trade, giving merchants from various countries a stake in his system.

Most importantly, Mongkut chose an English tutor for his son and heir, **Chulalongkorn**. After Chulalongkorn (choo-luh-awhn-korn) came to power in 1868, he installed Siamese advisers

who believed that their traditions and sovereignty could be preserved only through reform. Chulalongkorn modified the legal system to protect private property and abolish slavery and debt peonage, expanded access to education, and encouraged the introduction of telegraphs and railroads. Moreover, he centralized governmental power through a stream-lined bureaucracy that reached from the capital into the smallest villages.

Like his father, Chulalongkorn was an able diplomat who played Europeans off one another. Lacking a strong army, he gave up claims to parts of his empire, such as Laos, to protect

© W.&D. Downey/Getty Images.

King Chulalongkorn of Siam
This photograph from 1890 shows King Chulalongkorn of Siam with his son, the Crown Prince Vajiravudh Rama, who was studying in Britain. Chulalongkorn used deft diplomacy to maintain the independence of Siam (Thailand) during the height of the European scramble for colonial territory. Father and son are dressed in European style, but the warm embrace of their hands was a Southeast Asian touch. British males rarely showed such affection in Victorian portraits.

the core of his kingdom. Not only did this appease the French and the British, but it also gave his kingdom a more ethnically Thai character. While retaining advisers from various European countries, he oversaw policy with a new Council of State.

Chulalongkorn was fortunate that the British and the French wished to avoid a confrontation in Southeast Asia. Because their traders and missionaries were allowed to establish themselves in the kingdom, and because the Siamese leader was able to ensure peace and stability in his domain, the French and British agreed in 1896 to recognize the independence of the kingdom of Siam as a buffer between their empires (see Map 26.2).

As with Ethiopia, the independence of Siam was secured by internal reform, centralization of government power, and deft diplomatic maneuvering, all outcomes of effective political leadership. Nevertheless, had the British or French wished to conquer Ethiopia or Siam, they could have done so. The achievement of Menelik and Chulalongkorn in the 1890s was to position their countries to take advantage of inter-European rivalries.

In the age of the New Imperialism, African and Southeast Asian societies retained their sovereignty only under unusual circumstances. King Khama's situation was much more common. He did his best with the resources at his disposal, but his kingdom was too small and too poorly armed to survive as an independent state. Unlike Menelik and Chulalongkorn, most African and Southeast Asian rulers did not command sufficient resources to protect themselves from the New Imperialism. Even in Ethiopia and Siam, the ties of Western industrial capitalism bound their peoples to a global economy to which they contributed much, but received very little.

Chapter Review and Learning Activities

During the course of a life that lasted eighty-six years, King Khama III of the Bangwato witnessed the transformation of his society. When he was a young man, his people were independent farmers and pastoralists under the leadership of their own kings and elders. During his adulthood they were connected, as subjects of a great empire, to global, political, and economic networks. The New Imperialism was the final stage of a process that had begun in the sixteenth century when Europeans first established overseas maritime empires. With the force of the Industrial Revolution behind them, nineteenth-century Western imperialists spread those empires more widely than ever before, planting their flags across Africa and Southeast Asia and bringing the entire world, directly or indirectly, under their control.

What were the main causes of the New Imperialism?

While European colonial outposts had been established in the previous centuries, the period of the New Imperialism saw a dramatic expansion of empire building, encompassing the entire planet. Political competition within and between European states, increased activity by Christian missionaries, and the private ambitions of men like Cecil Rhodes and King Leopold II of Belgium were all important causes of the New Imperialism, but the most important factor was the rising demand for global economic resources resulting from technological and industrial developments in Europe and the United States. Imperialism was fueled by global economic competition for gold and diamonds in southern Africa, rubber in Central Africa and Southeast Asia, and other commodities like palm oil, tin, and coffee.

In what different ways did Africans respond to European imperialism?

For most Africans, European encroachment in the late nineteenth century occurred suddenly and unexpectedly. They responded by forming alliances with the powerful new outsiders against traditional rivals, using diplomatic initiatives, and practicing military resistance. The Europeans had great technological advantages, and only in Ethiopia was the military option successful. Resistance often took the form of guerilla warfare, as in the Asante kingdom, or called upon spiritual forces and religiously inspired organization, as with the Xhosa and followers of the Maji Maji.

What were the main outcomes of the New Imperialism in Southeast Asia?

In the Dutch East Indies, the New Imperialism meant tighter administrative control and more systematic economic exploitation by the Dutch colonialists over their Asian subjects. Elsewhere, formerly independent states were divided among European powers, with the French combining Vietnam, Cambodia, and Laos into French Indochina and the British taking control of Malaya and Burma. The former Spanish territory of the Philippines became a colony of the United States. The invaders established plantations and mines in their colonies to provide raw materials such as rubber and tin for their industries.

What connections and comparisons can be made between Africa and Southeast Asia in the late nineteenth century?

The history of rubber shows how the exploitation of colonial economies was connected to European industrial development. Production and consumption of rubber-based goods like boots and bicycle tires depended on the systematic extraction of raw materials and the coercive, and often violent, application of local labor in the forests of Central Africa and the plantations of Southeast Asia. In Ethiopia and Siam, able leaders were able to resist political incorporation, partially by playing on European rivalries. In both countries, however, political independence required that leaders like King Menelik II and King Chulalongkorn give European merchants and investors open access to their markets and raw materials.

FOR FURTHER REFERENCE

Headrick, Daniel. *The Tools of Empire: Technology and European Imperialism in the Nineteenth Century.* New York: Oxford University Press, 1981.

Hochschild, Adam. *King Leopold's Ghost: A Story of Greed, Terror and Heroism in Colonial Africa.* Boston: Houghton Mifflin, 1999.

Markus, Harold G. *The Life and Times of Menelik II: Ethiopia 1844–1913.* New York: Oxford University Press, 1975.

Martin, B. G., ed. *Muslim Brotherhoods in Nineteenth Century Africa.* New York: Cambridge University Press, 2003.

Owen, Norman G., ed. *The Emergence of Modern Southeast Asia.* Honolulu: University of Hawaii Press, 2004.

Packenham, Thomas. *The Scramble for Africa, 1876–1912.* 2d ed. London: Longman, 1999.

Parsons, Neil. *King Khama, Emperor Joe and the Great White Queen: Victorian Britain Through African Eyes.* Chicago: University of Chicago Press, 1998.

Peiers, J. B. *The Dead Will Arise: Nongqawuse and the Great Xhosa Cattle Killing Movement of 1856–1857.* London: James Currey, 1989.

Wyatt, David K. *A Short History of Thailand.* 2d ed. New Haven: Yale University Press, 2003.

KEY TERMS

King Khama III (578)
New Imperialism (579)
David Livingstone (580)
King Leopold II of Belgium (580)
Berlin Conference (581)
Asante kingdom (584)
Samori Toure (586)
Shaka (586)
Xhosa Cattle Killing (587)
Cecil Rhodes (587)
Union of South Africa (588)
Suez Canal (589)
The Mahdi, Muhammad Ahmad (589)
Federation of Indochina (592)
Menelik II (595)
Chulalongkorn (596)

VOYAGES ON THE WEB

Voyages: King Khama III

"Voyages" is a real time excursion to historical sites in this chapter and includes interactive activities and study tools such as audio summaries, animated maps, and flashcards.

Visual Evidence: National Flags

"Visual Evidence" features artifacts, works of art, or photographs, along with a brief descriptive essay and discussion questions to guide your analysis of visual sources.

World History in Today's World: Botswana: Diamond and AIDS

"World History in Today's World" makes the connection between features of modern life and their origins in the periods in this chapter.

 CourseMate

Go to the CourseMate website at www.cengagebrain.com for additional study tools and review materials—including audio and video clips—for this chapter.

27 War, Revolution, and Global Uncertainty, 1905–1928

...se Bryant
...n-Deutsch Collection/Corbis)

The violence and brutality of the First World War (1914–1918) made a mockery of the nineteenth-century idea of progress. Many people were left with doubt and pessimism about the future. Others, inspired by the revolutionary changes that accompanied the war, saw a brighter day dawning. Having witnessed the Russian Revolution of 1917 firsthand and interviewed many world leaders, the American journalist **Louise Bryant** (1885–1936) was in a good position to gauge the high stakes of the postwar world. She was entering the period of world history that one historian later called "the age of extremes." Bryant believed that the world was, for better or for worse, at a turning point:

On the grey horizon of human existence looms a great giant called Working Class Consciousness. He treads with thunderous step through all the countries of the world. There is no escape, we must go out and meet him. It all depends on us whether he will turn into a loathsome, ugly monster demanding human sacrifices or whether he shall be the savior of mankind.[1]

The Travels of Louise Bryant

→ Louise Bryant's journeys
→ Louise Bryant's 1919 speaking tour
• City visited by Bryant
• Other city

ATLANTIC OCEAN

Barents Sea

Vardø
Murmansk
Narvik
Haparanda Tornio

FINLAND (indep. 1917)

NORWAY
Oslo
SWEDEN Helsinki
Stockholm
Gothenburg
to NYC
ESTONIA
Riga
LATVIA
LITHUANIA

St. Petersburg (Petrograd, 1914–1924)

Moscow

RUSSIA (U.S.S.R. after 1922)

IRISH FREE STATE (indep. 1921)
UNITED KINGDOM
London
North Sea
DENMARK
Baltic Sea
NETHERLANDS
Berlin
BELGIUM
GERMANY
POLAND
Kiev

to/from New York City
Cherbourg
Paris
FRANCE
Bay of Biscay
SWITZERLAND
AUSTRIA
HUNGARY
Lake Garda
CZECHOSLOVAKIA
ROMANIA
YUGOSLAVIA
Danube

Caspian Sea

to Bukhara & Central Asian frontier

SPAIN
Corsica
Rome
ITALY
Sardinia
Adriatic Sea
BULGARIA
Constantinople
ALBANIA
GREECE
Athens
TURKEY

Mediterranean Sea
Sicily

AFRICA

to Paris

0   200   400 Km.
0   200   400 Mi.

Louise Bryant and John Reed witness Russian Revolution, 1917.

Bryant visits Central Asia, 1920.

UNITED STATES
Seattle
Portland
Yakima
Eugene
Reno
San Francisco
Salt Lake City
Los Angeles
Minneapolis
Detroit
Chicago
Provincetown
New York City

0   250   500 Km.
0   250   500 Mi.

Bryant goes on speaking tour across the U.S., 1919.

PACIFIC OCEAN

ATLANTIC OCEAN

Join this chapter's traveler on "Voyages," an interactive tour of historic sites and events: www.cengagebrain.com

	1900	1910	1920	1930	1940

Lifetime of Louise Bryant
(b. 1885)   1936

EUROPE

World War I   Paris Peace Conference
1914   1918   1919

October Revolution in Russia
1917

Union of Soviet Socialist Republics
1922   (to 1991)

Weimar Republic
1919   1933

THE MIDDLE EAST AND ASIA

Chinese Revolution and fall of the Qing dynasty
1911

End of the Ottoman Empire
1919

British mandate in Palestine
1920

NORTH AMERICA

Mexican Revolution
1910

United States enters World War I
1917

601

Louise Bryant (1885–1936) American journalist, traveler, feminist, and author of several books on the Russian Revolution.

Bryant was an exceptional woman for her times. Impatient with restrictive conventions and an ardent feminist, she was described as someone who "refuses to be bound … an artist, a joyous, rampant individualist, a poet and a revolutionary." She was a child of the American West, born in San Francisco and then, after her father's premature death, raised on a remote ranch in Nevada with only her grandfather, a Chinese cook, and her imagination for company. After graduating from the University of Oregon, Bryant wanted to be a serious journalist, but the only job she could get was as a "society" writer for a Portland newspaper. It was 1909, and women were not expected to be involved with "hard" news. She married a dentist but felt increasingly hemmed in by her middle-class surroundings.

Then a young journalist named John Reed swept into her life. She left with him for New York, experiencing the cultural and intellectual dynamism of Greenwich Village. This was the life she craved, full of adventure and purpose. After a series of stormy love affairs that nearly tore their relationship apart, Bryant and Reed were married, and together they traveled to Russia in the summer of 1917. Both left important records of that experience, but Reed overshadowed Bryant in historical memory. Given the gender perceptions of the time, Bryant's journalism was never taken as seriously as that of her husband.

During her lifetime Bryant witnessed remarkable changes. In the industrialized world telephones and electricity became commonplace, and the automobile and airplane were invented: Bryant saw the great aviator Amelia Earhart, a symbol of female emancipation, as a role model. In some places, women fought for and won the right to vote. The creativity of African American musicians led to the creation of jazz music, the first significant influence of the United States on global culture. Scientific advances continued, as physicists such as Albert Einstein made huge strides toward understanding nature at both cosmic and atomic levels, while Sigmund Freud, whom Bryant once interviewed, plumbed the depths of the human psyche.

But a shadow of uncertainty hung over these accomplishments. The industrially driven devastation of the First World War in Europe caused immense suffering not only for soldiers but also for civilians. In mobilizing their empires for the war effort, the European powers made their local conflict a genuinely global one, severely disrupting the lives of many Africans, Asians, and peoples of the Pacific. While the president of the United States, Woodrow Wilson, confidently proclaimed that this was "the war to end all wars," one that would "make the world safe for democracy," competing national interests destabilized the postwar world.

Meanwhile, both before and during the war, major world societies—Mexico, China, and Russia—were rocked by revolution. Louise Bryant, a socialist, saw hope in uncertainty, applauding downtrodden people who rose up against local oppressors or imperial masters. But she recognized as well the dangers that war and revolution had unleashed.

FOCUS QUESTIONS

▶ How can the First World War be regarded as a "total war," both for the domestic populations of the main combatants and for the entire world?

▶ How did the postwar settlements fail to resolve global political tensions?

▶ How did the outcomes of revolutions in Mexico, China, and Russia add to the uncertainty of the postwar world?

World War I as a "Total" War

World War I (1914–1918) represented a radical change in warfare. Requiring every national resource, it engaged masses of civilians. For each of the main combatants—Germany, Austria, Britain, France, Russia, and the United States—it strained social and political traditions to the breaking point. Nothing would remain the same. The British called it simply the Great War.

The global involvement of World War I was unprecedented. Young men from the United States shipped out to Europe, Indian soldiers marched to Baghdad, Southeast Asians worked behind the lines on the western front. This was a transformative mobilization of the whole world to battle: "total war."

Causes of World War I, 1890–1914

On June 28, 1914, Archduke Ferdinand, heir to the Austrian throne, was assassinated by a Serbian nationalist in the Balkan city of Sarajevo (see Map 27.1). The Balkan region had long been an unstable zone between the Austrian and Ottoman Empires. As the Ottomans declined, Austrians asserted themselves there, provoking local nationalists who did not want to escape one empire only to be dominated by another.

Despite their cultural similarities as Slavs and their long history of coexistence, the inhabitants of the Balkans vied with one another over religious differences. Serbian nationalists, members of the Orthodox Christian faith, looked to their co-religionists in Russia for support; Croatian nationalists allied themselves with Catholic Austria; Bosnian Muslims sided with the Ottoman Empire. These feuds gathered global importance when Germany supported the Austrians against the Serbs.

German support for Austria in the Balkans angered the Russians and also alarmed the British and the French, wary of Germany's global ambitions. Dismissing Otto von Bismarck in 1890, **Kaiser Wilhelm II** (r. 1888–1918) had undertaken a more aggressive foreign policy. His naval buildup caused Britain to reverse its practice of avoiding commitments on the continent. Likewise the French and Russian governments overcame their long-standing mutual distrust. A series of treaties produced a combination of alliances that divided Europe into two opposing blocs—the Triple Entente (ahn-tahnt) of France, Britain, and Russia against the Triple Alliance of Germany, Austria, and Italy—with no flexibility for the resolution of any crisis.

Thus the assassination of the Archduke Ferdinand detonated an explosive confrontation

Kaiser Wilhelm II (r. 1888–1918) German emperor whose foreign policy and military buildup changed the European balance of power and laid the foundation for the Triple Alliance and the Triple Entente.

Map 27.1 **World War I, 1914–1918**
By the end of World War I horrific violence along the western front in Belgium, Luxembourg, and northeastern France, and on the eastern front in the Russian Empire and eastern Europe, had led to the deaths of over 8 million soldiers, with 20 million wounded. On the southern front, defeat led to the dissolution of the Ottoman Empire. While these three theaters saw the fiercest fighting, the global effects of the conflict made this a truly world war. © Cengage Learning

between two hostile and heavily armed camps. The Austrian government threatened Serbia with war if it did not comply with a set of humiliating demands. The Serbs appealed to Russia, while the Germans backed up the Austrians. Thus war between Austria and Serbia meant war between Germany and Russia. The Ottoman Empire, fearful of Russian and British designs, allied itself with Germany. After a period of indecision, Italy joined with Britain, France, and Russia.

Public opinion compounded the war atmosphere. In urban, industrial societies foreign affairs were no longer the exclusive purview of diplomatic elites. Even in authoritarian Germany, public sentiment, as expressed in the opinion pages of daily newspapers, counted for much. Declarations of war were met with popular excitement and patriotic demonstrations. Only in Russia, where the tsar and his ministers customarily ignored public opinion, did the government act without a popular mandate. With remarkable naiveté, Europeans believed the war would be quick and conclusive, and that their side would win. (See the feature "Movement of Ideas: Emma Goldman's Critique of Militarism.")

Louise Bryant saw the war as nothing but a capitalist scheme. It seemed clear to her: French and German workers had common interests against their bosses; for them to fight each other under the banner of patriotism was irrational. Nevertheless, the German Social Democrats, who had long urged "workers of the world unite!" now favored war.

Total War in Europe: The Western and Eastern Fronts

Unlike 1870, when the Prussians took Paris quickly, in 1914 the German advance was stopped 20 miles (32.2 km) short (see Map 27.1). Stalemate on the **western front** resulted in a new tactic: *trench warfare*. On one side, French and British soldiers fortified entrenched positions with razor wire; on the other side, Germans did the same. Miserable in the muddy trenches, soldiers were called on to charge "over the top," braving harrowing gunfire in desperate attempts to overrun enemy positions. With bombs bursting around them, or choking on mustard gas (the first use of chemical weapons in history), they had little chance of survival, let alone victory. Immobilized, battle lines established early in Belgium and northern France hardly shifted. Military planners instead reinforced the trenches, connected them with tunnels, and built elaborate underground networks for supply and communications.

The casualties of trench warfare were horrific. At the Battle of Verdun in 1916, more than half a million French and German troops lost their lives. The same year, the Battle of the Somme killed nearly a million British and Germans. Slaughter brought no advantage to either side. Young men from the same neighborhood, school, or village who volunteered together were sometimes all wiped out in a single charge. Survivors lost not only their companions but also their physical and mental health. Some suffered "shell shock" for the rest of their lives from the intense trauma of their war experience.

To undermine the German war effort, the British navy blockaded Germany's seaports. Since Britain and Germany had been major trade partners before the war, the interruption of trade was harmful to both. The blockade elicited another relatively new military stratagem: the submarine, or "U-boat." Attacking without warning, German U-boats wrought havoc on British shipping early in the war.

Protracted total war transformed European government and society. Because all of a nation's energies had to be tapped in the interests of survival, governmental power expanded. Whereas large corporations and the state were already in close cooperation in Germany before the war, national economic planning represented a shift away from economic liberalism in France and Britain.

western front During World War I, the line separating the elaborate trenches of German and Allied positions, which soon became almost immobile. Trench warfare was characteristic of the western front.

Primary Source: Mud and Khaki, Memoirs of an Incomplete Soldier *Read from the memoirs of a British soldier, and imagine the horrors of trench warfare and poison gas in World War I.*

Emma Goldman's Critique of Militarism

"**P**reparedness, the Road to Universal Slaughter" was written by the anarchist Emma Goldman and published in New York in 1915. Emma Goldman (1869–1940) was born into a Jewish family in Lithuania, then part of the Russian Empire. As a teenager she moved to St. Petersburg, where she was first exposed to radical politics, and at sixteen she moved to New York. As a young woman she advocated violence and assassination, tactics that were deeply rooted in Russia's anarchist and revolutionary traditions. Later she became a pacifist, preferring mass organization as a means of countering the economic and political oppression of industrial capitalism. Louise Bryant, who attended a speech by Goldman in Portland in 1914, was just one of many young Americans stirred to radical political action by her oratory. The two became well acquainted, and Goldman attended the funeral of Bryant's husband John Reed in Moscow in 1921.

Goldman was arrested several times, once for heading an anticonscription campaign in the leadup to the First World War. After the Alien Act of 1918 allowed the deportation of "undesirable" immigrants without a trial, in 1919 the United States government deported her back to Russia. She left after two years, profoundly disappointed at the suppression of civil rights by Lenin and the Bolsheviks. Goldman then settled in Canada, traveling frequently to France and England, and continued to write and speak in defense of individual liberty.

Preparedness, the Road to Universal Slaughter

"Ammunition! Ammunition! O, Lord, thou who rulest heaven and earth, thou God of love, of mercy and of justice, provide us with enough ammunition to destroy our enemy." Such is the prayer which is ascending daily to the Christian heaven.... [All] of the European people have fallen over each other into the devouring flames of the furies of war, and America, pushed to the very brink by unscrupulous politicians, by ranting demagogues, and by military sharks, is preparing for the same terrible feat. In the face of this approaching disaster, it behooves men and women not yet overcome by the war madness to raise their voice of protest, to call the attention of the people to the crime and outrage which are about to be perpetrated upon them.

America is essentially the melting pot. No national unit composing it is in a position to boast of superior race purity, particular historic mission, or higher culture. Yet the jingoes and war speculators are filling the air with the sentimental slogan of hypocritical nationalism, "America for Americans," "America first, last, and all the time." This cry has caught the popular fancy from one end of the country to another. In order to maintain America, military preparedness must be engaged in at once. A billion dollars of the people's sweat and blood is to be expended for dreadnaughts and submarines for the army. The pathos of it all is that the America which is to be protected by a huge military force is not the America of the people, but that of the privileged class; the class which robs and exploits the masses, and controls their lives from the cradle to the grave. No less pathetic is it that so few people realize that preparedness never leads to peace, but that it is indeed the road to universal slaughter....

Forty years ago Germany proclaimed the slogan: "Germany above everything. Germany for the Germans, first, last and always. We want peace; therefore we must prepare for war. Only a

Though the French did little fighting outside Europe, they also looked to their empire for volunteers. When the number of volunteers was not enough to meet wartime demand, French colonial officials put pressure on local African leaders to produce more conscripts for the French army. The most famous regiment of colonial recruits was the **Senegalese Sharpshooters**. Many died or were maimed on the western front.

The scope of total war is evidenced in East
ica, where battles were fought between
rman East Africa and British-controlled
ya. On one side were African soldiers led by
rman officers, and on the other a largely
ian army commanded by the British. The
man commander's ambition was to tie
n British forces to keep them from being
eployed. He struck and then retreated into
countryside, requisitioning local food
ves for his army and burning what was left
eny sustenance to his opponents. Famine
disease stalked the land as total war reached
the remote interior of East Africa.
n Southeast Asia, the French recruited
namese villagers for the Indochinese Labor
s. These men dug fortifications and main-
d roads behind the lines on the western
s on the front line. At the same time
chinese rice and rubber were directed to
ort the French war effort.

Role of the United States

ntrance of the United States into the war
major turning point, again highlighting
obal nature of total war. In 1914, the
y had a small army, and Americans were
clined to follow George Washington's
that the republic should not "entangle
ace and prosperity in the toils of European
on." Initially, President **Woodrow Wilson**
3–1921) kept the United States out of the
ut neutrality proved impossible. With
ny's trade blocked by the British navy,

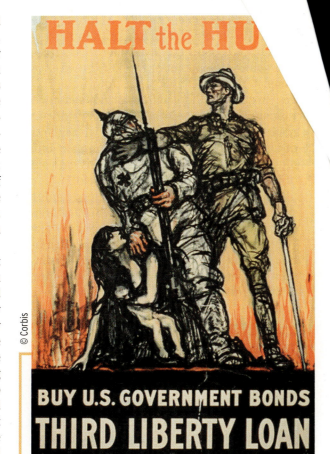

HALT the HU...

BUY U.S. GOVERNMENT BONDS
THIRD LIBERTY LOAN

© Corbis

Wartime Propaganda There is a strongly implied threat of sexual violence in this "liberty loan" poster, with a U.S. soldier protecting a mother and child who kneel helplessly before a German figure identified as a "Hun," or barbarian. Government attempts to arouse patriotism through such demonizing imagery were characteristic of twentieth-century "total war."

America supplied industrial and military provisions to France and Britain. Between 1914 and 1916 American exports to these two countries grew from $824 million to $3.2 billion.

America's entry into the war was catalyzed by Germany's use of submarine warfare. In 1915, the Germans sank the *Lusitania,* a passenger ship secretly carrying armaments from the United States to England. After President Wilson protested, the Germans promised to stop attacking ships without warning. Meanwhile, business

well armed and thoroughly prepared nation can maintain peace, can command respect, can be sure of its national integrity." And Germany continued to prepare, thereby forcing the other nations to do the same. The terrible European war is only the culminating fruition of the hydra-headed gospel, military preparedness....

But though America grows fat on the manufacture of munitions and war loans to the Allies to help crush Prussians the same cry is now being raised in America which, if carried into national action, would build up an American militarism far more terrible than German or Prussian militarism could ever be, and that because nowhere in the world has capitalism become so brazen in its greed and nowhere is the state so ready to kneel at the feet of capital.

"Americanization" societies with well known liberals as members, they who but yesterday decried the patriotic clap-trap of today, are now lending themselves to befog the minds of the people and to help build up the same destructive institutions in America which they are directly and indirectly helping to pull down in Germany— militarism, the destroyer of youth, the raper of women, the annihilator of the best in the race, the very mower of life....

The very proclaimers of "America first" have long before this betrayed the fundamental principles of real Americanism, of the kind of Americanism that Jefferson had in mind when he said that the best government is that which governs least; the kind of America that David Thoreau worked for when he proclaimed that the best government is the one that doesn't govern at all; or the other truly great Americans who aimed to make of this country a haven of refuge, who hoped that all the disinherited and oppressed people in coming to these shores would give character, quality and meaning to the country. That is not the America of the politician and munition speculators....

Supposedly, America is to prepare for peace; but in reality it will be the cause of war. It always has been thus—all through bloodstained history, and it will continue until nation will refuse to fight against nation, and until the people of the world will stop preparing for slaughter. Preparedness is like the seed of a poisonous plant; placed in the soil, it will bear poisonous fruit. The European mass destruction is the fruit of that poisonous seed. It is imperative that the American workers realize this before they are driven by the jingoes into the madness that is forever haunted by the specter of danger and invasion; they must know that to prepare for peace means to invite war, means to unloose the furies of death.

Source: Mother Earth 10, no. 10 (December 1915).

QUESTIONS FOR ANALYSIS

▶ **Based on these arguments, how would Goldman have responded to the criticism that as a Lithuanian Jew she had no right to question American patriotism?**

▶ **If we consider the actual experience of the United States during and after the war, were Goldman's warnings justified?**

The Western Front Trench warfare on the western front was a harrowing experience. When officers called for the troops to "go over the top," the men had to navigate a gauntlet of razor wire while facing exploding shells, constant gunfire, and sometimes poison gas. There were more than 1.5 million casualties in the Battle of the Somme alone, including, undoubtedly, some of the British soldiers shown here.

eastern front The front in Russia during World War I. The German army moved quickly across eastern Europe into Russia; low morale plagued the poorly equipped Russian army in the face of superior German technology.

Government bureaucracies expanded dramatically. Unions lost the right to strike. Imports declined. Factories converted from consumer to military production. The British Parliament even began to regulate the hours of the nation's "pubs"; less beer, it was thought, would improve industrial efficiency. Total war also meant restrictions on free speech and press censorship.

For women, the war brought opportunities as well as costs. The nursing profession expanded, and, with so many men absent, women became more important in factories as well. In France, many women ran family farms.

The idea that the woman's place was in the home, while men dominated the public sphere, was undermined. Before the war, British suffragists, campaigners for women's voting rights, used hunger strikes and public demonstrations to press their cause. The wartime contributions of British women helped swing public opinion, and in 1918 women over thirty possessing property and education were granted the right to vote.

In Russia, total war extracted a high price. On the **eastern front**, the tsar's forces were no match for the armaments and organization of the invading Germans. The invaders took hundreds of thousands of Russian prisoners and treated them with notable harshness. Morale among peasant conscripts was poor to begin

with and deteriorated rapidly. Mutinies were common: soldiers and sailors, mostly descendants of serfs, felt little loyalty for their aristocratic officers. Sometimes they killed their own commanders rather than head into futile battles; frequently they simply abandoned their weapons and walked home. Louise Bryant noticed them as she entered Russia, "great giants of men, mostly workers and peasants, in old, dirt-colored uniforms from which every emblem of Tsardom had been carefully removed."

As war disrupted food production, famine stalked the Russian countryside, while factories closed when industrialists lost access to the Western capital on which Russian industrialization depended. Despite deteriorating circumstances, Tsar Nicholas II rejected surrendering to the Germans. But by 1917, the Russians were exhausted.

Total War: Global Dimensions

Total war demanded the mobilization of global resources. Battles were fought in Africa and the Middle East; Japan declared war on Germany to seize German concessions in China; Britain and France depended on their Asian and African empires for manpower and materiel. By 1917, the Great War truly was a world war.

The decision by the Ottoman Empire to side with Germany opened a **southern front**. During the late nineteenth century, German banks, commercial houses, and manufacturers had invested heavily in the Ottoman economy, and the Ottomans saw a German alliance as protection against the French, British, and Russians. The most important strategic Ottoman position was the Dardanelles, a narrow strait connecting the Black Sea with the Mediterranean. In 1915, British forces, including many Australians, attacked the heavily fortified Ottoman position at Gallipoli. In a scene reminiscent of the carnage on the western front, thousands of Australian soldiers were mowed down. After a quarter of a million casualties, the British withdrew.

In the wake of Gallipoli, the British could spare neither men nor materiel to fight on the southern front, so they mobilized regiments from their African and Asian colonies. A force of Egyptian soldiers under British command moved toward Ottoman-controlled Palestine, while

Indian Soldier British a central role on the so the Ottoman Empire. T combines a traditional military clothing and g battle in Mesopotami His division was succe surrendered two days was taken.

Indian soldiers were br up to engage Ot counc forces in Mesopc still Knowing that many advic subjects of the Ot our p Empire were unhap ambi Turkish rule, the Brit (r. 19 forged an alliance w war, leaders. Germ

Senegalese Mostly Mus French Wes conscripted Empire in W developed a fearsome fig

Woodrow Wil 1921) Presid States during War I. Wilso view, enshrir Fourteen Poi end of the wa the spread of democracy.

A G Ke G In Ge do rec the res to an eve

Vie Cor tain fro troo Indo supp

The

The was the coun still advic our p ambi (r. 19 war, Germ

interests in the United States urged a rapid military buildup. While citing national security reasons, they were also aware, as critics like Louise Bryant pointed out, that military spending was highly profitable.

Early in 1917 the Germans, aiming to stop American arms shipments to Britain, resumed submarine attacks. By that time Wilson had decided on war, but he still had to convince Congress and the American people. To persuade Americans to overcome their hesitation, Wilson told Congress: "The world must be made safe for democracy. Its peace must be planted upon the tested foundations of political liberty."

Wilson's idealism swung public opinion in favor of war, and a draft was instituted. The mobilization of a vast national army gave the government unprecedented power. Economic and political life became more centralized while restrictions were placed on free speech, the right of workers to strike, and freedom of the press. Such were the mandates of total war.

The arrival of a million-strong American force helped turn the tide on the western front. On November 11, 1918, the war ended with the signing of an armistice. The United States was now in position to influence the peace talks that followed, along with the major European powers. But Asians and Africans, who were also deeply affected, gained no place in international affairs as a result of the war.

The Postwar Settlements

As diplomats headed to France to prepare the peace terms, an outbreak of influenza raced around the world, killing tens of millions. Wartime violence and dislocation had paved the way for an epidemic that further deepened the distress. The world seemed changed in some fundamental way, the future uncertain.

In this atmosphere, representatives of the Allied powers—Britain, France, Italy, and the United States—gathered at the **Paris Peace Conference** in 1919. In retrospect, the settlements negotiated in Paris seem clearly wrongheaded. France was intent on punishing Germany for the war, thus undermining its new liberal constitution. New national boundaries drawn in eastern Europe and the Mediterranean generated violence, instability, and dictatorship. Britain and France confiscated German colonies and Ottoman provinces for their own empires, thus stoking the flames of nationalism in Africa, the Middle East, and Asia. And the United States Senate voted against joining the new League of Nations that Woodrow Wilson had proposed precisely to avoid a catastrophic recurrence of total war.

The Paris Peace Conference

The principal leaders at the Paris Peace Conference—Woodrow Wilson of the United States, Georges Clemenceau of France, and David Lloyd George of Britain—faced an enormous task. Germany had somehow to be reincorporated into Europe. The Austrian and Ottoman Empires were in ruins, requiring the construction of entirely new political systems in central Europe and western Asia. Moreover, Germany had to relinquish its colonies in Africa and the Pacific. The world's map had to be redrawn (see Map 27.2).

Wilson brought to Paris the same high-minded attitude with which he earlier urged America's entry into the war. His Fourteen Points contained specific recommendations based on a few clear principles. Wilson stressed the importance of free trade, the right of peoples to national self-determination,

Paris Peace Conference
(1919) Conference that resulted in the Versailles treaty, which added to post–World War I tensions. A war guilt clause and reparations payments destabilized Germany, and efforts to create stable nations from former imperial provinces in eastern Europe were problematic.

Map 27.2   Territorial Changes in Europe After World War I

The map of Europe was altered dramatically by the Versailles treaty through the application of Woodrow Wilson's policy of "national self-determination." New nations appeared in central and eastern Europe, carved from the former Russian, Austro-Hungarian, and Ottoman Empires, though the complex ethnic composition of the region often made it impossible to draw clear lines between "peoples" and "states." The handover of the key regions of Alsace and Lorraine from Germany to France caused much bitterness among German nationalists.   © Cengage Learning   💻 Interactive Map

and the creation of a permanent international assembly to provide safeguards against future wars. The British goal, on the other hand, was to safeguard their imperial interests, while Clemenceau demanded Germany pay reparations as punishment for the war.

As the Allies negotiated, others sought to influence the outcome. At a Pan-African Congress also held in Paris in 1919, black leaders from Africa, the West Indies, and the United States spoke for the interests of Africans and peoples of African descent. A delegation of

612

Egyptians also planned to attend the conference to represent Arab and Muslim interests, but the British government refused them permission to travel. The Chinese delegation, upset by concessions made to Japan, angrily returned home. Also in Paris was a young Vietnamese man named Ho Chi Minh (hoh chee min), who petitioned the Western powers to apply the principle of self-determination to the Vietnamese people in French Indochina. Rebuffed, Ho became a member of the French Communist Party and later the leader of a Vietnamese insurgency against the French (see Chapter 29). Lacking a voice at the Paris Peace Conference, the world's people could only wait to see what the great powers would decide for them.

In the end, the Versailles treaty that resulted from the Paris Peace Conference fell far short of Wilson's goals. The Allies did agree to Wilson's plan for a **League of Nations**. But tensions resulted from French insistence on punishment for Germany; from the difficulty in creating coherent states in eastern Europe; from the imperial ambitions of Britain and France; and from the lack of participation in the League of Nations by both Russia, embroiled in revolution, and the United States, retreating into isolationism. The First World War was not a war to end all wars, and the world had not been made safe for democracy.

The Weimar Republic and Nation Building in Europe

After surrender and the abdication of Kaiser Wilhelm II, German liberals and socialists cooperated in the creation of the new **Weimar Republic**. Many years after the revolutions of 1848, Germany finally had a liberal, democratic constitution. But cultivating a liberal political culture was still difficult. A communist uprising in 1919 challenged the Weimar (vahy-mahr) leaders from the left, while on the right angry veterans blamed liberal weakness for the nation's defeat. At war's end, Germans were hungry and cold.

The harsh peace terms insisted upon by France made recovery more difficult than it had to be. First, the Weimar government was forced to sign a treaty that contained a "war guilt" clause. Germans did not believe that they were solely responsible for the war, and signing a treaty that said so diminished the credibility of the new government. The French also insisted on huge reparation payments that crippled the German financial system. One British economist warned that the economic punishment of Germany was simply foolish in an era of economic interdependence: everyone stood to lose. The treaty also called for the complete demilitarization of the Rhineland, the German province bordering France, and severe restrictions on German rearmament.

By 1923 the new Weimar Republic was foundering. It was unable to meet its reparation obligations, and the French occupied the Ruhr Valley, Germany's industrial heartland, in lieu of payment. As the government printed more money to make up for the shortfall in its treasury, inflation spiraled out of control. People needed a wheelbarrow full of bank notes to buy a loaf of bread, and the savings of the middle class were wiped out. Although an attempt by right-wing military forces to take over from elected politicians was thwarted, the rebellious officers had a good deal of public support.

Signs of recovery appeared in 1925. International agreements eased Germany's reparation payments and ended the occupation of the Ruhr Valley. The German economy finally came back to prewar levels, and Berlin regained its status as a major cultural, intellectual, and artistic center. Soon, however, another set of crises would undermine German liberalism.

In the meantime, postwar reconstruction was transforming eastern, central, and southeastern Europe. While the collapse of the Austrian and Ottoman Empires offered the opportunity to

League of Nations Assembly of sovereign states, advocated by Woodrow Wilson, that was intended to provide a permanent diplomatic forum in the hopes of avoiding future conflict.

Weimar Republic (1919–1933) After the abdication of Kaiser Wilhem II, the Weimar Republic created a new Germany based on a liberal constitution. However, the new republic was faced with huge war debts, political turmoil, and rising inflation.

Primary Source: Comments of the German Delegation to the Paris Peace Conference on the Conditions of Peace, October 1919 Read Germany's response to the Treaty of Versailles, which deprived it of its colonies, 13 percent of its land, and 10 percent of its population.

Mandate System System by which former Ottoman provinces and German colonies were redistributed. Based on the idea that some societies were not ready for national self-determination, it expanded the empires of Britain, France, Belgium, and Japan while angering African, Arab, and Chinese nationalists.

implement Wilson's ideal of national self-determination, nationalist sentiments led to conflict rather than consensus. The complex cultural geography of the region meant that ethnic, linguistic, and religious groups lived scattered among each other in many places. Along the German/Polish frontier, for example, German-speakers and Polish-speakers often lived side by side in the same towns and villages, along with a substantial Jewish population. Poland, which had disappeared from the map of Europe in the eighteenth century, was now restored as a nation-state. Polish nationalists felt that Germans living in the new Poland either had to be restricted or move to Germany, where they "belonged." The repression of Polish Jews was even more extreme.

Poland, like Germany, did not have democratic traditions. Tired of endless political squabbling, conservative army officers seized power in 1926 and imposed restrictions on free speech and political organization. The new Balkan state of Yugoslavia also moved toward authoritarianism and the repression of minorities.

The slide toward dictatorship in much of eastern, central, and southern Europe arose from a contradiction that Wilson had not recognized: nationalism is based on the rights of *groups,* while liberalism focuses on the rights of *individuals.* Nationalists with an "us versus them" mentality preferred to restrict the rights of minority groups. The problem was particularly acute for peoples with no state to protect them, such as Europe's Jews and the Roma (or Gypsies). As a basis for political reconstruction nationalism caused as many problems as it solved.

The Mandate System in Africa and the Middle East

The French and British considered their colonial interests paramount and rejected the concept that peoples in Africa and the Middle East might govern themselves. Rather than apply Wilson's concept of national self-determination, the Allies devised the **Mandate System**, whereby the great powers ruled over territories under

League of Nations auspices until their colonies might be "prepared" for self-government. Race was the unspoken determinant of who was deemed capable of self-rule: the Mandate System applied in Africa and Asia, but not in Europe.

In Africa, the Mandate System allowed the French, British, Belgian, and South African governments to take over former German colonies. With the addition of German East Africa (today's Tanzania) to her empire, Britain finally controlled a continuous stretch of territory "from Cape to Cairo." The French expanded their West African holdings, and the Belgians enlarged their Central African empire. While required to submit reports to the League of Nations showing that they were looking out for "native rights," the Europeans ruled the mandated territories like colonies, doing little to prepare them for eventual self-determination.

Despite such European skepticism that Africans would ever be capable of self-rule, leaders of the African National Congress in South Africa called for greater rights, including an extension of the right to vote to Western-educated African property owners. In West Africa, the consciousness of the continent's place in the wider world also increased. More African students studied in Europe and the United States and came back questioning the legitimacy of colonial rule. Thus, the seeds of African nationalism were sown.

The most complex application of the Mandate System came in the Middle East, where the collapse of Ottoman authority created a power vacuum. While the French and British wanted control of such rich and strategic areas as Turkey, Mesopotamia, Syria, and Palestine, they had to contend with well-organized forces of Turkish, Arab, and Jewish nationalism.

As the Ottoman Empire collapsed, some of its subject peoples sought to liberate themselves. Hoping for an independent state, Armenians had supported Russia during the war. Ottoman officials responded by forcibly relocating millions of Armenians; in that genocide as many as 1.5 million Armenians were killed. While Armenians did gain a state of their own in the postwar settlements, the Kurdish-speaking people of the Ottoman Empire did not. Kurds were scattered across several new postwar states (Turkey, Iraq, Syria, and Iran), their national aspirations unfulfilled.

In the Middle East the postwar situation was complicated by three contradictory promises made by the British during the war—to the Arabs, the French, and the Jews. In 1915, to gain Arab support against the Ottoman Empire, the British had promised the prominent Hashemite family to "recognize and support the independence of the Arabs." Contradicting that agreement, the British then signed a secret treaty with the French arranging to divide Ottoman provinces between themselves after the war.

A third agreement, difficult to reconcile with the previous two, was the **Balfour Declaration** of 1917, which committed the British government to support the creation of a "national home" for the Jewish people in Palestine. The government was seeking additional support for the war effort from financiers and industrialists in Britain who advocated the creation of a Jewish national state to represent Jewish interests in the world and offer Jews a refuge. These Zionists, as they called themselves, planned to build their new nation on the same site as the ancient Hebrew kingdoms. However, most Zionists had never been to the Middle East, and most of the people actually living in Palestine were Arab.

After the war, the British tried to use the Mandate System to reconcile these contradictory promises. True to their 1916 secret agreement, the British and the French divided the region between them. The French received a mandate over Syria and Lebanon, and the British stitched together three Ottoman provinces centered on the cities of Mosul, Baghdad, and Basra into a new entity they called Iraq. Members of the Hashemite family were installed in Syria and Iraq as political leaders. The British also drew a new line on the map at the Jordan River, separating Palestine, which they ruled directly, from the new kingdom of Jordan, where they installed yet another Hashemite ruler as king. Although Arab nationalists protested their status of a mandate, saying that Arabs "are not naturally less than other more advanced races" and that they did "not stand in need of a mandatory power," the lack of Arab unity still gave Europeans the upper hand. The French remained dominant in Syria, and the British in Iraq, even after they accelerated the transition from mandate status to fuller sovereignty.

The situation was more complicated in Palestine. Wartime anti-Semitism had increased the popularity of Zionism among American and European Jews, and even many who had no plans to move to Palestine contributed money to purchase land for those who did decide to move. Arab leaders were alarmed. While still the majority in Palestine, they feared becoming the minority in the land where many of their families had lived for over a thousand years.

It was impossible to please both sides. Support for a "national home" fell short of support for a Jewish state, and Arab nationalists viewed any immigration of Jews into Palestine with suspicion. When the British allowed such immigration in large numbers in the early 1920s, Arabs demonstrated. When they curtailed Jewish immigration in response, Zionist leaders were furious. The British were determined to keep Palestine because of its strategic location, but the political price was high.

With the Russians distracted by revolution, the Germans desperate and disarmed, and the Americans intent on returning to prewar normalcy, the British and French at first imagined that their empires would increase and endure. However, they were unable to dominate for long. Having liquidated many foreign investments to fight the war, Britain slipped from being the world's largest creditor to facing significant debts, especially to the United States. Meanwhile, the forces of anticolonial nationalism were gathering throughout Africa and Asia. As the twentieth century progressed, the United States and Russia, large nations rich in indigenous natural resources, would emerge as the dominant global players.

Balfour Declaration (1917) Declaration that committed the British government to helping create "a national home for the Jewish people" in Palestine. Britain made this declaration to court support from Zionists during World War I.

Primary Source: Letter from Turkey, Summer 1915 *Read an eyewitness account of the Armenian genocide by an American missionary from Massachusetts.*

Primary Source: The Balfour Declaration, Stating the British Government's Support for a Jewish Homeland in Palestine, and Discussions Leading to Issuing It in 1917 *Learn which questions were considered—and which were ignored—as Britain prepared to support the Zionist movement.*

Sun Yat-sen (1866–1925) The founding father of the Republic of China after the revolution of 1911; established the Guomindang, or Nationalist Party.

defense. Nationalists led by Sun Zhongshan, better known as **Sun Yat-sen** (1866–1925), declared a new Republic of China. Lacking an army, Sun was dependent on Yuan's support. In 1912, after serving as president for only a few weeks, he stepped aside and delegates to the new national assembly elected Yuan as president.

Sun Yat-sen (soon yot-SEN) grew up near Guangzhou, the center of European influence in south China. He earned a medical degree in Hong Kong in 1892 and then moved to Hawai'i, where he started the political organizing that would put him at the head of the Guomindang (gwo-min-DAHNG), or Nationalist Party. Sun envisioned a stable, modernized China, with a liberal legal system and a just distribution of resources, taking its rightful place among the world's great powers.

The new Republic of China faced daunting challenges. Japanese imperialists were already in formal control of Taiwan and exercised great power in Manchuria. In 1919 Japan was given control over Chinese territory on the Shandong peninsula formerly controlled by Germany, in acknowledgment of its wartime alliance with France and Britain. On May 4, 1919, Chinese university students demonstrated in Tiananmen Square in Beijing, appealing to the government to restore Chinese dignity in the face of Japanese aggression. Their May Fourth Movement led to strikes, demonstrations, and a boycott of Japanese goods. Chinese nationalism was on the rise, but the republican government had little power to respond to the students' appeals.

The domestic military situation was another challenge for Sun and the Guomindang. In 1916 Yuan broke with the Nationalists and declared the foundation of a new imperial dynasty. When regional generals rejected Yuan's imperial pretensions, formed their own armies, and began to act as warlords, the country descended into a decade of chaos. The only stable and prosperous parts of China were the foreign enclaves. Sun retreated to Guangzhou, where the Guomindang was rebuilt by his brother-in-law and successor Jiang Jieshi, known in the West as Chiang Kai-shek (1887–1975). After defeating or co-opting the warlords into the Guomindang, Chiang finally established central authority over most of the country in the mid-1920s. Under Chiang's authoritarian command, however, Sun's idealistic emphasis on reform was supplanted by a growing culture of corruption.

Meanwhile, in 1921, in the wake of the May Fourth Movement, the Chinese Communist Party was formed in Shanghai. At first, Sun and Chiang allied with the Communists. But in 1927, when Chiang felt more secure in power, he turned against them. Guomindang soldiers and street thugs killed thousands of Communists in the coastal cities, and those remaining fled to the countryside. One Chinese Communist, Mao Zedong (1893–1976), argued that this development was necessary because the peasants would lead the way to socialism. Rejecting the traditional Marxist emphasis on the leading role of the industrial workers, Mao wrote: "In a very short time … several hundred million peasants will rise like a tornado … and rush forward along the road to liberation. They will send all imperialists, warlords, corrupt officials, local bullies, and bad gentry to their graves." By allying with this elemental peasant force, Mao believed, the Communists could drive Chiang from power and bring about true revolution. It would be two decades before the conflict between the Guomindang and the Communists was finally resolved (see Chapter 30).

Russia's October Revolution

Even more than the Mexican and Chinese Revolutions, the Russian Revolution represented a fundamental change in world history. Indeed, the Bolsheviks and their leader V. I. Lenin saw themselves as fighting not just to control one country but also to change the destiny of all humanity.

Russia's first revolutionary crisis occurred in 1905, after Russia's defeat in the Russo-Japanese War. Protestors, converging on the Winter Palace in St. Petersburg to petition the tsar for reform, were mowed down by guards mounted on horseback, shattering old bonds of trust.

In the ensuing crisis Tsar Nicholas II (r. 1894–1917) conceded a series of reforms, including, for the first time, a representative assembly called the Duma. He also approved a crash program of industrialization that, though it achieved substantial progress by 1913, nevertheless also

May Fourth Movement May 4, 1919, was an important day in the development of Chinese nationalism. Hundreds of thousands of protesters gathered in Tiananmen Square in Beijing angered by the Versailles treaty, which had given Chinese territory to Japan. Demonstrations were held across the country, with students playing a large role. In this photograph residents of Shanghai are waving signs that say, "Down with the traitors who buy Japanese goods!"

created further social instability. The money for industrialization came largely from higher taxes on already miserable peasants, and the new industrial workers labored under much worse conditions and at much lower pay than their Western counterparts.

Although the Russian middle class could now express its desire for greater reform through the Duma, real power still lay with aristocrats, army officials, and the tsarist bureaucracy. While some reformers argued that the powers of the Duma could be expanded, others argued that a fresh start was needed. One of the revolutionary groups was the Social Democratic Party, communist followers of the Marxist tradition.

After 1903, the Social Democrats split into two factions. One group, the Mensheviks, adhered to the traditional Marxist belief that socialism could only be built on the foundation of capitalism. Before Russia's workers could seize power for themselves, a modern industrial economy would have to be built. The Mensheviks therefore favored an alliance with the Russian middle class leading to a multiparty constitutional republic.

V. I. Lenin (1870–1924), the leader of the opposing Bolshevik faction, had a different vision. Lenin's radicalism started in childhood, when his elder brother was hanged for plotting to assassinate the tsar. Lenin himself was exiled first to Siberia and then to western Europe. There he developed his theory that a "revolutionary vanguard," a small, dedicated group of professional revolutionists, could represent the interests of the industrial proletariat. Rather than waiting for Russia's industrial workers to increase in numbers and in political consciousness, the

V. I. Lenin (1870– 1924) Born Vladimir Ilyich Ulyanov, Lenin led the Bolsheviks to power during the Russian Revolution of 1917. Leader of the Communist Party until his death in 1924.

Bolshevik vanguard could seize power and rule in the name of the working class.

Lenin's opportunity to implement his ideas came as a result of the war. With soldiers fleeing the front, many blamed the tsar for the huge human and economic costs of war. Faced with mutiny and near anarchy across the country, Tsar Nicholas abdicated in February 1917. When Louise Bryant arrived in the summer of 1917, the Provisional Government that had replaced him was also losing legitimacy when it decided to continue to fight Germany, hoping to maintain access to foreign loans and to share in the division of Ottoman lands if the Allies won.

Russians, however, were sick and tired of war. Louise Bryant described the passionate appeal of one veteran for peace at a public meeting: "Comrades! I come from the place where men are digging their graves and calling them trenches! I tell you the army can't fight much longer!" A peasant delegate said that if they were not given sufficient land "they would go out and take it." "Over and over like the beat of the surf came the cry of all starving Russia," Bryant wrote, "'Peace, land and bread!'" The Provisional Government ignored those appeals.

As lines of tsarist authority broke down, they were spontaneously replaced by *soviets* (Russian for "committees"): soviets of workers in factories, of residents in urban neighborhoods, of railway workers, and even of soldiers and sailors in the military. It was a radical form of democracy in which participants had the right to speak and be represented, with decisions made through public discussion and consensus.

Lenin returned from exile as Russian society slid from dictatorship to near anarchy. His vision and organizational abilities put the Bolsheviks in a position to make a play for power. In Bryant's words, "Lenin is a master propagandist.... He possesses all the qualities of a 'chief', including the absolute moral indifference which is so necessary to such a part." In the summer of 1917 Lenin reduced the Bolshevik program to two simple slogans: "Peace, Land, and Bread!" and "All Power to the Soviets!" The fiery speeches and tireless organizing of another prominent Bolshevik, Leon Trotsky (1879–1940), did much to advance the Communist cause that summer.

In the fall, with the authority of the Provisional Government in decline, Lenin and the Bolsheviks planned and executed a coup d'état that later communists would celebrate as the October Revolution. Hardly a shot was fired in the Provisional Government's defense when Lenin disbanded the Constituent Assembly recently elected to write a new constitution. As Bryant wrote, "A big sailor marched into the elaborate red and gold assembly chamber and announced in a loud voice: 'Go along home!'" Russia's brief experiment with multiparty representative democracy had ended.

Civil War and the New Economic Policy, 1917–1924

The Communist Party, as the Bolsheviks were now called, considered the Constituent Assembly irrelevant. Defending the revolution was the first order of the day. To fulfill their promise to bring peace, they signed a treaty ceding to Germany rich Ukrainian and Belarusian lands in 1918. The Communists saw this unequal treaty as only a temporary setback, being certain that workers in Germany would soon rise up, overthrow their government, and establish a true and equitable peace with Russia. Their self-assurance was remarkable.

The Communists also contended with powerful counter-revolutionary forces, as aristocratic generals turning their attention from the Germans threatened to undo the revolution. The Russian Civil War of 1919–1921 pitted the Communist Red Army, commanded by Leon Trotsky, against the "White Armies" organized by former tsarist generals with the help of the United States and Great Britain. The Communists murdered the tsar and his family and then organized a secret police more terrifying than the old tsarist one.

By 1921, Lenin was securely in control and ruling with an iron hand. The anarchic democracy of freely elected soviets was replaced by strict party discipline in all facets of life. Even within the Communist Party Central Committee, dominated by Lenin, only limited debate was permitted. All other political organizations were banned.

Bryant believed that circumstances pushed the Communists toward dictatorship. "In the beginning," she wrote of Lenin, "he imagined he could maintain a free press, free speech and be liberal toward his enemies. But he found himself faced by a situation where iron discipline was the only method capable of carrying the day." Perhaps that was a naïve judgment: the free play of ideas and organizations was never part of Lenin's plan.

One achievement of Lenin and the Communists was to secure control over both Russia and the Russian Empire. Though they lost lands in the west (such as Poland, Finland, and Lithuania), they retained the rich lands of the Ukraine, the vastness of Siberia, the lands of Central Asia with their potential for agricultural development, and the strategic Caucasus Mountains in the south. These regions were brought together in 1922 in the Union of Soviet Socialist Republics (U.S.S.R.). Allegedly a federal republic, in reality the Soviet Union was a top-down dictatorship dominated by Moscow.

After the civil war ended, the country experienced a brief respite of relative peace and the beginnings of economic recovery when Lenin instituted the New Economic Policy (1921–1924). Peasants were allowed to keep the land they had recently won and to farm it as they saw fit. Restrictions on private business were lifted for all but the largest enterprises, such as transportation and heavy industry.

Stalin and "Socialism in One Country"

Louise Bryant never returned to Russia after Lenin's death in 1924, perhaps because she did not want to see how little her hopes for socialism were being realized after Joseph Stalin (r. 1926–1953) succeeded Lenin. Stalin lacked Lenin's intellectual brilliance. While the exiled Lenin was associating with European intellectuals, Stalin was robbing banks to raise funds for the party. Having spent time in jail, he knew the ways of the tsarist secret police from personal experience. *Stalin,* his chosen revolutionary name, means "man of steel."

From 1919 to 1924 Stalin was absolutely loyal to Lenin, who entrusted him with secret and sensitive tasks. He stayed in the background while other Communists argued about policies and sought positions of authority, and he served on all the important committees but was part of no faction. When Lenin died, he used divisions in the Central Committee to position himself as a safe and neutral choice for leadership. But once Stalin held power, he no longer acted as mediator. By 1926 Stalin had consolidated his authority and established a personal dictatorship, driving Leon Trotsky, his main competitor for the role of heir to Lenin, into exile.

More than personal ambition was at stake. Stalin had a vision of **"Socialism in One Country."** Some Communists, like Trotsky, thought socialism in Russia required the help of revolutions in advanced industrial nations; others believed that the moderate New Economic Policy was the correct course. Stalin rejected both. Instead, socialism would be built through top-down government control of every aspect of life.

In 1928 Stalin launched the first of his Five-Year Plans. The entire economy was nationalized in a crash policy of industrialization. Noting that Russia was far behind more advanced economies, Stalin said: "We must make good this lag in ten years … or we will be crushed." After the Soviet Union cut all ties with foreign economies, there was only one way Stalin could raise the capital needed for industrialization: by squeezing it out of the Soviet people. Low wages and harsh working conditions characterized new factories built to produce steel, electricity, chemicals, tractors, and other foundations of industrial growth. Especially productive workers received medals rather than higher wages, while poor performance could result in exile to a Siberian labor camp.

Faced with Stalin's brutal policies, people could no longer even turn to religion for solace. Denouncing the Orthodox Church as a foundation of the old, tsarist regime, Stalin turned churches into municipal buildings and heavily regulated the few remaining monasteries. In the world's first atheistic state, communist theory was the new orthodoxy.

Still, within ten years the successes of "Socialism in One Country" were notable. The Soviet Union had the fastest-growing industrial economy in the world, with production increasing as much as 14 percent a year. But the harshly repressive society Stalin created bore little resemblance to the hopeful scenario portrayed by Louise Bryant in the books she wrote during the early years of the revolution. Stalin's version of socialism was indeed a "loathsome, ugly monster demanding human sacrifices."

> **"Socialism in One Country"**
> Joseph Stalin's slogan declaring that Soviet socialism could be achieved without passing through a capitalist phase or revolutions in industrial societies. This policy led to an economy based on central planning for industrial growth and collectivization of agriculture.

Chapter Review and Learning Activities

Louise Bryant was part of a generation whose youthful idealism, inspired by the Mexican and Russian Revolutions, was crushed by the failure to create a more democratic and just postwar world. She spent the end of her life in Paris, where the earlier confidence of artists and intellectuals in human progress had been replaced by a much darker view of the human condition and a much grimmer set of expectations for the future. Their pessimism was justified: when Louise Bryant died in 1936, the drums of war were beating once again. Adolf Hitler had come to power in Germany.

How can the First World War be regarded as a "total war," both for the domestic populations of the main combatants and for the entire world?

Because industrial production was critical to the military balance of the First World War, it was essential for the combatant governments to mobilize their entire populations behind the war effort. Governments rationed consumer goods to prioritize the production of war materiel, placed limits on labor organization, and restricted free speech. Even in the most liberal societies, such as Great Britain, "total war" meant a much greater regimentation of daily life, bringing the war home to civilians. On a global scale, "total war" meant that colonial peoples were forced into the conflict by the imperial powers of Britain, France, and Germany. Africans and Southeast Asians fought in Europe, while Indian, Canadian, and Australian soldiers battled Ottoman armies in the Middle East. East Africa became a theater of war, and across the colonial world peasants and plantation workers stepped up production to feed the war machines of their colonial overlords.

How did the postwar settlements fail to resolve global political tensions?

Woodrow Wilson's vision that the war would "make the world safe for democracy" was not realized. At the Paris Peace Conference, the French delegation insisted on punishing Germany by inserting a "war guilt" clause and demanding financial reparations,

thus undercutting the chances of success for the liberal Weimar Republic. At the same time, Wilson's ideal of "national self-determination" proved an ineffective road map to stability and democracy in eastern Europe, a region with an exceptionally complex ethnic tapestry and with societies long dominated by the Russian and Austrian Empires and therefore lacking in liberal and democratic traditions. Reordering the former Ottoman Empire was even more complicated; the British and French divided up former Ottoman provinces, and Turkish, Arab, and Jewish nationalists pursued their own interests. While the framers of the Versailles treaty created the Mandate System to restore order in former German colonies and Ottoman provinces, nationalist groups competed in the Middle East, and Asian and African nationalists became angry at their second-class status. The failures of the postwar settlements were global in scope.

How did the outcomes of revolutions in Mexico, China, and Russia add to the uncertainty of the postwar world?

While the romance of revolution appealed to many observers of the Mexican, Chinese, and Russian Revolutions, each of them failed to live up to the highest ideals of their supporters. The exploits of Pancho Villa and Emiliano Zapata in Mexico showed that common people could rise up to claim their rights, but their failure, and the subsequent dominance of the corrupt and bureaucratic National Revolutionary Party, undermined hopes for change from the bottom. Likewise Sun Yat-sen's aspirations for the new Chinese Republic remained unfulfilled after warlord resistance, communist opposition, and corruption led the Guomindang in an authoritarian direction. Most important, in Russia the transition from tsarist autocracy to communist dictatorship had a deep impact on global politics. Some of those who were dissatisfied with their own societies, including some labor leaders and anticolonial nationalists, idealized the new Soviet Union. Especially after the rise of Stalin, however, it became clear that the Russian Revolution had only added to the cloud of uncertainty and anxiety that lay over the postwar world.

FOR FURTHER REFERENCE

Bryant, Louise. *Six Months in Red Russia*. Portland, Ore.: Powells, 2002.

Dearborn, Mary V. *Queen of Bohemia: The Life of Louise Bryant*. Bridgewater, N.J.: Replica, 1996.

Fromkin, David. *A Peace to End All Peace: The Fall of the Ottoman Empire and the Rise of the Modern Middle East.* New York: Holt, 2001.

Goldstone, Jack. *Revolutions: Theoretical, Comparative and Historical Studies*. Belmont, Calif.: Wadsworth, 2002.

Hart, John Mason. *Revolutionary Mexico*. Berkeley: University of California Press, 1997.

Keegan, John. *The First World War*. New York: Vintage, 2000.

Macmillan, Margaret. *Paris 1919: Six Months That Changed the World*. New York: Random House, 2003.

Neiberg, Michael S. *Fighting the Great War: A Global History*. New York: Cambridge University Press, 2005.

Service, Robert. *The Russian Revolution, 1900–1927*. 3d ed. New York: Palgrave Macmillan, 2007.

Strachan, Hew. *The First World War in Africa*. New York: Oxford University Press, 2004.

KEY TERMS

Louise Bryant (602)

Kaiser Wilhelm II (603)

western front (605)

eastern front (608)

southern front (609)

Senegalese Sharpshooters (610)

Woodrow Wilson (610)

Paris Peace Conference (611)

League of Nations (613)

Weimar Republic (613)

Mandate System (614)

Balfour Declaration (615)

Emiliano Zapata (616)

Sun Yat-sen (618)

V. I. Lenin (619)

"Socialism in One Country" (621)

VOYAGES ON THE WEB

Voyages: Louise Bryant

"Voyages" is a real time excursion to historical sites in this chapter and includes interactive activities and study tools such as audio summaries, animated maps, and flashcards.

Visual Evidence: History, Photography, and Power

"Visual Evidence" features artifacts, works of art, or photographs, along with a brief descriptive essay and discussion questions to guide your analysis of visual sources.

World History in Today's World: The Origins of Iraq

"World History in Today's World" makes the connection between features of modern life and their origins in the periods in this chapter.

CourseMate

Go to the CourseMate website at www.cengagebrain.com for additional study tools and review materials—including audio and video clips—for this chapter.

28 Responses to Global Crisis, 1920–1939

Halide Edib
(Memoirs of Halide Edib, New York and London; Century, 1926.)

After she had participated in the struggle for the creation of the new Turkey after the First World War, the novelist **Halide Edib** (1884–1964) was forced into exile in 1926 after falling out of favor with the country's president. For the next thirteen years she traveled to France, Britain, and the United States, writing books and lecturing at universities. In 1935 she went to India, a trip that resulted in the book *Inside India* and speculation about the future shape of the world. From her own experience in Turkey she understood the struggle of formerly powerful societies to overcome more recent Western domination and the difficulties in reconciling ancient cultures with modern influences. Edib's musings about the future importance of India and China were far-sighted:

[India] seemed to me like Allah's workshop: gods, men and nature abounded in their most beautiful and most hideous; ideas and all the arts in their ancient and most modern styles lay about pell-mell. Once I used to think that first-hand knowledge of Russia and America would enable one to sense the direction which the world was taking; but this India must certainly have its share in shaping the future. Not because of its immemorial age, but because of the new life throbbing in it! Perhaps the same is true of China.... How much must one see and understand before being able to have any idea of the working of history?[1]

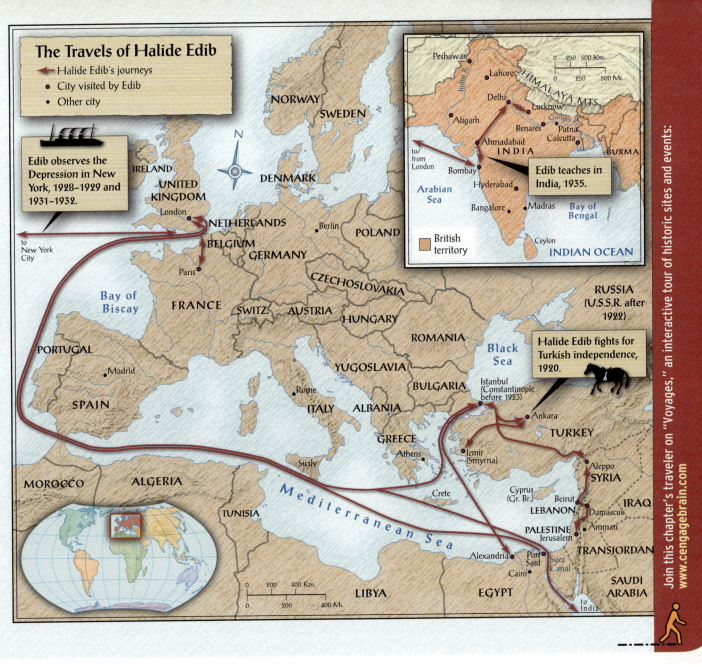

The Travels of Halide Edib

→ Halide Edib's journeys
• City visited by Edib
• Other city

Edib observes the Depression in New York, 1928–1929 and 1931–1932.

Edib teaches in India, 1935.

British territory

Halide Edib fights for Turkish independence, 1920.

RUSSIA (U.S.S.R. after 1922)

Join this chapter's traveler on "Voyages," an interactive tour of historic sites and events: www.cengagebrain.com

	1920	1925	1930	1935	1940

Lifetime of Halide Edib
(b. 1884)   (d. 1964)

AFRICA AND ASIA

Republic of Turkey
1923

Igbo Women's War
1929

Invasion of Manchuria
1931

Italian invasion of Ethiopia
1935

Rape of Nanjing
1937

Growth of Indian National Congress
1920s and 1930s

EUROPE

Mussolini controls Italy
1922

Soviet collectivization and Great Purges
1930s

Hitler takes power in Germany
1933

Spanish Civil War
1936   1939

Halide Edib (1884–1964) Turkish nationalist best known for her many popular works of fiction featuring women protagonists. Was part of the army that formed the Turkish nation and later served as a member of the Turkish parliament and as a professor of literature.

Halide Edib **(hall-ee-DEH eh-DEEP)** was the daughter of a progressive Ottoman official who made sure she learned Arabic and studied the Quran but also had her tutored by an English governess and sent her to a Greek-run school. In 1901, fluent in Turkish, English, Greek, and Arabic, Edib was the first Muslim girl to graduate from the American College for Girls in Istanbul. As a child of privilege, she had the luxury of exploring many different ideas and forming her identity in a safe and secure environment. She remained a practicing Muslim.

After graduation Edib married and had two children: "My life was confined within the walls of my apartment. I led the life of an old-fashioned Turkish woman." But over the next two decades her life was thrown into turmoil. She grew beyond traditional gender roles, publishing her first novel in 1908 and helping to found the Society for the Elevation of Women. In 1910 she left her husband after he married a second wife, in conformity with Muslim law but against her wishes. After her divorce Edib became even more active in public affairs. In 1912 she was involved with the Turkish Hearth Club, where, for the first time, men and women attended public lectures together. It was the outbreak of war in 1914, however, that thoroughly transformed her life.

The Ottoman government sent Edib west to Damascus and Beirut to organize schools and orphanages for girls. Before long, however, the Ottoman armies were in retreat, and she returned to Istanbul with her second husband, a medical doctor. After British forces occupied Istanbul, she fled east in disguise, wearing a veil and carefully concealing her manicured fingernails as she and her husband rode on horseback to join the Turkish nationalist army headquartered at Ankara. She was given official rank and served the cause as a translator and press officer.

Though the nationalists were victorious—Turkey was recognized internationally in 1923—Edib's voyages were not over. During her years of exile, from 1926 to 1939, the uncertainties of the postwar world were turning into genuine global crises. When she came to New York as a visiting professor of literature at Columbia University in 1931–1932, the United States was suffering from the economic collapse that became known as the Great Depression. She witnessed the global effects of that economic downturn in Britain and France, from where she also viewed the emergence of fascism with the rise to power of Benito Mussolini in Italy and Adolf Hitler in Germany. Under these fascist regimes the liberal tradition was under assault, with state power growing at the expense of individual liberties. In the Soviet Union, Joseph Stalin was further consolidating his communist dictatorship.

With the global economy in crisis and political tensions on the rise, fewer people defended liberal ideals such as free trade and free political association. Ideologies that magnified the role of the state grew in popularity, while extreme nationalism allowed authoritarian rulers in many parts of the world to concentrate ever greater power. Even the liberal institutions of democratic states were sorely tested by the challenges of the 1930s. Authoritarian tendencies were reinforced wherever liberalism was weak or absent, such as in Russia, the European colonial empires, and the new nation of Turkey.

Nationalism could also be a positive force, however, providing a source of hope for many colonized Africans and Asians. The great Indian nationalist leader Mohandas K. Gandhi personified these hopes, while giving the entire world a model of peaceful political change. Like Halide Edib, Gandhi saw the fight for national independence as inseparable from the fight for justice, including equality for women, who had few rights under colonialism. Gandhi's peaceful philosophy, a source of inspiration to many, stood in sharp contrast to the renewed militarism that would soon lead to another world war.

Focus Questions

▶ How did governments in different parts of the world respond to the crisis of the Great Depression?

▶ Why did liberal democracy decline in influence as fascism, communism, and other authoritarian regimes rose in power and popularity?

▶ How successful were anticolonial nationalists in Asia and Africa during this period?

▶ What major events led to the outbreak of the Second World War?

The Great Depression, 1929–1939

In October 1929 prices on the New York Stock Exchange plunged; within two months, stocks lost half their value. Bank failures across Europe and the Americas spread the turmoil, bringing the **Great Depression**. Unemployment surged, while agricultural prices plummeted. Ten years later, global markets still had not recovered.

The Great Depression in the Industrialized World

Historians continue to debate the causes of the Great Depression, but two factors clearly stand out: the speculative excesses of the American stock market and the international debt structure that emerged after the First World War.

Financial markets reflected the frenetic pace of life in the United States during the "jazz age" of the 1920s, with its glamorous movie stars, mass-produced automobiles, and sensational gangsters. Speculators bought stock on borrowed money and, trusting that markets would endlessly increase in value, used paper profits to extend themselves even further. When the bubble burst, investors and the bankers who had lent them money were ruined. As capital investment dried up, the stock market collapse turned into a general economic crisis.

The problem was magnified by a sharp division between rich and poor. By 1929, only 1 percent of the U.S. population controlled 20 percent of its wealth. Ordinary workers could no longer afford the products American factories produced, and the decrease in demand caused factories to close. By 1932, one-fourth of workers in the United States were unemployed.

Great Depression Depression beginning in 1929 with the crash of stock prices in New York followed by a series of bank failures in Europe. Was marked by sustained deflation, unemployment in industrial nations, and depressed crop prices.

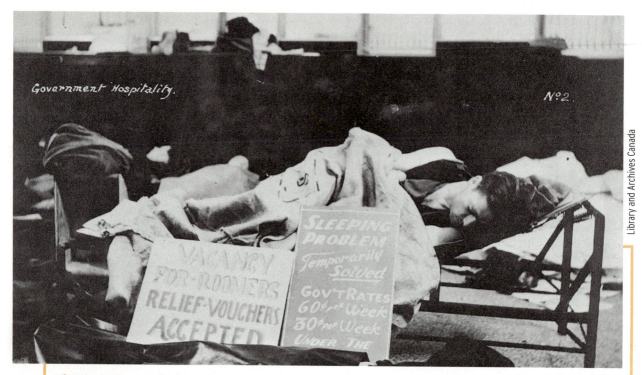

Library and Archives Canada

The Great Depression   Those left unemployed by the Great Depression were often left homeless. Here a Canadian man takes shelter on a cot in an office, his plight seemingly left unsolved by his government's efforts to provide relief vouchers to "temporarily solve" the problem.

During World War I the United States had replaced Great Britain as the world's leading source of investment capital, and European governments were in debt to American banks. The vulnerability of this system was revealed when the stock market crash led to a general run on banks. The banking crisis was particularly acute in Germany, which was borrowing heavily to make the huge payments to France required by the Versailles treaty. Financiers in the United States lent Germans money, which was then paid to France, which then sent the money back to the United States as French payments on American loans. After the stock market collapse, American investors called in their loans to German banks, driving them to bankruptcy. By 1933 German factories produced only half the goods they had manufactured in 1929, and half the workforce was idle.

Politicians exacerbated the crisis. In 1930 the United States imposed high tariffs to protect American manufacturing from foreign imports. Great Britain followed suit in 1932. Though intended to save jobs, protectionist measures caused steep declines in international trade and further job losses. By the early 1930s the world was trapped in a deflationary spiral, as wages and prices descended in a vicious cycle.

In the United States, France, and Britain, governments undertook much larger economic roles than before the war. In the United States President **Franklin Delano Roosevelt** (1887–1945) implemented his New Deal programs. Social Security created a "safety net" for many of the nation's elderly, and the Works Progress Administration put the unemployed to work on public infrastructure. Price subsidies helped stabilize farm prices while legislation strengthened workers'

Franklin Delano Roosevelt (r. 1933–1945) President of the United States during the Great Depression and World War II. Created the New Deal, which intended to stimulate the economy through government spending, financial sector reform, and a safety net for those most in need.

rights to unionize and strike. Government protection of depositors' accounts restored faith in the banking system. Although conservatives complained that Roosevelt was taking the country down the path of socialism, the New Deal was quite popular. But it did not get at the root of the economic problem, and in 1939 unemployment in the United States still stood at 16 percent.

The same pattern of government intervention unfolded in France and Britain, though the economic role of the state was most strongly developed in Sweden, Norway, and Denmark. Here Social Democrats pledged to construct a "welfare state" that would protect their citizens through comprehensive education, health care, housing subsidies, and unemployment insurance. But while such measures reduced suffering, they did not, any more than Roosevelt's policies, resolve underlying economic issues. No merely national solution could possibly solve the problem of depressed global markets caused by a shortage of credit.

The Great Depression in Global Perspective

Depressed agricultural prices hit hardest in those parts of the world most dependent on farming. In Africa, for example, agricultural commodities for export had been the norm. Small-scale family farms grew cash crops like cocoa, cotton, and coffee to buy imported goods like cloth, kerosene lamps, and bicycles as well as to pay taxes to European colonial governments. Parents with extra money often invested in school fees for their children. Thus in some areas, access to Western education was another stimulus for rural families to grow commercial crops.

When coffee and cocoa prices fell by over half in early 1930, many Africans were suddenly unable to meet their tax obligations or pay their debts. Since Western manufactures had increasingly displaced indigenous industries, Africans had come to depend on imported goods like iron hoes and cotton clothing, which they could no longer afford. A sensible strategy would have been to opt out of the market and grow their own food. But colonial governments, eager for tax revenues, forced African villagers to continue to plant cash crops for export. Years

of hardship followed during which school attendance declined.

Conditions were equally bleak where export commodities were produced on plantations. Brazil, the world's largest coffee producer, also experienced the steep fall in prices when coffee consumption in the United States and Europe declined. Exporters destroyed huge stockpiles of Brazilian coffee hoping that decreasing the supply would increase global prices. Agricultural workers left the plantations to scratch a living out of the soil or to join the destitute in the burgeoning *favelas,* or urban slums. The situation was similar in Southeast Asia, after a global decline in automobile and bicycle production caused rubber prices to crash. In Vietnam, as in Brazil, unemployed plantation workers were left destitute.

In the villages of India, the drop in crop prices further squeezed farmers who were already, in the words of Halide Edib, "at the mercy of rain, moneylender, and tax-gatherer." By 1932 peasant incomes had fallen by half. To avoid losing their land, many families sold the gold jewelry they were saving for their daughters' dowries. In the 1930s billions of rupees worth of such "distress gold" were sold, and many marriages were delayed or canceled. At the same time, many South Asian Muslims were forced to cancel plans to perform the *hajj,* the pilgrimage to Mecca and Medina that could take a lifetime of planning. As cotton prices plunged and textile factories in Europe and the United States cut production or closed, Egyptian farmers were struck equally hard. Whereas over 16,000 people a year traveled from Egypt to Arabia before 1929, only about 1,700 made the pilgrimage in 1933.

These were also troubled times in Halide Edib's native Turkey. To build up its own industrial base and make the country less dependent on foreign imports, the government pursued a policy of "import substitution," using high tariffs to protect local industries.. Also adopted in some Latin American countries, the import-substitution approach did create more light manufacturing enterprises in previously import-dependent countries like Turkey and Argentina, but was not a solution to the economic malaise caused by the steep drop in overall global trade, in fact contributing even further to its decline.

Fascism, Communism, and Authoritarianism

While economic crisis led to greater government intervention in democratic nations, liberalism was being directly challenged by authoritarian ideologies in Italy, Germany, and the Soviet Union, countries where it had much shallower roots.

Fascists, most notably Benito Mussolini in Italy and Adolf Hitler in Germany, were contemptuous of representative government. Weak, vain, and vacillating politicians should be replaced by strong leaders who represented not self-interested factions but the people as a whole. Only then, they promised, could national greatness be achieved. Unity of purpose and the role of the state in organizing the collective will were more important in fascist thinking than individual rights. Fascists were extreme nationalists, and while racism was strongly present across the world—from the segregated cities and schools of the United States to the racially based empires of Britain and France—the German Nazis imposed racial policies of unprecedented severity. Germany's Jews were the principal target.

Communists also had no use for liberal democracy. But in opposing an emphasis on individual rights, communists underplayed national unity while emphasizing class solidarity. The workers of each nation, after uniting to overthrow their oppressors, would unite to create global socialism. In reality, the Soviet Union was the only existing communist society in the 1930s. As Stalin collectivized agriculture, nationalized industrialization, and purged the state of his perceived enemies, the Soviet people lived in perpetual fear and deprivation.

Although fascists and communists hated each other passionately, they shared a common loathing for liberal democracy. Following the Great Depression, with the democratic nations struggling to restore their vitality without much success, many came to believe that fascism and communism were the cure.

Mussolini and the Rise of Fascism

For **Benito Mussolini** (1883–1945) the state bound the people together: "Everything for the state, nothing against the state, no one outside the state." The term *fascism* derives from an ancient symbol of authority: the Roman *fascio*, wood branches bound around an axe. Individual branches can be snapped, but together they are unbreakable. Mussolini was bitterly disappointed by the performance of the Italian government and military during World War I, and he was also offended by Italy's treatment at the Paris Peace Conference. In the postwar period he organized quasi-military groups made up largely of former soldiers, called Blackshirts, who assaulted socialists and communists in the streets. Their belligerence intimidated middle-class politicians, whose weakness, Mussolini thought, could allow Bolshevism to spread to Italy. Mussolini's supporters called him *Il Duce* **(ill DOO-chey)**, "the leader."

It was true that disunity made the country vulnerable. Social tensions accompanied industrialization in the north, while the south was still mired in the poverty that had driven many to emigrate abroad. The existing constitution seemed unable to reconcile regional and class divisions. The Catholic Church, though dominating the lives of most Italians, was also powerless to bridge such divides.

Mussolini stepped in, with supreme confidence and determination, offering order, discipline, and unity. His passion contrasted with the style of most politicians. Landowners and industrialists financed the fascists as his Blackshirts harassed union leaders, broke strikes, and kept disaffected farm laborers and tenants in line. In 1922 he maneuvered his way into the prime minister's position, and it seemed for a

Benito Mussolini (1883–1945) Prime minister of Italy and the world's first fascist leader. Also known as Il Duce, he founded the Italian Fascist Party and formed an alliance with Hitler's Germany.

fascism Authoritarian political doctrine based on extreme nationalism, elevation of the state at the expense of the individual, and replacement of independent social organization in civil society with state organizations.

time that the fascists would be willing to work within the framework of Italy's representative, democratic constitution. As the violence of fascist thugs continued, however, the Italian middle class became disillusioned. Mussolini responded by consolidating his power, arresting opponents and outlawing their political parties. After 1926 Mussolini ruled as dictator.

The foundation of liberty in liberal societies is free association: organizations formed voluntarily by people who share common interests. Mussolini had no sympathy with this idea. Instead, he installed a system of "corporations" by which all citizens involved in a common undertaking would be organized by the state. His government replaced independent unions with state-sanctioned ones and took over the nation's youth organizations. In theory, fascist government controlled the activities of everyone, though the fascists never actually achieved that level of intrusion. (See the feature "Movement of Ideas: Fascism and Youth.")

Mussolini's politics consisted of pageantry, singing, flag waving, marching, and stirring oratory. He often invoked Rome's imperial past and promised to make it once again the center of a mighty empire. In 1935, in defiance of the League of Nations, he invaded Ethiopia to avenge Italy's defeat at the Battle of Adowa by King Menelik's army in 1896 (see Chapter 26). Fervent patriotism was another way to bind the Italian people together.

Some Italians were active supporters of Mussolini's regime. Others paid for opposition to Mussolini with their lives, usually Italian communists. Most Italians did not care too much one way or the other, and simply went on with their daily lives.

Hitler and National Socialism in Germany

After World War I, Germany was both humiliated and financially devastated by the war and the punitive Versailles treaty. Although the Weimar Republic had brought liberal democracy to Germany in the 1920s, progress ended with the onset of the Great Depression. Germans were desperate for solutions. By the early 1930s the center was falling out of German politics, as communists on the far left and fascists on the extreme right gained popularity.

Into this environment stepped **Adolf Hitler** (1889–1945) and his National Socialist Party. Hitler had a very different idea than did liberals or socialists of what "the people" meant. Socialists believed that "the people" meant the masses of workers, and liberals believed that each individual was autonomous and that "the people" was simply the sum of those individuals. For Hitler, however, *das Volk* (**dahs vohlk**), "the people," was a single organism bound by history, tradition, and race. All Germans were connected by their racial destiny. Hitler defined Germans as an "Aryan" race superior to all others.

According to Nazism, any German who did not live up to the ideal of racial pride and racial purity needed to be excised. Nazi targets included communists, homosexuals, and the handicapped. Proponents of the racist pseudo-science of eugenics (also popular in the United States in the 1930s) argued that selective breeding could lead to superior human beings. If the smartest "Aryan" men and women married and had children, they could produce a "master race." Hitler was obsessed with what he saw as the "polluting" effects of racial mixing.

Looking for a scapegoat on which to blame the country's problems, he tapped into the centuries-old tradition of anti-Semitism. Although German Jews were thoroughly assimilated into national life, he identified them as the threat: "The personification of the devil as the symbol of all evil assumes the living shape of the Jew." For the Nazis, the characteristics of Jews illuminated the virtues of the German *Volk,* by contrast. Only by isolating the Jews could the goal of racial purity be achieved.

In the late 1920s such ideas were on the far fringe. But after the Great Depression, voters increasingly abandoned moderate views. Between 1928 and 1932 the National Socialist share of the vote jumped from 2.6 to 37.3 percent of the national total, and Hitler's deputies controlled more than a third of the seats in the Reichstag. His main supporters came from lower-middle-class people

Adolf Hitler (1889–1945) Leader of the National Socialist Party who became chancellor of Germany and dismantled the Weimar constitution. His ultranationalist policies led to persecution of communists and Jews, and his aggressive foreign policies started World War II.

Fascism and Youth

Fascists made a special appeal to youth, hoping to tap into the idealism of young people and their desire to be part of an exciting movement greater than themselves. Because fascism appealed to the emotions more than to reason, there were few philosophical statements of fascist principles. Perhaps the most coherent is the one extracted below, co-written by Benito Mussolini and the fascist political philosopher Giovanni Gentile in 1932.

The second document, published in a South African newspaper in 1938, shows how such fascist ideas spread to other parts of the world. It was an entry in a newspaper essay contest, written by a sixteen-year-old girl named Elsa Joubert. That year Afrikaner nationalists, descendants of the Boers who had claimed much of South Africa in the nineteenth century (see Chapter 26), staged an elaborate series of public ceremonies to mark the one-hundredth anniversary of the victory of "voortrekkers" ("pioneers") over a Zulu army. That miraculous victory, the nationalists claimed, had demonstrated God's covenant with the Afrikaner people to give them South Africa as their "promised land." Torches were carried by modern-day "voortrekkers" from across the country to the capital of Pretoria, where a bonfire was lit as part of the dedication of a nationalist museum, the Voortrekker Monument. In the 1930s Afrikaner nationalists used such rituals to unite their people against both South Africa's black majority and the English-speaking white immigrants who dominated the economy.

Benito Mussolini and Giovanni Gentile: "The Doctrine of Fascism"

Fascism sees in the world not only those superficial, material aspects in which man appears as an individual, standing by himself, self-centered, subject to natural law, which instinctively urges him toward a life of selfish and momentary pleasure; it sees not only the individual but the nation and the country; individuals and generations bound together by a moral law, with common traditions and a mission which suppressing the instinct for life closed in a brief circle of pleasure, builds up a higher life, founded on duty, a life free from the limitations of time and space, in which the individual, by self-sacrifice, the renunciation of self-interest, by death itself, can achieve that purely spiritual existence in which his value as a man consists....

Therefore life, as conceived of by the Fascist, is serious, austere, and religious; all its manifestations are poised in a world sustained by moral forces and subject to spiritual responsibilities. The Fascist disdains an "easy" life....

Anti-individualistic, the Fascist conception of life stresses the importance of the State and accepts the individual only in so far as his interests coincide with those of the State.... Liberalism denied the State in the name of the individual; Fascism reasserts the rights of the State as expressing the real essence of the individual.... Fascism stands for liberty, and for the only liberty worth having, the liberty of the State and of the individual within the State. The Fascist conception of the State is all embracing; outside of it no human or spiritual values can exist, much less have value. Thus understood, Fascism, is totalitarian, and the Fascist State ... interprets [and] develops ... the whole life of a people.

Source: Mussolini text from http://www.worldfuturefund. org/wffmaster/Reading/Germany/mussolini.htm, *Fascism Doctrine and Institutions*, 1935, pp. 7–42.

Elsa Joubert: "Young South Africa"

The hearts of three thousand Voortrekkers, each of whom in his own town had formed a link in the chain of the Torch Marathon, beat faster when they saw the light of the torch coming towards them over the hills in the dusk....

The hill is on fire; on fire with Afrikaner fire; on fire with the enthusiasm of Young South Africa! You are nothing—your People is all. One light in the dusk is puny and small. But three thousand flames. Three thousand! And more! There's hope for your future, South Africa!

The mighty procession brings the torches to the festival ground where thousands await them. A matchless, unprecedented enthusiasm in the darkness of the night. Numerous prayers of thanks for the torches rise up, many a quiet tear is wiped away. The torches get their "Welcome home."

Behind them, like a blazing snake in the night, the belt of fire coils down the hillside. On the festival grounds the two torches set alight a huge joyous fire. Around it march the three thousand Voortrekkers and each throws his small puny torch upon it—to form one great might Afrikaner fire.

The logs crackle as they burn. As they crackle so they exult—"The torches set us alight. Now we again set you alight, O youth of our South Africa! Come along there's work to do."

Source: Joubert quoted in T. Dunbar Moodie, *The Rise of Afrikanerdom: Power, Apartheid, and the Afrikaner Civil Religion* (Berkeley: University of California Press, 1975).

QUESTIONS FOR ANALYSIS

▶ According to Mussolini and Gentile, how are fascist values different from liberal ones?

▶ To what extent does the essay by a teenage South African girl reflect the fascist values promoted in the first document?

Mary Evans Picture Library/The Image Works

National Socialist Propaganda   The Nazi Party often used images of healthy blond children to emphasize German vitality and racial superiority and organized young people into party-based boys' and girls' clubs. This poster for the "League of German Girls" solicits donations to a fund to "Build Youth Hostels and Homes." In spite of her smile, and the flowers on the swastika-labeled collection tin, all of the money collected actually went into weapons production.

⧉ **Primary Source: The Centerpiece of Nazi Racial Legislation: The Nuremberg Laws** *These laws defined who was a Jew, forbade marriage between Germans and Jews, and paved the way for the Holocaust.*

Hitler, they thought he would be able to rally the public against communism. While President Hindenburg was reluctant to elevate Hitler, he needed Hitler's support to form a governing coalition, which Hitler would join only if he were made chancellor. In 1933 Hindenburg announced a new government with Hitler at its head.

A month after he took office, fire broke out in the Reichstag. The arson was likely the work of a single individual, but Hitler accused the Communist Party of treason and had all Communist members of the Reichstag arrested. The remaining representatives then passed a law that suspended constitutional protections of civil liberties for four years and allowed Hitler to rule as a dictator.

Hitler became the *Führer* (leader) of an industrial state of huge potential power. Changes to German society were sudden and extreme. The Nazis abolished all political parties other than the National Socialists and replaced Germany's federal structure with a centralized dictatorship emanating from Berlin. As in Italy, they took over or replaced independent organizations in civil society such as labor unions. Protestant churches came under tight state control. Hitler Youth replaced the Boy Scouts and church-sponsored youth groups as part of a plan, reinforced by a new school curriculum, to teach fascism to the next generation. Hitler promised a Third Reich ("Third Empire") that would last a thousand years.

Having sent the communists off to prison camps, the Führer **(FY-ruh-r)** turned to the "Jewish problem." In 1935 the Nazis imposed the Nuremberg Laws, which deprived Jews of all civil rights and forbade intermarriage between Jews and other Germans. Some Jews emigrated, but many felt so at home in Germany that they did not want to leave. They were further awakened to the threat they faced when, in 1938, the Nazis launched coordinated attacks against them throughout Germany and Austria. After this "Kristallnacht," named for the smashing of the windows of Jewish homes, synagogues, and stores, more Jews fled. Those who remained were forced into segregated ghettos.

Hitler's dictatorship, like Mussolini's, relied on either active support or passive consent from the majority of the population. Part of his appeal derived from his identification of scapegoats - communists and Jews - who could be

who did not have savings or job security, as well as from young people caught up in Hitler's emotional, patriotic appeals. Almost half the party members were under thirty.

German business leaders were alarmed when the Communist Party also gained strong support in the elections of 1932. Although most despised blamed for the country's problems. But Hitler's popularity also stemmed from his economic successes. While the Western democracies struggled with joblessness, German unemployment dropped from over 6 million to under 200,000 between 1932 and 1938. The government fixed prices and allocated resources in close coordination with Germany's largest corporations. Massive public works projects, such as the world's first superhighways and a large military buildup, put Germans back to work.

With communists and Jews out of the way, Hitler promised, traditional values of courage, order, and discipline would once again inspire and empower the German people. Women's highest calling was to stay in the home and nurture purebred Aryan children. The Nazis' massive rallies, with their precision marching, flag waving, and the spell-binding speeches by the Führer himself, turned politics into theater and gave people a sense of being part of something much larger than themselves. Radio broadcasts and expertly made propaganda films spread the excitement throughout the land.

Of course, not everyone was taken in. But outspoken opposition to Hitler meant imprisonment or death. Most Germans were content to go about their daily lives, appreciative of the relative order and prosperity.

Stalin: Collectivization and the Great Purges

For all the ambition of Mussolini and Hitler, neither could match the total control of society achieved by Joseph Stalin (1879–1953). While Stalin's totalitarian control predated the global depression and was independent of it, the Soviet Union also saw an escalation of state power in the 1930s.

Starting in 1928, Stalin launched the U.S.S.R. on a path of rapid industrialization based on centralized Five-Year Plans. Since most of the country was still agricultural, Stalin needed policies that applied to rural areas as well. Lenin had promised the peasants land, and his New Economic Policy allowed small-scale private ownership in the countryside. But for many communists this policy was an aberration, since private ownership would lead to agrarian capitalism. Instead, Stalin ordered the

collectivization of the rural sector and suddenly moved millions of peasants into barracks on collective farms.

There was substantial resistance to collectivization, which Stalin attributed to the *kulaks* (koo-LAHKS), rich peasants out to exploit their fellow villagers. When he sent the Red Army into the countryside, he said it was to help the masses defeat these kulaks. In reality, the Soviet state was waging war on its own people. In 1932–1933, Stalin's use of the army to impose collectivization resulted in famine. Ukrainians suffered the most, in punishment for their attempt to establish an independent republic after the First World War.

But the industrial sector continued to expand rapidly. The Communist Party bureaucracy treated the non-Russian parts of the Soviet Union, especially in Central Asia, in colonial fashion, as sources of raw material for industrial growth in the Russian heartland. In contrast with other industrial societies, there was no unemployment in the Soviet Union. But workers' wages were kept low to generate investment for further industrial expansion. Rapid industrialization also poisoned the air and water. A network of *gulags* (GOO-lahgs), or prison camps, became the destination for anyone who ran afoul of communist authority.

In the later 1930s Stalin, always paranoid about plots against him, stepped up his repression of the Old Bolsheviks. During the **Great Purges**, Stalin ordered the arrest of many former colleagues of Lenin and forced them to confess to supposed crimes. Movie cameras recorded their statements before they were taken out and shot. In 1937 alone, half of the officer corps of the army was imprisoned or executed. Even as he killed and imprisoned his generals, Stalin ordered a massive military buildup to protect the Soviet Union from the likelihood of yet another German invasion.

Primary Source: Speech to the National Socialist Women's Association, September 1935 *Learn what the Nazis believed were the proper roles for women in society—from the woman appointed to disseminate their beliefs.*

collectivization Stalin's replacement of peasant villages with large, state-run collective farms, following the idea of "Socialism in One Country." Millions died.

Great Purges The execution by Stalin in the late 1930s of many "Old Bolsheviks" he regarded as competitors for power. Public trials and forced confessions marked the Great Purges.

Authoritarian Regimes in Asia

In many other parts of the world where liberal traditions were absent or only weakly developed, the uncertainty of the postwar period and the economic crisis of the Great Depression strengthened authoritarianism. In Japan and Turkey, charismatic rulers gained authority, the state intervened more in the economy and society, and single-party states developed.

Ultranationalism in Japan

Although the Versailles treaty had rewarded Japan with territorial concessions at China's expense, nationalists remained dissatisfied:

> We are like a great crowd of people packed into a small and narrow room, and there are only three doors through which we might escape, namely, emigration, advance into world markets, and expansion of territory. The first door has been barred to us by the anti-Japanese immigration policies of other countries. The second is being pushed shut by tariff barriers…. It is quite natural that Japan should rush upon the last remaining door … of territorial expansion.[2]

The Great Depression strengthened the arguments of nationalists and militarists for a more aggressive foreign and imperial policy.

In the 1920s the country had shown signs of heading in a more democratic direction. Japan was a constitutional monarchy, with an emperor whose role was ceremonial. Voting rights were extended to more Japanese men, and the cabinet was no longer chosen by imperial advisers but by the party that gained the most votes in elections. But other factors limited liberal democracy in Japan. One was the power of civil service bureaucrats who controlled policy together with the *zaibatsu*, Japan's large industrial conglomerates.

Invasion of Manchuria (1931) Invasion that occurred when Japanese military officers defied the civilian government and League of Nations by occupying this northeastern Chinese province, leading to the further militarization of the Japanese government.

In 1926, when the new emperor Hirohito came to the throne, ultranationalists saw an opportunity to expand their influence. A new requirement stipulated that the minister of defense be an active military officer with power nearly equal to that of the prime minister. After the market collapse of 1930, the military role in government became even greater.

Ultranationalists in Japan envisioned a new Asian economic system that would combine Japanese management and capital with the resources and cheap labor of East and Southeast Asia. The turning point came in 1931 with the **Invasion of Manchuria**. As part of the postwar settlement, the Japanese had been allowed to keep soldiers in the Manchurian capital, though Manchuria was still formally a province of China. Then Japanese military commanders in Manchuria, in defiance of civilian politicians in Tokyo, ordered their soldiers to leave their barracks and occupy the main population centers and the transportation infrastructure. Brought to trial, the disobedient soldiers denounced the government and used the courtroom to whip up public support for the army's ambitions. As imperial fever grew, civilian politicians lost what little control they had over the military.

As in Italy and Germany, militarization brought Japanese corporations lucrative government contracts. And as in the fascist countries, Japan's economic policies seemed successful. Military spending, even if it required government borrowing, boosted the economy, as did the occupation of Manchuria. After 1932, expanding employment opportunities that benefited the Japanese working class further solidified the ultranationalists' political support.

The Rise of Modern Turkey

The new nation of Turkey emerged from the violent collapse of the Ottoman Empire in an exceptionally hostile environment. Without the leadership of **Mustafa Kemal** (1881–1938), a former Ottoman officer, Turkey may well have been partitioned. For his role, he earned the name Atatürk, "Father Turk." By 1923 the great powers agreed to recognize a sovereign Turkish republic that retained the core territories and population of the old empire.

Halide Edib played an important role. In 1919, as the Ottoman Empire crumbled before British and Greek invaders, she stood before a crowd of thousands and rallied them to the cause of Turkish nationalism. Her heart, she later wrote, "was beating in response to all Turkish hearts, warning of approaching disaster.... I was part of this sublime national madness.... Nothing else mattered for me in life at all." She and her husband then went to join Kemal's forces in Ankara, where she became one of the nationalist leader's closest confidantes. After independence was secured, however, they had a falling out. Whereas Edib and her husband led a party that favored the expansion of liberal democracy, Kemal intended to be the unchallenged leader of an absolutist state. "What I mean is this," he told her. "I want everyone to do as I wish.... I do not want any criticism or advice. I will have only my own way. All shall do as I command." According to her memoirs Edib responded, "I will obey you and do as you wish as long as I believe you are serving the cause." But Kemal ignored her and said, "You shall obey me and do as I wish." Shortly thereafter he banned her political party and she went into exile.

Having forged a new country through war, Mustafa Kemal put his personal stamp on the ideas that would guide Turkey for decades to come. His goal was to put Turkey on an equal economic and military footing with the European powers, and he ordered rapid modernization to achieve that end. In the nineteenth century, the Ottoman Empire had vacillated about how much it should adopt Western models. Kemal had no second thoughts in imposing a secular constitution with a strict line between mosque and state.

Kemal's drive to separate religion from politics included laws to improve the status of women. Girls and young women were given increased access to education, a move Edib

Turkey's New Alphabet   The Turkish leader Mustafa Kemal instituted a top-down program of modernization and westernization in the new nation of Turkey. In 1928, he declared that Turkish would no longer be written in Arabic script and that Latin characters would henceforth be used for all purposes, public and private. Here Kemal himself demonstrates the new alphabet.

strongly supported. Not surprisingly, after the emotional pain she suffered when her first husband took a second wife, she also favored the Turkish law abolishing polygamy. Edib applauded when, in 1930, Turkey became the first predominantly Muslim country in which women had the right to vote.

On the other hand, she critiqued the authoritarian means by which these reforms were attained. When Kemal banned Turkish women from wearing the veil in all government buildings,

Mustafa Kemal (1881–1938) Also known as Atatürk, an Ottoman officer who led the nationalist army that established the Republic of Turkey in 1923. A reformer who established the secular traditions of the modern Turkish state, he served as its leader until his death.

schools, and public spaces, Edib argued that while the veil should never be imposed on women, neither should it be banned by governments. "Wherever religion is interfered with by governments, it becomes a barrier, and an unremovable one, to peace and understanding."[3] Education and freedom to choose were the keys to reform. Impatient of gradual reform, Kemal simply imposed his own will on the nation.

Mustafa Kemal's modernization policies depended on centralized state power. After export prices fell in 1930, his government taxed the countryside heavily to finance state-sponsored industrialization. Along with imposing high tariffs on foreign products, this industrial policy sought to replace imported goods with domestic manufactures. But as long as trade was inhibited and the global economy remained stagnant, the shadow of the Great Depression would remain. When Mustafa Kemal died in 1938 and Halide Edib returned home the next year to become professor of English at the University of Istanbul, the problem remained unresolved.

Anticolonial Nationalism in Asia and Africa

Authoritarian colonial regimes were already well established in Africa, South Asia, and Southeast Asia in the 1920s. The economic crisis of the Great Depression, however, led colonial powers to exploit their colonies even more. Harsh policies, such as the use of forced labor, combined with the general decline in the global economy to spread distress throughout Africa and Asia. As a result, movements of anticolonial nationalism gathered strength.

These forces were strongest in India, where **Mohandas K. Gandhi** (1869–1948) and the Indian National Congress organized mass resistance to British rule. In Africa and most of Southeast Asia, mass nationalism was in an earlier stage of development. Nevertheless, by the 1930s a new generation of Western-educated leaders was forging links with mass supporters in both Africa and Asia.

Mohandas K. Gandhi (1869–1948) Indian political leader who organized mass support for the Indian National Congress against British rule. His political philosophy of nonviolent resistance had worldwide influence.

Gandhi and the Indian National Congress

Halide Edib traveled to India in 1935. Speaking before an audience at the National Muslim University, her thoughts were more on someone in the audience than on her own speech.

Looking out at the "fragile figure" before her, she wrote in her book *Inside India,* "I was thinking about the quality of Mahatma Gandhi's greatness." Gandhi had turned the Indian National Congress into the voice of India.

Before 1914, the Congress Party had been a reformist organization, seeking greater participation of Indians in their own governance but accepting the basic outlines of British rule. Given the contribution Indians had made to the British war effort, they expected to be rewarded with substantial political reform. But the British offered only modest proposals.

Then in 1919 the Amritsar Massacre shocked the nation. Although the British had banned public meetings, a crowd gathering for a religious ceremony was unaware of that order. To assert colonial authority, a British officer ordered his Indian troops to fire directly into the crowd, which was confined in a garden area. The soldiers fired 1,650 rounds of ammunition, leaving 400 dead and 1,200 wounded. Cooperation turned to confrontation, and in 1920 the Congress Party launched its first mass public protest to gain *Hind Swaraj,* Indian self-rule.

By then Gandhi, a Western-educated lawyer, had discarded European dress for the spare clothing of an ascetic Hindu holy man. His philosophy was in fact influenced by both traditions. Western ideals of equality informed his insistence that the so-called Untouchables, those considered outside and beneath the Hindu caste hierarchy, be given full rights and recognition as human beings. But his two main principles were from the South Asian tradition. *Ahimsa* (**uh-HIM-sah**), or absolute nonviolence, was at the center of Gandhi's moral philosophy. *Satyagraha* (**SUHT-yuh-gruh-huh**), or "soul force," was the application of that philosophy to politics. Gandhi believed that it is self-defeating to use violence to counter violence, no matter how just the cause. The moral force of his arguments earned him the title *Mahatma,* "Great Soul."

But in 1920, after the British threw Gandhi and other Congress leaders in jail, violence did accompany the first mass campaigns of civil disobedience. Deciding that the Indian people were not ready to achieve self-rule through satyagraha, Gandhi retreated to his *ashram* (**AHSH-ruhm**), a communal rural home, and spun cotton on a simple spinning wheel for hours at a time. The gentle clicking of the wheel stimulated meditation, and Gandhi stressed that Indians should produce their own simple cloth at home rather than import the British textiles that had, since the nineteenth century, represented imperial economic exploitation.

In 1930 Gandhi re-emerged to lead another campaign of mass civil disobedience. In his Salt March, he walked hundreds of miles to the sea to defy a British law that forbade Indians from using ocean water to make their own salt. While the Salt March galvanized his supporters and received international press coverage, the British responded with a combination of repression and concessions. After initially jailing Congress leaders, they then compromised with the Government of India Act of 1935, which called for elections of semirepresentative regional assemblies. The Congress Party won huge victories in the following elections, but the law was far short of complete self-government.

While Gandhi remained the symbol of Indian nationalism, other strong political actors emerged. In 1928 the young Jawaharlal Nehru (1889–1964), a British-educated son of a wealthy Congress leader, was elected president of the party. Although a follower of Gandhi, he did not think the moral transformation of Indian society was a necessary prerequisite for self-rule. Also, he was a socialist who believed in industrialization.

Whereas Gandhi idealized the simplicity of village life, Nehru saw the "backwardness" of rural India as an obstacle to progress.

Though Gandhi used Hindu symbols to rally mass support, he and Nehru agreed that the Indian National Congress should be open to members of all faiths. That did not reassure leaders of the new Muslim League, who feared that under self-rule they would be oppressed by the Hindu majority.

Gandhi did his best to reassure the Muslim community, and Nehru's vision was of a secular state in which religion would play no part. Based on her visit to India, Halide Edib was confident that nationalist unity could transcend religious differences. Nevertheless, distrust between the two communities increased. During the 1930s, Muslim League members conceived of a separate state for Muslim-majority areas. But in 1939 state power still rested with the British, who insisted that their presence as a neutral arbiter between India's diverse peoples would be necessary far into the future.

Colonialism in Africa and Southeast Asia

Nationalist movements were also developing in Africa and Southeast Asia during this period. As in India, Western-educated leaders were beginning to create political structures that could mobilize large numbers of people to challenge European authority. Nevertheless, European powers continued to rule Africa and most of Southeast Asia with confidence.

While the British, French, Dutch, Belgians, and Portuguese each developed particular modes of colonial rule, similar features prevailed. For example, it was too expensive to staff colonial administrations solely with European personnel. While the top positions were always reserved for Europeans, it made sense to educate members of the colonized society as clerks, nurses, and primary school teachers. However, in the process of being educated, young Africans and Southeast Asians also learned about the French Revolution and the traditional liberties of British subjects. They could not help but reflect on their own situations and aspire for greater freedom.

© Dinodia Photos/Alamy

Gandhi's Salt March   In 1930 Mohandas K. Gandhi received significant international press coverage when he and his followers marched 240 miles from his ashram to the sea to make salt. It was a perfect example of nonviolent civil disobedience, since the manufacture of salt was a legal monopoly of the British Indian government.

The gap between aspirations and realities for Western-educated members of colonized societies was stark. In the French colonies, for instance, despite studying French history, speaking French perfectly, and being immersed in French culture, *évolués* (**ay-vol-yoo-ay**) ("evolved ones") were still regarded as *indigenes* (**ihn-deh-JEN**), "natives" who were automatically inferior. The same dynamic was true in the Dutch East Indies, where people of mixed race, educated in Dutch schools, could never be social equals of the colonizers. The British, too, relied on Western-educated youth in places like Nigeria and Burma to carry out essential administrative tasks, yet there was no inkling of assimilation, no idea that Nigerians or Burmese could ever "become English." Still, Africans and Asians educated in English often emulated British cultural models, despite being rejected as equals.

The European policy of relying on indigenous figureheads spurred additional resentments that drove nationalist feelings among Western-educated Africans and Asians. In Southeast Asia, for example, the Vietnamese emperors of the Nguyen dynasty continued in office. Malaysian sultans were also given privileged positions. In Africa, the British brought the king of Asante back from exile. The British called their administrative structure "indirect rule," priding themselves on the respect they showed to local custom. In reality, European colonists forged alliances with traditional ruling elites to help maintain order and collect taxes. By the 1930s impatient nationalists increasingly saw such figures as hindrances to self-rule.

"Indirect rule" promoted local ethnic affiliations while forestalling the emergence of broader national identities. The British in particular divided Africans into discrete "tribes" and played their leaders against one another to secure continued control. One of the nationalists who deplored this policy was the Nigerian Nnamdi Azikiwe (NAHM-dee ah-zee-KEE-way) (1904–1996). From the largely Christian southeast, Azikiwe argued that only if all Nigerians identified themselves with the nation as a whole, whatever their ethnic and religious backgrounds, would they be able to struggle effectively for self-rule. Having stowed away on a ship to the United States in 1925 and then graduated from the University of Pennsylvania, Azikiwe returned to West Africa in 1937 and founded the Nigerian Youth Movement while editing the *West African Pilot,* a newspaper dedicated to inspiring Africans to challenge British colonial policies.

During the 1930s sporadic popular uprisings in Africa and Southeast Asia had only limited effect because they were not connected to larger political organizations. In the **Igbo Women's War** of 1929, for example, women in southeastern Nigeria rebelled against British household headcounts for tax purposes, which they saw as an invasion of privacy. Using traditional Igbo (ee-BWOH) means of protesting male abuse of authority, the women dressed up in special costumes, gathered in large numbers, and sang songs of derision to shame the African chiefs who acted as tax collectors. The British modified their tax system slightly in response, but there were no wider reforms. The women lacked a broader organization to connect their local efforts with a wider anticolonial struggle.

Colonial tensions were strongest where Europeans came as settlers, such as in South Africa and Kenya. Here Africans had lost not only their sovereignty but also their best farming and herding land. In East Africa in the 1920s, the British colony of Kenya saw the rise of a mass protest movement among Kikuyu farmers who had lost land to white settlers.

Igbo Women's War (1929) Rebellion led by women in colonial Nigeria who used traditional cultural practices to protest British taxation policies.

As in the Nigerian Women's War, however, the Kikuyu protests were too localized to secure substantial colonial reform. Meanwhile, however, a young Kenyan leader named Jomo Kenyatta (1895–1978) was earning a doctorate in anthropology from the London School of Economics. Only later, after the Second World War, would Kenyatta return and lead a nationalist movement that connected the ambitions of Western-educated Africans with the grievances of peasants and workers.

Across Africa and Southeast Asia, the Great Depression made the already difficult conditions of colonialism even worse. Colonial policies forced farmers in Africa to plant export crops, despite drops in world prices that made their crops virtually worthless. Such diversion from subsistence farming resulted in food shortages. Unemployment rose in Malaya, Vietnam, and the Dutch East Indies after 1929 when the drop in automobile manufacturing depressed the world market for rubber. Even where small-scale farmers stopped growing export crops and focused on food crops for their own consumption, colonial governments still required cash payment of taxes and were willing to use force to compel those payments. The French penalized Vietnamese peasants who did not pay taxes with forced labor on government projects and French-owned plantations. As in Africa, however, the peoples of French Indochina still lacked the organizational and ideological means for effective resistance.

Africa and Southeast Asia have been called the "quiescent colonies" during this period. But in larger historical perspective, the 1930s were merely a pause in the resistance to colonial occupation that began in the late nineteenth century. Nationalist leaders during this time were laying the foundations for the large-scale movements of mass nationalism that would emerge at the end of the new worldwide military conflict about to erupt.

The Road to War

In the 1930s numerous events in Asia, Africa, Asia, and Europe heralded a coming conflict. After the trauma of 1914–1918, the world's people barely had a chance to catch their breath before the coming of another, even more global and more violent total war.

Not content with the occupation of Manchuria, Japanese militarists sought a greater Asian empire. Having already left the League of Nations, they launched a savage attack on coastal China in 1937, in defiance of international law. Fighting between the Guomindang government of Chiang Kai-shek and Communist revolutionaries led by Mao Zedong had made China particularly vulnerable. Attacked in 1927 by their former Guomindang allies, the Communists had retreated to the interior. During the Long March of 1934–1936, they walked some 7,500 miles (12,000 km) to consolidate a base in the northeast. After the Japanese invaded, Chiang and Mao agreed to cease their hostilities and fight the common Japanese enemy, but they never combined forces or coordinated their efforts (see Map 28.1).

The Japanese invaders treated Chinese soldiers and civilians alike with callous brutality. During the **Rape of Nanjing**, Japanese soldiers killed hundreds of thousands of Chinese civilians, using tactics such as gang rape and mutilation of children to spread terror among the population. Total war, with its disregard of the distinction between soldiers and civilians, was being taken to a new level.

The inability of international institutions to counter military aggression was similarly demonstrated by the Italian occupation of Ethiopia in 1935, an attack that featured airplanes dropping poison gas on both civilians and soldiers. The Ethiopian emperor Hailie Selassie (1892–1975) went to the League of Nations for help:

> I ask the fifty-two nations, who have given the Ethiopian people a promise to help them in their resistance to the aggressor, what are they willing to do for Ethiopia? And the great Powers who have promised the guarantee of collective security to small States on whom weighs the threat that they may one day suffer the fate of Ethiopia, I ask what measures do you intend to take? Representatives of the world, I have come to Geneva to discharge in your midst the most painful of the duties of the head of a State. What reply shall I have to take back to my people?

The emperor warned that if the international community did not take effective action, no small nation would ever be safe. The League of Nations placed economic sanctions on Mussolini but took no further action. With access to colonial resources, such as Libyan oil, and with aid from the German government, the sanctions had little effect.

Meanwhile German and Italian fascists saw their movement gaining ground in Spain. In 1936, a democratically elected Spanish government was implementing socialist policies to deal with the crisis of the Great Depression. In reaction, Spanish conservatives took up arms under the leadership of General Francisco Franco (1892–1975) to overthrow the Republicans and the liberal constitution. During the **Spanish Civil War** (1936–1939) the Soviet Union supported the Republicans, while the Nazis supported Franco and his quasi-fascist movement. France, Britain, and the United States remained neutral. Mired in their own domestic concerns, they missed this chance to support democracy against fascism, although some young people in the Western democracies did form volunteer brigades to fight with the Spanish Republicans. Nevertheless, aided by the German air force, by 1939 Franco was victorious.

Rape of Nanjing   Slaughter in 1937 by the Japanese army of hundreds of thousands of Chinese civilians during their occupation of the city. The soldiers used tactics such as gang rape and child mutilation to spread terror among the Chinese population.

Spanish Civil War (1936–1939) Conflict between conservative nationalist forces, led by General Francisco Franco and backed by Germany, and Republican forces; also backed by the Soviet Union. The Spanish Civil War was seen by many as a prelude to renewed world war.

Map 28.1 The Japanese Invasion of China

Six years after the invasion of Manchuria (see Chapter 27), Japanese forces began conquest of coastal China in 1937, quickly taking Beijing, Shanghai, and other major cities. Chinese resistance, though extensive, was limited by divisions between the Guomindang government of Chiang Kai-shek and the Communists led by Mao Zedong. Expelled from coastal cities by the Guomindang after 1927, the Communists relocated first to the southern interior and then, after their dramatic Long March, established a new base in the northeastern Shaanxi Province. © Cengage Learning

■ Interactive Map

643

© Bettmann/CORBIS

The Rape of Nanjing   One of the most brutal episodes during the Japanese invasion of China was the Rape of Nanjing. Here Japanese soldiers are seen using live captives for bayonet practice, with fellow soldiers and future victims looking on. Though the Chinese have long remembered such atrocities, until recently Japanese schoolchildren learned nothing about them.

The Western democracies were slow to respond to Hitler's imperial ambitions. He had declared that the Germans needed *lebensraum* (**LEY-buhns-rowm**), "living space," in which to pursue their racial destiny. Jews had no role in this future, while the Slavic peoples of eastern Europe and Russia were looked upon as inferior peoples who would provide manual labor under German management. Hitler declared that the ethnic Germans scattered across eastern Europe needed to be reunited with the homeland. While Stalin took this threat seriously, most Western leaders thought that Hitler could be contained. In fact, some Westerners sympathized with Hitler's anti-Semitism and anticommunism.

In 1936 Hitler moved military forces into the Rhineland region bordering France, in violation of the Versailles treaty. In 1937 the British prime minister Neville Chamberlain (1869–1940) flew to Munich to deal directly with the German dictator. Chamberlain believed that Hitler could be mollified with minor concessions and that appeasement could prevent a major European war. The British public, still scarred by the trauma of the Great War, largely supported Chamberlain's policy.

Hitler, in turn, demanded that he be allowed to occupy the Sudetenland, a region of Czechoslovakia where, he claimed, ethnic Germans were being mistreated (see Map 28.2).

Map 28.2 The Growth of Nazi Germany, 1933–1939

The major turning point in the expansion of Nazi Germany was the annexation of the Sudetenland from Czechoslovakia in 1938. Joseph Stalin interpreted British diplomatic efforts to avoid renewed world war as a sign of weakness, and he agreed to a secret treaty to divide Poland between Hitler's Germany and his own Soviet Union. The German invasion of Poland from the west in 1939 therefore triggered the annexation of eastern Poland by the Soviet Union. © Cengage Learning   **Interactive Map**

Mistrustful and thoroughly alarmed, Stalin signed a nonaggression pact with Hitler in 1939, secretly dividing Poland between them. Hitler was merely delaying his planned attack on Russia, while Stalin was playing for time to ready his country for war.

When Hitler invaded Poland on September 1, 1939, Britain and France immediately declared war on Germany but took no active military steps to confront the German army. Meanwhile, in the United States public opinion was largely opposed to another intervention in European politics. Soon, however, peoples across Europe, Africa, Asia, and the Americas would be embroiled in a total war the likes of which humanity had never seen.

Chapter Review and Learning Activities

The decade of the 1930s was a harsh time, made harsher for Halide Edib by exile from Turkey, the country she loved and had helped to create. After her return in 1939, Edib continued to write novels, served one term as a member of parliament, and taught English literature at Istanbul University. It was a relatively peaceful life after her wartime adventures and later travels. The world context remained tense, however, as she lived to witness both the violence of the Second World War and, following that conflict, the bitter international divisions of the Cold War.

How did governments in different parts of the world respond to the crisis of the Great Depression?

Governments responded in a number of ways to the collapse of global markets. Liberal democracies like the United States, France, and Britain increased government involvement in the economy, trying to cushion their citizens from the effects of the depression while nudging their economies back to life. These attempts, which represented a compromise with the existing political, social, and economic order, were less effective than the more aggressive policies pursued in places like Germany and Japan, where more intensive state economic involvement and rapid military growth created millions of jobs. The governments of some recently industrializing economies, like Turkey and many Latin American nations, used import-substitution policies to stimulate modest increases in industrial activity. Meanwhile, the Soviet Union pursued a much more intensive policy of state industrial planning, resulting in rapid economic growth but no benefit for Soviet workers, while Stalin's policy of agricultural collectivization led to great hardship in the countryside.

Why did liberal democracy decline in influence as fascism, communism, and other authoritarian regimes rose in power and popularity?

In many countries, especially those that lacked strong liberal traditions, the economic crisis of the Great Depression weakened the political center as more people turned to ideologies of the extreme right and left in their search for solutions. Fascism in Italy and Germany, ultranationalism in Japan, and the authoritarianism of governments like that of Mustafa Kemal in Turkey are examples. China's conservative Nationalist government was challenged by communist forces, but in the 1930s the Soviet Union remained the world's only communist regime.

How successful were anticolonial nationalists in Asia and Africa during this period?

The authoritarian tradition of colonialism was reinforced when European powers used harsh measures such as forced labor to spur production among their imperial subjects in Africa and South and Southeast Asia, adding to the momentum of anticolonial nationalism. The most successful resistance was led by the Indian National Congress, where Western-educated leaders like Gandhi and Nehru organized millions of Indians in their campaign for self-government. By 1935 they had extracted an agreement that allowed provincial elections, but the British remained in secure control at the top. In Africa and Southeast Asia, anticolonial protests were largely confined to the local level. Here urban-based, Western-educated nationalists were just beginning to build the political infrastructure that would later allow them to more effectively connect local resistance to national movements.

What major events led to the outbreak of the Second World War?

Throughout the 1930s militarism was on the rise. Japanese expansion, first into Manchuria and then into coastal China, the Italian invasion of Ethiopia, and Hitler's remilitarization of the Rhineland all demonstrated that the League of Nations was incapable of guaranteeing international security. The reluctance of the Western democracies to face up to the possibility of another total war was demonstrated by their neutrality in the Spanish Civil War and by Britain's policy of appeasement toward Hitler. The American novelist Ernest Hemingway wrote *For Whom the Bell Tolls* based on his experiences fighting with the Republicans in Spain. The title comes from a seventeenth-century poem by Englishman John Donne: "No man is an island, entire of itself; every man is a piece of the continent, a part of the main.... Any man's death diminishes me, because I am involved in mankind; and therefore never send to know for whom the bell tolls; it tolls for thee...." The tolling bells of the 1930s, Hemingway warned, announced a looming catastrophe.

FOR FURTHER REFERENCE

Chang, Iris. *The Rape of Nanjing: The Forgotten Holocaust of World War II.* New York: Penguin, 1998.

Crozier, Andrew. *The Causes of the Second World War.* Malden, Mass.: Wiley-Blackwell, 1997.

Dalton, Dennis. *Mahatma Gandhi: Non-Violent Power in Action.* New York: Columbia University Press, 1993.

Edib, Halide. *House with Wisteria: Memoirs of Halide Edib.* Charlottesville, Va.: Leopolis Press, 2003.

Fitzpatrick, Sheila. *Stalin's Peasants: Resistance and Survival in the Russian Village After Collectivization.* New York: Oxford University Press, 1996.

Gellner, Ernest. *Nations and Nationalism.* Malden, Mass.: Wiley-Blackwell, 2006.

Hobsbawm, Eric. *The Age of Extremes: A History of the World, 1914–1991.* New York: Vintage, 1996.

Mango, Andrew. *Atatürk: The Biography of the Founder of Modern Turkey.* New York: Overlook, 2002.

Paxton, Robert. *The Anatomy of Fascism.* New York: Vintage, 2005.

Rothermund, Dietmar. *The Global Impact of the Great Depression, 1929–1939.* New York: Routledge, 1996.

KEY TERMS

Halide Edib (626)

Great Depression (627)

Franklin Delano Roosevelt (628)

Benito Mussolini (630)

fascism (630)

Adolf Hitler (631)

collectivization (635)

Great Purges (635)

Invasion of Manchuria (636)

Mustafa Kemal (637)

Mohandas K. Gandhi (638)

Igbo Women's War (641)

Rape of Nanjing (642)

Spanish Civil War (642)

VOYAGES ON THE WEB

Voyages: Halide Edib

"Voyages" is a real time excursion to historical sites in this chapter and includes interactive activities and study tools such as audio summaries, animated maps, and flashcards.

Visual Evidence: Guernica

"Visual Evidence" features artifacts, works of art, or photographs, along with a brief descriptive essay and discussion questions to guide your analysis of visual sources.

World History in Today's World: Caste and Affirmative Action in India

"World History in Today's World" makes the connection between features of modern life and their origins in the periods in this chapter.

29

The Second World War and the Origins of the Cold War, 1939–1949

cy Wake
ian War Memorial

By the spring of 1944, Nazi Germany had occupied France for nearly four years. In preparation for a British and American invasion at the Normandy coast, underground resistance fighters were being parachuted into the French countryside. **Nancy Wake** (b. 1912), a young Australian, was the only woman in her group. War can produce unlikely heroes, and Nancy Wake was one. While she had traveled to Paris in the 1930s looking for adventure, fun, and romance, now she was risking her life in the fight against Nazi Germany:

As the Liberator bomber circled over the dropping zone in France I could see lights flashing and huge bonfires burning. I hoped the field was manned by the Resistance and not by German ambushers. Huddled in the belly of the bomber, airsick and vomiting, I was hardly Hollywood's idea of a glamorous spy. I probably looked grotesque. Over civilian clothes, silk-stockinged and high-heeled, I wore overalls, [and] carried revolvers in the pockets.... Even more incongruous was the matronly handbag, full of cash and secret instructions for D-Day.... But I'd spent years in France working as an escape courier … and I was desperate to return to France and continue working against Hitler. Neither airsickness nor looking like a clumsily wrapped parcel was going to deter me.[*/1]

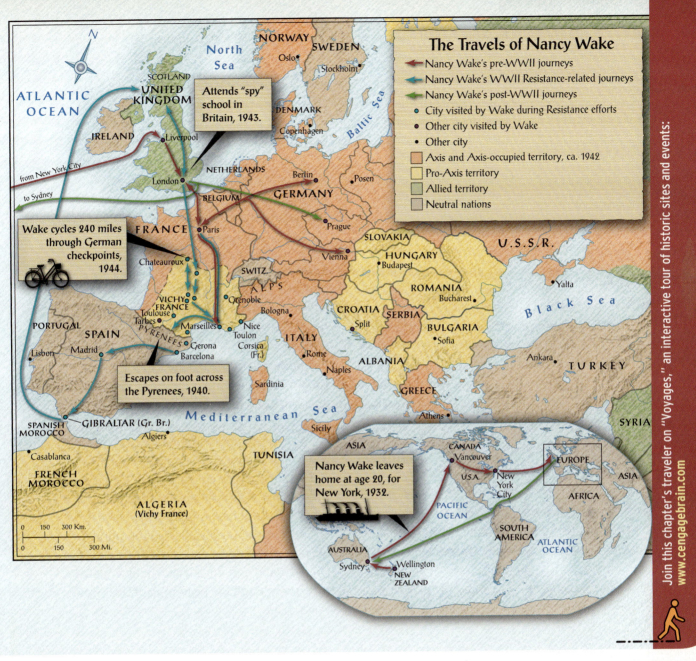

The Travels of Nancy Wake

- → Nancy Wake's pre-WWII journeys
- → Nancy Wake's WWII Resistance-related journeys
- → Nancy Wake's post-WWII journeys
- • City visited by Wake during Resistance efforts
- • Other city visited by Wake
- • Other city
- ▨ Axis and Axis-occupied territory, ca. 1942
- ▨ Pro-Axis territory
- ▨ Allied territory
- ▨ Neutral nations

ATLANTIC OCEAN

North Sea

NORWAY — Oslo
SWEDEN — Stockholm
SCOTLAND
UNITED KINGDOM

Attends "spy" school in Britain, 1943.

DENMARK — Copenhagen

Baltic Sea

IRELAND
• Liverpool

from New York City
to Sydney

NETHERLANDS
London
BELGIUM
GERMANY — Berlin
• Posen

Wake cycles 240 miles through German checkpoints, 1944.

FRANCE • Paris
Prague
SLOVAKIA
Vienna
U.S.S.R.

• Chateauroux
SWITZ.
ALPS
HUNGARY — • Budapest
ROMANIA — • Bucharest
• Yalta

VICHY FRANCE
• Grenoble
• Bologna
CROATIA
SERBIA
Black Sea

Toulouse
• Tarbes
• Marseilles
Nice
Toulon
Corsica (Fr.)
ITALY
• Rome
BULGARIA — • Sofia
ALBANIA
• Naples
TURKEY — • Ankara

PORTUGAL
SPAIN
PYRENEES
Gerona
Barcelona

Escapes on foot across the Pyrenees, 1940.

• Lisbon
• Madrid

Sardinia
GREECE
• Athens
SYRIA

Mediterranean Sea

SPANISH MOROCCO
GIBRALTAR (Gr. Br.)
• Algiers
Sicily

• Casablanca
FRENCH MOROCCO
TUNISIA

ALGERIA (Vichy France)

Nancy Wake leaves home at age 20, for New York, 1932.

ASIA
CANADA — Vancouver
U.S.A. — New York City
EUROPE
AFRICA
ASIA

PACIFIC OCEAN
SOUTH AMERICA
ATLANTIC OCEAN

AUSTRALIA
Sydney
Wellington
NEW ZEALAND

Scale:
0 150 300 Km.
0 150 300 Mi.

1935 — 1940 — 1945 — 1950

Lifetime of Nancy Wake (b. 1912)

EUROPE
- Invasion of Poland — 1939
- Siege of Leningrad — 1941–1944
- Firebombing of Dresden — 1945
- Berlin Airlift — 1948
- Battle for Britain — 1940
- Invasion of Soviet Union — 1942
- Soviet victory at Stalingrad — 1943

ASIA AND THE PACIFIC
- Pearl Harbor — 1941
- Battle of Midway — 1942
- Hiroshima and Nagasaki; end of World War II — 1945

NORTH AMERICA
- Atlantic Charter — 1941
- Bretton Woods Conference — 1944
- Foundation of United Nations — 1945
- Truman Doctrine — 1947

Nancy Wake (b. 1912)
Highly decorated Australian veteran of the Second World War. After serving as courier for the French underground resistance early in the war, she traveled to England for training and parachuted into central France in 1944 during the Allied reoccupation.

The German secret police, the Gestapo, called her "the White Mouse" and put her at the top of their "most wanted" list. But Wake evaded capture and went on to become the most highly decorated female veteran of the war.

Born in a family that was originally from New Zealand, Wake had both English and Maori ancestors. Even as a child she "dreamt of seeing the world," and at the age of twenty she sailed from Australia to Canada and traveled by train to New York; in 1934 she settled in Paris. At that time Wake was more interested in parties than in politics, but she had an awakening when she traveled to Vienna. After witnessing German Jews being publicly humiliated by Nazi sympathizers, she wrote, "I resolved then and there that if I ever had the chance I would do anything, however big or small, stupid or dangerous, to try and make things more difficult for their rotten party."

Wake became engaged to a wealthy French industrialist and lived an exciting life, with a wide circle of Parisian friends and frequent vacations to the Alps. But there was an undercurrent of tension. "In common with many others I feared war was inevitable and then where would we all be? When would laughter end and the tears begin?" By 1937, civil war was raging in neighboring Spain and the threat of Hitler's Germany was growing.

After Hitler attacked Poland in 1939, there was an ominous pause before Germany opened a western front against France. After that invasion came in 1940, Wake served as a courier for the underground resistance, passing messages and helping the *maquis* (mah-KEE)—the antifascist fighters—escape from both the Gestapo and collaborating French authorities. Soon there was too much heat on the "White Mouse"; she hiked to Spain over difficult and dangerous mountain passes, and from there went to England. After training in Britain, she parachuted into central France and joined the maquis, the only woman in her group.

Wake's story puts a human face on the concept of total war. The military mobilization, civilian involvement, and global reach of this conflict were even greater than in the First World War and had unprecedented global effects. The war deeply affected the world's peoples, and with its end came the rise of the United States and the Soviet Union as global superpowers and the beginning of their Cold War rivalry.

FOCUS QUESTIONS

▶ What factors contributed to early German and Japanese successes and later Allied ones?

▶ How did civilians in various parts of the world experience the Second World War as a total war?

▶ How did the outcome of the war affect the global balance of political and military power?

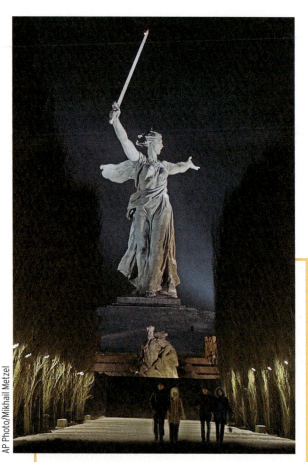

AP Photo/Mikhail Metzel

Stalingrad War Memorial   For Soviet citizens the Battle of Stalingrad symbolized their nation's toughness and resiliency in facing down the threat of fascism during the Great Patriotic Homeland War. The "Heroes of the Stalingrad Battle" complex, built on an epic scale, features this enormous "Mother of the Homeland" statue. It is still one of the most visited historical sites in Russia.

As the United States and the Soviet Union mobilized for war, momentum shifted toward the Allies. Apart from the "Big Three," the antifascist alliance also included both the Guomindang government of Chiang Kai-shek and communist partisans led by Mao Zedong. Britain and the United States supplied arms to Chiang to keep up the fight against the Japanese in Burma and in China, while Mao's forces harassed the Japanese in the north. By 1942 it was becoming clear that holding on to China required a huge Japanese investment of men and material.

The first decisive military reversal for the Axis came in North Africa, where the British finally gained the upper hand. Victory at the Battle of Al Alamein in Egypt (1942) not only protected Britain's control of the Suez Canal but also secured a base for a counterattack against Italy across the Mediterranean. By 1943 British and American forces were driving northward up the Italian peninsula, aided by Italian partisans. Mussolini's forces collapsed. Though Germany propped him up until 1945, he was eventually captured by the Italian resistance. To express their contempt, Mussolini's executioners hung his body by the heels from a public balcony.

In the Pacific, the Allies also gained momentum in 1942. In early summer American aircraft sunk four of Japan's six largest aircraft carriers at the Battle of Midway. Then the United States took the offensive at Guadalcanal, the beginning of an "island-hopping" campaign to drive back the Japanese. The fighting was tough, but with the huge U.S. economy now fully geared toward military production and with new ships and airplanes rolling off assembly lines at a staggering rate, American naval dominance in the Pacific was ensured.

Perhaps the single most important turning point of the war was the **Battle of Stalingrad**. Unable to take Moscow, in late 1942 the Germans swung south toward the Soviet

Battle of Stalingrad
(1942–1944) One of the major turning points of World War II, when the Soviet Army halted the German advance and annihilated the German Sixth Army. After victory at Stalingrad, the Soviets went on the offensive, driving the Germans out of Soviet territory.

and the harshness of winter to advantage. If the Germans had treated the Soviet people well, they might have found more allies among those who had suffered under Stalin. But by spring the Germans were bogged down, while Stalin's propagandists emphasized heroic stands against earlier invaders and rallied the Soviet peoples behind the "Great Patriotic Homeland War." Soviet resistance stiffened.

Hiroshima and Nagasaki
(1945) Two Japanese cities devastated by atomic bombs dropped by the United States in an attempt to end the Second World War. Hundreds of thousands were killed, many of slow radiation poisoning.

Union's strategic oil fields. House-by-house fighting in Stalingrad gave the Red Army time to organize a counter-offensive, and in 1943 they surrounded and annihilated the German Sixth Army. Galvanized by their victory, the Soviets launched a series of punishing attacks. In January 1944 the siege of Leningrad ended as Germans departed the city's outskirts, and in the spring Stalin's forces drove Hitler's army out of Soviet territory altogether.

The Japanese were also on the defensive by 1943. The Allies retook the Burma Road, their main supply line to Chiang Kai-shek's Nationalist forces in China. Matching the Soviet thrust to drive the German army back toward Berlin, by 1944 American forces were push-ing Japanese forces back toward their home islands. Local resistance in China, Vietnam, the Philippines, and the Dutch East Indies comple-mented British, Australian, Canadian, and American efforts.

When Churchill, Roosevelt, and Stalin met for the first time, in Teheran in 1943, they agreed to open a western front in addition to the front already opened in Italy. British and American commanders, led by General Dwight Eisenhower of the United States, began prepara-tions for a difficult landing on the beaches of Normandy in northwestern France. Meanwhile, Soviet forces drove the German army all the way back to Poland.

In anticipation of the Normandy invasion, Nancy Wake and her group parachuted into cen-tral France behind German lines. It was difficult and dangerous work. Once when her group lost their radio, and therefore con-tact with London, Wake bicycled more than a hun-dred miles over mountain-ous terrain to re-establish their communications link: "Every kilometer I pedaled was sheer agony. I knew if I ever got off the bike, I could never get on it again.... I couldn't stand up, I couldn't sit down, I couldn't walk and I couldn't sleep for days."

Primary Source: The Decision to Use the Atomic Bomb *Learn why President Truman was advised to drop atomic bombs on Japan—from the chair-man of the committee that gave him that advice.*

After assisting the Allied invasion of Normandy on D-Day, June 6, 1944, Wake reached Paris just as Allied forces drove the German army from the city she had once called home: "Paris was liberated on 25 August, 1944, and the whole country rejoiced.... After defeat and years of humiliation their beautiful capital was free. The aggressors were now the hunted.... The collaborators seemed to have vanished into thin air and the crowds in the street went wild with joy." But there was still hard fighting to do. A final German offensive in Belgium led to significant American casualties in the Battle of the Bulge in the winter of 1944 before British and U.S. forces regained the initiative. And Nancy Wake's happiness was tempered by per-sonal loss: the Nazis had executed her husband and many of her friends.

By early 1945 Allied forces were poised to invade Germany from both east and west. The European war ended in a final fury. As the Red Army moved into eastern Germany, Soviet troops took their vengeance by raping, looting, and executing German civilians. When British and American aircraft firebombed Dresden, tens of thousands of civilians who fled to underground shelters suffocated as the fire-storm above them sucked the oxygen from the air. As Soviet troops stormed Berlin, Hitler killed himself in a bunker beneath the city. His promise of a thousand year *reich* ended in hunger and homelessness for millions of German as, on May 8, 1945—V-E Day—Germany surrendered.

It took the rest of the summer, however, for American forces to defeat Japan. Once the United States retook the Philippines late in 1944, the path toward invasion lay open (see Map 29.2). American submarines blockaded Japan, starving its military of supplies, while U.S. aircraft dropped incendiary bombs on Tokyo and other cities, reducing them to ashes. Still, it seemed it would require a massive land-ing of troops to force a Japanese surrender.

After the death of Franklin Roosevelt in 1945, Harry S. Truman entered the presidency faced with a dreadful decision. Truman's choice to force a quick conclusion by dropping atomic bombs on Japan has been disputed ever since. The United States unleashed terrible devastation on **Hiroshima and Nagasaki**.

Map 29.2   World War II in Asia and the Pacific
The Japanese Empire, like the Axis powers in Europe, dominated the early stages of the war in Asia, overrunning British, French, Dutch, and Chinese positions in Southeast and East Asia in 1940–1942, and threatening British India. By 1943, however, with the United States fully mobilized to fight the Pacific war, momentum shifted to the Allies. The war ended in the summer of 1945 when President Harry Truman, afraid of fierce Japanese resistance on their home islands and suspicious of Soviet intentions as Stalin's forces moved into the region, ordered the use of the atomic weapons dropped on Hiroshima and Nagasaki. © Cengage Learning   ■ Interactive Map

Hundreds of thousands died, some instantly, others gradually from radiation poisoning. Meanwhile, the Soviet Union occupied Manchuria and northern Korea, raising fears of Soviet invasion. Calculating that immediate submission was Japan's best option, Emperor Hirohito (hee-ro-HEE-to), whose voice his subjects had never before heard, went on the radio and announced Japan's unconditional surrender. On September 2, 1945—V-J Day—that surrender was made official. Finally, the Second World War was over.

Total War and Civilian Life

The Second World War disrupted the lives of tens of millions of ordinary people; in that sense, Nancy Wake's experience was not untypical.

In addition to witnessing the horrors of war, civilian populations were affected in myriad ways. Governmental power intensified. Newspapers, radio, and film were censored and often incorporated state-sponsored misinformation and propaganda. Not only citizens of the great powers, but colonized peoples as well, participated directly in the war, were mobilized for wartime production, and had their destinies altered by the successes and failures of Allied and Axis armies.

Many suffered tragic losses. Warfare and famine killed tens of millions of Chinese and at least 25 million Soviet citizens. During the genocide known as the Holocaust, 6 million Jews were killed in concentration camps, death camps, and by other forms of abuse and execution. Of the entire European Jewish population, over 60 percent perished. The Nazis killed over 90 percent of Poland's Jews. Millions more people—homosexuals, disabled persons, Jehovah's Witnesses, and others deemed enemies of Aryan racial supremacy—were slaughtered as well. Eighty percent of Europe's Roma (Gypsies) were killed.

Civilians and Total War in the United States and Europe

The American people sacrificed in the fight against fascism. Families were disrupted, sons and husbands went to war, and basic consumer goods were rationed. But almost none of the fighting occurred on American soil, and the war actually benefited American society in a number of ways. Massive state spending on munitions put the country back to work, effectively ending the Great Depression. Secure employment boosted the spirits of those who had long been unemployed, even if there was relatively little to buy.

For Americans who had long been at the bottom of the job ladder, especially women and African Americans, mobilization brought new opportunities. "Rosie the Riveter" became the symbol of women in the labor market. Segregated African American military units, such as the famous "Tuskegee Airmen," distinguished themselves in combat, while other American blacks gained access to good industrial employment for the first time. More broadly, the camaraderie and discipline of a nation at war gave an entire generation of Americans a shared purpose.

The people of the Soviet Union also experienced "the Great Patriotic Homeland War" as a powerful collective endeavor; however, their suffering was much greater. Millions were killed or uprooted, the country's agricultural and industrial infrastructure destroyed. Soviet women bore a special burden, caring for children and the elderly while taking on dangerous jobs in mines and factories. Many Soviet women also served with distinction in the armed forces. Wartime suffering left the Soviet people with a deep determination never to allow such an invasion again.

The western European experience was more like the Soviet than the American one. Civilians throughout western Europe witnessed the horrors of war at their very doorsteps. In every nation, families were evacuated from cities under bombardment to safer rural areas, where farming families took them in. In countries under occupation by the Nazis, the slightest sign of anti-German feeling, or any display of sympathy for the Jews, could result in imprisonment, torture, and death. By war's end much of urban Europe lay in ruins.

The civilian experience of total war had long-term effects on Western political culture. In Europe, bitterness remained between those who resisted and those who collaborated with the Axis powers. Meanwhile, the Soviets sought to establish a zone of buffer states to insulate them from future invasion. And the people of the United States were, for the first time, fully willing to engage themselves as a great power in world affairs.

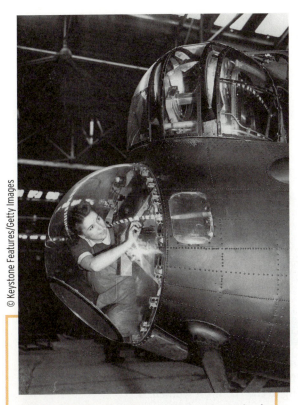

British War Production Total war required the complete mobilization of civilian populations behind a nation's military. As in the United States and Soviet Union, traditional gender roles in Britain were transformed as women factory workers replaced departed servicemen. Here a British worker finalizes assembly of the nose cone of an Avro Lancaster bomber in 1943.

Civilians and Total War in Asia and the Colonial World

At war, the Japanese state commanded all aspects of civilian life, regulating industry and commerce, while severely restricting speech and assembly. Even so, Japanese civilians did not experience the violence of war firsthand until 1944–1945 brought Allied aerial assaults and ultimately nuclear annihilation, a terrible price indeed for their nation's imperialist adventures.

In the Asian theater of war, on the other hand, European colonies were caught in the crossfire between the Allied powers and Japan from the very beginning. Early in the war, Japanese forces seized the colonial territories of the British, French, Dutch, and Americans. The European powers were intent on "liberating" their colonial territories by returning them to colonial rule. Local nationalists in places like Vietnam and Indonesia, however, saw the fight against the Japanese as a fight to throw off foreign rule altogether. Once the war against the Axis was over, multiple conflicts would arise between the European powers and local nationalists fighting for self-determination.

As in Europe, civilians in Asia suffered a war fought on their own soil. The Japanese regarded exploitation of Southeast Asia's natural resources as essential to their imperial mission. They treated local populations like slaves, even forcing Korean, Filipina, and other women into prostitution to service their troops. American, British, Canadian, and Australian prisoners of war were also cruelly treated and often died in captivity.

Hardship was the lot of Chinese civilians throughout the war. Those under Japanese occupation especially suffered, but even those living in zones controlled by Chiang Kai-shek's Guomindang Army lacked food and medicine. The rivalry between Chiang's Guomindang and Mao's Red Army hampered Chinese resistance to Japanese occupation, the two armies achieving little more than a temporary cease-fire. Once the Japanese were expelled, the fight between them for China's future would be renewed.

Communist resistance also arose in neighboring Vietnam, where guerillas led by Ho Chi Minh harassed Japanese occupation forces, with American and British assistance. In Southeast Asia the principal Allied concern was the Burma Road, the primary line of supply to Nationalist forces in China. Bitterly contested jungle warfare, engaging African and Australian troops supported by Allied bombing, caught many peasant villagers in its crossfire. Late in the war, forced replacement of food crops with industrial ones, Japanese hoarding of food, and American bombing of rail and road lines contributed to the starvation of 2 million Vietnamese.

The British were astonished when Mohandas K. Gandhi and his Indian National Congress refused to back the British Empire in the war. During World War I Gandhi and the Congress Party had supported the British, hoping to be rewarded with concrete steps toward Indian

© JAY DIRECTO/AFP/Getty Images

Filipina Women in Protest   Memories of Japan's wartime atrocities run deep in East and Southeast Asia. These Filipina women are protesting the Japanese government's lack of restitution for the suffering of the "comfort women"— girls and women from the Philippines and other Asian countries who were forced to provide sexual services to Japanese soldiers during the war.

self-government. But Congress leaders were frustrated when the British-controlled Government of India declared war on Germany and Japan without consulting them. Instead, the Congress launched a **"Quit India"** campaign, demanding immediate independence. Even more extreme was the Indian nationalist Subhas Bose (soob-ahs BOZ) (1897–1945) who advocated an Indo-Japanese alliance against the British and traveled to Tokyo to enlist captured Indian soldiers to fight alongside the Axis powers. Gandhi and other nationalist leaders were once again thrown into jail, and Bose died in a plane crash before British officials could charge him with treason. The Indian army remained the bulwark of British defense in Asia, and British India continued to contribute labor and economic resources to the Allied war effort. However, as in China and Vietnam, wartime economic policies led to great hardship for people in British India.

British war strategies also provoked backlash in Arab lands. Egyptian nationalists were outraged when the British mobilized their forces without seeking permission from the nominally independent government. As a result, Britain had to quell demonstrations in Cairo even as it prepared for desert war with Italy and Germany. Arab nationalists were also upset at the increased Jewish immigration to Palestine, while in Iraq anti-British feelings were so strong that the government actually declared its sympathies with the Axis powers, prompting the British to invade and occupy Baghdad in the spring of 1941.

Britain's African subjects, perhaps surprisingly, showed loyalty to the empire. For example, the British mustered the **King's African Rifles** from West African colonies such as Nigeria, and East African ones like Kenya, for service in Asia. Many of

"Quit India"   Campaign by Mohandas K. Gandhi and the Indian National Congress during World War II to demand independence. They refused to support the British war effort and instead launched a campaign of civil disobedience demanding that the British "quit India" immediately.

King's African Rifles   African regiment recruited by Britain during the Second World War. These soldiers saw action in Burma, fighting against the Japanese to save India for Britain.

these African soldiers had never traveled more than
a few days from home. Those who returned brought
an expanded view of the world and of Africa's place
in it. In addition, the liberation of Ethiopia from
Italian occupation in 1941, along with the return of
Hailie Selassie to his throne, became symbolic of a
restoration of African dignity.

Africans supported the Allies in the name of
ideals enshrined in the Atlantic Charter: liberty,
freedom, and national self-determination. In
South Africa, the African National Congress specifically pointed to this charter in its calls against
racial segregation and discrimination. In fact,
with many white working-class men conscripted
into the army and with blacks forbidden from
joining the military, some black South Africans
found new and better job opportunities in the
industrial sector, just as their counterparts did
in the United States. On the other side of the
racial divide, the war polarized South African
whites. While politicians loyal to the British
Empire brought South Africa into the war on
the Allied side, some Afrikaner nationalists organized a pro-Axis underground movement.

Some Africans in the French Empire also
helped in defeating fascism. While most colo-
nial officers allied with the Vichy government,
the governor of French equatorial Africa, Félix
Éboué (1884–1944), stood with de Gaulle.
Éboué was from French Guiana in South
America; a descendant of slaves, he had attained
French citizenship through educational achieve-
ment. Under his leadership, the colonial city of
Brazzaville became a staging ground for Free
French recruitment of African soldiers.

The Holocaust

In the midst of war, few grasped the magnitude
of Hitler's assault on the Jews of Europe. Only
when the death camps were liberated by Allied
forces in 1945 did the scale of the horror known
as the Holocaust become clear.

The ideology of racial superiority that drove
Hitler's National Socialism played to the insecu-
rities of Germans resentful of their losses after
World War I and frightened by the upheaval of
the Great Depression.

The Nazis regarded the peoples of eastern
Europe, especially the Slavs, as an inferior "race"
destined to work under the direction of their
"Aryan" superiors, the German "master race." But

Hitler identified two "races"
that he claimed played no
useful role at all. One was
the Roma, or Gypsies, a
traveling people whose
ancestors had come from
India. Clinging to their
own language and traditions, the Roma of central
Europe suffered prejudice and discrimination.
Hitler's other outsider group was the much larger
Jewish community. Thorough assimilation into
German culture and society gave the country's
Jews no protection from Hitler's racial obsession.

During the 1930s, the Nazis segregated Jews
into ghettos and then confined them to labor
camps. Early in 1942, Nazi officials met to
devise a "final solution" to the "Jewish problem." According to the minutes of the Wannsee
Conference, a bureaucracy would be set up to
"cleanse the German living space of Jews in a
legal manner." Jews "capable of work" would be
sent to camps in Poland, "whereby a large part
will undoubtedly disappear through natural
diminution." Those who were not worked to
death "will have to be appropriately dealt with."
That meant they would be murdered outright,
systematically liquidated in "death camps."
(See the feature "Movement of Ideas: Primo
Levi's Memories of Auschwitz.")

The Nazi extermination of the Jews was
methodical and cold-blooded. When a death
camp administrator observed that people died
faster if they were already short of breath when
they entered the "shower rooms" that were
actually gas chambers, he applied "the industrialist's logic" and forced Jewish captives to run to
the showers in a panic, saving gas as well as
time. Thus, thousands could be killed in a day.

Not all Jews went meekly, however. The most
militant resistance was the **Warsaw Ghetto
Uprising**. Shortly after occupying Warsaw, the
Nazis forced the city's Jews into a fenced-off
ghetto where they found no work and very little
food. In 1943, as the Nazis began to remove residents for transportation to the Treblinka death
camp, the sixty thousand
residents of the Warsaw
ghetto rose up in armed
revolt. Ten thousand paid
with their lives, and the
Nazis killed most of the
rest at Treblinka.

Warsaw Ghetto Uprising
(1943) Unsuccessful revolt of
Polish Jews confined to the
Warsaw ghetto who rose up to
resist being sent to the
Treblinka death camp.

**Primary Source:
Memoirs** *Read what the
man responsible for administering and overseeing the
Holocaust thought and felt
about his "work."*

Primo Levi's Memories of Auschwitz

Primo Levi (1919–1987) was an Italian Jew who joined the underground resistance to fascism in his home country. Like millions of other European Jews, he was sent to a Nazi concentration camp, but he survived and became one of the world's most renowned writers. The extract below is taken from an interview that appeared on Italian television in 1983. The interview took place as Levi was returning for the first time to Auschwitz on a Polish train. Primo Levi took his own life in 1987.

Return to Auschwitz

INTERVIEWER: Did you know where you were going [on the train to Auschwitz]?

PRIMO LEVI: We didn't know anything. We had seen on the cars at the station the writing "Auschwitz" but in those times, I don't think even the most informed people knew where Auschwitz was....

INTERVIEWER: What was your first [experience of] Auschwitz?

LEVI: It was night time, after a disastrous journey during which some of the people in the car had died, and arriving in a place where we didn't understand the language, the purpose.... It was really an alienating experience. It seemed we had abandoned the ability to reason, we didn't reason.

INTERVIEWER: And how was the journey, those five days?

LEVI: There were forty-five of us in a very small car. We could barely sit, but there wasn't enough room to lie down. And there was a young mother breast-feeding a baby. They had told us to bring food. Foolishly we hadn't brought water. No one had told us, and we suffered from a terrifying thirst even though it was winter. This was our first, tormenting pain, for five days. The temperature was below zero and our breath would freeze on the bolts and we would compete, scraping off the frost, full of mist as it was, to have a few drops with which to wet our lips. And the baby cried from morning to night because his mother had no milk left.

INTERVIEWER: What happened to the children and their mothers when [you arrived at Auschwitz]?

LEVI: Ah well, they were killed right away: out of the 650 of us on the train, 400–500 died the same evening we arrived or the next. They were immediately sorted out into the gas chambers, in these grim night scenes, with people screaming and yelling. They were yelling like I never heard before. They were yelling orders we didn't understand.... There was an officer ... who would ask each one of us, "Can you walk or not?" I consulted with the man next to me, a friend, from Padua. He was older than me and also in poor health. I told him I'll say I can work, and he answered, "You do as you please. For me, everything is the same." He had already abandoned any hope. In fact he said he couldn't work and didn't come into the camp. I never saw him again....

INTERVIEWER: And the food, how was it there?

LEVI: They gave us a minimal ration equivalent to about 1600–1700 calories a day, but ... there were thefts and we would always get less.... Now, as you know, a man who doesn't weigh much can live on 1600 calories without working, but just laying down. But we had to work, and in the cold, and at hard labor. Thus this ration of 1600 calories was a slow death by starvation. Later I read some research done by the Germans which said that a man could last, living off his own reserves and that diet, from two to three months.

INTERVIEWER: But in the concentration camps one would adapt to anything?

LEVI: Eh, the question is a curious one. The ones who adapted to everything are those who survived, but the majority did not adapt to everything, and died. They died because they were unable to adapt even to things which seem trivial to us. For example, they would throw a pair of mismatched shoes at you.... One was too tight, the other too big.... and those who were sensitive to infections would die.... The feet would swell, rub up against the shoes and one had to go to the hospital. But at the hospital swollen feet were not considered a disease. They were too common so those who had swollen feet would be sent to the gas chambers....

INTERVIEWER: For the Italians, there was the language problem....

LEVI: Understanding one another is very important. Between the man who makes himself understood and that one who doesn't there is an abysmal difference: the first saves himself.... The majority of Italians deported with me died in the first few days for being unable to understand. They didn't understand the orders, but there was no tolerance for those who didn't understand. An order was given once, yelled, and that was it. Afterwards there were beatings....

INTERVIEWER: We are about to return to our hotel in Kracow. In your opinion, what did the holocaust represent for the Jewish people?

LEVI: It represented a turning point.... [It] was perhaps the first time in which anti-Semitism had been planned by the state, not only condoned or allowed as in the Russia of the Czars. And there was no escape: all of Europe had become a huge trap. It entailed a turning point, not only for European Jews, but also for American Jews, for the Jews of the entire world.

INTERVIEWER: In your opinion, another Auschwitz, another massacre like the one which took place forty years ago, could it happen again?

LEVI: Not in Europe, for reasons of immunity. Some kind of immunization must exist. It is [possible] that in a fifty or a hundred years Nazism may be reborn in Germany; or Fascism in Italy.... But the world is much bigger than Europe. I also think that there are countries in which there would be the desire, but not the means. The idea is not dead. Nothing ever dies. Everything arises renewed.

INTERVIEWER: Is it possible to abolish man's humanity?

LEVI: Unfortunately, yes. Unfortunately, yes. And that is really the characteristic of the Nazi camps.... It is to abolish man's personality, inside and outside: not only of the prisoner, but also of the jailer. He too lost his personality in the concentration camp.... Thus it happened to all, a profound modification in their personality.... The memory of family had fallen into second place in face of urgent needs, of hunger, of the necessity to protect oneself against cold, beatings, fatigue ... all of this brought about some reactions which we could call animal-like. We were like work animals.

INTERVIEWER: Do you think that people today want to forget Auschwitz as soon as possible?

LEVI: Signs do exist that this is taking place: forgetting or even denying. This is meaningful. Those who deny Auschwitz would be ready to remake it.

Source: Interview with Daniel Toaff, *Sorgenti di Vita* (Springs of Life), a program on the *Unione Comunita Israelitiche Italiane, Radiotelevisione Italiana [RAI]*. From the transcript of a 1983 Italian radio broadcast, http://www.inch.com/~ari/ levi1.html. The English translation is by Mirto Stone, modified for clarity. (1983–04–25), trans. Mirto Stone.

QUESTIONS FOR ANALYSIS

▶ Apart from death itself, what were the effects of the physical and psychological torture endured by Levi and his fellow death camp inmates?

▶ Over two decades after this interview, how might we evaluate Levi's answer to the question of whether something like the horrors of Auschwitz might happen again?

During this time, the United States restricted Jewish immigration. In 1939, over nine hundred Jewish refugees seeking sanctuary were turned away at American ports and returned to Europe. (Many of them later died in the Holocaust.) Britain also restricted Jewish immigration to England and to Palestine. Zionists, seeking to create a Jewish state to be called Israel, formed guerilla groups and developed an underground network to aid illegal Jewish immigration to Palestine. After 1939, however, it was almost impossible for Jews under Nazi rule to escape. Those who did so were helped by people such as those in Denmark, who helped many Danish Jews flee to neutral Sweden, putting their own lives and livelihoods at risk. Nevertheless, neither resistance nor the heroism of people who tried to aid their Jewish neighbors was enough to prevent Hitler from carrying out his plans.

The Nazi death machine continued even after it became clear that the Allies would win the war. The Allied soldiers who liberated the emaciated victims were sickened by the sight of mass graves. Many Holocaust survivors found that their entire families had been killed. Sometimes, however, after scattering to different parts of the world after the war, survivors were lucky enough to find relatives who were still alive.

How could the Holocaust have happened? Anti-Semitism was strong across Europe, and Nazi collaborators from France, Italy, Hungary, Poland, and elsewhere helped send Jews to the camps. Moreover, the system could not have worked without the general acquiescence of the German people. There are still debates today about whether others could have done more to prevent the slaughter. For example, could Pope Pius XII, who sponsored humanitarian work for refugees and prisoners of war, have successfully confronted the German government? For her part Nancy Wake, appalled by the treatment of Jews in Austria before the war, did everything in her power to prevent Nazi ideas from spreading. Too many others simply looked the other way.

Origins of the Cold War, 1945–1949

At the end of the European war, Soviet and American troops met each other at the Elbe River in Germany. Roosevelt envisioned that Allied cooperation would continue after the war in the new **United Nations**, which was founded in San Francisco in the spring of 1945. Instead, the world divided into two hostile camps.

> **United Nations** Organization established near the end of the Second World War to guarantee international peace and security through permanent diplomacy. A Security Council of five members with veto power was created to enhance its authority.

The New United Nations and Postwar Challenges, 1945–1947

The United Nations was composed of a General Assembly of sovereign nations, plus a Security Council of the major war allies: Britain, France, China, the Soviet Union, and the United States. Since each member of the council had veto power, its decisions could only be reached through consensus. It was hoped that the Security Council's special powers would make the United Nations more effective than the League of Nations.

The spirit of Allied cooperation did not last. Soon the United States and the Soviet Union were "superpowers" dividing the globe in a bipolar struggle. But full-scale war between them never developed. This was a "cold" war, often fought by proxies (smaller nations on either side). The deployment of nuclear weapons, first by the United States in 1945 and then by the Soviet Union in 1949, raised the stakes of total war beyond what any leader was willing to wager.

Already before the end of the war, when Roosevelt, Churchill, and Stalin met at the Yalta Conference in early 1945, Europe was dividing into two opposing camps. The British, Americans, and de Gaulle's Free French controlled western Europe while Stalin's Red Army controlled eastern Europe. Churchill was suspicious of Stalin, a distrust rooted in both his hatred of communism and a traditional British fear of Russian imperial expansion. Roosevelt was more accommodating to Stalin's wishes, desperately hoping to lay the foundation for a safe and secure future.

One central issue was the fate of Poland. The British and Americans had promised the Polish government-in-exile elections after the war. Stalin, however, knew that any Polish government chosen through free elections would be hostile to the Soviet Union, and so he insisted that it must have a "friendly government." While the fighting continued, the conference participants papered over the difference. But as soon as the war was over, it became clear that Stalin intended to occupy eastern Europe and install communist governments there.

Stalin saw no contradiction, saying: "Everyone imposes his own system as far as his army can reach." In 1946, Churchill coined the term *iron curtain* to describe the imposition of communism in the Soviet sphere of influence:

> *From Stettin in the Baltic to Trieste in the Adriatic an iron curtain has descended across the Continent. Behind that line lie all the capitals of the ancient states of Central and Eastern Europe. Warsaw, Berlin, Prague, Vienna, Budapest, Belgrade, Bucharest and Sofia; all these famous cities and the populations around them … are subject, in one form or another, not only to Soviet influence but to a very high and in some cases increasing measure of control from Moscow.**

In many of these countries local communists were actually a strong political force after the war, having played important roles in the antifascist resistance. But Stalin was not interested in working with these communists. He wanted control through men of unquestioned loyalty to Moscow, whose rule would be enforced by the continued presence of the Soviet army.

Nancy Wake witnessed an example of Soviet domination when she traveled to Prague in 1947. Before the war, Czechoslovakia had been a prosperous society with a strong middle class and an emerging democratic tradition. But when Wake arrived to work at the British consulate, she found uneasiness: "Although the Russians

*Excerpt from Nancy Wake, *The Autobiography of the Woman the Gestapo Called the White Mouse.* Copyright © 1985 Pan Publishing.

were not visible, the majority of Czechs I met used to walk around looking over their shoulders in case someone was listening to their conversation."

Czechs saw themselves as a bridge between east and west. Local communists fared well in a free election held in 1946 and were part of a coalition government. But Stalin wanted firmer control. In 1948, Czech communists loyal to Moscow seized power. "Yes, the Germans had gone," Wake commented, "but who would liberate the country from the liberators?"

The United States, the Soviet Union, and the Origins of a Bipolar World

While Soviet ideology proclaimed the desirability and inevitability of socialist revolution on a global scale, Stalin was most concerned to protect the Russian core of the Soviet Union. With large, exposed land frontiers, Soviet Russia needed buffer states along its European and Asian borders to prevent invasions such as those staged by Napoleon and Hitler. Such "defensive expansion" had long been part of the grand strategy of the Russian Empire.

The American outlook was quite different. After the war, Americans retained their characteristic optimism and idealism and stood ready to project their ideals—personal liberty, democracy, technological progress, and market-driven economic efficiency—onto the world stage. But as Americans engaged the world, they found impediments to this global vision: not everyone seemed to share American ideals. Moreover, cynical observers saw American idealism as a smokescreen for the expansion of American capitalism and American imperialism.

The **Truman Doctrine** expressed America's intention to contain communism. The context

Truman Doctrine (1947) Declaration, by President Harry Truman, that the United States would aid all peoples threatened by communism. In reality, his doctrine of "containment" meant that the United States did not try to dislodge the Soviets from their sphere of influence.

Primary Source: The Long Telegram *This critique of the Soviet Union's ideology, authored by an American diplomat in 1946, profoundly influenced the foreign policy of the United States.*

Primary Source: Telegram, September 27, 1946 *Read what the Soviet ambassador wrote to his government regarding the foreign policy goals of the United States.*

was civil war in Greece. Communist partisans who had fought the Germans for control of their homeland did not disarm at the war's end but continued fighting to bring about a communist revolution. The Greek government and army were unable to put down this rebellion on their own, and in 1947 Truman stood before a joint meeting of Congress and promised American aid to suppress the "terrorist activities" of the Greek communists, while promising aid to Greece's neighbor and traditional enemy Turkey and to any nation struggling for freedom: "I believe that it must be the policy of the United States to support free peoples who are resisting attempted subjugation by armed minorities or by outside pressures." Despite Truman's strong language, his policy was actually one of "containment." The United States took no direct action in response to the Soviet takeover of Czechoslovakia, for example, but did install missiles in Turkey to deter the Soviets from advancing to the south. For his part, Stalin implicitly recognized America's sphere of influence by doing nothing to back the Greek communists.

The Cold War stalemate was most apparent in Germany, where the Soviets occupied the eastern part of the country and the British, Americans, and French occupied the west. The capital city of Berlin, which lay within the zone of Soviet occupation, was divided into four sectors. With the breakdown of wartime collaboration between the Soviet Union and the Western powers, no agreement could be reached on Germany's future. Border tensions escalated in 1948 when the Soviets cut off access to Berlin by land and the United States responded by dropping supplies by aircraft into West Berlin in what was called the Berlin Airlift. In 1949, the rift resulted in the creation of two separate states, the German Federal Republic (or West Germany) and the German Democratic Republic (or East Germany). Both sides blamed the other for preventing the reunification of Germany across the former Allied zones of occupation, but in reality neither neighboring France nor the Soviet Union was unhappy with the outcome of a divided, neutralized Germany. As long as the Cold War lasted, the division of Germany was its symbolic battle line.

Meanwhile, the United States took an active role in rebuilding war-ravaged western Europe, most famously through the **Marshall Plan**. Although some Americans wanted Germany to pay reparations, and others wanted the United States to withdraw from European affairs, Truman saw that the reconstruction of western European economies was essential. First, a revival of global trade, in which Europe would play a central role, was necessary for postwar American economic progress. Second, the communist parties of Italy and France were still quite strong, and continued economic difficulties might increase their popularity. In early 1948, the United States announced that $12 billion would be made available for European reconstruction.

In 1944, even before the war was over, the American-sponsored **Bretton Woods Conference** had formed a plan to prevent a repeat of the economic catastrophe that followed World War I. It created the World Bank to loan money to nations in need of a jumpstart, and the International Monetary Fund (IMF) to provide emergency loans to nations in danger of insolvency. The Marshall Plan and the Bretton Woods institutions were designed to enhance the stability of a free-market international economic order. Critics pointed out that the U.S. government was creating international institutions that favored American-style capitalism.

The Soviet Union and its eastern European satellites were invited to join the Marshall Plan, but Stalin refused. Thus, after 1948 the Cold War division of Europe would be economic, as well as political and military. While the U.S. sphere of influence consisted of market-based, industrialized economies, the Soviet Union dominated another sphere in which centralized planning shielded socialist economies from international market forces. To the weakest, least industrialized areas—Asian and African colonies, weak and dependent Latin American countries—the United States would promise development assistance, while the Soviet Union would advocate prosperity through socialist revolution.

Having undergone enormous industrial expansion during the war, the United States was in a much better position to aid its allies. The Soviet Union had suffered widespread destruction and was itself in need of reconstruction.

Marshall Plan   U.S. effort to rebuild war-ravaged Europe, named after the American secretary of state, George C. Marshall.

Bretton Woods Conference (1944) Conference that led to creation of the World Bank and the International Monetary Fund (IMF), designed to secure international capitalism by preventing global economic catastrophes.

AP Photo/Abe Fox

The Bretton Woods Conference   In 1944 delegates from forty-four countries met in New Hampshire to develop institutions to guide postwar economic reconstruction. The International Bank for Reconstruction and Development (part of today's World Bank) and the International Monetary Fund were designed to help the world avoid a repetition of the economic problems that followed from World War I. They were only partially successful, since the Soviet Union declined to join the IMF.

So while the United States offered the Marshall Plan, the Soviets exploited their eastern European satellites economically. Entire factories were dismantled and moved from Germany to the Soviet Union. While the United States could use a combination of military strength, diplomacy, and economic aid to gain allies during the Cold War, the Soviet Union more often relied on coercion.

Both sides also expanded their intelligence operations. The Soviet spy agency, known by the initials KGB, worked through local proxies, such as the East German *Stasi,* to maintain tight control over its satellites while trying to infiltrate Western political, military, and intelligence communities. The United States formed the Central Intelligence Agency (CIA) out of its wartime intelligence service. This was the first time a U.S. government agency was dedicated to collecting foreign intelligence and engaging in covert operations overseas. One of the CIA's first operations paid Italian journalists to write negative stories about communist parliamentary candidates.

As we will see in the next two chapters, the Cold War divided the globe. Outside Europe, communist regimes took power in the People's Republic of China, the Democratic People's Republic of Korea, the Democratic Republic of Vietnam, and the Republic of Cuba. As British and French empires declined in Asia and Africa, emerging new nations were often caught in the tension between the communist East and capitalist West. Some nations, such as India, were able to steer a middle course. But others, like Vietnam, Angola, Afghanistan, and Nicaragua, would be torn by Cold War rivalries. Two generations of humanity lived in the shadow of the Cold War, with the terrible knowledge that it could one day lead to a nuclear doomsday.

Chapter Review and Learning Activities

Nancy Wake is one of the most decorated women veterans in history, having earned the George Medal from the United Kingdom and the Medal of Freedom from the United States. She was made a Companion of the Order of Australia, and from France she received the Resistance Medal, the *Croix de Guerre* (War Cross), and the title of Chevalier in the Legion of Honor. Wake made extraordinary sacrifices in the fight against fascism. Because of her resistance activities, the Gestapo tortured her first husband to death. She symbolizes the heroism of the many who resisted, while her story stands as a reprimand to those who aided the fascist cause, either directly or through passive acquiescence.

What factors contributed to early German and Japanese successes and later Allied ones?

Having spent the 1930s building up their military capacities, Germany and Japan were in a strong position as the war began. Early Axis successes followed from the blitzkrieg tactics of the German army and from the ability of the imperial Japanese forces to overrun the European colonial positions in Southeast Asia after the surprise attack on Pearl Harbor. A key turning point was Adolf Hitler's decision to invade the Soviet Union in the summer of 1941. By early 1942, the huge productive potential of both the Soviet Union and the United States was fully mobilized. By 1943, victories by the British in the North African desert, the United States in the Pacific, and, most important, by the Soviets at Stalingrad paved the way for an American-led invasion of Italy. As the Soviets drove Hitler's army back toward Germany, the D-Day landing on the beaches of Normandy in 1944 created a pincer movement in which British and American troops moved east while the Soviets drove west. The enormous American naval effort in the Pacific stole the momentum from the Japanese, in concert with indigenous armies and resistance movements in China, the Philippines, the Dutch East Indies, and Vietnam. The Pacific war came to a swift and horrible conclusion soon after the United States dropped nuclear bombs on Hiroshima and Nagasaki.

How did civilians in various parts of the world experience the Second World War as a total war?

The Second World War caused tremendous hardship not only for the soldiers who fought in its battles but also for civilian populations. Even in the most liberal societies, political leaders restricted individual liberties and subjected their citizens to wartime propaganda and misinformation. The totalitarian nature of the fascist states and Stalin's Soviet Union was grotesquely exaggerated when wartime crises justified government intrusion in every domain of life. Even in those societies where the economy expanded, most notably the United States, the cause was government spending on the military, not prosperity based on free markets.

In Asia and Africa, total war meant the involvement of colonial societies. The harsh experiences of the Chinese, Filipinos, and others under imperial occupation showed the hollowness of the Japanese claim that their empire was a Co-Prosperity Sphere meant to liberate Asian societies from the European colonial yoke. Still, the Indian National Congress refused to support the British war effort even as Japanese forces entered neighboring Burma, and many Arab peoples responded with hostility to the operation of Allied forces in the Middle East. On the other hand, Africans served loyally and with distinction in both the British and Free French armies, and across East and Southeast Asia local partisans joined the fight against Japan. In Africa and Asia, civilians suffered as well as soldiers and resistance fighters: food scarcity was the norm, and millions died in the Asian famines that followed from economic dislocation.

The Jews and Roma of Europe faced the greatest disaster: a genocidal attempt to eliminate them entirely. After the nightmare of the Holocaust and the nuclear annihilation of Hiroshima and Nagasaki, the age of limited wars seemed over.

How did the outcome of the war affect the global balance of political and military power?

The formation of the United Nations in 1945 brought the prospect that the international community could learn its lesson and build a future of hope and security. That sense of optimism proved short-lived as tensions developed between the two new superpowers, the United States and the Soviet Union. Western Europeans, who previously controlled much of the globe through colonial empires and industrial strength, were no longer able to dominate the international order. The Cold War rivalry of the United States and the Soviet Union split the world into two mutually antagonistic camps, with the threat of nuclear annihilation hanging over their heads.

FOR FURTHER REFERENCE

Burleigh, Michael. *Third Reich: A New History*. New York: Hill and Wang, 2001.

Dower, John. *War Without Mercy: Race and Power in the Pacific War*. New York: Pantheon, 1987.

Higgonet, Margaret, ed. *Behind the Lines: Gender and the Two World Wars*. New Haven: Yale University Press, 1989.

Iriye, Akira. *Power and Culture: The Japanese-American War, 1941–1945*. 2d ed. Cambridge, Mass.: Harvard University Press, 2004.

Keegan, John. *The Second World War*. New York: Penguin, 2005.

LeFeber, Walter. *The United States, Russia and the Cold War*. Updated ed. New York: McGraw-Hill, 2002.

Leffler, Melvyn P., and David S. Painter. *Origins of the Cold War: An International History*. 2d ed. New York: Routledge, 2005.

Thurston, Robert W., and Bernd Bonwetsch, eds. *The People's War: Responses to World War II in the Soviet Union*. Champaign: University of Illinois Press, 2000.

Wake, Nancy. *The White Mouse*. Melbourne: Macmillan, 1986.

Yahil, Leni. *The Holocaust: The Fate of European Jewry*. New York: Schocken, 1987.

KEY TERMS

Nancy Wake (650)

Axis powers (651)

Winston Churchill (651)

Charles de Gaulle (653)

Atlantic Charter (654)

Pearl Harbor (654)

Allied powers (654)

Siege of Leningrad (654)

Battle of Stalingrad (655)

Hiroshima and Nagasaki (656)

"Quit India" (660)

King's African Rifles (660)

Warsaw Ghetto Uprising (661)

United Nations (664)

Truman Doctrine (665)

Marshall Plan (666)

Bretton Woods Conference (666)

VOYAGES ON THE WEB

Voyages: Nancy Wake

"Voyages" is a real time excursion to historical sites in this chapter and includes interactive activities and study tools such as audio summaries, animated maps, and flashcards.

Visual Evidence: Warfare and Racial Stereotypes

"Visual Evidence" features artifacts, works of art, or photographs, along with a brief descriptive essay and discussion questions to guide your analysis of visual sources.

World History in Today's World: Comfort Women

"World History in Today's World" makes the connection between features of modern life and their origins in the periods in this chapter.

CourseMate

Go to the CourseMate website at www.cengagebrain.com for additional study tools and review materials—including audio and video clips—for this chapter.

30

The Cold War and Decolonization, 1949–1975

Ernesto Guevara, 1951 (© Emiliano Rodriguez/ Alamy)

The Cold War and Revolution, 1949-1962   *(p. 674)*

Spheres of Influence: Old Empires and New Superpowers   *(p. 678)*

A Time of Upheaval, 1966-1974   *(p. 689)*

In 1952 Alberto Granado and **Ernesto Guevara** (1928–1967), two Argentine students with promising futures in medicine, decided to take an ambitious road trip across South America on an aging motorcycle. At first, their motive was fun and adventure, "not setting down roots in any land or staying long enough to see the substratum of things; the outer surface would suffice." Soon, however, their encounters with Indians, peasants, and miners changed the nature of Guevara's quest:

We made friends with a [Chilean] couple.... In his simple, expressive language he recounted his three months in prison ... his fruitless pilgrimage in search of work and his *compañeros*, mysteriously disappeared and said to be somewhere at the bottom of the sea. The couple, numb with cold, huddling against each other in the desert night, was a living representation of the proletariat in any part of the world. They had not one single miserable blanket to cover themselves with, so we gave them one of ours and Alberto and I wrapped the other around us as best we could.... The communism gnawing at [their]

670

Che Guevara crosses South America on his first trip, 1951.

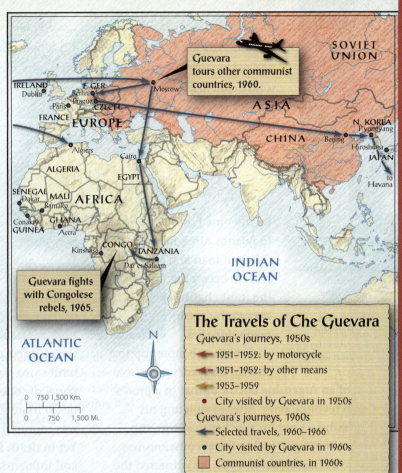

Guevara tours other communist countries, 1960.

Guevara fights with Congolese rebels, 1965.

The Travels of Che Guevara

Guevara's journeys, 1950s
➤ 1951–1952: by motorcycle
➤ 1951–1952: by other means
➤ 1953–1959
● City visited by Guevara in 1950s

Guevara's journeys, 1960s
➤ Selected travels, 1960–1966
● City visited by Guevara in 1960s
▮ Communist countries, in 1960s

liberati
betwee
States
reinfor

Thi
century
of new
of Euro
tionari

	1945	1950	1955	1960	1965	1970	1975
	Lifetime of Ernesto Guevara (b. 1928)				1967		
AMERICAS			Overthrow of Arbenz 1954	Cuban Revolution 1959	Cuban Missile Crisis 1962	Tlatelolco Massacre 1968	Overthrow of Allende 1973
ASIA		People's Republic of China 1949	Bandung Conference 1955	Great Leap Forward 1955	High point of Great Proletarian Cultural Revolution 1965—1970		
		Korean War 1950—1953			U.S. forces in Vietnam 1964—1975		
EUROPE			Hungarian Uprising 1956			Prague Spring 1968	
AFRICA AND THE MIDDLE EAST	Founding of Israel 1948		Algerian War 1954—1962		Six-Day War 1967		
			Suez Canal crisis 1956	Death of Patrice Lumumba 1961			

The Cold War and Revolution, 1949–1962

that (
siona
degre
time
Whil
overt
men
the I
to M
exile
tator
com
quick
Cub
Revo
the v
G
dow
Worl
poin
war
allies
the s
the S
indu
mad

By the 1950s, the United States and Soviet Union were amassing nuclear weapons many times more powerful than those dropped on Hiroshima and Nagasaki. Since any direct conflict between them threatened mutual annihilation, both sides were cautious not to push the other too far. Official U.S. policy remained one of "containment," of preventing an expansion of the Soviet sphere of influence but not intervening within it.

While the Cold War in Europe was a stand-off, communist revolutions elsewhere increased the potential sphere of Soviet influence. In 1949, after the victory of the People's Army, Mao Zedong stood in Tiananmen Square in Beijing and declared the foundation of the People's Republic of China. Ten years later Fidel Castro and Che Guevara led a rebel army into Havana and founded a socialist government in Cuba, an island just 90 miles (145 km) from Florida. From the perspective of anticommunists in the United States and elsewhere, the "Soviet menace" was increasing.

The People's Republic of China, 1949–1962

Almost immediately after Japan's defeat, contention between Chiang Kai-shek's Guomindang and Mao Zedong's Chinese Communist Party for control of China resumed. By the time war ended in 1949, the Communists were in charge of the People's Republic of China on the mainland, and Chiang Kai-shek and his Nationalist followers fled to the island of Taiwan, where they established the Republic of China (see Map 30.1).

The Communists succeeded even though the Nationalists started with a larger army, a stockpile of weapons supplied by the Allies during World War II, and control of China's largest cities. Mao's army had cultivated support among the Chinese peasantry while fighting Japanese invaders, and the People's Liberation Army had become a tough, disciplined organization. Mao used his popular base to advantage,

telling his soldiers to "swim like fishes in the sea" of rural China, camouflaging their activities amidst the routines of village life. Since the People's Liberation Army treated Chinese peasants with greater respect than did Chiang's Guomindang, they rode mass support to success.

Once in power, the Communists revolutionized China from the bottom up. They organized peasants into agricultural cooperatives, expanded educational opportunities, indoctrinated young people in youth organizations guided by the party, and enrolled workers in state-sponsored trade unions. Within the unions, the army, and other mass organizations, mandatory "thought reform" sessions focused on the study of "Mao Zedong Thought." Those accused of deviation from socialist thought were shamed and forced to publicly confess their "errors."

The repressive atmosphere of the People's Republic of China intensified during the Korean War (1950-1953). At the end of World War II, the Korean peninsula had been divided between a Soviet-backed Democratic Republic of Korea in the north and an American-allied Republic of Korea in the south. When North Korea invaded, the United States rushed to defend its South Korean ally. The Chinese government, fearing that the United States intended to attack them as well, then threw its massive forces into battle to reinforce North Korea. In the end, a stalemate ensued along the demilitarized zone that separated the communist regime in North Korea, which allowed no freedom at all, from the stern authoritarian regime in South Korea, which allowed very little.

Initially, the People's Republic of China followed Soviet-style economic policies of state-run heavy industry and collective farming. In 1953 the Chinese adopted a Five-Year Plan and sent engineers and state planners to Russia for training. But the results were disappointing. Not only was the growth of production slower

Map 30.1   China and Taiwan

After World War II, the Communist forces of Mao Zedong took the offensive against the Guomindang, or Nationalist army, of Chiang Kai-shek. The Nationalists were driven off the mainland to the island of Taiwan. In Beijing, Mao declared the creation of the People's Republic of China on October 1, 1949. The Communists and Nationalists agreed that there was only "one China," and their continuing animosity became another zone of conflict in the global Cold War.   © Cengage Learning

 Interactive Map

→ Nationalist retreat 1948–1949
- - - Boundary uncertain

than Mao expected, but the dull, bureaucratic socialism of the U.S.S.R. was uninspiring.

In 1956, Mao launched a public call for new ideas, using the phrase "Let a hundred flowers bloom." China's intellectuals responded by openly criticizing the Communist Party, and even Mao himself. Either the criticism was more than Mao had expected, or perhaps he had intended all along to trick opponents out into the open, but during the savage repression of 1957, intellectuals were arrested, imprisoned, and exiled. Independent thinking was now a "rightist" deviation to be purged.

Mao saw the Communist Party as divided into two factions, which he labeled "red" and "expert." The "experts" in charge of agricultural collectivization and industrial development were becoming an elite cut off from the masses. The "red" leadership, emphasizing socialist willpower rather than technical ability, would help China catch up with the world's dominant economic powers. If only the true revolutionary potential of China's peasants and workers could be unleashed, Mao thought, the people could move mountains.

In 1958 Mao launched the **Great Leap Forward**. Rather than relying on large steel factories, revolutionaries would set up small furnaces all across the country. The "masses" were directed to pour all their energy and enthusiasm into communal production. Meanwhile, property rights were restricted, and peasants lost access to the small plots they relied on to feed their families.

The Great Leap Forward was disastrous. The steel produced in small communal furnaces was virtually useless, and food production plunged. As many as 30 million people died in the famine that ensued. By 1961 the failure of the Great Leap Forward led the more pragmatic "experts" in the Communist Party to reduce Mao's authority behind the scenes (still publicly acknowledging his leadership) while reinstating rationality to economic planning.

Still, Mao's belief in the power of revolutionary enthusiasm would inspire a younger generation of revolutionaries. Che Guevara was among those attracted to the Chinese model as an alternative to both capitalism and the stodgy Soviet model of technocratic socialism.

The Cuban Revolution and the Cuban Missile Crisis

In the 1950s Cuba was an island of contrasts. Its capital Havana was famous for its beaches and nightclubs, its *mambo* a fusion of African and Latin musical traditions. But while Cuban culture was vibrant, there was a dark side as well. The Mafia controlled Havana's casinos and nightclubs, and prostitution flourished. While Havana was a playground for wealthy tourists, Cuban dictator Fulgencio Batista allowed no democratic freedoms, and most Cubans, the poorest of them descendants of slaves, without access to good employment, health care, or education, lived in desperate poverty.

Fidel Castro (b. 1926), like Ernesto Guevara, was an idealistic young man who renounced middle-class privilege in the name of revolution. In 1953 he was imprisoned for leading an attack on an army barracks, and after his release in 1955 he went into exile in Mexico City. There he formed a deep friendship with Che Guevara, newly arrived from Guatemala, who joined Castro's small rebel band for military training at a nearby secret base.

In 1956, Castro and Guevara left by boat for Cuba, finding sanctuary in the Sierra Maestra Mountains. Gradually they stockpiled ammunition by attacking police stations and military barracks. With recruits attracted from the peasant population, they were able to outmaneuver their government pursuers. During two years of hard fighting, Che's medical background came in handy for tending wounded colleagues, but his most important role was as commander and tactician. Conditions were ruthless, and Guevara had no second thoughts about executing suspected government agents. By 1958, the rebels were poised to attack Havana, and on New Year's Day 1959 Batista

Great Leap Forward (1958) Mao Zedong's attempt to harness the revolutionary zeal of the Chinese masses for rapid industrialization. The result was a massive economic collapse and millions of deaths from famine.

Fidel Castro (b. 1926) Cuban prime minister from 1959 to 1976 and president from 1976 to 2008. Led the successful revolution in 1959, after which his nationalization policies led to deteriorating relations with the United States and increasing dependence on Soviet support.

fled when Castro's forces marched triumphantly into the capital.

Neither Castro nor Guevara had ever joined the Cuban Communist Party, and many Cubans expected that the new government would redistribute wealth through a combination of socialist economics and liberal politics. But instead of civil liberty, Castro's immediate preoccupation became "defense of the revolution." The new leaders faced the threat of counter-revolution, as pro-Batista forces that fled to the United States were lobbying for an American-backed invasion.

Initially, President Eisenhower hoped that Castro might be someone he could work with, as the Cuban leader toured Washington and New York seeking both public and official support. But relations deteriorated after Cuba's Agrarian Reform Law nationalized land owned by American corporations. Both corporate lobbyists and Cold War hawks soon portrayed Castro as a Soviet threat on America's doorstep. As tensions increased, Castro sent Che Guevara to Moscow and Beijing to shore up support for his regime while the Eisenhower administration drew up plans for invasion.

In the spring of 1961 a U.S.-sponsored group of Cuban exiles stormed ashore at the Bay of Pigs. The new American president, John F. Kennedy (1917–1963), having had strong doubts about their prospects, had given the Cuban counter-revolutionaries only lukewarm support. Their invasion was a debacle and validated Castro's distrust of U.S. intentions, pushing him toward more repressive policies. In addition, the United States placed an economic embargo on Cuba that made diplomacy and compromise all but impossible. Castro turned to the Soviet Union for support.

In the fall of 1962 matters came to a head in the **Cuban Missile Crisis**. Convinced that the United States would never let his socialist experiment proceed in peace, Castro developed ever-closer ties with the Soviet Union. Soviet Premier Khrushchev took advantage of the situation to secretly ship nuclear missiles to Cuba. When American surveillance aircraft detected the missiles, Kennedy presented Khrushchev with an ultimatum: withdraw the missiles, or else. On the brink of nuclear war, both sides blinked: Khrushchev agreed to remove Soviet missiles from Cuba, Kennedy removed U.S. missiles from Turkey, and the world sighed in relief.

Feeling more vulnerable than ever, Castro threw himself into an even tighter alliance with Moscow. To help Cuba withstand the American trade embargo, the Soviets agreed to buy the island's entire sugar output at above-market prices and to subsidize the socialist transformation of the island with cheap fuel and agricultural machinery. By the mid-1960s, Cubans were better fed and better housed than they had been before the revolution; they also had free access to basic health care and were more likely to be able to read and write.

But underlying economic problems remained. As was common in Latin America, Cuba had long been a dependent economy, exporting agricultural produce (mostly sugar and tobacco) while importing higher-valued industrial goods. With the Soviet Union as an economic patron, Cuba's reliance on agricultural exports was as strong as ever. Economic development was further hampered by Cuba's Soviet-style command economy, characterized by bureaucratic inefficiency and low worker morale.

When Cuban workers agitated for higher wages, Che Guevara, as minister for industry, told them to be content knowing that their hard work supported the glorious cause of socialism. Himself willing to work long hours for almost no material reward, Guevara thought that others should do the same. But without material rewards for workers or incentives to inspire individual enterprise, the Cuban economy settled into lethargy.

A disappointed Guevara could not abide the endless meetings and plodding pace. The country's reliance on the Soviet Union bothered him, too, his distrust heightened by the Soviet suppression of popular uprisings in eastern Europe. In 1965 he left for Africa to pursue his revolutionary dreams on a global stage.

Cuban Missile Crisis Tense 1962 confrontation between the United States and the Soviet Union over placement of nuclear missiles in Cuba. A compromise led to withdrawal of Soviet missiles from Cuba and American missiles from Turkey.

Spheres of Influence: Old Empires and New Superpowers

The Cuban Missile Crisis illustrated the dangers of one superpower intervening in the other's sphere of influence. Usually such interventions took place within a superpower's own strategic domain, as when the United States helped overthrow the democratically elected government of Guatemala in 1953 or Soviet tanks crushed a prodemocracy uprising in Hungary in 1956.

But much of the world lay outside either sphere. In Asia and Africa, European empires were supplanted by decolonization movements. How would these new nations fit into the international system? In some countries, especially in Africa, colonial powers managed to retain substantial influence even after national independence. Elsewhere, however, new African and Asian nations became ensnared in the tensions of the Cold War. Some, like Congo and Vietnam, were pulled apart in the process.

Recognizing the danger that the superpower rivalry posed to recently decolonized nations, in 1955 a group of African and Asian leaders met to discuss ways to defend their sovereignty. Their goal in founding the Non-Aligned Movement was to avoid both neocolonial influence from Europe and, by refusing to associate themselves with either the Soviet Union or the United States, to avoid superpower intervention in their affairs. It was not a simple goal to achieve. The American intervention against Ho Chi Minh's communist forces after the French withdrawal from Vietnam showed how the decline of European power could lead to superpower intervention.

Superpower Interventions, 1953–1956

During the Cold War, both the United States and the Soviet Union presented themselves as champions of freedom. Of course, they had different interpretations of what that meant. The Soviets, identifying colonialism and imperialism as the main barriers to liberation, supported nationalists in the Third World who were fighting to throw off European colonialism, as well as socialists fighting against American political and economic domination in Latin America. But Moscow would not tolerate similar liberation movements within its own sphere. In the Soviet Union and its satellites (see Map 30.2), movements toward self-determination and freedom of speech, association, or religion were brutally crushed.

In eastern Europe, secret police networks kept people from openly expressing anticommunist or anti-Soviet views. In East Germany, for example, the *Stasi* planted informers at all levels of society and encouraged neighbors to spy on neighbors. Although the new Soviet leader Nikita Khrushchev (1894–1971) had denounced the excesses of Stalinism at a Communist Party congress, and subsequently promoted some limited reforms, the Soviets still would not tolerate popular movements for change.

When Soviet tanks crushed demonstrations in East Berlin, it became clear that the communist rule was based more on Soviet coercion than popular legitimacy. Over the next eight years, thousands of East Berliners fled to the West. Finally, in 1961 East Germany constructed the Berlin Wall to fence its people in. Now Churchill's metaphoric "iron curtain" took physical shape.

Poles detested the pro-Moscow government imposed on them by Stalin after the war. Being predominantly Catholic, they also resented the official atheism of the communist state. In 1956 a religious gathering attended by a million Poles turned into an antigovernment demonstration. Here the Soviet government compromised and allowed reforms, such as an end to the collectivization of agriculture and some religious freedom. But it was clear that attempts to further weaken Poland's ties to the Soviet Union would not be tolerated.

Map 30.2 Cold War Confrontations

Two military alliances, the North Atlantic Treaty Organization (NATO) led by the United States, and the Warsaw Pact, dominated by the Soviet Union, were the principal antagonists in the Cold War. Fearful of mutual nuclear annihilation, however, they never engaged in direct combat. Instead, the Cold War turned hot in proxy struggles around the world—in Central America and the Caribbean, Africa, the Middle East, and Southeast and East Asia. © Cengage Learning

Interactive Map

NATO nations
Warsaw Pact nations
Soviet military base
U.S. military base
U.S. Strategic Air Command base
U.S. Intercontinental Ballistic Missile base
U.S. naval fleet
Cold War point of conflict

CZECHOSLOVAKIA 1948,1968
EAST GERMANY 1948–1949, 1953,
POLAND 1956–1962
YUGOSLAVIA 1948–1953
HUNGARY 1956

The **Hungarian Uprising** showed the seriousness of the situation. In 1956 Hungarian students, factory workers, and middle-class professionals rose up to protest the Soviet-imposed communist dictatorship. The Hungarian government collapsed. The new provisional government feared a Soviet invasion but expected support from the Western democracies. Despite Voice of America broadcasts encouraging rebellion, however, the United States failed to intervene. Soviet tanks rolled in and crushed the revolt with mass arrests and executions.

Americans were quick to point out the obvious contradiction between Soviet rhetoric, which equated socialism with democracy, and their practice of suppressing freedom. But U.S. practices were also at odds with American ideals. Covert actions of the **Central Intelligence Agency** (CIA) often supported authoritarian leaders willing to oblige American interests. Since communism was evil, many thought, anyone who opposed Marxism-Leninism must be on the side of freedom. In reality, many anticommunist regimes were authoritarian dictatorships.

Iran was one example. In the early 1950s, Shah Muhammad Reza Pahlavi (**pahl-ah-vee**), a constitutional monarch, aspired to greater power. He was checked by parliament, led by a popular prime minister, Muhammad Mossadegh (**moh-sah-dehk**). Pahlavi, an ardent anticommunist, cultivated a close alliance with the United States. The Eisenhower administration was concerned that the Soviet Union, which had occupied northern Iran during World War II, still had designs on these oil-rich lands.

For their part, Mossadegh and his parliamentary allies were upset that Britain's Anglo-Iranian Oil Company reaped the lion's share of Iranian oil profits. Mossadegh tried to renegotiate Iran's contracts, and when negotiations failed he made plans to nationalize the oil industry. Then in 1953 the Iranian military, with the covert support of the CIA, arrested Mossadegh, expanding the shah's authority. Many Iranians now saw their king as an American puppet.

The next year the United States undermined democracy in Guatemala in similar fashion. Long ruled by authoritarian dictators, Guatemala had an economy dominated by the United Fruit Company, an American company that owned vast banana plantations, the only railroad, the only port, and the country's telephone system. A small Guatemalan elite benefited, but the country was a study in inequality: 72 percent of the land was owned by 2 percent of the population.

During World War II reformist army officers seized control and organized elections, and in 1946 a newly elected government promised land and labor reform. After another election in 1950,

Hungarian Uprising (1956) Popular revolt against the Soviet-controlled government of Hungary, leading to a Soviet invasion and reimposition of communist authority.

Central Intelligence Agency (CIA) U.S. federal agency created in 1947 whose responsibilities included coordinating intelligence activities abroad, including covert operations against the Soviet Union and its allies during the Cold War.

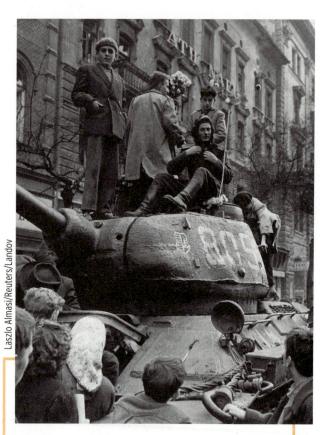

Laszlo Almasi/Reuters/Landov

The Hungarian Uprising A rebellion against their Communist regime brought thousands of Hungarians onto the streets of Budapest in 1956, provoking a Soviet invasion. Great courage was shown by the Hungarians in confronting Soviet tanks and troops, but they were bitterly disappointed when the United States and NATO provided no military support for their freedom struggle.

Ghana's Independence   In 1957 the British colony of the Gold Coast led the way toward continental decolonization when it became the independent state of Ghana, named after an ancient African kingdom. Here Prime Minister Kwame Nkrumah waves to a massive crowd during Ghana's independence ceremony. Nkrumah provided support for other anticolonial movements on the continent, and, through his emphasis on Pan-Africanism, became a spokesman for the ambitions of people of African descent around the world.

Bettmann/Corbis

the new president, **Jacobo Arbenz** (1913–1971), reaffirmed those policies. But the Eisenhower administration, thinking that the Arbenz government had been penetrated by Soviet agents, invoked the "domino theory." Claiming that the "loss" of Guatemala would lead to communist victories elsewhere in the Americas, the United States backed a rebel leader who overthrew Arbenz in 1954. Guatemala reverted to a caudillo-style dictatorship.

Witnessing these events first hand in Guatemala City further radicalized Ernesto Guevara, who fled to Mexico, affiliated himself with Castro, and dedicated himself to revolution. Though he distrusted the Soviet Union, his Guatemalan experience convinced him that the United States was the greater evil.

Decolonization and Neocolonialism in Africa, 1945–1964

During World War II, Africans became more aware of the wider world and increasingly dissatisfied with their colonial situation. The French, British, and Belgians underestimated African sentiments; entering the 1950s, colonial officials thought they were in Africa to stay. Yet by 1960, nationalist movements had freed most of the continent from colonial rule and many new African nations had been established (see Map 30.3). The Swahili word *uhuru,* "freedom," was heard around the world, and Kwame Nkrumah (1909–1972), first president of independent Ghana after 1957, became an international symbol of African aspirations and Pan-Africanism.

But reaping the fruits of independence proved difficult. For one thing, the economic structures of colonialism remained. Economic development required capital and expertise, and both had to be imported. This created ideal conditions for neocolonialism: the continuation of European dominance even after independence had been attained.

The French government was a clever practitioner of neocolonialism. Even before independence, the French had laid the foundations for neocolonial control of their former African colonies. Colonial policies of "assimilation" held out the promise of French citizenship for educated Africans, creating an African elite that identified with French culture. In 1958 President Charles de Gaulle announced a referendum to be held across French Africa. A "yes" vote meant that the former French colonies would receive control over their own internal affairs but

Jacobo Arbenz (1913–1971) President of Guatemala from 1951 to 1954. A moderate socialist, Arbenz enacted comprehensive land reforms that angered Guatemalan elites and U.S. corporations. Was deposed by rebel forces backed by the United States.

would remain part of a larger French "community" directed from Paris. A "no" vote meant complete and immediate independence, severing all ties to France.

All but one of the colonies voted to become members of the French community. The exception was Guinea, where trade union leader Sekou Toure (sey-koo too-rey) campaigned for complete independence. The French government responded to Guinea's "no" vote by withdrawing their administrators overnight, stopping economic aid, and even ripping telephones from the walls as they vacated their offices. Other African leaders learned the lesson and cooperated with France. There were actually more French soldiers in the Ivory Coast after independence than before; with their currencies pegged to the value of the French franc, new nations such as Senegal and Mali had little control over their own economic policies.

Elsewhere, Africans were forced to take up arms to liberate themselves, especially where Europeans had come as settlers. For instance, over a million French men and women lived in Algeria. After the Second World War, Algerian nationalists, some of whom had fought for de Gaulle's Free French Army, demanded rights equal to French settlers and a voice in their own governance. Harshly repressed, these nationalists formed the National Liberation Front and, in 1954, began their armed struggle. It was a brutal war, with the FLN (the French acronym) sometimes launching terrorist attacks on French civilians and the French military systematically using torture in its counter-insurgency campaign. Over time French public opinion soured on the violence, and in 1962 an agreement recognizing Algerian independence was finally negotiated. (See the feature "Movement of Ideas: *The Wretched of the Earth*.")

Primary Source: Comments on Algeria, April 11, 1961 *Read excerpts of a press conference held by Charles de Gaulle, in which he declares France's willingness to accept Algerian independence.*

Like Algeria, Kenya in East Africa was a country with a large settler population (see Chapter 29). The main nationalist leader, Jomo Kenyatta (joh-moh ken-yah-tuh), hoped to develop a mass organization to force the British into negotiations. But a group of African rebels took a more militant stand, forming a secret society, stealing arms from police stations, assassinating a collaborationist chief, and naming themselves the Land and Freedom Army. The British called them the Mau Mau and depicted them as "savages" who had returned to a "primitive" state of irrationality. Hopelessly outgunned by colonial forces, the rebels used their knowledge of the forest and the support of the local population to carry on their fight. By the late 1950s the Kenyan rebellion was contained, after over twelve thousand Africans and one hundred Europeans had been killed. The British government was now determined to make the settlers compromise with moderate African nationalists. In 1964, Jomo Kenyatta became the first president of an independent Kenya.

In southern Africa, compromise between white settlers and African nationalists was impossible. The white settlers of Rhodesia declared their independence from Britain in 1965 rather than enter into negotiations over sharing power, while in South Africa the apartheid regime was deeply entrenched. Because the Rhodesian and South African leaders were adamantly anticommunist, governments in London and Washington were willing to overlook their repressive policies. In 1964, when Nelson Mandela was sentenced to life in prison, hopes for transforming South Africa were at an all-time low.

The former Belgian Congo was one place where the difficulties of the postcolonial transition were compounded by superpower interference. After King Leopold's reign (see Chapter 26), the Belgian government created a tightly centralized, racially divided colonial administration. Yet it did little to prepare Africans for independence: after eighty years of Belgian rule, only sixteen Africans in the entire Congo had university degrees. Still, with Congo caught up in the nationalist excitement spreading across the continent, in 1960 the Belgians made hasty plans for independence, believing that the weakness of the new Congolese government would make it susceptible to neocolonial control.

The election was won by the Congolese National Movement, and a government was

Map 30.3 Decolonization

In the three decades following Indian independence in 1947, the European colonial empires in Asia and Africa unraveled, adding many new "Third World" representatives to the United Nations. Their aspirations of dignity and development were frequently thwarted, however, by Cold War politics, continued Western economic domination, poor leadership, and ethnic and religious rivalry. © Cengage Learning   **Interactive Map**

1960 Year independence achieved

Former ruler

Great Britain	Belgium
France	Portugal
Netherlands	United States
Italy	Other

GREAT BRITAIN
PORTUGAL
SPAIN
FRANCE
NETHERLANDS
BELGIUM
ITALY
JAPAN

MOROCCO 1956
WESTERN SAHARA 1975 (Morocco)
MAURITANIA 1960
CAPE VERDE 1975 (From Port.)
SENEGAL 1960
GAMBIA 1965
GUINEA-BISSAU 1974
GUINEA 1958
SIERRA LEONE 1961
LIBERIA 1820s
CÔTE D'IVOIRE 1960
GHANA 1957
BURKINA FASO 1960
MALI 1960
ALGERIA 1962
TUNISIA 1957
MALTA 1964 (From Gr. Br.)
LIBYA 1951
NIGER 1960
BENIN 1960
TOGO 1960
NIGERIA 1960
EQUATORIAL GUINEA 1968 (From Spain)
SÃO TOMÉ AND PRÍNCIPE 1975 (From Port.)
CAMEROON 1960
GABON 1960
REPUBLIC OF CONGO 1960
CENTRAL AFRICAN REPUBLIC 1960
CHAD 1960
EGYPT 1922
SUDAN 1956
ERITREA 1993 (From Ethiopia)
ETHIOPIA
DJIBOUTI 1977
SOMALIA 1960
CYPRUS 1960
LEBANON 1944
ISRAEL 1948
SYRIA 1944
IRAQ 1932
JORDAN 1946
KUWAIT 1961
BAHRAIN 1971
QATAR 1971
UNITED ARAB EMIRATES 1971
OMAN 1971
P.D.R. OF YEMEN 1967 (Unified 1990) YEMEN
DEM. REP. OF CONGO 1960
UGANDA 1962
RWANDA 1962
BURUNDI 1962
KENYA 1963
TANZANIA 1964
ANGOLA 1975
ZAMBIA 1964
MALAWI 1964
MOZAMBIQUE 1974
ZIMBABWE 1980
NAMIBIA 1990 (From South Africa)
BOTSWANA 1966
SWAZILAND 1968
LESOTHO 1966
SOUTH AFRICA (Republic 1961)
MADAGASCAR 1960
COMOROS 1975 (From France)
SEYCHELLES 1976 (From Gr. Br.)
MAURITIUS 1968 (From Gr. Br.)

PAKISTAN 1947
INDIA 1947
MALDIVES 1975 (From Gr. Br.)
SRI LANKA (CEYLON) 1948
PAKISTAN 1947, BANGLADESH 1973
MYANMAR (BURMA) 1947
LAOS 1949
NORTH VIETNAM 1954 (Unified 1974)
SOUTH VIETNAM 1954
CAMBODIA 1953
MALAYSIA 1963
SINGAPORE 1965 (From Malaysia)
BRUNEI 1984 (From Gr. Br.)
INDONESIA 1949
TIMOR-LESTE 1999 (From Indonesia)
PHILIPPINES 1946
NORTH KOREA 1948 (From Japan)
SOUTH KOREA 1948
JAPAN
PAPUA NEW GUINEA 1975 (from Australia)

ATLANTIC OCEAN
PACIFIC OCEAN
INDIAN OCEAN
Mediterranean Sea
Black Sea
Caspian Sea
Arabian Sea
Bay of Bengal

Tropic of Cancer
Tropic of Capricorn
Equator

40°N 20°N 0° 20°S
20°W 0° 20°E 40°E 60°E 80°E 100°E 120°E

0   1,000   2,000 Km.
0   1,000   2,000 Mi.

N

The Wretched of the Earth

Frantz Fanon (1925–1961) was an advocate of Third World revolution, guerilla warfare, and socialism. Born on the Caribbean island of Martinique, in the French West Indies, Fanon volunteered for service in the Free French Army and was wounded during the liberation of France in 1944. After training in Paris as a psychiatrist, he was stationed in North Africa. During the Algerian war Fanon's medical practice included psychiatric treatment of both French practitioners and Arab and Berber victims of torture. From this experience he concluded that colonialism was intrinsically violent and could only be removed by violence. He joined the Algerian National Liberation Front and became a prominent spokesman for their cause. Fanon was dying of leukemia in 1961 while writing his most bitter indictment of colonialism, *The Wretched of the Earth* (1961).

Decolonization is the meeting of two forces, opposed to each other by their very nature.... Their first encounter was marked by violence and their existence together—that is to say the exploitation of the native by the settler—was carried on by dint of a great array of bayonets and cannons....

The naked truth of decolonization evokes for us the searing bullets and bloodstained knives which emanate from it. For if the last shall be first, this will only come to pass after a murderous and decisive struggle between the two protagonists....

The settlers' town is a strongly built town, all made of stone and steel. It is a brightly lit town; the streets are all covered with asphalt, and the garbage cans swallow all the leavings, unseen, unknown, and hardly thought about.... The settlers' town is a town of white people, of foreigners....

The native town is a hungry town, starved for bread, of meat, of shoes, of coal, of light. The native town is a crouching village, a town on its knees, a town wallowing in the mire.... The look that the native turns on the settlers' town is a look of lust, a look of envy; it expresses his dreams of possession—all manner of possession: to sit at the settler's table, to sleep in the settler's bed, with his wife if possible. The colonized man is an envious man....

The violence which has ruled over the ordering of the colonial world, which has ceaselessly drummed the rhythm for the destruction of native social forms and broken up without reserve the systems of reference of the economy ... that same violence will be claimed and taken over by the native at the moment when, deciding to embody history in his own person, he surges into the forbidden quarters....

As if to show the totalitarian character of colonial exploitation the settler paints the native as the quintessence of evil. Native society is not simply described as a society lacking in values.... The native is declared insensible to ethics; he represents not only the absence of values, but the negation of values ... and in this sense he is the absolute evil....

The violence with which the supremacy of white values is affirmed and the aggressiveness which has permeated the victory of these values over the ways of life and thought of the native mean that, in revenge, the native laughs in mockery when Western values are mentioned in front of him…. In the period of decolonization, the colonized masses mock at these very values, insult them, and vomit them up….

[When the urban militants] get into the habit of talking to the peasants they discover that the rural masses have never ceased to pose the problem of their liberation in terms of violence, of taking back the land from the foreigners, in terms of a national struggle. Everything is simple…. They discover a generous people prepared to make sacrifices, willing to give of itself, impatient and with a stony pride. One can understand that the encounter between militants who are being hunted by the police and these impatient masses, who are instinctually rebellious, can produce an explosive mixture of unexpected power….

Come, then, comrades, the European game has finally ended; we must find something different. We today can do everything so long as we do not imitate Europe, so long as we are not obsessed with desire to catch up with Europe…. European achievements, European techniques, and European style ought to no longer tempt us and to throw us off our balance.

When I search for Man in the technique and style of Europe, I see only a succession of negations of man, and an avalanche of murders…. It is a question of the Third World starting a new history of Man, a history which will have regard to the sometimes prodigious theses Europe has put forward, but which will also not forget Europe's crimes…. For Europe, for ourselves, for humanity, comrades, we must turn over a new leaf, we must work out new concepts, and try to set afoot a new man.

Source: From Frantz Fanon, *The Wretched of the Earth* (New York Grove, 1963), pp. 36, 39–41, 43, 45, 59, 61, 312, 315–316. Reprinted by permssion.

QUESTIONS FOR ANALYSIS

▶ **What is similar and what is different between Fanon's ideas and those of Mohandas K. Gandhi (see Chapter 28)?**

▶ **What is Fanon's critique of European society, and how does he find hope in Third World revolution?**

formed by Prime Minister **Patrice Lumumba (loo-MOOM-buh)** (1925–1961). The independence ceremony in 1960 was fraught with tension. After the Belgian king made a patronizing speech praising his country's "civilizing mission" in Africa, Lumumba responded with a catalogue of Belgian crimes against Africans. "Our wounds," he said, "are still too fresh and painful for us to be able to erase them from our memories." The speech made Lumumba a hero to African nationalists, but he was now regarded as a dangerous radical in Brussels and Washington.

Lumumba faced immediate challenges. African soldiers mutinied against their Belgian officers, and the mineral-rich province of Katanga seceded. When the United Nations sent in peacekeeping forces, Lumumba suspected their real purpose was to defend Western interests. After turning to the Soviet Union for military aid, Lumumba was branded a "communist," and—with the complicity of the CIA—he was arrested, beaten, and murdered by rivals. Rebel armies arose in several provinces. Finally Joseph Mobutu **(mo-BOO-too)**, an army officer long on the CIA payroll, seized dictatorial power.

Che Guevara was among those who regarded Lumumba as a fallen hero and Mobutu as an American puppet. In 1965, Che joined up with Congolese rebels in the eastern part of the country. It was a disappointing experience, since the rebels were lacking in both discipline and ideological commitment: "I felt entirely alone," he later wrote, "in a way that I had never experienced before, neither in Cuba nor anywhere else, throughout my long pilgrimage across the world."[2]

When Che returned to Cuba in 1966, the Congo was firmly under Joseph Mobutu's authoritarian control. The United States was the main power broker in Central Africa, allied with Mobutu to secure the mineral riches of the Congo, some of which, such as cobalt, were vital to the aerospace industry.

Patrice Lumumba (1925–1961) The first prime minister of the Democratic Republic of Congo in 1960. Was deposed and assassinated by political rivals in 1961.

Ahmed Sukarno (1901–1970) Leader in the struggle for Indonesian independence from Holland, achieved in 1949. Indonesian military leaders, backed by the United States, thought Sukarno incapable of battling communism and removed him from power.

Jawaharlal Nehru (1889–1964) Statesman who helped negotiate the end of British colonial rule and served as independent India's first prime minister from 1947 to 1964. Nehru was an influential advocate of the Non-Aligned Movement, refusing to choose sides in the Cold War.

The Bandung Generation, 1955–1965

Neocolonialism and superpower intervention were exactly what the leaders of former colonial states who met in Bandung **(bahn-doong)**, Indonesia, for the first Asia-Africa conference in 1955 wished to avoid. The careers of the Indonesian, Indian, and Egyptian representatives at the Bandung Conference illustrate how difficult it was to remain nonaligned with either the United States or the Soviet Union.

Ahmed Sukarno (1901–1970) first emerged as a nationalist fighting against Dutch colonialism in the 1920s. In 1945 he and his party declared Indonesia free of both the Dutch and the Japanese, but it was not until 1950 and the defeat of Dutch reoccupation forces that independence became a reality. The new country was a scattering of hundreds of islands across thousands of miles. Sukarno promoted the development of an Indonesian language with a simplified grammar to unify Indonesia's great diversity of peoples.

Sukarno was widely popular at first, but he had no experience running a country. Priding himself as the key to Indonesia's development, he became erratic and declared himself "president-for-life" in 1963. As his popularity waned, he faced a potent communist insurgency. Suspecting that Sukarno was either sympathetic to the communists or too weak to stave them off, the Indonesian military launched a murderous crackdown in 1964 to wipe them out. In 1967 General Suharto, a military commander backed by the United States, suspended the constitution and took power. American administrations turned a blind eye to the authoritarianism and corruption of Suharto's regime. As in Mobutu's Congo, they were glad to have a dependable ally in the struggle against communism.

India's prime minister **Jawaharlal Nehru (juh-wah-her-lahl NAY-roo)** (1889–1964) was more successful than Sukarno in securing his country's nonalignment during the Cold War, though the partition of India at independence had been a wrenching experience. In the 1930s the Muslim League began to challenge the dominance of the Indian National Congress by arguing for a separate Muslim nation to be carved out of British India. In 1947, when the British did finally grant British India independence, they partitioned their colony into two separate independent states: India and Pakistan.

However, a substantial Hindu minority resided in Pakistan and an even larger Muslim minority remained in the new state of India. In a climate of fear and uncertainty, millions of people tried desperately to cross to the country where they "belonged." In the intercommunal violence that followed, as many as 10 million people were dislocated, perhaps seventy-five thousand women were raped or abducted, and more than 1 million people lost their lives.

Despite its violent birth and the enduring challenges of poverty and illiteracy, India emerged as the world's largest democracy. Though military tensions emerged on India's borders with Pakistan and China, Nehru kept his country stable and nonaligned by purchasing military hardware from both the United States and the Soviet Union and by building up India's own defense industries. In Pakistan, by contrast, corruption and misrule led to a military seizure of power. In 1958, Pakistan's military government entered into a defense agreement with the United States, which was concerned about India's military ties with the Soviet Union and anxious to have a reliably anticommunist ally in this strategic region. These agreements meant that, in spite of India's nonalignment, the Cold War deeply affected South Asian politics.

Another prominent figure at Bandung was **Gamal Abdel Nasser** (1918–1970). In 1952 he had led a military coup to overthrow Egypt's King Farouk, whom he saw as a pawn of foreign interests. Nasser argued that Arabs should unite to fight European neocolonialism and American imperialism. He embraced secular Arab nationalism while rejecting religion as a basis for politics and banning competing political parties such as the Egyptian Communist Party and the Muslim Brotherhood.

In 1954 Nasser successfully negotiated the withdrawal of British troops from the Suez Canal Zone and began plans for building a giant dam on the Nile River to provide electricity for industrialization. He approached Britain and the United States but refused to join an anti-Soviet alliance as a condition of their assistance. Instead, in 1956 Nasser proclaimed the nationalization of the Suez Canal to finance the dam. The British government was outraged.

The Suez Crisis of 1956 developed further when the British, French, and Israelis hatched a secret plan: the British and the French would send "peacekeeping" troops to the Canal Zone in response to a prearranged Israeli incursion across the Egyptian border. However, the plan lacked American support, and the British and Israelis withdrew when faced with Egyptian opposition and international criticism. For Nasser, it was a triumph. He became a hero across the Arab world for facing down British imperialism and Israeli aggression, and the Aswan Dam was later completed with Soviet aid.

Nasser's reputation in the Arab world was grounded in his support of the Palestinian cause and belligerence toward Israel. In 1947, as the British withdrew their forces from Palestine, diplomats at the United Nations finalized a plan to partition Palestine into separate Arab and Jewish states. In 1948, with Arab states refusing to accept the partition plan, Zionist leaders declared the independence of Israel. Egypt, Lebanon, Syria, Jordan, and Iraq immediately attacked Israel; Nasser himself fought in the Pan-Arab army.

As Arab refugees fled the fighting, some driven from their homes by Israeli soldiers, the Israeli government expanded its borders beyond what the United Nations plan had envisioned; the Israelis routed the Arab armies. Shocked and humiliated, Arabs thereafter looked to Nasser as their best hope to destroy Israel and return Palestinian refugees to their native land.

Nasser's reputation, however, was severely damaged after he made a series of threatening moves that prompted a pre-emptive Israeli attack. In the Six-Day War of 1967, virtually the entire Egyptian air force was destroyed as Israeli forces occupied Egypt's Sinai Desert, Syria's Golan Heights, and the West Bank of the Jordan River. Israeli occupation of predominantly Arab East Jerusalem was particularly galling. U.S. support had helped make Israeli victory possible, a cause of resentment across the Muslim world. The Soviet Union gave rhetorical support to the Palestinians, but no military aid.

Sukarno, Nehru, and Nasser had all grown up in European-dominated colonial worlds and had dedicated themselves to the liberation of their peoples. While they were all aware that Cold War entanglements would compromise their ability to move their nations forward,

Gamal Abdel Nasser (1918–1970) Prime minister of Egypt from 1954 to 1956 and president from 1956 to 1970. The nationalization of the Suez Canal in 1956 made Nasser a Pan-Arab hero, though the loss of the Six-Day War to Israel in 1967 badly damaged that reputation.

they had different levels of success in achieving the nonalignment to which they had dedicated themselves at Bandung. Sukarno was the least successful; his fall brought to power a military dictatorship allied with the United States. Nehru was by far the most successful, maintaining India's status as a genuinely nonaligned democracy throughout this period. Nasser chose to ally Egypt with the Soviet Union simply because the Soviets were enemies of the United States, Israel's main ally.

Vietnam: The Cold War in Southeast Asia, 1956–1974

As in Indonesia, Vietnamese nationalists had to fight colonial reoccupation forces to win their independence. After helping drive the Japanese from Indochina during World War II, Ho Chi Minh had declared an independent Democratic Republic of Vietnam in 1945, explicitly referring to the American Declaration of Independence in asserting the right of the Vietnamese people to be free from foreign rule. That claim was disputed by France, which sent forces to re-establish colonial control.

Ho's Viet Minh fighters had developed their skills in war against the Japanese. In 1954, the Viet Minh victory at Dien Bien Phu (dyen byen foo) proved to be too much for France. French military officers told their government that they could not wage two counter-insurgencies—in Algeria and Vietnam—simultaneously. Since Algeria was home to a million French citizens, it was the greater priority, and the French withdrew from Indochina.

At the Geneva Conference, Vietnam was temporarily partitioned into north and south, pending national elections. Fearing that Ho Chi Minh's communists would win those elections, the United States supported the formation of a separate South Vietnamese regime. Conflict between the two Vietnams intensified as the United States supplied the south with weapons and military training, while North Vietnam sponsored a southern-based rebel army, the National Front for the Liberation of South Vietnam, or Vietcong. In 1964, President Lyndon Johnson sought congressional approval for launching a full-scale war against the communist regime in Hanoi,

Primary Source: Letter to the French Chamber of Deputies *Read what the chairman of the Vietnamese Nationalist Party, twenty-six years old and awaiting execution, wrote to the parliament of France.*

claiming that North Vietnamese ships had launched an unprovoked attack on American gunboats; in reality the American ships were within North Vietnamese waters on an intelligence-gathering mission. Congress gave Johnson authority to wage war, and by 1965 there were 200,000 American combatants in Vietnam.

In spite of massive bombing attacks on North Vietnam, the Vietcong grew in strength. American soldiers were often unable to distinguish guerilla soldiers from civilians. At home, Americans were incredulous when their troops brutally slaughtered the villagers of My Lai (**mee lie**) in 1969 and spread poisonous clouds of defoliating chemicals across the Vietnamese countryside. Images of burning children fleeing napalm bomb blasts sickened global audiences. In this first "televised war," images of death and destruction were transmitted around the world.

In 1968, the Vietcong took the fight straight to the South Vietnamese capital of Saigon during the Tet Offensive. In 1969, as antiwar protests spread across American college campuses and anti-American feelings arose in much of Europe, Asia, Africa, and Latin America, the new administration of Richard Nixon promised a "secret plan" to win the war: even more intensive bombing of North Vietnam and the replacement of American ground forces with South Vietnamese ones. Demoralized and corrupt, the South Vietnamese government and military were not up to the task. On April 30, 1975, after the United States withdrew its ground forces, communist forces entered Saigon, renamed it Ho Chi Minh City, and reunified the country under their dictatorship.

Entering the Vietnam War, Americans were inclined to think in simple terms: democracy was good, communism was evil, and any fight against communism was necessarily a fight for freedom. In the course of the Vietnam War they discovered that the world was more complicated. While the Viet Minh were dedicated Marxist-Leninist revolutionaries, their movement had its roots in Vietnam's long history of resistance to foreign intrusion: China in former times, Japan and France in more recent times, and now the United States.

In many parts of the world, the Cold War disrupted the transition from colonialism to national independence. While outcomes in Vietnam, Indonesia, and the Congo varied, they had one thing in common: by the mid-1970s not one of them was a democracy.

Vietnamese Protest On June 11, 1963, Quang Duc, a Vietnamese Buddhist monk, burned himself to death on a Saigon street. His self-immolation was a protest of the policies of the U.S.-backed South Vietnamese government, which many Buddhists thought favored the Catholic minority.

A Time of Upheaval, 1966–1974

Americans who grew up during "the Sixties" remember it as a time of political, social, and cultural turmoil. The Civil Rights Movement under the leadership of figures like Dr. Martin Luther King paralleled other liberation movements taking place around the world. Young people took center stage, proclaiming that the world could, and should, be made a far better place of peace, love, and justice. In 1963, the poet-musician Bob Dylan captured the spirit of the time:

Come mothers and fathers throughout the land
And don't criticize what you can't understand
Your sons and your daughters are beyond your command
Your old road is rapidly aging
Please get out of the new one if you can't lend your hand
For the times they are a-changing. *

This global trend toward greater youth involvement in politics and society arose among students who had come of age after the Second World War. In dormitory rooms across the world, posters of Che Guevara symbolized the revolutionary fervor of youth. In most places, youth movements arose in opposition to traditional authority. In China, however, Mao Zedong harnessed the power of young people to drive his final experiment in radical revolutionary transformation.

In the end, global youth in the 1960s did not change the world. In the United States, Europe, China, and Latin America, authorities reasserted control, and the bipolarity of the Cold War continued.

*Bob Dylan lyrics from "The Times They Are A-Changing." Reprinted with permission of Special Rider Music.

The Great Proletarian Cultural Revolution, 1965–1974

After the disaster of the Great Leap Forward, the People's Republic of China returned to a more conventional planned economy. But the Soviet model of top-down economic planning had never appealed to Mao, who felt that it stifled the revolutionary enthusiasm of the masses. In 1965, Mao mobilized the **Red Guards**, who were taught that Mao himself was the source of all wisdom. His thoughts were collected in a "little red book" that became the bible of the Red Guard movement, waved enthusiastically in the air by the millions of young people who came to Beijing to pay homage to the "Great Helmsman."

Mao used the Red Guards to attack his enemies within the Communist Party, the "rightists" and "experts" who had resisted him during the Great Leap Forward. Soon the Red Guards had created an atmosphere of anarchy, attacking party offices, publicly humiliating their teachers, destroying cultural artifacts that linked China to its past, and harassing anyone they thought needed "re-education." Educated Chinese were sent to farms and factories, where they were expected to humble themselves and absorb the authentic revolutionary spirit of the masses. Many died.

By 1968 the country was near anarchy and its economy was at a standstill. Pragmatic communist leaders convinced Mao to allow the People's Liberation Army to restore governmental authority. Now, Red Guards themselves faced "downward transfer" to remote villages and labor camps. But while the worst excesses of the Cultural Revolution were curbed, a bitter power struggle took place behind the scenes. A radical faction called the "Gang of Four," led by Mao's wife, Jiang Qing (jyahng ching), schemed to restore the Cultural Revolution. Jiang was a former actress who used her power to purge Chinese art and intellectual life of Western influences and to take vengeance on her many enemies. On the other side were pragmatists like Deng Xiaoping (dung shee-yao-ping), an "expert" who was struggling to regain his influence. With the Cultural Revolution reined in and an aging Mao no longer in complete command, Deng and the "expert" faction gradually reasserted themselves.

The pragmatists scored a victory in 1972 when the American president Richard Nixon came to Beijing. Relations between the two countries had long been tense, partly because the Americans supported the Nationalist government of Chiang Kai-shek on the island of Taiwan, which the communists regarded as a rebel province of China. But the Chinese were also worried about their long border with the Soviet Union, where armed confrontations had recently taken place. Although a die-hard anticommunist, Nixon judged that better relations with communist China would increase his own bargaining power with the U.S.S.R. and might help the United States extricate itself from Vietnam.

In spite of thawing relations with the United States, the restoration of party and army control, and the return of moderates to positions of influence, the shadow of the Cultural Revolution still hung over China at the time of Mao's death in 1976. But the eventual victory of Deng Xiaoping's pragmatic faction over the Gang of Four sent the People's Republic of China in a new direction. The people of China had paid a terrible price for Mao's political adventures: the Great Leap Forward and the Great Proletarian Cultural Revolution had killed tens of millions of people.

1968: A Year of Revolution

In 1968, just when the Chinese Communist Party was suppressing the Red Guard movement, the political power of youth was escalating elsewhere in the world. In the United States, the "hippie" movement was in full flower. During the "summer of love" in 1967, long hair, psychedelic art and music, and slogans such as "make love, not war" emanated from college campuses. Eastern religion and consciousness-altering drugs became part of the quest to remake the mind while remaking the world.

New thinking about gender roles transformed women's rights. Even though women had achieved legal equality in much of the world, opportunities for women remained sharply limited; the common expectation was that young women need not advance in their careers because they would quickly marry and

Red Guards   Young people who rallied to the cause of Maoism during the Great Proletarian Cultural Revolution. As their enthusiasm got out of control, the Red Guards spread anarchy across the People's Republic of China.

Bettmann/Corbis

Nixon in China   A lifelong anticommunist, President Richard Nixon nevertheless seized the chance for global realignment by visiting China in 1972, hoping that better relations with China would aid U.S. diplomacy with the Soviet Union. The agenda for the meeting was the work of Premier Chou En-lai (*far left*) and Nixon's national security adviser Henry Kissinger (*far right*), who were both practitioners of *realpolitik* ("realistic politics").

devote themselves to motherhood. In the 1960s, the founders of the modern feminist movement demanded equal social and economic rights for women.

However, the hopes of feminists, civil rights advocates, and student leaders in the early 1960s were soon tempered by harsher realities. Drug use ruined lives, peace marches turned violent, demonstrations resulted in mass arrests, and in 1968 two voices for peace and moderation—civil rights leader Martin Luther King, Jr. and Democratic presidential candidate Robert F. Kennedy—were assassinated. Violence spread through American cities.

During the 1968 Democratic National Convention, American television viewers watched in horror as Chicago police bludgeoned youthful protestors; a few months later Republican Richard Nixon won the presidency. To those Americans appalled by the ferment of the sixties, Nixon was an experienced, thoughtful anticommunist who would restore order. To those who dreamt of a new age of peace and justice, Nixon represented everything that was wrong with "the establishment." The nation became even more bitterly divided after Ohio Army National Guardsmen shot four student protestors to death at Kent State University in the spring of 1970.

In Europe, Paris was a major center of student unrest. As in the United States, the number of university students had risen sharply in the post-1945

period. After three college students were arrested for occupying a dean's office, students all over France rose to their defense. By May the Sorbonne University in Paris was festooned with portraits of Che Guevara and other revolutionary heroes. Student marchers, assaulted by riot police, built barricades of overturned cars and garbage cans.

Whereas in the United States most working Americans, including most union members, tended to side with the forces of "law and order," in France the major trade unions joined the protests. Two million French workers went on strike, taking over factories and proclaiming that their bosses were unnecessary. Art students expressed this philosophy on posters they plastered around Paris, with slogans such as "Be realistic, ask for the impossible," "The boss needs you, you don't need him," and "It is forbidden to forbid."

In response, French president Charles de Gaulle appeared on television to proclaim: "The whole French people … are being prevented from living a normal existence by those elements, Reds and Anarchists, that are preventing students from studying, workers from working." But he also offered concessions. The minimum wage was raised, and new elections were organized. De Gaulle's re-election in late 1968, like the election of Richard Nixon in the United States, made it clear that most voters wanted a return to "normal existence." After workers were appeased with new contracts, French students

Prague Spring (1968) An attempt by political reformers in Czechoslovakia to reform the communist government and create "socialism with a human face." The Soviet Union invaded Czechoslovakia, ending this attempt at reform and reimposing communist orthodoxy.

Tlatelolco Massacre (1968) Massacre that occurred when ten thousand university students, faculty, and other supporters gathered in Tlatelolco Plaza to protest the closing of the Mexican National University; government forces opened fire and killed three hundred people.

lost their working-class allies and the forces of "law and order" reasserted themselves.

In eastern Europe, students also played a prominent role in the **Prague Spring**. In 1948 Czechoslovakia had been forced by Stalin's Red Army to give up its fledgling democracy. By the mid-1960s, discontent with the stifling conditions of communism was growing. Early in 1968 workers' strikes and students' protests forced the resignation of the hard-line communist leadership.

The new head of the Czechoslovak Communist Party, Alexander Dubček (**doob-chek**), promised "socialism with a human face," including freedom of speech and association as well as more liberal, market-oriented economic policies. The Czech public rallied to Dubček's cause, and students and teachers took advantage of the new atmosphere to discuss how economic justice and democratic freedoms could be achieved in their country.

Fearing that the movement toward liberalization would spread, the Soviet leadership ordered a half-million Soviet and Warsaw Pact troops into Czechoslovakia, replacing Dubček with a more compliant Czech Communist leader. There was no substantial resistance. Reformers in Czechoslovakia, as well as in Poland, Hungary, and the Soviet Union itself, were put on notice: no changes to the status quo would be allowed.

Mexico was another country where a large school-age population aspired to a better life. But while Mexican society was changing rapidly, Mexican politics were not. The Party of Institutional Revolution (PRI) was the elitist, bureaucratic, and corrupt descendant of the old National Revolutionary Party (see Chapter 27). Since the PRI did not allow free elections, Mexican advocates of political change had no choice but to go to the streets.

The tensions of 1968 began when riot police used force to break up a fight between two student groups. Over a hundred thousand students, with support from many of their teachers and parents, went on strike, marching through the city shouting "*¡Mexico, Libertad!*" ("Mexico,

Liberty!"). The timing of the protests was particularly awkward. The Summer Olympic Games were to be held in Mexico City in October, and the government wanted to project a positive image to the worldwide television audience. The government decided to crack down.

The result was the **Tlatelolco Massacre**. The government said the protestors fired first, a contention contradicted by many eyewitnesses watching from apartments lining the square. Hundreds were killed, but the Olympic Games went on as planned, and most of the world heard nothing about the bloodshed at Tlatelolco (**tlah-tel-OHL-koh**).

Despite their passionate commitment, student protestors in the United States, France, Czechoslovakia, and Mexico were unable to radically change the status quo. In the longer view of history, however, the impact of this generation seems unmistakable. The spirit of the 1960s informed social movements in the decades to come, bringing idealism and activism to music and arts, educational reform, environmental sustainability, and gender equality.

Death and Dictatorship in Latin America, 1967–1975

After his failed sojourn to Central Africa, Che Guevara was still looking for a place where a band of rebels could provide the spark for revolution. In 1967 he headed for Bolivia, convinced that its corrupt government would fall swiftly once the oppressed indigenous population rose against it. But Guevara did not attract the support he expected. Long exploited, Andeans were wary of Spanish-speaking outsiders who claimed to be fighting on their behalf. Short on rations, Che's rebel band wandered in the frigid mountains, and in September 1967 Guevara was captured by Bolivian soldiers and executed as an agent of the CIA stood by.

Che's death occurred as dictatorships arose throughout Latin America, with authoritarian governments justifying repression in the name of anticommunism. Chile's relatively strong democratic tradition came under assault after an alliance of center-left and left-wing parties led by the Marxist **Salvador Allende** (**uh-YEN-day**) (1908–1973) won a bitterly contested election in 1970. Allende's effort to build a socialist economy was strongly opposed by Chilean businessmen and landowners, and his nationalization of the copper mines alarmed American economic interests. In the fall of 1973, with the backing of the United States, the military staged a coup. Salvador Allende committed suicide as a force commanded by General Augusto Pinochet (ah-GOOS-toh pin-oh-CHET) stormed the Presidential Palace in Santiago. Pinochet instituted free-market economic policies and invited foreign investment. But economic liberalism was not matched by political openness, as Pinochet dismantled the institutions of Chilean democracy. Like the couple Che had once met on the road, thousands of students and union leaders were jailed or killed.

In the mid-1970s military government prevailed across South America. In Argentina thousands of students vanished, their mothers holding silent vigils for months and years for these *desaparecidos* (deh-say-pah-re-see-dohs) ("disappeared ones"), not knowing that in many cases their sons and daughters had been killed, some drugged and pushed out of airplanes over the open sea. In Brazil as well, military authorities used anticommunism to limit freedom of speech and freedom of association. Successive administrations in Washington, ever fearful that communism might gain advantage in "America's own backyard" following the Cuban example, were generally supportive of the right-wing regimes that repressed popular democracy.

Détente and Challenges to Bipolarity

Relations between the United States and the Soviet Union were particularly strained at the time of the Cuban Revolution and the Cuban Missile Crisis. Images from the time include Soviet premier Nikita Khrushchev banging his shoe on a table at the United Nations while angrily denouncing American imperialism, and President John F. Kennedy pledging to put American astronauts on the moon before the end of the decade. In 1957 the Soviets had launched *Sputnik* (spuht-nick), the first artificial satellite to orbit the earth. In response America developed the Apollo space program, accomplishing the first manned mission to the moon in 1969. Indeed, the Cold War propelled continuous technological innovation, as each side poured huge resources into applied scientific research.

By the mid-1960s a state of reluctant coexistence between the superpowers was becoming the norm. Both "nations faced increasing challenges, domestic and foreign. While the United States was dealing with social discord related to the Civil Rights Movement and increasing opposition to the Vietnam War, in the Soviet Union poor living standards were the issue. The Soviet people had guaranteed employment, universal education, and health care, but they faced persistent shortages of consumer goods, and those available were often shoddy. Moscow was looking for some breathing space in which to develop its domestic economy.

In theory, the division between East and West, between capitalism and communism, was absolute. In reality, both the United States and the U.S.S.R. were having increasing difficulty controlling their respective blocs. After 1960 relations between Moscow and Beijing were strained. It was this Sino-Soviet split that gave Richard Nixon an opening with the People's Republic of China. At the same time, the Western alliance was no longer subject to complete American domination. In 1957, the Treaty of Rome laid the foundation for what would become the European Economic Community. While shielded from Soviet aggression by the North Atlantic Treaty Organization and the still powerful American military presence, in the 1960s and early 1970s western European leaders began to emerge from under the economic and political umbrella of the United States.

Although the Cold War division of the world appeared likely to remain for the foreseeable future, the two superpowers began to soften their rhetoric and seek ways to live together in a spirit of **détente** (day-tahnt). The greatest achievement was the Strategic Arms Limitation Treaty (SALT) of 1972, which froze the number of ballistic missiles in the possession of the United States and the Soviet Union. The specter of nuclear war never disappeared, but in the mid-1970s it began to recede.

Salvador Allende (1908–1973) Socialist leader elected president of Chile in 1970. His government was overthrown in a U.S.-backed military coup in 1973, during which Allende took his own life.

détente The easing of hostility between nations, specifically the movement in the 1970s to negotiate arms limitations treaties to reduce tensions between the Eastern and Western blocs during the Cold War.

Chapter Review and Learning Activities

Long after his death, Che Guevara remains an iconic figure. Staring out from millions of tee-shirts and posters, his youthful image evokes romantic qualities: idealism, self-sacrifice, and a restless yearning to transform the world. Whether the real Ernesto Guevara, medical student turned revolutionary, is worthy of such latter-day worship remains an open question. What is beyond dispute is that the bitter divisions of the Cold War made the realization of global justice and equality all the more difficult to achieve.

What were the implications of successful revolutions in China and Cuba for the Cold War rivalry of the United States and the Soviet Union?

The establishment of the People's Republic of China in 1949 by the Chinese Communist Party under Mao Zedong added to the global power and prestige of communism and intensified fears in the United States and elsewhere of Soviet domination. In reality, however, Mao resisted Soviet models of development, and Sino-Soviet relations deteriorated. The Cuban Revolution in 1959 gave the Soviet Union another opportunity to expand its sphere of influence, but the Cuban Missile Crisis of 1961 showed just how dangerous the Soviet military alliance with Cuba was to the global balance of power, as both of the superpowers sought a face-saving compromise. More generally, the United States and the Soviet Union stayed within their own spheres of influence.

How were democratization and decolonization movements in the mid-twentieth century affected by the Cold War?

In many regions, such as Central Africa and Southeast Asia, decolonization took place in a political environment filled with Cold War tensions. The leaders who had gathered at the Bandung Conference pledged to create a world in which formerly colonized societies would maintain their nonalignment in the East/West power struggle. The difficulty of doing so was confirmed by the long war in Vietnam. Meanwhile, the United States and the Soviet Union undercut struggles for national independence, democracy, and social reform in countries from Guatemala to Hungary and from Congo to Poland.

What was the role of youth in the global upheavals of 1965–1974?

The "sixties" brought to the fore the cultural influence of the generation born during and just after World War II. In China, students responded enthusiastically to Mao Zedong's call for a Great Proletarian Cultural Revolution, and violence and disorder spread with the influence of the Red Guards. In many other parts of the world, students, while also politically active, organized against the established authorities. In 1968, student activists took to the streets of cities like Chicago, Paris, Prague, and Mexico City demanding change. Though the global youth movement of the 1960s certainly had long-term influence, the political aspirations of student activists were not achieved. In the United States, France, Czechoslovakia, Mexico, and elsewhere, leaders representing traditional institutions reasserted control. By 1974 the youth revolution had largely run its course. In the age of détente, the Cold War status quo of global division remained.

FOR FURTHER REFERENCE

Gaddis, John Lewis. *The Cold War: A New History*. New York: Penguin, 2005.

Guevara, Ernesto. *The Motorcycle Diaries: Notes on a Latin American Journey*. Edited and translated by Alexandra Keeble. Melbourne: Ocean Press, 2003.

Hart, Joseph, ed. *Che: The Life, Death and Afterlife of a Revolutionary*. New York: Thunder's Mouth Press, 2003.

Hunt, Michael. *The World Transformed: 1945 to the Present*. New York: Bedford/St. Martin's, 2004.

Jeffrey, Robin, ed. *Asia: The Winning of Independence*. London: Macmillan, 1981.

Kurlansky, Mark. *1968: The Year That Rocked the World*. New York: Random House, 2005.

McMahon, Robert J. *The Cold War: A Very Short Introduction*. New York: Oxford University Press, 2003.

Prashad, Vijay. *The Darker Nations: A People's History of the Third World*. New York: New Press, 2007.

Spence, Jonathan. *Mao Zedong*. New York: Viking Penguin, 1999.

Westad, Odd Arne. *The Global Cold War: Third World Interventions and the Making of Our Times*. New York: Cambridge University Press, 2007.

KEY TERMS

Ernesto Guevara (672)
Great Leap Forward (676)
Fidel Castro (676)
Cuban Missile Crisis (677)
Hungarian Uprising (680)
Central Intelligence Agency (680)
Jacobo Arbenz (681)
Patrice Lumumba (686)

Ahmed Sukarno (686)
Jawaharlal Nehru (686)
Gamal Abdel Nasser (687)
Red Guards (690)
Prague Spring (692)
Tlatelolco Massacre (692)
Salvador Allende (693)
détente (693)

VOYAGES ON THE WEB

Voyages: Ernesto Guevara

"Voyages" is a real time excursion to historical sites in this chapter and includes interactive activities and study tools such as audio summaries, animated maps, and flashcards.

Visual Evidence: Sergeant Pepper's Lonely Hearts Club Band

"Visual Evidence" features artifacts, works of art, or photographs, along with a brief descriptive essay and discussion questions to guide your analysis of visual sources.

World History in Today's World: The Doomsday Clock

"World History in Today's World" makes the connection between features of modern life and their origins in the periods in this chapter.

CourseMate

Go to the CourseMate website at www.cengagebrain.com for additional study tools and review materials—including audio and video clips—for this chapter.

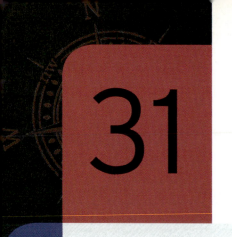

31

Toward a New World Order, 1975–2000

Nelson Mandela
(© David Tunley/Corbis)

Throughout the 1950s **Nelson Mandela** (b. 1918) had campaigned for racial justice and democracy as a member of the African National Congress (ANC). Forced underground in 1961 when the South African government banned the ANC, Mandela then traveled across Africa seeking support for the creation of a guerilla army. After returning to South Africa, he was captured and, in 1964, tried and sentenced to life in prison.

Finally, in early 1990, after decades of repression and violence, South Africa's white leaders responded to international calls for Mandela's release. A few hours after he walked through the prison gates, he spoke before a large crowd in Cape Town and before a global television audience:

Today, the majority of South Africans, black and white, recognize that apartheid has no future.... Negotiations on the dismantling of apartheid will have to address the overwhelming demand of our people for a democratic, nonracial, and unitary South Africa. There must be an end to white monopoly on political power and a fundamental restructuring of our political and economic systems to ensure that the inequalities of apartheid are addressed and our society thoroughly democratized.... I wish to quote my own words during my trial in 1964. They are as true today as they were then: "I have fought against white domination and I have fought against black domination. I have cherished

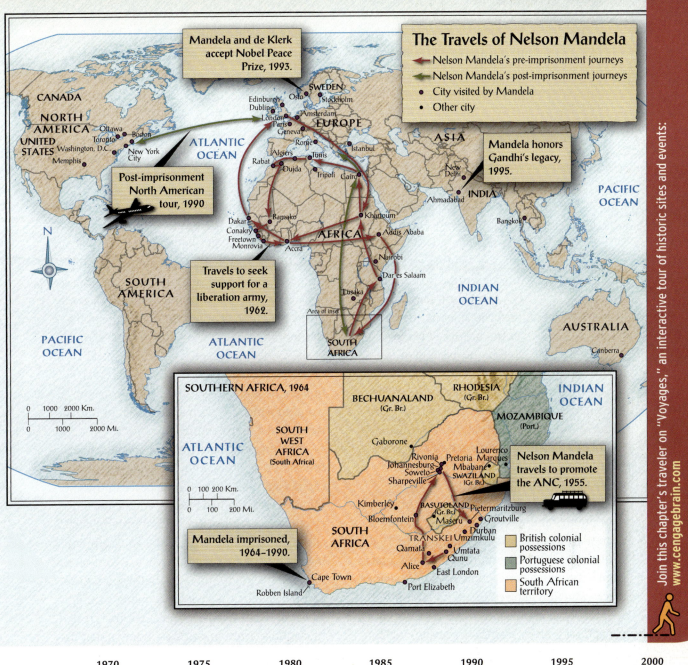

The Travels of Nelson Mandela

← Nelson Mandela's pre-imprisonment journeys
← Nelson Mandela's post-imprisonment journeys
• City visited by Mandela
• Other city

Mandela and de Klerk accept Nobel Peace Prize, 1993.

Mandela honors Gandhi's legacy, 1995.

Post-imprisonment North American tour, 1990

Travels to seek support for a liberation army, 1962.

CANADA

NORTH AMERICA

UNITED STATES

Ottawa
Toronto
Boston
Washington, D.C.
New York City
Memphis

ATLANTIC OCEAN

SOUTH AMERICA

PACIFIC OCEAN

ATLANTIC OCEAN

SWEDEN
Edinburgh
Dublin
Oslo
Stockholm
London
Amsterdam
Paris
Geneva
EUROPE
Rome
Istanbul
Algiers
Tunis
Rabat
Oujda
Tripoli
Cairo
ASIA
New Delhi
Ahmadabad
INDIA
PACIFIC OCEAN

Dakar
Conakry
Freetown
Monrovia
Bamako
Accra
AFRICA
Khartoum
Addis Ababa
Nairobi
Dar es Salaam
Lusaka
SOUTH AFRICA
Area of inset

Bangkok

INDIAN OCEAN

AUSTRALIA
Canberra

N

0 1000 2000 Km.
0 1000 2000 Mi.

Southern Africa Inset

SOUTHERN AFRICA, 1964

Nelson Mandela travels to promote the ANC, 1955.

Mandela imprisoned, 1964–1990.

ATLANTIC OCEAN

SOUTH WEST AFRICA (South Africa)

BECHUANALAND (Gr. Br.)

RHODESIA (Gr. Br.)

MOZAMBIQUE (Port.)

INDIAN OCEAN

Gaborone
Rivonia
Johannesburg
Soweto
Sharpeville
Pretoria
Lourenço Marques
Mbabane
SWAZILAND (Gr. Br.)

Kimberley
Bloemfontein
BASUTOLAND (Gr. Br.)
Maseru
Pietermaritzburg
Groutville
Durban
Umzimkulu
TRANSKEI
Qamata
Umtata
Qunu
Alice
East London
Port Elizabeth

SOUTH AFRICA

Cape Town
Robben Island

0 100 200 Km.
0 100 200 Mi.

British colonial possessions
Portuguese colonial possessions
South African territory

Join this chapter's traveler on "Voyages," an interactive tour of historic sites and events:
www.cengagebrain.com

	1970	1975	1980	1985	1990	1995	2000

Lifetime of Nelson Mandela (b. 1918)

AFRICA AND THE MIDDLE EAST
- Soweto Uprising 1976
- Iranian Revolution 1979
- Mandela released 1990
- Mandela elected president of South Africa 1994
- Persian Gulf War 1991
- Rwandan genocide 1994

AMERICAS
- Sandinistas fight for power in Nicaragua 1970 – 1979
- Ronald Reagan president of United States 1981 – 1989
- NAFTA passed 1994

EUROPE AND ASIA
- Helsinki Accords 1975
- Fall of communism in eastern Europe 1989
- Tiananmen Massacre 1989
- Dissolution of Soviet Union 1991

the ideal of a democratic and free society in which all persons live together in harmony and with equal opportunities. It is an ideal which I hope to live for and to achieve. But if needs be, it is an ideal for which I am prepared to die."[1]

Nelson Mandela (b. 1918) South African leader of the African National Congress and opponent of apartheid. Sentenced to life in prison in 1964; released in 1990. After winning the Nobel Peace Prize in 1993, he became the country's first democratically elected president in 1994.

None of Mandela's many journeys before and after his imprisonment were as significant as his short walk through those prison gates.

As a youth, Mandela received an early education in the history of his own Tembu people and in the protocols of the chief's court while also attending an English-language primary school. There a teacher assigned him the "proper" English name of Nelson; before that, he was called Rolihlahla ("pulling the branch of a tree," or "troublemaker"). He lived up to his African name at the all-black Methodist college he attended when he became embroiled in student politics and was expelled after leading a protest against the bad cafeteria food. In 1940 he headed for Johannesburg and earned a law degree through a correspondence course (since blacks were not allowed to attend law school).

Mandela combined his practice of law with a passion for politics, taking a leadership role in the African National Congress, the party that had, since 1912, worked for racial equality in South Africa (see Chapters 27 and 29). When their nonviolent campaign was met with police brutality and escalating repression, Mandela was set on the path that led to his imprisonment and his later triumph. In 1994 he became the country's first democratically elected president.

The world had changed dramatically in the period of Mandela's confinement. In 1964 Cold War tensions dominated international affairs. But with the collapse of the Soviet Union in the early 1990s, new possibilities emerged. Hopes for democracy spread not only across Russia and the former Soviet sphere but also in many other parts of the world, like South Africa, where Cold War alliances had empowered authoritarian regimes. Latin America, for example, was swept by a wave of democratization in the last decade of the twentieth century. Capturing the optimism of the time, President George H. W. Bush of the United States spoke of a "new world order." With the stalemate of the Cold War broken, he said in 1991, the path lay open to "a world in which freedom and respect for human rights find a home among all nations."

Still, myriad challenges remained unresolved. Russia's transition to democracy and capitalism was a difficult one, peace in the Middle East remained elusive, and democratic elections in South Africa did not instantly or automatically remove the social and economic inequalities of apartheid. The liberal association between free trade and democratic politics was contradicted by the People's Republic of China, where market-driven economic reforms created the world's fastest-growing economy under the control of the communist government. Some critics of the United States equated "globalization" with "Americanization" and saw the "new world order" as a means of expanding American power. Among them were Islamist activists, who, inspired by the Iranian Revolution, joined the struggle against what they saw as the decadent West. While the last decade of the twentieth century therefore offered hope, and in some places genuine progress toward freedom and security, the "new world order" did not offer a clear and agreed-upon road map as humanity entered the twenty-first century.

FOCUS QUESTIONS

▶ What were the major causes of the collapse of the Soviet Union?

▶ How successful were free markets and political reforms in bringing stability and democracy to different world regions?

▶ At the end of the twentieth century, in what ways were major conflicts in the Middle East still unresolved?

▶ What were the major effects of economic globalization?

The Late Cold War and the Collapse of the Soviet Union, 1975–1991

Abandoning Vietnam in 1975, the United States was divided and weary of war. Sensing America's weakness, Soviet leaders expanded their navy and their support for rebel movements globally. In 1981, however, the United States reasserted an aggressively anti-Soviet posture, menacing the Soviet regime with intensified military spending. In eastern Europe, as well, simmering discontent was threatening outright rebellion against Soviet overrule. After 1985 a new Soviet leader, Mikhail Gorbachev, tried to save communism by initiating reforms. Still, in 1989 the Berlin Wall fell, and in 1991 the Soviet Union dissolved.

After communism's collapse, Germany reunified while Poland and the Czech Republic became stable democracies. But in Russia and some other nations that emerged from the U.S.S.R.'s breakup, establishing democratic institutions proved difficult. Where authoritarian traditions persisted, sharp inequalities attended the introduction of capitalist markets.

The United States in the Post-Vietnam Era, 1975–1990

Misadventure in Vietnam and the resignation in 1974 of President Nixon in the Watergate scandal left U.S. society in disarray. At the same time, a steep rise in oil prices engineered by the Organization of Petroleum Exporting Countries (OPEC) shocked Americans into realizing how much their standard of living depended on foreign oil. *Stagflation* was a term coined to describe the combination of slow growth and inflation that afflicted the U.S. economy in the 1970s.

When Iranian revolutionaries seized American hostages in late 1979 and a rescue attempt the following spring failed to free them, Americans felt powerless and angry. In the 1980 presidential campaign, Republican **Ronald Reagan** (1911–2004) promised to restore American power and confidence. His sweeping victory brought a brash, nationalistic, and sternly anticommunist tone to American foreign policy. Huge tax cuts combined with sharp increases in military spending sent the federal budget into deficit. Nevertheless, after a harsh recession in 1981–1982, economic recovery provided the popular support Reagan needed for re-election in 1984, promising that it was "morning in America."

Ronald Reagan (1911–2004) Fortieth president of the United States. A staunchly anticommunist Republican, he used harsh rhetoric toward the Soviet Union and increased American military spending but compromised when negotiating arms limitations agreements.

Reagan's refusal to use the diplomatic language of détente alarmed Europe. Europeans rallied for peace, and except for British prime minister Margaret Thatcher, their leaders had misgivings about Reagan calling the Soviet Union an "evil empire." Reagan's harsh tone was offset by his optimism, however, and in 1986 he and Gorbachev met in Iceland, where they made unexpected progress on arms limitation. Even so, Reagan kept up the pressure, traveling to Germany in 1987 where he stood before the Berlin Wall and demanded, "Mr. Gorbachev, tear down this wall!" Few guessed how soon the wall would indeed come down.

From Leonid Brezhnev to Mikhail Gorbachev

The period from 1964 to 1982, when Leonid Brezhnev led the Soviet Union, was a time of relative stability for Soviet citizens. While their standard of living was low, employment, education, and health care were guaranteed. They might never own a car, but they could take an annual vacation. While they had no freedom of speech, religion, or assembly, they did have old-age pensions.

Détente with the United States led to the **Helsinki Accords**. The accords emboldened eastern European dissidents to speak out, among them Russian physicist Andrei Sakharov (1921–1989), the man most responsible for the development of the Soviet hydrogen bomb. In 1975, Sakharov won the Nobel Peace Prize for his writings in defense of civil rights and democracy. In response, Brezhnev cut off Sakharov's communications with the outside world. Soviet promises to protect human rights meant nothing in practice.

A large gap existed between the Soviet Union's ambitions and its accomplishments. When Brezhnev

Helsinki Accords A 1975 agreement made during the Cold War that gave recognition to the borders of communist bloc countries in eastern Europe in return for a Soviet promise, never fulfilled, to respect basic human rights.

Mikhail Gorbachev (b. 1931) Leader of the Soviet Union from 1985 to 1991 who introduced "openness" to Soviet politics and "restructuring" to the Soviet economy. Unable to control calls for even greater changes, Gorbachev presided over the collapse of the Soviet Union.

Primary Source: The Last Heir of Lenin Explains His Reform Plans: Perestroika and Glasnost *Read President Gorbachev's analysis of the Soviet Union's decline and his prescriptions for reform.*

sensed a lack of American resolve after its withdrawal from Vietnam, he made major new military commitments, such as expanding his country's nuclear submarine program and its Indian Ocean fleet. However, when Reagan subsequently stepped up American military spending in the 1980s, the Soviets could not keep pace.

War in Afghanistan took an especially heavy toll on Brezhnev's regime. After Afghan communists seized power in Kabul in 1978 with the help of Soviet Special Forces, a Soviet occupation faced tough resistance from Islamic guerilla fighters known as *mujahaddin* (moo-jah-ha-DEEN). Aided by the United States and Pakistan, the mujahaddin used their familiarity with the land and the populace to counter superior Soviet firepower. The Soviet people grew weary of war in Afghanistan, like Americans had in Vietnam.

When Brezhnev died in 1982, the party functionaries who replaced him were old and out of touch. Then in 1985 came a startling change when **Mikhail Gorbachev** (b. 1931) consolidated power. Knowing that Russia's younger generation was impatient for reform, Gorbachev withdrew from Afghanistan, introducing policies of "restructuring" and "openness." *Perestroika*, "restructuring," brought an end to massive economic centralization. While the state would still dominate, industry would now use market incentives rather than bureaucratic command to manage production. *Glasnost,* "openness," allowed formerly taboo subjects to be discussed. Gorbachev's new policy was tested in 1986, when officials tried to cover up the Chernobyl disaster, the worst nuclear accident in history. Both the Soviet people and their European neighbors were enraged, and Gorbachev promised that the old lies would be replaced by honesty and openness.

While Gorbachev's attempts to combine the Marxist-Leninist tradition with market principles and political transparency did lead to reform and greater openness, they also produced dissatisfaction and instability. Meanwhile, with Moscow having loosened its grip on power, the forces of repressed nationalism exploded in various Soviet republics. The Soviet Union began to break apart. Soon, Gorbachev felt forced to agree to a treaty giving the republics of the U.S.S.R. their de facto independence

Map 31.1   The Dissolution of the Soviet Union

In the 1990s, the collapse of the Soviet Union led to the creation of new states across eastern Europe, the Caucasus Mountains, and Central Asia, regions that in the nineteenth century had been part of the Russian Empire. The Baltic states of Estonia, Latvia, and Lithuania emerged as thriving democracies. Conflict was endemic in the Caucasus, however, where Russia battled separatists in Chechnya, and Armenia and Azerbaijan fought for control of territory. The new nations of former Soviet Central Asia were dominated by strong-armed dictators.   © Cengage Learning   🖥 **Interactive Map**

as part of a commonwealth led from Moscow (see Map 31.1).

This proposal being too much for hard-line conservatives in the Communist Party, in the summer of 1991 they attempted a coup d'état. But the people were against them. Huge crowds rallied to protect the newly elected government of the Russian Republic; the Communist Party could no longer dominate. Having failed to find a middle ground between reform and revolution, Gorbachev's political career was over.

Revolution in Eastern Europe

As the Hungarian uprising in 1956 and the Prague Spring in 1968 had shown, force was necessary to keep eastern Europe in Moscow's orbit. By the mid-1980s, however, the Soviet Union was losing its grip. The Roman Catholic majority in Poland, for example, despised the atheism of their rulers. Catholicism was a touchstone of Polish nationalism, and the surprise announcement in 1978 that the Polish cardinal Karol Wojtyla would become

Solidarity   Polish trade union created in 1980 that organized opposition to communist rule. In 1989, Solidarity leader Lech Walesa was elected president of Poland as the communists lost their hold on power.

Boris Yeltsin   (1931–2007) First president of the Russian Federation, from 1991 to 1999. Rallied the people of Moscow to defend their elected government during the attempted communist coup of 1991, but his presidency was marred by financial scandals and war in Chechnya.

Pope John Paul II powerfully affirmed that feeling.

In 1980 discontent with the communist regime reached a turning point with the formation of **Solidarity**, the first independent trade union in the Soviet bloc. In a direct challenge to the authority of the Communist Party, nearly a third of Poland's population joined Solidarity. Faced with increasing unrest, the government agreed to an election in 1989. The result was a massive victory for Solidarity and the election of its leader Lech Walesa to the position of president.

In Czechoslovakia the young rebels of the Prague Spring, now adults, began pushing for a new constitution. They had an additional grievance: the terrible pollution and environmental degradation caused by communist industrial policies. Despite police crackdowns, Czech authorities were unable to control events, and this time no Soviet forces arrived to keep them in power. Communism's fall went so smoothly in Czechoslovakia that it has been called the "Velvet Revolution."

In Romania in 1989, transition to democracy was sudden and violent. Dictator Nicolae Ceauşescu (chow-shehs-koo) had ruled with an iron fist, building sumptuous palaces and promoting family members to increase his personal control while the Romanian people went hungry. Isolated in his palace, Ceauşescu did not realize the depth of public anger. At a large public rally in the capital of Bucharest organized to reaffirm his position, Ceauşescu stepped forward to receive the accolades of the crowd; instead, he was loudly jeered. Television showed Ceauşescu's confusion as he heard, for the first time, his people's true opinion of him. His own security officials turned on him, and he and his wife were summarily executed.

The most evocative image of the fall of communism in eastern Europe was the destruction of the Berlin Wall. Since 1961 the wall had symbolized the Cold War divide, but in 1989, as part of the larger wave of revolution in central Europe, huge crowds of East Berliners streamed toward it. The next year the East German government relented and opened the gates, allowing tearful reunions of long-separated families. Soon after, the Berlin Wall was demolished by euphoric Berliners. The Cold War was truly over.

Post-Soviet Struggles for Democracy and Prosperity

The final stage in the dissolution of the Soviet Union came in 1991, after Soviet hard-liners attempted a coup d'état and the people rose against them, rallied by the newly elected Russian **Boris Yeltsin** (1931–2007).

Advised by American economists that free markets would bring prosperity to the new Russia, Yeltsin instituted bold economic reforms. However, Russia was ill prepared to shift to a capitalist system rapidly. State assets were auctioned off into the hands of a small elite, who behaved more like gangsters than corporate executives. The old securities of the Soviet system—free education and health care, guaranteed employment, old-age pensions—disappeared, but the market system failed to boost productivity and wages. While more consumer products might be available, workers lacked the means to purchase them. By the end of the 1990s, life expectancy and fertility rates were in decline, the population was shrinking, and Russians were often hungry and cold.

Yeltsin's problems were compounded by unrest in the southern Caucasus region, where Muslim guerillas organized a separatist movement in Chechnya (CHECH-nee-yah). Though Yeltsin used massive military force against them, he was unable to suppress the uprising. Ailing, Yeltsin handed power to Vladimir Putin (b. 1952) in 1999.

A former intelligence officer, Putin was returned to office in 2000 by a Russian electorate anxious to embrace an authority figure who promised a return to order. Putin reined in capitalism by restoring state authority over the economy and the media, using control of oil revenues and television as bases of power. He crushed the Chechnya rebellion, stood up to the United States in global forums, and restored order to the Russian Republic. Stability was achieved, but at the expense of democracy and civil rights.

The former Central Asian republics of the U.S.S.R. faced equally difficult transitions. Located on the borderlands between China, Russia, and the Muslim world, these newly independent nations had plentiful natural resources, especially oil and gas. However, unlike in eastern Europe, regime change came from the top down rather than through popular mobilization. In Kazakhstan and Uzbekistan, independence was overseen by former communist officials who paid lip service to democracy while keeping a tight rein on power.

In general, the transition to liberal governance and market economics was smoother in eastern Europe. Hungary, the Czech Republic, and Poland all experienced political and economic progress in the 1990s, with a blossoming of the free associations that characterize civil society. The reunification of Germany, however, was more difficult because East Germans were much poorer than West Germans and usually lacked competitive job skills. The first decade after the fall of the Berlin Wall brought freedom and opportunity to eastern Germany, but also unemployment and insecurity.

Though it is still too soon to assess its implications for history, the fall of the Soviet Union was clearly momentous. It marked not only the failure of the world's longest experiment with communism but also the breakup of the formerly great Russian Empire.

The Late Cold War in Africa and Latin America: Crisis and Opportunity

During the late stages of the Cold War (1975–1990), political crises afflicted many parts of Africa and Latin America. With the end of the Cold War and the fall of communism, however, opportunities arose to heal political divisions and bring greater democracy. In Central America, violence between leftist insurgents and military regimes gave way in the 1990s to elections and new hope for democracy and stability. Likewise in southern Africa, warfare gave way to elections and the promise of a brighter future. But civil war and genocide in Central Africa demonstrated that the destructive legacies of colonialism and superpower intervention were still powerful.

The Late Stages of the Cold War in Central America

Events in Chile in 1973 were a preview of things to come. That year a group of Chilean military officers, with U.S. backing, launched a successful coup against President Salvador Allende, the leader of a left-wing coalition. The new military dictator, General Augusto Pinochet, denounced communism, protected U.S. investments, and brought down Chile's once-powerful labor unions, remaking Chile's economy along free-market lines by authoritarian means. Like dictators elsewhere, Pinochet was supported by the U.S. government because of his anticommunist credentials.

In the 1980s the main battleground between leftist rebels and military forces backed by the United States was Central America. Nicaragua, for example, had long been ruled by the Somoza family, anticommunist dictators aligned with American economic interests. Resistance to the Somoza dictatorship was organized by the rebel Sandinista National Liberation Front. When a major earthquake occurred in 1972, the Somoza family and its friends in government stole millions of the dollars of relief aid sent to Nicaragua by international donors, pushing many Nicaraguans toward sympathy with the rebels. In 1979 the Sandinistas ousted the Somoza family and formed a new government.

After Ronald Reagan took office in 1981, the U.S. government threw its support behind anti-Sandinista insurgents known as *Contras*,

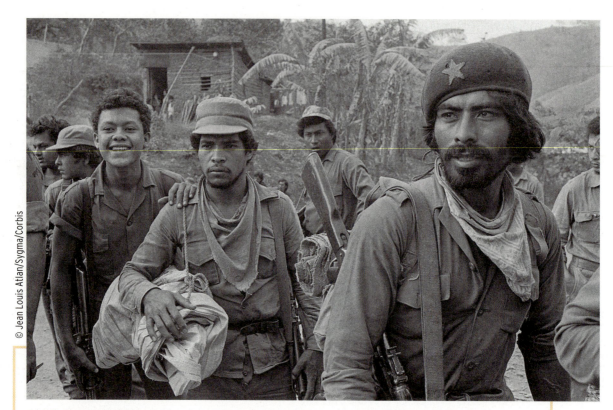

© Jean Louis Atlan/Sygma/Corbis

Sandinistas   The Sandinistas were victorious in 1979, but their control over Nicaragua was then challenged by U.S.-backed *Contra* rebels. The Sandinistas modeled themselves on Cuban revolutionary heroes; the soldier on the right wears a red-starred beret like that of Che Guevara.

led by military men associated with the previous regime. The Sandinistas then clamped down on civil liberties, justifying their dictatorship in the name of saving the revolution.

Reagan's support for the Contras was politically divisive domestically; in the Iran-Contra scandal, administration officials evaded congressional oversight by illegally selling arms to Iran to get funds for the Nicaraguan rebels. But the Central American dynamic changed when Gorbachev phased out Soviet subsidies of the Cuban economy. Cuba could no longer aid the Sandinistas, and with the communist threat diminished U.S. leaders no longer saw the Contras as necessary allies. Free elections were held in Nicaragua in 1989. The defeated Sandinistas respected the election results by peacefully handing over power, a major step forward for Nicaraguan democracy.

Guatemalan society was also marred by violence in the 1980s. Paramilitary death squads

aligned with the right-wing government targeted hundreds of thousands of Guatemalans, mostly indigenous Maya people, suspected of collusion with rebel armies. Often the killers were children kidnapped by the army and forced into service. As many as a million refugees fled from the mountains to the cities or across the border into Mexico. Guatemalan leaders either denied their connection to the death squads or justified the violence as necessary to defeat communism. Four decades after Che Guevara had witnessed the destruction of Guatemalan democracy, the position of the country's poor was worse than ever.

After the Cold War, the United States brought pressure on the Guatemalan government and military to work toward a solution. But a peace deal was not brokered until 1996, when the rebels agreed to lay down their arms in exchange for land. For the first time since 1952 Guatemalans went to the polls to vote in free elections. Wounds from the violence remained deep, however, and a government panel was set up to investigate paramilitary atrocities.

Elsewhere in Latin America the trend was the same. In Chile, prodemocracy activists removed General Pinochet from power. In Argentina, the turning point was defeat in the Falklands War against Great Britain in 1982, when the incompetence of Argentine generals brought about irresistible calls for change. A short time later, in 1985, elections swept the military from power in Brazil as well.

In Mexico, the problem was neither military governments nor Cold War alignments, but rather the monopoly power of the Party of Institutional Revolution (PRI), which constrained Mexican political freedom and bound the country to incompetence and corruption. Finally, in 1989, a conservative opposition party won gubernatorial elections in the state of Baja California, the first time the PRI had lost control of a statehouse since the 1920s. The stage was then set for more open electoral competition at the national level. In 2000 the election of Vicente Fox of the National Action Party (PAN) finally ended the PRI monopoly on Mexican presidential politics.

The Congolese Conflict and Rwandan Genocide

In Africa, the big Cold War prize had been the former Belgian Congo. America's ally Joseph Mobutu changed his name to Mobutu Sese Seko and took dictatorial control over the vast nation he renamed Zaire. In return for facilitating Western access to Zaire's strategic minerals and for allowing American use of his military bases, he amassed large sums of American foreign aid in his private accounts. Mobutu's regime was so corrupt that a new term was coined to describe it: *kleptocracy,* or "government by theft."

With the fall of the Soviet Union and the release of Nelson Mandela, the United States' affiliation with Mobutu Sese Seko became an embarrassment, and in 1990 Congress cut off direct aid to Zaire and supported efforts to democratize the country. Those efforts failed for two reasons. First, the political opponents of Mobutu were themselves bitterly divided. Second, the region was destabilized by the shock of genocide in Rwanda.

The Rwandan genocide is often presented as having "tribal" or "ethnic" roots, but Rwandans, Hutu as well as Tutsi, speak the same language, participate in the same culture, and mostly share a common Roman Catholic faith. As colonial rulers, however, the Belgians had sharply differentiated the two groups, favoring the Tutsi. Resentments surfaced at independence in 1960, when the previously disenfranchised Hutu took power and expelled many Tutsi, who then organized a rebel army in neighboring Uganda. In early 1994, the plane carrying the Rwandan president was shot from the sky, unleashing Hutu death squads. Within a few months nearly a million people were slaughtered, many cut with machetes, while another million fled to neighboring countries. United Nations peacekeepers stood by, unwilling to intervene.

As a Tutsi army re-entered Rwanda to establish a new government, Hutu extremists who had perpetrated the horrible violence fled to refugee camps in neighboring Zaire. By this time Mobutu was old and sick and no longer able to hold the country together. As in the early 1960s, Zaire (which restored the name Congo in 1997) fractured along ethnic and regional lines. The aftermath of Mobutu's authoritarian rule was not freedom but a nation of multiple militias verging on anarchy. Neighboring African countries compounded problems by sending in armies to back the various factions.

Although the "new world order" of democracy and civil rights did not arrive in Congo, after 1995 Rwanda did make strides toward restoring peace and civility. But the dream of African democracy rising from the ashes of Cold War conflict came closer to fulfillment further south.

South African Liberation

During Nelson Mandela's many years in prison, South African apartheid became more and more extreme. The government oversaw a "Bantu education" system that prepared blacks for menial jobs only. Residential segregation was strictly enforced, making it illegal for blacks to be in "white" areas unless they could prove they were there for employment. Meanwhile, white South Africans enjoyed a First World standard of living.

To complete the racial separation, the South African government developed the system of **Bantustans**, arguing that Tswana, Zulu, Xhosa, and other peoples did not belong to a common South Africa but to "tribal" enclaves (Bantustans) where they should seek their rights. The Bantustan system was developed on the foundation of the old "native reserves," where inadequate land and overcrowding had long forced blacks to seek work in white-controlled cities and mines. According to apartheid, these impoverished and scattered territories would form the basis for independent "nations." In reality, the Bantustans were simply a device to subjugate black Africans.

While African National Congress (ANC) leaders languished in jail or left South Africa to seek foreign allies, in the 1970s a new generation of leaders emerged. The Black Consciousness Movement was led by Steve Biko, who argued that black South Africans faced not only the external challenge of apartheid but also an inner challenge to surmount the psychological damage it caused. The first step toward liberation, Biko said, was for blacks to eliminate their own sense of inferiority.

Many black South African youths heeded his call, culminating in the 1976 **Soweto Uprising**, in which black students protested the inferiority of their education. When marchers refused an order to disband, police fired into the crowd, killing dozens of children. As protests spread across the country, authorities responded with their usual brutality. But this time resistance endured. Black consciousness stayed alive in the Soweto generation even after 1977, when Steve Biko's jailers beat him to death.

By 1983 black trade unions, church groups, and student organizations had formed a nationwide United Democratic Front. Schoolchildren boycotted the apartheid schools. Resistance on the streets became violent. Blacks accused of collaborating with apartheid had tires put around their necks and set ablaze. Nelson Mandela's own wife, Winnie Mandela, was implicated in the violence. In 1986 the government declared a state of emergency.

Critics outside South Africa argued that economic sanctions could force meaningful change. College students in the United States and Britain demanded that their institutions sell off investments in companies that did business in South Africa. In 1986 the U.S. Congress passed a comprehensive bill limiting trade with and investment in South Africa. President Reagan, viewing the South African government as an ally against communism, vetoed the bill, but Congress overrode his veto.

Pressured, the South African government offered to release Mandela if he renounced the ANC. His daughter Zindzi read his response at a packed soccer stadium: "I will remain a member of the African National Congress until the day I die.… Your freedom and mine cannot be separated. I will return."[2] Finally, as the decline of the Soviet Union undercut the government's claim that Mandela and the ANC represented a communist threat, and as sanctions undermined its already weak economy, South African president F. W. de Klerk granted Mandela an unconditional release in 1990. Despite ongoing violence, elections were held in 1994. Mandela was easily elected president, and the ANC became the dominant political force in the new South Africa.

True to the words he had spoken at his trial in 1964, Mandela emphasized inclusiveness in his government. South Africa, christened the "rainbow nation," had a new flag, a new sense of self-identity, a multiracial Olympic team, and one of the world's most democratic constitutions. A Truth and Reconciliation Commission was instituted to uncover the abuses of apartheid, while offering amnesty to those who publicly acknowledged their crimes.

Despite the new dawn for South Africa, its legacies of racism would take a long time to overcome. A severe crime wave and the rapid spread of HIV/AIDS posed difficult challenges for the Mandela administration. But at least all South Africans were empowered to help find solutions.

Bantustans Term used by apartheid planners for "tribal regions" in which Africans, denied citizenship in a common South Africa, were expected to live when not working for whites. They were not internationally recognized and were later reabsorbed into democratic South Africa.

Soweto Uprising (1976) Youth demonstrations in South Africa that were met with police violence. The Soweto Uprising brought a new generation of activists, inspired by Steve Biko's Black Consciousness Movement, to the forefront of resistance to apartheid.

Primary Source: The Rivonia Trial Speech to the Court *Read how Nelson Mandela defended himself against charges of treason before an all-white South African court in 1964.*

Bettmann/Corbis

Soweto Uprising   In 1976 schoolchildren in South Africa protested the compulsory teaching of the Dutch-based Afrikaans language in their schools. When police fired into the crowd, made up mostly of teenagers, hundreds were killed and thousands injured. The Soweto generation played a central role in bringing down apartheid over the next fifteen years.

Enduring Challenges in the Middle East

Throughout the twentieth century the Middle East had been politically unsettled, with tensions magnified by its strategic importance as a primary source of fossil fuels. Ethnic and religious rivalries combined with the involvement of external powers in a combustible mixture.

The Iranian Revolution of 1979 represented the first time in the postcolonial era that a state would be ruled under a constitution derived explicitly from Islamic law. Iran provided inspiration to **Islamists** throughout the Middle East and across the Muslim world. The path toward a just society, Islamists argued, was not through absorption of Western influences and modernity but through a return to the guiding precepts of their religion.

Islamists Muslims who believe that laws and constitutions should be guided by Islamic principles and that religious authorities should be directly involved in governance.

The rise to power of the Islamists in Iran, and their increasing influence elsewhere, accelerated conflicts in the Middle East. Regimes founded on the principles of secular Arab nationalism, such as Egypt, Syria, Iraq, and Jordan, were threatened by the popular appeal of this new ideology. The Iranian Revolution also provided inspiration and support for Islamist revolutionaries in Afghanistan.

Meanwhile the Israeli-Palestinian conflict endured. In spite of occasional signs of compromise, no resolution was forthcoming, although it seemed impossible that any meaningful "new world order" could ever be constructed without one.

Iran and Iraq

In the 1950s the shah of Iran had been supported by American intervention. For over twenty years, the shah used oil money to modernize the country while his secret police repressed the students, workers, and religious leaders who accused him of promoting decadent Western values and serving as a tool of U.S. power.

With riots and demonstrations spreading, the shah fled to the United States early in 1979. Returning from exile in Paris at the same time was **Ayatollah Khomeini** (1902–1989), whose authority was recognized by the ninety-thousand-member *ulama* (**oo-leh-MAH**), or community of Shi'ite religious scholars. Some of these scholars argued that while the ulama should advise political authorities on proper Islamic practice, they should not themselves wield governmental power. But Khomeini envisioned a tighter connection between religious and governmental authority. Though the radicals who seized the American Embassy in Teheran and held its employees hostage were motivated more by nationalism than by religion, they responded to Khomeini's assessment of the United States as "the great Satan."

Under Iran's new constitution, adopted in a 1979 referendum, the president and parliament were subject to strict oversight by a council of Islamic legal experts. A Ministry of Islamic Guidance was formed to supervise the new legal system, and vigilante groups patrolled the streets enforcing regulations on Islamic dress. The schools, which had been primarily secular under the shah, now emphasized religious education.

After Iraq invaded Iran, a surge of nationalism further consolidated support for Khomeini's government. The political divide between the two countries also had religious overtones. While the vast majority of Iranians are Shi'ites, in Iraq a Sunni minority had ruled over the Shi'ite majority since the days of the Ottoman Empire. During eight years of brutal fighting (1980–1988), as many as a million people died; Iranian civilians and soldiers also suffered terribly when the Iraqi army illegally used chemical weapons.

As the war dragged on, Iran's economic problems became acute. Starved of investment capital, the economy foundered. By the 1990s employment prospects for Iran's growing population of graduates were bleak, and dissatisfaction with the regime was growing. Even with the election of a moderate reformist candidate as president in 1997, ultimate power still rested with religious leaders who inherited Khomeini's authority after his death in 1989.

After reaching a stalemate with Iran, Iraqi president Saddam Hussein turned his expansionist ambitions toward Kuwait, a small, oil-rich state on the Persian Gulf. Hussein considered Kuwait part of Iraq's rightful patrimony, taken away from Baghdad's control by the British in 1919, and accused the Kuwaitis of reaching below Iraqi soil to steal its oil. Miscalculating that the United States would not oppose him, Hussein invaded Kuwait in the summer of 1990.

Though the United States had aided Iraq during its war with Iran, President George H. W. Bush reacted to Hussein's gambit by forging an international coalition against him. In the past, Hussein might have tried to counterbalance the United States by seeking an alliance with the Soviet Union, but that option no longer existed. Early in 1991 the **Persian Gulf War** began with the devastating bombing of Baghdad by the United States, after which the coalition swiftly liberated Kuwait. Hussein's army melted away under the onslaught, many killed by aerial bombardment. While the path to Baghdad was

Ayatollah Khomeini (1902–1989) Shi'ite cleric who led the Islamic Revolution in Iran in 1979 and became Supreme Leader of the Islamic Republic of Iran.

Persian Gulf War (1991) War that occurred when an international coalition led by the United States expelled Iraqi forces from Kuwait. Iraq was not invaded, and Saddam Hussein remained in power.

open, the Bush administration calculated that removing Hussein would upset the delicate Middle Eastern balance of power. As Americans withdrew, Hussein brutally crushed a rebellion in the largely Shi'ite south.

Afterwards, Hussein's regime was subjected to United Nations sanctions intended to force his disarmament. The burden of sanctions, however, fell on the common people rather than the governing elite, and officials in the West grew skeptical about having left the regime in power. The "new world order" promised by President George H. W. Bush had yet to emerge.

Afghanistan and Al-Qaeda

Beginning in 1993, the administration of a new U.S. president, William Jefferson Clinton (b. 1946), was increasingly concerned about Afghanistan. In the aftermath of the Soviet withdrawal, Afghanistan had come under the control of an Islamist group known as the Taliban that imposed a legal system even harsher than that of neighboring Iran. Women especially suffered; education for girls was eliminated completely. Joining the Afghani mujahaddin were other Muslims who entered the fight against the Soviets in the 1980s inspired by the call to holy war. After the Soviet withdrawal, many of them returned home to places like Egypt and Saudi Arabia determined to bring Islamic revolution to their own societies. Others found refuge under the Taliban.

The most notorious was **Osama bin Laden** (1957-2011), a member of a rich and powerful Saudi family. Though formerly allied with the United States against the Soviets, Osama bin Laden saw the Americans as the leading power in a global system where the West played on Arab and Muslim disunity to prop up illegitimate and exploitative regimes in return for a flow of cheap oil. Bin Laden and his followers in al-Qaeda (el-ka-aye-dah) were willing to use terrorism to advance

Osama bin Laden (b. 1957–2011) Saudi Arabian leader of the Islamist group al-Qaeda whose goal is to replace existing governments of Muslim countries with a purified caliphate. He was killed during a U.S. raid on his home in Pakistan.

Kuwait Oil Fields   In 1991, near the end of the Persian Gulf War, retreating Iraqi soldiers set fire to Kuwait's oil fields, causing significant environmental damage. That damage was compounded when the Iraqis purposely dumped hundreds of millions of barrels of oil into the Gulf.

Nicolas Kamm/AFP/Getty Images

© Reuters/Corbis

Hope for Middle East Peace   This 1993 handshake between Israeli prime minister Yitzhak Rabin and Yasser Arafat, chairman of the Palestine Liberation Organization, gave the world hope for a Middle East peace. However, negotiations for an Israeli-PLO peace accord, mediated by U.S. president Bill Clinton, proved unsuccessful. Some Israelis and their allies regarded Arafat as nothing more than a terrorist, and Rabin was later assassinated by an Israeli extremist for his role in the negotiations.

their cause, as shown by attacks on American embassies in the East African nations of Kenya and Tanzania in 1998. In retaliation, the Clinton administration bombed southeastern Afghanistan in an unsuccessful attempt to kill Osama bin Laden and destroy al-Qaeda's base of operations.

The link between extreme versions of Islamist theology and international terrorism had been made. While only a minority of the world's Muslims believed in the establishment of Islamic states or condoned violence against civilians in the name of jihad, some were proud to see someone standing up to the forces they blamed for their social, political, and economic ills. The unresolved Israeli-Palestinian issue added fuel to those flames.

Primary Source Declaration of Jihad Against Americans Occupying the Land of the Two Holy Mosques   *Read a speech given by Osama bin Laden to his followers in Afghanistan, and soon published worldwide.*

The Israeli-Palestinian Conflict

The unresolved Israeli-Palestinian conflict further fueled Arab and Muslim resentments. Israel kept the territories it had occupied during the Six-Day War of 1967, arguing that their continued control, especially in the West Bank and Gaza, ensured security; but a vicious cycle of violence persisted. Some Israelis believed that these lands, as part of the ancient Hebrew kingdom, should be permanently annexed. To this end, the conservative Likud (lih-kood) Party, in power in Israel for much of the period after 1977, sponsored the construction of Jewish settlements on half of the land on the West Bank in defiance of international law. Return of the territory to its Arab inhabitants was becoming much more difficult (see Map 31.2).

The Palestine Liberation Organization (PLO), under the leadership of Yasir Arafat (1929–2004), felt justified in using any means

The map contains the following labels and annotations:

BULGARIA, Black Sea, RUSSIA, KAZAKHSTAN, UZBEKISTAN, CHINA

Soviet occupation, 1979–1989
U.S. aid to rebels, 1980s
International and Northern Alliance
forces defeat Taliban, 2001

GEORGIA, Ankara, ARMENIA, AZERBAIJAN, Caspian Sea, TURKMENISTAN, TURKEY

Mediterranean Sea, Crete, CYPRUS, SYRIA, Tikrit, Kirkuk, Tehran, AFGHANISTAN, Herat, Mazar e Sharif, Kabul, Islamabad

U.S. troops, 1958, 1983–1984

U.S. arms sales, 1955–1978:
$20.8 billion
Shah overthrown, 1979
American hostages taken,
1979–1981

LEBANON, Damascus, ISRAEL, Tel Aviv, Amman, JORDAN, Fallujah, Baghdad, IRAQ, IRAN, Kandahar, Quetta, PAKISTAN, INDIA, Indus R.

Cairo, Basra, U.S. and allies launch First U.S.-Iraq War, 1991, Kuwait, KUWAIT, Karachi

LIBYA, EGYPT, Nile R., U.S. arms sales, 1980s, during Iran-Iraq War, Iraq invades Kuwait, 1990, Second U.S.-Iraq War, 2003, Manama, BAHRAIN, QATAR, Doha, Dubayy, Abu Dhabi, Muscat, Persian Gulf, Strait of Hormuz, UNITED ARAB EMIRATES

Tropic of Cancer, Aswan Dam, Red Sea, Riyadh, SAUDI ARABIA, OMAN, Arabian Sea

Al-Qaeda headquarters, 1992–1996, SUDAN, Mecca, Oil embargo, 1973, Source of 17% of U.S. oil imports in 1975, Largest buyer of U.S. arms, 1978

ERITREA, Sana, YEMEN, Mukalla

Map legend (inset):
- Jewish state after UN partition of Palestine, 1947
- Israel after War of 1948–1949
- Area controlled by Israel after Six-Day War, 1967
- Israeli-occupied area after Yom Kippur War, 1973

By Egyptian-Israeli agreements of 1975 and 1979, Israel withdrew from the Sinai in 1982. In 1981 Israel annexed the Golan Heights. Through negotiations between Israel and the PLO, Jericho and the Gaza Strip were placed under Palestinian self-rule, and Israeli troops were withdrawn in 1994. In 1994 Israel and Jordan signed an agreement opening their borders and normalizing their relations.

LEBANON, Beirut, Damascus, SYRIA, Haifa, GOLAN HEIGHTS, Sea of Galilee, WEST BANK, Tel Aviv, ISRAEL, Jerusalem, Amman, Gaza, Dead Sea, JORDAN, Mediterranean Sea, Port Said, Suez Canal, EGYPT, Cairo, Suez, SINAI PENINSULA, Elath, Gulf of Suez, Gulf of Aqaba, SAUDI ARABIA, Sharm el-Sheikh, Red Sea, Nile R.

ARAB-ISRAELI CONFLICT

Aden, Gulf of Aden, Socotra (Yemen), Bombing of USS *Cole* by al-Qaeda, 2000, DJIBOUTI, Djibouti

ETHIOPIA, SOMALIA, U.S. troops assist in relief of famine, 1992–1993. U.S. troops withdrawn, 1994. U.S.-backed Ethiopian invasion removes Islamist government, 2006

INDIAN OCEAN

Mogadishu, Equator

Members of the Organization of Petroleum Exporting Countries (OPEC)
Oil fields

Scale: 0–250–500 Km. / 0–250–500 Mi.

Map 31.2   Middle East Oil and the Arab-Israeli Conflict

Not all Arabs and Arab states benefit from Middle Eastern oil reserves, which are highly concentrated in Arabia and the Persian Gulf. Farther west, Israel, born into a state of war when attacked by its Arab neighbors in 1948, ruled over significant Palestinian populations after taking the West Bank from Jordan and the Gaza Strip from Egypt during the Six-Day War in 1967. Whatever their other disagreements, Arabs have been unified in their denunciation of the Israeli occupation of the West Bank.   © Cengage Learning   Interactive Map to resist the Israeli occupation, including terrorist attacks on civilians. In 1982, Israel invaded Lebanon to root out the bases from which they faced constant attacks and to drive out the PLO, which had its headquarters in Beirut. The international community was horrified by the savage attacks on Palestinian refugee camps by Lebanese militias allied with Israel. Support for Islamist organizations grew both in Lebanon, with the increasing influence of Hezbollah ("Party of God"), and in Palestine, where Hamas (the "Islamic Resistance Movement") arose as an alternative to the secular PLO.

Violence flared in Palestine in 1987 with the beginning of the first *intifada,* "ceaseless struggle," against the Israeli occupation of Gaza and the West Bank. The Israelis responded with security regulations restricting Palestinian mobility.

In 1991, under European and American sponsorship, Israeli and Palestinian diplomats met to discuss possibilities for compromise, and in 1993 the Oslo Accords laid out a mutually agreed-upon "road map" for peace based on the idea of two separate and secure nations living side by side. President Clinton then invited Yasir Arafat **(yah-seer ahr-ah-fat)** and Israeli prime minister Yitzhak Rabin **(yit-shak rah-BEEN)** to Washington, where the two men, formerly implacable enemies, shook hands before a worldwide television audience.

In 2000 Clinton hosted Arafat and another Israeli prime minister, Ehud Barak, for direct negotiations. While Barak offered to return 90 percent of the West Bank for a new Palestinian state, Arafat refused to compromise on the right of Palestinian refugees to return to lands within Israel from which they had fled in 1948. In spite of the new possibilities offered by the end of the Cold War, the Israeli-Palestinian conflict remained at an impasse.

The Economics of Globalization

With the fall of the Soviet Union and communism, globalization increased. Expanding global trade led to unprecedented growth and international economic integration. Some Asian economies surged, with Taiwan, South Korea, and Singapore, the so-called "Asian Tigers," leading the way. Overcoming the disruptions of the Cultural Revolution, the People's Republic of China became the world's fastest-growing economy by adopting market principles. Likewise India embraced the market, purging old socialist and bureaucratic institutions to achieve stunning rates of growth.

Western Europe was consolidated when the European Economic Community transformed into the European Union (EU). By the late 1990s the EU had expanded into the former Soviet sphere, attaining a market size larger than that of the United States, to constitute one of the three major centers of the global economy along with China and the United States. At the same time, however, economic globalization led to imbalances. Both within nations and between them, the benefits of economic growth were not shared equally, and the gap between the global haves and have-nots increased.

Japan and the "Asian Tigers"

Japan rose quickly from the battering it took in 1945. Under occupation by the United States, Japanese leaders renounced militarism and accepted the democratic constitution Americans drafted for them. The energy and drive that had earlier gone into empire building was now focused on domestic rebirth. Fukuzawa Yûkichi (see Chapter 24) would have been proud as Japanese products came to surpass those of Europe and the United States in both quality and price.

Several factors facilitated Japanese economic success. American military protection relieved the country of the financial burden of military spending, and close collaboration between the government bureaucracy and large corporations brought planning and coordination to the national economy. Japanese employees, famous for their work ethic, were also willing to accept policies that favored savings and investment over consumption. Old corporations, like Mitsui, and new ones, like Sony, developed organizational structures that emphasized long-term loyalty between employer and employee, leading to relatively harmonious labor relations and an absence of strikes. However, company loyalty entailed endless work hours, and Japanese women lived confining lives, raising children while rarely seeing their husbands.

In the 1970s, Japan enjoyed a rapid increase in automobile exports, especially to the United States. Japanese models first targeted consumers of inexpensive yet well-built cars. Meanwhile, manufacturers in the United States built large vehicles of indifferent quality. After oil prices surged in 1973, demand for the more fuel-efficient Japanese cars skyrocketed.

As other Asian nations began to follow the same industrial export strategy with even lower labor costs, Japanese manufacturing transitioned to knowledge-intensive sectors such as computers and telecommunications. Backed by large government subsidies for research and development, and coordinating their efforts with the Ministry for International Trade and Industry, Japanese corporations in the 1980s increasingly focused on such high-profit activities while relocating factories to countries with lower labor costs.

Then, at the height of Japan's success, the bubble burst. In 1989 the Tokyo Stock Exchange collapsed. Real estate speculation, political corruption, and a banking crisis caused by bad loans were to blame. To reignite the economy, the government began to emphasize leisure and consumption over savings, hoping that the country could spend its way out of crisis; but, while the Japanese economy stabilized, Asian growth moved elsewhere.

The South Korean government emulated the export-oriented industrial model of Japan, including close coordination between the state administration and the emerging Korean *chaebols,* economic conglomerates such as Hyundai. The South Korean government was fiercely anticommunist, led by authoritarian personalities with close ties to the military, and student and worker protests were often met with fatal force by paramilitary police. Then in 1988, with South Korea preparing to host the Summer Olympics, liberal political reforms were finally instituted, with a peaceful transfer of power between political parties in 1992. The liberal political equation of rule of law, democratic process, and free markets was achieved.

Taiwan was another Asian country characterized by economic growth and authoritarian government. The island's government was dominated by exiles from the mainland who controlled the bureaucracy, the military, and the economy. As in South Korea, popular discontent grew during the 1980s, especially among those who had been born on the island. By 1988, as part of the general trend toward democratization, free elections had laid the foundation of Taiwanese democracy. Meanwhile, the economy blossomed.

By the 1980s Taiwan, along with South Korea, Singapore, and British-ruled Hong Kong, was counted as one of the "Asian tigers," adding high technology to its existing industrial infrastructure. South Korea became a leader in telecommunications technology, while Taiwan became a major supplier of microchips for the expanding market in home computers. Some thought that "Confucian capitalism," based on group consensus and hierarchy rather than individualism and class conflict, offered an alternative to the Western model. But no generalizations about Asian capitalism could be made without taking into account the transformation of the People's Republic of China.

Deng Xiaoping's China and Its Imitators

At the start of the nineteenth century China produced about one-third of the world's industrial output. But in 1949, after a century and a half of European economic dominance, that percentage had shrunk to less than 3 percent.

The country's astonishing economic growth in the last two decades of the twentieth century restored China's historical role as a global center of manufacturing.

That turnabout resulted from the policies of **Deng Xiaoping** (1904–1997), one of the pragmatic "experts" who had opposed the excesses of the Great Leap Forward and the Cultural Revolution. After Mao's death and the defeat of the "Gang of Four," Deng put China on a new economic path by adopting market incentives. The first step was to grant peasants their own farm plots for private production. Food production surged. Deng became a hero to millions of Chinese farming families, who could now afford small luxuries for the first time. When asked how he, a lifelong communist, justified adopting capitalist principles, Deng replied: "It does not matter whether the cat is black or white, as long as she catches mice."

The second stage in Deng's reforms was to provide legal and institutional mechanisms for the development of the industrial sector. In the southern region of Guangzhou, near the British-controlled territory of Hong Kong, foreign investors were invited to build manufacturing plants to take advantage of China's cheap labor. Chinese banks funded local investors with connections to the Communist Party. The Red Army itself became a major economic power, controlling one of the world's largest shipping lines. As manufacturing spread from Guangzhou throughout eastern and central China, a vast flow of finished goods crossed the Pacific destined for American markets. China's cities experienced a huge construction boom, attracting millions of rural migrants. The coastal city of Shanghai became a glittering cosmopolitan center as billboards and traffic jams replaced bicycles and moralistic party posters.

Although Deng Xiaoping resigned from his posts in 1987, he remained a dominant power behind the scenes until his death in 1997. During that period, Hong Kong was returned to Chinese control. Communist leaders promised that the people of Hong Kong would retain their accustomed civil liberties such as rights of free speech and assembly, but some were suspicious that Beijing would impose its system of open markets and closed politics.

The big test to Deng's legacy came in 1989. Student activists, yearning for political change to match the economic transformation of their country, organized a large antigovernment rally, erecting a replica of the Statue of Liberty in the heart of Beijing to symbolize their goal of greater freedom. This student-led prodemocracy movement ended with the **Tiananmen Massacre** during which hundreds of students were killed and thousands arrested. The Chinese Communist Party would not risk its political monopoly.

China's economic transformation also created other challenges. Environmental problems multiplied. The gap between rich and poor increased, as did imbalances between wealthier coastal regions and China's interior. As corruption spread, protests increased among the same rural population that Mao had made the center of his revolution. Nevertheless, the economic policies of Deng Xiaoping raised China to the status of a great power after two centuries of humiliation by the West and Japan.

China's competitive advantage was its political stability combined with low-cost labor. By the 1990s other Asian countries were also able to build up export-oriented manufacturing centers. For much of the twentieth century, nationalist leaders in Thailand, Malaysia, Indonesia, and Vietnam had dreamed of catching up with the West through industrialization. Now, like China, they were moving toward that goal.

The nature of the global economy, however, was shifting. Industry was being overtaken by marketing, financial services, and other "knowledge industries" as the highest value-producing activities. Chinese leaders worked to develop and borrow high technology as part the country's economic mix. But for many Asian workers, especially in Southeast Asia, industrialization brought little benefit. Young women with few skills other than manual dexterity made up much of the industrial workforce, and

Deng Xiaoping (1904–1997) Chinese Communist Party leader who brought dramatic economic reforms after the death of Mao Zedong.

Tiananmen Massacre Massacre in a public square in Beijing, where, in 1989, students and workers demanded freedom and democracy. On order from the Communist Party, the Chinese military cleared Tiananmen Square with tanks and gunfire.

child labor was all too common. As global consumers demanded ever-cheaper products, wages fell in China, Southeast Asia, and other industrial economies.

The European Union

Beginning in the 1980s, western European leaders, especially in France and Germany, sought to deepen the level of cooperation already in place throughout the European Economic Community. A European Parliament, with little real authority but great symbolic importance, was elected. Negotiations were begun to open borders, to create a single internal market free of tariffs, and to move toward a common European currency. While these negotiations were taking place, the Soviet Union began to dissolve and talk turned to the possibility of incorporating new members from the former Eastern bloc.

In 1992 the Treaty on European Union was signed at the Dutch city of Maastricht. It set a date of January 1, 1999, for the introduction of the euro (the EU's currency), limited the amount of public debt that a nation could hold to be admitted to the union, and created a European Central Bank to control monetary policy. Critics complained that a European "superstate" run by bureaucrats in Brussels would undermine national sovereignty, and Great Britain, Denmark, and Sweden all rejected the euro, refusing to surrender control of their own currencies. But other provisions of the Maastricht Treaty were approved (see Map 31.3).

Uniting member states with complementary economic and human resources, the European Union was a major success, accounting for over 18 percent of global exports by century's end. Growth rates were especially high in poorer countries thanks to loans and subsidies from wealthier EU members. Spain, Greece, and Portugal, all of which had suffered from authoritarian governments, became modern democracies with better educated populations. Their debt-driven economies would later falter, however, along with that of Ireland, which in the 1990s was haild as a "Celtic Tiger" for its prowess in technology.

The European Union arose partly in reaction to the United States. Many Europeans saw the materialism of American society as a threat to their own more leisurely mode of life and generous social policies. In the 1990s, leaders of traditionally socialist parties, such as Tony Blair in Great Britain and Gerhard Schroeder in Germany, advocated a "third way" to growth and stability. Rejecting both the relatively unfettered capitalism of the United States and the inefficiencies of state socialism, they advocated a combination of market incentives and social investment. In France, the government reflected popular feeling when it took advantage of globalization while criticizing the "new world order" of cultural Americanization. (See the feature "Movement of Ideas: Jihad vs. McWorld.")

On balance, the European Union represented optimism and growth. In 2000 negotiations began to bring former Soviet satellites such as Poland, the Czech Republic, and Hungary into the EU.

Structural Adjustment and Free Trade in the Third World

As we have seen, the "new world order" based on democracy and free markets had a mixed record. During the 1980s many indebted Third World governments were forced to accept the terms of a **structural adjustment** in order to get loans from the International Monetary Fund (IMF) or the World Bank, two institutions that had been set up after the Second World War to guarantee global economic stability. These institutions insisted that only when state expenditures were slashed could developing countries reach sustainable levels of growth. Especially in Africa and Latin America, structural adjustment led to steep spending cuts that threatened advances in health and education.

In Mexico, structural adjustment meant cutting government subsidies on the price of maize meal. In

structural adjustment Economic policy imposed by the International Monetary Fund and World Bank on debtor nations, requiring significant cuts in government spending and reduced economic intervention in markets to create conditions for long-term growth.

Map 31.3 **The European Union**

The European Union (EU) developed from the more limited European Economic Community, dominated by France and the Federal Republic of Germany and to which the United Kingdom, Ireland, Denmark, Spain, Portugal, and Greece were added in the 1970s and 1980s. The collapse of the Soviet Union led to a dramatic EU expansion into eastern Germany, central and southeastern Europe, and the Nordic and Baltic countries. Turkey's application for membership has proved controversial, while Russia has resisted the inclusion of Georgia and Ukraine.

© Cengage Learning

Interactive Map

the long run, economists argued, the "magic of the market" would align production and consumption and lead to greater prosperity. In the short run it meant a sharp rise in the price of tortillas and thus more hungry children. When the East African nation of Tanzania accepted an IMF loan in 1987, it was forced to lay off thousands of teachers to help balance its books, suspending the country's goal to provide universal primary education. Still, advocates of structural adjustment argued that, in the long term, free markets were the only way to create abundance for the people of countries like Mexico and Tanzania.

Flag of the European Union   During the 1990s, the flag of the European Union was often flown alongside the national flags of member nations. The twelve stars represent the peoples of Europe regardless of nationality; the circle symbolizes the union of these peoples to achieve a common purpose.

Chris Cheadle/Photographer's Choice RF/Getty Images

The economics of liberal free trade also guided the development and passage, in 1994, of the North American Free Trade Association (NAFTA), uniting Canada, the United States, and Mexico in a market even larger than that of the European Union. NAFTA was controversial. In the United States, critics warned that the removal of tariffs on Mexican imports would mean the loss of high-paying industrial jobs as manufacturers seeking to pay lower wages moved south of the border. In Mexico, farmers worried that they would be ruined by open competition with U.S. farmers, who were heavily subsidized by their government. Then even as previously high-wage industrial jobs moved south, rural Mexicans would flee north because of falling crop prices.

In the southern state of Chiapas, rebels calling themselves Zapatistas (after the Mexican revolutionary Emiliano Zapata) declared "war on the Mexican state" in 1994, with NAFTA as one of their principal grievances. The Zapatistas sought to reassert their collective welfare against the free-market onslaught and to protect their locally based cultural and political identity against the wave of globalization. Such efforts would continue, but for better or worse, capitalism was now the only game being played in the global economy.

Jihad vs. McWorld

For half a century, all discussions of the global balance of power had been based on Cold War bipolarity. In the 1990s, lively debates took place over what "new world order" would replace that old one. One optimistic author trumpeted the fall of the Soviet Union as "the end point of mankind's ideological evolution and the universalization of Western liberal democracy as the final form of human government."* Another, more pessimistic observer predicted a looming "clash of civilizations."†

As part of this dialogue, Benjamin Barber has explained a complex scenario in which "globalism," which he labels "McWorld," and reactions against those forces, which he calls "Jihad," exist in critical balance with one another. Barber claims that across the world (including the United States) "McWorld" threatens local autonomy. Fearful of globalization, people rally around ethnic or religious differences for self-protection. According to Barber, neither "McWorld" nor "Jihad" is conducive to democracy.

Just beyond the horizon of current events lie two possible political futures—both bleak, neither democratic. The first is a retribalization of large swaths of humankind by war and bloodshed ... in which culture is pitted against culture, people against people, tribe against tribe—a Jihad in the name of a hundred narrowly conceived faiths against every kind of interdependence, every kind of artificial social cooperation and civic mutuality.

The second is being borne in on us by the onrush of economic and ecological forces that demand integration and uniformity and that mesmerize the world with fast music, fast computers, and fast food—with MTV, Macintosh, and McDonald's, pressing nations into one commercially homogenous global network: one McWorld tied together by technology, ecology, communications, and commerce. The planet is falling precipitantly apart AND coming reluctantly together at the very same moment....

Four imperatives make up the dynamic of McWorld:

THE MARKET IMPERATIVE. All national economies are now vulnerable to the inroads of larger, transnational markets within which trade is free, currencies are convertible, access to banking is open, and contracts are enforceable under law.... [S]uch markets are eroding national sovereignty—international banks, trade associations, transnational lobbies like OPEC and Greenpeace, world news services like CNN and the BBC, and multinational corporations that increasingly lack a meaningful national identity—that neither reflect nor respect nationhood as an organizing or regulative principle.

THE RESOURCE IMPERATIVE. Every nation, it turns out, needs something another nation has; some nations have almost nothing they need.

THE INFORMATION-TECHNOLOGY IMPERATIVE. Scientific progress embodies and depends on open communication, a common discourse rooted in rationality, collaboration, and an easy and regular flow and exchange of information....

THE ECOLOGICAL IMPERATIVE. We know well enough that ... Brazilian farmers want to

*Francis Fukuyama, "The End of History?" *The National Interest,* Summer 1989.
†Samuel Huntington, "The Clash of Civilizations?" *Foreign Affairs,* Summer 1993.

be part of the twentieth century and are burning down tropical rain forests to clear a little land to plough ... upsetting the delicate oxygen balance and in effect puncturing our global lungs. Yet this ecological consciousness has meant not only greater awareness but also greater inequality, as modernized nations try to slam the door behind them, saying to developing nations, "The world cannot afford your modernization; ours has wrung it dry!"

The movement toward McWorld is in competition with forces of global breakdown, national dissolution, and centrifugal corruption. These forces, working in the opposite direction, are the essence of what I call Jihad.

... The passing of communism has torn away the thin veneer of internationalism ... to reveal ethnic prejudices that are not only ugly and deepseated but increasingly murderous. Europe's old scourge, anti-Semitism, is back with a vengeance, but it is only one of many antagonisms. It appears all too easy to throw the historical gears into reverse and pass from a Communist dictatorship back into a tribal state.

Among the tribes, religion is also a battlefield.... [T]he new expressions of religious fundamentalism are fractious and pulverizing, never integrating. This is religion as the Crusaders knew it: a battle to the death for souls that if not saved will be forever lost.

The atmospherics of Jihad have resulted in a breakdown of civility in the name of identity, of comity in the name of community. International relations have sometimes taken on the aspect of gang war—cultural turf battles featuring tribal factions that were supposed to be sublimated as integral parts of large national, economic, postcolonial, and constitutional entities.

McWorld does manage to look pretty seductive in a world obsessed with Jihad. It delivers peace, prosperity, and relative unity—if at the cost of independence, community, and identity (which is generally based on difference). The primary political values required by the global market are order and tranquility....

Jihad delivers a different set of virtues: a vibrant local identity, a sense of community, solidarity among kinsmen, neighbors, and countrymen, narrowly conceived. But it also guarantees parochialism and is grounded in exclusion. Solidarity is secured through war against outsiders. And solidarity often means obedience to a hierarchy in governance, fanaticism in beliefs, and the obliteration of individual selves in the name of the group....

Source: From Benjamin Barber, "Jihad vs. McWorld," *The Atlantic Monthly*, March 1992. Reprinted by permission.

QUESTIONS FOR ANALYSIS

▶ How does Barber argue that increasing globalization leads to the development and expansion of the movements he labels as "Jihad"?

▶ In the world today, which forces seem stronger, those of "Jihad" or those of "McWorld"?

Chapter Review and Learning Activities

The world changed in dramatic ways during Nelson Mandela's decades of incarceration. When he walked free in 1990, the Cold War, at its height when he was convicted of treason in 1964, was coming to an end. New possibilities for democracy marked the emerging "new world order," a trend shown by the election of Nelson Mandela as president of South Africa in 1994. The high hopes of that period were only partially fulfilled, however. Global society entered the twenty-first century with no solution to enduring issues such as the Israeli-Palestinian conflict and with new challenges, such as economic globalization, still to be resolved.

What were the major causes of the collapse of the Soviet Union?

The collapse of the Soviet Union in the late 1980s was completely unexpected, yet in retrospect the weaknesses that brought it down are apparent. An upsurge in international commitments and military spending in the 1970s was not matched by equivalent advances in economic productivity, and in the renewed arms race of the 1980s the Soviets could not keep pace with the United States. The invasion of Afghanistan put tremendous strains on Soviet society. The long-suppressed nationalism of non-Russian minorities within the U.S.S.R. and of captive peoples in its eastern European satellites was ready to boil over at a moment's notice. Ironically, it was Mikhail Gorbachev's reform policies that doomed the Soviet Union. Once "restructuring" and "openness" came to Russia, calls for more radical change cascaded throughout the Soviet sphere and Gorbachev was unwilling to use force to stop them.

How successful were free markets and political reforms in bringing stability and democracy to different world regions?

The new nations formed from the old Soviet Union, and the eastern European ones liberated from Moscow's control, had a mixed record of democratization. European nations like Poland, which were liberated through an authentic popular movement, were more successful than the Central Asian ones where authoritarian rulers controlled the process of independence. Globally, the disappearance of Soviet sponsorship for left-wing insurgencies in Africa, Asia, and Latin America created new opportunities for democratization, especially when the United States withdrew its support from authoritarian, anticommunist regimes and backed international efforts at conciliation and democracy. In other areas, such as the Congo, historical legacies of division were so strong that the weakening of authoritarianism brought instability and civil war rather than freedom and democracy.

At the end of the twentieth century, in what ways were major conflicts in the Middle East still unresolved?

Progress toward a "new world order" was most difficult in the Middle East. Although the Israeli occupation of the West Bank and Gaza was explained as a security measure, Israelis began to build permanent settlements, further angering Arab nationalists in Palestine and elsewhere. The international coalition that ousted Saddam Hussein from Kuwait in 1991 overcame some of the divisions within the Islamic world, but only temporarily. Some Arabs became disenchanted with secular nationalism and turned to religion for their political ideals.

What were the major effects of economic globalization?

The economic forces of globalization were relentless. The economies of Japan and the "Asian Tigers" grew at unprecedented rates, and free-market reforms in the People's Republic of China made it, in the 1990s, the world's fastest-growing industrial economy. Both Europe, through the European Union, and the United States, through the North American Free Trade Association, expanded their free-trade zones in response to globalization. Both the EU and NAFTA had their critics. Some worried about the potential loss of sovereign decision-making power in their nations when, for example, the euro was adopted as a common currency, and some worried over the possible movement of industrial jobs to low-wage markets like Mexico.

While citizens of wealthy nations debated the pros and cons of globalization, the transition to the new market regime was even more difficult for developing countries. Structural adjustment promised long-term benefits, but in the short term the deregulation of markets often had a negative impact on people's lives. Globalization also affected world culture in ways that left many people uneasy. Entering the twenty-first century, the political, social, cultural, and environmental consequences of globalization would be at the top of the world's agenda.

FOR FURTHER REFERENCE

Barber, Benjamin. *Jihad vs. McWorld: How Globalism and Tribalism Are Reshaping the World.* New York: Times Book, 1995.

Garthoff, Raymond. *The Great Transition: American-Soviet Relations at the End of the Cold War.* Washington, D.C.: Brookings, 1994.

Hoffman, David. *The Oligarchs: Wealth and Power in the New Russia.* New York: Public Affairs, 2002.

Kagan, Robert. *Of Paradise and Power: America and Europe in the New World Order.* New York: Knopf, 2003.

Kenney, Padaric. *A Carnival of Revolution: Central Europe, 1989.* Princeton: Princeton University Press, 2002.

Kepel, Gilles. *The War for Muslim Minds: Islam and the West.* Cambridge, Mass.: Harvard University Press, 2004.

Mandela, Nelson. *Long Walk to Freedom: The Autobiography of Nelson Mandela.* Boston: Little Brown, 1996.

Marti, Michael. *China and the Legacy of Deng Xiaoping: From Communist Revolution to Capitalist Evolution.* Washington, D.C.: Potomac, 2002.

Smith, Charles D. *Palestine and the Arab-Israeli Conflict.* 6th ed. New York: Bedford/St. Martin's, 2006.

Smith, Peter H. *Democracy in Latin America: Political Change in Comparative Context.* New York: Oxford University Press, 2005.

KEY TERMS

Nelson Mandela (698)

Ronald Reagan (699)

Helsinki Accords (700)

Mikhail Gorbachev (700)

Solidarity (702)

Boris Yeltsin (702)

Bantustans (706)

Soweto Uprising (706)

Islamists (707)

Ayatollah Khomeini (708)

Persian Gulf War (708)

Osama bin Laden (709)

Deng Xiaoping (714)

Tiananmen Massacre (714)

structural adjustment (715)

VOYAGES ON THE WEB

Voyages: Nelson Mandela

"Voyages" is a real time excursion to historical sites in this chapter and includes interactive activities and study tools such as audio summaries, animated maps, and flashcards.

Visual Evidence: Tanks and Protests in Moscow and Beijing

"Visual Evidence" features artifacts, works of art, or photographs, along with a brief descriptive essay and discussion questions to guide your analysis of visual sources.

World History in Today's World: Truth, Justice, and Human Rights

"World History in Today's World" makes the connection between features of modern life and their origins in the periods in this chapter.

Go to the CourseMate website at www.cengagebrain.com for additional study tools and review materials—including audio and video clips—for this chapter.

32 Voyage into the Twenty-First Century

Nair
Mira Nair)

Filmmaker **Mira Nair** (b. 1957) grew up with a variety of cross-cultural influences. Although her family was from the Punjab in India's northwest, she was raised in the different language and culture of the far eastern state of Orissa. She listened to the Beatles and also to the soundtracks from "Bollywood," the Indian film industry centered in Bombay (now called Mumbai). As a student she experienced boarding school in the tranquil foothills of the Himalayas, frequent visits to the bustling streets of Kolkata (Calcutta), and, finally, studies focused on photography and film at Harvard University. Nair now lives a tri-continental life, with a home and office in New York City, a film institute in Kampala, Uganda, and frequent trips to India. While her work deals with global influences, her emphasis is on the local and personal:

[In] this post 9/11 world, where the schisms of the world are being cemented into huge walls between one belief and way of life and another, now more than ever we need cinema to reveal our tiny local worlds in all their glorious particularity. In my limited experience, it's when I've made a film that's done full-blown justice to the truths and idiosyncrasies of the specifically local, that it crosses over to become surprisingly universal....

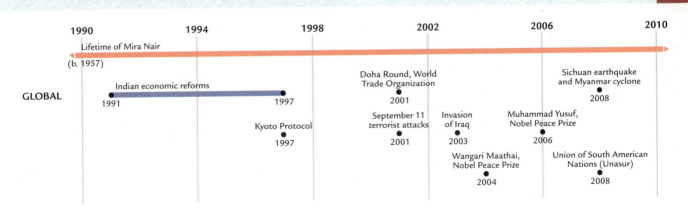

Map: Selected Travels of Mira Nair

Mira Nair attends Harvard University, 1988.

Wins Golden Camera award at Cannes for Salaam Bombay!, 1988.

Nair founds film training program in Uganda, 2005.

Main map labels

- Vanity Fair
- ASIA
- London
- Utrecht
- Venice
- Cannes
- UNITED STATES
- Toronto
- Hanover
- Cambridge
- New York City
- Los Angeles
- Greenwood
- Mississippi Masala
- Miami
- CUBA
- So Far From India
- Hysterical Blindness
- The Namesake
- The Perez Family
- Caribbean Sea
- ATLANTIC OCEAN
- PACIFIC OCEAN
- SOUTH AMERICA
- AFRICA
- Area of inset
- Delhi
- INDIA
- Mumbai
- Kampala
- Mississippi Masala
- INDIAN OCEAN
- Cape Town
- N

Scale: 0 1,000 2,000 Km. / 0 1,000 2,000 Mi.

Inset map labels

- AFGHANISTAN
- Jama Masjid Street Journal / Monsoon Wedding
- CHINA
- Shimla
- PUNJAB
- BHUTAN
- PAKISTAN
- Delhi
- NEPAL
- Varanasi
- INDIA
- Kolkata (Calcutta)
- Ahmadabad
- The Namesake
- ORISSA
- Bhubaneswar
- MYANMAR (BURMA)
- Mumbai (Bombay)
- Salaam Bombay!
- BANGLADESH
- Hyderabad
- Arabian Sea
- Bay of Bengal
- Bengaluru (Bangalore)
- Chennai (Madras)
- SRI LANKA

Scale: 0 250 500 Km. / 0 250 500 Mi.

Legend

Selected Travels of Mira Nair

- → Mira Nair's selected journeys
- Vanity Fair — Setting for selected feature films of Nair, and name of film
- • City visited by Nair
- • Other city

Timeline

1990   1994   1998   2002   2006   2010

Lifetime of Mira Nair (b. 1957)

GLOBAL

- Indian economic reforms 1991–1997
- Kyoto Protocol 1997
- Doha Round, World Trade Organization 2001
- September 11 terrorist attacks 2001
- Invasion of Iraq 2003
- Wangari Maathai, Nobel Peace Prize 2004
- Muhammad Yusuf, Nobel Peace Prize 2006
- Sichuan earthquake and Myanmar cyclone 2008
- Union of South American Nations (Unasur) 2008

I've seen that the Indian films' influence—specifically that unabashed emotional directness, the freewheeling use of music, that emphasis on elemental motivations and values—is a thread running consistently through every one of my films; even when exploring foreign worlds, I have taken the bones and flesh of those societies and tried to infuse them with the spirit of where I'm from.... I find myself applying an Eastern gaze to Western contexts now, and enjoying the reversal.[1]

Mira Nair (b. 1957)
Influential New York–based Indian filmmaker and cultural critic, director of *Monsoon Wedding, My Own Country, Salaam Bombay!, Mississippi Masala, The Namesake, Hysterical Blindness, Vanity Fair,* and other films.

If current trends continue, there will likely be increasing commercial and aesthetic cross-fertilization between Hollywood and Bollywood and other global cultural institutions, even as each retains distinctive local elements.

As with cultural influences, economic and political influences are also moving in multiple directions. The bipolarity of the Cold War was followed in the 1990s by the rise of the United States as the sole remaining superpower. In what one analyst calls the twenty-first-century "post-American world," however, the global role of the United States is offset not only by the growth of the European Union and the continuing economic importance of Japan, but also by the rapid development of Brazil, Russia, India, and China, countries that are using their human capacities and natural resources to benefit from globalization.

When international financial markets collapsed in the autumn of 2008, with global capital markets freezing up as a result, the interrelationship of national and international economies was more forcefully highlighted than ever before. Nations across Europe, Asia, and the Americas struggled to stabilize their financial sectors and to find ways to coordinate their responses internationally. Watching from the sidelines were those billion people left behind by globalization—those who, according to the World Bank, subsist on less than $1 a day.

To one author, India expresses the hopes and challenges of the contemporary world: "No other country matters more to the future of our planet than India.... From combating global terror to finding cures for dangerous pandemics, from dealing with the energy crisis to averting the worse scenarios of global warming, from rebalancing stark global inequalities to spurring the vital innovation to create jobs and improve lives—India is now a pivotal player."[2] This concluding chapter will use the films of Mira Nair **(meer-uh nah-eer)** and the situation of contemporary India to frame a discussion of some of the most important issues facing humanity: economic globalization and global economic crisis; global security and democratization; health and the environment; demography and population movement; questions of identity, gender and human rights; and global culture.

Our survey of world history has given us some tools for assessing trends in each of these areas, especially for connecting local developments with broader patterns. Still, we cannot fully understand the most recent past because we cannot see far enough ahead to draw conclusions with the confidence that comes with evidence. Inevitably, then, our conclusions in this final chapter can be only tentative.

FOCUS QUESTIONS

▶ How is globalization affecting the world economy and global security?

▶ What are the most important environmental and demographic trends of the twenty-first century?

▶ To what extent is the world moving forward in gender equality, human rights, and democracy?

Economic Globalization and Global Economic Crisis

The Indian family at the heart of Mira Nair's *Monsoon Wedding* (2001) is emblematic of global consumer culture. Late-model cars clog their New Delhi driveway, the latest electronics fill their home, and cell phones interrupt their conversations. But Aditi Verma feels conflicted. Working as a television journalist, she is used to an independent lifestyle, including a torrid romance with a married producer. Her upcoming arranged marriage, in true Indian fashion, would change all that. Hundreds of people, including family flying in from Europe and the United States, will attend the lavish wedding ceremony and banquet. After various complications, including confronting a sexually abusive uncle, the marriage finally takes place, a riotous celebration of Punjabi tradition.

A parallel love story in *Monsoon Wedding* follows the relationship of Dubey, the Vermas' wedding contactor, and Alice, one of their servants. A restless entrepreneur, Dubey shares a modest apartment with his mother, who constantly plies him with stock tips while he arranges deals on his cell phone. The happy, if modest, marriage of Dubey and Alice shows that even those without much education or family connections can find a path to success in India's newly globalized, consumer-focused economy. At multiple levels of society, *Monsoon Wedding* presents globalization with a happy ending.

Indeed, the twenty-first century began with strong global economic growth. The economic fundamentals of the United States and Europe seemed strong (though Japan's economy remained sluggish), but spectacular growth rates were achieved in China and India, with other Asian, African, and Latin American economies showing strength as well. Economists coined the term BRIC—for Brazil, Russia, India, and China—to describe the world's surging growth points. In fact, the dramatic collapse of the financial sectors in the United States and Europe in 2008 sent a sharp signal that the age of western economic dominance might be over.

For India, the starting point of a new economy came in 1991 when India's finance minister, **Manmohan Singh** (b. 1932), lowered business taxes and relaxed government regulations. Combined with further reforms in 1997, the results were truly impressive. Annual economic growth rates surged toward 10 percent, and India's steel, chemical, automotive, and pharmaceutical industries, once bound by state regulation, made major strides in

Manmohan Singh Finance minister (1991–1996) and prime minister of India (from 2004) whose liberal reforms lessened government regulation of the economy, leading to rapid economic growth.

Map 32.1 Per Capita Income

In spite of recent surges in the economies of countries such as India, China, and Russia, the global economy is still dominated by the United States, western Europe, Canada, Australia, and Japan. Per capita income gives only a rough estimate of people's quality of life, however. The United Nations Development Program (UNDP) uses a Human Development Report that takes account a variety of factors in addition to income—such as education, health care, environmental standards, and gender equality—in its rankings. According to the UNDP, the island nation of Iceland ranks first in human development, Canada fourth, Japan eighth, France tenth, and the United States twelfth.[3] © Cengage Learning

Interactive Map

Over $30,000
Andorra
Australia
Austria
Bahrain
Belgium
Bermuda
Brunei
Canada
Denmark
Equatorial Guinea
Finland
France
Germany
Greece
Iceland
Ireland
Italy
Japan
Kuwait
Luxembourg
Netherlands
Norway
Qatar
Singapore
Spain
Sweden
Switzerland
United Arab Emirates
United Kingdom
United States

$12,001–$30,000
Argentina
Bahamas
Barbados
Botswana
Chile
Costa Rica
Croatia
Czech Republic
Estonia
Gabon
Hungary
Iran
Israel
Korea, South
Latvia
Libya
Liechtenstein
Lithuania
Malaysia
Malta
Mexico
Monaco
New Zealand
Oman
Poland
Portugal
Russia
Saudi Arabia

$5,001–$12,000
Seychelles
Slovakia
Slovenia
Taiwan
Trinidad and Tobago
Venezuela
Albania
Algeria
Angola
Antigua and Barbuda
Armenia
Azerbaijan
Belarus
Belize
Bosnia and Herzegovina
Brazil
Bulgaria
Cape Verde

$3,001–$5,000
China
Colombia
Dominican Republic
Ecuador
Egypt
El Salvador
Guatemala
Guyana
Kazakhstan
Lebanon
Macedonia
Mauritius
Namibia
Panama
Peru
Romania
St. Kitts and Nevis
Serbia
South Africa
Suriname
Thailand
Tunisia
Turkey
Turkmenistan
Ukraine
Uruguay
Bolivia
Congo, Republic
Cuba
Dominica
Fiji
Georgia
Grenada
Honduras
Indonesia
Iraq
Jamaica
Jordan
Maldives

$1,001–$3,000
Montenegro
Morocco
Nauru
Nicaragua
Paraguay
Philippines
St. Lucia
St. Vincent and Grenadines
Samoa
São Tomé and Príncipe
Senegal
Sudan
Tajikistan
Tanzania
Timor-Leste
Tonga
Tuvalu
Uganda
Uzbekistan
Vanuatu
Vietnam
Yemen
Zambia
Côte d'Ivoire
Ghana
India
Kenya
Kiribati
Korea, North
Kyrgyzstan
Laos
Lesotho
Marshall Is.
Mauritania
Moldova
Mongolia
Myanmar (Burma)
Nepal
Nigeria
Pakistan
Papua New Guinea
Sri Lanka
Swaziland
Syria

$0–$1,000
Comoros
Congo, Democratic Republic
Djibouti
Eritrea
Ethiopia
Gambia
Guinea
Guinea-Bissau
Liberia
Madagascar
Malawi
Mozambique
Niger
Rwanda
Sierra Leone
Solomon Is.
Somalia
Togo
Zimbabwe
Afghanistan
Burundi
Central African Republic

0 1,500 3,000 Km.
0 1,500 3,000 Mi.

726

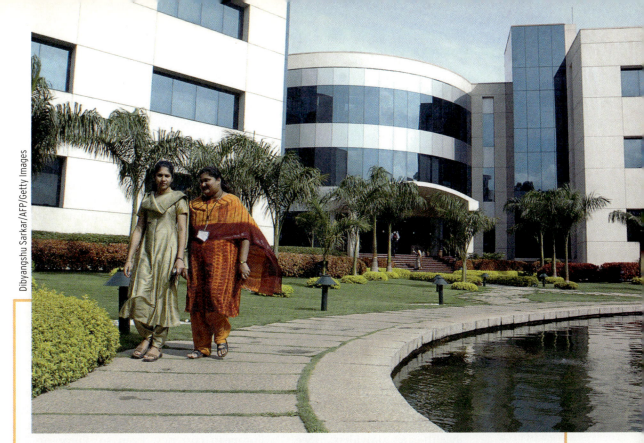

India's High-Technology Sector The southern Indian city of Bangalore is home to the headquarters of software giant Infosys Technologies, which reported over $3 billion in revenue for 2007. The beautiful Infosys campus and the middle-class lifestyles of its employees contrast sharply with the conditions faced by the hundreds of millions who have yet to share in the economic dynamism of the New India.

national, regional, and global markets. Middle-class families no longer spent years waiting to buy a car; now they could choose among multiple models and use credit for their purchases. At the same time, India became a major player in the software industry, especially as concerns about a "millennium virus" caused Western companies to seek inexpensive ways to back up electronic data. Firms like Infosys, based in the southern city of Bangalore, became shining stars of India's new economy.

While such has been the good news for India, many have been left behind. In the world's largest democracy, hundreds of millions of Indian citizens still live without access to clean water, let alone computers. Is it just a matter of time before they too will enjoy plenty? Or is inequality a necessary outcome of globalization?

Data from India, China, Brazil, the United States, and elsewhere show a strong correlation between global economic growth and rising inequality. Critics contend that, in their haste to liberalize their economies, governments have abandoned the health and educational needs of their citizens. As one economist argues, "The ancient question of how market forces need to be tempered for the greater good of the economy and the society is now a global one (see Map 32.1)."[4]

The solution in Russia was to use increased revenue from oil and gas to restore the country's optimism by investing in physical infrastructure and social services, with Vladimir Putin and his United Russia party keeping a tight grip on the media and politics. India and China, lacking self-sufficiency in energy, have been aggressively pursuing access to African energy resources, extending lines of credit, technical assistance, and trade preferences to African petroleum-producing countries. Meanwhile, in 2008 the growth of India and China helped drive up petroleum prices, past $140 a barrel for the first time in history. Because of high levels of corruption, however, citizens of oil-producing countries such as Nigeria saw little benefit from the boom.

Globalization exposes more people to capitalism's "creative destruction." Rapid innovation renders old skills obsolete, and wages get undercut by workers in other countries who can do the same work for less—called **outsourcing**. Here too, India has become a pioneer. Falling telecommunications prices combine with relatively high skills and low wages to move American customer service jobs to India. The same process affects other service sectors as well. Thailand, for example, is building a reputation for quality health facilities that charge far lower rates than American health-care providers. (See the feature "Movement of Ideas: The World Is Flat.") While low-wage jobs are outsourced to poorer countries, the most talented and educated from poor countries often leave to seek opportunity elsewhere. This "brain drain" makes it more difficult for the poorest nations to benefit from globalization.

Regional trading blocs that first arose during the 1990s continue to be important, but balancing regional goals with national interests often entails controversy and tough bargaining. The United States, Canada, and Mexico have all had complaints about the North Atlantic Free Trade Association (NAFTA). The Mexican government, for example, worried that American agricultural subsidies made it impossible for Mexico's farmers to compete, while union members in the United States thought that losing industrial jobs to Mexico was too high a price to pay for free trade. Political disputes have also hampered the effectiveness of **Mercosur**, a South American common market, especially tensions between Colombia, closely allied with the United States, and Venezuela, where President Hugo Chávez accused the United States of interfering in his country's internal affairs.

The European Union was the most mature and successful of the regional blocs, even as it members haggled over the balance of power between national governments and the European Parliament and over the protection of local interests against continental ones. In 2011, opinion was also divided over the degree to which the wealthier EU countries should "bail out" the troubled economies of Greece and Ireland; Germans in particular were concerned that they were having to pay the price for the fiscal irresponsibility of others.

Significant debates had surrounded the adoption of the euro as a common currency after 1998. States that adopted the euro were willing to sacrifice some degree of national economic control for the trade advantages of a common European currency. Even so, European Union membership has expanded dramatically, with twelve new countries added between 2004 and 2007 alone—Cyprus, Czech Republic, Estonia, Hungary, Latvia, Lithuania, Malta, Poland, Slovakia, Slovenia, Bulgaria, and Romania—many of them formerly part of the Soviet sphere. The new Balkan states formed from the breakup of Yugoslavia—Serbia, Croatia, Bosnia and Herzegovina, Montenegro, and Kosovo—all applied for EU membership.

More ambitious than regional agreements was the attempt by members of the **World Trade Organization** (WTO), founded by former signatories of the General Agreement on Tariffs and Trade (GATT), to establish rules for global trade. Organized opposition to the WTO began at once. The Global People's Network, allying environmentalists and campaigners for social justice, directs its criticism not only at the WTO but also at multinational corporations that gain from the loosening of global trade restrictions. In particular, detractors object to corporations avoiding labor protections and environmental regulations. Just as labor unions once arose in individual nations to counterbalance the power of industrialists, advocates of the Global People's Network argue for the need to reduce the excesses of multinational corporate power.

outsourcing Obtaining goods or services from an outside supplier. The term commonly refers to Western companies that contract work to providers in lower-wage markets, lowering their costs and increasing their competitiveness.

Mercosur The Common Market of the South, a South American regional trade association that was the foundation for Unasur, the Union of South American Nations.

World Trade Organization (WTO) Membership organization founded in 1995 to establish rules for international trade, with an emphasis on lowering tariffs and other barriers to the free movement of goods.

Protests did not stop the World Trade Organization from beginning negotiations toward a comprehensive global trade pact at Doha, Qatar, in 2001. The importance of the Doha round of negotiations was magnified when the People's Republic of China, previously excluded from GATT because of perceived unfair trade practices, was accepted for WTO membership. Progress was slow, however, and the agreement remains unsigned. One controversial point has been the insistence on retaining tariffs to protect member state agricultural sectors. When the U.S. Congress passed a farm bill in 2008 that continued subsidies and tariffs to protect American agriculture from global competition, it was clear that even the nation expressing the strongest commitment to free trade was constrained by national politics. The European Union has also defended its farm subsidies, to the frustration of less developed countries seeking access to Western markets.

While defenders and opponents debated the merits of free-market globalization, **Muhammad Yusuf** (b. 1940) was thinking of practical solutions for those left behind. His Grameen ("Village") Bank pioneered microfinance: lending small amounts of money. Poor borrowers proved to be trustworthy clients even when they had no collateral to secure the loans, and small investments often led to big returns when they pooled their resources, energy, and ideas to start new enterprises. Yusuf's model, even if sometimes plagued by corruption and hurt by his firing as Chairman of Grameen in 2011, still showed promise as a means of spreading the benefits of free markets more widely across the globe.

Attention shifted to the world's largest financial corporations when, in the autumn of 2008, the sudden bankruptcy of Lehman Brothers revealed the insolvency of most of the world's dominant banks and brokerages. Their balance sheets near default, banks suddenly lost trust in each other, and international finance collapsed like a house of cards. As nations around the world struggled to put their financial houses in order, it became clear that the relative absence of regulation was inadequate to safeguard the global flow of free-market capital.

The initial reaction of the United States and Britain was to use governments' borrowing ability to prop up the financial sector while hoping to stimulate economic growth with tax cuts and increased government spending. However, while the United States continued to advocate that policy as a way to revive global demand, a rift appeared at the G-20 meeting of the world's wealthiest nations in 2010. The German government in particular became concerned about growing government deficits, and the new conservative government in Britain changed course with deep spending cuts and tax increases. Economists were divided, some seeing a continuing need for fiscal stimulus, especially in countries with high unemployment like the United States, others arguing that deficit spending was unsustainable and threatening to future growth. Britain's change of policy, as well as the extreme cost-cutting measures in the worst-hit European nations, Greece and Ireland, made the less austere policies of the Obama administration in the United States seem out of the mainstream. Meanwhile, growth rates in India and China remain stronger than those in the West.

Whatever policies predominate, every nation must face balancing economic growth and social equity. The potential for progress is naturally greatest in developing nations such as India, where the benefits of a growing economy can still be extended to millions more people. If India can reform its state sector and make its operations more open and transparent, use the energies of its civil society, reinvigorate the tradition of social responsibility bequeathed by Mohandas K. Gandhi, harness private philanthropy, and invest in the education of its rural and urban poor, then it will justify the optimism at the heart of *Monsoon Wedding*.

Primary Source: Free Trade and the Decline of Democracy *Read a cogent critique by Ralph Nader, a consumer advocate and political activist, of international free-trade agreements.*

Muhammad Yusuf (b. 1940) Bangladeshi pioneer of microfinance whose Grameen ("Village") Bank gives small loans to the poor, usually women, to start small enterprises. His bank became a global model for microfinance, and in 2006 he was awarded the Nobel Peace Prize.

Primary Source: Selection from a Roundtable Discussion of Globalization and Its Impact on Arab Culture *An Arab intellectual discusses the challenges and opportunities of globalization for Arab culture.*

The World Is Flat

"It's a Flat World, After All" is an influential essay written by Thomas Friedman in 2005. Friedman, a *New York Times* columnist and Pulitzer Prize winner, portrays globalization as an opportunity for India, China, and other parts of the world; however, the technological and educational requirements for success in a "flat world," he argues, present a looming challenge for the United States of America.

I encountered the flattening of the world quite by accident [when] … I interviewed Indian entrepreneurs who wanted to prepare my taxes from Bangalore, read my X-rays from Bangalore, trace my lost luggage from Bangalore and write my new software from Bangalore.… Nandan Nilekani, the Infosys C.E.O., was showing me his global video-conference room.… Infosys, he explained, could hold a virtual meeting of the key players from its entire global supply chain for any project at any time … its American designers could be on the screen speaking with their Indian software writers and their Asian manufacturers all at once.… Above the screen there were eight clocks that pretty well summed up the Infosys workday: 24/7/365.…

Nilekani explained, "[O]ver the last years … hundreds of millions of dollars were invested in putting broadband connectivity around the world.…" At the same time … there was an explosion of e-mail software, search engines like Google and proprietary software that can chop up any piece of work and send one part to Boston, one part to Bangalore and one part to Beijing, making it easy for anyone to do remote development. When all of these things suddenly came together around 2000, Nilekani said, they "'created a platform where intellectual work, intellectual capital, could be delivered from anywhere. It could be disaggregated, delivered, distributed, produced and put back together again—and this gave a whole new degree of freedom to the way we do work.…'"

This has been building for a long time. Globalization 1.0 (1492 to 1800) shrank the world from a size large to a size medium, and the dynamic force in that era was countries globalizing for resources and imperial conquest. Globalization 2.0 (1800 to 2000) shrank the world from a size medium to a size small, and it was spearheaded by companies globalizing for markets and labor. Globalization 3.0 (which started around 2000) is shrinking the world from a size small to a size tiny and flattening the playing field at the same time.… But Globalization 3.0 [is] different in that Globalization 1.0 and 2.0 were driven primarily by European and American companies and countries. But going forward, this will be less and less true. Globalization 3.0 is going to be driven … by a much more diverse—non-Western, nonwhite—group of individuals.…

"Today, the most profound thing to me is the fact that a 14-year-old in Romania or Bangalore or the Soviet Union or Vietnam has all the information, all the tools, all the software easily available to apply knowledge however they want," said Marc Andreessen, a co-founder of Netscape and creator of the first commercial Internet browser.… "As bioscience becomes more computational and less about wet labs and as all the genomic data becomes easily available on the Internet, at some point you will be able to design vaccines on your laptop."

… [W]e are now in the process of connecting all the knowledge pools in the world together.

We've tasted some of the downsides of that in the way that Osama bin Laden has connected terrorist knowledge pools together through his Qaeda network, not to mention the work of teenage hackers spinning off more and more lethal computer viruses that affect us all. But the upside is that by connecting all these knowledge pools we are on the cusp of an incredible new era of innovation.... Only 30 years ago, if you had a choice of being born a B student in Boston or a genius in Bangalore or Beijing, you probably would have chosen Boston, because a genius in Beijing or Bangalore could not really take advantage of his or her talent. They could not plug and play globally. Not anymore. Not when the world is flat, and anyone with smarts, access to Google and a cheap wireless laptop can join the innovation fray.... And be advised: the Indians and Chinese are not racing us to the bottom. They are racing us to the top. What China's leaders really want is that the next generation of underwear and airplane wings not just be "made in China" but also be "designed in China...."

Rajesh Rao, a young Indian entrepreneur who started an electronic-game company from Bangalore [said], "We can't relax.... That is gone. There are dozens of people who are doing the same thing you are doing, and they are trying to do it better.... That is what is going to happen to so many jobs—they will go to that corner of the world where there is the least resistance and the most opportunity. If there is a skilled person in Timbuktu, he will get work if he knows how to access the rest of the world, which is quite easy today...."

... There is no sugar-coating this: in a flat world, every individual is going to have to run a little faster if he or she wants to advance his or her standard of living. When I was growing up, my parents used to say to me, "Tom, finish your dinner—people in China are starving." But after sailing to the edges of the flat world for a year, I am now telling my own daughters, "Girls, finish your homework—people in China and India are starving for your jobs."

Source: From Thomas Friedman, "It's a Flat World After All," *New York Times*, April 3, 2005. Reprinted with permission of PARS International Corp.

QUESTIONS FOR ANALYSIS

▶ What are the implications of Friedman's argument for college students in various parts of the world?

▶ How might the developing "flat earth" affect those hundreds of millions of people lacking in economic resources or access to education?

Global Security

The events of **September 11, 2001**, shocked the world. Thousands were killed, and international sympathy for the people of the United States was nearly universal.

As a resident of New York, Mira Nair was deeply affected and joined in an international collaboration of eleven directors, each of whom made a short film of exactly eleven minutes, nine seconds, and one extra frame. For her contribution to *11"9'01*, Nair focused on the true story of Mrs. Hamdani, a Pakistani American who lost her son that day. Salman Hamdani was a young paramedic who on that morning noticed smoke rising from Lower Manhattan and rushed to help, not pausing to tell his mother or anyone else where he was going; Nair shows his mother's devastating uncertainty when he failed to come home. Salman's remains were later salvaged from ground zero, where he had died rendering assistance to 9/11 victims.

Mrs. Hamdani's fear and pain were amplified by the suspicion of her neighbors. The film shows how previously friendly people on her block began to look at her strangely and turn away when she approached, wondering if her missing son had been involved in the attack. Indeed, the shock of 9/11 caused some Americans to suspect and stigmatize all Muslims; Nair was critiquing prejudices that surfaced after 9/11.

Muslims in India have also been affected by recent terrorist attacks over the status of the northern province of Kashmir, unresolved since partition in 1947. In May 2008 a series of coordinated explosions in the city of Jaipur killed eighty people; Indian authorities suspected that local extremists carried out the bombings with aid from Islamist organizations in Pakistan. The terrorists focused the explosions on a Hindu temple and surrounding markets, and some in India have repeated the mistake of Mrs. Hamdani's neighbors by equating "Muslim" with "terrorist."

The people of India therefore paid close attention when President George W. Bush declared a "war on terror" and then invaded Taliban-controlled Afghanistan in October 2001 and Saddam Hussein's Iraq in April 2003. The invasion of Afghanistan had broad international backing because Taliban leaders had given Osama bin Laden sanctuary. Even Iran, Russia, and China—nations usually suspicious of American military ventures—supported the American-led effort to remove the Taliban from power.

The U.S. invasion of Iraq, however, generated controversy, unlike in 1991, when evicting Iraqi forces from Kuwait enjoyed a broad global consensus. While some Americans incorrectly believed that Iraq was complicit in the 9/11 attacks, others argued that Iraq had no connection to al-Qaeda and that Afghanistan should remain the priority. Many Americans, and even more members of the international community, doubted the Bush administration's claims that Iraq possessed "weapons of mass destruction."

In 2002, United Nations weapons inspectors assigned to Iraq ascertained that earlier chemical, biological, and nuclear weapons programs were no longer active. U.S. and British intelligence services, however, disputed the weapons inspectors' reports, suggesting that the UN inspectors were being deceived. With the support of British prime minister Tony Blair, President George W. Bush insisted that Iraq represented an imminent threat: "Facing clear evidence of peril, we cannot wait for the final proof—the smoking gun—that could come in the form of a mushroom cloud." Without United Nations sanction, Bush assembled a "coalition of the willing," invaded Iraq in April 2003, and deposed Saddam Hussein.

The Bush advisers who initiated the Iraq War rejected the moderate internationalism of the first Bush administration and argued for a more

September 11, 2001   Date of the al-Qaeda terrorist attacks on the United States in which two hijacked planes were used to destroy the two towers of the World Trade Center in New York City. Another hijacked plane crashed into the Pentagon, and a fourth fell in a Pennsylvania field.

Primary Source: The Last Night   *Read a list of instructions meant to be reviewed on September 10, 2001, by the terrorists who attacked the United States the next morning.*

proactive and, if necessary, unilateral policy toward the Middle East. The "new world order" might still be achieved, they argued, but only if the United States took a more aggressive role in bringing democracy to the Middle East. In their view, Iraq would become a model of democracy and free enterprise, an inspiration to the people of the Arab world and a bulwark against terrorism.

But, after removing the authoritarian power that held Iraq together, the region seemed less rather than more secure. By the fifth anniversary of the invasion, over 130,000 U.S. troops were still in Iraq; almost all the "coalition of the willing" had left, and even the British had begun drawing down their troops. Although the Shi'ite majority of the country had political control for the first time in over a thousand years, Iraq remained divided not just between Kurdish, Sunni, and Shi'ite interests but also between armed Shi'ite factions (see Map 32.2).

Map 32.2   Iraq in Transition
After the regime of Saddam Hussein, dominated by Iraq's Sunni Arab minority, fell to U.S.-led forces in 2003, some Sunnis took up arms against the U.S. coalition, independent Shia Arab militias, and the now Shi'ite-dominated Iraqi government itself. By 2007, however, violence abated as an increasing number of Sunni leaders rejected the terrorist tactics of the militants and as the United States increased its troop levels. The question remained whether the Iraqi government—with a Shi'ite prime minister, Kurdish president, and Sunni leader of Parliament—could effectively balance the complex regional, religious, and ethnic divisions of the country.   © Cengage Learning   **Interactive Map**

There was no evidence of the quick transformation that Bush and his advisers had promised.

Although waged in the name of democracy and human rights, the "war on terror" sometimes had an opposite effect. Constitutionally protected civil liberties were undermined both by wiretaps without warrant or court approval and by the detention of terrorism suspects without charges or trial. And once again, the United States was supporting foreign regimes, such as Egypt and Pakistan, based on their strategic usefulness rather than their democratic credentials. In 2006 it backed an Ethiopian invasion of Somalia to remove an Islamist government in Mogadishu. Meanwhile, other capitals, including Moscow and Beijing, borrowed Washington's antiterror rhetoric to justify crackdowns, especially in areas with large Muslim populations, such as the Caucasus region in the southern Russian Federation and China's western Xinjiang province.

The 9/11 terrorists showed the great damage that could be done by small, dedicated groups using minimal technology, while the Iraq War showed once again that sophisticated military forces could have difficulty containing and policing civil uprisings. The death of Osama bin Laden in an American raid in Pakistan in 2011 did revive confidence in the effectiveness of superior training and technology. Even with Bin Laden's death, however, there still remained the frightening prospect of massive death and destruction were terrorists ever able to gain access to more deadly biological, chemical, or nuclear weapons. Even if that danger were avoided, nuclear proliferation remained a difficult challenge to global security.

In Europe the threat of nuclear weapons seemed to have diminished after the fall of the Soviet Union. Still, there was reason to be worried that nuclear devices and technology in post-Soviet states might enter the global arms trade and find their way into the hands of extremist organizations or irresponsible governments. Russian leaders bristled at the expansion of the North Atlantic Treaty Organization into former Soviet satellites such as Poland. Their response came with the invasion of independent Georgia in the summer of 2008. Vladimir Putin's resurgent Russia, like the Soviet Union

and the tsarist empire before it, regarded the Caucasus Mountain region as part of its "near abroad," where Russian interests must hold sway. The invasion was a lesson not only to Georgia, but also to any other contiguous republic contemplating membership in the North Atlantic Treaty Organization and the European Union.

Russian security anxieties had been heightened in 2007 when the United States announced plans to station antimissile defenses in eastern Europe, purportedly to contain a future Iranian nuclear threat but also with the capacity to shoot down Russian missiles. A nuclear exchange was even more worrisome between India and Pakistan; both nations (along with Israel) have developed such devices while refusing to sign the international Treaty on the Non-Proliferation of Nuclear Weapons. In 2007 the Bush administration agreed to allow the transfer of civilian nuclear technology to New Delhi despite its potential for military purposes. At the same time, the United States drew a firm line against Iran's nuclear program. While Tehran claimed merely to be advancing its civilian energy potential, President Bush argued that Iran was such a threat to world peace that it should not be allowed a civilian program that could be converted to military use. Using the same rationale, Israeli aircraft destroyed a Syrian nuclear power plant in 2007. A year earlier, the communist government of North Korea had snubbed international opinion by openly testing a nuclear bomb.

North Korean and Iranian scientists had made substantial strides after the chief of Pakistan's nuclear program shared his technology with them. South Asia has thus been a possible flashpoint for armed conflict between nuclear states and a focal point for the proliferation of nuclear technology beyond the relatively small club—the United States, France, the United Kingdom, Russia, Israel, Pakistan, India, China, and North Korea—already in possession of nuclear weapons. Meanwhile, with so much attention fixed on terrorism and nuclear proliferation, insufficient progress has been made on other issues also vital to long-term global security.

Health and the Environment

Global issues of health arise when we consider Mira Nair's film on the HIV/AIDS crisis, *My Own Country* (1998). The film was based on the memoir of Dr. Abraham Verghese, an Indian doctor whose family fled their home in Ethiopia to avoid civil strife. After completing his medical degree in India, Dr. Verghese began working as a Veterans Administration doctor in Johnson City, Tennessee. *My Own Country* shows the strains that affect this small town when a native son returns from the city, his body wracked with AIDS. The year was 1985, before the development of retroviral drug treatments, and there was little medical help Dr. Verghese could offer. Yet, even though he faced prejudice and hostility for taking in patients ostracized by the community, Dr. Verghese persevered with dignity and kindness.

The presence of an Indian doctor in the rural United States is one of *My Own Country*'s global links. Small American towns must often look far afield to find doctors, and those trained abroad are more likely than their American-trained counterparts to work as general practitioners for modest salaries. Another global dimension of the film is HIV/AIDS itself. When it was first diagnosed in the 1980s, the disease was associated with two particular groups, homosexual men and intravenous drug users. Today, Africa has the largest number of AIDS victims, and there are more women than men among them. While medical advances have decreased suffering and extended life spans for those who can afford them, most of the world's HIV victims die without the benefit of any effective medical intervention. And while infection rates have stabilized in wealthier nations, many global health experts fear that India and China are now joining Africa as frontiers in the expansion of the disease.

In India, hundreds of millions lack access to the most basic health care, and older scourges like tuberculosis, polio, cholera, and malnutrition have yet to be effectively addressed. If HIV were to spread there as quickly as it did in South Africa in the 1990s (growing from 1 to 25 percent of the population between 1990 and 2005), the Indian society would be overwhelmed. Unlike most epidemic diseases, which are deadliest for the very young and very old, AIDS carries people away in the prime of their productive and reproductive lives, adding huge social and developmental costs.

HIV is just one of the diseases that exploit increased human mobility to spread quickly. Virulent new strains of traditional killers like malaria, which until recently were confined to small geographic areas, now hop from continent to continent courtesy of mosquito hosts aboard jet airplanes. New strains of influenza, such as the avian flu virus from East Asia and the deadly Ebola (ee-BOH-lah) virus from Central Africa, threaten to create uncontrollable global epidemics. Meanwhile, the worldwide use of antibiotics has spawned resistant strains of bacteria that make the suppression of diseases like tuberculosis more difficult. So far, viruses and bacteria that ignore national borders are straining the global health-care system.

Health threats are compounded by global climate change. Approximately 60,000 people are killed every year in natural disasters that scientists believe are related to increasing global temperatures, including a massive European heat wave in 2003, Hurricane Katrina in the United States in 2005, the huge cyclone that hit Myanmar in 2008, and unprecedented cycles of drought and flooding in many parts of Africa and Asia. Though climate change is not always a factor in natural disasters (the devastating Indian Ocean tsunami that claimed almost 250,000 casualties in 2004 was caused by an earthquake), many suspect that humans are a principal cause of the increasing tempo of such events. Scientists predict that melting polar ice

Global Warming Average temperatures in the Arctic are rising twice as fast as elsewhere in the world. The rapid melting of the polar ice cap is an outcome of global warming and also a further cause: in the future there will be less snow and ice in the Arctic to absorb the sun's heat and cool the planet. The peril faced by this polar bear mother and her cubs is immediate; the threat to humanity from rising sea levels is ominous.

caps will soon disrupt the world's highly populated coastal areas, especially Bangladesh, where 55 million people would be displaced by even a modest rise in sea levels.

Global climate change is also affecting the spread of infectious diseases. The director general of the World Health Organization, Dr. Margaret Chan, argues: "Many of the most important global killers are highly sensitive to climatic conditions. Malaria, diarrhea and malnutrition kill millions of people every year, most of them children. Without effective action to mitigate and adapt to climate change, the burden of these conditions will be greater, and they will be more difficult and more costly to control."[5] Violent monsoons and hurricanes generate conditions for the spread of water-borne disease, while warmer weather allows the spread of tropical diseases like malaria and dengue fever to formerly temperate regions. "No country can shield itself," Dr. Chan said, "from an invasion by a pathogen in an airplane passenger or an insect hiding in a cargo hold." Increasingly, anyone's health issue is everyone's health issue.

The most significant international effort to address global warming is the **Kyoto Protocol**. For the first time, nations agreed to mandatory limits on emissions of the "greenhouse gases" that pump carbon dioxide into the atmosphere and contribute to increased temperatures. The effectiveness of the Kyoto (kee-oh-toh) Protocol was undermined, however, by the

Kyoto Protocol (1997) International agreement adopted in Kyoto, Japan, under the United Nations Framework Agreement on Climate Change in an effort to reduce greenhouse gas emissions linked to global warming. The Kyoto accords were not accepted by the United States.

refusal of the United States to ratify the treaty. The most contentious question was how to share the global burden. The largest contributors to global climate change historically have been the United States, Canada, western Europe, and Japan. Now the surging and largely unregulated Chinese and Indian economies threaten to offset progress elsewhere in the world.

China and India have argued that since most greenhouse gases are still produced in the United States and Europe, those countries should shoulder the largest burden in their reduction. Western governments, meanwhile, have argued that rapidly developing China and India should begin immediately to cut greenhouse gas emissions. In 2008, China became the world's largest producer of carbon dioxide emissions, much of it from coal-fired power stations. In fact, China brings on line two power stations every week. On the other hand, its per capita power consumption is only one-third that of the United States and western Europe, and its leaders say Chinese citizens are entitled to a standard of living equivalent to that of the most developed nations. The goal of **sustainable development** is nowhere within reach.

Deforestation magnifies the effect of the world's rising output of greenhouse gases. Tropical forests play a large role in cleansing the atmosphere of carbon dioxide and replenishing

it with oxygen. High prices and sustained demand for tropical hardwoods from Central Africa and Indonesia, however, have led lumber companies to fell vast areas of forest, sometimes bribing politicians to evade environmental regulations. In Brazil, farmers clear the forests for agriculture, especially where they can grow sugar cane for ethanol. In 2008 the minister for the environment, Marina Silva, resigned when she was unable to block transportation projects that hasten the demise of the rainforest.

On environmental issues, India is a source of both worry and hope. On the one hand, the Indian economy is generating consumption that makes the environmental challenges of the subcontinent many times more daunting. On the other hand, Indian scientists and entrepreneurs are already finding solutions in renewable energy sources such as wind power. The capital city of New Delhi has a sparkling, energy-efficient new subway system and has converted much of its public transportation to run on cleaner natural gas.

Work is needed on every front to resolve the health and environmental challenges of our times. Meanwhile, rising population, urbanization, and global migration make the search for solutions all the more urgent.

sustainable development
Economic growth that can be sustained without causing environmental damage.

Demography and Population Movement

India is crowded, a realization that emerges from *Salaam Bombay!* (1988), the film with which Mira Nair first made her international reputation. It is a heartbreaking tale of poverty in India's largest city, with a cast made up largely of homeless children. Their presence gives an unmistakable authenticity to this story about "children who have never experienced childhood."[6]

We first meet the child protagonist Krishna as he returns to find that the circus where he worked has left without him. He had left his home village to earn five hundred rupees to replace his brother's bicycle, which he had destroyed. Krishna does not know exactly where Bombay is located, but like so many in the countryside, he sees the big city as a land of opportunity. At the train station, the ticket seller leaves Krishna with the advice that he should return as a movie star. Alas, the glamour of Bollywood is not Krishna's future. He takes up residence as a tea boy in a brothel. In this harsh world, those at the bottom band together to form a community and cherish opportunities for laughter and comradeship.

Krishna's story touches on the size and composition of the world's population, and the movement of that population from villages into cities. India contains by far the largest youth population in the world, with over 600 million people (half the population) under the age of twenty-five. By 2035 India is expected to surpass China as the most populous nation on earth, with 1.6 billion people. The move toward cities is a part of that growth. For the planet as a whole, 2008 was the first year when the majority of humankind lived in cities.[7] So far, only about 28 percent of Indians live in urban environments. Yet, especially in remote hamlets, television raises expectations among the young, with portrayals of the urban "good life." The pressure driving migrants into the cities increases, as does the already immense pressure on urban infrastructure: transport, water, education, and sanitation.

Expressed on a global scale, these trends are alarming. While the population of wealthier countries grows old and in some cases (for example, Italy, Japan, and Russia) fertility rates are below the level needed to replace the current population, surging growth rates in Latin America, Africa, and much of Asia have created an enormous population of young people whose ambitions exceed their chances to fulfill them. Creating opportunities to tap the creativity and intelligence of these hundreds of millions of young people is a matter of urgent concern.

In the 1980s, leaders of the People's Republic of China adopted a radical **One Child Policy** that punishes parents who have a second child with heavy penalties and even prosecution, enforcement being strictest in urban areas. Within a single generation, population growth leveled off. Without siblings, the younger generation receives the full attention and financial support of their parents, who usually focus on

One Child Policy   In China, most parents are restricted by this policy to a single child to curb population growth. The policy has led to significant gender imbalance.

education. When the massive earthquake of 2008 toppled schools in the Sichuan province, many Chinese parents lost their only child.

Commonly, when people attain greater wealth and security they tend to have fewer children. Today, population growth is slowing not just in richer countries but also across much of the world. Unfortunately, in much of Africa and elsewhere, high mortality from disease is partly accountable. If current trends hold, total global population will reach equilibrium sometime later in this century, perhaps at a level of 9 billion people.

There is currently a demographic imbalance between world regions. On the one hand, countries like India have many underemployed young people of productive age; on the other, societies like Japan have aging populations but insufficient workers to support them. Through immigration, affluent societies can maintain a stable mix of working-age and senior citizens, but nations that snub immigration, such as Japan, will need other solutions (such as robotics) to help care for their graying populations. Even China is looking to a future where eventually there may not be enough workers to support the current working-age population when they retire. In 2008 the Communist Party began re-evaluating its One Child Policy.

Migrants leave home, and often family, in search of higher wages. Migrants move, not only to cities, but also across national borders. Not surprisingly, India reflects this wider trend. India sends not only doctors to Europe and the United States, but also construction workers and domestic servants to the Persian Gulf. The government of the southern state of Kerala, for example, relies heavily on remittances sent home by migrant workers from the United Arab Emirates. Migrant workers are often abused by unscrupulous employers, who subject them to unsafe conditions and withhold their pay.

Immigration also causes controversies. Since immigrants often work for less, they drive down wages for native workers. In 2008, South African gangs killed twelve immigrants from other African countries, claiming that the outsiders were taking their jobs. In Italy, the government cracked down on illegal Roma (Gypsy) immigrants from southeastern Europe, claiming that they were responsible for an increase in crime. In the United States, immigration from Latin America has shifted the cultural and linguistic balance of American society.

Many western Europeans are alarmed by Muslim immigration to their countries. In 2005 and 2007, Arabs and Africans rioted in the suburbs of Paris. Conservatives called for law and order and restrictions on immigration; those with more liberal views cited racism as the cause of the riots and demanded greater educational and employment prospects for immigrant youth. The Netherlands was rocked in 2004 when Theo van Gogh, who had made a film critical of the treatment of women in Islam, was stabbed to death by a Dutch citizen of North African ancestry. Muslims in the United Kingdom and the United States, sensing a hostile atmosphere after 9/11, cluster even more closely into separate ethnic and religious communities.

In the past, immigrants gradually assimilated. Today's transportation and communications, however, make it easy to remain connected to familial and cultural networks on the other side of the globe. Mira Nair maintains homes on multiple continents and moves freely between them. This shrinking of the globe amplifies issues of national, ethnic, racial, gender, religious, and other modes of self-identification.

Questions of Identity

Questions of identity—especially multiple, overlapping identities—are frequently at the heart of Mira Nair's films. In *Mississippi Masala* (1991), Jay Patel is unable to settle down and appreciate the success his family is having in the motel business in the rural American South. Though his origins lie in India, the home he longs for is in Uganda, from which his family had been expelled in the 1970s, along with the entire Ugandan Indian community, by the dictator Idi Amin. Self-identifying as an African, Patel writes letter after letter trying to have his property restored.

Meanwhile, his daughter Mina is developing a relationship with Demetrius, an African American carpet cleaner. Their relationship is frowned on by both the Indian and African American communities, even though both of them are "colored" in the eyes of the town's white population. In these circumstances, what does it mean to be "black," "Indian," "African," or "American"? The complexity of that question was recognized by the U.S. Census in 2000 when, for the first time, citizens were given the option to check more than one racial box.

On November 4, 2008, Barack Hussein Obama was elected as 44th president of the United States. As the country's first African American leader, Obama brought America's evolving identity conversation to the fore. His mother was from Kansas and his father from Kenya, and he was educated in settings as diverse as Honolulu, Jakarta (Indonesia), Los Angeles, and New York. After growing up in Hawaii as "Barry" Obama, he later stressed the black dimension of his identity by reclaiming his father's first name (which means "blessings" in Swahili) and by moving to Chicago to work as a community organizer on the city's heavily African American south side. As with the golf legend Tiger Woods, whose mother was from Thailand and whose black father had African, European, and Native American ancestry, complex global influences meant that Obama's identity could scarcely be captured by a single hyphen between "African" and "American."

In India as well, all the migrants, invaders, and rulers that have passed through over the millennia have left their trace. One marker of that history is the hundreds of different languages spoken in India. Hindi, the most widely understood, is used by only 40 percent of the population. Though English is the language of

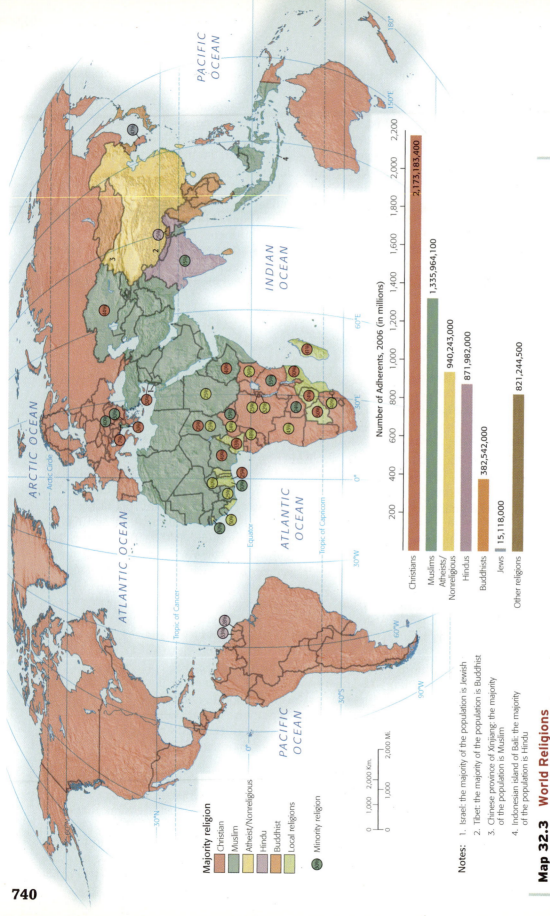

Majority religion

- Christian
- Muslim
- Atheist/Nonreligious
- Hindu
- Buddhist
- Local religions

⦿ Minority religion

PACIFIC OCEAN

ARCTIC OCEAN

Arctic Circle

ATLANTIC OCEAN

Equator

Tropic of Cancer

Tropic of Capricorn

PACIFIC OCEAN

INDIAN OCEAN

ATLANTIC OCEAN

0   1,000   2,000 Km.
0   1,000   2,000 Mi.

Number of Adherents, 2006 (in millions)

Christians	2,173,183,400
Muslims	1,335,964,100
Atheists/Nonreligious	940,243,000
Hindus	871,982,000
Buddhists	382,542,000
Jews	15,118,000
Other religions	821,244,500

200 400 600 800 1,000 1,200 1,400 1,600 1,800 2,000 2,200

© Cengage Learning

Notes:

1. Israel: the majority of the population is Jewish
2. Tibet: the majority of the population is Buddhist
3. Chinese province of Xinjiang: the majority of the population is Muslim
4. Indonesian island of Bali: the majority of the population is Hindu

Map 32.3   World Religions

Christianity, Islam, Hinduism, and Buddhism are the four major world religions, with "atheists/nonreligious" forming a majority in Communist-ruled China. The religious map of Africa is especially complex. While Muslims predominate in the north and west, and Christians in the east and south, there is a great deal of mixing along the boundaries between them, and local religions are still strong in many areas. In much of Europe and Russia, where Christian majorities are indicated, secularism is also strong and rates of church attendance quite low. While Islam predominates in North Africa and the Middle East, the nation with the largest Muslim population in the world is Indonesia, in Southeast Asia.

▶ Interactive Map

the elite, fewer than 10 percent of all Indians understand it. What can hold this vast and diverse country together?

In the past two decades the **Bharatiya Janata Party** (BJP) has attempted to use Hinduism as a unifying principle. While in power, the BJP proved competent custodians of the Indian economy, but many Indians are uneasy about their use of Hinduism. Some groups within the BJP have long histories of promoting intolerance against minority groups, especially Muslims. During intercommunal violence in the western state of Gujarat in 2002, fifty-eight Hindu nationalists were burned alive on a train heading for the contested site of a former Mughal mosque. Hindus claiming that Muslims had set the fire were actively aided by the BJP state government as they took vengeance, systematically raping Muslim women and dousing children with kerosene before setting them alight. Calm was restored, and the BJP lost the next elections. Some worried, however, that the infusion of religion into politics was threatening India's secular democracy.

Issues of identity in India go far beyond religious differences (see Map 32.3). Traditionally, identities were intensely local, tied to intimate networks of family, village, and caste. That local focus made sense for people whose work and daily routines were not much different from those of their forebears. Now, however, accelerated connections with the larger world create contexts that emphasize broader identities and affiliations. Television plays a powerful role. Before the 1990s few people had televisions and the government controlled all the programming. Now hundreds of millions of people watch domestic programs like soap operas and cricket matches, as well as imported channels like the Cable News Network (CNN) and the British Broadcasting Company (BBC).

Confusion over identity causes severe anxiety for Gogol Ganguli, the main character in Mira Nair's film *The Namesake* (2006), based on the novel by Jhumpa Lahiri. Gogol is the son of Indian immigrants to the United States. Named for a nineteenth-century Russian author for reasons known only to his father, Gogol spends his early life trying to piece together an identity from the cultural fragments around him, alternately rejecting and reconciling himself to his parents' Bengali traditions, while moving between Kolkata and New York. As so often in Nair's films, this intensely personal story points toward a broader thesis. Confronted with a complex menu of identities from which to choose, Gogol's solution, which makes him whole, is to embrace them all.

Bharatiya Janata Party (BJP) Nationalist political party in India that emphasizes the country's Hindu identity, in contrast to the secular Congress Party. The BJP led the federal government from 1998 to 2004.

Gender, Human Rights, and Democracy

The theme of gender pervades Mira Nair's work. One of the saddest moments in her films occurs in *Salaam Bombay!* when a teenage girl named Solasaal arrives at the brothel where Krishna lives; the adults nickname her "Sweet Sixteen" and expect to make a big profit by selling her virginity.

Globalization offers a world of new possibilities to women who have an education. It might seem that gender progress only requires a general improvement in living standards. Unfortunately, prosperity and technology cause new problems even as they ease others. In India, the **dowry system** has become a major problem. A girl's dowry has traditionally been the largest expense faced by Indian parents, sometimes leading the poor to lifelong indebtedness.

dowry system Traditional Indian marriage system in which a bride brings substantial gifts to the household of her new husband. Though illegal, it has expanded as the country's wealth has grown, leading to chronic indebtedness and the frequent murder of young brides.

The dowry system is now more widespread than ever, and the greater availability of consumer goods has had an inflationary effect. Families demand ever-greater payments in return for marriage to their sons, including refrigerators, houses, cars, and even business capital. Newspapers abound in reports of young brides murdered by their in-laws after their dowry payments have been made. Officially there were 6,787 dowry murders in India in 2005; experts suspect that the actual number is much higher.

Because of the dowry system, the birth of a girl can seem a tragedy, ruining the family's financial prospects. One ancient tradition has been female infanticide, leading to a long-term gender imbalance in India favoring males. Modern technology makes the process more efficient. Across India, medical clinics advertise sonogram services to determine the gender of a fetus, leading to the selective abortion of female fetuses. In the Punjab there are fewer than 800 girls for every 1,000 boys.

In China as well, some parents practice selective abortion using ultrasound technology. Here the traditional preference for boys has been magnified by the government's One Child Policy, since the birth of a girl means no male offspring. Demographers estimate that there are as many as 70 million more males than females in the country, an imbalance that makes it more difficult to find brides: tens of millions of Chinese men face a lifetime of bachelorhood.

Overcoming legacies of male dominance and rebalancing power more evenly between men and women require more than material prosperity, technological progress, or government intervention. Addressing patriarchal attitudes requires attention to local circumstances.

Connecting the local to the global is a hallmark of the work of **Wangari Maathai (wahn-gah-ree mah-TIE)**. Alarmed by environmental degradation in the region of East Africa where she grew up, Dr. Maathai organized rural women into collectives to plant trees, inspiring

Wangari Maathai (b. 1940) Kenyan biologist, environmentalist, and human rights campaigner who founded the Green Belt Movement in Kenya, empowering rural women to plant trees and take leadership roles. Was awarded the Nobel Peace Prize in 2004.

affiliated organizations in other developing countries. Her success did not come without a fight, however. While women planting trees may not sound daring, in patriarchal Kenya it took great courage. These women, Maathai explains, have learned that "planting trees or fighting to save forests from being chopped down is part of a larger mission to create a society that respects democracy, decency, adherence to the rule of law, human rights, and the rights of women."[8] Reflecting on the path that led from environmental activism to a Nobel Peace Prize, Dr. Maathai envisions peace as the stable top of an African stool, supported by the three stout legs of human rights, democracy, and protection of the environment.

Unfortunately, Africa's path toward democracy has not been smooth. In early 2008 disputed election results in Kenya led to widespread ethnic violence. The situation was even worse in Zimbabwe, where agents of the aged dictator Robert Mugabe falsified election results, used violence to suppress opposition parties, and rendered 700,000 people homeless in a slum clearance program called "Operation Drive Out Trash." Sudanese authorities evaded responsibility for arming militias who killed thousands and displaced millions in Darfur, while Somalia remained a "failed state" without any effective government at all. Stable, multiparty democracies in Tanzania, Ghana, and Botswana were hopeful exceptions to the continent's general disorder.

In Asia as well, the record of democratization remained mixed. Indonesia, the world's fourth most populous and largest Muslim-majority nation, successfully adapted to democracy, with relatively clean elections and smooth transitions of power between parties. In Vietnam and the People's Republic of China, by contrast, communist parties monopolized power even as they introduced market economics. It remains to be seen whether economic growth can trigger political reform.

Less promising is the military dictatorship of Myanmar (Burma), ruled since 1962 by secretive generals without any restraint. The callousness of the generals shocked the world when they refused to allow international agencies to

AP Photo/Sayyid Azim

Wangari Maathai   The Green Belt Movement led by Wangari Maathai stresses environmental renewal, women's empowerment, and human rights. Here Dr. Maathai (*right*) plants a tree in Nairobi's Uhuru Park with U.S. Senator Barack Obama, later elected president of the United States, who traveled to Kenya in 2006 to visit his father's homeland.

come to the aid of desperate victims of the catastrophic cyclone of 2008. At least Aung San Suu Kyi **(awng san soo key)**, Myanmar's courageous human rights campaigner, was finally released from house arrest in 2010, only after rigged elections, however, that kept the military elite in power.

Today's world has no lack of female role models, as Aung San Suu Kyi, Mira Nair, and Wangari Maathai all demonstrate. In Nair's film *Hysterical Blindness* (2002), the character of Debby is trapped in a narrow and stifling world; she has no idea how to escape from boredom and despair other than the futile hope that a man will come along and rescue her. Nair uses the recurrent image of a bridge to Manhattan seen from below to indicate the path to a wider and more hopeful world, though Debby never looks up to see it. Education is key, not just to provide skills but also to promote empowerment. The issue is how to spread opportunity within and between societies equitably.

Global Culture

When Mira Nair was growing up in India, the influence of the British Empire was still strong. One of the novels she enjoyed as a teenager was William Thackeray's *Vanity Fair,* the story of a young woman using all her intelligence and guile to improve her station in class-bound early-nineteenth-century England. In Nair's version of *Vanity Fair,* silk outfits, "oriental" furniture, and Indian servants suggest how the British Empire infiltrates English life. Nair hired a Bollywood choreographer for a scene in which Becky does a titillating dance for her love interest, embellishing Victorian life with Bollywood style.

Though the global film industry is vast and diverse, the two most influential players by far are Hollywood and Bollywood, and Mira Nair personifies the synergy between them. In fact, Reliance Big Entertainment, a subsidiary of India's largest telecommunications company, has invested over $1 billion in Hollywood, while in 2008 American rapper Snoop Dogg was signed to perform "Singh Is King," the title song for a Bollywood movie.

AP Photo/Rafiq Maqbool

Bollywood Goes Global   This 2004 street scene from Kabul, Afghanistan, with a video shop in the foreground, shows the increasing international influence of India's massive film industry. The Islamist Taliban regime (1996–2001) banned Bollywood films, objecting to their romantic leading men and women, lavish sets, and boisterous singing and dancing.

Although globalization has been a mixed blessing, the potential for cultural globalization still seems immense. Some equate globalization with Americanization, fearing that fast foods will replace local cuisines or that the global film industry will be homogenized through the dominance of Hollywood. But music and sport indicate that there is good reason to be optimistic.

The African experience shows the enduring cultural power of music. Even under colonialism, Africans adapted their music to new circumstances, instruments, and cultural influences. In the 1950s, African musicians responded to the Afro-Latin rhythms of the Cuban *mambo* and other American musical idioms that retained deep African roots, reimporting these styles and adding their own modern voice to re-create global African music all over again. Listening to great masters of African popular music—such as Angelique Kidjo (Benin), Salif Keita (Mali), and the late Fela Anikulapo Kuti (Nigeria)—will leave little doubt that the creative power of African music has never been diminished.

Sport, especially football (or soccer), is another positive area. During the 1990s, one writer notes, "You could see globalization on the pitch…. Basque teams, under the stewardship of Welsh coaches, stocked up on Dutch and Turkish players; Moldavian squads imported Nigerians. Everywhere you looked, it suddenly seemed, national borders and national identities had been swept into the dustbin of soccer history.[9] As with film and music, global interaction unleashes untapped creative potential.

Mira Nair's commitment to increasing cultural connections is also clear from her sponsorship of the Maisha Film Makers Lab. Based in Kampala, Uganda, Maisha ("life" in Swahili) gives new screenwriters and film directors from East Africa and South Asia access to professional training and mentoring. The Maisha (mah-EE-sha) program's goal is to "unleash local voices from these regions … motivated by the belief that a film which explores the truths and idiosyncrasies of the specifically local often has the power to cross over and become significantly universal."[10] Artists like Mira Nair help make the local and global connect.

Chapter Review and Learning Activities

The films of Mira Nair, though deeply personal, touch on universal themes. Serving as a bridge between Hollywood and Bollywood, Nair shows the creativity that often accompanies global cultural interaction. Globalization, while it has in many ways raised international stress and discord, has also given vast numbers of people a chance to discover the power and beauty of the world's cultural traditions. The optimistic view is that as the flow of world cultures increases, lives will be enriched, perhaps even helping lay foundations for peace.

How is globalization affecting the world economy and global security?

The increased pace of economic interchange and transfer of technologies in the twenty-first century has presented people across the world with new opportunities. As the emergence of the new India and the increased economic importance of Brazil, Russia, and China all show, globalization can result in rapid economic growth. The question remains, however, how equitably the benefits will be shared within societies and between nations. Meanwhile, terrorism has created uncertainty in international affairs, a landscape also altered by the emergence of China and the resurgence of Russia as great powers and by the growth of regional blocs like the European Union. These developments, combined with the extended war in Iraq, have resulted in the relative weakening of the United States as the main arbiter of international affairs, with unknown consequences for global security.

What are the most important environmental and demographic trends of the twenty-first century?

In the twenty-first century, the world's people became increasingly aware that the environmental damage caused by human activity, especially the release of the greenhouse gases that cause global warming, was a problem requiring global solutions. With every nation striving to maximize economic growth, however, remedies such as those proposed in the Kyoto Protocol remained hard to implement. Although most scientists no longer believe that it is simply the rising number of people that will place our planet at risk, economic and demographic imbalances still present a challenge. In some parts of the world, such as India and Africa, great numbers of young people seek access to education and opportunity, while in mature industrial countries graying populations might have insufficient workers to support them in old age. These

trends, combined with faster telecommunications and better transportation, have led to an unprecedented movement of peoples. Most of the world's people now live in cities, which strain to provide them services, while in many countries tensions over immigration have increased.

To what extent is the world moving forward in gender equality, human rights, and democracy?

Disparities in education and income determine whether women experience globalization as an opportunity or a threat, though entrenched structures of male dominance everywhere hamper the drive toward gender equality. As in the 1990s following the collapse of the Soviet Union, the world's record on human rights and democracy has remained mixed. Democracy came to former military dictatorships like Brazil and Indonesia and former communist countries like Poland, but brutal dictators resisted change in places like Zimbabwe and Myanmar, and communist regimes in China and Vietnam were slow to match their free-market reforms with political openness. While many of the world's people have focused solely on ethnic and national interests and identities, a growing number have become aware of themselves as global citizens. Perhaps the best hope for the advancement of democracy, human rights, and gender equality lies with them.

FOR FURTHER REFERENCE

Appiah, Kwame Anthony. *Cosmopolitanism: Ethics Is a World of Strangers*. New York: W.W. Norton, 2007.
Connelly, Matthew. *Fatal Misconception: The Struggle to Control World Population*. Cambridge, Mass.: Belknap Press, 2008.
Foer, Franklin. *How Soccer Explains the World: An Unlikely Theory of Globalization*. New York: HarperCollins, 2004.
Friedman, Thomas. *Hot, Flat and Crowded: Why We Need a Green Revolution*. New York: Farrar, Straus and Giroux, 2008.

Kamdar, Mira. *Planet India: How the Fastest Growing Democracy Is Changing America and the World.* New York: Scribner, 2007.

Luce, Edward. *In Spite of the Gods: The Strange Rise of Modern India.* London: Abacus, 2006.

Maathai, Wangari. *Unbowed: A Memoir.* New York: Knopf, 2006.

Muir, John Kenneth. *Mercy in Her Eyes: The Films of Mira Nair.* New York: Applause, 2006.

Obama, Barack. *Dreams from My Father: A Story of Race and Inheritance.* New York: Times Books, 1995.

Sen, Amartya. *Identity and Violence: The Illusion of Destiny.* New York: W.W. Norton, 2007.

Zakaria, Fareed. *The Post-American World.* New York: W.W. Norton, 2008.

KEY TERMS

Mira Nair (724)

Manmohan Singh (725)

outsourcing (728)

Mercosur (728)

World Trade Organization (728)

Muhammad Yusuf (729)

September 11, 2001 (732)

Kyoto Protocol (736)

sustainable development (737)

One Child Policy (738)

Bharatiya Janata Party (741)

dowry system (741)

Wangari Maathai (742)

VOYAGES ON THE WEB

Voyages: Mira Nair

"Voyages" is a real time excursion to historical sites in this chapter and includes interactive activities and study tools such as audio summaries, animated maps, and flashcards.

Visual Evidence: The Fall of Saddam Hussein

"Visual Evidence" features artifacts, works of art, or photographs, along with a brief descriptive essay and discussion questions to guide your analysis of visual sources.

World History in Today's World: Studying World History

"World History in Today's World" makes the connection between features of modern life and their origins in the periods in this chapter.

CourseMate

Go to the CourseMate website at www.cengagebrain.com for additional study tools and review materials—including audio and video clips—for this chapter.

Notes

Chapter 15

1. J. M. Cohen, trans., *The Four Voyages of Christopher Columbus* (New York: Penguin, 1969): description of Hispaniola, pp. 117–118; giving trifles, 35.
2. Michael E. Smith, *The Aztecs* (Malden, Mass.: Blackwell Publishing, 1996), p. 62, says 4 to 6 million.
3. Cassandra Fedele, "Oration to the University of Padua (1487)," in *The Renaissance in Europe: An Anthology*, ed. Peter Elmer et al. (New Haven: Yale University Press, in association with the Open University, 2000), pp. 52–56.
4. Peter Russell, *Prince Henry "the Navigator": A Life* (New Haven: Yale University Press, 2000), pp. 242–243, n. 8, citing *Crónica dos Feitos na Conquista de Guiné*, II: 145–148.
5. Michael Wood, *Conquistadors* (Berkeley: University of California Press, 2000), p. 81, citing the *Florentine Codex*.
6. Alfred W. Crosby, *The Columbian Exchange: Biological and Cultural Consequences of 1492* (Westport, Conn.: Greenwood Press, 1972), p. 4, n.2, citing Christopher Columbus, *Journals and Other Documents on the Life and Voyages of Christopher Columbus*, trans. Samuel Eliot Morison (New York: The Heritage Press, 1963), pp. 72–73, 84.

Chapter 16

1. *The Diary of Matthew Ricci*, in Matthew Ricci, *China in the Sixteenth Century*, trans. Louis Gallagher (New York: Random House, 1942, 1970), pp. 54–55.
2. E. Mungello, *The Great Encounter of China and the West, 1500–1800*, 2d ed. (Lanham, Md.: Rowman and Littlefield, 2005).
3. Michael Pearson, *The Indian Ocean* (London: Routledge, 2003), p. 121.
4. James D. Tracy, *The Political Economy of Merchant Empires* (New York: Cambridge University Press, 1991), p. 1.
5. Cited in John Reader, *Africa: A Biography of the Continent* (New York: Vintage, 1999), pp. 374–375.
6. Matteo Ricci, *The True Meaning of the Lord of Heaven*, trans. Douglas Lancashire and Peter Hu Kuo-chen, S.J. (Paris: Institut Ricci-Centre d'études chinoises, 1985), p. 99.

Chapter 17

1. Sir John Chardin, *Travels in Persia, 1673–1677, an abridged English version of Voyages du chevalier Chardin en Perse, et autres lieux de l'Orient* (New York: Dover Press, 1988), p. 70. Spelling and usage have been modernized.
2. *The Turkish Letters of Ogier Ghiselin de Busbecq, Imperial Ambassador at Constantinople, 1554–1562*, trans. Edward S. Foster (New York: Oxford University Press).
3. Cited in Ronald W. Ferrier, *A Journey to Persia: Jean Chardin's Portrait of a Seventeenth Century Empire* (London: I. B. Tauris, 1996), p. 44.
4. William Shakespeare, *King Richard II*, Act 2, Scene 1.

Chapter 18

1. Catalina de Erauso, *Lieutenant Nun: Memoir of a Basque Transvestite in the New World*, trans. Michele Stepto and Gabriel Stepto (Boston: Beacon Press, 1996), pp. 33–34. Other quotations in the chapter from pages 4, 6, 16, 28–29, 39.

2. Quoted in Octavio Paz, *Sor Juana*, trans. Margaret Sayers Peden (Cambridge: Harvard University Press, 1988), p. 219.
3. Quoted in George Fredrickson, *White Supremacy: A Comparative Study in American and South African History* (New York: Oxford University Press, 1981), p. 100.
4. Octavio Paz, *The Labyrinth of Solitude* (New York: Grove Press, 1961), pp. 101–102.

Chapter 19

1. Olaudah Equiano, *The Interesting Narrative of the Life of Olaudah Equiano, or Gustavus Vassa, the African*, ed. Vincent Carretta, 2d ed. (New York: Penguin Putnam, 2003).
2. Quoted in David Northrup, *The Atlantic Slave Trade*, 2d ed. (Boston: Houghton Mifflin, 2001), p. 53.
3. *A Letter to a Member of Parliament, Concerning the Importance of Our Sugar-Colonies to Great Britain, by a Gentleman, Who Resided Many Years in the Island of Jamaica* (London: J. Taylor, 1745).
4. Quoted in *Equiano*, p. 83, spelling modernized.
5. Mark Kurlansky, *Cod: A Biography of the Fish That Changed the World* (New York: Penguin Books, 1997), p. 75.

Chapter 20

1. Xie Qinggao, *Hailu jiaoyi*, ed. An Jing (Beijing: Shangwu yingshugan, 2002).
2. Susan Mann, *Precious Records: Women in China's Long Eighteenth Century* (Stanford: Stanford University Press, 1997), p. 149.
3. J. L. Cranmer-Byng, ed., *An Embassy to China: Lord Macartney's Journal, 1793–1794* (Hamden, Conn.: Archon Books, 1963), p. 340.
4. Horace Walpole, speech quoted in *Cambridge History of India* (Cambridge: Cambridge University Press, 1929), vol. 5, p. 187.
5. Quoted in Francis Watson, *A Concise History of India* (London: Thames and Hudson, 1979), p. 131.
6. Xie, p. 63.
7. Quoted in Ryusaku Tsunoda et al., *Sources of the Japanese Tradition* (New York: Columbia University Press, 1958), pp. 399–400.

Chapter 21

1. J. C. Beaglehole, ed., *The Endeavour Journal of Joseph Banks*, 2d ed. (Sydney: Halsted Press, 1962), vol. 1, p. 252. Here as elsewhere, some revisions of Banks's punctuation and usage have been made.
2. Quoted in Patrick O'Brien, *Joseph Banks: A Life* (Chicago: University of Chicago Press, 1987), pp. 105 and 264.
3. Immanuel Kant, *The Critique of Pure Reason* (Garden City: Doubleday, 1966).
4. Sir Francis Bacon, *The Advancement of Learning* (London: Oxford University Press, 1960).
5. Alexander Pope, "Epitaph intended for Sir Isaac Newton."
6. Quoted in Richard Drayton, *Nature's Government: Science, Imperial Britain, and the 'Improvement' of the World* (New Haven: Yale University Press, 2000), p. 108.
7. Quoted in ibid., p. 55.

8. Quoted in ibid., p. 118.
9. Thomas Hobbes, *The Leviathan.*
10. Quoted in Moira Ferguson, ed., *First Feminists: British Women Writers, 1578–1799* (Bloomington: Indiana University Press, 1985), p. 86.
11. Kant, *Critique of Pure Reason.*
12. Quoted in Dava Sorbel and Willam J. H. Andrews, *The Illustrated Longitude: The True Story of a Lone Genius Who Solved the Greatest Scientific Problem of His Time* (New York: Walker & Co., 1998), p. 176.
13. Laura Hostetler, *Qing Colonial Enterprise: Ethnography and Cartography in Early Modern China* (Chicago: University of Chicago Press, 2001), p. 24.
14. Matthew H. Edney, *Mapping an Empire: The Geographical Construction of British India, 1765–1843* (Chicago: University of Chicago Press, 1990), p. 1.
15. Quoted in O'Brien, p. 94.
16. Ibid., p. 95.

Chapter 22

1. Simón Bolívar, "Oath Taken at Rome, 15 August 1805," trans. Frederick H. Fornoff, in *El Libertador: Writings of Simón Bolívar,* ed. David Bushnell (New York: Oxford University Press, 2003), pp. 113–144.
2. David Bushnell, *Simón Bolívar: Liberation and Disappointment* (New York: Perason Longman, 2004).
3. Olympe de Gouges, *Écrits politiques, 1788–1791,* trans. Tracey Rizzo (Paris: Côtes Femmes, 1993), p. 209. Reprinted in Tracy Rizzo and Laura Mason, eds., *The French Revolution: A Document Collection* (Boston: Houghton Mifflin, 1999), p. 111.
4. Quoted in Bushnell, p. 77.

Chapter 23

1. Alexander Herzen, *My Past and Thoughts,* trans. Constance Garnett (Berkeley: University of California Press, 1982), p. 313.
2. Quoted in *Edward Acton, Alexander Herzen and the Role of the Intellectual Revolutionary* (Cambridge: Cambridge University Press, 1979), p. 29.
3. Alexander Herzen, "An Open Letter to Jules Michelet," in *From the Other Shore and the Russian People and Socialism* (New York: George Braziller, 1956), pp. 189–190.
4. Herzen, *My Past and Thoughts,* p. 462.
5. Ibid., p. 414.
6. Friedrich Engels, *The Condition of the Working Class in England,* in *The Marx-Engels Reader,* ed. Richard C. Tucker, 2d ed. (New York: W.W. Norton, 1978), pp. 580–581.
7. John Stuart Mill, *On Liberty* (London: Longman, Roberts & Green, 1869), p. 5.
8. Herzen, *My Past and Thoughts,* pp. 333–334.
9. Quoted in Otto Pflanze, *Bismarck and the Development of Germany* (Princeton: Princeton University Press, 1990), vol. 1, p. 184.
10. Karl Marx and Friedrich Engels, *Manifesto of the Communist Party,* in *The Marx-Engels Reader,* ed. Richard C. Tucker, 2d ed. (New York: W.W. Norton, 1978), p. 500.
11. Ibid., p. 477.
12. Ibid., p. 474.
13. Ibid., pp. 476–477.
14. Herzen, *My Past and Thoughts,* p. 321.

Chapter 24

1. Fukuzawa Yûkichi, *The Autobiography of Yukichi Fukuzawa,* trans. Eiichi Kiyooka (New York: Columbia University Press, 1960), pp. 112–116.
2. Ibid., p. 277.
3. William H. McNeill and Mitsuko Iriye, *Modern Asia and Africa* (Oxford: Oxford University Press, 1971).
4. Franz Michael and Chang Chung-li, *The Taiping Rebellion: History and Documents* (Seattle: University of Washington Press, 1971), vol. 2, p. 314.
5. Jen Yu-Wen, *The Taiping Revolutionary Moment* (New Haven: Yale University Press, 1973), pp. 93–94.
6. Michael and Chang, vol. 3, p. 767.
7. Teng Ssu-yü and John K. Fairbank, *China's Response to the West: A Documentary Survey, 1839–1923* (Cambridge, Mass.: Harvard University Press, 1954), pp. 53–54.
8. Quoted in Patricia Buckley Ebrey, *Cambridge Illustrated History of China* (London: Cambridge University Press, 1996), p. 245.
9. Victor Purcell, *The Boxer Uprising: A Background Study* (New York: Cambridge University Press, 1963), p. 224.
10. Fukuzawa, p. 18.
11. Ibid., p. 164.
12. Ibid., p. 210.
13. Fukuzawa Yûkichi, *The Speeches of Fukuzawa: A Translation and Critical Study,* ed. Wayne Oxford (Tokyo: Hokuseido House, 1973), p. 93.
14. Fukuzawa Yûkichi, *Fukuzawa Yukichi on Japanese Women: Selected Works* (Tokyo: University of Tokyo Press, 1988), p. 138.
15. http://womenshistory.about.com/library/qu/blqutosh.htm?pid=2765&cob=home.
16. Quoted in Helen M. Hopper, *Fukuzawa Yûkichi: From Samurai to Capitalist* (New York: Pearson Longman, 2005), p. 120.
17. Stanley Wolpert, *India* (Berkeley: University of California Press, 1991), p. 51.
18. Quoted in Stanley A. Wolpert, *Tilak and Gokhale: Revolution and Reform in the Making of Modern India* (Berkeley: University of California Press, 1991, p. 191.

Chapter 25

1. Pauline Johnson-Tekahionwake, "A Cry from an Indian Wife," in *Flint and Feather: The Complete Poems of E. Pauline Johnson* (Tekahionwake) (Toronto: Hodder and Stoughton, 1969).
2. Cited in Thomas Bender, *A Nation Among Nations: America's Place in World History* (New York: Hill and Wang, 2006), p. 121.
3. *Aberdeen Saturday Pioneer,* December 20, 1890.

Chapter 26

1. King Khama of the Bangwato, quoted in Neil Parsons, *King Khama, Emperor Joe and the Great White Queen: Victorian Britain Through African Eyes* (Chicago: University of Chicago Press, 1998), p. 103.
2. W. E. B. Du Bois, *The Souls of Black Folk* (New York: Vintage, 1990).

Chapter 27

1. Louise Bryant, *Six Red Months in Moscow* (London: Heinemann, 1919), p. xx.

Chapter 28

1. Halide Edib, *Inside India* (New York: Oxford University Press, 2002).
2. Hashimoto Kingoro, "Address to Young Men," in *Sources of Japanese Tradition,* ed. William Theodore de Bary (New York: Columbia University Press, 1958), vol. 2, p. 289.
3. Ibid, p. 231.

Chapter 29

1. All quotations from Nancy Wake, *The White Mouse* (Melbourne: Australian Large Print, 1987).

Chapter 30

1. Ernesto Guevara, *The Motorcycle Diaries: Notes on a Latin American Journey,* ed. and trans. Alexandra Keeble (Melbourne: Ocean Press, 2003), pp. 75–78.
2. Quoted in David Sandison, *Che Guevara* (New York: St. Martin's Griffin, 1997), pp. 105 and 108.

Chapter 31

1. Nelson Mandela, *Nelson Mandela in His Own Words,* ed. Kader Asmal, David Chidester, and Wilmot James (New York: Little Brown, 2003), pp. 59–62.
2. Nelson Mandela, "I Will Return," ibid., pp. 46–47.

Chapter 32

1. Mira Nair, "Create the World You Know," Variety Cinema Militans Lecture delivered at the Netherlands Film Festival in Utrecht on September 29, 2002; http://mirabaifilms.com/wordpress/?page_id=42.
2. Mira Kamdar, *Planet India: How the Fastest-Growing Democracy Is Transforming America and the World* (New York: Scribner, 2007), p. 4.
3. Caption data from http://hdr.undp.org/en/statistics. Map data from *The World Almanac and Book of Facts, 2008,* ed. C. Alan Joyce (World Almanac Books, 2008).
4. Robert Kuttner, "The Role of Governments in the Global Economy," in *Global Capitalism,* ed. Will Hutton and Anthony Giddens (New York: New Press, 2000), p. 163.
5. Dr. Margaret Chan, "Health in a Changing Environment," http://www.who.int/mediacentre/news/statements/2007/s11/en/index.html.
6. Mira Nair and Sooni Taraporevala, *Salaam Bombay!* (New York: Penguin Books, 1988), p. 7.
7. United Nations, *World Urbanization Prospects* (New York: United Nations, 2006).
8. *The Greenbelt Movement,* "Question and Answer Session with Prof. Wangari Maathai," http://www.greenbelt-movement.org/a.php?id=27.
9. Franklin Foer, *How Soccer Explains the World*: *An Unlikely Theory of Globalization* (New York: HarperCollins, 2004), pp. 2–3.
10. http://www.maishafilmlab.com/index.php.

Index

Poland and, 441; enlightened despots of, 467; ethnic minorities in, 498; French armies and, 488, 489; Nazis in, 634

Austrian Empire (1867–1919): in World War I, 603, 604(map), 605; collapse of, 611, 612(map), 613

Authoritarianism. *See* Dictatorship (authoritarian rule)

Automobile industry, 641; Indian, 727; Japanese, 713

Axis Powers (Germany, Italy, Japan), 651, 652(map), 654, 655, 658, 660

Ayacucho, Battle of (1824), 494(map), 495

Ayllu (Andean kin group), 328

Azerbaijan, 701(map)

Azikiwe, Nnamdi, 641

Azores Islands, 332

Aztec Empire (Mexico), 325–328; military and conquests of, 327–328; religion and society, 326–327; Spanish conquest of, 334, 337–339 and illus.; Tenochtitlan and, 325–326 and map, 338–339

Aztlan, 325

Bacon, Francis, 458, 463, 464

Baghdad, 373, 376; British occupation of, 660, 708; United States' bombing of, 708

Balance of power: in Western Eurasia, 370, 381–386; in Europe, 382–384, 498, 520; New Imperialism and, 581; in Middle East, 709; in European Union, 728

Balboa, Vasco Núñez de, 337

Balfour Declaration (1917), 615

Bali, Hindu rebellion on, 593

Balkans, 513; Ottoman rule in, 382, 523; World War I and, 603; after World War I, 614; in World War II, 652 and map, 653; new states in, 728

Baltic Sea region, 386, 441, 701(map); European Union and, 716(map)

Bandas Islands, 352

Bandung Generation (1955–1965), 686–688

Bangalore, India, 731; software industry in, 727 and illus., 730

Bangladesh, 736

Bangwato people, 576, 580, 587. *See also* Botswana; Khama III (Bangwato)

Banks, Joseph, 455(map), 468; agricultural revolution of, 462, 505; Australian settlement and, 456, 473, 474–475; economic botany and, 456, 459, 462, 463; Kew Gardens and, 462, 469, 475; Royal Society and, 456, 458, 470, 505; in Tahiti, 454, 474

Banks and banking: Bank of France, 489; failures, in Great Depression, 628; protection for depositors, 629; Japanese crisis, 713; European, 715; microfinance and, 729

Banner system, in Qing China, 435

Bantu-speakers, migrations of, 413, 586

Bantustans, 706

Barak, Ehud, 712

Barbados, sugar plantations on, 399, 417

Basques, 392; fisheries of, 428

Basra, 373, 376

Bastille, storming of (1789), 486

Bataan death march (1942), 654

Batista, Fulgencio, 676–677

Baum, L. Frank, 569

Bay of Pigs invasion (Cuba, 1961), 677

Beethoven, Ludwig von, 489, 509

Beijing, 435, 437; Forbidden City in, 354, 356, 529, 530, 533; French-British invasion of, 530; tribute missions to, 439; protest in (1919), 533, 618, 619(illus.); Nixon in, 690; protest and massacre in (1989), 714

Belarus, 620; Jews of, 444, 445

Belgian Congo, 580–581, 585(map); terror in, 594–595 and illus.; nationalism in, 682, 686

Belgium: African empire of, 580–581, 585(map), 614; industrialization in, 506, 507(map); terror in colonies of, 594–595 and illus.; World War I in, 604(map), 605; World War II in, 651, 653(illus.); decolonization and, 683(map)

The Bell (Herzen), 521

Belloc, Hillaire, 576

Bengal, 353; British rule in, 434, 448, 540; famine in, 448; partition of, 546–547; Roy and, 541 and illus.

Bentham, Jeremy, 511

Berber, Benjamin, 718–719

Bering expedition, 441

Berlin, 613, 656; airlift (1949), 666; revolution of 1848 in, 509, 514

Berlin Conference (1884), 581

Berlin Wall, 678; destruction of, 699, 700, 702

Bharatiya Janata Party (India), 741

Bible: authority of, 335; book of Genesis, 361; in German language, 359; Gutenberg and, 332; human sacrifice in, 340–341; in India, 361 and illus.

Bicycles, women and, 572 and illus., 656

Biko, Steven, 706

Bill of Rights: in England (1689), 385; in United States (1791), 485; in Mexico (1857), 563

Bin Laden, Osama, 709–710, 731; death of, 734; September (2001) terrorism and, 732

Bipolar World. *See* Cold War (Bipolar World)

Bird guano, as fertilizer, 564–565

Bishops: *See also* Priests; corruption of, 359; in Spanish America, 393; Anglican, 380, 381, 580, 581(illus.); West African, 580, 581(illus.); African American, 582–583

Bismarck, Otto von, 515, 537, 538, 603; New Imperialism and, 579, 581

Black Americans. *See* African Americans

Black Consciousness Movement, 706

"Black legend," Spain and, 405

Black Seminoles, 420

Blackshirts (fascists), 630

Blair, Tony, 715, 732

Blake, William, 510

Blanc, Louis, 512

Blitzkrieg (lightning war), 651, 653(illus.). *See also* Nazi Germany

Boer republics (South Africa), 632; Great Trek (1834–1836), 587; war with Britain, 588

Bolívar, Simón: "Jamaica" letter of, 493, 496–497; Napoleon and, 489, 490; in Rome, 478; South American independence and, 492–493, 494(map); travels of, 479(map); Gran Colombia and, 493, 498

Bolivia: War of the Pacific and, 564–565, 566(map); Guevara's death in, 672, 692

Bollywood films, 722, 724, 744 and illus.

Bolsheviks, 606, 618, 619–620. *See also* Communist Party (Soviet Union)

Bombay (Mumbai), 449, 540; film industry in, 722, 724, 744 and illus.; homeless children in, 737–738

Bombs and bombing: *See also* Nuclear weapons; World War I, 605; World War II, 654, 656–657, 658, 659; of Vietnam, 688; of Afghanistan, 710; of Baghdad, 708; in India, 732

Bonaparte. *See* Napoleon I (Napoleon Bonaparte)

Books: *See also* Printing technology; in Korea, 357; libraries, 332, 398, 414; in Timbuktu, 414

Knowledge industries, 714

Kobayashi, Kiyochika, 539(illus.)

Kolkata. *See* Calcutta (Kolkata)

Kongo kingdom, 416(map); Christianity in, 352. 413; slave trade and, 399

Korea. *See also* North Korea; South Korea; Chosôn dynasty, 357, 533; printing technology in, 332; literacy in, 357; China and, 353, 354, 439, 450; Japan and, 528, 533, 539–540; navy of, 358; comfort women, World War II, 659

Korean language, 357

Korean War (1950–1953), 674

Kowtow (bow), 356, 440

Krupp Steelworks, 514(illus.)

Kulaks (peasants), 635

Kumasi (Asante capital), 589

Kurds: in Iraq, 733 and map; nationalism, 614

Kuwait, Iraqi invasion of, 708, 709(illus.), 732

Kyoto Protocol (1991), 736–737

Labor: *See also* Slaves and slavery; Working class; of Amerindians, 337, 393, 395 and illus.; Inca, 330, 395 and illus.; indentured, 402, 417; division of, 464, 504, 506; for South African mines, 587; outsourcing of, 728

Labor, gendered division of: Huron people, 400; in China, 438; in Britain, 506

Labor camps, in Siberia, 521, 621

Labor unions. *See* Trade unions

Ladino language, 372

Lahiri, Jhumpa, 741

Laissez faire, 464–465. *See also* Free market

Lakota Sioux, 568

Land and Freedom Army (Kenya), 682

Land and landowners: *See also* Gentry; French, 486; reclamation of, 462; speculators, 484; in Latin America, 396, 403–404, 498; Japanese, 538; Mexican, 563; Brazilian, 567; Canada, 554, 556; South African, 588; Palestinian, 615; Italian fascists and, 630

Land grants, in Ottoman Empire, 372

Land reform: in Vietnam, 358; in Cuba, 677; in Guatemala, 680–681; in Mexico, 616–617

Languages: Arabic, 372, 376; Arawak, 335; German, 359, 614; Greek, 331; Korean, 357; Latin, 331, 462; Turkish, 372; vernacular, 331; Nahuatl, 325, 326, 327(illus.), 338,

339, 340–341, 342; Sanskrit, 362; Slavic, 441; Persian, 372, 376; Yiddish, 444; Spanish, 372, 493; Quechua, 329, 495; English, 541, 543, 640, 739; French, 554, 570; Indonesian, 686

Laos, 591, 596, 652

La Plata, viceroyalty of, 393, 394(map)

Latin alphabet, in Turkey, 637(illus.)

Latin America: colonial era (*See* Brazil, Portuguese and; Spanish America); cattle raising in, 343; Iberian conquest of, 337–339 and illus.; colonial era, 334, 342; silver from, 352, 355(map); landowner class in, 396, 403–404, 498; wars of independence in, 480, 492–498; raw materials from, 508, 567; elites and state building in, 492, 495, 564; reform and reaction in, 562–565, 567; ca. 1895, 566(map); import substitution in, 629; United States' domination of, 678; death and dictatorship in, 692–693; democratization in, 698; late Cold War in, 703–705; population growth in, 738; structural adjustment in, 715; immigration from, 739

Latin language: humanists and, 331; in botanical binomials, 462

Latvia, 701(map), 728

Laws and legal codes: Amerindians and, 393; free blacks and, 421; in British India, 448–449; Napoleonic, 489; Prussian reforms, 467; Islamic law, 353, 371, 544, 584, 707, 708; Ottoman reforms, 523

League of Nations, 611, 613; Mandate System and, 614; Mussolini's defiance of, 631, 642; United Nations and, 664

Lebanon, 615, 687

"Lecture on Teaching and Learning" (al-Afghani), 518

Lê dynasty (Vietnam), 358

Legislative Assembly (France), 487, 488

Lehman Brothers, bankruptcy of, 729

Lenin, Vladimir I., 619–621; Bolsheviks and, 606, 618, 619–620; New Economic Policy of, 621, 635; death of, 621

Leningrad, Siege of (1941–1944), 654. *See also* St. Petersburg

Leonardo da Vinci, 331(illus.)

Leopold II (Belgium), Congo and, 580–581, 588; violence under, 594–595 and illus.

Lepanto, Battle of (1571), 372–373

Levi, Primo, 662–663

Lewis, Meriwether, 472(map), 473

Lewis and Clark Expedition, 472(map), 473, 498

Liberal Party (Britain), 579

Liberal Party (Canada), 556

Liberals and liberalism, 504; in Britain, 508, 511; in British India, 541; in Japan, 538; in Mexico, 563, 616; nationalism and, 614; New Imperialism and, 580; authoritarian rule and, 626, 630; in Chile, 693

Liberia, emigration to, 582

Libraries: *See also* Books; Literacy; of Columbus, 332; of Sor Cruz, 398; in Timbuktu, 414

Libya, oil of, 642

Likud Party (Israel), 710

Lima, Peru, 396, 494(map)

Lincoln, Abraham, 557, 560

Lineage: matrilineage, 328; slave origins and, 425

Linnaeus, Carl, 459, 462

Lin Zexu, 530

Literacy: *See also* Education; in Europe, 359; of Chinese women, 362; in Korea, 357; Enlightenment and, 465

Lithuania, 701(map), 728

Little Big Horn, Battle of (1876), 568, 569(illus.)

Livestock: *See also* Cattle; in Columbian Exchange, 343; crossbreeding of sheep, 462–463, 475

Livingstone, David, 580

Llamas, 330, 393, 395, 396

Llaneros (cowboys), Bolívar and, 492, 493

Lloyd George, David, 611

Loans: *See also* Debt; in World War I, 628; "lend lease" World War II, 653; international banks and, 666; microfinance, 729

Locke, John, 464, 465, 483

London, 505; cholera in, 510; bombing of, in World War II, 651

London Missionary Society, 580

Longitude problem, 468–469

Long March (China, 1934–1936), 642, 643(map)

Louisiana Purchase, 472(map), 498, 556, 557(map)

Louis Napoleon. *See* Napoleon III (France)

Louis Philippe (France), 512

Louis XIV (France), 380 and illus.; absolutism of, 383, 466; Catholicism and, 382, 383

Louis XV (France), 467